THE ETHICAL JOURNALIST

GENE FOREMAN

THE ETHICAL JOURNALIST

MAKING RESPONSIBLE DECISIONS
IN THE DIGITAL AGE

Second Edition

WILEY Blackwell

Registered Office
John Wiley & Sons Ltd, The Atrium, Southern Gate, Chichester, West Sussex, PO19 8SQ, UK

Editorial Offices
350 Main Street, Malden, MA 02148-5020, USA
9600 Garsington Road, Oxford, OX4 2DQ, UK
The Atrium, Southern Gate, Chichester, West Sussex, PO19 8SQ, UK

For details of our global editorial offices, for customer services, and for information about how to apply for permission to reuse the copyright material in this book please see our website at www.wiley.com/wiley-blackwell.

Library of Congress Cataloging-in-Publication Data
Foreman, Gene.
  The ethical journalist : making responsible decisions in the digital age/Gene Foreman. – Second edition.
    pages cm
  Includes bibliographical references and index.
    ISBN 978-1-119-03173-4 (paperback)
  1. Journalistic ethics. 2. Reporters and reporting. 3. Journalistic ethics–Case studies. 4. Reporters and reporting–Case studies. I. Title.
  PN4756.F67 2015
  174'.907–dc23
                                                                                2015004142

A catalogue record for this book is available from the British Library.

Cover image: © ansonsaw/Getty Images

Set in 10.5/13 pt Bembo Std by Aptara, India

Printed in Singapore by C.O.S. Printers Pte Ltd

5   2017

*In memory of Jim Naughton,
who personified The Ethical Journalist*

Contents

Detailed Contents

Our society needs news professionals who do the right thing

- Contemporary journalists are keenly aware of the ethics of the profession; they deal frequently with ethics questions in their working lives.
- In a profession that cannot be regulated because of the First Amendment, responsible journalists adhere voluntarily to high standards of conduct.
- The goal of this book and course is to teach you how to make ethically sound decisions.
- Discussing case studies in class is crucial to learning the decision-making process.
- The digital era, which has radically changed the way the news is gathered and delivered, has provoked controversy over whether ethics should radically change as well.
- Confronted with a daily deluge of information, the public depends on ethical journalists for news that can be trusted.

Point of View: A "Tribal Ferocity" Enforces the Code (*John Carroll*)

An introduction to terms and concepts in an applied-ethics course

- Ethics is about discerning between right and wrong – and then doing what is right.
- Ancient societies developed systems of ethics that still influence human behavior.
- Ethics and law may be related, but they are not the same; law prescribes minimum standards of conduct, while ethics prescribes exemplary conduct.
- A member of a society absorbs its ethical precepts through a process of socialization.
- A person's values shape the choices he or she makes.
- When ethical values conflict, an ethical dilemma results.
- The ethical person learns how to make decisions when facing ethical dilemmas.

12   Getting the Story Right and Being Fair

Newswriting skills of accuracy and fairness are ethical skills, too

- Accuracy and fairness are journalism's fundamental ethical values.
- The digital era, with its emphasis on speed, entices reporters to take shortcuts – and thus to make mistakes.
- Social media have become an essential tool for news reporting, but professional journalists must verify everything.
- Journalists have to be alert for hoaxes, especially on the Web.
- Journalists should promptly and clearly correct any mistakes they make.

Point of View: Declaring What You *Won't* Report (*Craig Silverman*)
Point of View: Decision-Making in the Digital Age (*James M. Naughton*)
Case Study: Richard Jewell: He Really Was a Hero
Case Study: A Story of Rape at Mr. Jefferson's University
Case Study: The Football Star's Fictitious Girlfriend
Case Study: Verifying a Key Boston Video (*Malachy Browne*)

13   Dealing with Sources of Information

The fine line between getting close but not too close

- Ethical issues arise in the reporter's efforts to cultivate sources while maintaining an independence from those sources.
- If a journalist agrees to protect a source who provides information on condition of anonymity, honoring that agreement is a solemn ethical duty.
- This chapter examines recurring situations in which ethics issues arise in source relationships.

Point of View: Sometimes, Different Rules Apply (*Jeffrey Fleishman*)

14   Making News Decisions about Privacy

The public may need to know what individuals want hidden

- Journalists often have to decide between the public's legitimate need to have certain information and the desire for privacy by the individuals involved.
- Although there are certain legal restraints on publicizing private information, most decisions are made on the basis of ethics rather than law.
- A three-step template can help you make decisions in privacy cases.
- This chapter examines reporting situations in which privacy is central to decision-making.

Case Study: Tracing the Source of Web Comments
Case Study: Mapping the Locations of Gun Owners
Case Study: Identifying a 13-Year-Old Rape Victim

- Requests from the public to "unpublish" archival content creates an ethical dilemma. News organizations should resist deleting the digital record while also being considerate of the human problems stemming from the permanence of that record.
- Although the Internet empowers the audience to be heard, news organizations need to find ways to curb incivility.
- Hyperlinks in online news stories help journalists be transparent about their sources.
- Social-media participation and blogging provide benefits, but journalists have to be careful not to undermine their credibility as impartial observers.

Point of View: Let's Have Rules for Online Comment (*Edward Wasserman*)
Case Study: For a Reporter-Blogger, Two Personalities

19 Ethics Issues Specific to Visual Journalism 349
Seeking truth with the camera while minimizing harm

- The public must be able to trust the truthfulness of the news media's photographs and video.
- An image can be distorted either by stage-managing the scene or by manipulating the image.
- Photojournalists have adopted standards to ensure the integrity of their images.
- Recognizing that some images can offend, journalists weigh these images' news value against the likely offense.
- The presence of photojournalists and their cameras can cause psychological harm, whether or not the images are disseminated.

Case Study: The Falling Man, World Trade Center, 2001
Case Study: Photographing a Man Pushed to His Death
Case Study: A Marine Is Mortally Wounded

20 Some Thoughts to Take with You 374
Capsules of advice for aspiring journalists

- This chapter summarizes the lessons learned in your course in journalism ethics.

Foreword
Journalism Genes

When Gene Roberts left *The New York Times* in 1972 to begin elevating one of America's worst newspapers, *The Philadelphia Inquirer*, he quickly realized he needed help. "I was looking," he recalls, "for someone who was everything I was not." Roy Reed, then a national reporter for *The Times*, and others who knew Roberts well told him they had just the right person to be his managing editor: Gene Clemons Foreman.

Gene Foreman.
PHOTO BY
JOHN BEALE.

And so the two editors became Gene and Gene, or as the staff in Philadelphia dubbed them, The Chromosomes. They were indeed an odd couple – Roberts an unmade bed of an intuitive strategist and Foreman a conscientious pillar of reasoned exactitude – and they were a perfect match. Roberts always has been given, rightly, credit for the development of a literate *Inquirer* staff that may well have been, pound for pound, the most enterprising in American newspapering. In his 18 years in Philly, the staff was awarded 17 Pulitzer Prizes. Yet Roberts would be the first to say, and others of us who had the privilege of helping improve *The Inquirer* would echo, that it was Gene Foreman whose standards were at the center of the remarkable transformation.

It was Foreman who commissioned, edited, and published newspapering's most thorough and high-minded policy manual. It was Foreman who established and conducted standards and procedures training sessions for every staff member. It was Foreman who encountered Michael Josephson, a lawyer who was creating an ethics institute in Los Angeles, and tutored him in news issues so that Josephson could train journalists anywhere – including *The Inquirer* – in news ethics. It was Foreman who defined what the paper should look like and made sure it did. It was Foreman who built an exceptional core of copy editors, in part by creating a pre-employment editing test that became a model for the industry. It was Foreman who relentlessly examined each issue of the newspaper and delivered detailed guidance about where there was room for improvement. Never has there been a newspaper editor more focused on fact, honesty, reality, ethics, truth, accuracy, style.

Without either of the Genes, the remaking of *The Inquirer* likely would have collapsed. With the two as a team, yin and yang, it prospered as we performed a little more enterprisingly and a little more carefully each day. Many of us came to regard working for the Genes as the golden era of our careers. Plus it was great fun. They fostered the kind of newsroom in which on one of Gene Foreman's birthdays his fanatical devotion to the Philadelphia Phillies could be celebrated by creating a huge sheet cake on which there was a deliberate typo in the icing spelling Foreman's name. Just as Gene was about to cut the "cake," it popped open and up came Larry Bowa, the Phillies' shortstop. I've often thought Foreman identified with Bowa because both did their utmost to perform

at a high level without error. Gene certainly deserved a gold glove for editing. When Gene Foreman retired in 1998 after a quarter-century at *The Inquirer*, the staff threw a huge family picnic in his honor. One of the mementoes was a "baseball" card celebrating how much he loved both journalism and his baseball team.

As Gene's editing career wound down, Penn State arranged for him to continue to advocate best practices by joining the journalism faculty. Every week, Foreman made the rigorous round-trip from his home outside Philadelphia to the main campus in State College.

Students aspiring to careers in journalism came to revere him for his meticulous teaching and his energetic mentoring. Here's how Leann Frola Wendell, class of '06 and now a copy editor at the *Dallas Morning News*, put it:

> Professor Foreman was my most influential teacher at Penn State. Not only did he give me a solid foundation for copy editing and ethical journalism, he went above and beyond to help me with my career. Inside the classroom, he was impeccably organized and made each grading point count. He taught in a way that challenged us to intimately learn the material. And he was sure to explain why what we learned mattered. Professor Foreman was also a great resource outside the classroom. He made me aware of editing opportunities and encouraged me to work hard and apply for them. At his urging, I applied for a program that led me to the job I have today.

In preparing to teach ethics, Gene concluded that there were people in the craft and the academy who advocated high-minded practices, but no single text that explained to his satisfaction why and how journalism should be done right. Over nearly a decade he kept pulling together material from everywhere he could find it – accounts of best practices, case studies of news coverage gone awry, quotations from exemplars of the craft, and breaking news about how news was being broken in print, on the air, and online.

And he has put all of it, and more, into this book. *The Ethical Journalist* is like GPS for sound decision-making. It will not tell you what path to take but rather where you are on the journey to an ethical decision. It is invaluable for anyone who practices or cares about the craft. It is up to the minute in relevance. It will serve not merely to teach but to exemplify Gene Foreman's conviction that while there are immutable principles to guide the honest and careful delivery of news, ethical values are not static but alive. Standards cannot merely be proclaimed; they must be experienced, for every day, every broadcast, every edition, every deadline brings some unforeseen wrinkle in the who, what, when, where, why, and how of the world.

James M. Naughton

James M. Naughton (1938–2012) headed the Poynter Institute of Media Studies at St. Petersburg, Florida, from 1996 to 2003 and on retirement became its president emeritus. He joined *The Philadelphia Inquirer* in 1977 and was the paper's executive editor when he left for Poynter. Before his work at *The Inquirer*, he was *The New York Times'* White House correspondent during the Nixon and Ford administrations.

Preface

I am pleased to present this second edition of *The Ethical Journalist*. The content has been thoroughly updated to reflect the changing news environment of the digital age.

Like the first edition, issued in 2009, this book is intended to inform your professional life. Technically, it is published as a textbook for college courses in journalism ethics and communications ethics, and as the ethics textbook in a course combining journalism ethics and law. I hope that practicing journalists – especially young men and women who did not take journalism courses in college – will also find it useful for its comprehensive discussion of the standards of the profession.

If you fit those categories of student journalist and practicing journalist, you will find yourself addressed directly in this book. I reach out to you in two ways: first, to help you learn to make ethically defensible decisions in the practice of journalism; and, second, to give you the benefit of the thinking of generations of professionals and scholars that resulted in today's consensus guidelines for ethical conduct.

With these goals in mind, I have divided the book into two parts. Part I examines ethics in a general way, shows the relevance of ethics to journalism, and outlines a decision-making strategy. Part II discusses specific subject areas in which journalists frequently confront ethical problems.

Throughout the book, the consensus guidelines are explained, not to dictate your decision-making but to offer a starting point for thinking through the issues. The idea is that you don't have to start from a zero base; you can build on the best thinking of those who have gone before. Where there is disagreement in the profession, I have noted that, too. In several instances I advocate for what I consider to be best practice. All this is fodder for classroom discussion.

The book is largely the product of my half-century in journalism – more than 41 years in the newsroom and more than eight as a college professor. Although my approach is an entirely practical one of trying to improve decision-making in the profession, I have been influenced by ethics scholars as well as newsroom colleagues. One theme of the book is the value of ethical theory as a resource in the decision process. As a longtime newspaper managing editor, I acknowledge that the newsroom has benefited from the scholars' thoughtful analysis of issues whose nuances we practicing journalists sometimes overlooked as we focused on the next deadline.

To learn journalistic techniques like writing headlines for a website, I presume that you will take other courses and read other textbooks. In contrast, the purpose of this book is to encourage you to ponder the ethical ramifications of what journalists do, whether the consumer gets the news from a newspaper or a TV set or a computer screen or a mobile device.

The case studies and other actual experiences of journalists recounted in this book illustrate the ethical choices you may have to make. Those experiences have occurred in all types of news media – print, broadcast, and digital.

The timeless values of journalism are explained in the book's first 17 chapters. Although news delivered digitally is referenced throughout those chapters, there remain certain ethics issues that apply specifically to digital journalism. These are discussed in Chapter 18. Visual journalism, too, has its own specific issues, and these are the topic of Chapter 19. Summarizing the book's lessons, Chapter 20 offers capsules of ethics advice for aspiring journalists. In this new edition there is a Glossary at the back of the book; terms included in the Glossary are printed in bold when they are introduced in the text.

On the website accompanying *The Ethical Journalist*, you will find additional resources: more readings in print and online, and more case studies. The texts of reports and articles cited in the chapters can be accessed by clicking on the hyperlinks. You can expand the book's content to an almost infinite degree by following the links – much in the way that digital journalists offer their audience the ability to read the documents underpinning their reporting. Where readings have been posted on the book's website, their availability is noted in the chapter endnotes. We intend to refresh the website's content regularly so that *The Ethical Journalist* will continue to be up to date. You can find the website here: www.wiley.com\go\foreman\theethicaljournalist.

The journalists' decisions in the book's examples are open to debate, which is precisely why you should study them. If you decide that the journalist involved in a case study made a mistake, bear in mind that, nearly always, those were mistakes of the head and not of the heart. In teaching the journalism ethics course for 16 semesters, I frequently told my students of my own decisions that I would do differently if given a second chance. In many ways, learning journalism ethics is about learning from our mistakes.

Gene Foreman
Keswick, Virginia
September 2014

Acknowledgments

In preparing this second edition of *The Ethical Journalist*, I once again drew on the wisdom of colleagues whose friendship I enjoyed in my careers in the newsroom and in the classroom.

Four colleagues read all, or much, of the manuscript: Steve Seplow, Katie O'Toole, Jim Davis, and Avery Rome. Others reviewed at least one chapter: John Affleck, John Beale, Curt Chandler, Bill Connolly, Rick Edmonds, Russ Eshleman, Russell Frank, Maxwell King, Malcolm Moran, and Jeff Price. They were valued sounding boards, offering many suggestions that improved the book. I thank them all.

As I outlined the content revisions for this edition, I consulted with the folks named above and also with Doug Anderson, Malachy Browne, John Carroll, Tom Kent, Hank Klibanoff, Carol Knopes, Santiago Lyon, Arlene Morgan, Gene Roberts, Craig Silverman, Bob Steele, Al Tompkins, and Stacey Woelfel. I am grateful to them for their guidance.

I thank Bill Marsh, who again prepared the book's graphics, and John Beale, who collected the photographs that appear in these pages.

I extend special thanks to Marie Hardin, dean of the College of Communications at Pennsylvania State University, who arranged research support for the second edition. I was privileged to have taught eight years at Penn State as the inaugural Larry and Ellen Foster Professor, and I am proud to continue my relationship with the university as a visiting professor. Dean Hardin assigned two graduate students, Steve Bien-Aime and Roger Van Scyoc, to help in my project. I thank Steve and Roger for their dedicated assistance.

I express my appreciation to the journalists who graciously allowed their work to be used in the book as Point of View essays, as case studies, or as illustrations. Their contributions are acknowledged where they appear in the book.

I am grateful to Elizabeth Swayze at John Wiley & Sons, the acquisitions editor who commissioned both editions, and to the Wiley Blackwell editors who guided my manuscript into print, Julia Kirk, Leah Morin, and Jacqueline Harvey.

I thank my wife, JoAnn, and our children and grandchildren, for their continued support of my work – and for being who they are. I love you all.

Gene Foreman
Keswick, Virginia
September 2014

Part I   A Foundation for Making Ethical Decisions

This part of the book will prepare you to make ethical decisions in journalism.

Chapter 1 explains why journalists should understand ethics and apply ethical principles in their decision-making.

Chapter 2 explores the history of ethics and the way that members of society develop their ethical values.

Chapters 3, 4, and 5 discuss journalism's role in society, the shared values of the profession, and the often tenuous relationship of journalism and the public.

Chapters 6, 7, and 8 lay the foundation for moral decision-making in journalism, which is the goal of a course in applied ethics. Chapter 6 discusses classic ethics theories, Chapter 7 codes of ethics, and Chapter 8 the decision process.

1 Why Ethics Matters in Journalism

Our society needs news professionals who do the right thing

Learning Goals

This chapter will help you understand:

- why ethics is vitally important in a journalist's everyday work;
- why responsible journalists adhere voluntarily to high standards of conduct;
- how journalists should make ethically sound decisions;
- how discussing the case studies in class is crucial to learning the decision-making process;
- how the digital era, in revolutionizing the way the news is gathered and delivered, has provoked a controversy over ethical standards; and
- why the public depends on ethical journalists more than ever.

Lovelle Svart, a 62-year-old woman with short, sandy hair, faced the video camera and calmly talked about dying. "This is my medication," she said, holding an orange bottle of clear liquid. "Everyone has told me … I look better than I did ten years ago, but inside, I hurt like nobody's business." On that afternoon of September 28, 2007, after she had danced the polka one last time and said her goodbyes to family and close friends, the contents of the orange bottle quietly killed her.[1]

Svart's death came three months after her doctor informed her she would die of lung cancer within six months. The former research librarian disclosed the grim prognosis to a reporter friend at *The Oregonian* in Portland, the newspaper where she had worked. She said she had decided to avail herself of Oregon's assisted-suicide law. Svart also said she wanted to talk to people frankly about death and dying, hoping she could help them come to grips with the subject themselves. Out of that conversation grew an extraordinary mutual decision: On its website and in print, *The Oregonian* would chronicle Lovelle Svart's final months on earth (Figure 1.1).

Figure 1.1
Lovelle Svart faces the camera during one of her "Living to the End" video diaries on *The Oregonian*'s website.
PHOTO BY ROB FINCH. REPRINTED BY PERMISSION OF *THE OREGONIAN*.

The Ethical Journalist: Making Responsible Decisions in the Digital Age, Second Edition. Gene Foreman.
© 2016 John Wiley & Sons, Inc. Published 2016 by John Wiley & Sons, Inc.

In her series of tasteful "video diaries," she talked about living with a fatal disease and about her dwindling reservoir of time. In response, hundreds of people messaged her on the website, addressing her as if they were old friends.

But before Svart taped her diaries, journalists at *The Oregonian* talked earnestly about what they were considering. Most of all, they asked themselves questions about ethics.

The threshold question was whether their actions might influence what Svart did. Would she feel free to change her mind? After all the attention, would she feel obligated to go ahead and take the lethal dose? On this topic, they were comforted by their relationship to this story subject. Familiarity was reassuring, although in the abstract they would have preferred to be reporting on someone who had never been involved with the paper. In 20 years of working with her, they knew Svart was strong-willed; nobody would tell her what to do. Even so, the journalists constantly reminded her that whatever she decided would be fine with them. Michael Arrieta-Walden, a project leader, personally sat down with her and made that clear. The story would be about death and dying, not about Svart's assisted suicide.

Would the video diaries make a statement in favor of the controversial state law? No, they decided. The debate was over; the law had been enacted and it had passed court tests. Irrespective of how they and members of the audience felt about assisted suicide, they would just be showing how the law actually worked – a journalistic purpose. They posted links to stories that they had done earlier reflecting different points of view about the law itself. Other links guided readers to organizations that supported people in time of grief.

In debates among themselves and in teleconferences with an ethicist, they raised countless other questions and tried to arrive at answers that met the test of their collective conscience. For example, a question that caused much soul-searching was what to do if Svart collapsed while they were alone with her. It was a fact that she had posted "do not resuscitate" signs in her bedroom and always carried a document stating her wishes. Still, this possibility made them very uncomfortable – they were journalists, not doctors. Finally they resolved that, if they were alone with her in her bedroom and she lost consciousness, they would pull the emergency cord and let medical personnel handle the situation. As Svart's health declined, they made another decision: They would not go alone with her outside the assisted-living center where she lived. From then on, if they accompanied her outside, there would also be another person along, someone who clearly had the duty of looking out for Svart's interests.[2]

The self-questioning in the *Oregonian* newsroom illustrates ethics awareness in contemporary **journalism**. "Twenty years ago, an ethical question might come up when someone walked into the editor's office at the last minute," said Sandra Rowe, then the editor of *The Oregonian*. "We've gone through a culture change. Now an ethical question comes up once or twice a week at our daily news meeting, where everyone can join the discussion. We are confident we can reach a sound decision if everyone has a say."[3]

The Incentives for Ethical Behavior

Most journalists see theirs as a noble profession serving the public interest. They *want* to behave ethically.

Why should journalists practice sound ethics? If you ask that question in a crowd of journalists, you would probably get as many answers as there are people in the room. But, while the answers may vary, their essence can be distilled into two broad categories. One, logically enough, is moral; the other could be called practical.

- *The moral incentive.* Journalists should be ethical because they, like most other human beings, want to see themselves as decent and honest. It is natural to crave self-esteem, not to mention the respect of others. There is a psychic reward in knowing that you have tried to do the right thing. As much as they like getting a good story, journalists don't want to be known for having exploited someone in the process.
- *The practical incentive.* In the long term, ethical journalism promotes the news organization's credibility and thus its acceptance by the public. This translates into commercial success. What journalists have to sell is the news – and if the public does not believe their reporting, they have nothing to sell. Consumers of the news are more likely to believe journalists' reporting if they see the journalists as ethical in the way they treat the public and the subjects of news coverage. Just as a wise consumer would choose a product with a respected brand name over a no-name alternative when seeking quality, journalists hope that consumers will choose their news organization because it behaves responsibly – because it can be *trusted*.

Why Ethics Standards Are Needed

There are also practical arguments for ethical behavior that flow from journalism's special role in American life.

The First Amendment guarantee of a free press means that, unlike other professionals, such as those in medicine and the law, journalists are not regulated by the state and are not subject to an enforceable ethics code. And that is a good thing, of course. The First Amendment insulates journalists from retribution from office holders who want to control the flow of information to the public and who often resent the way they are covered in the media. If a state board licensed journalists, it is a safe bet that some members of the board would abuse their power to rid themselves of journalists who offend them. The public would be the loser if journalists could be expelled from the profession by adversaries in government.

But there is a downside to press freedom: Anybody, no matter how unqualified or unscrupulous, can become a journalist. It is a tolerable downside, given the immense benefit of an independent news media, but bad journalists taint the reputation of everyone in the profession. Because they are not subject to legally enforceable standards, honest journalists have an individual obligation to adhere voluntarily to high standards of professional conduct. Ethical journalists do not use the Constitution's protection to be socially destructive.

Yet another argument for sound ethics is the dual nature of a news organization. Journalism serves the public by providing reliable information that people need to make governing decisions about their community, state, and nation. This is a news organization's quasi-civic function. But the news organization has another responsibility, too — and that is to make a profit. Like any other business, the newspaper, broadcast station, or digital news site must survive in the marketplace.

The seeming conflict of those two functions — serving the public, yet making money — is often regarded cynically. Decisions about news coverage tend to be portrayed by critics as calculated to sell newspapers, raise broadcast ratings, or draw Web traffic rather than to give the citizens the information they need. The truth is that good journalism is expensive, and the best news organizations invest significant sums in deeply reported projects that could never be justified in an accountant's profit-and-loss ledger. If there is a pragmatic return in such projects, it is in the hope that they build the organization's reputation as a source of reliable information.

Journalists cannot expect their work to be universally acclaimed. But they have an obligation to themselves and their colleagues to never deliberately conduct themselves in a way that would justify the criticism. They have an obligation to practice sound ethics.

The Growth of Ethics Codes

For reasons that are explored in Chapter 3, journalism matured in the second half of the twentieth century. During this period, it became common for individual news organizations to articulate their ethics standards in comprehensive codes, which can be useful guides in decision-making about the news. Today, not only professional organizations of journalists, but also individual newspapers, broadcast stations, and digital news sites typically have ethics codes.

There is a distinct difference in the effect of these two different kinds of codes. Although the codes of professional organizations fulfill an important purpose of establishing profession-wide standards, they are voluntary and cannot be enforced. But, when a newsroom adopts a code, violations can be enforced by suspension or dismissal of the violators. Of course, codes are valuable only to the extent that they are practiced, and newsroom leaders have a responsibility both to enforce their codes and to set an example of propriety.

Journalists new to the profession may be surprised to find that the rank-and-file reporters, editors, and photojournalists often are more effective than their bosses in enforcing the code. John Carroll, former editor of the *Los Angeles Times*, says that among journalists "certain beliefs are very deeply held," and that the core of these beliefs is a newspaper's duty to the reader. "Those who transgress against the reader will pay dearly," Carroll says, adding that this intensity usually is masked by a laid-back newsroom demeanor. "There's informality and humor, but beneath the surface lies something deadly serious. It is a code. Sometimes the code is not even written down, but it is deeply believed in."[4] See his Point of View essay, "A 'Tribal Ferocity' Enforces the Code," at the end of this chapter for more of John Carroll's thoughts on the subject.

The Goal: Make Ethically Sound Decisions

In this text and in the ethics course you are studying, you will continue your preparation for a journalism career by examining how good journalists make responsible decisions. The text will identify and discuss the principles of applied ethics that are a foundation for sound decision-making. As the course progresses, you will practice your decision-making skill in case studies. The goal is to encourage you to think critically and in concrete terms about the situation confronting you – to employ logic rather than respond reflexively.

You should know that there are capable, intelligent journalists who reject the idea that journalism ethics can be taught in a college course. They argue that journalists, and journalism students, either are honorable, or they are not. If they are honorable, this hypothesis continues, they will automatically make the right decision and so do not need this course. If they are not honorable, no college course is going to straighten them out. As an esteemed editor remarked to a college audience, "If your mom didn't teach you right from wrong, your college teacher is not going to be able to."

Although there is truth to that statement, it misses the point. The author of this textbook assumes that you *did* learn honesty and propriety in your early life. In fact, this course is intended to build on your own sense of right and wrong and to show how to apply that sense to solving ethics problems in the profession.

Journalism prizes essentially the same values as the rest of society – values like honesty and compassion – but sometimes journalists have conflicts in values that their fellow citizens do not. For example, your mom would instruct you to *always* go to the aid of someone in need. However, journalists might have to weigh intervention to help one person against their duty to inform the public about thousands of other people in the same sort of adversity. If they intervene, they destroy the story's authenticity – and they fail to inform the public.

Another flaw in the critics' argument is the presumption that honorable journalists will reflexively do the right thing. Your mom may not have taught you a decision-making procedure. As you will discover, "the right thing" is not always obvious. You will see that sound decision-making goes beyond instinct and carefully considers – in a process called critical thinking – the pros and cons of various courses of action.

Honing Decision Skills through Case Studies

The case-study method gives you a chance to work through difficult decisions in the classroom without consequences and without deadline pressure. The experience will prepare you for making on-the-spot ethical decisions in the real world. Each of the case studies selected for class discussion is intended to teach an important nuance about news media ethics.

In addition to explaining the principles of journalism ethics and teaching a decision-making process, this course in journalism ethics gives you two valuable opportunities:

- You can study the thinking of academics and experienced practitioners on recurring problems that journalists face. While you should always do your own critical thinking, you don't have to start with a blank slate. You can draw on the trial-and-error efforts of people who have gone before you in the profession. Their experiences can help you think clearly about the issues.
- You can practice your decision-making technique in a classroom setting where no one is hurt if a decision proves to be flawed. Just as a musician, an actor, or an athlete improves through practice, you benefit by thinking through the courses of action you might take in the case studies. You should emerge from the course with a deeper understanding of the challenges of the profession and with infinitely more confidence about your own decision-making.

You should also keep in mind that an applied-ethics course prepares you for a career in which you will be dealing with people who want to influence the way you report the news. Because journalists work for the public, it would be a betrayal of the public's trust to allow themselves to be diverted from the truth. The ethicist Bob Steele describes the manipulators:

> You will be stonewalled by powerful people who will deter you from getting to the truth. You will be manipulated by savvy sources who do their best to unduly influence your stories. You will be used by those with ulterior motives who demand the cover of confidentiality in exchange for their information. You will be swayed by seemingly well-intentioned people who want to show you some favor in hopes that you, in return, will show them favoritism in the way you tell their story.[5]

A cautionary note is in order. Although ethical considerations may occasionally cost you a story, being an aggressive reporter and being ethical are not mutually exclusive. Keep in mind that your job is to inform your **audience**, and that means being a good, resourceful reporter who gets the story into the paper, on the air, or on the Web.

Given the real-life problems you will study in this course, it could be easy to conclude that the ethical choice is simple: Decide *against* publishing, broadcasting, or posting any news story that is the least bit questionable. But such a choice would itself be unethical. It would signify a failure to fulfill the journalist's mission of informing the public.

The 21st-Century Debate over Ethics

As the new century arrived, the news industry entered a tumultuous period of transition as it reacted to a revolution in the technology of gathering and delivering the news.

Digital journalism is rapidly becoming the dominant news medium. And no wonder: The Web matches radio and television's speed; it can far exceed newspapers' depth of content; and it adds the unique dimension of an instantaneous conversation with the audience. With prose, video, still images, and audio available at the consumer's demand, the Web offers exciting opportunities. Not the least of these is the ability to involve the audience itself in reporting the news.

The statistics confirm the increasing popularity of digital as a source of news (Figure 1.2). In 2012 the Pew Research Center's biennial news consumption survey showed that 39 percent of respondents answered "online/mobile" to the question "Where did you get news yesterday?" That was more than the percentage who received news from radio (33) or newspapers (29) and second only to television (55). (The percentages add up to more than 100 because some respondents received news from multiple sources.)[6]

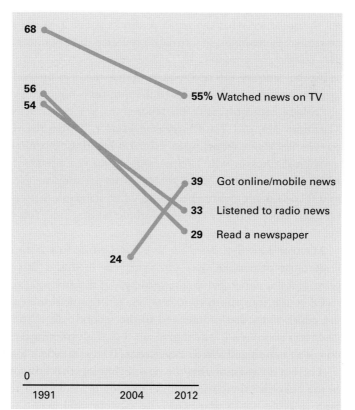

Figure 1.2
Digital surpasses print as source of news, 1991–2012. Survey respondents were asked, "Where did you get news yesterday?"
GRAPHIC COURTESY OF BILL MARSH. DATA REPRINTED BY PERMISSION OF THE PEW RESEARCH CENTER.

Unfortunately, online and mobile sites have been less successful in attracting advertising dollars. The revenue shortage threatens the credibility of digital news in two ways. First, websites have tended to skimp on staffing, which can translate into lapses in accuracy in covering the news, especially on a news-delivery medium based on speed. Second, the money crunch has led some business executives to experiment with revenue-producing ideas that blur the line between news and advertising.

Given the pervasive presence of the Internet and social media today, it is astonishing to realize that the digital era in journalism dates only to the mid-1990s. Students reading this textbook have literally grown up with digital journalism – along with texting, tweeting, and Facebook friending – and that is how their generation predominantly receives the news. But, in the context of 400 years of journalism history, the digital era is a blink of the eye.

Right now, in newsrooms across the country, the standards are being forged for digital journalism. Typically, the decision process is about a feverish rush to post a news story before someone else does, or about an expedient solution to a short-term, money-related problem such as a shortage of staff. Collectively, whether they realize it or not, the decision-makers are creating a template for the future of journalism.

At the same time, a controversy over ethical standards has exploded. In an environment in which so much has changed, we increasingly hear arguments that our professional principles must change as well. Some journalists propose that the neutral point of view should be replaced with news stories that both describe the event and tell the audience what the reporter thinks about it. Some say it would improve the news media's credibility if journalists revealed their opinions of the people and events they cover.

To the contrary, this textbook contends that it is precisely in a period of technological transition that we should adhere to time-honored principles.

"Ethical standards can't be tailored to a specific delivery medium," said Bill Marimow, editor of *The Philadelphia Inquirer*. "Doing the right thing can't be based on whether you're reporting in print, on broadcast or online."[7]

Michael Oreskes, who later became senior vice president and editorial director of NPR, observed early in the digital era that "pressures are great at times of change, and so it follows that times of change are when standards matter most." Having a website, Oreskes wrote, "doesn't change a simple editing rule: You shouldn't run something before you know it's true."[8]

Maureen Dowd of *The New York Times* wrote in a 2013 column emphasizing the importance of content over news-delivery medium: "It is not about pixels versus print. It is not about *how* you're reading – it is about *what* you're reading."[9]

Of course, journalism ethics evolves, as the profession demonstrated in formulating the ethics codes that proliferated in the second half of the twentieth century. That evolution continues in the digital age, but the evolutionary process should be based on collaboration and shared experience. It should reflect logic rather than reflex.

There is no question that the new technology has brought new ethical challenges. In the old order, there was nothing like social media, in which journalists participate both as professionals and as private citizens. Still, traditional ethical standards can guide us. For example, social media make it easier for journalists to gather facts and images from citizens who either possess specialized knowledge or have witnessed and possibly photographed breaking news. The time-honored standard of verification still applies to this content. As another example, an old standard – that journalists should not publicly reveal their opinions on controversial matters – applies to the journalists' personal Facebook pages, which are manifestly public.

As this new edition of *The Ethical Journalist* was being prepared, the orderly evolution of journalism ethics was continuing as three professional organizations engaged in a collegial discussion of the subject. The ethics committee of the Society of Professional Journalists was examining its 1996 code and formulating revisions that were adopted in 2014 (its new code appears in Chapter 7). The Online News Association was producing an analysis of about 40 topics as a smorgasbord from which journalists could choose to create do-it-yourself ethics codes. The Radio Television Digital News Association was revising the code it adopted in 2000 when "Digital" did not appear in its name.

Journalism rests on three principles: First, it is an *independent act* of gathering and disseminating information. Second, the practitioner *owes first loyalty to the citizens who consume the news*. Third, the practitioner *is dedicated to truth-seeking and a discipline of verification*.

In the view of this textbook's author, those broad principles define journalism.[10] The definition could serve as a job description for anybody who aspires to be a journalist, provided he or she is committed to meeting the high standards that the definition implies. Such a person could be a staff member of a mainstream print, broadcast, or online organization – or a citizen blogger or tweeter or anyone else who purports to report and comment on the news, even as a hobby.

This text's purpose is to identify and discuss the ethics standards that dedicated journalists live by. Those standards help journalists gain *the trust* of citizens who are seeking the reliable information they need to be self-governing in a democracy. Ethical journalists, regardless of whether they are a part of an established news organization or reporting on their own, must be *credible*.

A Different Role for Journalists

Today's news consumer can draw on a vast array of information sources. The day is long past when editors in a distant newsroom decided what information was worthy of passing along to the public, and what was not. "Journalists can no longer be information gatekeepers in a world in which gates on information no longer exist," Cecilia Friend and Jane B. Singer wrote in *Online Journalism Ethics*.[11] Twenty-first-century journalism requires a different interpretation of the gatekeeper role. A democratic society now depends on journalists to be its surrogates in sifting the huge volume of information available, testing it for accuracy, and helping citizens understand it. "**Gatekeeping** in this world is not about keeping an item out of circulation,"

Friend and Singer wrote. "[I]t is about vetting items for their veracity and placing them within the broader context that is easily lost under the daily tidal wave of 'new' information."[12]

In *The Elements of Journalism,* Bill Kovach and Tom Rosenstiel wrote that, in the new environment, a journalist must play the roles of Authenticator and Sense Maker. As Authenticator, the journalist works with audiences to sort through the different accounts of a news event and help them "know which of the facts they have encountered they should believe and which to discount." As Sense Maker, the journalist puts "events in context in a way that turns information into knowledge."[13]

Although the technology for delivering the news is changing radically, the public's need for reliable information is the same. Confronting a daily deluge of information, citizens will look for sources they can trust to be accurate and fair, to be independent, and to be loyal above all to the citizens themselves.

More than ever, they will depend on ethical journalists.

Point of View

A "Tribal Ferocity" Enforces the Code

John Carroll

One reason I was drawn to my chosen career is its informality, in contrast to the real professions. Unlike doctors, lawyers or even jockeys, journalists have no entrance exams, no licenses, no governing board to pass solemn judgment when they transgress. Indeed, it is the constitutional right of every citizen, no matter how ignorant or how depraved, to be a journalist. This wild liberty, this official laxity, is one of journalism's appeals.

I was always taken, too, by the kinds of people who practiced journalism. My father, Wallace Carroll, was editor and publisher of a regional newspaper, in Winston-Salem, North Carolina. The people he worked with seemed more vital and engaged than your normal run of adults. They talked animatedly about things

they were learning – things that were important, things that were absurd. They told hilarious jokes. I understood little about the work they did, except that it entailed typing, but I felt I'd like to hang around with such people when I grew up. Much later, after I'd been a journalist for years, I became aware of an utterance by Walter Lippmann that captured something I especially liked about life in the newsroom. "Journalism," he declared, "is the last refuge of the vaguely talented."

Here is something else I've come to realize: The looseness of the journalistic life, the seeming laxity of the newsroom, is an illusion. Yes, there's informality and humor, but beneath the surface lies something deadly serious. It is a code. Sometimes the code is not even written down, but it is deeply believed in. And, when violated, it is enforced with tribal ferocity.

Consider, for example, the recent events at *The New York Times*.

Before it was discovered that the young reporter Jayson Blair had fabricated several dozen stories, the news staff of *The Times* was already unhappy. Many members felt aggrieved at what they considered a high-handed style of editing. I know this because some were applying to me for jobs at the *Los Angeles Times*. But until Jayson Blair came along, the rumble of discontent remained just that, a low rumble.

When the staff learned that the paper had repeatedly misled its readers, the rumble became something more formidable: an insurrection. The aggrieved party was no longer merely the staff. It was the reader, and that meant the difference between a misdemeanor and a felony. Because the reader had been betrayed, the discontent acquired a moral force so great that it could only be answered by the dismissal of the ranking editors. The Blair scandal was a terrible event, but it also said something very positive about *The Times*, for it demonstrated beyond question the staff's commitment to the reader.

Several years ago, at the *Los Angeles Times*, we too had an insurrection. To outsiders the issue seemed arcane, but to the staff it was starkly obvious. The paper had published a fat edition of its Sunday magazine devoted to the opening of the city's new sports and entertainment arena, called the Staples Center. Unknown to its readers – and to the newsroom staff – the paper had formed a secret partnership with Staples. The agreement was as follows: The newspaper would publish a special edition of the Sunday magazine; the developer would help the newspaper sell ads in it; and the two would split the proceeds. Thus was the independence of the newspaper compromised – and the reader betrayed.

I was not working at the newspaper at the time, but I've heard many accounts of a confrontation in the cafeteria between the staff and the publisher. It was not a civil discussion among respectful colleagues. Several people who told me about it invoked the image of a lynch mob. The Staples episode, too, led to the departure of the newspaper's top brass.

What does all this say about newspaper ethics? It says that certain beliefs are very deeply held. It says that a newspaper's duty to the reader is at the core of those beliefs. And it says that those who transgress against the reader will pay dearly.

This essay is excerpted from the Ruhl Lecture on Ethics delivered at the University of Oregon, May 6, 2004. John Carroll was then the editor of the *Los Angeles Times*.

Notes

1   Svart video diary, *The Oregonian*, Sept. 28, 2007.
2   Author's telephone interviews with Michael Arrieta-Walden, Nov. 15 and Dec. 7, 2007.
3   Author's telephone interview with Sandra Rowe, Sept. 21, 2007.
4   John Carroll, Ruhl Lecture on Ethics, University of Oregon, May 6, 2004.
5   Bob Steele, "Why ethics matters," Poynter, 2002.
6   "In changing news landscape, even television is vulnerable," Pew Research Center, Sept. 27, 2012. The survey was conducted May 9–June 3, 2012, among 3,003 adults.
7   Bill Marimow, email exchange with the author, March 2013.

8   Michael Oreskes, "Navigating a minefield," *American Journalism Review*, Nov. 1999, 23.

9   Maureen Dowd, "As *Time* goes bye," *The New York Times*, Mar. 9, 2013.

10 In composing his definition of journalism, the author derived its components from Bill Kovach and Tom Rosenstiel, *The Elements of Journalism: What Newspeople Should Know and the Public*

Should Expect, 3rd edn. (New York: Three Rivers Press, 2014).

11 Cecilia Friend and Jane B. Singer, *Online Journalism Ethics: Traditions and Transitions* (Armonk, NY: M. E. Sharpe, 2007), 218.

12 Ibid., 218.

13 Kovach and Rosenstiel, *The Elements of Journalism*, 27.

2 Ethics, the Bedrock of a Society

An introduction to terms and concepts in an applied-ethics course

---

Learning Goals

This chapter will help you understand:

- the definition of ethics — discern what is right and wrong, then act on what is right;
- how ancient societies developed systems of ethics;
- how ethics and the law are similar, and how they differ;
- how a member of a society absorbs its ethical precepts;
- how a person's values shape the choices he or she makes; and
- the meaning of the term *ethical dilemma*; and how the ethical person makes decisions.

Virginia Gerst knows something about ethics. In May 2003, when she was arts and entertainment editor for the Pioneer Press chain of weeklies in the Chicago area, she ran a critical review of a restaurant. (The baby back ribs "tasted more fatty than meaty"; several other dishes were "rather run-of-the-mill.")

That displeased the restaurant owner, who was both a prospective advertiser and county president of the restaurant owners' association. To placate the restaurateur, the Pioneer Press publisher had an advertising executive write a second review – one that would be positive. Gerst was ordered to run it. Instead, she quit.

"I understand that these are tough times for newspapers," she wrote in her letter of resignation. "But economic concerns are not sufficient to make me sacrifice the integrity of a section I have worked for, cared about and worried over for two decades."[1]

John Cruickshank understands ethics, too. In the midst of a management upheaval in November 2003, this career journalist was thrust into the job of publisher of the *Chicago Sun-Times* (owned by the same company as the Pioneer Press weeklies). Months later, he discovered a breach of trust that astonished and angered him. Using accounting ruses that fooled even the agency responsible for auditing newspaper circulations, departed executives had been overstating the paper's circulation by up to 50,000 copies a day, or 11 percent. Cruickshank did not hesitate to go public with his discovery. This was not just a commendable display of candor; it was costly to a paper

The Ethical Journalist: Making Responsible Decisions in the Digital Age, Second Edition. Gene Foreman.
© 2016 John Wiley & Sons, Inc. Published 2016 by John Wiley & Sons, Inc.

already a distant second to the *Chicago Tribune*. The paper was acknowledging that its advertisers had not been getting the exposure they had paid for, and it eventually had to repay those advertisers millions of dollars.[2]

Defining Ethics: Action Is Required

Ethics is a set of moral principles, a code – often unwritten – that guides a person's conduct. But more than that, as Gerst and Cruickshank demonstrated, ethics requires action.

"There are two aspects to ethics," the ethicist Michael Josephson says. "The first involves the ability to discern right from wrong, good from evil, and propriety from impropriety. The second involves the commitment to do what is right, good, and proper." As a practical matter, Josephson says, "ethics is about how we meet the challenge of doing the right thing when that will cost more than we want to pay."[3] Or, in the words of Keith Woods, former dean of faculty of the Poynter Institute, "ethics is the pursuit of right when wrong is a strong possibility."[4]

Gerst and Cruickshank were practicing **applied ethics**, the branch of moral philosophy that deals with making decisions about concrete cases in a profession or occupation.[5] That is what this text is about. Your study of applied ethics in journalism is intended to help you solve the challenges you may face in your career. To do so, you need to draw on your own sense of right and wrong, enhanced by an understanding of ethical theory and a systematic way of making decisions. The idea is to put ethics into action.

Although some scholars see a fine distinction between *ethics* and *morals*, the terms are used interchangeably in this text. *The Cambridge Dictionary of Philosophy* defines *ethics* as "the philosophical study of morality" and says *ethics* "is commonly used interchangeably with *morality*" to mean the subject matter of such a philosophical study.[6]

The Origins of Ethical Theory

Tracing the origins of ethical thinking underscores the importance of ethics as a society's bedrock foundation. Ethical theory evolved in ancient societies as a basis for justice and the orderly functioning of the group, a purpose it still serves today.

The most familiar example is the Ten Commandments from the Judeo-Christian heritage, which sets forth the rules that would govern the Hebrews freed from Egyptian captivity in about 1500 BCE. Among other things, they were admonished not to kill, steal, or lie.

An earlier example is Babylonia's Code of Hammurabi. The laws promulgated by the ruler Hammurabi (1728–1646 BCE) directed that "the strong might not oppress the weak" and outlined a system of justice that meant "the straight thing." Hammurabi's justice centered on rules governing property and contracts. A surgeon who caused the blindness of a man of standing would have his hand cut off, but if he caused the blindness of a slave, he could set things right by paying the owner half the value of the slave.[7]

Ancient Greece gave the English language the word *ethics*, which is derived from the Greek *ethos*, meaning character. The citizens of Athens created the concept that an ethical reasoning system should be based on an individual's virtue and character, rather than rules. Because virtue was to be practiced as a lifelong habit, a Greek citizen would be honest simply because it would be unthinkable to be dishonest. The virtue philosophers of Athens – Socrates (469–399 BCE), Plato (427–347 BCE), and Aristotle (384–322 BCE) – believed that "the individual, in living a virtuous life, would form part of an overall virtuous community."[8]

Socrates, who made the famous declaration that "the unexamined life is not worth living," established a line of questioning intended to provoke thought. He "roamed Greece probing and challenging his brethren's ideas about such abstract concepts as justice and goodness," ethics scholar Louis A. Day wrote. "This Socratic method of inquiry, consisting of relentless questions and answers about the nature of moral conduct, has proved to be a durable commodity, continuing to touch off heated discussions about morality in barrooms and classrooms alike."[9]

Ethical thinking evolved in societies around the world. A common thread is found in how various cultures articulated what is best known as the Golden Rule. This rule defines the essence of being an ethical person, which is to consider the needs of others. Today we state it as "Do unto others as you would have them do unto you." The author Rushworth M. Kidder traced the "criterion of reversibility":

> This rule, familiar to students of the Bible, is often thought of as a narrowly Christian dictum. To be sure, it appears in the book of Matthew: "All things whatsoever ye would that men should do to you, do ye even so to them: for this is the law and the prophets." But Jews find it in the Talmud, which says, "That which you hold as detestable, do not do to your neighbor. That is the whole law: the rest is but commentary." Or, as it appears in the teachings of Islam, "None of you is a believer if he does not desire for his brother that which he desires for himself." … The label "golden" was applied by Confucius (551–479 BCE), who wrote: "Here certainly is the golden maxim: Do not do to others which we do not want them to do to us."[10]

The Relationship of Ethics and the Law

Some laws are based on ethical precepts, such as those forbidding murder and stealing, and civil lawsuits can be filed to require someone to live up to contractual promises. However, ethics and law emphatically are not the same. Law sets forth minimal standards of conduct. Law states what a person *is required* to do; ethics suggests what a person *ought* to do. An ethical person, as Michael Josephson says, "often chooses to do more than the law requires and less than it allows."[11] Potter Stewart, a former US Supreme Court justice, put it this way: "Ethics is knowing the difference between what you have a right to do and what is right to do."

Some laws of the past are universally regarded today as morally wrong. The Supreme Court, in *Dred Scott v. Sandford* (1857), upheld the principle of slavery and, in *Plessy v. Ferguson* (1896), the principle of racial segregation. Courageous leaders like Martin Luther King Jr. defied state segregation laws in the South in the civil rights movement of the 1950s and 1960s. Theirs were acts of *civil disobedience*, in which the person who disobeys is convinced of the laws' immorality, is nonviolent, and is willing to pay the price for disobedience.[12]

In the late 1940s trials of Germans accused of war crimes, the Nuremberg tribunals representing the victorious Allied powers established the principle that the crimes cannot be excused on the grounds that they are committed under orders of the state. An individual has the moral duty to reject blatantly criminal orders.

Transmitting a Society's Ethical Precepts

Through the centuries, societies have passed down ethical precepts from one generation to the next. Over time, through a process called **socialization**, the new generation absorbs the values of the community. Louis A. Day identified four main conduits for transmitting values, in this chronological sequence: family, peer groups, role models, and societal institutions.

Think about how each group influenced you as you grew up. You should be aware, too, that the process continues throughout adulthood.

Consider the influence of family. When parents urge toddlers to share with their siblings or friends, they get their first exposure to the idea of considering the needs of others. Not all lessons learned in the home are positive, of course. Day points out that a parent who writes a phony excuse to a teacher saying that "Johnny was sick yesterday" signals to the child that lying is permissible, even though the parent would never state such a thing.

Next are peer groups. As children grow older, the values instilled in the home are exposed, for good or ill, to the influence of friends in the neighborhood and in school. There is a powerful urge to "go with the crowd."

Then there are role models. They could be famous people, living or dead, such as athletes or musicians. Or they could be people one knows personally, such as teachers and ministers, or drug dealers. What these disparate individuals have in common is the fact that they occupy a prominent place in the minds of impressionable young people who want to emulate them.

The fourth source of influence is societal institutions. Through drama, television and the cinema transmit ethical standards — as well as standards that some would say are *not* ethical. When you graduate and go into the workforce, you will find that companies, too, are influential societal institutions. "Within each organization there is a moral culture, reflected both in written policies and the examples set by top management, that inspires the ethical behavior of the members," Day wrote.[13]

In the process of socialization, members of the new generation learn that benefits flow from living in a society in which people *generally* behave morally – they treat each other civilly, they keep promises, they help a person in distress, and so on. These are moral duties that the young learn to embrace. They also become aware that there are consequences for violating the group culture. These consequences, depending on the seriousness of the violation, range from being snubbed to being criminally prosecuted.

Though they still have moral duties that other humans have, people in certain occupations are permitted to function by different standards in some respects. The rights of the individual prevail over the needs of the community in conversations between lawyer and client, doctor and patient, minister and parishioner. In making the exceptions, society recognizes that those conversations need to be extremely candid. Indeed, through "shield laws" adopted in nearly every state, journalists are given similar protection to keep secret their conversations with confidential sources. This protection, however, is far from absolute, and it does not exist in federal law.

How Values Determine a Person's Choices

A person's **values** shape how he or she will react when confronted with a choice. Josephson defines values as "core beliefs or desires that guide or motivate attitudes and actions."[14] Our values, Josephson has written, "are what we prize and our value system is the order in which we prize them. Because it ranks our likes and dislikes, our value system determines how we will behave in certain situations. … The values we consistently rank higher than others are our core values, which define character and personality."[15] These values may or may not be ethical values.

Ethical values directly relate to beliefs about what is right and proper: honesty, promise-keeping, fairness, compassion, respect for the privacy of others. **Nonethical values** relate not to moral duty but to desire: wealth, status, happiness. Josephson labels them *non*ethical (not *un*ethical) because they are ethically neutral. Pursuing nonethical values is not morally wrong so long as ethical values are not violated in the process.[16] Nonethical values that a journalist might hold include selling more newspapers, raising broadcast ratings, or increasing a website's traffic count – values achieved mainly by getting interesting stories ahead of the competition. Those are worthy values, but the crucial question is how they are achieved.

The controversy over abortion, the most divisive domestic issue in the United States, is illustrative here because it reflects the core values of people on both sides. To the abortion opponent, the core value is the sanctity of life, and that person believes life begins at conception. To the abortion-rights advocate, the core value is the autonomy of the individual, and that person believes the state has no right to tell a woman what she must do with her body.

The Ethical Dilemma: A Conflict in Ethical Values

Inevitably, a person faces a situation in which his or her ethical values conflict. The result is an **ethical dilemma**. The person confronted with the dilemma has to weigh the conflicting ethical values and choose one over the other.

A classic hypothetical story devised by the ethics scholar Lawrence Kohlberg illustrates the ethical dilemma: Heinz's wife is dying from cancer. A druggist has a life-saving drug but wants $2,000 for it. Heinz, who has only $1,000, pleads with the druggist to sell it for that amount. When the druggist refuses, Heinz has to decide between ethical values – honesty (not stealing the drug) or compassion (not letting his wife die). Choosing one ethical value means that he must violate the other. In Kohlberg's story, Heinz breaks into the store and steals the drug. Kohlberg asks: "Should the husband have done that? Was it right or wrong? … If you think it is morally right to steal the drug, you must face the fact that it is legally wrong."[17]

The ethical dilemma, pitting one ethical value against another, is distinguished from what Josephson calls a **false ethical dilemma**. In such equations only one side has an ethical value. On the other side is a nonethical value. The clear choice for the ethical person is to reject the nonethical value and act on the ethical value, to "choose ethics over expediency."[18]

This is not to say that such choices are easy. To the contrary, these choices often result in self-sacrifice. In journalism, for example, a reporter might have to give up doing a story that will raise broadcast ratings (a nonethical value) if it requires invading someone's privacy (an ethical value). This underscores the point made at the beginning of this chapter – that doing the right thing requires action, and it often entails a heavy cost.

When Virginia Gerst quit her job over a principle and John Cruickshank acknowledged to advertisers that they had been short-changed, they were making sacrifices in order to the right thing. To do nothing, to go along, might have been an easier choice – but it would have been wrong. Gerst and Cruickshank were confronted not with an ethical dilemma (which Rushworth Kidder labels a right-versus-right choice) but with a false ethical dilemma (right versus wrong). This observation takes nothing away from the courage of either Gerst or Cruickshank.

How the Ethical Person Makes Decisions

The person who makes a decision in a given situation is called the **moral agent**. To be an effective moral agent, you can't decide on a whim. Clear thinking is needed. Ultimately, your decision must be one that you can defend as having been rationally chosen by a caring individual.

Josephson described the complexity of the process:

Most decisions have to be made in the context of economic, professional and social pressures which can sometimes challenge our ethical goals and conceal or confuse the moral issues. In addition, making ethical choices is complex because in many situations there are a multitude of competing interests and values. Other times, crucial facts are unknown or ambiguous. Since many actions are likely to benefit some people at the expense of others, the decision maker must prioritize competing moral claims and must be proficient at predicting the likely consequences of various choices.[19]

With practice, you will be more confident and consistent in your decision-making. This does not mean that you will not make mistakes. Everyone does.

"We need to acknowledge the mistakes, figure out how and why mistakes are made, and then try to do better," ethics scholars Deni Elliott and Paul Martin Lester have written. In their view, professionals who take ethics seriously will "stay conscious of the power that they have and the responsibility that they have to use that power judiciously." They will treat people fairly, with respect and compassion; they will keep an open mind to alternatives.[20]

Elliott and Lester suggested a final check. If you think you have made your decision in a rational way, would you be willing to allow your decision process to be published on the front page or run in the first news segment on television?[21] If you wince at that prospect, you ought to think again.

Notes

1 Michael Miner, "Pioneer Press aims at foot, fires," *Chicago Reader*, Sept. 5, 2003, and "Yes, Virginia, some people still care about ethics," *Chicago Reader*, May 7, 2004.

2 Eric Herman, "Paper sales inflated up to 50,000 a day," *Chicago Sun-Times*, Oct. 6, 2004, and Jacques Steinberg, "Sun-Times managers said to defraud advertisers," *The New York Times*, Oct. 6, 2004.

3 Michael Josephson, "Definitions in ethics," unpublished paper (2001). (*The paper is available in the Student Resources section of the website.*)

4 Keith Woods, Oweida Lecture in Journalism Ethics, Pennsylvania State University, Apr. 11, 2006.

5 Louis A. Day, *Ethics in Media Communications: Cases and Controversies*, 5th edn. (Belmont, CA: Thomson Wadsworth, 2006), 5.

6 Robert Audi (ed.), *The Cambridge Dictionary of Philosophy* (Cambridge: Cambridge University Press, 1999), 284.

7 Gerald A. LaRue, "Ancient ethics," in Peter Singer (ed.), *A Companion to Ethics* (Oxford: Blackwell, 1991), 32.

8 Elaine E. Englehardt and Ralph D. Barney, *Media and Ethics: Principles for Moral Decisions* (Belmont, CA: Thomson Wadsworth, 2002), 25.

9 Day, *Ethics in Media Communications*, 3.

10 Rushworth M. Kidder, *How Good People Make Tough Choices: Resolving the Dilemmas of Ethical Living* (New York: HarperCollins, 1995), 159.

11 Michael Josephson, *Making Ethical Decisions* (Los Angeles: Josephson Institute, 2002), 5.

12 This definition of civil disobedience appears in Day, *Ethics in Media Communications*, 34.

13 Ibid., 15–16.

14 Josephson, "Definitions in ethics."

15 Josephson, *Making Ethical Decisions*, 4.

16 Michael Josephson, *Becoming an Exemplary Police Officer* (Los Angeles: Josephson Institute, 2007), 21.

Although the book was written for police officers, it offers Josephson's thinking on ethics in a general sense. (*The paper is available in the Student Resources section of the website.*)

17   Lawrence Kohlberg, *Essays in Moral Development*, vol. 1, *The Philosophy of Moral Development: Moral Stages and the Idea of Justice* (New York: Harper & Row, 1981), 12.

18   Michael Josephson, *Ethical Issues and Opportunities in Journalism* (Marina del Rey, CA: Josephson Institute, 1991), 26.

19   Michael Josephson, unpublished paper on ethical decision-making (2001).

20   Deni Elliott and Paul Martin Lester, "Taking ethics seriously: to err is human," *News Photographer*, May 2004.

21   Ibid.

3 The News Media's Role in Society

The profession has matured and accepted social responsibility

---

Learning Goals

This chapter will help you understand:

- journalism's purpose and its guiding principles;
- the meaning of the term *social responsibility*;
- how journalism was practiced in an earlier era;
- how the Hutchins Commission defined social responsibility for journalism;
- the ethical awakening that occurred in the decade beginning in the mid-1970s;
- the reasons for this period of reform; and
- how today's practice of journalism reflects decades of rising professionalism.

In the horror of September 11, 2001, many journalists risked their lives to do their jobs. Through the day, television, radio, and Internet news sites reassured Americans by providing reliable information about the stunning events at the World Trade Center, the Pentagon, and a field in Shanksville, Pennsylvania. Wire services sent bulletin after bulletin around the world. The next day, newspapers added context and analysis. Newsmagazines published special editions. "In those early defining moments of mid-September, the nation's news media conducted themselves with the courage, honesty, grace, and dedication a free society deserves," Gloria Cooper wrote in *Columbia Journalism Review*.[1]

There were casualties. A photojournalist and six television transmission engineers were killed at the World Trade Center.

"On this day of unimaginable fear and terror, journalists acted on instinct," Cathy Trost and Alicia C. Shepard wrote in a 2002 oral history that documents the heroism: "They commandeered taxis, hitched rides with strangers, rode bikes, walked miles, even sprinted to crash sites." Appropriately, the book's title is *Running toward Danger*.

It wasn't competition that motivated these men and women – cable and broadcast networks, for example, shared video that day. It wasn't profit – the networks aired no commercials for 93 hours, and all news organizations broke their budgets to cover the

---

The Ethical Journalist: Making Responsible Decisions in the Digital Age, Second Edition. Gene Foreman.
© 2016 John Wiley & Sons, Inc. Published 2016 by John Wiley & Sons, Inc.

story. As Trost and Shepard concluded, it could only be instinct that drove these journalists, an ingrained conviction that their profession is a high calling to public service.[2]

In *The Elements of Journalism*, Bill Kovach and Tom Rosenstiel wrote about a craving for news that humans have had throughout history. They call it "the Awareness Instinct" – people's need "to be aware of events beyond their direct experience." Knowledge of the unknown, the authors wrote, gives people a sense of security.[3] Contemporary society needs reliable information to satisfy the Awareness Instinct, and it was especially in demand on September 11.

Journalism's Purpose and Guiding Principles

In 1997 Kovach and Rosenstiel began two years of interviews, forums, and surveys intended to define journalism's purpose. There were clues in the ethics codes adopted by national journalism organizations. Those codes asserted that journalists serve the public and that they are dedicated to truth and fairness.

Beyond writing the codes, journalists had not spent much time analyzing what their guiding principles were. For one thing, they thought it was evident that they worked in the public interest and that the news they published or broadcast defined their standards. For another, their lawyers had cautioned against putting these standards in writing, lest they be used against them in court. And, finally, meeting the deadlines for today's newscast or tomorrow's newspaper always seemed to take priority over the intellectual exercise of writing down their professional beliefs.

However, as Kovach and Rosenstiel's research proceeded, it became clear that certain beliefs were widely and strongly held. These beliefs guided the authors to a definition of journalism's primary purpose: "to provide citizens with the information they need to be free and self-governing." They elaborated in *The Elements of Journalism*: "The news media help us define our communities, and help us create a common language and common knowledge rooted in reality. Journalism also helps identify a community's goals, heroes and villains."[4]

An affirming statement of journalism's purpose was crafted by Leonard Downie Jr., editor of *The Washington Post*, and Robert G. Kaiser, *The Post*'s managing editor, in their 2002 book *The News about the News*. Downie and Kaiser wrote:

> Citizens cannot function together as a community unless they share a common body of information about their surroundings, their neighbors, their governing bodies, their sports teams, even their weather. Those are all the stuff of news. The best journalism digs into it, makes sense of it, and makes it accessible to everyone.[5]

Kovach and Rosenstiel identified the key principles – which they called the "elements" – of journalism. Six of those are listed here:

- *Journalism's first obligation is to the truth.* Although **truth** is difficult to define, there was unanimity among journalists that the first step is "getting the facts right."

Kovach and Rosenstiel concluded that "the disinterested pursuit of truth" is what distinguishes journalism from other forms of communication, like propaganda and entertainment.[6]

- *Journalism's first loyalty is to citizens.* The authors described "an implied covenant with the public" that the work is honest. The covenant, they wrote, "tells the audience that the movie reviews are straight, that the restaurant reviews are not influenced by who buys an ad, that the coverage is not self-interested or slanted for friends." This first allegiance to the readers, viewers, and listeners is the basis for journalistic **independence**. Journalists are most valuable to their employers if they put their duty to the audience ahead of the employer's short-term financial interests.[7]
- *Journalism's essence is a discipline of verification.* This principle is the basis of techniques that reporters and editors rely on to get the facts right, such as "seeking multiple witnesses to an event, disclosing as much as possible about sources, and asking many sides for comment."[8]
- *Journalists must maintain an independence from those they cover.* Journalists are observers, not players. For their reporting to be trusted, reporters have to be detached from the people and events they cover. They also have to be sure there is not an *appearance* of a relationship that would conflict with their journalistic duties.[9]
- *Journalists must serve as an independent monitor of power.* News media have a watchdog role, "watching over the powerful few in society on behalf of the many to guard against tyranny." Essentially, journalism is a court of last resort when the systems of government and business break down. Kovach and Rosenstiel also note that the media should report when powerful institutions are working effectively, as well as when they are not.[10]
- *Journalists must provide a forum for public criticism and compromise.* The news media have an obligation to amplify the community conversation, allowing citizens a voice in letters to the editor, op-ed essays, radio and television talk shows, and comments on news websites. The authors caution that the journalist has to be "an honest broker and referee" who insists that the debate is based on facts, because "a forum without facts fails to inform and a debate steeped in prejudice and supposition only inflames."[11]

Defining the Term *Social Responsibility*

For more than a century before *The Elements of Journalism* articulated them, journalism standards had been steadily improving. Underlying this trend was the news media's growing acceptance of **social responsibility** – a concept that, in its application to commerce, imposes on business enterprises a moral duty to make their communities better. This is a duty that goes beyond merely obeying laws. Although social responsibility is not discussed here as a religious matter, a principle in Judaism known as *tikkun olam* seems to define it. *Tikkun olam* (pronounced tee-KOON oh-LUHM) is Hebrew for "repairing the world" – an obligation to fix the problems of society, including violence, disease, poverty, and injustice.[12]

In the world of commerce, a company's acts of social responsibility might involve contributing money and executive time to charities, hiring the disabled, or going beyond legal requirements to prevent pollution. A classic business example is the straightforward way in which Johnson & Johnson responded to the Tylenol tragedy of 1982. Someone tampered with containers of Tylenol on store shelves in Chicago, inserting cyanide that eventually killed seven people. Through the news media, the company immediately warned the public not to buy or use Tylenol until the source of the contamination had been found. Next, Johnson & Johnson recalled every container of the pain reliever. The company did not put the product back on the market until its containers had been made tamper-proof. A lesser corporate response might have doomed the popular pain reliever, but Tylenol's sales quickly rebounded.[13]

In journalism, Adolph Ochs embraced the idea of social responsibility when he bought *The New York Times* in 1896 and immediately published a pledge "to give the news impartially, without fear or favor, regardless of party, sect or interests involved."[14] Eugene Meyer, who bought *The Washington Post* in 1933, similarly adopted a business plan based on journalistic independence: "In pursuit of the truth, the newspaper shall be prepared to make sacrifices of its material fortunes, if such a course be necessary for public good."[15]

One impetus for social responsibility in the news media was commerce. America's first newspapers were political organs, but in the 1830s that was changing, "stimulated by industrial growth, the development of larger cities, and technological innovations including steam-driven printing presses." Publishers and editors began aiming at a mass market, one in which it made economic sense to report the news neutrally instead of from a party perspective.[16] By the 1880s, the concept of neutral reporting was well established.

By the first half of the twentieth century, journalists' aspirations for professionalism were growing. Better-educated people were joining the workforce, and the world's first journalism school was launched in 1908 at the University of Missouri.[17] Newly formed organizations of journalists quickly adopted codes expressing their responsibility to report the truth and to be fair. The first of these codes was the Canons of Journalism ratified by the new American Society of Newspaper Editors in 1923.[18]

The Journalism of an Earlier Era

In spite of these signs of growing awareness of press responsibility, the historical record shows examples of journalism practiced through the mid-twentieth century that would horrify today's practitioners and news consumers alike.

Fabrication was not uncommon. In an article in *Columbia Journalism Review* in 1984, Cassandra Tate described one telling episode. *The New York World* established a Bureau of Accuracy and Fair Play in 1913, and the bureau's director noticed a peculiar pattern in the newspaper's reporting on shipwrecks: Each story mentioned a cat that had survived. When the director asked the reporter, he was told:

> One of those wrecked ships had a cat, and the crew went back to save it. I made the cat a feature of my story, while the other reporters failed to mention the cat, and were called down by their city editors for being beaten. The next time there was a shipwreck, there was no cat, but the other ship news reporters did not wish to take a chance, and put the cat in. I wrote the report, leaving out the cat, and then I was severely chided for being beaten. Now when there is a shipwreck all of us always put in the cat.[19]

Some news photography similarly was suspicious. In his final column for *The Wall Street Journal*, which he had served as managing editor, Paul E. Steiger reminisced about a photographer colleague at a California paper who carried "a well-preserved but very dead bird" in his car trunk:

> The bird, he explained, was for feature shots on holidays like Memorial Day. He'd perch it on a gravestone or tree limb in a veterans' cemetery to get the right mood. Nowadays such a trick would get him fired, but in the 1950s, this guy said, there was no time to wait for a live bird to flutter into the frame.[20]

Impersonation was an accepted reporting technique in some places. As an 18-year-old rookie police reporter in Chicago, Jack Fuller followed the lead of his elders and told a crime victim on the phone that he was a police officer. His ruse was exposed when the victim called back with a few additional details – on the police desk sergeant's line. A few years later, when Fuller returned to Chicago journalism after school and military service, he stopped misrepresenting himself. He explained in his book *News Values*: "Times simply had changed, and so had I." The reformed impersonator went on to win a Pulitzer Prize and become editor of the *Chicago Tribune*.[21]

Racism permeated the news and editorial columns of newspapers. In 1921 in Tulsa, Oklahoma, a black teenager was accused of assaulting a white female elevator operator. *The Tulsa Tribune* published a news story headlined "Nab Negro for attacking girl in elevator," and an editorial headlined "To lynch a Negro tonight." The inflammatory notices set off a chain of events that led to a week of terror and violence in which up to 300 people were killed. More than 10,000 residents were left homeless when a mob of whites burned nearly the entire black residential district of 35 square blocks.[22]

Reporters did not always distance themselves from the people and agencies they covered. An extraordinary conflict of interest was described by Robert J. Lifton and Greg Mitchell in their 1995 book *Hiroshima in America: Fifty Years of Denial*. The authors wrote that William L. Laurence of *The New York Times* was on the payroll of the Pentagon in 1945, having been hired at a secret meeting at *The Times'* offices.

Laurence wrote many of the government press releases that followed the August 6, 1945, bombing of Hiroshima. For *The Times*, Laurence wrote a news story casting doubt on Japanese descriptions of radiation poisoning. However, the authors said, he had witnessed the July 16, 1945, atomic test in New Mexico and was aware of radioactive fallout that poisoned residents and livestock in the desert.[23] Laurence was awarded the Pulitzer Prize in 1946 "for his eye-witness account of the atom-bombing of Nagasaki and his subsequent ten articles on the development, production, and significance of the atomic bomb."[24]

The Hutchins Commission Defines Journalistic Duty

Ironically, social responsibility in journalism was defined most persuasively not by journalists but by a panel of intellectuals. Robert Maynard Hutchins, chancellor of the University of Chicago, was asked in 1942 by Henry Luce, publisher of *Time* magazine, to "find out about freedom of the press and what my obligations are." Luce put up $200,000 (about $2.9 million in 2014 currency). Hutchins assembled a dozen men from universities, government, and finance to join him on what was formally titled the Commission on Freedom of the Press but was to become better known as the Hutchins Commission.

In 1947 the commission issued its conclusions. The report was an indictment of journalism as it was practiced in that era. As the commission saw it, the press was neglecting its social responsibility – reporting accurately on news important to society – and choosing instead to focus on sensational stories designed to attract readers rather than inform them. The report warned that if the press did not reform, it could face government intervention.[25]

In the passage that was to have the most enduring influence on journalism, the commission declared that the press has the responsibility of providing "the current intelligence needed by a free society." It then identified five things that American society needed from the press:[26]

1 *A truthful, comprehensive, and intelligent account of the day's events in a context that gives them meaning.* The commission was saying that being accurate is essential but not enough. The commission then made a statement that journalists and the public recognize today as an important duty of the news media, and that is to distinguish between fact and opinion: "There is not fact without a context and no factual report which is uncolored by the opinions of the reporter."

2 *A forum for the exchange of comment and criticism.* "The great agencies of mass communication," the commission said, "should regard themselves as common carriers of public discussion." They should publish "significant ideas contrary to their own," using such devices as letters to the editor (or columnists offering a wide range of commentary, which would become a standard practice). The commission, which lamented that some ideas could be stifled because their authors had

no access to newspaper printing presses, presumably would be gratified today by the ease with which ideas are spread on the Internet.

3   *The projection of a representative picture of the constituent groups in society.* The commission denounced stereotypes and "hate words." It observed that, "when the images [the media] portray fail to present the social group truly, they tend to subvert judgment." The commission thus prodded the era's news media, composed almost entirely of white males, to cover the entire community. The admonition was not taken seriously until the 1950s and 1960s, when the civil rights movement awakened the media to the need to broaden their news coverage.

4   *The presentation and clarification of the goals and values of society.* The media "must assume a responsibility like that of educators in stating and clarifying the ideals toward which the community should strive." Sketching an agenda for the community has become a function that editorial pages and television panel discussions typically perform.

5   *Full access to the day's intelligence.* The commission urged "the wide distribution of news and opinion" so that citizens could choose what they wanted to use. In the decades that followed, news outlets broadened the definition of "full access." As surrogates for the citizens, they campaigned for legislation and court orders to compel governments to open meetings and records. They took the position that citizens should know how their business was being transacted.

The press didn't like the Hutchins Commission's report. Critics pointed to the fact that not a single journalist was on the commission. Columnist George Sokolsky said that having this commission critique the press was like having "a jury of saloonkeepers" assess the quality of education.[27] Luce himself was unimpressed, saying the report suffered from a "most appalling lack of even high school logic."[28]

Journalists also recoiled at the commission's suggestion that citizen panels should be set up to monitor their performance. They didn't like the idea of outsiders judging their work, and warned that voluntary commissions could lead to regulatory agencies with legal powers. It was not until 1973 that a National News Council was established to investigate complaints against the news media. It died a decade later, having failed to gain the support of either the public or the industry.[29]

An Ethical Awakening in the Profession

Press criticism did not begin or end with the Hutchins Commission, as George Seldes, I. F. Stone, and others were publishing press critiques in the decades before and after the commission made its study. Over the years, however, the Hutchins report was debated in journalism schools. The commission's findings were elaborated on by scholars, notably in the 1956 book *Four Theories of the Press* by Frederick S. Siebert, Theodore Peterson, and Wilbur Schramm.[30]

In time, the commission's definition of journalism's social responsibility made an impression on journalists, even though they rarely acknowledged the source. This was borne out at the end of the century when Kovach and Rosenstiel grilled journalists on what they stood for. Reading the purpose of journalism and the principles of journalism defined in *The Elements of Journalism*, one cannot miss the influence of the Hutchins Commission.

Somehow, journalists absorbed the ideas of Hutchins' intellectuals and made them their own. These ideas found their way into the codes of ethics adopted by organizations of journalists. New, stronger codes were adopted in 1966 by the Radio Television News Directors Association, in 1973 by the Society of Professional Journalists, in 1974 by the Associated Press Managing Editors, and in 1975 by the American Society of Newspaper Editors. The Hutchins influence can also be seen in the revised code adopted in 2014 by the Society of Professional Journalists, and discussed in detail in Chapter 7.

In an activist decade between the mid-1970s and the mid-1980s, many newspapers and broadcast stations formulated their own codes. The growth of newsroom codes during this period is documented by two surveys. An inquiry in 1974 by the Associated Press Managing Editors (APME) found that fewer than one in ten newspapers had ethics codes. Nine years later, journalism professor Ralph Izard of Ohio University found that three out of four newspapers and broadcast stations had written policies on newsroom standards and practices.[31]

These newsroom codes aimed at improving credibility by eliminating conflicts of interest. Broadly defined, a **conflict of interest** is anything that could divert a journalist – or a news outlet – from performing the mission of providing reliable, unbiased information to the public. Journalists can be conflicted by accepting gifts from the people being covered, by their personal political or civic interests, or by part-time jobs that create divided loyalties. News outlets are conflicted if they allow their commercial interests to interfere with gathering the news, such as killing a story under pressure from an advertiser. To their credit, many have resisted this pressure and done their journalistic duty even at a cost of millions of dollars in withheld advertising.

Initially, ethics reform centered on the practice of accepting gifts. As the 1970s began, one might see cases of liquor being carted into the newsroom just before Christmas. If a reporter needed to buy a car, the automobile manufacturer would be pleased to provide a discount. A press pass entitled the bearer and his (nearly everybody in the newsroom was male) family to so-called freebies – free admittance to ball games, circuses, and amusement parks, and gifts of all kinds from business executives and politicians.

Typically, the journalists protested that they wouldn't slant news coverage to get a bottle of free liquor. This rationalization "underestimates the subtle ways in which gratitude, friendship, and the anticipation of future favors affect judgment," the ethicist Michael Josephson wrote in his book *Making Ethical Decisions*: "Does the person providing you with the benefit believe that it will in no way affect your judgment? Would the person still provide the benefit if you were in no position to help?"[32]

At the time, an argument for accepting freebies was that it was a way of supplementing salaries, which were notoriously low in most places. In fact, when the *Madison* (Wisconsin) *Capital Times* in 1974 promulgated an ethics code forbidding staff members from accepting gifts and discounts, the journalists' union complained that the paper had committed an unfair labor practice. After hearing testimony in the case, a National Labor Relations Board judge ruled in 1975 in favor of the union. The judge said the paper could not unilaterally impose an ethics code on its employees but must instead bargain with the union. Fifteen months later, the hearing judge was overruled by the NLRB. The board held that newspapers do not have to bargain with unions over whether employees may accept gifts from news sources, but any discipline for violating an ethics code would have to be bargained.[33]

Initially, many ranking editors and news directors were unconvinced that freebies were a problem. A 1972 study by APME found that two out of three managing editors themselves would accept an expenses-paid overseas trip if offered. Almost half of the editors permitted their sports writers to serve in jobs as official scorers or announcers at professional sports events, jobs in which they were paid by the teams they covered.[34] The late Paul Poorman, managing editor of *The Detroit News*, ordered his staff in 1973 to stop accepting gifts, but he was not encouraged that reform would occur. He lamented, "The whole issue is greeted with tightly controlled apathy on the part of many newspapermen."[35]

A decade later, newsroom attitudes had changed drastically, and any journalist who valued the respect of colleagues would turn down freebies. The conflict-of-interest standards were not just about freebies. The codes also warned journalists not to take secondary jobs with competitors or businesses they might cover, not to engage in political activity other than voting, and not to state publicly their opinions on controversial issues in the news.

Some of those standards met resistance. In 1985 two Detroit journalists acknowledged in a *Columbia Journalism Review* article that a ban on gifts was "noncontroversial" but argued that the codes went too far when they kept staff members from exercising "their rights as citizens." They wrote that a journalist should be allowed to participate in civic activities, including being a candidate for an office the journalist is not assigned to cover. They warned: "The danger is that news organizations, in their zeal to demonstrate their purity, will reach too far into the personal lives of their employees by regulating outside activities that pose no real conflict."[36]

Today, journalists are more accepting of the premise that the public always sees them in their professional role, whether they are on or off duty. This text discusses conflicts of interest for individual journalists in Chapter 10 and for news outlets in Chapter 11.

In many newsrooms, there was a second wave of code-writing in the 1980s. Spelling out rules on conflicts of interest had addressed the most glaring ethical abuses. Now, journalists decided that it was even more important to define best practices for covering the news.

The process of staff committees used in formulating the conflict-of-interest guidelines was put to work on news policies. This made media lawyers uncomfortable.

They feared that if the policies were subpoenaed by the attorney for someone suing for libel, they could be used to show that a news organization was negligent by its own standard. Ultimately, many lawyers worked with newsrooms to forge a compromise. Mainly, this was achieved by hedging the codes' language: "shall" became "should," and "always" became "in most cases." Also, the codes made clear that their provisions were guidelines, not absolute rules, and that sometimes the circumstances would dictate a course of action different from that stated in the guidelines.

In Part II of this book, you can consider some of the thinking of journalism practitioners and scholars that evolved over the decades to deal with recurring ethical issues in news coverage. These topics include:

- Achieving fairness and accuracy in gathering the news (Chapter 12).
- Striking the right balance in how reporters deal with their sources (Chapter 13).
- Deciding between an individual's entitlement to privacy and the public's entitlement to information it needs (Chapter 14).
- Deciding when it is appropriate to print or broadcast content that is likely to offend the audience (Chapter 15).
- Deciding when, if ever, deception in reporting is justified (Chapter 16).

What Prompted the Ethical Awareness?

The code-writing in the 1970s and 1980s was a manifestation of greater ethical awareness in the newsroom, a maturing of the profession. Why did the phenomenon occur when it did? These are some likely reasons:

- *Embarrassment.* Scandals were rocking the industry, the most noteworthy being the Janet Cooke case at *The Washington Post. The Post* had to give back a Pulitzer Prize in 1981 after Cooke, under intense questioning, admitted that she had made up her prize-winning story of an eight-year-old heroin addict named in the paper only as Jimmy. Roy Peter Clark of the Poynter Institute calls this episode "the alpha event in the history of media ethics." The Cooke scandal, Clark has written, "did not invent the field of media ethics, but it certainly fertilized it. Articles, seminars, programs, journals sprang up everywhere."[37]
- *A new generation of journalists.* As older journalists retired, the traditions of their era faded. The new generation, better educated and more idealistic, had come into the profession in the decades after the Hutchins Commission defined social responsibility. The drive for professionalism came not just from newsroom leaders but also from the rank-and-file newsroom staff.
- *The nature of the news.* Journalists were covering government and society's institutions more critically than ever, and they were reporting on officials who lied to the public. The Vietnam War and Watergate were prime examples. If you are going

to point out transgressions by people in public life, it follows that you need to get your own house in order.

- *More scrutiny.* The media watchdogs were themselves being increasingly watched. Back then, the scrutiny came from *Columbia Journalism Review, Washington Journalism Review* (later renamed *American Journalism Review,* which shifted to online only in fall 2013), alternative weeklies, and a handful of mainstream media critics. In more recent times, this function has also become the province of all manner of critics who have the capacity through the Internet to call the media to account.

- *Chain ownership.* The shift from local ownership of newspapers and broadcast stations was not without its negative effects, but many papers and stations improved under chain ownership. The new corporate owners tended to be attuned to industry trends, including ethics awareness, unlike some local owners who had often been isolated and arbitrary. Under a local owner, the *Lexington* (Kentucky) *Herald* and its sister *Lexington Leader* ignored the 1960s civil rights demonstrations that were changing the city's social fabric.[38] In 1985, under the ownership of Knight Ridder, the merged *Herald Leader* courageously reported cash payoffs to University of Kentucky basketball players in violation of National Collegiate Athletic Association (NCAA) regulations, enduring a storm of criticism from the state's basketball fans.

- *Fear of libel lawsuits.* The news industry was reeling from big libel judgments. Gil Cranberg of the University of Iowa, after surveying 164 libel plaintiffs for a study published in 1987, concluded that if journalists are seen as ethical they are less likely to be sued. Most of the plaintiffs in the survey told Cranberg that they would not have sued if the newspaper or station had taken their complaints seriously and run a correction.[39]

Whatever its origins, the emphasis on written professional standards produced yet more awareness of ethics. It became common in the newsroom to talk about ethics and to raise questions — the process that Sandra Rowe, editor of *The Oregonian*, described in Chapter 1. These discussions often were facilitated by outside ethicists like those at the Poynter Institute in St. Petersburg, Florida, which was established in 1975 and has become journalism's leading in-service training center and think tank. Over time, newsrooms placed the stress on having a process for discussing and deciding ethics issues rather than on trying to envision a comprehensive set of commandments.

For all that, there is still mild debate about whether journalism is a profession. This text takes the position that it is, while conceding that it lacks a few of the distinguishing characteristics of a profession. The most significant of these differences is that journalists are not governed by a formal organization with authority to set educational requirements for entering the profession and performance standards for continuing in it.[40] The First Amendment prohibits such regulation. To distinguish themselves from the pretenders, responsible journalists subscribe voluntarily to standards of accuracy, fairness, and independence.

Overall, Decades of Improvement

The journalism of the twenty-first century reflects the reforms that occurred over more than a half-century of rising professionalism.

- *Journalists are better educated.* A journalist without a college degree is a rarity in newsrooms today. According to a 2013 survey of journalists by the Indiana University School of Journalism, 92 percent have at least a bachelor's degree.[41] Although possessing a diploma does not automatically make someone a better journalist, the rising education level signifies better preparation for the challenges of a complex profession.
- *Newsrooms have diversified.* Diversity in the news staffs is reflected in news coverage that is more likely to examine the whole community. The journalists of the mid-twentieth century, nearly all white men, tended to write for people like themselves. The profession has been profoundly changed by the influx of women and people of color into the workforce in the second half of the twentieth century. The transition remains a work in progress, however. The Indiana University survey showed that the percentage of minority-group journalists decreased from 9.5 in 2002, the year of the last previous survey, to 8.5 in 2013. In contrast, the survey noted, the overall percentage of minority-group members in the US population stood at 36.6 percent in 2012. The IU survey showed that the number of women in journalism increased 4.5 percent between 2002 and 2013. Yet women still represent about one-third of newsroom staffs, as has been the case since the 1980s, "even though more women than ever are graduating from journalism schools."[42]
- *Journalists have accepted a duty to be accountable to the public.* A news organization's social responsibility is to provide honest, impartial, and reliable information about current events that their fellow citizens need to make democratic institutions work. This responsibility entails being responsive to questions and complaints from the audience – the readers, viewers, listeners, and online users. It means a commitment to the principle of **transparency** – a spirit of openness, one that acknowledges journalists' mistakes and explains news decisions rather than arrogantly asserting that the decisions speak for themselves. The Internet has made **accountability** more important than ever, for two reasons: first, citizens form an army of fact-checkers calling attention to journalists' mistakes, and, second, the Web's interactivity fosters a conversation between journalists and the audience. In this chapter's Point of View essay, "The Case for Transparency," Jane B. Singer writes about how adhering to the principle of transparency helps journalists embrace the new culture that the Internet has created.
- *Journalists have embraced compassion.*   Where many journalists of the mid-century liked to project an image of toughness toward the people they covered, today's journalists generally show empathy. They are concerned not just with reporting the news but also with how their reporting will affect the people involved. "Minimizing harm" is one of the four cornerstone principles of the Society of Professional Journalists' code of ethics and is, as well, a key component of a course in journalism ethics.

- *"Watchdog" journalism has flourished.*   Journalists, especially through investigative reporting, use their platform to expose wrongdoing and to illuminate solutions to public ills. When the government's democratic system of checks and balances breaks down, journalists have stepped in to investigate and report to the public on the system failure. In February 2007, for example, Dana Priest, Anne Hull, and Michel duCille of *The Washington Post* documented neglect by Walter Reed Army Medical Center in caring for outpatients – soldiers and marines who had been physically and psychologically damaged in the wars in Iraq and Afghanistan. Congress and the White House immediately responded by promising sweeping reforms and by firing the officials who they thought should have prevented the failure. Although officials and the citizenry do not always respond so forcefully, that has not deterred responsible journalists from continuing to try to raise the public conscience when they discover civic dysfunction.

The Challenges of Contemporary Journalism

As outlined in Chapter 1, journalism in the early twenty-first century is undergoing an economic and technological transition that raises significant ethical challenges. Those contemporary issues – such as questions of how journalism will be paid for as news consumers move online, and the unresolved issues of Internet journalism – are discussed in detail elsewhere in this book.

As formidable as they are, the profession's challenges can be solved by the next generation of journalists, including those of you reading this text. Remember that journalism remains a high calling. Whether they are covering 9/11 or the city council meeting, ethical journalists provide the kind of information that society cannot do without.

Point of View
The Case for Transparency
Jane B. Singer

In today's networked environment, the structural change in the relationship between practitioners and the public is having a profound effect on newsroom culture. In the past, virtually all of a journalist's working relationships were with sources and colleagues; the newsroom walls (and at larger papers, the security guard in the lobby) meant control over who entered the physical workspace, and ownership of the printing press or broadcast transmitter ensured even firmer control over who or what entered the news space. Aside from the occasional

(Continued)

phone call to the news desk or letter to the editor, which might or might not be edited and then published, actual readers or viewers rarely touched the working lives of most journalists, particularly at large news organizations.

Today, interaction with audience members has become integral to the journalistic process. Consider the notion of objectivity. One of the most hotly debated issues in the industry is whether objectivity remains valuable (or even plausible) or whether it is being superseded by an ethical zeitgeist better suited to the rise of a relativistic medium. An emerging consensus seems to suggest that journalistic credibility in an unfettered information environment remains crucial and rests to a significant extent on independence from partisan or factional interests.[1] The ethical value in both objectivity and independence lies in underscoring the need for journalists to remain free from outside pressures to shape information toward ends that serve vested, rather than public, interests. That said, journalists are either naïve or just plain wrong to think that protestations of independence and high-minded impartiality will suffice when every word they write (or fail to write) is open to scrutiny and speculation in the rowdiest, most rapid-fire, and least restricted marketplace of ideas ever created.

Instead, the ethical buzzword of the Internet is "transparency," and it addresses a wide range of real and imagined journalistic sins. It is most closely connected with the traditional journalist norm of *accountability*. Aside from a few dictatorships, most nations around the world have at least one code of press ethics that delineates the nature of accountability to peers, sources, subjects, and audience members; the US Society of Professional Journalists' newly updated Code of Ethics, for example, urges journalists to "explain ethical choices and processes to audiences; encourage a civil dialogue with the public about journalistic practices, coverage, and news content." The Internet, with its unlimited space and inherently interactive structure, offers the ideal platform for both explanation and conversation.

In a traditional environment, journalists tend simply to ask audiences to trust them: to trust that they are being truthful, that they have been diligent and open-minded in gathering information, that they have captured the most important details of a story in the ten inches or two minutes allocated to it. It is a lot to ask. Perhaps, as the declining reputation of the news media suggests, it is too much.[2] The online environment, though, offers the opportunity to actively foster trust, not just demand it.

Transparency can take various forms. Using links to back up story references, for example, is essentially an aspect of the new narrative structure; a story is no longer self-contained but can be extended outward to connect to other material anywhere on the Internet. Although linking decisions require judgment about the appropriateness of what's at the other end of a click, most raise few ethical alarms for journalists, who see them as offering readers relatively straightforward options to obtain more information about a story topic.

Offering more information about oneself, another crucial aspect of transparency, is a thornier issue for journalists steeped in a culture that prizes the maintenance of professional distance. Many harbor a not-irrational fear that such information could provide ammunition for those looking for bias behind every byline. However, other members of the vast Internet community, including many bloggers, have given precisely this element of transparency a central place in their idea of how life in a network should function. Journalists themselves are finding blogs an optimal format for this sort of disclosure.

More broadly, the Internet encourages the construction of closer relationships with news audiences than in the past. For journalists, serving the public becomes about more than telling people what information exists; it is also about sharing in its discovery, verification, and interpretation, as well as providing help with its synthesis into meaningful knowledge – the interpretive function. As journalists' control over the flow of information is significantly loosened, and as the process of "making news" becomes more openly iterative, the enterprise becomes necessarily collaborative.

Sometimes the closeness is uncomfortable. Sociologists have long recognized that one of the hallmarks of a profession – and most journalists either believe themselves to be professionals or aspire to be, depending on whom you ask – is the right to devise and enforce their own ethical standards.[3] But online, oversight of journalists' behavior has become a team sport, and here, too, the newsroom no longer controls who gets to play.

Many have been startled by the intensity of the scrutiny – and by the fact that so few seem to think journalists are as ethical as they believe (or hope) themselves to be. The criticism is valuable for a variety of reasons, not least because it provides an impetus for the attention to ethical issues and efforts to make changes where they are needed. Perhaps less predictably, new relationship structures also are encouraging journalists to think about what, exactly, it is that they do, and why (or if) it retains any value in a world in which anyone can be a publisher.

Jane B. Singer is Professor of Entrepreneurial Journalism at City University London. This passage is excerpted, with permission, from her article "Journalism ethics amid structural change," *Daedalus*, 139:2 (Spring 2010), 95–96. © 2010 by the American Academy of Arts and Sciences. Reprinted with permission of MIT Press Journals.

Notes

1　Bill Kovach and Tom Rosenstiel, *The Elements of Journalism: What Newspeople Should Know and the Public Should Expect* (New York: Crown, 2001).

2　Arthur S. Hayes, Jane B. Singer, and Jerry Ceppos, "Shifting roles, enduring values: the credible journalist in a digital age," *Journal of Mass Media Ethics*, 22:4 (2007): 262–279.

3　Margali Sarfetti Larson, *The Rise of Professionalism: A Sociological Analysis* (Berkeley: University of California Press, 1977).

Notes

1　Gloria Cooper, "Laurel," *Columbia Journalism Review*, Nov.–Dec. 2001.

2　Cathy Trost and Alicia C. Shepard for the Newseum, *Running toward Danger: Stories behind the Breaking News of 9/11* (Lanham, MD: Rowman & Littlefield, 2002), ix–xiii.

3　Bill Kovach and Tom Rosenstiel, *The Elements of Journalism: What Newspeople Should Know and the Public Should Expect*, 3rd edn. (New York: Three Rivers Press, 2014), 22.

4　Ibid., 17.

5　Leonard Downie Jr. and Robert G. Kaiser, *The News about the News: American Journalism in Peril* (New York: Alfred A. Knopf, 2002), 6.

6　Kovach and Rosenstiel, *The Elements of Journalism*, 49–56.

7　Ibid., 72–77.

8　Ibid., 98.

9　Ibid., 142.

10　Ibid., 171–175.

11　Ibid., 197–201.

12   David Shatz, Chaim I. Waxman, and Nathan J. Diament (eds.), *Tikkun Olam: Social Responsibility in Jewish Thought and Law* (Lanham, MD: Jason Aronson, 1997).

13   Conrad C. Fink, *Media Ethics: In the Newsroom and Beyond* (New York: McGraw-Hill, 1998), 246–247.

14   Susan E. Tifft and Alex S. Jones, *The Trust: The Private and Powerful Family behind The New York Times* (London: Little, Brown, 1999), xix.

15   Downie and Kaiser, *The News about the News*, 13.

16   W. David Sloan and L. M. Parcell (eds.), *American Journalism: History, Principles and Practices* (Jefferson, NC: McFarland, 2002), 46.

17   "History of the Missouri School of Journalism," Mizzou: University of Missouri, http://www.missouri.edu/about/history/journalism.php, accessed Jan. 15, 2015.

18   See the American Society of News Editors website at http//asne.org.

19   Cassandra Tate, "What *do* ombudsmen do?," *Columbia Journalism Review*, May–June 1984. Tate's article cited "a 1916 issue of *American Magazine*." The reporter's response was quoted by Kovach and Rosenstiel in *The Elements of Journalism*, 52–53.

20   Paul E. Steiger, "Read all about it," *The Wall Street Journal*, Dec. 29, 2007.

21   Jack Fuller, *News Values* (Chicago: University of Chicago Press, 1996), 45–46.

22   Neil Henry, *American Carnival: Journalism under Siege in an Age of New Media* (Berkeley: University of California Press, 2007), 76.

23   Robert J. Lifton and Greg Mitchell, *Hiroshima in America: Fifty Years of Denial* (New York: Putnam, 1995), 10–22, 51–52.

24   "Reporting," The Pulitzer Prizes, http://www.pulitzer.org/bycat/Reporting, accessed Jan. 15, 2015.

25   Steven K. Knowlton and Patrick Parsons, *The Journalist's Moral Compass* (Westport, CT: Praeger, 1995), 207–208.

26   Commission on Freedom of the Press, *A Free and Responsible Press: A General Report on Mass Communication: Newspapers, Radio, Motion Pictures, Magazines, and Books* (Chicago: University of Chicago Press, 1947), 20–30.

27   George Sokolsky, "Dumb professors," essay included in a collection of reaction to the Hutchins Report, *Nieman Reports*, July 1947, 18.

28   Charlene J. Brown, Trevor R. Brown, and William L. Rivers, *The Media and the People* (Huntington, NY: R. E. Krieger, 1978), 178.

29   A. David Gordon and John Michael Kittross, *Controversies in Media Ethics*, 2nd edn. (New York: Longman, 1999), 97.

30   Frederick S. Siebert, Theodore Peterson, and Wilbur Schramm, *Four Theories of the Press* (Urbana: University of Illinois Press, 1956).

31   Karen Schneider and Marc Gunther, "Those newsroom ethics codes," *Columbia Journalism Review*, July–Aug. 1985. Through his work in the Associated Press Managing Editors, the author also observed the exponential growth of newsroom codes in the 1970s and 1980s.

32   Michael Josephson, *Making Ethical Decisions* (Los Angeles: Josephson Institute, 2002), 29.

33   Mark A. Nelson, "Newspaper ethics code and the NLRB," Freedom of Information Center Report No. 353, Columbia, MO.

34   George N. Gill, "It's your move, publishers," *Quill*, Aug. 1973.

35   Poorman was quoted in "Junketing journalists," *Time*, Jan. 28, 1974.

36   Schneider and Gunther, "Those newsroom ethics codes."

37   Roy Peter Clark, "Red light, green light: a plea for balance in media ethics," Poynter, May 17, 2005.

38   The author is indebted to the following for their insights into the reasons for increased ethical awareness during this period: John Carroll, Bob Giles, Bill Marimow, Jim Naughton, Mike Pride, Steve Seplow, and Bob Steele.

39   Alicia C. Shepard, "To err is human, to correct divine," *American Journalism Review*, June 1998.

40   Wilbert E. Moore, "Is journalism a profession?," in *The Professions: Roles and Rules* (New York: Russell Sage, 1970), 4–22.

41   Lars Willnat and David H. Weaver, *The American Journalist in the Digital Age: Key Findings* (Bloomington: School of Journalism, Indiana University, 2014), 9. The findings come from online interviews conducted Aug. 7–Dec. 20, 2013, with 1,080 US journalists working in print, broadcast, and online media.

42   Ibid.

4 For Journalists, a Clash of Moral Duties

Responsibilities as professionals and as human beings can conflict

---

Learning Goals

This chapter will help you understand:

- how journalists sometimes find that their journalistic duties are in conflict with their moral obligations as citizens and human beings;
- why journalists should, in the abstract, avoid being involved with the events and the people they cover;
- the kinds of situations in which journalists have to decide whether they are going to stop being observers and become participants; and
- guidelines that can help journalists make those decisions.

When Hurricane Katrina struck New Orleans and the Gulf Coast in late August 2005, journalists arriving to report the disaster often felt morally obliged to assume the role of relief workers. Assessing their experience a few months later in *American Journalism Review*, Rachel Smolkin found

> countless acts of kindness by journalists who handed out food and water to victims, pulled them aboard rescue boats or out of flooded cars, offered them rides to safer ground, lent them cell phones to reassure frantic family members, and flagged down doctors and emergency workers to treat them.[1]

At first glance the decision to stop reporting and help may seem obvious – journalists, after all, are human beings. However, their professional responsibility makes the decision more complex. To be blunt, the reason these journalists were sent to the scene was to report the news, not to give aid. If they had chosen to do so, the journalists could have spent all their time helping victims, but then they could not have done their reporting. The public, including the victims of the hurricane, desperately needed reliable information that only journalists could provide.

Generally speaking, journalists should be detached observers who do not intervene in the events they are covering. There are two good reasons for this:

1 **Intervention** changes the nature of the event, rendering it no longer authentic.
2 Intervention can lead the audience to perceive bias on the journalist's part.

The Ethical Journalist: Making Responsible Decisions in the Digital Age, Second Edition. Gene Foreman.
© 2016 John Wiley & Sons, Inc. Published 2016 by John Wiley & Sons, Inc.

However, to say that the journalists' choices in Katrina were complex rather than obvious does not mean that their decisions to give aid were wrong. They were temporarily subordinating the moral obligations of their profession to their moral obligations as human beings. If they hadn't given aid, suffering or death might have resulted.

The ethicist Michael Josephson told Smolkin flatly that the journalist's primary obligation is to act as a human being. "We shouldn't be too finicky about the notion that rendering some simple assistance would compromise objectivity." He said that, when people are in dire straits, "the more obligated someone is, regardless of who they are, to render assistance. The other factor is whether there are others there who can render assistance." Sometimes, he said, journalists could fulfill their moral duty by summoning help.[2]

In contrast, Paul McMasters of the Freedom Forum's First Amendment Center was equivocal. He said factors to consider before getting involved were "how natural or instinctive the journalist's impulse is and whether or not there is a potential for immediate harm or injury without the journalist's involvement." McMasters cautioned that when a journalist acts as a relief worker, "you're not observing, you're not taking notes; you're not seeing the larger picture." It is very important, he said, that the journalist return to his or her professional role "as soon as the moment passes."[3]

In most situations in Katrina, the journalists were not reporting on the people they helped, or their plight was tangential to the larger stories they were writing. But, for Anne Hull of *The Washington Post*, intervention would have kept her from reporting the story. That made her decision heartbreaking.

Hull wrote about Adrienne Picou and her six-year-old grandson in a poignant *Post* article headlined "Hitchhiking from squalor to anywhere else." She found the pair near an interstate exit ramp and told how they had twice become homeless, once from the flood and then from "the dire conditions of the city Convention Center." On the boy's red Spider-man shirt his grandmother had written, "Eddie Picou, DOB 10/9/98," just in case they became separated or his body was found.

After the interview, Adrienne Picou asked the reporter for a ride to Baton Rouge. Although Hull did not have a car, she knew a colleague who did. But Hull explained to Picou that she had to sit down to start writing. As Hull sat under an interstate overpass typing the story on her laptop, a medic in a rescue truck asked her for directions. Hull pointed to the Picous. "See that woman and child over there? She will know, and she needs your help."

The medic initially declined, but Hull pleaded, and the Picous were given the first ride on their journey out of New Orleans. That journey led to a shelter in northern Louisiana to a cattle ranch in Texas to a new job in Smyrna, Georgia.

Hull, who had handed out water and PowerBars to hurricane victims, felt torn over refusing to give the Picous a ride. "How can you explain to somebody you can't take them to a shelter?" But she also told Smolkin, "I believe journalists should have an ethical framework to guide them, and in the case of covering catastrophe or hardship, we must try to remember that we are journalists trying to cover a story. That is our role in the world, and if we perform it well, it is an absolutely unique service: helping the world understand something as it happens."[4]

When journalists do intervene, they also have to decide whether to reveal their actions to their audience. That is another conundrum: Will this disclosure be accepted by the audience as a well-intentioned effort to be transparent? Or will it come across as self-aggrandizement? One television producer who helped a driver escape from a flooded car in New Orleans was videotaped by colleagues as he did so, and the dramatic rescue was aired repeatedly.[5]

On the question of disclosing the intervention, Smolkin's ethicists disagreed. Jeffrey Dvorkin, then the ombudsman for National Public Radio, said that broadcasting the journalist's involvement "ends up looking, sounding self-serving and manipulative," and that it should not be part of the story unless it changes the outcome. Josephson would report the involvement and let the readers decide whether it's grandstanding: "If you take the hit, well, that's unfortunate, but the alternative is you let somebody suffer."[6]

More than four years after Katrina, journalists covering the January 2010 earthquake in Haiti were confronted with similar conflicts. The Society of Professional Journalists, while praising the journalists for their humane acts, cautioned that they should "avoid making themselves part of the stories they are reporting." Kevin Smith, then the SPJ president, said in a statement:

> Advocacy, self-promotion, offering favors for news and interviews, injecting oneself into the story or creating news events for coverage is not objective reporting, and it ultimately calls into question the ability of a journalist to be independent …
>
> No one wants to see human suffering, and reporting on these events can certainly take on a personal dimension. But participating in events, even with the intention of dramatizing the humanity of the situation, takes news reporting in a different direction and places journalists in a situation they should not be in, and that is one of forgoing their roles as informants.[7]

Front-Line Decisions: Observer or Participant?

In the episodes described below, journalists had to decide instantly whether they would step out of their roles as detached observers. They illustrate the importance of ethical preparation by journalists: thinking through the situations they might face and deciding – often in consultation with other journalists – how they will respond. This is the kind of preparation that editor Sandra Rowe of *The Oregonian* mentioned in Chapter 1.

"Fly-on-the-wall" reporting

Sonia Nazario envisioned worst-case scenarios she might encounter in doing the arduous fieldwork for "Enrique's Journey," a 2002 *Los Angeles Times* series that told the story of young Latinos who traveled from Central America to join parents working in the United States. Nazario is the *Times* reporter who wrote the "Orphans of

Addiction" series discussed in the Case Study "The Journalist as a Witness to Suffering." In preparing for "Enrique's Journey," Nazario drew on lessons learned in the earlier series. "Enrique's Journey" won Pulitzer Prizes for both Nazario and photographer Don Bartletti.

To report realistically on the 48,000 Latino children who have made the lonely journey, the *Times* journalists followed a boy from Honduras who was trying to reach his mother. Enrique was five years old when his mother left; he was seventeen when they were reunited in North Carolina.

Nazario and Bartletti followed Enrique and other children, observing them through the majority of the trip, most notably as they rode on the tops of freight trains in Mexico. Nazario followed in Enrique's footsteps to conduct interviews and make observations that would enable her to reconstruct parts of the journey that she did not witness.

In an article in *Nieman Reports* magazine, Nazario defined her journalistic purpose:

> to try to give an unflinching look at what this journey is like for these children and what these separations are like through one thread, through one child. I wanted to take the audience into this world, which I assume most readers would never see otherwise. I tried to bring it to them as vividly as possible so they could smell what it's like to be on top of the train. They could feel it. They could see it. They literally would feel like they were alongside him.[8]

Nazario knew that she would be confronted with difficult decisions about whether to continue to observe or to intervene to make the journey easier for Enrique and the other children. "You have to think these things out ahead of time," Nazario wrote, "because things can happen so quickly that it's too late to react in an appropriate way if you're not prepared." As part of the preparation, Nazario spent time at Immigration and Naturalization Service shelters and jails along the border, and interviewed children who had made the entire journey.

She realized that if she did intervene on Enrique's behalf, she could not use him in the story, because her intervention would destroy the authenticity of the account of his journey. She wrote that reporters have to accept that they are going to see a lot of misery in such an assignment. This is an emotional struggle, especially when children are involved. For example, Enrique realized that he did not have a telephone number for his mother in North Carolina, so he had to work for two weeks to raise enough money to make a telephone call to Honduras to get the number. All the while, Nazario had a cell phone, which she kept out of sight. "Sometimes you need to watch that play out to be able to write a really powerful story. Those aren't often things the public understands very well. I got some emails that basically said, 'Aren't you a human being? How could you do this?'"

Nazario devised a test for an intervention decision:

> The dividing line was whether or not I felt the child was in imminent danger. Not discomfort, not "things are going really badly," not "I haven't eaten in twenty-four hours." … The bottom line on all this is that I try not to do anything I can't live with.

Riding on top of a freight train, the *Times* journalists shared danger with the children they were observing. Of course, they had resources that their subjects did not – resources they did not flaunt. Nazario wrote:

> When I was on top of the train I would refrain from calling my husband until I could go to a part of the train that was empty. I would never eat in front of the kids. I would never drink water in front of the kids.

Ultimately the reporter did not accompany Enrique on the Rio Grande crossing. Here, ethical questions were intertwined with legal ones. "If I was with a child and was viewed as helping him across, then that would be aiding and abetting, which is a felony," Nazario wrote. But she did think in advance of what she might do if she were in the water with Enrique:

> Crossing the Rio Grande is a very dangerous challenge. Hundreds of people drown there, sucked under by whirlpools. … I was going to have an inner tube, even though I'm a former lifeguard. … If the kid's in trouble in the water I was obviously going to help him, but short of that I was not going to help him. He would not use my inner tube because that would be altering reality, and I didn't want to do that, if at all possible.

In the Point of View essay at the end of this chapter, Halle Stockton of Public-Source describes how reporters Wendy Ruderman and Barbara Laker of the *Philadelphia Daily News* immediately reported to authorities in November 2013 when they suspected that a 47-year-old disabled man was being regularly beaten by his "caretaker." In response to a neighbor's tip, they visited the apartment where the man lived with his presumed assailant, a 48-year-old woman who was the payee for his disability payments and food-stamp allowance. Finding the man bruised and apparently ill, Ruderman and Laker called a state-run hotline, and the man eventually was relocated. The reporters followed developments in the case and published their story in January 2014.

It is instructive to compare this case to the Case Study at the end of this chapter, "The Journalist as a Witness to Suffering." In the Philadelphia case, the reporters notified authorities two months before publishing anything; in the Los Angeles case, involving neglected children living with adult addicts, the authorities learned of the situation when the story was published. In each case the authorities came to the aid of the victims, and in each case the journalists called the public's attention to systemic problems in the social welfare system.

The cases differ in two significant ways that could influence a journalist's intervention decision. First, the *Los Angeles Times* journalists had arranged to observe life in the addicts' homes over an extended period so that they could meticulously document the problems of children living under those conditions, and reporting the case immediately would have made it impossible to deliver that evidence to their readers. *The Philadelphia Daily News* reporters had made no such arrangements with the subjects of their story; acting on a citizen's tip, they went to the apartment and determined that the evidence appeared to corroborate the tip. Second, the Philadelphia case indicated imminent danger to the victim; the children in the Los Angeles case, though horribly neglected, were not in that kind of danger.

When Eli Saslow spent time in the homes of poor families to report his Pulitzer Prize-winning series on the food-stamp program, he occasionally bought a meal for the people he was writing about. *The Washington Post*'s ethics policy restrained him from helping his subjects more than that. In an article in *Columbia Journalism Review*, Saslow was quoted as being conflicted:

> My job is not to advocate, and I'm not there to feed people. But it's difficult sometimes. Maybe I'm spending all day with a family as their fridge is nearly empty, and as they're trying to figure out what to do, and then I go back to my hotel and have a microbrew and take down notes about the day. There's something about that that feels not quite satisfying, obviously, and a little bit not right.[9]

Helping the police catch a suspect

When photographer Russ Dillingham of the Lewiston (Maine) *Sun Journal* heard on the police radio that officers had cornered a fugitive in an apartment building, he rushed to the scene. He watched from the ground while police searched the third floor. "I've been doing this a long time," the 25-year veteran said later. "I kind of figured he'd be where the cops weren't."

His calculation was correct. He started taking pictures as the fugitive, Norman Thompson, leaped from the building's balcony onto a garage roof next door (Figure 4.1). From there, Thompson jumped to the ground – "like a cat," Dillingham remembered later.

"Tackle him, Russ! Tackle him!" Detective Sergeant Adam Higgins called down.

Dropping his camera, Dillingham chased Thompson, tackled him, and held him down until the officers could catch up. Then he retrieved his camera and photographed Thompson as he was handcuffed and taken to jail on multiple charges of automobile theft and fleeing police in high-speed car chases. Thompson was not armed, but Dillingham hadn't known that when he made his tackle.

Police praised Dillingham, saying they could not have made the arrest without the photographer's help. The *Sun Journal*'s executive editor, Rex Rhoades, also was effusive: "We're all very proud of Russ. He's a stud."[10]

However, in a column in *News Photographer* magazine, ethics scholar Paul Martin Lester raised questions about the 2007 incident, including: What if Dillingham had been severely injured? What if the suspect had been injured and sued Dillingham? What if the suspect was innocent? What happens the next time Dillingham is asked by police for help? What if a more dangerous suspect mistakes him for a cop?

Lester noted that the ethics code of the National Press Photographers Association says photographers should not "intentionally contribute to, alter, or seek to alter or influence events." He recommended that Dillingham and his colleagues

Figure 4.1 After taking this picture of a fugitive fleeing police, newspaper photographer Russ Dillingham tackled him at the officer's request. PHOTO BY RUSS DILLINGHAM. REPRINTED BY PERMISSION OF THE SUN JOURNAL.

meet with the police to make clear that tackling suspects is not something journalists will do in the future, and that officers should not take it personally when they refuse.[11]

Dillingham's decision was instinctive. "In a split second, I made a decision to be a citizen, a community member, an American," he said. "I did what I thought was right and would do it again in a heartbeat."[12] "You don't even think about it," Dillingham said. "You just react." In his column Lester made it clear he wasn't criticizing Dillingham but urging that journalists think in advance about how to respond to situations they might face, much as a baseball fielder anticipates what he will do if the ball is hit in his direction.[13]

Dillingham was not confronted with saving someone from death, injury, or suffering. Instead, the photographer was asked to help the police do their jobs. Lester made a case for saying no.

Yet, refusing to tackle the suspect would have almost certainly subjected Dillingham and the journalism profession to scorn not only from the police but from the public as well. What kind of citizen would not stop someone fleeing from police officers, especially when the officers are asking him to do so?

Both the police and the journalists who cover them have important missions in the community, and sometimes those missions are in conflict. Such a conflict occurs when, after a riot, the police ask the news media to turn over photographs and videos that have not been published or broadcast. They want to use the images to identify and prosecute wrongdoers.

Philip Seib and Kathy Fitzpatrick framed this journalist's dilemma in their book *Journalism Ethics*:

> The "good citizen" response might be: "Sure; use our tapes. We're not pro-looter here. If we can help you lock up criminals, we'll be glad to do so." That reply sounds noble, but it contains a significant problem. Journalists were able to do their reporting after police had left the riot area because the rioters were angry with the police but not with the news media. If, however, the news gatherers turn out to have been evidence gatherers, the next time a similar event occurs the public may not treat police and reporters differently. The journalists might not be able to cover the event from the vantage points they previously enjoyed, and they may even find themselves in danger.[14]

In his book *Don't Shoot the Messenger*, media lawyer Bruce W. Sanford wrote:

> The media have long opposed these attempts to press them into service as a sort of litigation resource or video library for the prosecution or defense. Reporters fear that they seem to take sides when their testimony or work product becomes the subject of a trial. And when confidential sources are involved, compelling reporters to testify or to surrender their notes, video- or audiotapes may reveal identities and dry up important sources of information.[15]

Giving criminals access to the news media

Even so, when law enforcement asks for help, the choice can be difficult. Journalists at KKTV in Colorado Springs, Colorado, helped authorities in January 2001 because they thought their cooperation could defuse a threat of lethal violence.

Two heavily armed Texas prison escapees were holed up in a Colorado Springs hotel room. They told negotiators they would surrender if they could be interviewed on live television and were allowed to vent their complaints about the Texas prison system. The negotiators agreed to ask the station to give them five minutes each.

The station went along, and the interviews were carried live with the video showing anchor Eric Singer at a desk talking with the men on a telephone. Singer allowed them to make opening statements and then asked questions. An FBI agent sat off-camera and kept time.[16]

Singer said that, before the interviews began, he briefed officers on the questions he planned to ask. He said he agreed to "stay away from hot-button words," so he did not ask the fugitives what happened when they allegedly shot a police officer in Texas. The limitations on his interview did not disturb Singer. In his experience, he said, it is not uncommon for people being interviewed to "dictate how they want it done." He said interview subjects frequently specify "what questions will be on or off limits."

Singer said the viewers were told what was happening before the interviews were aired. Afterward, he said, the station made sure that the viewers "were clear about the questions that I came up with and the ones that weren't asked. … There was nothing hidden."[17] After the interviews, at about 3:45 a.m., the fugitives surrendered.[18]

Singer expressed satisfaction with the station's role in the event. "We are in the business to know things and report on them," he said. "These two men were the hottest stories of the day. We got to interview them and also helped keep the community safe."[19]

The episode ended well, but ethical questions remain – questions that other broadcasters should consider *before* they face similar requests.

The situation faced by the Colorado Springs station replicated the issues that the publishers of *The New York Times* and *The Washington Post* faced in 1995. A person known only as the Unabomber had been mailing bombs that in the previous 17 years had killed three people and injured 23. Now he demanded that the two newspapers publish his 35,000-word manifesto denouncing "the industrial system" and advocating a revolution to wreck that system. If the publishers refused, he wrote, he would resume bombing.

The newspapers complied, even though some in journalism warned that they were setting a precedent and leaving the media open to further blackmail. "You print and he doesn't kill anybody else, that's a pretty good deal," *Times* publisher Arthur O. Sulzberger Jr. said in a message to his staff. "You print it, and he continues to kill people, what have you lost? The cost of newsprint?"

The publication of the manifesto led to the arrest and conviction of Theodore Kaczynski, the Unabomber. His brother David recognized the writing style and informed authorities, who tracked down Theodore Kaczynski in a mountain cabin in Montana.[20]

Intervention at Central High

September 4, 1957, was to have been the day that 15-year-old Elizabeth Eckford would be among the first African American students admitted to the previously all-white Central High School in Little Rock. But when Eckford arrived by bus at Central High that morning, she found herself the only African American in a sea of angry white people. Her path to the school was quickly blocked by the raised rifles of National Guardsmen, who had been sent by Governor Orval E. Faubus ostensibly to prevent disorder.

Eckford and the eight other African American students turned away later that morning would earn a place in history as the Little Rock Nine. Because her family did not have a telephone, she had failed to receive instructions to go to Central with the others. So she was terrified and alone as she sat on a bench awaiting a bus to take her away from a jeering crowd that appeared to be on the verge of a riot.

In different ways and for very different reasons, two journalists intervened in the event they were covering.

Robert Schakne, a CBS News television and radio reporter, discovered that his network's cameras had not captured the yelling and Confederate flag-waving as Eckford walked the distance of a city block to the bus stop. What Schakne did next was described by Gene Roberts and Hank Klibanoff in *The Race Beat*, the Pulitzer Prize-winning history of the news media's coverage of the civil rights movement:

> He did something that revealed the raw immaturity of this relatively new medium of newsgathering: he ordered up an artificial retake. He urged the crowd, which had fallen quieter, to demonstrate its anger again, this time for the cameras. "Yell again," Schakne implored as his cameraman started filming.
>
> The television reporter had carried journalism across a sacrosanct line. … [H]ere in Little Rock, where a domestic confrontation of unsurpassable importance was unfolding, where journalistic propriety and lack of it were being put on public display, reporters who were inches from the drama found themselves making up the rules as they went along and doing it in front of everyone in a volatile situation with a hot, erratic new technology.[21]

The second journalist to intervene was reporter Benjamin Fine of *The New York Times*. Roberts and Klibanoff write that, as Fine observed tears stream down Eckford's cheeks behind her sunglasses, he

> began thinking about his own fifteen-year-old daughter. His emotions carried him beyond the traditional journalistic role of detached observer. He moved toward Eckford and sat beside her. He put his arm around her, gently lifted her chin, and said, "Don't let them see you cry."

Soon afterward, a white woman named Grace Lorch, whose husband was a teacher at a local college for African Americans, joined Fine and Eckford. When the girl boarded a bus a few minutes later, Lorch went with her.

Fine's effort to comfort Eckford, the authors of *The Race Beat* wrote,

> was seen by many around him as humane but completely inappropriate and probably provocative. [Fine] had inserted himself into a live story – only to remove himself from it when he wrote about the day's events a few hours later for The Times.[22]

Other reporters at the scene felt compassion for Eckford, too. Jerry Dhonau and Ray Moseley of the *Arkansas Gazette* and Paul Welch of *Life* magazine arranged themselves in an informal protective cordon around her as she sat at the bus stop. "It was all that they, as professionals, felt they could do," David Margolick wrote a half-century later on VanityFair.com.[23]

Lessons from the battlefield

The experience of journalists who cover wars is also instructive, because the violence and danger define the intervention question in stark terms. Most of the reporters and photographers who covered the combat in Iraq in 2003 were "embedded" with American military units. The Defense Department guidelines on embedding stated, "Embedded media operate as a part of their assigned unit," and required that, for security reasons, the journalists agree in advance to ground rules placing restrictions on their ability to report.[24] Journalists' alternative to embedding was to work as "unilaterals" – on their own – and that was far more dangerous.

The embedded journalists often bonded with the soldiers and, more important, depended on them for protection when the shooting began. When soldiers in his unit sneaked off and got drunk, Jules Crittenden of the *Boston Herald* reassured their sergeant: "Don't sweat it. That didn't happen." Later he reconsidered, and went back to the sergeant to let him know of his change of heart and get his agreement to let the story be told.[25]

Crittenden explained afterward why he had initially told the sergeant he would not write about the incident: "I didn't intend to ruin my relationship with the unit and its leadership on the first night … by humiliating them in the international press over a disciplinary issue." As for why he changed his mind, he said:

> I witnessed the discipline being meted out – a remarkably open handling of sensitive personnel matters that would have never happened in the civilian world. … My story in the Herald was not about a soldier getting drunk, but about the platoon sergeant's leadership in a period immediately prior to hostilities. I took the unusual step of seeking [the sergeant's] permission and gave him the courtesy of a veto because I had made a commitment to him, and it was important for him to understand in our ongoing relationship under difficult circumstances that I could be expected to do what I said I was going to do.[26]

On another occasion, Crittenden gave the unit the location of Iraqi military positions he had spotted. In the resulting firefight, three enemy soldiers were killed. Shortly afterward, he wrote: "I'm sure there are some people who will question my ethics, my objectivity, and so forth. I'll keep the argument short. Screw them, they weren't there."[27]

Meg Laughlin, a Knight Ridder reporter, took a different view of her role as a noncombatant. When she was offered an M16 rifle and asked to take a place in her unit's perimeter defense, she declined. "Are you crazy?" she asked. "We're all in trouble if you're depending on me to guard you."[28] Crittenden said he did pick up a rifle once when the enemy ambushed the unit he was accompanying, but he intended to use it only for self-defense and put it down without firing.

Crittenden disputes any assumption that embedded reporters are "automatically influenced" by the security provided by the soldiers. "Reporters in war zones typically operate on goodwill and good sense," he said, and they "share whatever security is enjoyed by whichever group they happen to be with." He acknowledged that "eating, sleeping, and enduring hardship with generally likeable and well-behaved young men day in and day out creates personal relationships."[29]

For Crittenden, the context of the war itself is relevant in a discussion of American journalists' conduct. He said:

> We were riding with the United States Army as it was engaged in removing a dangerous, murderous despot and his forces. Any question of objectivity and balance has to be objectively balanced against those facts. Applying any kind of moral equivalence to the United States Army and the Iraqi Republican Guard or the Saddam Fedayeen in that situation would be immoral.[30]

In his gripping account of the US Army's capture of Baghdad, author David Zucchino told how reporter Ron Martz of *The Atlanta Journal-Constitution* helped a medic administer aid to two soldiers gravely wounded in an armored personnel carrier as they drove into the capital. His was a humane intervention, even though the soldiers were actors in the drama he was covering.[31] "Once we crawl inside the Abrams tank and trundle our way to Baghdad with the boys, we should not kid ourselves about 'objectivity,'" Julie McCarthy of National Public Radio said.[32]

Covering the fighting in Afghanistan in 2002, *The Wall Street Journal* reporter Alan Cullison went shopping in Kabul for spare parts for his damaged laptop. He bought a hard drive that turned out to have been used by an al-Qaeda agent. *The Journal* turned the hard drive over to the American military, which downloaded its contents, including information about the agent's target-scouting mission. *The Journal* also reported the find to its readers.

Paul E. Steiger, then *The Journal's* managing editor, said the decision to turn over the hard drive was an easy one. "In moral terms, we would have been devastated if we had withheld information that could have saved the lives of our servicemen or of civilians."[33]

The Search for Intervention Guidelines

So, when do you stop reporting and get involved in the story? The answer to this question — and many other ethical questions presented in this book — is: "It depends." Every situation is different. There are no absolute answers.

Even so, you will benefit from the framework of guidelines to help you make your decision in a rational way. Note the word *guidelines*. Not rules.

Over the years, journalism practitioners and scholars have reached a consensus guideline:

A journalist should act to save a life or prevent injury if he or she is the best person or the only person in a position to intervene.

Amplifying that guideline, Bob Steele of Poynter outlined a four-question process:

1   Is the danger imminent?
2   Is the danger profound?
3   Is there anyone else present who can help?
4   Do you, the journalist, possess special skills needed in the situation?

To illustrate, Steele offered a hypothetical example: You arrive after a car has gone off a bridge and into the river. It is about to sink. Thus the answers to questions 1 and 2 are yes — there is imminent danger, and it is profound.

If paramedics and divers are already in action, you can do your journalist's job in good conscience, shooting pictures and gathering facts. The answer to question 3 is yes — others on the scene are in a better position to help.

But the situation changes if the answer to question 3 is no. If you're the only one at the scene or there are only a few others, you might go into the river to attempt a rescue. But only if you're an expert swimmer. In that case the answer to question 4 is yes: you possess the special skill desperately needed in this situation. If you are not a skilled swimmer, to try to make a rescue would likely be futile and perhaps suicidal. You still have a duty to intervene, and you do so by summoning help.[34]

As useful as the guideline and Steele's questions are in framing the decision-making, the journalist may still need to make a dire judgment call. This can be especially painful if the judgment involves a medical decision that the journalist is technically unqualified to make. In the Case Study "The Journalist as a Witness to Suffering," for example, the reporter had to decide whether the girl's fever from the spider bite was serious enough to warrant stepping out of her journalist role to drive her to hospital.

Rachel Smolkin, who wrote about journalists who intervened in Katrina's aftermath, offers this guidance:

- Follow your conscience. Your humanity — your ability to empathize with pain and suffering, and your desire to prevent it — does not conflict with your professional standards. Those impulses make you a better journalist, more attuned to the stories you are tasked with telling.
- If you change an outcome through responsible and necessary intervention because there's no one else around to help, so be it. Tell your bosses, and when it's essential to a story, tell your readers and viewers, too.
- Remember, though, that your primary — and unique — role as a journalist is to bear witness. If you decide to act, do so quickly, then get out of the way.[35]

Point of View
Journalists Are Humans, Too
Halle Stockton

Journalists are taught to avoid conflicts of interest, and we try to learn how to observe a situation like a fly on the wall.

Even so, reporters occasionally become part of the story.

The public usually hears about plagiarism scandals and journalists refusing to name sources (or complaining about their hotel arrangements at the Olympics).

(Continued)

But there are reporters in communities across the nation who are faced with less-publicized challenges of how to abide by a code of ethics while also remaining human.

An example of this occurred in Pennsylvania with two *Philadelphia Daily News* reporters. Wendy Ruderman and Barbara Laker were contacted by an anonymous caller with concerns about the safety of Clarence Shuford, a 47-year-old man with physical and intellectual disabilities.

They learned Shuford and the actions of his caregiver, Barbara Floods, were not being supervised closely, so they visited the home and asked to go inside.

> Floods invited the reporters up to her second-floor apartment, where a barefoot Shuford, dressed in a plaid shirt and gray denim pants, sat meekly on a leather sofa next to a table covered with dusty prescription-pill bottles and an open bag of adult diapers.
> His eyes were bloodshot and puffy, rimmed underneath with inky black circles. His bottom lip appeared swollen. He looked unkempt, with bits of white lint stuck to his closely cropped hair. Small flies circled his head.

Ruderman and Laker toured the apartment, noting the food in the refrigerator, the sleeping arrangements and Shuford's nervous demeanor when checking to see if Floods was listening to what he said.

They left uneasy, a feeling quickly confirmed by neighbors.

> A group of men stood on a nearby street corner. In hushed tones, without giving their names, they said that Floods repeatedly beat Shuford. It was no secret – she treated him like "a punching bag," one man said.

> "You gotta get him outta there," he said, stealing a look at Floods' house.

The journalists called about Shuford to a state-run hotline established under the Adult Protective Services Act to field reports of abuse or neglect of adults ages 18 to 59 with physical or intellectual disabilities.

Investigators with the Department of Public Welfare and the Philadelphia Police Department got involved, and Shuford was removed from the home about a week later.

He revealed scars, whip marks and other injuries that he said were a result of his caretaker's abuse.

At the time of the story, Shuford had moved in with his brother.

The reporters' actions were certainly not characteristic of a fly on the wall, but they got a vulnerable person out of harm's way.

Though the caretaker is not a politician or a company CEO, she still held a position of power, and their reporting held her accountable.

And with this reporting, they also illuminated some deficiencies in the state's enactment of the law meant to protect this population.

All characteristics of great journalism.

This essay by Halle Stockton was published on February 20, 2014, on PublicSource.org. PublicSource is an independent online news organization based in Pittsburgh. It produces original, in-depth reporting on social issues, criminal justice, money and politics, and the environment in Pennsylvania. The quotations in the essay are from Wendy Ruderman and Barbara Laker, "Disabled man kept virtual hostage – until one phone call," *Philadelphia Daily News*, Jan. 31, 2014.

Case Study

The Journalist as a Witness to Suffering

When writer Sonia Nazario and photographer Clarence Williams set out in 1997 to document the lives of children in homes where the adults were drug and alcohol addicts, they wanted to show the suffering of these children with what Nazario called "grab-you-by-the-throat" reality.

Only by being detached, "fly-on-the-wall" observers, the *Los Angeles Times* journalists reasoned, could they report with power what life is like, day in and day out, for the millions of American children who grow up in these dire circumstances. And only powerful journalism could motivate citizens and their elected representatives to alleviate their suffering.

For three months Nazario and Williams spent long days with two Long Beach families, one with a three-year-old girl named Tamika and the other with siblings, eight-year-old Kevin and ten-year-old Ashley. In a two-part series in November 1997, "Orphans of Addiction," Nazario described some of the scenes the journalists watched:

- Tamika going 24 hours without eating, while her mother focuses on her own hunger for drugs.
- With her mother out looking for drugs, Tamika passing the time alone in the kitchen, "where she steps on shards from a broken jar. The toddler hobbles to the sofa, sits down, and digs two pieces of glass from her bleeding feet. Not a tear is shed."
- The mother so "intent on smoking the last crumbs of crack, she gently lowers her girl onto a mattress moist with urine and semen.

As Mom inhales, Tamika sleeps, her pink and white sundress absorbing the fluids of unknown grownups."
- Kevin and Ashley missing school for four months because their father worries that enrolling them "might bring too much attention to them – and to him – from campus officials." Sometimes, Nazario wrote, Ashley "walks to a nearby elementary school so she can watch the children spill out onto the playground."
- Kevin's father disparaging his emotionally troubled, rebellious son as a "retard" and disciplining him by letting his hand fly. He "beats me all the time," Kevin said. "I don't want to be like him. He's nasty. He'd be nice if he didn't use drugs."
- Kevin and Ashley going weeks without bathing, in part because the bathtub "brims with dirty clothes alive with fleas." At one point Kevin rummages through a dumpster looking for clothes for his sister, finding a pair of canvas shoes. When the shoes turn out to be too small, "a familiar look of disappointment crosses her face."

In the spring of 1997, looking for subjects for their story, Nazario approached about 50 parents in the social services office of a university before settling on the mother of Tamika and the father of Kevin and Ashley.

The editor directing the *Times* investigation, Joel Sappell, told Susan Paterno of *American Journalism Review* in 1998: "My only instruction was: Don't tamper with reality. ... We're making

(Continued)

a documentary here ... Don't intrude into it. Because that changes it."

Reflecting on the assignment a decade later, Nazario wrote: "I believe that witnessing some suffering, even by children, was acceptable *if those children were not in imminent danger* and if I thought the telling of their story in the most powerful way possible might lead to a greater good." The italics are Nazario's.

She said: "I was clear in my mind about one thing. If I felt these children were in imminent danger, I would immediately report them to child welfare authorities. Yes, they were clearly being neglected. Yet I never felt the three children I spent time with were *in imminent danger*."

One factor that gave Nazario confidence was that at least two individuals, a neighbor and a nearby pastor, were keeping "a careful eye" on the children. "When the children got hungry, or needed help, they would often go a few blocks away to Pastor Bill Thomas in Long Beach and ask for food or assistance or advice." She said Pastor Thomas agreed with her that the children were not in imminent danger.

Nazario pointed out that if she and Williams had immediately told authorities about the neglect of the children they observed, there would have been no story. Not only would they have been ejected from the homes they were observing, but word would have quickly spread in the neighborhood, and it would have been "very difficult or impossible for me to gain the trust of another family." Sometimes, she said, "it is necessary to witness some harm to be able to tell a story in the most powerful way. Your goal is to move people to act in a way that might bring about positive change."

But the *Times* did not make clear the surveillance of the neighbor or pastor, nor did it explain to readers any ground rules that

the reporter and photographer had set for themselves. When the story came out, readers blistered the *Times* for callously allowing children to suffer so the paper could have a good story.

Nazario recounted the criticism: "I had watched a girl go hungry for 24 hours and done nothing. I had allowed these children to be neglected. Someone who claimed to be a child abuse investigator called three times to let me know he had urged police to arrest me. ... [One reader said], 'Was winning an award so important to you that you would risk the life of a three-year-old child to do so?'"

One of Williams' photographs and its caption especially outraged readers. It showed Tamika's teeth being brushed by her mother's boyfriend. The caption read: "Johnny brushes Tamika's teeth with a toothbrush she is sharing this day with Theodora [the mother], who is HIV-positive. After noticing that her own gums were bleeding, Theodora asked him to clean Tamika's teeth first."

Williams said he took only a couple of frames of the toothbrushing scene. "It all happened so quickly. After it was over, I was, like, whoa, that's screwed up."

On at least two occasions, the journalists did intervene, but those actions were not reported to readers.

Williams told Susan Paterno for the *American Journalism Review* article that he saw a baby, left alone in a room, was about to bite down on an electrical cord. "I made one frame, but at that point, it's crazy. I just ended up holding the baby that afternoon." When a life is in danger, he said in a 2008 interview, "you help."

Nazario told Paterno that she arrived one morning to find Tamika screaming in pain from infected spider bites. She "didn't think twice" when the mother asked her for a ride to the hospital. "I got into the car and drove her."

Both journalists spoke of the anguish they felt during the assignment. "I never cried so much doing a piece," Williams said in 2008. "I would come home at night and just stare in the mirror and cry." Nazario told Paterno in 1998: "I think you would not be a human being if you didn't go into these situations, seeking some of these things, and not coming home with a knot in your stomach."

At a seminar at the Poynter Institute in 2002, Nazario said she had to "buffer" herself in the manner that police officers and social workers detach themselves emotionally from the suffering they see. Otherwise, she said, "you couldn't function day to day doing these kinds of stories. … It is a real balancing act."

Describing how she watched Tamika go 24 hours without eating, Nazario told the Poynter seminar:

> There were times when I purposefully allowed hunger to play out. I knew that this girl often went 24 hours without eating and I wanted to see that. I was willing to watch that happen. … I was reporting the neglect that occurred to these kids in the most powerful way I could, by putting it on the front page of a major newspaper.

After the *Times* series was published, the county's child-abuse hotline registered a 45 percent increase in reports from the public of children being abused or neglected. More important, the series led to systemic reforms. One of those was a revamping of Los Angeles County's child-abuse hotline after reports surfaced that four people, including a doctor, had reported Tamika's situation to the hotline without anything being done. More money was put into federal and state programs to provide treatment for addicted women with children.

A task force representing 20 agencies was set up to identify and help endangered children through the schools and police. Schools in the county changed policies to identify children like Kevin and Ashley who had dropped out of one school but never enrolled in another.

Even though use of email in 1997 was a fraction of today's traffic, Nazario received more than 1,000 phone calls and emails. The majority of reader comments were words of praise. One man thanked Nazario on behalf of the three children she had written about: "You may have saved not just their lives, but the lives of millions of other innocent children throughout the country."

Tamika was picked up and put in foster care the day the story was published.

Her mother, Theodora, got free drug-rehabilitation treatment at a residential facility whose director had read the story. She lived, clean and sober, at the facility for 18 months only to go back to drugs a few weeks before she was to have regained custody of Tamika. Ultimately, Tamika was adopted by a foster-care family.

Kevin and Ashley had moved with their father to central California before the *Times* published its report. They came under scrutiny of the social-welfare system as a result of the publicity, but authorities decided not to remove the children from their father's custody.

Nazario wrote in 2008 that although she would have reported and written the story in much the same way, there are some things she would do differently.

First, she would write the story in less than the two months she took in 1997, after the three months of observation. "I should have taken greater care to drop in on the children and monitor their situation much more closely during the writing phase."

(Continued)

Second, the *Times* would run a note explaining to readers the rationale for why the journalists chose not to intervene. The *Times* did consider such a note but decided against it because of an aversion to writing about itself and concerns that a note would detract from the story's power. For her 2002 series, "Enrique's Journey" [a Honduran boy's odyssey described in this chapter], Nazario wrote 7,000 words of footnotes "in an effort to provide greater transparency."

Third, she would be much more methodical in thinking through potential ethical dilemmas and deciding in advance how she would react. What are the worst things that could happen? How would I react in an instant?

After Nazario's seminar at the Poynter Institute in 2002, Poynter faculty member Bob Steele said the *Times* journalists had faced a dilemma in which there were competing principles. One principle was the "obligation for the newspaper to reveal the truth about this issue to readers," Steele told reporter Tran Ha of the Poynter website. Steele continued:

There also is the journalistic principle that journalists do not become overly involved with their sources or subjects in ways that change the story or that will make the newspaper seem as if it is an arm of law enforcement or the government. The third principle is one of minimizing harm and what obligation the journalist has in preventing further harm or profound harm to vulnerable people.

Sources

Ha, Tran, "A journey through the 'ethical minefield,'" Poynter, Aug. 1, 2002, updated Mar. 2, 2011.

Kahle, Shannon, telephone interview with Clarence Williams, Aug. 15, 2008.

Nazario, Sonia, reporter, and Clarence Williams, photographer, "Orphans of addiction," *Los Angeles Times*, Nov. 16–17, 1997.

Nazario, Sonia, email to the author, July 17, 2008.

Paterno, Susan, "The intervention dilemma," *American Journalism Review*, Mar. 1998.

Steele, Bob, "Journey through the 'ethical minefield,' part 2," Poynter, Aug. 1, 2002, updated Mar. 2, 2011.

Questions for Class Discussion

- How did the project editor, Joel Sappell, explain the decision to have the reporter and photographer avoid involvement in the story? How do you react to the decision?
- Should the journalists have agreed in advance on the kinds of situations that would compel them to intervene? Should they have informed readers of those ground rules?
- On at least two occasions the journalists did intervene to protect the children. Did their actions violate their instructions to avoid involvement? Did they damage the story's authenticity? Should these interventions have been disclosed to the readers?
- Do you agree with the three things Nazario said she would do differently if she were doing the story over? Are there any other things you would change?

Notes

1 Rachel Smolkin, "Off the sidelines," *American Journalism Review*, Dec.–Jan. 2006.

2 Ibid.

3 Ibid.

4 Ibid.

5 Ibid.

6 Ibid.

7 Society of Professional Journalists, "SPJ cautions journalists: report the story; don't become a part of it," news release issued Jan. 22, 2010.

8 This section of the chapter is based on Sonia Nazario, "Ethical dilemmas in telling Enrique's story," *Nieman Reports*, Fall 2006, 27–29.

9 Alexis Sobel Fitts and Nicola Print, "Are we journalists first?," *Columbia Journalism Review*, July–Aug. 2014.

10 Mark LaFlamme, "Fugitive caught in flash," Lewiston (Maine) *Sun Journal*, Oct. 4, 2007.

11 Paul Martin Lester, "Think fast," *News Photographer*, Nov. 2007.

12 Russ Dillingham, email to Shannon Kahle, Apr. 30, 2008.

13 Lester, "Think fast."

14 Philip Seib and Kathy Fitzpatrick, *Journalism Ethics* (Fort Worth, TX: Harcourt Brace, 1997), 122.

15 Bruce W. Sanford, *Don't Shoot the Messenger: How Our Growing Hatred of the Media Threatens Free Speech for All of Us* (New York: Free Press, 1999), 128.

16 "TV interview helps end Texas escape standoff," The Associated Press, Jan. 24, 2001.

17 Eric Singer, email to Shannon Kahle, July 8, 2008.

18 "TV interview helps end Texas escape standoff."

19 Singer, email to Kahle.

20 Clifford G. Christians, Kim B. Rotzoll, Mark Fackler, Kathy Brittain McKee, and Robert H. Woods Jr., *Media Ethics: Cases and Moral Reasoning*, 7th edn. (Boston: Allyn & Bacon, 2005), 61.

21 Gene Roberts and Hank Klibanoff, *The Race Beat: The Press, the Civil Rights Struggle, and the Awakening of a Nation* (New York: Alfred A. Knopf, 2006), 159–160.

22 Ibid., 161.

23 David Margolick, "Through a lens, darkly," VanityFair.com, Sept. 24, 2007.

24 Department of Defense memorandum, "Subject: Public Affairs guidance on embedding media during possible future operations/deployments in the US Central Commands (CENTCOM) area of responsibility (AOR)," Feb. 10, 2003.

25 Jim Bettinger of the Knight Fellowships Program at Stanford University, "Detail provided by embedding was invaluable, and haunting," a report for the American Society of Newspaper Editors, June 4, 2004.

26 Jules Crittenden, email to Shannon Kahle, Apr. 6, 2008.

27 Ibid.

28 Bettinger, "Detail provided by embedding was invaluable, and haunting."

29 Crittenden, email to Kahle.

30 Crittenden, email to the author, July 16, 2008.

31 David Zucchino, *Thunder Run: The Armored Strike to Capture Baghdad* (New York: Atlantic Monthly Press, 2004), 57–58.

32 Bettinger, "Detail provided by embedding was invaluable, and haunting."

33 Felicity Barringer, "Why reporter's discovery was shared with officials," *The New York Times*, Jan. 21, 2002.

34 Author's telephone interview with Bob Steele, Jan. 15, 2008.

35 Smolkin, "Off the sidelines."

5 The Public and the Media: Love and Hate

The goal for the journalist should be respect, not popularity

---

Learning Goals

This chapter will help you understand:

- the widespread public hostility to the news media, which has been documented repeatedly in surveys;
- the possible reasons for the hostility;
- how journalists should respond to criticism;
- the types of complaints that the public most often makes about the news media, and the lessons that can be learned from these complaints; and
- how to apply perspective to the complaints.

When the Red River overflowed in the spring of 1997 and flooded Grand Forks and East Grand Forks, North Dakota, the *Grand Forks Herald* surmounted one obstacle after another to keep the community informed. *The Herald*'s printing plant was flooded and then destroyed by fire, inspiring the newspaper's grim headline "Hell and High Water."

Still, the papers kept coming. The newsroom was moved to an elementary school, where the news was transmitted to the *St. Paul* (Minnesota) *Pioneer Press*. The papers were printed there and flown to Grand Forks for free distribution to the beleaguered North Dakotans.[1]

That was public service in journalism's finest tradition.

But the goodwill soon dissipated in a torrent of criticism. What angered many of the *Herald*'s readers was its decision to disclose the identity of the donor who had given the towns $15 million and requested anonymity. From that gift, $2,000 was distributed to each of the 7,500 households hardest hit by the flood.

The disclosure was the result of a visit by Joan Kroc, widow of McDonald's founder, Ray Kroc. When *Herald* reporters learned that the donor was being given a tour of the flood area, they drove to the airport and established her identity from the tail markings on her private jet, from fuel receipts, and from interviews with airport employees.[2] The story began: "Angel was in town Saturday night. So was Joan Kroc's jet. This appears to be no coincidence."[3]

"You owe the community and state an apology, as well as Mrs. Kroc," one reader wrote in a letter to the editor. Another wrote, "If she was nice enough to give that

---

The Ethical Journalist: Making Responsible Decisions in the Digital Age, Second Edition. Gene Foreman.
© 2016 John Wiley & Sons, Inc. Published 2016 by John Wiley & Sons, Inc.

much money, her wishes should have been respected." A man who called in to a radio station's talk show lamented: "The *Herald* has been wonderful through this whole thing, keeping the paper printed and distributing it for free. ... This has ruined it all."[4] The newspaper's own poll showed that 85 percent of respondents thought Kroc's name should not have been published.[5]

The *Herald's* decision to name the Angel is addressed here to illustrate the mercurial nature of the public's attitudes toward the news media. Whether the *Herald* was right or wrong can be — and has been — debated in journalism circles. It should be noted, however, that the paper did not pursue the matter until the Angel toured the flood area. At that point, her identity became widely known in the community — knowledge shared by political and civic leaders but shielded from the average citizen.

The *Herald* explained in a front-page statement: "[W]e believe printing the news is part of the bargain we have made with the community. We'd be breaking the bargain if we didn't print the news."[6] Reflecting on that statement later, *Herald* editor Mike Jacobs told an audience of journalists: "News, we said, is timely information of general interest. The Angel's identity was clearly news. Besides, we said, if she really wanted to remain anonymous she should have driven into Grand Forks in a pickup truck. With a gun rack."[7]

The controversy in Grand Forks did, in Jacobs' words, "blow over." But the newspaper's precipitous fall from community hero to community villain demonstrates a paradox in American society: People *do* rely on the information that independent news media provide — and even praise it in times of crisis like September 11 and the flood in Grand Forks. Yet, the people who value the information also like to complain — and they are apt to react in anger when they think the media's agenda differs from their own.

The public's relationship with the news media is, indeed, one of love and hate.

Documented Evidence of Public Hostility

It is an irony that, even as the news media mature and strive to fulfill an obligation of social responsibility, the public has grown hostile. The hostility is painfully evident to anyone answering the telephone or reviewing incoming email at news outlets, or perusing the reader comments appended to online news stories.

There also is empirical proof. With occasional upticks, the public's declining trust has been documented in surveys since the 1980s.

The Project for Excellence in Journalism (now the Pew Research Center, Journalism & Media), a research organization and think tank, addressed the public's perception in 2004 in one of its annual reports on *The State of the News Media*: "Americans think journalists are sloppier, less professional, less moral, less caring, more biased, less honest about their mistakes, and generally more harmful to democracy than they did in the 1980s."[8]

Figure 5.1
Survey respondents who said they have "a great deal" or "quite a lot" of confidence in the news media (%).
GRAPHIC COURTESY OF BILL MARSH. DATA © 2014 GALLUP, INC. ALL RIGHTS RESERVED. CONTENT USED WITH PERMISSION. GALLUP RETAINS ALL RIGHTS OF REPUBLICATION.

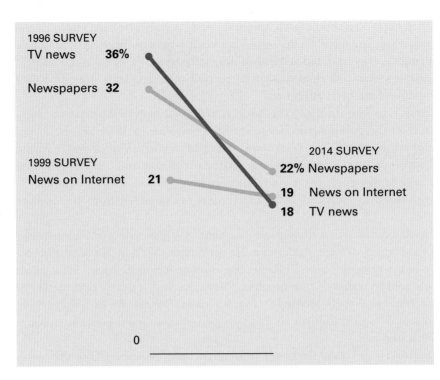

The Pew researchers saw a disconnect between the public and the news media over motive. Their report observed that, while journalists think they are working in the public interest and trying to be fair and independent, the public thinks otherwise. In the public's eyes, news organizations are operating largely to make money and their journalists are primarily motivated by professional ambition and self-interest.

A Gallup Poll reported in 2014 that only about one in five people trusted the news media. Twenty-two percent of those surveyed said they had "a great deal" or "quite a lot" of confidence in newspapers, 19 percent in news on the Internet, and 18 percent in television news (Figure 5.1). The survey asked people for their level of confidence in 17 institutions, and the three sources of news ranked in the bottom third of those institutions. Gallup said confidence in newspapers peaked at 51 percent in 1979 and television at 46 percent in 1993, the first year the survey asked about television. For Internet news, the question was first asked about Internet news in 1999, when the confidence level was 21 percent.[9]

In a survey conducted in 2013 by the Pew Research Center, 67 percent said news stories are often inaccurate. In contrast, 44 percent made that judgment in 1985. Since the 1990s, consistent majorities have expressed the belief that news stories are often inaccurate.

The Pew Center also reported, "Overwhelming majorities express doubt about news organizations' independence: 76 percent say news organizations tend to favor one side and 75 percent say they are influenced by powerful people and organizations."[10]

All that research is important to journalists because it underscores a threat to credibility – whether their reporting is believed. "The bottom line … is believability.

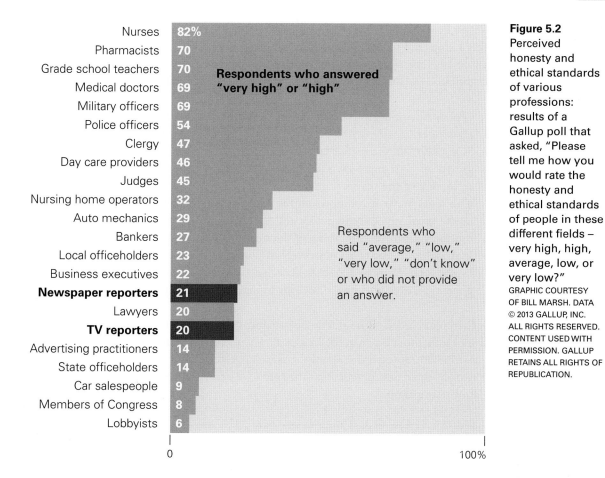

Figure 5.2
Perceived honesty and ethical standards of various professions: results of a Gallup poll that asked, "Please tell me how you would rate the honesty and ethical standards of people in these different fields – very high, high, average, low, or very low?"

Trust is the lifeblood of the media's relationship with the people," the Pew Center wrote in an analysis of its surveys in 2005.[11]

The public is skeptical of journalists' ethics. When a Gallup Poll ranked the "honesty and ethical standards" of various occupations in 2013, reporters placed in the bottom half (Figure 5.2). Only 21 percent of respondents thought newspaper reporters had "very high" or "high" ethical standards, and only 20 percent thought that highly of television reporters. The ratings have declined in recent decades.[12] In Gallup's survey in 1981, 36 percent of respondents thought television journalists had "high" or "very high" ethical standards, and 30 percent rated newspaper journalists that highly.[13]

Possible Explanations for the Hostility

Although public hostility to the news media has been well documented, the reasons for the hostility have not been. Thus the question is open to speculation.

Roy Peter Clark of the Poynter Institute sees a correlation between the low credibility ratings and relentless attacks on the news media. He says the attacks are coming from many directions, with a persuasive cumulative effect on "a public that has been conditioned to hate us." In a column in January 2008, Clark gave these examples:

- "Politicians under pressure – from every political party – try to kill the media messenger."
- "On radio talk show after talk show, in best-seller after best-seller, an industry has grown up with many agendas. Among the greatest of the agendas is to destroy the credibility of the mainstream press."
- The "geek news revolution" on the Internet has undermined public confidence in the press, not only by endorsing the attacks of partisan bloggers, but also by routinely dismissing the value of the mainstream news media.
- Journalists are portrayed negatively in films and television dramas, as exemplified by the long-running TV show *Law and Order* in which reporters and photographers typically appear as "slimeballs or part of the wolf pack."

Clark concluded: "The public bias against the press is a more serious problem for American democracy than the bias (real or perceived) of the press itself."

As one antidote to the assaults, Clark suggested that the news media find ways to explain their best practices to the public. Essentially, he was proposing a public-relations campaign:

> Let's remind them of the journalists who have risked their lives as war correspondents, or who have worked hard to create an environment on the home front (I'm thinking of *The Washington Post*'s investigation of Walter Reed Army Medical Center) where returning military men and women can get the physical and mental health care they might need. [14]

Over the longer term, suspicion of the news media has been fueled by the media's dual nature – stations, newspapers, and news websites have to make a profit at the same time that they fulfill their quasi-civic function of informing the community. It is easy for cynics to ask: Are they reporting this story because it is news the public needs, or are they just trying to sell papers, raise broadcast ratings, or attract Web traffic?

Another chronic problem, discussed by the authors of *Doing Ethics in Journalism,* is the way journalists explain their newsgathering decisions to the public. Rather than reflexively citing their legal right to publish the information, they should be emphasizing their moral obligation to report the news, the authors wrote. "There is a tendency by journalists to wrongly assume the public understands the rationale behind First Amendment protections." [15]

The late William F. Woo, a newspaper editor and later a Stanford University professor, wrote that journalists had to take some of the blame for the public's lack of sympathy with the First Amendment. In *Letters from the Editor,* he wrote:

> Many of us seem to think that the amendment was written for the press, rather than for the people, and that it confers upon us special privileges or rights that are not given

to others. … There is almost no phrase used by journalists that I dislike more than "the public's right to know," for it so often justifies not courage and independence but excess, intrusion and abuse."[16]

Sometimes, the public misunderstands journalism's mission, which quite likely was a factor in the reaction to the *Grand Forks Herald*'s outing of Joan Kroc as the Angel. In another common misunderstanding of journalism's purpose, people watching televised interviews and news conferences perceive that journalists are being discourteous when they ask tough but appropriate questions of public officials.

Another cause of tension, for newspapers at least, is that the editorial pages express opinions about the people and events covered on the news pages. Even though the news and editorials are written by separate staffs (or at least they should be), readers may conclude that a paper's editorial position influences its news coverage. In addition, some people may refuse to buy a paper whose editorials they disagree with. Unquestionably, these are downsides, but journalists generally think it is important that the newspaper offer informed opinion on issues in the news and stand up for what its editorial board thinks is sound public policy, especially when the issues have a moral dimension.

In 2009, after surveying its readers, *The Atlanta Journal-Constitution* stopped running editorials except on Sundays. Julia Wallace, then the paper's editor, told David Folkenflik of National Public Radio (NPR):

> What we found is they don't want us to be a newspaper with a strong point of view. But what they do want is, they want balance. If we have a view to the right, they want a balance of a view to the left. And they want us to be transparent about how we go about our work.[17]

The paper still runs opinion columns, both national and local, but they are ideologically balanced against each other.

Ironically, it was as editor of *The Constitution*, one of *The Journal-Constitution*'s predecessors, that Ralph McGill wrote fearless editorials urging his fellow white Southerners to accept the end of racial segregation and Jim Crow rule in the late 1940s, the 1950s, and the 1960s. He drew the ire of many in his lifetime, but now a boulevard in Atlanta bears his name.

How Journalists Should Respond to Criticism

The incessant criticism in the surveys might tempt journalists to conclude that, since there is no way to please the public, why even try?

That would be a mistake. Journalists have to take their credibility very seriously. Whether they think readers, viewers, and listeners are right or wrong, they ignore the audience's opinions at their peril.

People who make complaints about the news ultimately may not get satisfaction. The owners of some department stores tell their employees that "the customer is always right" – a policy that may be smart in retailing but not in news. The final resolution of a complaint is determined by the facts, not by what would make the customer happy.

Of course, the customer isn't always wrong, either. A reasonable customer – not one who calls for the sole purpose of mindless screaming – is entitled to serious consideration of a complaint of inaccuracy. The news organization's proper response is: "We'll check it out."

If the complaint proves valid, the news organization should speedily correct the record. In addition, the journalists ought to analyze how the error occurred. That could lead them to improve their procedures of gathering and presenting the news.

If, however, the investigation shows the original report was correct, the news organization should explain its decision-making. The explanation could be delivered in a telephone conversation, an email message, or a private letter. Citizen critics often are astonished, and pleased, that the news organization would take the time to address their complaints in a thoughtful way. If the critic's point of view is widely shared, a way could be found – a letter to the editor or a comment posted online – to accommodate a customer who wants to explain his or her perspective.

In his Point of View essay at the end of this chapter, "Connecting with the Audience in a Digital Dialogue," Mark Bowden relates how, while he was writing his 29-part "Black Hawk Down" series for *The Philadelphia Inquirer* in 1997, the Web gave readers all over the world a chance to make his story better by correcting errors and offering information. It also let the readers see that the reporter was eager to get the story right.

No matter how their motives are misunderstood, journalists must not consciously do anything that would validate the criticism and justify the lack of trust.

Nor should journalists pander to the public – shaping the news to fit the perceived desires of the audience. In the first place, the public is far from monolithic, and no one can precisely determine what it wants to be told about a news event. Far more important, journalists would be betraying their audience's trust by making popularity their goal instead of an honest search for truth.

In short, journalists:

- have to accept that they are not going to be loved by their audience, but …
- can't stop trying to improve their credibility in the eyes of the public.

Nobody said this job was going to be easy!

Learning from the Complaints

The rational way to deal with citizen complaints to the news media is to look beyond the vitriol to find the constructive criticism. This requires keeping an open mind. "We're too thin-skinned," said Kathleen Carroll, executive editor of the Associated Press, speaking of the industry as a whole. "We should not take questioning by the public as an assault."[18]

So it is useful to compile a list of what – according to the surveys – irritates the public the most. Like market research in the business world, the complaints can identify patterns that need attention.

In some cases, this exercise might suggest that, instead of changing their news-gathering techniques, journalists should do a better job of explaining themselves – in other words, being transparent. "We have not been good at explaining our methodology – the reasons why we do the things we do," said the late James M. Naughton, president emeritus of the Poynter Institute. "There is less fear of conspiracy if the newsgathering process is open."[19]

What follows is a discussion of the recurring themes found in the surveys.[20]

Too many mistakes

Although journalists are far better educated today, the public thinks they still don't know enough. When the Freedom Forum invited members of the public to a series of forums to discuss media credibility in the late 1990s, the guests expressed concern that journalists "don't have an authoritative understanding of the complicated world they have to explain to the public."[21]

The results were similar when the American Society of Newspaper Editors conducted a survey in 1998 to discern the reasons for public distrust of newspapers. The biggest reason turned out to be mistakes – not just factual errors but sloppiness in grammar and punctuation as well. The public was saying that, if journalists can't get the little things right, how can they be trusted on the larger issues?[22]

The twenty-first-century surveys by Gallup, Pew, and others confirm that those suspicions continue to be strongly held. The findings should challenge journalists to work harder than ever to report accurately, fairly, and in context.

The surveys show that it helps credibility if news organizations run corrections, but the public thinks news organizations, especially television, are reluctant to acknowledge their mistakes. They also think newspaper corrections should be published more prominently.

Accuracy in the news is discussed in more detail in Chapter 12.

Bias

This complaint is undoubtedly overstated in the surveys. Most often, bias is perceived in political coverage, and what a news consumer ascribes to media bias might well be a report that is factual but at odds with the citizen's own biases. However, it is one thing to discount the degree of bias the public perceives in news reporting, and quite another to deny that bias exists at all.

Bias exists in part because journalism is a subjective art. Its practitioners continually make decisions about the news – what stories to cover, what facts to use, what facts to highlight in the stories, and what stories to present most prominently. Each decision is an opportunity for opinions to seep in. Conscientious journalists adopt an attitude of professional detachment, blocking out their opinions and following where the facts lead.

The Editorial Eye, an editing text, described the process:

> "The facts speak for themselves," the heroes of detective novels like to say. Honest journalists, however, acknowledge that the facts alone say little. What delivers the message is the writer's selection and arrangement of those facts. By using one fact and omitting another, by juxtaposing facts in a certain way, the writer illuminates the news ... Editors help ensure that the choosing hasn't resulted in inaccuracy and unfairness.[23]

Much of the bias in supposedly neutral news accounts results from an unconscious failure of the journalist to block out opinions. These opinions are sometimes manifest in word selection.

A more egregious ethical transgression is to decide what the story is going to say before the facts are reported. In her Point of View essay at the end of this chapter, "Journalism, Seen from the Other Side," Jane Shoemaker, a veteran journalist who became a business executive, writes about reporters she has seen doing this: "They had already drawn a conclusion and were simply collecting facts to dress it up."

The vocabulary of the news should be neutral — no pejoratives, no stereotypes, no code words. "Ethical journalists use language ethically, considering the truthfulness, the precision, the impact, and the long-term consequences of the words used. Unethical journalists, on the other hand, are careless with the language," ethics scholar John C. Merrill wrote in *Journalism Ethics*.[24]

Keith Woods of the Poynter Institute identified some of the errant language:

> Inference substitutes for fact. Language is loaded. Euphemisms reign. A man "admits" that he is gay. A pregnant woman "peddles" her story to the press. Richard Jewell "bounces" from job to job. "Inner-city" replaces black or Hispanic. "Conservative," "suburban," or "blue-collar" replace white.[25]

Gerald Jordan, a former *Philadelphia Inquirer* reporter and editor who teaches journalism at the University of Arkansas, sees a problem not just in word choice, but also in how reporters frame, or establish the context of, their stories. The framing, too, can reflect journalist bias. "The command to 'make sense' and 'write with authority' is an invitation to surmise and analyze," Jordan said.[26]

Story framing can be flawed if the reporter, perhaps without realizing it, adopts the position of one side in a conflict. An example: To reduce chronic delays for travelers at a metropolitan airport, the Federal Aviation Administration orders new takeoff patterns that will cause aircraft noise over certain neighborhoods near the airport. The news coverage emphasizes the neighbors" protests and barely mentions the benefits of the new takeoff patterns. The fair approach is to offer thoughtful, detailed treatment of both the protests and the benefits, allowing the audience to judge the wisdom of the tradeoffs the FAA made.

A recurring complaint from the public is the media's focus on bad news. The public thinks "the press is biased – not with a liberal bias, but with a negative one," Robert H. Giles wrote after the Freedom Forum's study of news consumers' attitudes. "There is too much focus on what is wrong and what is in conflict, and not enough on reporting and explaining what is working and succeeding."[27]

Negativity, of course, is part of the nature of news because one of its definitions is an event that deviates from the norm. Although the hundred planes that land safely at the airport today are not news, the one that crashes becomes the top story on the evening newscast. Yet the traditional definition of news also validates the point Giles was making. If a dozen towns in the region have an identical problem and one of them discovers an innovative solution, the success story deserves media attention.

Stephen Seplow, retired reporter and editor for *The Philadelphia Inquirer*, suggested yet another bias – a bias toward the front page or the opening story on the newscast:

> Reporters and editors understandably want the best possible play for the stories they write and edit. I think we are all sometimes guilty of hyping stories by moving less important – but more sexy – details higher in the story than they deserve. There is nothing inaccurate in the reporting, but it distorts reality a little by emphasizing the wrong thing.[28]

The public's focus on perceived ideological bias led to the birth in 1996 of a cable network that would unabashedly filter the news the way people wanted it – or at least those who saw themselves as conservatives. As a 27-year-old with a degree in broadcasting, Roger Ailes persuaded Richard M. Nixon of the importance that television should play in his 1968 presidential campaign. After a career split between politics and television, Ailes created the Fox News Channel.[29]

Today, Fox is a huge money-maker for its owner, Rupert Murdoch's News Corporation. "If you're a cable subscriber, you pay roughly 89 cents per month for Fox News Channel," Jesse Holcomb wrote for Pew Research Center in 2013. MSNBC, Fox's mirror image on the liberal side of the political spectrum, was costing subscribers 18 cents a month.

Fox's 1.7 million viewers each evening in 2013 made it by far the leader among the cable news-and-commentary channels. Holcomb wrote that the Fox audience was more ideologically skewed than MSNBC's. According to a 2012 survey by Pew Research Center, 60 percent of Fox viewers described themselves as conservatives, 23 percent as moderates, and 10 percent as liberals. In the MSNBC audience, 32 percent saw themselves as conservatives, 23 percent as moderates, and 36 percent as liberal. (The totals do not add up to 100 because they exclude people who did not respond to the question.)[30]

In one sense, the growth of "news we can choose"[31] harks back to the party-line newspapers in the early years of the American republic. In the more complex twenty-first century, however, there is the possibility that citizens will be misinformed if they get their news only from news outlets that tell it the way they want to hear it. David Carr of *The New York Times* laments "a media ecosystem" in which "news consumers select and assemble a worldview from sources that may please them, but rarely challenge them." In a column, he observed that a tendency to converse only with like minds extends as well to social media communities:

> [T]hink of your Facebook feed or your Twitter account, if you have either. When you pick people to follow, do you select from all over the map, or mostly from among those whose views on culture and politics tend to align with your own? Thought so.
>
> Unless you make a conscious effort to diversify your feeds, what you see in your social media stream is often a reflection, even amplification, of what you already believe. It's a choir that preaches to itself.[32]

Insensitivity

News consumers may be interested in how victims of tragedy are coping with their ordeals, but they are disgusted when reporters, especially those on television, appear to trample on the victims' feelings. Unlike public officials and business executives who are accustomed to media questioning, these ordinary citizens are thrust involuntarily into the news. They are vulnerable to exploitation and have a right to be left alone. When they approaching traumatized people for interviews, reporters should be aware of their vulnerability.

In *Best Practices for Newspaper Journalists*, Robert J. Haiman quoted an editor as telling his staff:

> The mayor, the police chief, the people who run the big companies in town … they deal with us all of the time and they are all big boys and girls who can take care of themselves. But let's not treat somebody's old Uncle Harry or Aunt Millie the same way we treat the pols and the pros.[33]

These are among the guidelines developed by Michigan State University's Victims and the Media Program:

- Switch out of investigative reporter mode. Don't be afraid to open the conversation with "I'm sorry for your loss" or "I'm sorry for what happened to you."
- In cases of death, celebrate the life. Inform the family that an interview will allow your article to go beyond the facts on the official record provided by the police or hospitals.
- Tell their side of the story. There are times when victims want to put their version on the record (the warning light wasn't flashing, the attacker threatened to kill her if she called the police, etc.). Many victims complain that initial articles contained glaring errors that they were not given the opportunity to correct.
- Discuss the ground rules. Make sure that victims know you are there as a reporter, not their friend, but that your goal is to help them tell their stories.[34]

In the Case Study at the end of this chapter, "Roughed Up at Recess," a lesson was learned by the television station whose stunning video made the public aware of child-on-child playground assaults at local schools. The video crews often tried to stop the fighting, but they did not realize the importance of telling the audience how they intervened. When the video was aired, much of the public's anger was directed at the messenger instead of at the school employees who were responsible for patrolling the playgrounds.

Unnamed sources

When journalists use anonymous sources, they are asking their audience – proved in the surveys to be skeptical – to trust their judgment that the sources know what they are talking about. Without the source's name and position, the public has no way to assess the validity of the information or its possible bias.

Thus the use of an anonymous source places a special burden on the reporter, because the news organization effectively is vouching for the accuracy of what is attributed to the source.

News accounts are more authoritative when sources are identified. Journalists in the abstract tend to agree that they should get their sources to go on the record by name. In practice, it is a different matter, as reporters are tempted to trade anonymity for information that is not vital but merely interesting.

Anonymity should be granted to protect a whistleblower – someone with inside knowledge of wrongdoing who is willing to come forward but would be in jeopardy if identified. Protecting such a source enables journalists to give the public information that it otherwise would not receive.

This topic is discussed in more detail in Chapter 13.

Sensationalism

The public thinks journalists chase stories about sex, scandal, and celebrities not because they are important but because they think they will sell newspapers, build broadcast ratings, or attract Web traffic.

Sensationalism is indeed a problem in the news media, although it seems to be less pervasive than it was in the early years of the twenty-first century.

A classic example of the genre was the coverage of Anna Nicole Smith's death in a Florida hotel-casino on February 8, 2007. For two days, the cable networks devoted 50 percent of their news coverage to the saga of the *Playboy* centerfold model who had become a rich widow and then a star on reality TV.[35]

The Smith story – "what killed her, who fathered her infant, where her money would go" – dominated cable television for nearly a month, absorbing nearly one-fourth of the available news time. The network morning shows also covered the story intensively.[36]

Mark Jurkowitz, who analyzed the coverage for the Project for Excellence in Journalism, pronounced the Smith coverage "one of those stories the media feel compelled to both cover and apologize for." Although many other news outlets "treated Smith's death as a blip on the radar screen," Jurkowitz concluded that the episode "speaks to cable's ability to magnify an event until it feels like the only story on the entire media agenda."[37]

The phenomenon illustrated by the Smith coverage is a blending of entertainment and information to yield "**infotainment**," a label that applies despite the morbid nature of this particular story.

Michael Schudson and Susan Tifft, in an essay in the 2005 book *The Press*, saw an uninformed citizenry and placed at least part of the blame on infotainment. "Today, Americans are saturated with images, interviews, facts, and analysis, yet have a surprisingly superficial knowledge of the machinery of democracy or the rest of the world," Schudson and Tifft wrote. "Paradoxically, there is more quality news available than ever before, but it is often overwhelmed by the sheer volume of entertainment, consumer features, crime, and sensation."[38]

Infotainment has ethical implications for journalism, whose primary purpose is to give citizens the information they need to be free and self-governing.[39] If lighter fare gets more of the news media's resources, important civic topics get less.

Journalists' ethics

Although many of the complaints that the public makes about journalists are exaggerated, this one is outrageously so.

As a journalism ethicist for the Poynter Institute, Kelly McBride is used to being gibed by nonjournalists who view her job description as a contradiction in terms. On an airliner, when a row neighbor finds out what she does for a living, the response is often: "Isn't that an oxymoron?"[40]

Based on a career's worth of observation, the author of this text is convinced that journalists take ethical standards seriously. Most get into the profession because they want to make a difference; they see a noble calling in journalism's mission of public service.

Ethics might be yet another area in which journalists should do a better job of explaining themselves. One way news organizations might do this is to post their ethics codes online and invite their audience to hold them to those standards.

In contrast to the Gallup Poll that shows little public respect for journalists' ethics, a study of moral development by two professors showed that journalists are skilled at working through the ethical dimensions of problems in their profession. The professors, Lee Wilkins of the University of Missouri and Renita Coleman of Louisiana State University, reported that their study of 249 journalists placed them fourth among 20 groups that had taken the Defined Issues Test, designed to assess moral development.[41] "Thinking like a journalist requires moral reflection, both done dynamically and at a level that in most instances equals or exceeds that of members of the other learned professions," Wilkins and Coleman wrote.[42]

Advertisers' influence

As mentioned above, the dual nature of newspapers and broadcast stations creates an unavoidable appearance of a conflict of interest. The media perform a quasi-civic function of providing information to the public, but they cannot survive in the marketplace if they don't make a profit. Nearly all their income is derived from selling advertisements to businesses that want their messages to reach the news organization's audience.

Given that reality, it is easy for a skeptical consumer to assume that the news organization will slant the news to cater to the wishes of an advertiser. This has happened, but journalists are zealous about guarding against such occurrences or blowing the whistle on them if they do occur. Time and again, news organizations have rebuffed advertisers' pressure at great financial sacrifice.

The commercial aspect of news organizations, along with its implications for journalism ethics, is explored in Chapter 11.

Applying Perspective to the Complaints

It is well to conclude this chapter by trying to put the public criticism in perspective. Despite the complaints, people do say good things about the news media in the surveys. They like local television news, network news, cable television news, and the newspapers they know best[43] – notwithstanding the *Grand Forks Herald*'s experience in the Angel controversy.

Media scholar Lawrence T. McGill, in a 1997 analysis of surveys about press fairness, made the same point:

> Questions referring to specific news organizations ask people something they know about firsthand. For example, when people are asked about CNN, they can describe what they think of CNN because they've watched it themselves. If people are asked about their local newspaper, they can describe what they think about it because they've read it themselves. But questions about "news organizations in general" ask people about something they know about only secondhand, either through conversations with others about "the media," or, ironically, through news reports about "the media."[44]

For that matter, "the media" is a nebulous, inaccurate term that contributes to public misunderstanding about journalism. *The New York Times* and the *New York Post* have little in common. Likewise, Rush Limbaugh differs from NPR. Likewise, partisan blogs differ from the websites of the mainstream newspapers and broadcast networks.

Significantly, the public continues to support journalism's watchdog role. The Pew Research Center reported in 2013:

> In the wake of revelations about government activities, including the NSA surveillance program and the IRS targeting of political groups, nearly seven-in-ten (68%) say press

criticism of political leaders keeps them from doing things that should not be done, while just 21% say press criticism keeps leaders from doing their job. Support for the media's watchdog role has risen 10 points since 2011 even as other press ratings have shown little sign of improvement.[45]

Although it is true that credibility has fallen sharply since the 1980s, you should bear in mind that complaints about journalists are nothing new.

Consider these complaints: "News is distorted. Some newspapers invade privacy. Scandal and 'sex' stories are printed solely to sell papers. Innocent persons are made to suffer needlessly by publicity. The real interest of the press is money-grubbing."

Those appeared in Leon Nelson Flynt's book, *The Conscience of the Newspaper*.[46] It came out in 1925.

Point of View

Connecting with the Audience in a Digital Dialogue

Mark Bowden

When I was paring down the first draft of my book *Black Hawk Down* to run as a 29-part *Philadelphia Inquirer* serial in 1997, editor Jennifer Musser introduced herself and asked for help.

Musser said she was going to prepare the series for publication on *philly.com*, *The Inquirer's* website. I assumed that she planned to simply run each day's installment, and assured her that she would receive each day's copy promptly.

"No," she said. "I'm interested in more than that. What kind of source material do you have?"

That was the first clue that Musser's understanding of Internet journalism was a generation ahead of my own. She turned my newspaper story into an Internet phenomenon, packaging it with graphics, video, audio, maps, documents, and a Q&A with its readers. The unfolding series drew in hundreds of thousands of online readers from all over the world. At its height, the electronic version of the story was getting 46,000 hits every day. Her work opened my eyes to the marvelous potential of the Web to merge all forms of journalism, and to add something entirely new.

When we invited readers to participate in a Q&A, I had anticipated maybe a dozen or so notes, which would have been a solid response for most newspaper articles. Instead, they flowed in by the hundreds daily, from men who had fought in the battle, from soldiers at military bases all over the world, from appreciative and critical readers. I sat for hours every morning while the series ran, answering them one by one. The author of this textbook, then *The Inquirer's* managing editor, concerned that the final parts of the series had not been finished, walked by my desk one morning and announced how pleased he was to see me writing away so furiously.

"Is that the last part?" he asked, hopefully (no doubt with visions of my being hit by a truck and the paper being left with its highly popular story unfinished).

"No, Gene, I'm answering the email. If I don't do this every morning I'll never keep up with it."

For the rest of the month I was completely swept up in this digital dialogue. One critical way it vastly improved the story was by giving readers all over the world a chance to instantly correct my mistakes. Military experts are notoriously finicky about getting the details of weaponry and equipment exactly right, and because the format was digital, mistakes were fixed immediately. Readers who received an apology and thanks from me saw that they had contributed directly to the story's accuracy.

This greatly enhanced the account's credibility. Instead of dealing with the reporter as a distant "expert," and speculating on the reasons for mistakes or omissions, readers saw my own eagerness to simply get the story right, something which in my experience is the primary motivation of most reporters. Those who sent email messages offering more information on key points in the story were contacted immediately, by phone or email. Interactivity helped to break down the normal wall of suspicion between soldiers and reporters, and I found myself suddenly offered whole new sources of information.

I struggled to take advantage of them as the series unfolded and later spent months plumbing these new sources for the book version. Instead of leaning back and wondering how the work was being received, I was in an arena with my readers, explaining, defending, and correcting the story as it unfolded. I never had so much fun with a story.

Mark Bowden is the author of *Black Hawk Down* and nine other books, the most recent of which is *The Finish: The Killing of Osama bin Laden*. He writes regularly for *The Atlantic* and *Vanity Fair*.

Point of View

Journalism, Seen from the Other Side
Jane Shoemaker

After a quarter-century as a reporter and editor, I became head of communications for a regional brokerage and investment-banking firm. When I switched to the other side, it was an eye-opener to see the wide variance in standards and ethics from one reporter to the next.

To my distress, I found that far too many journalists are lazy. The lazy ones did not come to an interview prepared, and their shallow questions reflected that. Lazy reporters accepted whatever we told them, not questioning anything. Trade publications and smaller newspapers were alarmingly willing to take my writing and publish it as fact. My news releases often were printed word for word as news stories by publications short of help and eager to fill space. I could have written self-serving drivel, and readers would not have had any way to know it.

(Continued)

And it was a great surprise to learn how many reporters, particularly those who consider themselves specialists, came to interviews with an obvious bias. They had already drawn a conclusion and were simply collecting facts to dress it up. A telltale sign was questioning intended to back the interviewee into a corner: "Don't you agree that …?" "Isn't it true that …?"

Even worse were those who tried to push their own words onto the unwitting subject. I warned executives to be wary of any reporter who said, "So what you're saying is …" or "In other words …" That was a red flag that the reporter was choosing the words he or she wanted to attribute to the subject.

We found that many reporters want stories to be black or white. Good guys or bad guys.

Right or wrong. The truth is that most events are in shades of gray and need to be presented in perspective. That was particularly difficult when working with television reporters, who hate anything gray because it takes too much time on the air to explain.

The most challenging situation for us was to continue to work with reporters we knew to be lazy or to have a strong point of view. The best was the opportunity to work with reporters who were prepared, ready to listen, willing to learn, and balanced and fair in their stories. Fortunately, there were plenty of them.

Jane Shoemaker, now retired, was a reporter for United Press International; a reporter, foreign correspondent and departmental editor for *The Philadelphia Inquirer*; and managing editor of *The Charlotte Observer*.

Case Study

Roughed Up
at Recess

The investigative team at WITI-TV in Milwaukee received multiple phone calls from viewers who reported their children had been bullied and "beaten up" by classmates on school playgrounds.

Bob Clinkingbeard, WITI's vice president and news director, was impressed by the volume of calls the station had received on the topic. Soon after the school year began in fall 2003, reporter Bob Segall began investigating the issue by conducting surveillance at area elementary schools. He went alone, carrying a home video camera, to sit in his car and watch children play on randomly selected schoolyard playgrounds.

At the first stop, Segall videotaped children taunting, hitting, and kicking each other. In one case, a seven-year-old boy was repeatedly hit, kicked, and dragged by a group of older students on the playground. The boy tried to escape his elementary-aged assailants by climbing a tall chain-link fence, but when the boy climbed down, he was hit and kicked some more.

Segall found the same kind of physical violence on schoolyard after schoolyard across the Milwaukee area. In 37 of 52 schools the station visited over a few weeks, WITI recorded kids hitting and/or kicking other kids during recess on what were supposed to be supervised school playgrounds.

The station aired its findings in a special sweeps story, "Roughed Up at Recess." Clinkingbeard said:

> I thought viewers would be shocked and angry that this was going on in schools. We thought we knew how people would react. The reporter who did the story has children. An editor with children put the story together, and the photographers who shot the story have children. Other people in the newsroom who have children saw the story and while they were amazed – and maybe it is because they were journalists – nobody said to Segall, "Why didn't you do something to stop the attacks?"

Because the story was a lengthy one – 13 minutes – the station divided it into two segments within the same newscast, separated by a commercial break. Before the first segment ended, the assignment desk began getting phone calls from viewers who were angry because they thought the journalists had not intervened. These calls intensified during the commercial break.

Segall said, "We decided the best way to handle the dilemma was for a news anchor to address the issue by asking me a question" during the live "tag" that followed the second segment. The anchor asked, "Bob, what would you say to parents who are calling our newsroom now saying, 'Why didn't you step in and alert a teacher or break up the fight yourself?'" Segall responded by explaining what he did – and did not do – at the time he witnessed the incidents.

"In retrospect," Segall said, "this fell far short of the thorough explanation and broader context viewers needed to better understand the ethical issues we faced while reporting the story."

Segall said he and his colleagues had underestimated the importance of informing viewers about what he had done to intervene. About the first little boy he witnessed being attacked, Segall said:

> I put down my video camera to intervene three times. The first time the boys ran off before I got ten steps from my car. The second time I got as far as the street before the fighting broke up, and the kids ran off. On occasion number three, I didn't even have a chance to get out of the car before they ran away.

Segall said he called the school district's safety director, whose cell phone number he had programmed into his phone, and the director in turn called the principal. "I thought the school would act more quickly getting a call from him, than by getting a call from a stranger. The safety director did respond right away, so I think it was a good decision." In suburban districts, school districts were also notified – some as soon as 15 minutes after an altercation, and all of them within a week.

As Clinkingbeard pointed out, the powerful video overwhelmed the problem the station had exposed. Segall agreed: "Everything that followed – the additional detail, insight, and resolution – did not matter to some of our viewers. They did not hear any of it because they were just too angry."

Segall said the actions of the journalists were not a part of the original report because the focus was intended to be on the behavior of the children, and there was concern that a lengthy explanation would detract from the pacing of the report and shift the focus onto the journalists instead of the students. "What we failed to realize was, without providing at least some of that context to accompany the video, *my* action and perceived inaction became the focus for some viewers," he said.

Clinkingbeard said that in retrospect he wished he and Segall had given more thought to what their protocol would be if the station witnessed abuse on the playground. "I had no idea that we would catch something that awful on camera," he said.

(Continued)

Such up-front conversations, Segall later said, might have included instructions to "look at each child on the playground as if it were your own child. Make sure the decisions you make about when to intervene would be the same decisions you would make if that child were your own."

The video was edited to obscure the identities of children involved in the fights, both the assailants and the victims. The finished report showed how WITI-TV crews videotaped the fighting.

The investigation and an ensuing community-service project resulted in extensive reforms. The Wisconsin Department of Health conducted a statewide bullying education program. The state's largest school districts carried out comprehensive bullying prevention programs, and another program trained school police officers statewide. The Milwaukee Public Library set up a Bully Project resource center with books, videos, and other resources for teachers, students, and parents.

Reprinted courtesy of the Radio Television Digital News Foundation. This case is adapted from *Newsroom Ethics: Decision-Making for Quality Coverage*, 4th edn. (Washington, DC: Radio Television News Directors Foundation, 2006), 20–21. Additional reporting by the author includes email exchanges with Bob Segall, May 28–29, 2008, and a telephone interview with Segall, May 30, 2008.

Questions for Class Discussion

- Was it appropriate for the WITI-TV crews to intervene in the playground fighting?
- What kind of "front-end" instructions should have been given to crews in advance of reporting this story?

- What should WITI-TV have told its viewers about what its crew members did to stop the fighting and to notify school officials?
- Why do you think the news staff underestimated the viewers' reaction to the video?

Notes

1   Mike Jacobs, editor of the *Grand Forks Herald*, in remarks made publicly at the 2003 convention of the American Society of Newspaper Editors.

2   Jay Black, Bob Steele, and Ralph Barney, *Doing Ethics in Journalism: A Handbook with Case Studies*, 3rd edn. (Boston: Allyn & Bacon, 1999), 245–246.

3   "Angel appears in GF, EGF; Angel's wings registered to Kroc," *Grand Forks Herald*, May 19, 1997.

4   "Flood of complaints follows newspaper's disclosure of donor" and "On the radio waves," *Grand Forks Herald*, May 20, 1997.

5   Black, Steele, and Barney, *Doing Ethics in Journalism*, 246.

6   "The Herald's first commandment: never hold the news," *Grand Forks Herald*, May 20, 1997.

7   Jacobs, remarks at the American Society of Newspaper Editors convention, 2003.

8   Pew Research Center, *The State of the News Media 2004*.

9   Andrew Dugan, "Americans' confidence in news media remains low," Gallup, June 19, 2014. Dugan reported on a national telephone poll of 1,027 adults between June 5 and 8, 2014.

10 "Amid criticism, support for media's 'watchdog' role stands out," Pew Research Center, Aug. 8, 2013. Pew surveyed 1,480 adults between July 17 and 21, 2013.

11 "The media: more voices, less credibility," Pew Research Center, Jan. 25, 2005, 49.

12 "Honesty/ethics in professions," Gallup, Dec. 5–8, 2013. Gallup conducted a national telephone survey of 1,031 adults.

13 Ibid.

14 Roy Peter Clark, "The public bias against the press," Poynter, Jan. 28, 2008.

15 Black, Steele, and Barney, *Doing Ethics in Journalism*, 17–18.

16 William F. Woo, *Letters from the Editor: Lessons on Journalism and Life* (Columbia: University of Missouri Press, 2007), 24.

17 David Folkenflik, "Bias or balance? Media wrestle with faltering trust," NPR, Apr. 23, 2010.

18 Author's telephone interview with Kathleen Carroll, Nov. 2, 2007.

19 Author's telephone interview with James M. Naughton, Sept. 14, 2007.

20 This list is derived from one created in November 1997 by Lawrence T. McGill, then director of research for the Freedom Forum Media Studies Center.

21 Robert H. Giles, "Introduction," in Robert J. Haiman, *Best Practices for Newspaper Journalists* (Arlington, VA: Freedom Forum's Free Press/Fair Press Project, 2000), 2.

22 "Examining our credibility: perspectives of the public and the press," a report by Urban & Associates for the American Society of Newspaper Editors, 1999. The telephone survey of 3,000 people was conducted in April and May 1998.

23 Jane T. Harrigan and Karen Brown Dunlap, *The Editorial Eye*, 2nd edn. (Boston: Bedford/St. Martin's Press, 2004), 118.

24 John C. Merrill, *Journalism Ethics: Philosophical Foundations for News Media* (New York: St. Martin's Press, 1997), 167.

25 Keith Woods, "Transmitting values: a guide to fairer journalism," in Michele McLellan, *The Newspaper Credibility Handbook* (Reston, VA: American Society of Newspaper Editors, 2001), 107.

26 Author's telephone interview with Gerald Jordan, Sept. 17, 2007.

27 Giles, "Introduction," 2.

28 Stephen Seplow, email to the author, Feb. 4, 2008.

29 David Carr and Tim Arango, "A Fox chief at the pinnacle of media and politics," *The New York Times*, Jan. 10, 2010.

30 Jesse Holcomb, "5 facts about Fox News," Pew Research Center, Jan. 14, 2014.

31 The phrase is taken from the headline over an essay by Ted Koppel in *The Washington Post*, Nov. 14, 2010: "The case against news we can choose."

32 David Carr, "The media equation: it's not just political districts. Our news is gerrymandered, too," *The New York Times*, Oct. 11, 2013.

33 Haiman, *Best Practices for Newspaper Journalists, 32.*

34 Bonnie Bucqueroux and Sue Carter (of Michigan State University's Victims and the Media Program), "Interviewing victims," *Quill*, Dec. 1999.

35 Mark Jurkowitz, "Anna and the astronaut trigger a week of tabloid news," Pew Research Center, Feb. 12, 2007; "Anna Nicole Smith – anatomy of a feeding frenzy," Pew Research Center, Apr. 4, 2007. For its weekly content index, PEJ analyzes content from 48 news outlets representing five media sectors: newspapers, network television, cable television, websites, and radio

36 Jurkowitz, "Anna and the astronaut trigger a week of tabloid news."

37 Ibid.

38 Michael E. Schudson and Susan E. Tifft, "American journalism in historical perspective," in Geneva Overholser and Kathleen Hall Jamieson (eds.), *The Press* (Oxford: Oxford University Press 2005), 40.

39 Bill Kovach and Tom Rosenstiel, *The Elements of Journalism: What Newspeople Should Know and the Public Should Expect*, 3rd edn. (New York: Three Rivers Press, 2014), 17.

40 McBride's experience is related in Kristen Hare, "Still slip-sliding: Gallup Poll ranks journalists low on honesty, ethics," Poynter, Dec. 17, 2013.

41 Renita Coleman and Lee Wilkins, *The Moral Media: How Journalists Reason about Ethics* (Mahwah, NJ: Lawrence Erlbaum, 2005), 39.

42 Ibid., 136.

43 "Internet news audience highly critical of news organizations: views of press values and performance: 1985–2007," Pew Research Center, Aug. 9, 2007.

44 Lawrence T. McGill, "The history of public perception that the press is unfair," in Haiman, *Best Practices for Newspaper Journalists*, 68.

45 "Amid criticism, support for media's 'watchdog' role stands out," Pew Research Center.

46 Leon Nelson Flynt, *The Conscience of the Newspaper: A Case Book in the Principles and Problems of Journalism* (New York: Appleton, 1925), 7–11.

6 Applying Four Classic Theories of Ethics

Ancient philosophy can help you make sound decisions

Learning Goals

This chapter will help you understand:

- four classic theories that can be tools in making decisions;
- rule-based thinking and its strengths and weaknesses;
- ends-based thinking and its strengths and weaknesses;
- the Golden Rule and its strengths and weaknesses;
- Aristotle's Golden Mean and its strengths and weaknesses;
- the value of blending rule-based thinking and ends-based thinking in the practice of journalism; and
- how editors used ends-based thinking to decide twenty-first-century cases of whether to publish government secrets.

In the spring of 1971 a fierce debate was being waged in the executive conference rooms of *The New York Times*. The paper had its hands on a historic exclusive: a 7,000-page Pentagon document revealing that, over three decades, the government had lied to American citizens about how their country got increasingly involved in the fighting in Vietnam.

There were two problems with what was to become known as the Pentagon Papers. First, the document had been stolen from the government by one of its authors, Daniel Ellsberg, a military analyst working for the Rand Corporation think tank. Ellsberg had handed it over to *Times* reporters. Second, it was classified "top secret."

Publishing the Pentagon Papers would be a crime.

The paper's editors argued unanimously that the citizens were entitled to the information in the Pentagon history of the war, stolen or not, classified or not. Their lawyers, nearly unanimously, pointed to the law violations and warned that publishing could lead to criminal prosecution that could ruin *The Times*.

Finally, the debate was decided by the one person whose vote counted. Arthur Ochs Sulzberger, the publisher, wanted to leave no doubt about his decision, so he put it in a formal memorandum: "I have reviewed once again the Vietnam story and documents that will appear on Sunday, and I am prepared to authorize their publication ..."[1]

The Ethical Journalist: Making Responsible Decisions in the Digital Age, Second Edition. Gene Foreman.
© 2016 John Wiley & Sons, Inc. Published 2016 by John Wiley & Sons, Inc.

That Sunday, June 13, 1971, *The Times* published the first of a series of articles under the purposely understated headline "Vietnam Archive: Pentagon Study Traces 3 Decades of Growing U.S. Involvement." On Tuesday, after three installments, the government got a court order to halt *The Times'* series. With *The Times* silenced, *The Washington Post, The Boston Globe,* and the *St. Louis Post-Dispatch* obtained copies of the Pentagon Papers from Ellsberg and defiantly began publishing their own reports.[2]

On June 30, the United States Supreme Court handed down a decision that has stood as a landmark affirmation of press freedom. The court, by a vote of six to three, held that the government was unjustified in exercising "prior restraint" to prevent *The Times* from continuing its series.[3] Siding with the majority, Justice Hugo Black referred to the nation's founding principles: "The press was protected so that it could bare the secrets of government and inform the people. Only a free and unrestrained press can effectively expose deception in government."[4]

Max Frankel, in 1971 the chief of *The Times'* Washington bureau and later the paper's top editor, reflected after a quarter of a century: "As the prosecutors of the case confessed decades later, no damage was done. No military battles were lost. The national security bureaucracy had fought not to protect information from aliens but to enlarge its authority to deny information to Americans."[5]

In the weeks-long debate at *The Times* that spring, ends-based thinking triumphed over rule-based thinking.

Most of the lawyers argued in favor of following *the rule*. Embodied in the law, the rule says that citizens don't use stolen property. And they certainly don't publicize information that the government has legally declared to be "top secret."

The editors argued for looking beyond the rule and focusing on *the ends*. The citizens of the United States have sacrificed blood and treasure in the Vietnam War, they were saying, and now we have a document that shows their government has repeatedly lied to them about that war. The people deserve to know what is in the document. *The Times* has a moral obligation to tell them.

The publisher ultimately decided that the editors were right. Less than three weeks later, so did the Supreme Court majority. "In revealing the workings of government that led to the Vietnam War," Justice Black wrote, "the newspapers nobly did precisely that which the founders hoped and trusted they would do."[6]

How Ethical Theories Influence Decisions

Although there is no evidence that either the editors or the lawyers cited those classic theories of ethics in *The Times'* debate, the case has significance in terms of news media ethics, as it does in news media law. It illustrates the role that the classic theories of ethics, consciously or not, play in journalists' decision-making.

This chapter discusses four classic theories as tools in the decision process: rule-based thinking, ends-based thinking, the Golden Rule, and Aristotle's Golden Mean. The descriptions that follow are summarized from ethics scholars' analysis of the four theories.

Rule-Based Thinking
(Deontology, Duty-Based Thinking)

Rule-based thinking is absolutist. A person has a duty to do the right thing – no excuses, no exceptions, and no worrying about the consequences. Ethical obligations must be obeyed regardless of the situation and, as ethicist Michael Josephson has written, "in spite of social conventions and natural inclinations to the contrary."[7]

The champion of rule-based thinking was Immanuel Kant (1724–1804), a German philosopher whose concept of *the categorical imperative* is central to the theory. The categorical imperative, as Kant articulated it, is: "I ought never to act except in such a way that I can also will that my maxim should become universal law." Kant was saying that a person should act as if he or she were setting a standard for other people to follow, and that, if everyone followed that standard, the world would be a better place.[8]

Kant believed that people should live up to standards of conduct "because they are good, not because of the consequences that might result," Louis A. Day wrote in *Ethics in Media Communications: Cases and Controversies*. Although people are free to make their own choices – a fundamental requirement of ethics – "they have a responsibility to live up to moral principles." Truthfulness is a universal good, so everyone should always tell the truth. It doesn't matter that sometimes the truth can cause harm.[9]

Kant also urged respect for all. Every person is intrinsically important as a human being. People should treat others with dignity and grant others the same autonomy they enjoy.

Rule-based thinking is sometimes called *duty-based thinking* because of its emphasis on an individual's moral duty. Philosophers label it *deontology*, derived from the Greek word *deon* (duty). A person who adheres to rule-based thinking is a deontologist.

The strength of rule-based thinking lies in its simplicity. "If we follow the rules, we are ethical; if we break them, we are unethical," John C. Merrill wrote in *Journalism Ethics: Philosophical Foundations for News Media*.[10] Using rule-based thinking, a decision-maker (called *a moral agent* by the philosophers) does not have to calculate the consequences of the decision.

The weakness of rule-based thinking is that it is rigid. A person confronted with two or more competing ethical values – by definition, an ethical dilemma – has no way to make a choice. Think of the Heinz dilemma in Chapter 2: Heinz has to decide whether to steal the drug or allow his wife to die; choosing one value would mean rejecting the other. If Heinz were a deontologist, he would be paralyzed by indecision.

A journalist who is a strict deontologist would never quote a source anonymously because the source's identity is a truth that the journalist would be morally obligated to report, John C. Merrill wrote. Similarly, a deontologist would always identify a rape victim. Such a journalist

> feels a loyalty to the integrity of the story and not to any person connected to the story. This journalist is not concerned with all the possible consequences that might result from the story; these are considered irrelevant to good journalism. Just tell the truth and let the chips fall where they will.[11]

In the Pentagon Papers case, deontology would have guided *The Times* to a decision not to publish. The law embodies a universal rule that people should refuse to accept property that they know is stolen; otherwise, they aid and abet thievery. Also, in the abstract, it is essential to national security that the government be allowed to protect secrets.

Ends-Based Thinking (Consequentialism, Utilitarianism, Teleology)

Ends-based thinking is flexible. It allows the decision-maker to weigh competing values according to the consequences that might occur. "In essence," Michael Josephson wrote, "the ends can justify the means."[12]

Ends-based thinking directs a choice in favor of the course of action that brings the most good to the most people. It is a calculation of the preponderance of good over evil, or benefits over harm – a sort of "cost–benefit analysis," as the author Rushworth M. Kidder phrased it in *How Good People Make Tough Choices*.[13]

Jeremy Bentham (1748–1832) and John Stuart Mill (1806–73), British philosophers, were the champions of this theory. Mill held that people should choose the greatest happiness for the greatest number of people – the greatest balance of pleasure over pain. Later adherents of this theory argued that happiness is not the only desirable value, so it is more commonly known today as the greatest good for the greatest number, as Clifford G. Christians and his co-authors explained in *Media Ethics: Cases and Moral Reasoning*.[14]

Ends-based thinking requires thoughtful consideration of who will be helped and who will be harmed by a decision, and to what degree. These people are commonly called stakeholders, because they have a stake in the decision.

Not to be overlooked in examining ends-based thinking is its principle that the rights of a minority are to be respected. "In a society of ten people, nine sadists cannot justly persecute the tenth person even though it yields the greatest happiness," Christians and his associates wrote.[15] In the United States, the constitutional guarantee of a fair trial cannot be disregarded because most of the people in a town have already concluded the guilt of the accused.

Since Bentham and Mill called their ethical system *the theory of utility*, it is known in philosophy as *utilitarianism*. Another name is *consequentialism*, derived from the theory's focus on the consequences of a decision. In contrast to deontology, ends-based thinking is called teleology, from the Greek word *telos* (end).

The strength of ends-based thinking is that its flexibility permits a person to make a choice between competing ethical principles. Heinz could decide, for example, that the principle of compassion for his wife's well-being is more important than the moral rule (and law) prohibiting theft.

Ends-based thinking directs the decision-maker to consider all the possible courses of action and to weigh the benefits and harms likely to result from each alternative.[16] If the process is carried out thoughtfully, this can contribute to a sound decision.

The flexibility of ends-based thinking is also its main weakness. In Michael Josephson's view, the theory can be "manipulated by self-serving rationalizations to produce ... an end-justifies-the-means credo that elevates expediency over principle."[17] Another problem with ends-based thinking is that sometimes it is difficult or impossible to predict the consequences of a decision.

The journalist who is a teleologist might deceive a source if the journalist judges that the deception will elicit important information. In such a case the journalist would contend that the harm of deception is outweighed by the good of informing the public – that the end justifies the means. A deontologist, on the other hand, would reject all forms of deception.

Teleology permits compassion to influence decisions. Unconcerned about the consequences, a deontologist would not omit any verified fact from a news story that is embarrassing to a private individual. In contrast, a teleologist would likely discard harmful facts if they are irrelevant to the story's point. The teleologist thus would "inflict only the harm required to put the story in perspective," Louis A. Day wrote. "To do more would be merely an appeal to the morbid curiosity of the public."[18]

In deciding to publish the Pentagon Papers, *The Times* concluded that the document's value to the public outweighed the principles of refusing stolen property and respecting the top-secret classification. The decision was a model of teleology in action.

The Golden Rule

Do unto others as you would have them do unto you. This rule of reversibility, found in the teachings of the world's great religions, is the best single rule of ethical decision-making. Imagine yourself in the place of the person affected by your decision and, from that perspective, assess the fairness of the decision. No wonder that it is the only rule of ethics many people profess to know.[19]

Consider how instructive the **Golden Rule** is. As Michael Josephson wrote, "If you don't want to be lied to or deceived, don't lie to or deceive others. If you want others to keep their commitments to you, keep your commitments to them."[20] Applying the Golden Rule tells you which of your contemplated actions are ethical and which are not. The Golden Rule counsels people to use restraint and self-discipline to avoid inflicting harm. It stresses love, not self-interest, as the moral base of conduct.[21] People are to be treated with dignity, as ends in themselves, not as the means to an end.

The Golden Rule has broad application to journalism. A reporter following the Golden Rule would not write a story subjecting people to ridicule and voyeurism, because the reporter would not want to be exploited if the tables were turned. Such a reporter would not secretly record a source, because he or she would not want to be secretly recorded.

However, if a journalist is reporting on a situation in which two or more stakeholders have competing interests, the Golden Rule alone is not a sufficient guide. The Golden Rule cannot tell the journalist how to decide between the competing stakeholders. That is the Golden Rule's singular weakness.

There were a multitude of stakeholders in the decision facing publisher Arthur Ochs Sulzberger in the Pentagon Papers case. His fellow owners depended on his judgment to shield the paper from financial harm, which could have been a consequence of prosecution. The thousands of employees likewise looked to his stewardship of a business that provided a livelihood for them and their families. Among those employees, however, were newsroom staff members who likely would have agreed with their editors that the paper would be failing its journalistic duty if it did not publish. And, finally, there were the millions of American citizens who, depending on Sulzberger's decision, would either be informed or kept in the dark about what their government had done in Vietnam. As good as it is, the Golden Rule could not have guided Sulzberger's decision.

Aristotle's Golden Mean

The ancient Greek philosophers emphasized a virtuous character. Aristotle (384–322 BCE) saw virtue in moderation – finding the mean, or intermediate, between an excess and a deficiency. He saw *courage* as the mean between *recklessness* and *cowardice*, and *proper pride* as the mean between *empty vanity* and *undue humility*.[22]

From Aristotle's virtue ethics, contemporary moral agents can draw on his theory of the Golden Mean (not to be confused with the Golden Rule). He believed that the virtuous person learns to avoid the extremes in a given situation. Thus, "the Golden Mean provides a moderate solution in those cases where there are identifiable extreme positions, neither of which is likely to produce satisfactory results," Louis A. Day wrote.[23]

"Aristotle was not advocating a bland, weak-minded consensus or the proverbial middle-of-the-road compromise," Clifford G. Christians and his co-authors wrote. "Although the word *mean* has a mathematical flavor and a sense of average, a precise equal distance from two extremes is not intended."[24]

Aristotle's Golden Mean is at work in the decisions of the Federal Trade Commission on tobacco sales and advertising. The FTC could have chosen one extreme of allowing tobacco, as a legal product, to be sold and advertised without regulation. Or, in the face of medical evidence of tobacco's hazards, it could have gone to the opposite extreme and prohibited tobacco sales. Instead, the FTC has taken moderate steps like prohibiting sales to minors, banning cigarette ads on television, and requiring health warnings on cigarette packages.[25]

Journalists can often find a Golden Mean to guide their decisions. As an example, consider a highly newsworthy video or still photograph whose graphic nature is certain to offend a segment of the audience. For television, the Golden Mean might lead to a decision to warn the audience before showing the video, and not to show it in the daytime or early evening when children likely will be in the audience. For a newspaper or magazine, the Golden Mean might result in publishing the photo in black and white rather than in color, on an inside page rather than the front, or in a smaller size rather than a larger one. A digital news site could offer a cautionary description of the photo and require users to click on a link in order to see it.

Not every situation offers a Golden Mean. For example, there was no compromise available for publisher Sulzberger in the Pentagon Papers case. Either *The Times* would publish the document or it would not.

Blending Rule- and Ends-Based Thinking

Taken as a whole, the classic ethical theories give you a solid foundation for decision-making in journalism. You should not feel compelled to align yourself with a single theory. In particular, you do not have to choose between being a strict deontologist or a strict teleologist. You can benefit from the wisdom of an ethics code laid out in advance (rule-based thinking), but you also need to sense when the circumstances call for a different solution (ends-based thinking).

The Golden Rule deserves consideration in every situation. This overarching ethical guideline is a revealing test of the fairness of your proposed course of action. It may not be the ultimate solution of an ethical problem you face, but it is a step in that direction.

Rule-based thinking provides structure in the decision-making process. Your newsroom may have a policy that applies to a particular situation you are facing in gathering the news. In the absence of a newsroom policy, consider the accepted standards of the profession, such as those in the ethics code of the Society of Professional Journalists.

Policies and standards are useful because they are the product of thoughtful, off-deadline discussions and reflect the wisdom of experience. They are what the news organization has decided is "best practice" in given situations. They help a news organization be consistent and fair.

But no policy can anticipate every situation that might arise. Departing from the teaching of Kant, journalists should view policies as guidelines, not rules. In developing your skills as a moral agent, learn to analyze the circumstances. There may be reasons *not* to follow the policy in a given situation.

That does not mean that you set aside a policy on a whim, or on your own authority. To the contrary, you conduct a careful analysis that prepares you to articulate the reasons for choosing a different course of action. Except in rare cases, there is time for you to discuss your reasoning with a newsroom supervisor. You will need to argue convincingly that departing from the policy is the best choice.

The process illustrates the constructive tension between rule-based thinking and ends-based thinking. Start with the policy, consider the circumstances, consult with experienced colleagues, and decide with them which should prevail.

Aristotle's Golden Mean comes into play when other courses of action would likely result in unacceptable consequences. When that happens, search for an ethical compromise.

In your analysis of the case studies in the rest of this book — and in the decisions you will make in your journalism career — you should find the four classic ethical theories to be important tools in your decision-making process.

Rushworth M. Kidder saw these principles as useful not because they are "part of a magic answer kit that produces infallible solutions," but because they help us reason. The principles, Kidder wrote, "give us a way to exercise our moral rationality. They provide different lenses through which to see our dilemmas, different screens to use in assessing them."[26]

Postscript: Publishing 21st-Century Secrets

In the years after the terrorism of September 11, 2001, the US government sent combat troops to fight in Afghanistan and Iraq while simultaneously waging a secret war intended to prevent any enemy from mounting such an attack again.

The news media, when they have obtained information about some aspects of that secret war, have concluded that the information deserved the public's attention. These include seizing and torturing presumed terrorists, allowing the abuse of prisoners held after the Iraq War, and carrying out air strikes in Yemen that were falsely attributed to the Yemeni military. They also include bold intrusions into privacy, such as monitoring international banking records and collecting vast amounts of data about the telephone calls of average Americans.

In reporting to the public, the news media contended that citizens were entitled to know about questionable moral behavior by agents of the American government, and about the tradeoffs of privacy rights being made in the name of national security. Most of the reporting was protested by government officials who argued that divulging the secrets would make the nation vulnerable to attack.

As a result of the Supreme Court's ruling in the Pentagon Papers case in 1971, the media's legal right to publish secret government information was never in doubt. Yet the new cases imposed a heavy ethical responsibility on the editors and news directors who made the decisions. The twenty-first-century cases required newsroom leaders to weigh the benefit of the information to the public against the possibility that publishing would aid America's enemies.

In terms of the ethical theories discussed earlier in this chapter, these were exercises in ends-based thinking. And they are instructive to students of journalism ethics.

Everyone who works any length of time in journalism can expect to be confronted by a public official, a business executive, or an ordinary citizen who fiercely opposes a course of action that the journalist thinks is in the public interest. When that happens, the journalist has a duty to give a carefully reasoned response — to show, in the terms of this textbook's statement in Chapter 2, that the decision had been rationally made by a caring individual. For most of us, these confrontations do not take place in the Oval Office, nor are we likely to receive a phone call from the director of national intelligence, as a former executive editor of *The New York Times* did, saying, "Jill Abramson, you will have blood on your hands if *The Times* publishes this story." (Abramson didn't publish the information – about how US intelligence had intercepted a message between two Al Qaeda leaders – in the next day's paper, but she did a month later.)[27]

In the 2010 publication of information gleaned from the intercepts by WikiLeaks, an activist organization that disdains government secrecy and seeks to reveal all government secrets, editors demonstrated a decision-making process that was both meticulous and transparent.

Bill Keller, then *The New York Times'* editor, and his colleagues alerted Obama administration officials before his paper published selections from thousands of intercepted messages providing new details about the wars in Afghanistan and Iraq and the US anti-terrorism campaign. WikiLeaks, headed by an Australian national named Julian Assange, had made its information available to *The Guardian* and other European news organizations, and *The Guardian* had decided to share with *The New York Times*. In turn, WikiLeaks' source was believed to be a US Army private first class, Bradley (now Chelsea) Manning, who had gained access to the data as an intelligence analyst in Iraq. Manning was convicted in a court martial in 2013 and sentenced to 35 years.

As Keller related later in *The New York Times*, the government objections fell into three categories. One was "the importance of protecting individuals who had spoken candidly to American diplomats in oppressive countries." *The Times* agreed to redact nearly all of those. The second category involved "sensitive American programs, usually related to intelligence." The journalists agreed to withhold some of this information, such as the description of "an intelligence-sharing program that took years to arrange and might be lost if exposed," but they concluded that in other instances "publication would cause some embarrassment but no real harm." The third category consisted of messages in which American diplomats had written candidly about foreign leaders. To the State Department's argument that publication would sour US relations with those countries, the journalists were mostly unconvinced.[28] When the WikiLeaks stories were published, *The Times* explained its thinking in a note to readers.[29]

In 2013 a former National Security Agency contractor, Edward Snowden, gave *The Guardian* and *The Washington Post* a far more significant trove of government secrets he had downloaded with computers in a National Security Agency office in Hawaii.

Snowden's key revelation was that secret court orders allowed the NSA to obtain the telephone records of customers of most American communications companies. Other documents showed that the NSA could request user data from companies like Google, Facebook, Microsoft, and Apple, and the companies would be obliged to comply. Among other revelations was that the NSA was spying on dozens of world leaders.[30]

Snowden handed over the documents to *Guardian* and *Post* journalists in Hong Kong. Facing prosecution in the United States, he then flew to Moscow, where Russia granted him temporary asylum.

While American public opinion was divided over whether Snowden was a whistleblower or a traitor, there was no question that he had created a legitimate debate over privacy rights in the post-9/11 era. Responding to the widespread protest after the Snowden disclosures, President Obama took steps to protect privacy, reining in the NSA's surveillance of customer telephone records as well as its monitoring of foreign leaders. In a column in *USA Today*, media critic Rem Rieder wrote that the president's agreeing to "reforms, however modest, was entirely due to the Snowden disclosures. And it underscores the value of what Snowden has done."[31]

The news media have drawn criticism, of course, for publicizing secrets in the face of dire warnings from officials. Typically, citizens' objections have been expressed in rhetorical questions: What right do these editors have to do this? Who elected them?

In a joint message to their readers in 2006, the editors of two newspapers tried to answer those questions. Dean Baquet of the *Los Angeles Times* and Bill Keller of *The New York Times* explained why the two newspapers had just published secret information about the US government's monitoring of international banking records. They described how they had proceeded when they came into possession of secrets that, arguably, the public should know about:

> The process begins with reporting. … We double-check and triple-check. We seek out sources with different points of view. We challenge our sources when contradictory information emerges.
>
> Then we listen. No article on a classified program gets published until the responsible officials have been given a fair opportunity to comment. And if they want to argue that publication represents a danger to national security, we put things on hold and give them a respectful hearing. …
>
> Finally, we weigh the merits of publishing against the risks of publishing. There is no magic formula, no neat metric for either the public's interest or the dangers of publishing sensitive information. We make our own best judgment. …
>
> We understand that honorable people may disagree with any of these choices – to publish or not to publish. But making those decisions is the responsibility that falls to editors, a corollary of the great gift of our independence. It is not a decision we take lightly. And it is not one we can surrender to the government.[32]

Notes

1   Susan E. Tifft and Alex S. Jones, *The Trust: The Private and Powerful Family behind The New York Times* (London: Little, Brown, 1999), 482.

2   Ibid., 480–493.

3   "Supreme Court, 6–3, upholds newspapers on publication of Pentagon report," *The New York Times,* July 1, 1971.

4   Bill Kovach and Tom Rosenstiel, *The Elements of Journalism: What Newspeople Should Know and the Public Should Expect* (New York: Crown, 2001), 113.

5   Max Frankel, "Top secret," *The New York Times,* June 16, 1996.

6   *The New York Times,* July 1, 1971.

7   Michael Josephson, *Ethical Issues and Opportunities in Journalism* (Marina del Rey, CA: Josephson Institute, 1991), 21.

8   Rushworth M. Kidder, *How Good People Make Tough Choices: Resolving the Dilemmas of Ethical Living* (New York: HarperCollins, 1995), 24.

9   Louis A. Day, *Ethics in Media Communications: Cases and Controversies*, 5th edn. (Belmont, CA: Thomson Wadsworth, 2006), 58.

10   John C. Merrill, *Journalism Ethics: Philosophical Foundations for News Media* (New York: St. Martin's Press, 1997), 62.

11   Ibid.

12   Josephson, *Making Ethical Decisions* (Los Angeles: Josephson Institute, 1999).

13   Kidder, *How Good People Make Tough Choices*, 24.

14   Clifford G. Christians, Kim B. Rotzoll, Mark Fackler, Kathy Brittain McKee, and Robert H. Woods Jr., *Media Ethics: Cases and Moral Reasoning*, 7th edn. (Boston: Allyn & Bacon, 2005), 16–17.

15   Ibid., 17.

16   Day, *Ethics in Media Communications,* 63.

17   Josephson, *Ethical Issues and Opportunities in Journalism*, 22.

18   Day, *Ethics in Media Communications*, 63.

19   Kidder, *How Good People Make Tough Choices*, 25.

20   Josephson, *Making Ethical Decisions* (Los Angeles: Josephson Institute, 2002), 22. (The 2002 edition is a revision of the booklet that was first published in 1999.)

21   Josephson, *Making Ethical Decisions* (1999).

22   Kidder, *How Good People Make Tough Choices*, 70.

23   Day, *Ethics in Media Communications*, 64.

24   Christians et al., *Media Ethics*, 13–14.

25   Ibid., 13.

26   Kidder, *How Good People Make Tough Choices*, 26.

27   Michael Calderone, "James Clapper warned ex-*New York Times* editor Jill Abramson of 'blood on your hands,'" *The Huffington Post*, July 14, 2014. Abramson related the phone conversation with Clapper in a speech at the Chautauqua Institution in upstate New York.

28   Bill Keller, "Dealing with Assange and the WikiLeaks secrets," *The New York Times*, Jan. 26, 2011.

29   "A note to readers: the decision to publish diplomatic documents," *The New York Times*, Nov. 26, 2010.

30   Lorenzo Franceschi-Bierchierai, "The 10 biggest revelations from Edward Snowden's leaks," Mashable, June 5, 2014.

31   Rem Rieder, "Edward Snowden's powerful impact," *USA Today*, Jan. 17, 2014.

32   Dean Baquet and Bill Keller, "When do we publish a secret?," *Los Angeles Times* and *The New York Times*, July 1, 2006.

7 Using a Code of Ethics as a Decision Tool

Written professional standards are valuable in resolving dilemmas

---

Learning Goals

This chapter will help you understand:

- the history of codes of ethics for journalists;
- the arguments for and against ethics codes;
- how an ethics code can be a useful tool in decision-making;
- the four guiding principles of the code adopted in 2014 by the Society of Professional Journalists:
  1 Seek truth and report it.
  2 Minimize harm.
  3 Act independently.
  4 Be accountable and transparent.

When magazine writer Will Irwin surveyed the state of American newspapers in 1911, he concluded that the best reporters followed unwritten rules. These rules commanded them to be honest with their sources and empathetic toward the people they wrote about.

Irwin wrote that these reporters would "never, without special permission, print information which you learn at your friend's house, or in your club"; that sources would always be advised what newspaper the reporter represented; and that, unless the source was a criminal, nothing would be printed without prior consent. In addition, he wrote, good reporters "remember that when the suicide lies dead in the chamber there are wretched hearts in the hall, that when the son is newly in jail intrusion is torment to the mother."

The word-of-mouth standards Irwin described in his critique of the press for *Collier's Weekly* formed a sort of code of ethics. As journalism embraced professionalism in those early decades of the twentieth century, ethical guidelines would soon be put in writing.[1]

After the founding in 1922 of the American Society of Newspaper Editors (ASNE, now the American Society of News Editors), one of its first actions was to draw up its Canons of Journalism. ASNE's canons were revised in 1975 and renamed the Statement of Principles.

The Ethical Journalist: Making Responsible Decisions in the Digital Age, Second Edition. Gene Foreman.
© 2016 John Wiley & Sons, Inc. Published 2016 by John Wiley & Sons, Inc.

Sigma Delta Chi, the forerunner of today's Society of Professional Journalists, adopted ASNE's canons in 1926 and wrote its own code in 1973. That code has been revised in 1984, 1987, 1996, and 2014.

The 1923 canons of ASNE directed that newspapers be independent of "all obligations except that of fidelity to the public interest," to be accurate and truthful, to distinguish between news reports and expressions of opinion, to give subjects of news coverage a chance to reply to charges against them, and to avoid reporting in detail on crime and vice and thereby "pandering to vicious instincts."[2]

In 1946 the new National Association of Radio News Directors adopted a resolution calling for stations to have autonomous news departments staffed by trained journalists. The next year, the radio directors resolved that commercials should be clearly separated from news content and preferably not be read by the newscaster. These resolutions evolved into the code of ethics of the Radio Television News Directors Association, last revised in 2000.[3] The organization is now called the Radio Television Digital News Association (RTDNA). As this edition of *The Ethical Journalist* was being prepared, an RTDNA committee was at work drafting a new round of code revisions.

The Online News Association (ONA), formed in 1999, pledged to uphold the "traditional high principles in reporting original news" and to make clear the distinction between news and "paid promotional information and other non-news." In 2014 ONA was compiling a series of essays on ethics topics to help individual journalists and news outlets create "do-it-yourself" codes.[4]

A crucial aspect shared by all these codes – and the codes adopted by other national associations of journalists – is that compliance is voluntary.

The Society of Professional Journalists (SPJ) briefly tried to put teeth in its code, calling in 1973 for journalists to "actively censure" violators. Fourteen years later, SPJ retreated, mainly because sanctioning journalists could invite costly litigation. The 1987 amendment deleted the "censure" clause and substituted an education program to encourage journalists to adhere to the code's ideals. SPJ says on its website that its code "is not, nor can it be under the First Amendment, legally enforceable."[5]

In contrast to the voluntary codes, the standards adopted by individual newspapers, broadcast stations, and websites can be enforced, to the point of firing violators. In unionized newsrooms, that discipline is subject to collective-bargaining agreements.

As noted in Chapter 3, the number of newsrooms with written codes increased exponentially in the 1970s and 1980s. Editors' and news directors' insistence on providing *a priori* guidance to their staffs overcame the resistance of their lawyers, who feared that written codes would make it easier for plaintiffs' attorneys to prove negligence in libel cases by showing that a journalist had failed to live up to the organization's own standards.

The ethics statements by national organizations like ASNE, SPJ, RTDNA, and ONA give journalists broad guidance for avoiding conflicts of interest and for covering the news accurately, fairly, and compassionately. The codes of individual newsrooms tend to be more specific in identifying unacceptable conflicts of interest. In addition, the newsroom codes may spell out policies for recurring news-coverage situations such as whether to identify rape victims or juveniles accused of crimes.

The Debate over the Value of Codes

Although codes are well established in the profession, journalism scholars and practitioners continue to debate their worth. Critics make these arguments:

- *The codes are too vague.* Since the codes can't cover every conceivable situation, they dwell on lofty ideals that no serious journalist disagrees with. In a nod to the lawyers, the language might be hedged further. This results in a lack of clarity that defeats the purpose of written instructions.
- *The codes discourage thoughtful decision-making.* Some journalists, intimidated by the code, follow its directions slavishly instead of engaging in the kind of critical thinking needed to resolve ethical dilemmas. Edmund B. Lambeth wrote in his book *Committed Journalism*: "[A] strong case can be made that a combination of moral imagination, professional ingenuity, and interpersonal communication skills is more effective in establishing and maintaining ethical standards in the newsroom than codes of ethics."[6]
- *The codes are mere public-relations ploys.* Instead of setting an example of probity, newsroom leaders may signal through their behavior that the organization's published codes really don't count. The late John C. Merrill, a pioneering ethics scholar, dismissed an ethics code as something to put in a frame to cover a hole in the wall.[7]
- *The owners don't follow the codes.* Most codes "are aimed entirely wrong, in focusing on journalists rather than on owners, who are the ones with real autonomy and decision-making power," journalism professor Carol Reuss wrote.[8] As an example, newsroom staff members scrupulously avoid involvement in outside activities that the organization may have to cover, but company executives routinely take on active civic roles. The executives maintain that this kind of involvement is in the spirit of the company's social responsibility to the community.

All of those criticisms have some degree of validity. For some critics, the minuses of ethics codes outweigh the pluses, so they reject codes altogether. As autonomous moral agents, they are entitled to that conclusion.

Another assessment, however, is that the negatives demonstrate only that codes of ethics are not *absolute* solutions to ethical problems.

Ethics Codes as a Decision-Making Tool

This text takes the position that a code is a useful tool in decision-making. Journalists benefit from the guidance found in well-thought-out codes such as the one adopted in 2014 by the Society of Professional Journalists.

The key is to view the code as part of a step-by-step process in making news-coverage decisions, not as a substitute for the process.

Thanks to the code, a journalist does not have to begin the decision process with a blank canvas. The code offers conventional wisdom – best practices as defined by experienced journalists thinking together in a relaxed, off-deadline setting. Defining best practices helps a news organization be fair and consistent in the way it covers the news. The late James M. Naughton, a member of a staff committee that drafted *The Philadelphia Inquirer's* code in 1978, remembered the process as a useful exercise because it provided "a baseline for collegial understanding of what the standards are." It is important, Naughton said, that staff members understand the strengths and weaknesses of codes.[9]

Newsroom leaders have an obligation to be fair and consistent in dealing with conflicts of interest that they consider unacceptable. An important step toward fairness and consistency is informing staff members in advance about what those conflicts are. A written code does that.

The authors of *Doing Ethics in Journalism* wrote that ethics codes are

> supposed to act as the conscience of the professional, of the organization, of the enterprise. … The strength of an ethics code is a function not only of its various principles and mandates, but of its legitimacy and power in the eyes of those for whom it is written.[10]

Codes can be counterproductive if they focus only on what journalists should *not* do. Roy Peter Clark of the Poynter Institute views such an approach as "Red Light" ethics, placing obstacles in the path of journalists who are trying to report stories the public needs. Clark's preference is "Green Light" ethics, which helps journalists figure out how to do those stories while behaving decently.[11]

Newsroom codes vary drastically in degree of detail. *The New York Times* published a 54-page "handbook of values and practices for the news and editorial departments" in September 2004. It is a model of clear, carefully explained guidelines. No one expects a staff member to memorize the book, but it is reasonable to expect that journalists *be familiar with* the guidelines and consult them when the need arises. (The author recommends the ethics codes of *The New York Times*,[12] the Associated Press,[13] and NPR[14] as supplemental text material for a journalism ethics course. All are available online.)

Commenting on the detailed *Times* code, public editor Manning Pynn of the *Orlando Sentinel* wrote a column playfully suggesting an alternative – a code that would fit on a wallet card. His succinct code also is a model of good counsel: "Don't accept free stuff. Don't cover friends, families – or enemies. Don't use your position for personal benefit. Don't make stuff up. Explain where you got your information. Don't steal other people's work. Don't alter photographs."[15]

SPJ's Four Fundamental Principles

The revised code that the Society of Professional Journalists adopted at its 2014 convention is based on four fundamental principles: seek truth and report it; minimize harm; act independently; and be accountable and transparent. In drafting the revisions, the SPJ ethics committee kept the four cornerstones of the code adopted

18 years earlier while adding "transparent" to the fourth. This is how the SPJ leadership summarized the most important of the 2014 changes:

- "The code isn't filled with specific references to social or digital media or special forms of emerging media such as entrepreneurial, point-of-view and citizen journalism. Instead, it is made clear that the code is applicable to all forms of journalism and the people who work within them."
- "The idea of transparency makes a debut in this code. Although this code does not abdicate the principle of being independent of conflicts that may compromise integrity or damage credibility, it does note more strongly that when these conflicts can't be avoided, it is imperative the journalists make every effort to be transparent about their actions. It acknowledges the importance of corrections, engaging the public in discourse over journalism issues, and it tells journalists they should uphold the highest ethical standards in all engagements with the public."[16]

In the SPJ code, the four fundamental *principles* appear in large type. Below each principle, in smaller type, are *standards of practice* to guide journalists as they try to live up to the principle. Each standard represents a consensus of the profession.

SPJ strengthened certain standards in 2014. The revised code emphasizes verification of information, which the ethics committee said is intended to "address the growing trend to repeat information without independent verification, even when that information is from another news outlet." In a reference to the competitive pressure of journalism in the digital age, the code stresses that neither speed nor format excuses inaccuracy. The code drops the 1996 admonition "to avoid bidding for news" and declares flatly that journalists "do not pay for access to news." A new standard advises journalists that "legal access to information differs from an ethical justification to publish or broadcast."[17]

The four guiding principles are intended to work in tandem, not in isolation. A journalist might have to balance two or more of the principles in making a decision. Journalists should start their decision-making with the "truth" principle, because it is their job to convey information to the public, not to suppress it. Then, in recognition that telling the truth can hurt, "minimize harm" enters the process. In the Case Study "The Death of a Boy," the tragic accident needed to be reported, even though reading it would deepen the family's pain. However, you should explore how useful it was to publish the photograph of the boy's distraught mother or to report irrelevant details in the news story, such as the fact that the parents were married in a civil ceremony.

As part of your reading for this chapter, review the SPJ code's small-type standards beneath the four large-type guiding principles. To help you in your decision-making in case studies that appear in Part II of this textbook, you should be familiar with the standards. As a reference, the 2014 SPJ code is reprinted in Box 7.1.

The four guiding principles chosen by the SPJ code-makers are worthy of class discussion because they articulate fundamental beliefs of journalists. The sections below are intended to stimulate that discussion. (Except where the SPJ code and other sources are quoted, the commentary is the author's.)

Box 7.1   Society of Professional Journalists' Ethics Code

Preamble

Members of the Society of Professional Journalists believe that public enlightenment is the forerunner of justice and the foundation of democracy. Ethical journalism strives to ensure the free exchange of information that is accurate, fair and thorough. An ethical journalist acts with integrity.

The Society declares these four principles as the foundation of ethical journalism and encourages their use in its practice by all people in all media.

Seek truth and report it

Ethical journalism should be accurate and fair. Journalists should be honest and courageous in gathering, reporting and interpreting information.

Journalists should:

- Take responsibility for the accuracy of their work. Verify information before releasing it. Use original sources whenever possible.
- Remember that neither speed nor format excuses inaccuracy.
- Provide context. Take special care not to misrepresent or oversimplify in promoting, previewing or summarizing a story.
- Gather, update and correct information throughout the life of a news story.
- Be cautious when making promises, but keep the promises they make.
- Identify sources clearly. The public is entitled to as much information as possible to judge the reliability and motivations of sources.
- Consider sources' motives before promising anonymity. Reserve anonymity for sources who may face danger, retribution or other harm, and have information that cannot be obtained elsewhere. Explain why anonymity was granted.
- Diligently seek subjects of news coverage to allow them to respond to criticism or allegations of wrongdoing.
- Avoid undercover or other surreptitious methods of gathering information unless traditional, open methods will not yield information vital to the public.
- Be vigilant and courageous about holding those with power accountable. Give voice to the voiceless.
- Support the open and civil exchange of views, even views they find repugnant.
- Recognize a special obligation to serve as watchdogs over public affairs and government. Seek to ensure that the public's business is conducted in the open, and that public records are open to all.
- Provide access to source material when it is relevant and appropriate.
- Boldly tell the story of the diversity and magnitude of the human experience. Seek sources whose voices we seldom hear.
- Avoid stereotyping. Journalists should examine the ways their values and experiences may shape their reporting.
- Label advocacy and commentary.
- Never deliberately distort facts or context, including visual information. Clearly label illustrations and re-enactments.
- Never plagiarize. Always attribute.

Minimize harm

Ethical journalism treats sources, subjects, colleagues and members of the public as human beings deserving of respect.

Journalists should:

- Balance the public's need for information against potential harm or discomfort. Pursuit of the news is not a license for arrogance or undue intrusiveness.
- Show compassion for those who may be affected by news coverage. Use heightened sensitivity when dealing with juveniles, victims of sex crimes, and sources or subjects who are inexperienced or unable to give consent. Consider cultural differences in approach and treatment.
- Recognize that legal access to information differs from an ethical justification to publish or broadcast.
- Realize that private people have a greater right to control information about themselves than public figures and others who seek power, influence or attention. Weigh the consequences of publishing or broadcasting personal information.
- Avoid pandering to lurid curiosity, even if others do.
- Balance a suspect's right to a fair trial with the public's right to know. Consider the implications of identifying criminal suspects before they face legal charges.
- Consider the long-term implications of the extended reach and permanence of publication. Provide updated and more complete information as appropriate.

Act independently

The highest and primary obligation of ethical journalism is to serve the public.
Journalists should:

- Avoid conflicts of interest, real or perceived. Disclose unavoidable conflicts.

- Refuse gifts, favors, fees, free travel and special treatment, and avoid political and other outside activities that may compromise integrity or impartiality, or may damage credibility.
- Be wary of sources offering information for favors or money; do not pay for access to news. Identify content provided by outside sources, whether paid or not.
- Deny favored treatment to advertisers, donors or any other special interests, and resist internal and external pressure to influence coverage.
- Distinguish news from advertising and shun hybrids that blur the lines between the two. Prominently label sponsored content.

Be accountable and transparent

Ethical journalism means taking responsibility for one's work and explaining one's decisions to the public.
Journalists should:

- Explain ethical choices and processes to audiences. Encourage a civil dialogue with the public about journalistic practices, coverage and news content.
- Respond quickly to questions about accuracy, clarity and fairness.
- Acknowledge mistakes and correct them promptly and prominently. Explain corrections and clarifications carefully and clearly.
- Expose unethical conduct in journalism, including within their organizations.
- Abide by the same high standards they expect of others.

Reprinted with the permission of the Society of Professional Journalists.

Seek truth and report it

From the SPJ code: "Ethical journalism should be accurate and fair. Journalists should be honest and courageous in gathering, reporting and interpreting information."

As you read the standards beneath the "truth" principle in the SPJ code, notice the emphasis on sound techniques of newsgathering and verification.

Any discussion of truth in journalism leads to the overarching question of how to define truth. Indeed, some would argue that truth is an abstract – an ideal to be strived for but not achievable because the facts can be viewed from so many perspectives.

The elusiveness of truth is illustrated in the Case Study "A Double Disaster at the Sago Mine," in which a town celebrated – and the governor seemingly confirmed – the rescue of 12 trapped miners. Only hours later did the townspeople and the reporters learn that all but one of the miners had perished.

Each day, journalists struggle to piece together a semblance of truth from fragments of information. *The Washington Post*'s longtime politics writer, the late David Broder, succinctly expressed the difficulty of their mission in this famous summary:

> [T]he newspaper that drops on your doorstep is a partial, hasty, incomplete, inevitably somewhat flawed and inaccurate rendering of some of the things we have heard about in the past twenty-four hours – distorted, despite our best efforts to eliminate gross bias, by the very process of compression that makes it possible for you to lift it from the doorstep and read it in about an hour.[18]

Journalists today tend to agree that truth cannot be achieved through what has been called *objectivity*. In the first half of the twentieth century, so-called objective reporting was the accepted practice. Supposedly bias-free, it stated the surface facts without interpretation or analysis.

Senator Joseph McCarthy of Wisconsin exploited the flaws of objective reporting in the early 1950s with his reckless accusations of communist influence in government. Though he never documented the charges, he reaped the publicity he sought. To objective reporters, statements made by a US senator met the definition of news whether they were substantiated or not. Though the reporters sought out McCarthy's targets to record their denials, by the time they were published they had been overshadowed by new accusations by the senator. Amazingly, some reporters were aware, through their private conversations with McCarthy, that the charges lacked documentation. That did not keep those reporters from continuing to be conduits for his character assassination.[19]

The McCarthy debacle led journalists to the realization that they fail in their mission if they simply write what they are told. Tom Goldstein, a former reporter and educator, has written that reporters have "a greater responsibility than to just transcribe what someone in authority has to say. ... They must dig beneath the rhetoric to get at the primary sources."[20]

"Objectivity" has always been a misnomer. Reporting is a subjective process, not an objective one, and journalists are continually making judgments about how to cover and present the news. A more accurate description of what objectivity was supposed to deliver is "impartial journalism." In his Point of View essay accompanying this chapter, Thomas Kent of the Associated Press explains impartial journalism's enduring value.

As ethical journalists go beyond the surface facts to discover context, they draw on their background knowledge while consciously filtering out their biases. They go where the facts lead, not where their private opinions would take the story. Dick Polman, former *Philadelphia Inquirer* politics analyst, is guided by a song lyric by the rock group Steely Dan: "Let's take it where it goes." The journalist, Polman says,

> is a lot like an emergency-room doctor. There is a patient on the table in front of him. The patient could be a thief or a saint, but it doesn't matter to the doctor, because if the doctor is to perform professionally, he or she will suspend personal feelings and take the case wherever it needs to go.[21]

People trying to inform themselves about the news should not have to consult a variety of partisan sources and then try to piece together an accurate account, as news consumers did in the early decades of the Republic. Impartial news coverage, authoritatively produced by disciplined journalists, gives today's news consumers the information they need in a single location.

There is, of course, a place in journalism for opinion that, as the SPJ code recommends, is clearly labeled to distinguish it from the impartial accounts the public expects in news reporting. However, the oft-quoted admonition of the late Senator Daniel Patrick Moynihan is apt: "Everyone is entitled to his own opinion, but not his own facts." Thus, commentators have an ethical duty to establish the facts before expressing their opinions. They also have a duty to be fair.

In addition, to maintain the clear line between news reporting and commentary, the same journalist should not be assigned to produce both. When reporters write columns, **op-ed** commentaries, or opinionated blogs, they risk losing the confidence of the news audience and the people they cover. Once people become aware of a journalist's opinions, they may be less likely to trust the supposedly impartial accounts the journalist produces while in reporter mode.

Impartial journalism is under attack by critics who argue that, in the digital era, the public wants a different approach – reporters who simultaneously report the news and tell their audience what to think about it. In this construct, opinion would be integrated into the news coverage instead of being separate and labeled. Also, reporters would disclose their personal biases in the interest of transparency.

Critics of impartial journalism deplore two common failings in the way that impartial journalism is practiced. First, reporters create a *false balance* by simply reporting what adversaries say, ignoring that in many cases one side has a valid argument and the other side does not. Second, when the subjects of news stories misstate facts, the reporters do not challenge them and simply pass along the misstatements.

Although these are indeed problems, they can be corrected without abandoning the principles of impartial journalism.

Balance can be a virtue in framing a story if it leads a reporter to examine all sides of a controversy instead of emphasizing a single perspective or the polar opposites. But, as the critics point out, reflexively seeking balance can cause distortion. In his book and film *An Inconvenient Truth*, former presidential candidate Al Gore chastised journalists for giving the public the impression that scientists were divided over whether human behavior was causing global warming. Mentioning a scientific study, he wrote that peer-reviewed articles by scientists showed zero disagreement on the subject, while half of journalists' accounts managed to find dissenting voices.[22]

Likewise, an impartial journalist can challenge misstatements. For example, in the aftermath of Hurricane Katrina's devastation of New Orleans in 2005, Chris Wallace of Fox News asked Homeland Security Secretary Michael Chertoff:

> How is it possible that you could not have known on late Thursday, for instance, that there were thousands of people in the convention center who didn't have food, who didn't have water, who didn't have security, when that was being reported on national television?[23]

Rem Rieder, then the editor of *American Journalism Review*, wrote a 2011 column asserting that journalists shouldn't shrink from making judgments, as long as their conclusions are "shaped by hard-edged reporting, by facts, not by political point of view":

> For too long, mainstream journalism has pulled its punches. Admirably dedicated to fairness, balance, not picking winners and losers, it too often settled for "on the one hand, on the other hand" stories that left readers in the dark. Clearly it's important to be impartial, to represent main points of view, to give each side its say. But that doesn't mean treating both sides of the argument equally when one is demonstrably false, or even deeply flawed. The world isn't flat, no matter how many times some misguided soul might say it is.[24]

The growth of fact-checking units is another affirmation of journalists' duty to point out what's truth and what's fiction. Cary Spivak wrote in *American Journalism Review* that at least two dozen news outlets launched fact-checking operations in 2010 alone. They assess the statements politicians make, and some of them dispense a feared "Pants on Fire" rating to the most outlandish claims. Fact-checking by journalists has been influenced by the example of the FactCheck.org site established in 2003 at the Annenberg Public Policy Center of the University of Pennsylvania. Brooks Jackson, director of FactCheck.org, told Spivak that citizens need that kind of service because they are "awash in all sorts of unverified, false, misleading information."[25]

The opposing viewpoints of how the news should be reported were articulated in a remarkable debate in 2013 between two leading journalists. Bill Keller, former executive editor of *The New York Times* and then a columnist for the paper, invited Glenn Greenwald to join him in an online exchange to be published in *The Times*. (Greenwald is the journalist who reported for the British newspaper *The Guardian* on what Edward Snowden revealed about surveillance by the US National Security

Agency.) Journalism students would be enlightened by reading the complete text, which is available on the Web. Following are excerpts:

KELLER: Journalists in [the mainstream] tradition have plenty of opinions, but by setting them aside to follow the facts – as a judge in court is expected to set aside prejudices to follow the law and the evidence – they can often produce results that are more substantial and credible.

GREENWALD: A journalist who is petrified of appearing to express any opinions will often steer clear of declarative sentences about what is true, opting instead for a cowardly and unhelpful "here's-what-both-sides-say-and-I-won't-resolve-the-conflicts" formulation. That rewards dishonesty on the part of political and corporate officials who know they can rely on "objective" reporters to amplify their falsehoods without challenge.

KELLER   I don't think of it as reporters pretending they have no opinions. I think of it as reporters, as an occupational discipline, suspending their opinions and letting the evidence speak for itself.

GREENWALD: Why would reporters who hide their opinions be less tempted by human nature to manipulate their reporting than those who are honest about their opinions? If anything, hiding one's views gives a reporter more latitude to manipulate their reporting because the reader is unaware of those hidden views and thus unable to take them into account.

KELLER: I believe that impartiality is a worthwhile aspiration in journalism, even if it is not perfectly achieved. I believe that in most cases it gets you closer to the truth, because it imposes a discipline of testing all assumptions, very much including your own. … I believe journalism that starts from a publicly declared predisposition is less likely to get to the truth, and less likely to be convincing to those who are not already convinced.

GREENWALD   My view of journalism absolutely requires both fairness and rigorous adherence to facts. But I think those values are promoted by being honest about one's perspective and subjective assumptions.[26]

Minimize harm

From the SPJ code: "Ethical journalism treats sources, subjects, colleagues and members of the public as human beings deserving of respect."

The authors of *Doing Ethics in Journalism* wrote that minimizing harm is connected to the values of humaneness – values like fairness, compassion, empathy, kindness, respect: "It is based on our responsibility to treat others with decency and to allow them their dignity even in the worst of circumstances. It is connected to a concern for the consequences of our actions."[27]

Compassion could prompt a journalist to omit a detail from a story if its news value does not justify the harm caused by reporting it. For example, newspaper writers routinely consult the electronic archives to see if the subject of an obituary has been in the news. But if the search reveals a single embarrassing incident, recounting that incident in the obituary of an ordinary citizen could be an injustice. (In contrast, the careers of public officials and public figures should be evaluated critically in obituaries. Imagine an obituary of President Richard M. Nixon without mention of the Watergate scandal.)

The concept of minimizing harm might lead to a decision *not* to publish a news development, though most journalists are troubled by the notion of withholding information from the audience.

If law-enforcement officers ask journalists to withhold a certain fact because it might put a kidnapping victim in jeopardy, the journalists are morally obliged to take the request seriously. The ethicist Bob Steele recommends that journalists would do well to seek the advice of a "rabbi" – in this case, an authority on police matters – to help them assess such a request. Ideally, withholding information should be temporary.

In certain situations, information is withheld routinely. Combat correspondents do not report troop movements because doing so would endanger the soldiers. In covering a police siege, broadcast journalists must assume that the hostage-taker has access to a radio or television and for this reason they do not disclose the location of police assault teams. Journalists usually shield the identity of sex-crime victims, juvenile defendants, and jurors.

Late in 2007, all major news organizations operating in Britain – including the US-based Associated Press and CNN – agreed not to report that Prince Harry had been deployed to combat in Afghanistan. The news organizations agreed to the blackout to avoid jeopardizing the prince, who was third in line to the throne, and members of his unit. They also were promised "special access" to Harry before, during, and after his deployment, and an opportunity to share pooled interviews, video, and photographs taken while he was in the combat zone. Harry's presence in Afghanistan was reported first in an Australian magazine and then on Feb. 28, 2008, by the Drudge Report website. The day after Drudge posted the news, the British military brought Harry home, four weeks before the scheduled end of his 14-week tour.[28]

By their very presence, journalists can cause harm. Compassion should be a priority when interviewing ordinary people who find themselves thrust into the news – as, for example, the kin of someone who has been killed in a tragic accident. Even experienced newsmakers are entitled to common courtesy.

Mirthala Salinas, a television newscaster, was herself the subject of media pursuit in 2007 when her affair with Los Angeles mayor Antonio Villaraigosa became public knowledge (see the Case Study in Chapter 10, "A Love Triangle on the Evening News"). Shawn Hubler, who interviewed Salinas for *Los Angeles Magazine*, described the experience:

> At her condo complex, reporters trooped past the swimming pool, stood on her doormat, and pounded on her door. The doormat said LEAVE. She had bought it as a novelty, but now the joke wasn't funny. "I'd be in my bedroom watching TV, trying not to know they were knocking," she says. Her dogs grew hoarse from barking. "I couldn't leave my house. They would sit at the front door for hours, one reporter in the front, and the other in the back. I wasn't going to come out and be rude, and I wasn't going to come out and give them what they wanted. ... I just let them knock on the door. I thought eventually they would get tired." She pauses for a beat. "It took them a long time to get tired. Months."[29]

Act independently

From the SPJ code: "The highest and primary obligation of ethical journalism is to serve the public."

The SPJ standards call for avoiding both real and perceived conflicts that would interfere, or appear to interfere, with carrying out journalists' ethical duty to the public. Specifically, journalists are urged to refuse gifts and other favors they might be offered to influence them in performing their professional duties.

If a conflict cannot be avoided, the standards say, a journalist should publicly disclose it. Note that **disclosure** is a solution only for *unavoidable* conflicts. Most conflicts can be avoided, and a journalist is not entitled to absolution simply by letting the audience know about those conflicts.

Tim McGuire, former editor of the *Star-Tribune* in Minneapolis and now a professor at Arizona State University, wrote in his blog that "disclosure is not enough for the crooks and charlatans who want to argue their news should be respected as much as anyone else's." He explained:

> Let's say I am a reporter and I take $25,000 from a prominent health insurance company to write a story about health insurance. Let's also say that I meet all the disclosure requirements of transparency. Not enough. Even if the reader knows I took the $25,000 to feather my own nest, I have committed an egregious ethical violation.[30]

At a forum on journalism ethics in New York in 2013, senior managing editor Michael Oreskes of the Associated Press made the point that, valuable as transparency may be, it is not a substitute for independence. "Disclosing connections, conflicts or partisan affiliations is important for journalists who have them," he said; "[b]ut in a world inundated with information of various levels of credibility, it's more important than ever that at least some of our journalism be thoroughly independent."[31]

Journalists are observers, not players. They serve a vital role in society by providing reliable information. If journalists take part in the events they cover, they rightfully lose credibility in the eyes of their audience, and the public no longer benefits from the unique service of a neutral observer.

In the days after the September 11 attacks, some journalists – especially on television – started wearing American-flag pins on their lapels. Other journalists worried that their colleagues were sending an ambiguous message. Did the flags mean that the journalists were demonstrating patriotism, concern for the families who lost loved ones in the attack, and support for the troops? Or did the flags represent unquestioning support for whatever military or domestic response the government might take? Bob Steele wrote presciently on September 20, 2001:

> There is nothing wrong with journalists loving their country. And displays of patriotism can be a natural expression of that loyalty, particularly during these trying times. But the true measure of journalism's worth to our democracy will be measured not by our outward displays of patriotism, but by the work we produce. Our contributions to the

United States of America – and in many respects the global community beyond our borders – will be gauged not by any ribbons and flags we wear, but by the vigor and rigor we bring to our coverage and our commentary.[32]

Possibly because they did not want to be seen as unpatriotic, most of the news media failed to deliver a critical examination of President George W. Bush's rationale for invading Iraq in 2003. The rationale was that the Iraqi dictator, Saddam Hussein, posed a threat to the United States because he possessed weapons of mass destruction and because he was allied with al-Qaeda, the group responsible for the September 11 attacks. After the combat phase ended, no such weapons were found and no link to al-Qaeda was proved. Ultimately, *The New York Times* and *The Washington Post* acknowledged to their readers that they should have asked tougher questions before the invasion.[33] As the costly war extended into years and as an Iraqi insurgency resulted in thousands of American casualties, the public's support for the war ebbed. Would the course of history have been changed if the media had asked probing questions in 2002 and early 2003?

Be accountable and transparent

From the SPJ code: "Ethical journalism means taking responsibility for one's work and explaining one's decisions to the public."

This principle is about treating the audience with respect and responding constructively to criticism. In particular, it means being responsive to allegations of factual error or unfairness in reporting the news.

"The quality-driven news organization," Jack Fuller wrote in *News Values*,

examines each serious complaint of error, open to the possibility that it may have been wrong, and takes the time to be sure before either correcting itself or reaffirming the truth of what it said. … [W]hen it errs, such a newspaper quickly and without defensiveness acknowledges its mistake and corrects it.[34]

In the spirit of transparency – the principle that Professor Jane B. Singer explained in her Point of View essay accompanying Chapter 3 – the SPJ code tells journalists to be willing to explain how they made their news-coverage decisions. They should be open to a "civil dialogue" about their work. They are expected to expose unethical conduct, including lapses in their own organizations. They must "abide by the same high standards they expect of others."

Elsewhere in the code, transparency directs journalists to be clear about where they got their information and to "provide access to source material when it is relevant and appropriate." To be transparent, journalists routinely provide hyperlinks to related news stories, even those on competing websites. They do not hesitate to tell their audience that another news outlet broke a story first. They acknowledge gaps in their reporting.

The emphasis on transparency in journalism is a phenomenon of the digital age. In the past, journalists tended to be opaque about what they did and, if they explained at all, it was often to say "we stand by our story" or "our work speaks for itself."

The Commission on Freedom of the Press (also known as the Hutchins Commission), the panel of intellectuals who defined social responsibility of the press in a 1947 report, proposed that journalists "engage in vigorous mutual criticism." The commission wrote: "Professional standards are not likely to be achieved as long as the mistakes and errors, the frauds and crimes, committed by units of the press are passed over in silence by other members of the profession." It called on journalists to discipline each other "by the only means they have available, namely, public criticism."[35]

Today, *Columbia Journalism Review*, *Nieman Reports*, and the online-only *American Journalism Review* analyze issues in the news media. Journalists keep abreast of news and commentary about the profession through the daily posts of Jim Romenesko, the Poynter Institute, and the Pew Research Center's Journalism & Media site. The annual *State of the News Media* report by Pew's Journalism Project offers a penetrating analysis of trends.

However, only a handful of media critics work in the news media, and fewer than 20 news organizations have ombudsmen, or public editors, to assess citizen complaints.[36] Ombudsmen have varying degrees of independence to criticize their news organizations. But, at minimum, these positions mean that there is someone at those organizations who is dedicated to listening and responding to the public.

News organizations beset by scandal have sometimes unstintingly reported on their own embarrassments.

In 1977 Laura Foreman (no relation to this book's author) was found to have been involved in a romantic relationship with a leading political figure while she was covering politics for *The Philadelphia Inquirer*. The editors assigned their Pulitzer Prize-winning team, Donald L. Barlett and James B. Steele, to investigate. The paper published their 17,000-word report.

William Green, who was *The Washington Post*'s ombudsman in 1981, produced an 18,000-word examination – reported and written in just four days – after the paper determined that Janet Cooke had fabricated her Pulitzer Prize-winning story about an 8-year-old heroin addict. Other exhaustive examples of the genre include: the *Los Angeles Times*' 14-page special section reporting on its Staples Center fiasco in 1999; *The New York Times*' 14,000-word analysis and correction of stories that Jayson Blair had fabricated or plagiarized, which ran in 2003 under the headline "*Times* Reporter who Resigned Leaves Long Trail of Deception"; *USA Today*'s multiple-story report in 2004 detailing the serial fabrications of its reporter Jack Kelley between 1993 and 2003; CNN's analysis of its "Valley of Death" documentary in 1998, which concluded that the evidence did not support the program's premise that the US military used nerve gas against American defectors in the Vietnam War; and CBS's study of how its 2004 report on President George W. Bush's wartime National Guard record was based on documents whose authenticity could not be proved.

A monitoring institution favored by the Hutchins Commission was an independent panel to review accusations against the news media and to render a report that would be published. The National News Council was formed in 1973 for such a purpose, but it died ten years later without ever gaining significant support from the media. The Minnesota News Council, founded in 1970 and the oldest organization monitoring the news media, closed in 2013. The only surviving state organizations were in Hawaii and Washington.

When the Minnesota council closed, Tony Carideo, chairman of the Minnesota Council's board of directors, blamed the declining number of complaints, a "brutal recession" that eroded its financial support, and the advent of the Internet. Carideo told Greg Masters of *American Journalism Review*, "The news council was very effective at a time when complaints were delivered in envelopes," and that changed when people had the ability to complain instantaneously through blogs, Twitter, email, and the like. "I don't think people were quite as sophisticated as they are now about the media," Carideo said, but he also saw a downside. Whereas the council's hearings produced thoughtful conversation about media performance, online comments "often veer quickly into acrimonious, unsubstantiated and unbridled invective," especially if they are anonymous.[37]

Despite the tendency toward acrimony that Carideo mentioned, email does offer a convenient way for journalists and citizens to communicate. In pre-Internet days, a citizen who wanted to offer a comment to a journalist usually wrote a letter, addressed the envelope, put a stamp on it, and took the missive to a mailbox. The alternative, hardly more user-friendly, was to try to navigate the company's telephone system. Today, many news organizations post the email addresses and telephone numbers of staff members on websites and beneath their bylines in newspapers. Serious inquiries get the attention of conscientious journalists. The resulting "conversation" not only makes journalism more transparent to the citizen, but it can also result in an exchange of information that improves the quality of the news coverage.

Another way that news organizations are trying to be accountable is by inviting questions from the audience that are then answered by staff members online. At some news organizations, virtual conversations are conducted in real time; at others, journalists select questions submitted by the audience and write responses that are posted later.

The instant critiques of citizen bloggers are yet another source of audience feedback. Although those critiques may be needlessly abusive, they often have substance that journalists should heed.

The concept that the media should be accountable raises questions of definition. What do *responsibility* and *accountability* mean?

As Professor Louis W. Hodges of Washington and Lee University defined them in a 2004 essay, "responsibility has to do with defining proper conduct, accountability with compelling it":

> The distinction is clearly reflected in our common language. Notice the prepositions: we talk about being *responsible for* but *accountable to*. For example, we may be *responsible for* the accuracy of the information we deliver, for informing the reader about government,

for not invading privacy or inflicting further hurt on victims of a tragedy. However, we are *accountable to* a government, an editor, a court, or a reader.

Hodges theorized that confusion about the two words may have led the news media to reject the Hutchins Commission's theory of social responsibility in 1947: "The commission addressed press *responsibility*, but the working press read *accountability*. Journalists and news organizations did not want to be accountable to a bunch of intellectuals on the commission who would judge their performance."[38]

To whom, then, does a journalist owe accountability? Hodges' answer is: "All those whose lives and well-being are significantly affected by the professional's conduct." For journalists, he wrote, that list of stakeholders includes the audience, the sources and subjects of news stories, and the journalism profession at large. Journalists owe moral accountability to anyone they can harm through their work. It doesn't make any difference whether those people have the power to demand accountability. They are still entitled to it.[39]

Point of View

Reporting a Fact, Causing Harm

William F. Woo

Let me tell you about a man named Frank Prince. I should say, with some relief, that all of this took place before I had anything to do with editing the *Post-Dispatch*.

Prince was a prominent St. Louis businessman and chief stockholder in the Universal Match Company. He gave $500,000 to Washington University, back in the days when half a million meant something. The grateful university decided to name a building after him, and the *Post-Dispatch* assigned a reporter to write a story about the benefactor.

The reporter found that the 71-year-old Prince had served 10 years in prison when he was a young man on charges of bad checks, forgery, and larceny – white-collar crimes. Very few people in the community knew that, and when the story appeared, with all the awful details about a life long ago, readers were outraged. Speak about no good deed going unpunished.

Readers thought the story was a piece of vandalism – destructive, irrelevant, and certainly not newsworthy. The public did not need to know that Prince had done time to understand his generosity.

The journalistic justification for this trashing was what you might expect. The story was relevant to understanding Frank Prince and why, now many years later, he was giving back to society. Put another way, that argument declares journalists are psychologists and are qualified to assert why people act the way they do.

Another journalistic justification was the newsworthiness of the story. When somebody is in the news, as Prince was, people want to

(Continued)

know more about them. If Prince didn't wish to have information about his life made public, he could have made an anonymous donation to the university.

You can decide for yourself which of these responses – the criticism or the justification – seems most reasonable to you. My view, as you can gather, is that the readers had it right.

William F. Woo was editor of the *St. Louis Post-Dispatch* from 1986 to 1996, the culmination of a 34-year career at the paper. For the next 10 years, until his death in 2006, he was the Lorry I. Lokey Professor of Journalism at Stanford University. This excerpt is from *Letters from the Editor: Lessons from Journalism and Life* (Columbia: University of Missouri Press, 2007), 160–161, a compilation from the letters he wrote to his Stanford students. Reprinted with permission of Martha Shirk, widow of William Woo.

Point of View

Impartial Journalism's Enduring Value

Thomas Kent

For years now, advocates of new forms of journalism have been blasting away at impartiality as a hopeless goal. They're still blasting.

Yet impartial journalism is remarkably resilient, despite the mocking and stereotyping it has endured. There's plenty of room for other models, but it's worth recognizing the value impartiality delivers.

Critics of impartiality often start by saying everyone has an opinion. Trying to write without one, they say, yields mushy he-said, she-said reporting[1] with no clear conclusions.

Critics propose this alternative: journalists should flaunt their biases – posting their beliefs and acknowledging they may be reflected in their stories.

Both assertions reflect stereotypes of how impartial journalism works.

First, impartial journalism is a profession. That means exercising a skill that's separate from personal beliefs.

Doctors may not like their patients' politics, but they don't kill them in the operating room. Lawyers eloquently defend even the sleaziest clients. Journalists who seek to be impartial should be able to cover people and events irrespective of personal feelings.

Critics also confuse impartial reporting with impartial conclusions. Just because a reporter canvasses all points of view doesn't mean her completed story will be a mishmash of he-said, she-said.

When the *Sun Sentinel* of Fort Lauderdale, Fla., exposed police officers as among the worst speeders on south Florida roads, the paper's data-driven conclusions were unambiguous. When AP discovered negligence and cheating in America's nuclear forces, its stories were hardly wishy-washy.

At the same time, not every story needs to be written like an indictment. Sometimes, fairly presenting diverse points of view isn't shrinking from the truth, but the only honest way to report:

- A story may still be developing, or we may not have the resources available to reach a bottom line. In such cases, it's absolutely better to present what we know on all sides than to be either silent, or pressured into picking a villain by the next newscast.

- "What is true" may be just unknowable. How often have we seen common wisdom turned on its head: peak oil found not to be peak oil, healthy eating redefined, powerful-looking regimes suddenly collapsing? Reporters can't judge and predict everything. We shouldn't pretend we can.

How much bias do journalists have to begin with? It's true that any culture has beliefs that permeate everyone's soul. In many places, for instance, people share a belief that governments should not oppress citizens and the powerful should not undermine the common good. It's because of these beliefs that reporters consider it newsworthy when governments and the powerful overreach.

The more cultural diversity our newsrooms have, the more stories we'll perceive as worthy of coverage.

But while cultural perspectives help identify stories to cover, they don't make it impossible to present them fairly. And not every story risks biased reporting to begin with. Sometimes spot news – a wildfire, a tsunami – simply is what it is.

Clearly, journalists with personal beliefs that are truly going to affect their stories or photos should disclose them. Jay Rosen[2] advocates experimenting with systems where clicking on a byline takes you to "a disclosure page where there is a bio, a kind of mission statement, and a creative attempt to say: Here's where I'm coming from …" (My disclosure: I'm involved in an Online News Association project to help journalists be transparent about factors that may influence their coverage.)

But we need to accept that not every journalist is the prisoner of beliefs that skew his reporting. By one measure, half of U.S. journalists are political independents,[3] up about 18 percentage points in 11 years. Little will come from trying to beat political confessions out of them.

And nothing guarantees that a mission statement will be honest, or that a reporter's biography will tell you whether he is trustworthy. If a reporter used to work for the chemical industry, does that mean he's a propagandist for his former employers? Or that with his inside information, he's the best source around?

Ultimately a journalist's credibility rests not on what he says about his beliefs or his past, but on the correctness over time of what he reports.

That's why millions of busy people who have limited time for news expect it quickly and compactly from a journalist or news brand they've previously found reliable and impartial. Try following links to a reporter's mission statement when you're listening to the news in the car.

There's room out there both for defenders of impartial journalism and those who continue to insist it should be replaced by opinion-with-transparency. In a world that already has enough intolerance and polarization, we should keep testing and improving all approaches to journalism instead of slamming the door on techniques that retain significant value.

Thomas Kent, deputy managing editor and standards editor of The Associated Press, posted this essay on June 25, 2014. It is used by permission.

Notes

1 Mathew Ingram, "He said/she said isn't just a failure of journalism, it's a failure to understand the media market," GigaOm, May 12, 2014.

2 Jay Rosen, "The view from nowhere: questions and answers," Pressthink, Nov. 10, 2010,

3 Indiana University School of Journalism, "Press release: survey finds U.S. journalists less satisfied, have less autonomy," May 1, 2014.

Case Study
The Death of a Boy

On June 6, 1996, *The St. Petersburg Times* (now the *Tampa Bay Times*) published a story on the front of its metro section about a 4-year-old boy who was crushed when a large piece of furniture fell on him in his family's living room. The story was accompanied by a photo of the boy's distraught mother, Marilyn Sue Puniska, 39, as she waited for a helicopter to meet the ambulance carrying her son (Figure 7.1).

The story quoted sheriff's deputies speculating that the boy, Brett Puniska, was eager to play a videotape in the family's new entertainment center. As he climbed it, they said, he pulled the 400-pound unit on top of himself. The furniture still had casters that workers were to remove the next day. The unit was delivered Saturday, "but there was a problem with it and the family had not permanently placed it, pending repairs," a sheriff's spokesman said.

The Times' story related how Brett's 12-year-old sister, in the dining room talking on the telephone, heard the crash and screamed for her mother, who was taking a bath. Mrs Puniska rushed from the bathroom and attempted CPR while Jessica called 911. *The Times'* story also reported:

> Neighbors said the Puniskas had moved into the corner house just weeks ago. Marilyn and her husband, Gabriel J. Puniska Jr., 49, were married in a civil ceremony in Pasco on Valentine's Day 1991, records show.
>
> "I hadn't ever met them," said Karen Kuebler, 36, who lives next door. "They never came over. They never asked for anything." …
>
> Mrs Puniska was distraught while awaiting the medical helicopter. She asked authorities

to remove news reporters from the scene, and at one photographer she screamed: "My son's inside half-dead, and you're taking my picture!"

Sheriff's officials said Brett suffered head injuries, though the exact cause of death will be determined by the medical examiner's office. Officials characterized the event as an accident, though the investigation is continuing.

"At this point there is nothing to indicate the tragic incident was anything but accidental," said [the sheriff's spokesman].

The next day, *The Times* published a feature story about Brett, an active child who loved sports, and told how his parents and sister were coping with their loss. But some readers were still upset by the photograph the paper used with its news story about the accident, the one of Mrs Puniska waiting for the helicopter.

In a column on June 10, Bill Stevens, editor of the regional edition in which the coverage appeared, defended the use of that photograph and similar photographs of tragedies. Below the headline "Powerful images can also be lifesavers," Stevens wrote that they were dramatic, "the kind that tug at your heart." He continued:

> And, yes, they were taken over the objections of Mrs Puniska. These were frantic, terrible moments, and the last thing she needed was reporters and photographers swarming to the scene.
>
> One caller challenged me to put myself in the Puniskas' position. How would I feel if my child had just been killed, and a photographer was taking my wife's picture? "Have you no heart?"
>
> I understand the reaction completely. I understand that aggressive, deadline reporting

Pasco boy, 4, dies after furniture crushes him

■ Sheriff's officials say the child was trying to climb a 400-pound entertainment center when it fell on him.

By JOHN HILL
Times Staff Writer

NEW PORT RICHEY — A 4-year-old boy, possibly eager to play a videotape, tried to climb his family's new entertainment center Wednesday.

Instead, young Brett Puniska pulled the 400-pound, 6- by 4-foot unit on top of himself, sheriff's officials said. Despite attempts to revive him, he was pronounced dead at 6 p.m.

The furniture still had casters that workers were to remove today. The unit was delivered Saturday, "but there was a problem with it and the family had not permanently placed it, pending repairs," sheriff's spokesman Jon Powers said.

Officials would not speculate whether the absence of wheels would have prevented the accident.

The tragedy happened about 4:45 p.m. as the boy was alone in the living room of his family's home at 7705 Bass Lane, sheriff's officials said.

Brett's 12-year-old sister, Jessica, was in the dining room talking on the phone. She heard the crash and screamed for the pair's mother, Marilyn Sue Puniska, 39.

Mrs. Puniska, who records show has been a licensed practical nurse, rushed from the bathroom and attempted CPR. Jessica called 911.

At 5:15 p.m., rescue workers took Brett from the peach single-story house and drove him to a golf driving range across the street.

Please see **BOY** 8B

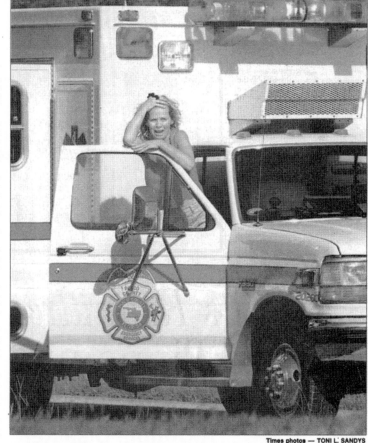

Times photos — TONI L. SANDYS

Marilyn Sue Puniska, the mother of the boy, waits Wednesday for a helicopter to meet the ambulance carrying her son. He was pronounced dead shortly afterward.

Figure 7.1   A mother's anguish.
REPRINTED BY PERMISSION OF THE *TAMPA BAY TIMES*.

of breaking news often puts us in the position of defending our actions. But I also believe a newspaper is expected to cover major events in its community thoroughly and accurately.

Almost 20 years ago, we responded to a similar tragedy in New Port Richey when a young boy suffocated in a backyard dirt cave-in. Our photographer captured the parents

(Continued)

from a distance near the dirt pile, and many callers expressed their anger the next day when we published the picture and story.

They didn't know that the editor in charge had himself lost a young son to a similar accident while at play. He didn't tell them. Time passed and we moved on to other stories.

Then last year, a woman called me to complain that somebody had left a large pile of dirt near the New Port Richey Recreation Center. She was worried that a child might be killed there, because she remembered a photo and story that we carried all those years ago.

Powerful images.

I regret that our words and images can cause such anguish. In the case of the Puniskas, I am grateful that they welcomed us into their home the next day for detailed discussion of their child. And I am convinced that their decision to share the details … will save another child's life.

This case is excerpted from Michele McLellan, *The Newspaper Credibility Handbook*, with a discussion guide by Bob Steele (Washington, DC: American Society of Newspaper Editors, 2001), 182–187.

Questions for Class Discussion

- What arguments can be made for and against publishing the photograph of the distraught mother at the ambulance? Do you think the photograph should have been published? Note that the photographer was on a public street and had a legal right to take the picture, and that it was taken over the mother's objections.
- The story includes details about the victim's family. Do any of these details raise fairness questions?

- Some journalists think that, by publishing stories and photographs about tragedy, the news media help others by sounding what might be called a "warning bell." Stevens ends his column by saying: "I am convinced that their decision to share the details … will save another child's life." How do you respond to that justification? Does it work in this case?

Case Study

A Double Disaster at the Sago Mine

The scene was Sago, West Virginia, just before midnight on January 3, 2006. Forty-one hours after an explosion had killed one coal miner underground and trapped 12 others, church bells pealed and jubilation filled the town: "They're alive!" A dozen ambulances surged toward the mine entrance. Police cars' sirens screamed in triumph.

West Virginia governor Joe Manchin III was at the Sago Baptist Church speaking with family members of the trapped miners. He immediately left for the command center. On the way to his car, strangers hugged him and, as he related later, "I hugged them back." As he drove away, reporters said they asked him if the report was true, and he answered, "Miracles do happen." (Later, the governor's communications director said that what the governor told the reporters was: "I don't know. I'm heading up there right now to find out what's going on, but believe in miracles.")

If you are a reporter, what do you report?

Those who were at Sago that night reported that the 12 miners had survived. Most attributed the information to family members, and some also mentioned the apparent corroboration from the governor. But the attributions went largely unnoticed in the news stories while the headlines heralded the euphoric report of a "miracle" rescue.

We know now that the news was tragically wrong – and that it would not be corrected for three hours, by which time most American news consumers were asleep and after many newspapers had printed editions heralding the wrong report. A day later, the *Los Angeles Times* reconstructed the events that led to the mistake:

> Two and a half miles into the mountain, twelve men were clustered behind a makeshift shelter, and one of them was moaning.
>
> The rescue crew swarmed him. In the dim light and slowed by their protective gear, they scrambled to assess the man's injuries, administer oxygen and find the best way to carry him through the debris-filled tunnels.
>
> In the feverish rush, one or more rescuers spoke into the radio transmitters inside their oxygen masks. They needed to get word to a base camp nearer the mouth of the mine: They had found all 12 men. One was alive.
>
> At 11:45 p.m., the base camp staff heard the transmission and passed it on to rescue teams at the surface.
>
> But somewhere along the way, the message got garbled. …

Base camp was on the line, on speakerphone – and the news was better than anyone dared hope. Not one miracle, but a dozen: "It came across," said Gene Kitts, senior vice president [of the mining company], "as 12 alive."

Mine officials had warned everyone in the command center to keep any news bulletins to themselves until they could be confirmed. But this was incredible news. Such an uproar swept the office that the command staff couldn't hear further reports from base camp. They ordered all nonessential personnel to leave.

The joyous crowd spilled into the parking lot, and disregarding their earlier instructions, began dialing their cell phones.

When he heard the rejoicing at the church, Governor Manchin asked members of his staff whether they had confirmation of the rescue. They said they did not. He did not tell the crowd this. It was easy to interpret his euphoria, and his comment about "miracles," as corroboration. Manchin said later that, when he reached the command post, he saw professionals celebrating just as the families had. He said he himself began to think there truly had been a miracle.

At 12:30 a.m., base camp called the command center to report that the rescue crew had arrived with just one survivor. Ben Hatfield, president and chief executive of the mining company, said later that he and others clung to "the fervent hope" that the others, still in the mine, might be just comatose. He did not send word to the families that the earlier report might be wrong. "We didn't believe there was any productive benefit of saying, 'It could be one, could be twelve, we have conflicting reports,'" Hatfield said later. He acknowledged that he had made a mistake in allowing the erroneous report to go unchallenged.

The mining company remained silent for three hours. Finally, at 3 a.m., Hatfield came to the church and told the family members

(Continued)

there was only one survivor. The crowd angrily refused to believe him. One man had to be restrained by police.

At Sago, journalists had struggled to ascertain the truth when everybody they saw was convinced that the miners had been saved. They reported what they heard, and from whom they had heard it.

The command-post spokesman was Joe Thornton, deputy secretary for the West Virginia Department of Military Affairs and Public Safety. He told *Editor & Publisher* magazine that he had fielded more than a hundred phone calls from journalists that night, most of them in the first half-hour after the celebration began. He said his response to each was: "We are hearing that twelve miners were found alive – but that has not been confirmed." However, *Editor & Publisher* noted that *The New York Times* quoted Thornton by name as saying that 12 miners had been found alive and that "the miners were being examined at the mine shortly before midnight and soon would be taken to nearby hospitals." Thornton told the magazine he had not said that, but the *Times* reporter, James Dao, was certain that "what I wrote was what I understood him to tell me. . . . He didn't say that he couldn't confirm."

Television reports by CNN and Fox News went uncorrected for three hours; CNN's Anderson Cooper was interrupted on camera by people bearing the horrible correction. Newspapers in eastern and central states went to press with the wrong reports. *The Philadelphia Inquirer* was able to print the erroneous report of the rescue only because it had held its presses well past the normal start time in order to cover the Penn State–Florida State triple-overtime game at the Orange Bowl; the paper ran with that wrong story the rest of the night. *The New York Times* had incorrect stories in all its print editions. *The Pittsburgh Post-Gazette* stopped its

presses at 3:18 a.m. to remove front pages with the headline "Miracle at Sago, 12 Miners Alive," which had run in 132,000 papers, and to insert the right story into the remaining 114,000 papers. Benefiting from the three-hour time difference, the *Los Angeles Times* got the correct story to its readers, but only after recalling delivery trucks and discarding 204,861 newspapers with the wrong story.

Later, news organizations assessed the damage. Criticism within the profession was restrained; many journalists who were not there were reluctant to blame those who were. *The Houston Chronicle* wrote: "If there is such a thing as a pardonable news media sin, this story offers the example." Managing editor Mike Silverman of the Associated Press said, "AP was reporting accurately the information that we were provided by credible sources – family members and the governor." Leonard Downie Jr., executive editor of *The Washington Post*, defended his reporters' sourcing and said, "The mistake was not ours, it was the authorities at the scene."

Still, the public had been misinformed, and those who depended on newspaper reports were the most likely to have received the wrong information. The timing of the wrong report, right on deadline for the morning papers, meant that many copies had gone out with the wrong story. And, unlike broadcast and online outlets, newspapers could not correct their mistake in print for 24 hours.

"The question that a lot of journalists probably wish had been asked of the governor is, 'How do you know that?'" Butch Ward, distinguished senior fellow at the Poynter Institute, told *The Philadelphia Inquirer*, the paper he had served as managing editor: "The national press corps is asking it more often to officials in Washington and being called arrogant for asking. But it's an important question to ask."

Tom Rosenstiel, then director of the Project for Excellence in Journalism, told *The Houston Chronicle*:

I think that when you're not sure about something, but you've got to go with the best you've got, that's when we should be as circumspect as possible. The way to do that is to be as clear as possible with the public about what we have and what we don't have and what the sourcing is. Under the circumstances, it's hard to imagine that reporters at the scene would be skeptical. On the other hand, that is what we are supposed to do.

Howard Kurtz, then the media writer for *The Washington Post*, was blunt:

While the mining company's refusal to correct the misinformation for hours is inexplicable, the situation was exacerbated by the journalistic reluctance to say the facts are unconfirmed and we just don't know. Experienced journalists should have understood that early, fragmentary information in times of crisis is often wrong.

Sources

Abcarian, Robin, and Matea Gold, "Media take a hard look at what went wrong," *Los Angeles Times*, Jan. 5, 2006.

Campbell, James T., "Miners' story an example of a pardonable media sin," *The Houston Chronicle*, Jan. 8, 2006.

Eichel, Larry, "How the media got it wrong," *The Philadelphia Inquirer*, Jan. 5, 2006.

Flannery, Mary, "Not a miracle at all," *Philadelphia Daily News*, Jan. 5, 2006.

Kurtz, Howard, "Mine disaster's terrible irony: a failure to look deeper," *The Washington Post*, Jan. 9, 2006.

Moore, Tina, and Jeff Shields, "Joy at mine: 12 are alive," *The Philadelphia Inquirer*, Jan. 4, 2006.

Peterson, Jonathan, and Stephanie Simon, "West Virginia mine tragedy: cruel hope began with a garbled message," *Los Angeles Times*, Jan. 5, 2006.

Ramsburg, Lara, director of communications for Governor Joe Manchin III, email exchange with author.

Simonich, Milan, "Mangled message created heartbreak," *Pittsburgh Post-Gazette*, Jan. 5, 2006.

Strupp, Joe, "Editors explain why they announced 'miracle rescue,'" *Editor & Publisher*, Jan. 4, 2006.

Strupp, Joe, "Spokesman in miner tragedy says he never confirmed miracle rescue," *Editor & Publisher*, Jan. 8, 2006.

Thornton, Joseph C., deputy secretary for the West Virginia Department of Military Affairs and Public Safety, email exchange with author.

Questions for Class Discussion

- Imagine that you were a reporter covering the Sago mine disaster. Knowing what you know now, what would you have reported when the celebration began?
- Should the newspaper headlines have contained attribution?
- Did any of the people celebrating in the town *really* know that the trapped miners were alive?
- Did the governor *really* confirm the rescue?
- Why is it important for reporters to ask the follow-up question "How do you know that?"
- Journalism teachers like to say, "If your mother says she loves you, check it out." Why is it important for journalists to maintain professional skepticism at all times? How does skepticism differ from cynicism?

Notes

1 Will Irwin, *The American Newspaper: A Series First Appearing in Colliers January–July, 1911* (Ames: University of Iowa Press, 1969), 47–48.

2 Craig Branson, "A look at the formation of ASNE," ASNE, Apr. 25, 2002.

3 Vernon Stone, "RTNDA codes of ethics and standards across half a century," University of Missouri.

4 "Build your own ethics code," Online News Association.

5 The text of the 2014 ethics code of the Society of Professional Journalists, along with the enforcement disclaimer, is on the SPJ website.

6 Edmund B. Lambeth, *Committed Journalism: An Ethic for the Profession* (Bloomington: University of Indiana Press, 1986), 76.

7 Dr. Merrill made this statement while delivering a guest lecture in the author's journalism ethics class at Pennsylvania State University in 2000.

8 Carol Reuss, "Media codes of ethics are impotent, and too often they are facades that imply ethical behavior," in A. David Gordon and John Michael Kittross (eds.), *Controversies in Media Ethics*, 2nd edn. (Boston: Allyn & Bacon, 1998), 58.

9 Author's telephone interview with James M. Naughton, Sept. 14, 2007.

10 Jay Black, Bob Steele, and Ralph Barney, *Doing Ethics in Journalism: A Handbook with Case Studies*, 3rd edn. (Boston: Allyn & Bacon, 1999), 24–25.

11 Roy Peter Clark, "Red Light, Green Light: a plea for balance in media ethics," Poynter, May 17, 2005.

12 *Ethical Journalism: A Handbook of Values and Practices for the News and Editorial Departments* (New York: The New York Times, 2004).

13 "AP news values and principles," The Associated Press.

14 NPR Ethics Handbook, "This is NPR: and these are the standards of our journalism."

15 Manning Pynn, "Ethical guidelines keep journalists on track," *Orlando Sentinel*, Feb. 3, 2008.

16 "SPJ updates code of ethics," Society of Professional Journalists, news release, Sept. 6, 2014.

17 Ibid.

18 David Broder, *Behind the Front Page* (New York: Simon & Schuster, 1987), 14.

19 John Herbers, "McCarthyism, 1950–1954," in Tom Rosenstiel and Amy S. Mitchell (eds.), *Thinking*

Clearly: Cases in Journalistic Decision-Making (New York: Columbia University Press, 2003), 6–22.

20 Tom Goldstein, *Journalism and Truth: Strange Bedfellows* (Evanston, IL: Northwestern University Press, 2007), 21, 70.

21 Dick Polman, "Writing a news analysis," unpublished essay (2001). (*The paper is available in the Student Resources section of the website.*)

22 Al Gore, *An Inconvenient Truth* (Emmaus, PA: Rodale, 2006), 262–263. The scientific study mentioned by Gore is Naomi Oreskes, "The scientific consensus on climate change," *Science*, 306 (Dec. 3, 2004), 1686.

23 Alessandra Stanley, "Reporters turn from deference to outrage," *The New York Times*, Sept. 5, 2005.

24 Rem Rieder, "Reporting to conclusions: journalists shouldn't shrink from making judgments about factual disputes," *American Journalism Review*, Feb. 16, 2011.

25 Cary Spivak, "The fact-checking explosion," *American Journalism Review*, Dec. 2010–Jan. 2011.

26 Bill Keller, "Is Glenn Greenwald the future of news?," *The New York Times*, Oct. 27, 2013.

27 Black, Steele, and Barney, *Doing Ethics in Journalism*, 40.

28 "Prince Harry fights on frontlines in Afghanistan; 3 month tour," Drudge Report, Feb. 28, 2008; Kevin Sullivan, "Prince Harry's seeing combat and British media kept quiet," *The Washington Post*, Feb. 29, 2008; Bob Satchwell, "Why we agreed to a media blackout on Harry," *The Guardian*, Feb. 29, 2008; Tariq Panja, "Britain's Prince Harry in Afghanistan," The Associated Press, Feb. 28, 2008; "Prince Harry: my withdrawal is a shame," CNN, Mar. 1, 2008.

29 Shawn Hubler, "The mayor and his mistress," *Los Angeles Magazine*, May 2008.

30 Tim McGuire, "Three new ethical principles are important, positive step, but independence needs to stay," McGuire on Media, Oct. 2, 2013.

31 Quoted in Thomas Kent, "New journalism ethics," The Definitive Source, Nov. 14, 2013.

32 Bob Steele, "A pledge of allegiance for journalists," Poynter, Sept. 20, 2001.

33 "*The Times* and Iraq," *The New York Times*, May 26, 2004; Howard Kurtz, "The Post on WMDs: an inside story: prewar articles questioning threat

often didn't make front page," *The Washington Post*, Aug. 11, 2004.

34   Jack Fuller, *News Values* (Chicago: University of Chicago Press, 1996), 14.

35   Commission on Freedom of the Press, *A Free and Responsible Press: A General Report on Mass Communication: Newspapers, Radio, Motion Pictures, Magazines, and Books* (Chicago: University of Chicago Press, 1947), 94.

36   Jeffrey Dvorkin is quoted on the number of ombudsmen in Rem Rieder, "A disappointing move by *The Washington Post*," *American Journalism Review*, Mar. 4, 2013.

37   Greg Masters, "Fading away," *American Journalism Review*, Mar. 2, 2011.

38   Louis W. Hodges, "Accountability in journalism," in Lisa H. Newton, Louis Hodges, and Susan Keith, "Accountability in the professions: accountability in journalism," *Journal of Mass Media Ethics*, 19:3–4, 173–180.

39   Ibid.

8 Making Moral Decisions You Can Defend

The key ingredients are critical thinking and a decision template

---

Learning Goals

This chapter will help you understand:

- how journalists' decision-making can draw on their practical skills in gathering facts, analyzing them, and making judgments;
- how critical thinking, or thoughtful analysis, is better than a reflexive response to an ethical question;
- how a step-by-step decision template can guide you to a better decision;
- how to test your decision to see if it can be defended on rational grounds; and
- how to approach the case studies as a laboratory for decision-making.

Think for a moment about what makes journalists so good at what they do.

The distinctive occupational skill they possess – rare in the population at large – is their ability to size up a complicated situation and swiftly produce a summary that is accurate, clear, and engaging.

For the seasoned journalist, it seems intuitive, but it's actually a logical process that requires three steps. First, collect facts. Second, analyze the facts. Third, make judgments – about what facts to include and what to discard, what facts to highlight and what to subordinate.

As an aspiring journalist, you've performed this process in your courses in reporting and editing. You've also learned that practice makes you better.

Now think about making ethical decisions in journalism.

The same skill that serves journalists so well in reporting the news can also be a valuable asset in resolving the ethical challenges of the profession. It, too, is a skill that can be developed through practice in the classroom, which is why this course is taught through case studies.

At this point in your study of applied ethics in journalism, you're ready to start making decisions.

In Chapters 6 and 7, you became familiar with the classic ethical theories and professional codes of ethics. The ethical theories give you different perspectives for studying an ethical problem and considering how to respond. The professional codes

---

The Ethical Journalist: Making Responsible Decisions in the Digital Age, Second Edition. Gene Foreman.
© 2016 John Wiley & Sons, Inc. Published 2016 by John Wiley & Sons, Inc.

give you the benefit of the conventional wisdom for dealing with the kind of problem you are facing.

Think of the ethical theories and the professional codes as tools in the process you will use to make your decisions. Now you need to add two last items to your toolbox: critical thinking and a step-by-step template.

Critical thinking is a systematic way of analyzing ethical problems; it involves applying logic to the available information. Critical thinking is the opposite of reflexive response. Stopping to think, the ethicist Michael Josephson has written, "is a powerful tonic against poor choices. … It prevents rash decisions. It prepares us for more thoughtful discernment. And it can allow us to mobilize our discipline."[1]

Having a step-by-step template helps you stay on task as you progress toward your decision. The value of a template, as editor Joann Byrd has described it, is that, "when a dilemma falls out of the sky, which most of them have a habit of doing, your decision-making is faster, more efficient and more reliable."[2]

You need all of the decision-making tools because you will face complex moral challenges in journalism. Making decisions is not just deciding between two choices, right and wrong, as the authors of *Doing Ethics in Journalism* wrote:

> True ethical decision making is … about developing a range of acceptable actions and choosing from among them. It's about considering the consequences of those actions. And it's about basing decisions on obligation, on the principles of the journalist's duty to the public.[3]

Applying Critical Thinking

A journalist's gut feeling of right and wrong has a place in this process, but it's not the *whole* process. If you're morally repelled by a course of action your news organization is considering, don't ignore your instincts. If something *seems* wrong, it may well *be* wrong. This preliminary test is what the author Rushworth Kidder called the stench test:

> Does this course of action have about it an indefinable odor of corruption that makes you (and perhaps others) recoil and look askance? The stench test really asks whether this action goes against the grain of your moral principles – even though you can't quite put your finger on the problem.[4]

However, you need to be able to state your case with logic rather than emotion. As a journalist, you will be called on again and again to explain why you made a certain choice. Members of the audience may confront you and demand an explanation. So might your boss, a colleague, the subject of your story, or a source – any stakeholder in the decision you made. You owe them a better answer than "It seemed like a good idea at the time."

Thus the goal of ethical decision-making is to produce a decision that can be defended on rational grounds. Such a decision may not be embraced by everyone, but a reasonable critic would be obliged to concede that you have deliberated conscientiously and that your arguments are plausible.

The authors of *The Virtuous Journalist* wrote that "no system of ethics can provide full, ready-made solutions to all the perplexing moral problems that confront us, in life or in journalism": all that can be asked is that decision-makers take "a reasoned and systematic approach" to finding solutions.[5] That's critical thinking.

In *Committed Journalism*, scholar Edmund B. Lambeth wrote that journalism requires "a capacity for self-detachment, deliberative thought, and reflective scrutiny of events, people and circumstances."[6]

Author Barry Beyer defined critical thinking as "making reasoned judgments." He further defined "reasoned" as *arrived at by logical thinking*, and "judgment" as *determining the degree to which something meets a standard*. The word *critical* is derived from the Greek word *kriterion*, a standard for judging. In his book *Critical Thinking*, Beyer wrote:

> In the broadest sense, critical thinking is judging the quality of anything. Whenever we evaluate our own cooking, someone else's performance of a task, the accuracy of a newspaper or TV account, a work of art, or a researcher's conclusion, we are applying criteria to make a judgment – we are engaged in critical, or criterial, thinking.[7]

Applying a Step-By-Step Template

To carry out that "reasoned and systematic approach," various scholars have created templates outlining an orderly decision process. These templates all have merit, and they all have a great deal in common. They explicitly or implicitly invoke the classic ethical theories and the accepted standards of journalism stated in the codes. They tell the moral agent (decision-maker) to gather facts and use critical thinking to analyze those facts. They prod the decision-maker to identify and evaluate multiple ways to solve the problem. They require the decision-maker not just to state a solution but to defend it as well.

In short, the templates replicate the three-step process that guides the journalists in reporting the news: gathering facts, analyzing them, and making judgments.[8]

The template (see Box 8.1) that this text will use is the straightforward series of 10 questions devised by the ethicist Bob Steele:

1   What do I know? What do I need to know?
2   What is my journalistic purpose?
3   What are my ethical concerns?
4   What organizational policies and professional guidelines should I consider?
5   How can I include other people, with different perspectives and diverse ideas, in the decision-making process?
6   Who are the stakeholders – those affected by my decision? What are their motivations? Which are legitimate?

7   What if the roles were reversed? How would I feel if I were in the shoes of one of the stakeholders?

8   What are the possible consequences of my actions? Short term? Long term?

9   What are my alternatives to maximize my truth-telling responsibility and minimize harm?

10 Can I clearly and fully justify my thinking and my decision? To my colleagues? To the stakeholders? To the public?[9]

Look again at Steele's 10 questions. As you do, think about the three-step process of reporting the news and about the contents of your decision-making toolbox. For the purpose of this discussion, Steele's 10 questions can be divided between the three steps (Steele himself does not compartmentalize them).

Box 8.1   A Template for Making Decisions in Journalism

Step 1: Collect the information

1   What do I know? What do I need to know?
2   What is my journalistic purpose?
3   What are my ethical concerns?

Step 2: Analyze the information

4   What organizational policies and professional guidelines should I consider? *Resources: rule-based thinking; codes of ethics.*
5   How can I include other people, with different perspectives and diverse ideas, in the decision-making process?
6   Who are the stakeholders – those affected by my decision? What are their motivations? Which are legitimate? *Resource: ends-based thinking.*

7   What if the roles were reversed? How would I feel if I were in the shoes of one of the stakeholders? *Resource: Golden Rule.*
8   What are the possible consequences of my actions? Short term? Long term? *Resource: ends-based thinking.*
9   What are my alternatives to maximize my truth-telling responsibility and minimize harm? *Resource: Aristotle's Golden Mean.*

Step 3: Make a judgment and defend it

10 Can I clearly and fully justify my thinking and my decision? To my colleagues? To the stakeholders? To the public? *Resources: front-page test, Mom test, and God-is-my-witness test.*

Step 1: Collect the information (Questions 1–3)

If you do a half-hearted job of assembling facts to answer Question 1 (yes, it's actually two questions), the rest of the process will be flawed. It will be like playing a card game without a full deck.

In Question 2, you articulate the journalistic purpose you are trying to achieve.

That leads you to Question 3, in which you define the ethical issues presented by your answers to the first two questions.

As you define those issues, it may become clear that you are not facing an ethical dilemma at all. The situation could instead be a *false ethical dilemma*, a concept of the ethicist Michael Josephson that was described in Chapter 2. Instead of *ethical* values on both sides of the equation – the definition of a true ethical dilemma – one side might have only a *nonethical* value.

Ethical values in journalism include telling the truth, keeping a promise, respecting confidentiality and the right of privacy, fostering fairness and justice, minimizing harm, avoiding conflicts of interest, and fulfilling the journalist's responsibility to inform the public about relevant information even when it is unpopular to do so.

Nonethical values include beating the competition and getting an interesting story that raises circulation, broadcast ratings, or the number of online hits. There is nothing wrong with achieving nonethical values except where you do so at the expense of fulfilling ethical values.

The false ethical dilemma can also be expressed as a clash between what you *should* do and what you *would like* to do.

If you conclude that you are dealing with a false ethical dilemma, you already know your ethical duty. That, however, may not make your decision any easier, because you now have to decide whether you are willing to make a sacrifice to do the right thing.

Step 2: Analyze the information (Questions 4–9)

Your answers to these questions constitute a step-by-step analysis of the information you gathered in Step 1. Here, the ethical theories and ethics codes come into play. Remember the strengths and weaknesses of each of the ethical theories.

To answer Question 4 about professional standards, you can consult your newsroom's code or advisory codes like the one written by the Society of Professional Journalists. This process also reminds you of the value of *rule-based thinking* – how it provides a structure for decision-making. You think about the "best practices" embodied in the codes, and consider whether these apply to the case at hand. You keep in mind the SPJ code's guiding principles of seeking and reporting truth, minimizing harm, acting independently, and being accountable and transparent.

Question 5 suggests that you involve other people in your decision-making process, taking advantage of their experience, expertise, and unique perspectives. Some journalists would argue there just isn't time for this kind of discussion. To the contrary, there usually *is* time – and you would be short-changing yourself by making the decision alone. Although you remain responsible for the decision, why not tap into the best advice available?

Sometimes ethical questions can be anticipated and discussed thoroughly before there is a crisis, as the journalists at *The Oregonian* did in preparing to cover Lovelle

Svart's last weeks of life (Chapter 1). Ethics scholar Paul Martin Lester's advice (Chapter 4) also is apt: Think like a defensive player in baseball, who ponders choices *before* the ball is hit to him.

Questions 6 (about stakeholders) and 8 (about consequences) ask you to apply *ends-based thinking*. Think about who will be helped by your decision and who will be harmed.

Question 7 sharpens that process by introducing the Golden Rule and its telling test of empathy – how you would feel if you were a person affected by your decision.

As you consider the benefits and consequences of your decision, you also need to be sensitive to how **rationalizations** can tempt you to make a self-serving decision instead of an ethically defensible one. That is a dangerous trap. In his Point of View essay in this chapter, "Rationalizations in Decision-Making," Michael Josephson describes the most common rationalizations.

Question 9 directs you to assess the multiple responses you could make to resolve the ethical question, possibly including an Aristotle's Golden Mean. "If you can think of only one or two choices, you're probably not thinking hard enough," Josephson has written.[10]

Step 3: Make a judgment and defend it (Question 10)

This defense is the essence of applied ethics, because you are obliged to explain your decision to the stakeholders. You sift the alternatives and settle on the one you will adopt as your course of action.

To help you evaluate your own arguments, measure your decision against this checklist from Michael Josephson:

- All decisions take into account the well-being of others.
- Ethical values always take precedence over nonethical ones.
- It is ethically proper to violate one ethical principle only when it is clearly necessary to advance another in the given situation.[11]

Then take these three easy tests:

1 *The front-page test.*   How would you feel if what you are about to do showed up tomorrow morning on the front pages of the nation's newspapers? If you are rationalizing a decision on the basis that people will never know what you did, this test exposes a moral flaw. What has been a private process now becomes public.[12] As Rushworth Kidder observed, "The truly consistent individual, the one who generally wins our highest praise as an exemplar of virtue, is one whose actions in public and in private are morally identical."[13]

2 *The Mom test.*   What would your mother think about your decision? Kidder explained that "the focus here is not only on your mother, of course, but on

any moral exemplar who cares deeply about you and means a lot to you." If this test makes you uneasy, "think again about what you are on the verge of doing."[14]

3   *The God-is-my-witness test.*   Imagine you have just sworn, hand on a Bible, to tell the whole truth and nothing but the truth, and now you must explain your decision in open court. Donald L. Barlett, winner of two Pulitzer Prizes, concluded that, "whatever you are going to write, you need to be comfortable with the idea of relating your story to twelve strangers. If you're comfortable telling your story to a jury, that's the gut check."[15]

Practicing Decision Skills in Case Studies

In the Case Study "Deciding Whether to Identify a CIA Agent," you can practice the above decision template. Then you will be ready to move on to Part II of this book, studying areas of journalism in which ethical issues frequently occur and examining how journalists have sought to resolve those issues.

In this case, the ethical theory of ends-based thinking is prominently involved as the journalists weigh the needs of the stakeholders – the public's need for information and the CIA agent's need to protect his identity. The journalists could apply the Golden Rule and imagine themselves in the position of the agent, who is concerned about his safety and that of his family, as well as his privacy. Aristotle's Golden Mean comes into play as the journalists decide to omit the agent's given first name (using his nickname and surname), and in cautioning him about potentially dangerous personal information he has posted on the Web.

The SPJ code's guiding principles of seeking truth and minimizing harm are in conflict in this case. Naming the agent makes the news account more credible and informative, but at the possible cost of endangering the agent and his family. The SPJ code's principle of acting independently comes into play as the journalists deal with government pressure to omit the agent's name. The fourth SPJ principle, being accountable and transparent, is applied as the editors explain their decision in an editors' note and later in responses to the public editor's questions for his column.

The case studies in this text will help you prepare for the decisions you will make in your journalism career, particularly since you have a duty to justify your choices to your instructor and classmates. The ethicist Deni Elliott has written that the case-study approach of studying ethics will help you:

• appreciate the complexity of newsroom decision making;
• understand the context within which difficult decisions are made;
• track the consequences of choosing one action over another; and
• learn both how and when to reconcile and how and when to tolerate divergent points of view.[16]

There are traps in a class discussion of case studies, but these traps can be avoided. Elliott has identified two of them:[17]

1 *Every opinion is equally valid.*   As you debate the choices proposed in your class, it should become clear that some choices are more likely than others to result in benefits for the stakeholders. At the other extreme, some choices are quite likely to result in harm without significant benefit to anybody. In addition, some choices might fail the test of logic – they cannot be reasonably justified by the facts. So there is going to be a difference in the validity of the opinions offered on a case.

2 *Since we can't agree on an answer, there is no right answer.*   Although it is true that there may be more than one ethically acceptable solution to a case, one will probably emerge from the debate as being more logically defensible than the others. More important, certain solutions can and should be ruled out on moral grounds. These wrong answers should be rejected because they cause unjustified harm to stakeholders, or because they violate the shared values of the journalism profession. These values are outlined in *The Elements of Journalism*, the Society of Professional Journalists ethics code, and other statements of professional standards. Deni Elliott has listed three values as essential:
   • giving readers, viewers, and digital users the information they need;
   • striving for news accounts that are accurate, balanced, relevant, and complete;
   • avoiding unnecessary harm in the course of reporting the news.[18]

So, while your discussions can be highly subjective, everyone should recognize that certain values are nonnegotiable. These values include not just journalistic values but basic human values as well.

Ethics professor Christina Hoff Sommers wrote that a typical course in applied ethics (like this one) concentrates on problems and dilemmas in which there can be well-argued positions on all sides. That creates a problem: "the atmosphere of argument and counterargument" reinforces the idea that "*all* moral questions have at least two sides, i.e., that all of ethics is controversial." To the contrary, Sommers maintained that some things are clearly right and some are clearly wrong. When a television interviewer challenged her to name some uncontroversial ethical truths, she replied:

> It is wrong to mistreat a child, to humiliate someone, to torment an animal. To think only of yourself, to steal, to lie, to break promises. And on the positive side, it is right to be considerate and respectful of others, to be charitable and generous.[19]

In addition to avoiding the traps discussed above, keep in mind that the case studies in this book tend to focus on journalist decisions that are questionable. While that is what makes the cases useful for aspiring journalists to study, remember that the journalists involved were trying to do the right thing. You should remember, too, that the overwhelming majority of journalists' decisions, day in and day out, conform to the ethical standards you are studying in this course.

Point of View

Rationalizations in Decision-Making

Michael Josephson

1 *If it's necessary, it's ethical.* This rationalization is based on the false assumption that necessity breeds propriety. The approach often leads to ends-justify-the-means reasoning and treating nonethical tasks or goals as moral imperatives.

2 *If it's legal and permissible, it's proper.* This substitutes legal requirements (which establish minimal standards of behavior) for personal moral judgment. This alternative does not embrace the full range of ethical obligations, especially for those involved in upholding the public trust. Ethical people often choose to do less than the maximally allowable but more than the minimally acceptable.

3 *It's just part of the job.* Conscientious people who want to do their jobs well often fail to adequately consider the morality of their professional behavior. They tend to compartmentalize ethics into two domains: private and occupational. Fundamentally decent people thereby feel justified doing things at work that they know to be wrong in other contexts. They forget that everyone's first job is to be a good person.

4 *I was just doing it for you.* This is a primary justification of committing "little white lies" or withholding important information in personal or professional relationships, such as performance reviews. This rationalization pits the values of honesty and respect against the value of caring. An individual deserves the truth because he has a moral right to make decisions about his own life based on accurate information. This rationalization overestimates other people's desire to be "protected" from the truth, when in fact most people would rather know unpleasant information than believe soothing falsehoods. Consider the perspective of people lied to: If they discovered the lie, would they thank you for being thoughtful or would they feel betrayed, patronized or manipulated?

5 *I'm just fighting fire with fire.* This is based on the false assumption that promise-breaking, lying and deceit are justified if they are routinely engaged in by those with whom you are dealing.

6 *It doesn't hurt anyone.* Used to excuse misconduct, this rationalization is based on the false assumption that one can violate ethical principles so long as there is no clear and immediate harm to others. It treats ethical obligations simply as factors to be considered in decision-making rather than as ground rules. Problem areas: Asking for or giving special favors to family, friends or public officials; disclosing nonpublic information to benefit others; using one's position for personal advantage.

7 *Everyone's doing it.* This is a false, "safety in numbers" rationale fed by the tendency to treat cultural, organizational or occupational behaviors uncritically as if they were ethical norms, just because they are norms.

8 *It's OK if I don't gain personally.* This justifies improper conduct done for others or for institutional purposes on the false assumption that personal gain is the only test of impropriety. A related but narrower view is that only behavior resulting in improper financial gain warrants ethical criticism.

9 *I've got it coming.* People who feel they are overworked or underpaid rationalize that minor "perks" – acceptance of favors, discounts or gratuities – are nothing more than fair compensation for services rendered. This is also used as an excuse to abuse sick time, insurance claims, overtime, personal phone calls, and personal use of office supplies.

10 *I can still be objective.* By definition, if you've lost your objectivity, you can't see that you've lost your objectivity! This rationalization also underestimates the subtle ways in which gratitude, friendship, anticipation of future favors and the like affect judgment. Does the person providing you with the benefit believe that it will in no way affect your judgment? Would the person still provide the benefit if you were in no position to help?

This list is excerpted from Michael Josephson, *Making Ethical Decisions*, edited by Wes Hanson (Los Angeles: Josephson Institute, 2002), 27–29. © Michael Josephson. Reprinted with permission.

Case Study

Deciding Whether to Identify a CIA Agent

Readers of *The New York Times* learned on June 22, 2008, about the success of an obscure CIA interrogator in prying secrets from a captured al-Qaeda leader who was believed to have masterminded the September 11 attacks in New York City and Washington.

The interrogator, according to reporter Scott Shane's front-page story in *The Times*, asked his questions of Khalid Shaikh Mohammed only after the captive had been subjected by other CIA operatives to cold, sleeplessness, pain, and fear – tactics intended to force him to talk. The interrogator "came in after the rough stuff, the ultimate good cop with the classic skills: an unimposing presence, inexhaustible patience and a willingness to listen to the gripes and musings of a pitiless killer in rambling, imperfect English."

In addition to providing fascinating detail about the interrogation, which occurred in a CIA prison in Poland 18 months after the 2001 attacks, Shane's account created controversy. It named the CIA analyst who had persuaded Mohammed to talk: Deuce Martinez.

In an editors' note accompanying the story, *The Times* explained its decision to identify Martinez over the objections of the CIA and Martinez's own attorney, who protested that naming the interrogator "would invade his privacy and would put him at risk from terrorists or harassment from critics of the agency."

(Continued)

The Times said the name was "necessary for the credibility and completeness of the article." It noted that Martinez "had never worked under cover and that others involved in the campaign against Al Qaeda have been named in news stories and books." Martinez was a 36-year-old CIA analyst at the time of the 2003 interrogation. By the time the 2008 article was published, he had taken a job with a consulting company and was coaching other CIA analysts in their efforts to track terrorists.

The Times' article described how Martinez would bring Mohammed snacks, usually dates, and listen attentively as his adversary complained about his accommodations and described his despair over the likelihood that he would never again see his children. To establish rapport, Martinez also exploited their common experiences: They were about the same age, they had both attended public universities in the American South (Mohammed at North Carolina A&T and Martinez at James Madison University in Virginia); they were both religious (Mohammed follows Islam; Martinez Catholicism); and they were both fathers.

Eventually, Mohammed "grew loquacious" and, in a gesture of respect to Martinez, wrote poems to Martinez's wife. He also divulged information about plots, past and planned. He revealed that he himself had beheaded *Wall Street Journal* reporter Daniel Pearl, a claim that the CIA believed because of the detail he provided. On June 5, 2008, at his arraignment at the American military prison at Guantanamo Bay, Cuba, Mohammed demanded that he be granted his wish for execution and martyrdom.

After *The Times* published its story, many readers wrote to object that the use of Martinez's name had needlessly endangered him and his family. In a column about the controversy on July 6, public editor Clark Hoyt quoted one of those letters. Suzanne Dupre of Evanston,

Illinois, wrote that Martinez "was loyally serving his country in a dangerous job. *The Times* has made him a marked man."

The ethical decision that *The Times* faced in the Martinez case illustrates the tension that frequently exists between the guiding principles of *seeking truth and reporting it* and *minimizing harm*. Hoyt's column framed the controversy:

> The episode involved the clash of two cultures, journalism and government intelligence, with almost diametrically opposed views about openness. It raised the difficult question of how to weigh the public's right to know about one of the most controversial aspects of the war on terror, the interrogation of prisoners, against the potential harm in naming an honorable public servant.

One aspect of reporting truth is to offer details that make a news account credible to the audience, and *The Times* feared that its story would not be seen as authentic if its central character went nameless.

Hoyt's column elaborated on the arguments the paper had made in the editors' note that accompanied the original story:

> The reporter and his editors said that nobody provided evidence that Martinez would be in any greater danger than the scores of others who have been identified in the news media for their roles in the war against Al Qaeda. These include other former CIA officers, the warden at Guantanamo, military prosecutors, the lawyer who wrote the Justice Department memos justifying harsh interrogation techniques, and even a New York Port Authority policeman who helped arrest a terrorist.

Hoyt also disclosed that the paper had decided that, since Martinez was so worried, it would not use his first name, only his nickname. In addition, *The Times* had alerted Martinez to the easy accessibility of a website where he had posted considerable personal information, which was removed before *The Times* published its story.

Hoyt interviewed Martinez's lawyer, Robert Bennett, who told him Martinez had been threatened repeatedly by Mohammed and others he interrogated. Until the *Times* story, they did not know his identity, Hoyt wrote, but "now their friends do, at least to some degree."

"*The Times* and other news organizations have been asked over the years to withhold stories for fear of harm," Hoyt wrote:

> And they have done so when a persuasive case has been made that the danger – whether to national security or an individual – is real and imminent. In this case, there is no history of Al Qaeda hunting down individuals in the United States for retribution. It prefers dramatic attacks that kill indiscriminately. And *The Times* took reasonable precautions to prevent Martinez from being easily found.

As *The Times*' independent public editor, Hoyt sometimes was at odds with the paper's news-coverage decisions. This time he found himself in agreement. He concluded his column:

> I can understand how readers can think that if there is any risk at all, a person like Martinez should never be identified. But going in that direction, especially in this age of increasing government secrecy, would leave news organizations hobbled when trying to tell the public about some of the government's most important and controversial actions.

In preparing his column, Hoyt consulted Bob Steele, who posted his own analysis of the case on the Poynter website, arguing that the case "powerfully exemplifies the essence of ethics and ethical decision-making process." As he saw it, *The Times* journalists were wrestling with these competing principles:

- A duty to report accurate, precise and substantive information about a significant issue or event.
- An obligation to seriously consider and weigh the consequences to a key stakeholder (Martinez) who is described as very vulnerable to harm.
- A responsibility to protect journalist independence in the face of pressure to withhold a key element (Martinez's name) from the story.

Steele gave considerable weight to the importance of the story. He said *The Times* made a compelling argument of that importance in the seventh paragraph of the story itself. There, Shane observed that the description of Martinez's role "provides the closest look to date beneath the blanket of secrecy that hides the program from terrorists and from critics who accuse the agency of torture."

Using Martinez's name, Steele pointed out, "gives readers a clear focal point. Using his name – rather than a pseudonym or just referring to him by title – also heightens the reliability and validity in the reporting process. The story is more believable."

Steele saw little merit in the arguments made by the CIA and Martinez's lawyer that the *Times*' story invaded his privacy or damaged his career. If there are any negative consequences in those areas, he argued, they "don't appear to me to outweigh a duty to publish the story with Martinez's name included."

A far more serious concern, in Steele's opinion, was the potential safety risk to Martinez and his family. To make that assessment, Steele outlined a process:

> Gather all the facts possible. Verify and scrutinize and make sense of those facts. Consider any missing pieces of the puzzle and how they could change things if known. Hear as many

(Continued)

opinions as possible from diverse sources. Identify and recognize various motives of the stakeholders, including the journalists. Examine and challenge any assumptions.

Steele wondered whether, in addition to considering the pleas of the CIA and Martinez's attorney, *The Times* could have consulted with experts who could have independently assessed the danger to Martinez and his family.

"In the end," Steele wrote, "this case comes down to a judgment call":

> *Times* executive editor Bill Keller and his colleagues had to make an ethical decision based on which principle deserved the greatest weight. They chose publishing an accurate, precise and substantive account of an important issue that included Deuce Martinez's name. Additionally, they honored the principle of independence

through their process of including various key stakeholders in the deliberations. They were transparent and accountable in giving readers information on why and how they made their decisions. Ethics is about principles and process. Well-intentioned, thoughtful people can and will disagree.

Sources

Hoyt, Clark, "Weighing the risk," *The New York Times*, July 6, 2008.

The New York Times, "Editors' Note," June 22, 2008.

Shane, Scott, "Inside a 9/11 mastermind's interrogation," *The New York Times*, June 22, 2008.

Steele, Bob, "When principles collide: the *NYT* and the CIA interrogator," Poynter, July 5, 2008.

Questions for Class Discussion

- Visualize how Scott Shane's story would have read if its central character had gone nameless or been given a pseudonym. Do you agree that the story would have been less credible to readers? Do you agree that this particular story's importance gives added significance to the issue of credibility?
- Analyze the arguments that the CIA and Martinez's attorney made for keeping his name out of the story. Do you agree that the story invades Martinez's privacy or damages his career? Or that it placed him and his family in danger?
- Now, considering the arguments you have analyzed in the first two questions, put yourself in the place of *Times* executive editor, Bill Keller. Would you have included Martinez's name in the story?

Notes

1 Michael Josephson, *Making Ethical Decisions* (Los Angeles: Josephson Institute, 2002), 21.

2 Joann Byrd, comments at the American Society of Newspaper Editors conference in 2003.

3 Jay Black, Bob Steele, and Ralph Barney, *Doing Ethics in Journalism: A Handbook with Case Studies*, 3rd edn. (Boston: Allyn & Bacon, 1999), 51.

4 Rushworth M. Kidder, *How Good People Make Tough Choices: Resolving the Dilemmas of Ethical Living* (New York: HarperCollins, 1995), 159.

5 Stephen Klaidman and Tom L. Beauchamp, *The Virtuous Journalist* (New York: Oxford University Press, 1987), 20.

6 Edmund B. Lambeth, *Committed Journalism: An Ethic for the Profession* (Bloomington: Indiana University Press, 1986), 152.

7 Barry Beyer, *Critical Thinking* (Bloomington, IN: Phi Delta Kappa Educational Foundation, 1995), 8–9.

8 In *Ethics in Media Communications: Cases and Controversies*, 5th edn., Louis A. Day also divides the decision

process into three steps, for which he uses the acronym SAD: situation definition, analysis, and decision.

9   Bob Steele, "Ask these 10 questions to make good ethical decisions," Poynter, Feb. 29, 2000.

10   Josephson, *Making Ethical Decisions*, 23.

11   Michael Josephson, *Ethical Issues and Opportunities in Journalism* (Marina del Rey, CA: Josephson Institute, 1991), 23–24.

12   Kidder, *How Good People Make Tough Choices*, 184.

13   Ibid., 193.

14   Ibid., 184.

15   Author's telephone interview with Donald L. Barlett, Oct. 10, 2007.

16   Deni Elliott, "Cases and moral systems," in Philip Patterson and Lee Wilkins, *Media Ethics: Issues and Cases*, 6th edn. (New York: McGraw-Hill, 2008), 18.

17   Ibid.

18   Deni Elliott, "All is not relative: essential shared values of the press," *Journal of Mass Media Ethics*, 3:1 (1988), 28–32.

19   Christina Hoff Sommers, "Teaching the virtues," *Public Interest*, 111 (Spring 1993), 3–13.

Part II Exploring Themes of Ethics Issues in Journalism

This part of the book challenges you to practice the decision-making skills you learned in Part I.

Each of the chapters 9 through 17 discusses a topic in which all journalists – print, broadcast, digital – confront ethics issues:

Chapters 18 and 19 discuss ethics issues that are specific to the following specialized areas:

Chapter 20 offers capsules of advice for aspiring journalists

9 Stolen Words, Invented Facts ... or Worse

Plagiarism, fabrication, and other mistakes that can kill a career

Learning Goals

This chapter will help you understand:

- plagiarism and fabrication are morally wrong – plagiarism is stealing the creative work of another; fabrication is making things up and presenting them as fact;
- the offenses of plagiarism and fabrication destroy journalism's credibility and can cost offenders their jobs and their careers;
- illegal acts are unacceptable in the pursuit of news;
- journalists should follow sound work practices to avoid any hint of impropriety; and
- newsroom leaders have a duty to establish clear rules about journalistic malpractice and to enforce them.

Leonard Pitts Jr. of *The Miami Herald* devoted his nationally syndicated column on March 11, 2005, to lending support to the outspoken comedian Bill Cosby, who was then embattled over an allegation of sexual misconduct. "I like hypocrites," Pitts began his column.

> You would, too, if you had this job. A hypocrite is the next best thing to a day off. Some pious moralizer contradicts his words with his deeds and the column all but writes itself. It's different with Bill Cosby.

On May 12, *The Daily Tribune News* in Carterville, Georgia, published a column under the byline of its associate managing editor, Chris Cecil. "I like hypocrites," it began.

> You would, too, if you had this job. A hypocrite is the next best thing to a day off. Some pious moralizer contradicts his words with his deeds and the column all but writes itself. It's different with Bill Cosby.

Alerted by one of his readers, Pitts checked *The Daily Tribune News'* website and found eight of Cecil's columns in the preceding three months that replicated Pitts'

The Ethical Journalist: Making Responsible Decisions in the Digital Age, Second Edition. Gene Foreman.
© 2016 John Wiley & Sons, Inc. Published 2016 by John Wiley & Sons, Inc.

prose. The Pulitzer Prize-winner's next column was an indignant open letter to Cecil. Pitts called the Cosby column "a wholesale heist" in which "you essentially took my name off and slapped yours on." The dictionary, Pitts wrote, "is a big book. Get your own damn words." When *The Daily Tribune News'* publisher learned of the plagiarism, he immediately fired Cecil.[1]

Compared with high-profile miscreants like Jayson Blair and Jack Kelley, Chris Cecil is an obscure entry in the annals of journalistic malpractice. But Cecil nevertheless finds himself in rare company: His is one of only four known cases of *appropriation plagiarism* committed by full-time journalists in American daily newspapers in an entire decade, from 1997 through 2006.

The statistic and the term are from Norman P. Lewis' 2007 doctoral dissertation at the University of Maryland. Appropriation plagiarism, Lewis wrote, is "blatantly taking another's work without any pretense or uncertainty of what the rules are." He further described appropriation plagiarism as either "serial" or "brazen," or both.[2]

Altogether, Lewis identified 76 cases of plagiarism during the 10 years. He limited his study to full-time employees because "newspapers are most heavily invested in those workers, and an evaluation of full-timers would more accurately reflect how newspapers respond to plagiarism cases." His study thus excluded weekly newspapers, college newspapers, and cases at daily newspapers involving part-timers, nonstaff correspondents, freelancers, or college interns.[3]

Of Lewis' cases, 67 were "research plagiarism" – "blending someone else's words with original reporting or failing to sufficiently paraphrase to disguise the copying."[4]

Lewis also identified three cases of "idea plagiarism," involving the borrowing of the ideas for editorial cartoons or editorials.[5] The remaining two cases were "self-plagiarism," in which writers recycled material they had written for previous employers, without crediting the original publisher.[6]

Defining Plagiarism and Fabrication

Plagiarism is one of two offenses that journalists regard as egregious sins worthy of dismissal. The other is **fabrication**, which is making things up and passing them off as genuine.

Plagiarism and fabrication both transgress against the audience. They destroy the credibility of the journalist and the news organization.

Plagiarists take credit for phrases, sentences, paragraphs, or even an entire story that someone else has created. In "The Unoriginal Sin," his seminal essay on the subject in 1983, Roy Peter Clark of the Poynter Institute wrote that plagiarism is "a form of deception … a violation of language … a substitute for reporting."[7]

To fabricate, print reporters can invent scenes, characters (including composites of real characters), and quotations to embellish stories. Print photographers can manipulate images or present posed photographs as "found moments." Broadcast journalists can distort what happened by indiscriminately adding sound effects and music, staging misleading re-enactments, or abusing special visual effects. Given the wide range of techniques at their disposal, digital journalists can deceive in any of those ways.

When they occur, plagiarism and fabrication tend to be committed by journalists who find themselves under pressure to meet high expectations, either their bosses' or their own. Deadlines exacerbate the stress of relentless competition with other media outlets or with their own colleagues. Plagiarists and fabricators give in to delusions: that the pressure is so great that they have no choice; that no one will ever know of their moral shortcut; or even that fictional technique can express a greater truth.

Like many journalism professors, Cynthia Gorney thought the rules were so fundamental that she did not need to spell them out for her students in the Graduate School of Journalism at the University of California, Berkeley. After reading about a spate of plagiarism and fabrication incidents, she changed her mind.

"In the interest of clarity, and with a heavy heart," she wrote in an open letter to her students, "I articulate them now":

> Don't steal.
> Don't lie.
> Don't make things up and pretend that's reporting.[8]

Some perspective is in order. To read the journals and blogs that discuss journalism issues, one could assume that malpractice is common in the profession. The Internet and its search engines ensure that any offense, irrespective of degree, becomes common knowledge everywhere. "In the Internet age, there's no rug under which to sweep these problems," media critic Howard Kurtz wrote in *The Washington Post* in 2005.[9]

Thomas Kunkel, then dean of the University of Maryland's Philip Merrill College of Journalism, told Kurtz that

> because we are self-policing so much better, it makes it seem like there's a tremendous cascade of ethical violations. There used to be a lot more in the way of shenanigans and monkey business that we either didn't know about or, if it was caught, it was winked at. There was a boys-will-be-boys quality about it – they were mostly boys – and they would get a slap on the wrist at best.[10]

Roy Peter Clark of the Poynter Institute elaborated on that point in an online essay in 2013:

> I see no persuasive evidence that literary abuse is more common today than in yesteryear. In the cut-and-paste culture of digital technology, plagiarism may be easier to commit, but it is also easier to detect. Standards may appear in decline when, in fact, media crime fighters … are simply more assertive and armed with better Geiger counters.[11]

Jim Romenesko's blog, which since 1999 has been reporting news in the news media, is so widely read in the profession that his influence has been labeled by media critic Jack Shafer as "the Romenesko effect." Shafer praised Romenesko for improving journalism by casting light on its misdeeds: "The site functions brilliantly as an ad hoc, post-publication, peer-review mechanism for the journalistic profession."[12]

The instant peer reviews, as well as the tendency of news organizations to make a public disclosure of ethical breaches by their staffs, fulfill one of the "be account-able and transparent" standards of the Society of Professional Journalists' code. That standard says, "Expose unethical conduct in journalism, including within their organ-izations."

A side effect of the disclosures – or perhaps it is just another manifestation of the cynicism discussed in Chapter 5 – is that what journalists see as departures from the norm is seen by the public as the norm. In the Freedom Forum's Free Press/Fair Press surveys in 1998, 76 percent of the respondents thought that journalists often or sometimes plagiarize, and 66 percent that journalists often or sometimes make up stories and pass them off as real.[13]

More subtly, the public expresses its mistrust by *not* calling news organizations to account when scenes and quotations have been blatantly invented. After Jayson Blair's fabrication and plagiarism in *The New York Times* were exposed in 2003 (see below), Harvard media analyst Alex Jones told *USA Today*'s Peter Johnson that he was trou-bled because people who were quoted by Blair didn't contact *The Times* to say they had never talked with the reporter. "They didn't say, 'Holy cow, this is somebody who is clearly unscrupulous.' Instead, their response was to shrug their shoulders and say, 'Hey, what do you expect?'"[14]

After the Blair episode, the Associated Press Managing Editors assigned 15 news-papers to contact readers through mass emails to ask why people would fail to tell the papers about obvious errors. One reader wrote back, "What's the point? Do they really care?" The most common explanations readers gave for not contacting the paper were that surely someone in the newsroom would correct obvious errors; that it would take too much time to navigate the newspaper's corrections system; and that the readers thought inaccuracies were intentional in a journalism "that glosses over the fine points and hypes storytelling."[15]

In contrast to the public's perceptions of widespread malpractice, the 76 instances of plagiarism identified in Norman Lewis' study took place over an entire decade in a total workforce of 55,000 journalists in America's daily newspapers. Even allowing for incidents not detected or reported, that is relatively small. (A comparable statistical study of fabrication has not been performed.)

News organizations treat plagiarism and fabrication as more serious offenses than factual mistakes in reporting. These offenses frequently result in firing or forced resig-nation; 43 of the 76 journalists involved in Norman Lewis' plagiarism study lost their jobs.[16] In addition to disciplining the staff member, the news organizations usually disclose the offense. Their reasoning is that the audience, having been deceived, is entitled to know.

In the profession, there is a consensus: Although both plagiarism and fabrica-tion vary in degree of seriousness and of intent to deceive, they are *always* morally wrong. And they always give the audience a reason to doubt the work of journal-ists. Roy Peter Clark, referring to cases of plagiarism, wrote: "Like defensive pass interference in football, they may be blatant or accidental, but they always deserve the yellow flag."[17]

Cautionary Examples of Plagiarism and Fabrication

When journalists talk about plagiarism and fabrication, these are the cases they usually bring up.

Janet Cooke, *The Washington Post* (fabrication, 1980)

"Jimmy is 8 years old and a third-generation heroin addict," Cooke wrote in *The Washington Post* on September 28, 1980. Every day, someone "fires up Jimmy, plunging a needle into his bony arm, sending the fourth grader into a hypnotic nod."[18] When Washington authorities asked *The Post* to identify Jimmy so that they could help him, *The Post* refused, saying it was protecting its sources.

On April 13, 1981, Cooke's story won the Pulitzer Prize for feature writing. The Associated Press story about the prize reported that she was a Phi Beta Kappa graduate of Vassar and had attended the Sorbonne in Paris, academic achievements she had listed on her Pulitzer entry form. When the AP story was read by staff members at *The Blade* in Toledo, Ohio, where she had formerly worked, they told *The Post* that the statements about her education were untrue.

In lengthy questioning, Cooke broke down and confessed. The next day, she submitted her resignation and a statement in longhand that included the admission, "I never encountered or interviewed an 8-year-old heroin addict." *The Post* returned the Pulitzer Prize.[19]

Stephen Glass, *The New Republic* (fabrication, 1998)

In his two-and-a-half-year career, Stephen Glass was a prolific magazine writer who wrote fantastic stories. Having worked as a fact-checker at *The New Republic*, he knew how to fool the people assigned to contact his sources and authenticate his reporting. He escaped detection when he made up stories like the ones about "The First Church of George Herbert Walker Christ" and a "get-naked" room at a conservative political conference.

On May 18, 1998, *The New Republic* published Glass' "Hack Heaven," a story about a 15-year-old hacker who had extorted a high-paying job with Jukt Micronics in exchange for not penetrating its databases. Forbes Digital Tool, a website covering the industry, thought that was an interesting story and assigned a reporter to check it out. The Forbes reporter could find no evidence that Jukt Micronics existed. His editor called *The New Republic*'s newly appointed editor, Charles Lane, who demanded verification from his writer. Glass offered a phone number – that of his brother, who then posed as a Jukt executive in his conversation with Lane – and a Jukt website Glass had created himself. Lane discovered the ruse and fired Glass.

Later, the magazine acknowledged fabrications in 27 of the 41 articles Glass had written.[20]

Glass graduated in 2000 from Georgetown University's law school, where he had started attending evening classes while working at *The New Republic*. He sought admission to the New York bar in 2002 but withdrew his application two years later on learning that his "moral character" application would be rejected. Glass passed the California bar examination in 2006, but the California Supreme Court turned him down in 2014, saying he "has not sustained his heavy burden of demonstrating rehabilitation and fitness for the practice of law."[21]

Patricia Smith, *The Boston Globe* (fabrication, 1998)

In four years as a metro columnist, Smith turned out beautifully written essays about characters who said amazing things. Like the woman named Claire who learns that a drug has cured cancer in mice and wants it to cure her own cancer: "Hell, if I could get my hands on it, I'd swallow the whole … mouse." Superbly talented in both prose and poetry, she was in demand as a speaker at writing workshops.

Doubts about the veracity of her columns had been raised in the *Globe* newsroom for at least three years. After the Claire column, and after others in which the paper could not locate people she described, an editor confronted her about six suspicious characters. She admitted that four of the six were made up. With that, Smith resigned.

In a farewell column on June 19, 1998, Smith wrote:

> From time to time in my metro column, to create the desired impact or slam home a salient point, I attributed quotes to people who didn't exist. I could give them names, even occupations, but I couldn't give them what they needed most – a heartbeat.[22]

Smith has since built an acclaimed career as an author, poet, and professor of creative writing. Among her six books are *Shoulda Been Jimi Savannah*, winner of the 2013 Lenore Marshall Poetry Prize, and *Blood Dazzler*, a finalist for the 2008 National Book Award.

Mike Barnicle, *The Boston Globe* (plagiarism and fabrication, 1998)

In a 25-year run as a columnist, Barnicle was a favorite of the paper's working-class readers. He frequently came under suspicion that he was fabricating. It was plagiarism, however, that set in motion the events that led to his departure from the paper. His August 2, 1998, column contained jokes similar to those in comedian George Carlin's 1997 book *Brain Droppings*. The columnist said he hadn't read Carlin's book, but then a Boston television station showed a video clip of Barnicle promoting the book. When Barnicle refused to resign, *Globe* editor Matthew V. Storin suspended him for two months.

In the midst of that controversy, *The Globe* heard from the retired editor-in-chief of *Reader's Digest*, Kenneth Tomlinson. Three years earlier, the *Digest* had wanted to reprint a Barnicle column about two young cancer patients who formed a friendship in hospital, but the *Digest's* fact-checkers had been unable to confirm the story. Tomlinson now told *The Globe* that he had rejected Barnicle's article as a fabrication. When Barnicle could not authenticate the cancer victims' story, Storin again demanded Barnicle's resignation. This time he got it.[23]

The cases of Barnicle, a white man, and Patricia Smith, an African American woman, are linked because some critics, including the famous lawyer Alan Dershowitz, accused *The Globe* of a double standard in the handling of their cases.[24] Afterward, Storin acknowledged concern about giving that impression. He said editors had held off confronting Smith because there had been "allegations over the years that Barnicle had engaged in some fictions," but the allegations had not been proved.[25]

Since leaving *The Globe*, Barnicle has been successful on the national scene, appearing regularly on MSNBC's *Morning Joe* program and writing for a variety of magazines and websites.

Jayson Blair, *The New York Times* (plagiarism and fabrication, 2003)

Blair, hired as a reporter at *The Times* at age 23, resigned under pressure four years later as the paper investigated the stories he had written. The triggering incident was a purported interview in Los Fresnos, Texas, with the mother of a soldier who had died in Iraq.

On April 18, reporter Macarena Hernandez had written for *The San Antonio Express-News*:

> So the single mother, a teacher's aide, points to the ceiling fan he installed in her small living room. She points to the pinstriped couches, the tennis bracelet still in its red velvet case and the Martha Stewart patio furniture, all gifts from her first born and only son.

Blair's story for *The Times* on April 26 began:

> Juanita Anguiano points proudly to the pinstriped couches, the tennis bracelet in its red case and the Martha Stewart furniture out on the patio. She proudly points up to the ceiling fan, the lamp for Mother's Day, the entertainment center that arrived last Christmas and all the other gifts from her only son, Edward.

In addition to the similarities in the two stories, there was a problem with the Martha Stewart furniture: Still in boxes, it had never been placed on the patio. After Hernandez's editor notified *The Times*, Blair's story and ultimately his reporting career unraveled. Mrs. Anguiano said Blair had never visited her.[26]

On May 11, *The Times* issued a report on its investigation that started on the front page and covered four full pages inside. The report said Blair

> misled readers and *Times* colleagues with dispatches that purported to be from Maryland, Texas and other states, when often he was far away, in New York. He fabricated comments. He concocted scenes. He lifted material from other newspapers and wire services. He selected details from photographs to create the impression he had been somewhere or seen someone, when he had not.

He was found to have plagiarized or fabricated in at least 36 articles.[27]

Journalists on *The Times'* staff and elsewhere demanded to know how Blair's deceptions could have gone undetected for so long. The internal investigation showed that the paper had frequently run corrections of Blair's stories and that several supervisors had raised questions about his performance, including metropolitan editor Jonathan Landman, who in 2002 sent an email to newsroom administrators: "We have to stop Jayson from writing for *The Times*. Now."[28] The scandal led to the resignation of the newsroom's top two leaders, executive editor Howell Raines and managing editor Gerald Boyd.

Jack Kelley, *USA Today* (plagiarism and fabrication, 2004)

Kelley, who joined *USA Today* during its founding year of 1982 as an editorial assistant, rose quickly to become the paper's star reporter. For years he roamed the world, sending back eyewitness accounts of stunning sights. In his report on the 2001 bombing of a pizzeria in Jerusalem, he wrote: "Three men, who had been eating pizza inside, were catapulted out of the chairs they had been sitting on. When they hit the ground, their heads separated from their bodies and rolled down the street." A *USA Today* investigation later showed that Kelley was 90 feet from the pizzeria, that he had his back turned when the bomb went off, and that none of the adult victims were decapitated.[29]

Eventually the paper decided to check the veracity of his stories. Kelley was forced to resign in January 2004 after *USA Today* investigators confronted him over a deception. The investigators had discovered that Kelley, trying to persuade them of the truth of a story from the Balkans, had arranged for a Russian translator to impersonate a Serbian translator. In a telephone call to *USA Today*, the impersonator said she had witnessed Kelley's interview with a Yugoslav human-rights activist.[30]

The newspaper reported on March 21, 2004, that Kelley's

> most egregious misdeed occurred in 2000, when he used a snapshot he took of a Cuban hotel worker to authenticate a story he made up about a woman who died fleeing Cuba by boat. The woman in the photo neither fled by boat nor died, and a *USA Today* reporter located her this month.

USA Today also said evidence contradicted numerous other accounts of intrepid reporting by Kelley, including going on a high-speed hunt for Osama bin Laden in 2003.[31] In addition, *USA Today* said Kelley had on dozens of occasions used "material from other news organizations or wire services without crediting them."[32]

Besides its detailed report on the results of the investigation, *USA Today* made public an internal report by a team of three distinguished retired editors who had been asked to determine how Kelley's deceptions could have gone undetected. The team said that Kelley's editors had failed to be vigilant and diligent and that some staff members had reported being "scolded and insulted" when they voiced suspicions about his stories.[33] In the wake of the Kelley disclosures, *USA Today* editor Karen Jurgensen retired from the job she had held in the last five years of Kelley's time at the paper. Managing editor Hal Ritter resigned.

Jonah Lehrer, *The New Yorker* and Wired.com (plagiarism and fabrication, 2012)

At age 31, Lehrer was a successful author of three books and a magazine writer. Then Jim Romenesko reported in his news-media blog on June 19, 2012, that a post Lehrer wrote for *The New Yorker*'s website was almost identical to what Lehrer had written for *The Wall Street Journal* in October 2011.[34] Later that day, *New York* magazine reported online that Lehrer had frequently lifted his previously published material for other *New Yorker* posts.[35] *The New Yorker* acknowledged Lehrer's recycling by adding an editor's note to five of his posts: "We regret duplication of material." The editor of the website said, "This is wrong. He knows it's a mistake. It's not going to happen again."[36] In an interview with *The Wall Street Journal*'s MarketWatch, David Remnick, editor of *The New Yorker*, said, "There are all kinds of crimes and misdemeanors in this business, and if he were making things up or appropriating other people's work, that's one level of crime."[37]

A month later, Lehrer stood accused of exactly that "level of crime." Michael Moynihan of *Tablet* magazine wrote that Lehrer's new book, *Imagine: How Creativity Works*, fabricated quotations attributed to the singer Bob Dylan.[38] Lehrer quickly resigned from *The New Yorker*, and his publisher, Houghton Mifflin Harcourt, recalled the book. Lehrer apologized in a prepared statement, saying, "The lies are over now."[39] In 2013 the publisher, "after completing our fact-checking process," decided to stop selling another Lehrer book, *How We Decide*.[40]

Lehrer's posts for Wired.com were also challenged in the summer of 2012 by Charles Seife, a New York University journalism professor. At the request of the website, Seife analyzed 18 of Lehrer's posts on Wired.com and concluded that 17 of them "revealed evidence of some journalistic misdeed." Most of the misdeeds were recycling, but Seife also found examples of plagiarism of others, altering quotations, and factual errors.[41] In severing Lehrer's relationship with Wired.com, editor Evan Hanson said, "Lehrer's failure to meet WIRED editorial standards leaves us no choice."[42]

Cases in Which Journalists Broke the Law

In rare cases journalists have broken the law in the course of their work. The following are noteworthy episodes.

R. Foster Winans, *The Wall Street Journal*

A writer of the "Heard on the Street" column in *The Journal* in the early 1980s, Winans realized that mentioning a company favorably or unfavorably in the column could cause the company's stock to rise or fall. He then became involved in an illegal conspiracy using his – and *The Journal's* – ability to move markets. He would tip off a broker about what he was going to write, the broker would invest before publication, and then the broker would share the profits with Winans and his roommate. Federal regulators became aware of the scheme, which they said netted a total of $675,000, only $31,000 of which went to Winans and his roommate. Winans and the others were convicted in 1985 of mail and wire fraud and securities fraud. Winans served eight months in prison.[43]

Mike Gallagher, *The Cincinnati Enquirer*

Under the headline "Chiquita Secrets Revealed," *The Enquirer* published an 18-page investigation report on May 3, 1998, charging that the Cincinnati-based fruit conglomerate had bribed foreign officials and had mistreated its Central American workers. On June 28, *The Enquirer* published another huge headline, "An Apology to Chiquita," at the top of its front page, and beneath it the newspaper expressed regret for "creating a false and misleading impression of Chiquita's business practices."

What happened in the interim was that Chiquita convinced executives of *The Enquirer* and its owner, Gannett, that reporter Mike Gallagher had illegally tapped into the voicemail of Chiquita executives. Gannett also paid $14 million to Chiquita and fired Gallagher. On September 24, 1998, Gallagher pleaded guilty to unlawful interception of communications and unauthorized access to computer systems. He avoided jail – he was sentenced to five years' probation and 200 hours of community service – by cooperating in the prosecution of a Chiquita lawyer who had given him the voicemail passwords. On June 30, 1999, the lawyer, George Ventura, pleaded "no contest" to misdemeanor counts of attempted unauthorized access to computer systems. He received two years of unsupervised probation and 40 hours of community service.[44] In 2012 a judge in Cincinnati expunged Gallagher's criminal record, giving him a clean slate.[45]

The *News of the World*'s phone-hacking scandal

In Rupert Murdoch's best-selling weekly tabloid, gossipy items about the British royal family were keeping readers informed in late 2005: Prince William had pulled a tendon in his knee, and his younger brother, Harry, had visited a strip club, which amused William but upset Harry's girlfriend. The revelations puzzled the family's senior aides. Since the information was not known outside "a small, discreet circle," they suspected eavesdropping on private conversations. Scotland Yard investigated.[46]

By January 2006, *The New York Times* reported later,

> an unambiguous trail led to Clive Goodman, the *News of the World* reporter who covered the royal family, and a private investigator, Glenn Mulcaire, who also worked for the paper. The two men had somehow obtained the PIN codes needed to access the voicemail of the royal aides.[47]

As the investigation continued, detectives learned that Goodman and Mulcaire were listening to the voicemail messages of the two princes, William and Harry. They also "collected evidence indicating that reporters at the *News of the World* might have hacked the phone messages of hundreds of celebrities, government officials, soccer stars – anyone whose personal secrets could be tabloid fodder."[48]

In January 2007 Goodman and Mulcaire pleaded guilty to one count of conspiracy to intercept the royal family's communications. In a London courtroom, the defendants apologized to the princes and their aides for the "gross invasion of privacy."[49] That was followed by the resignation of Andy Coulson, the editor of *News of the World*.

A shocking new dimension of the scandal emerged on July 4, 2011, when *The Guardian* reported that *News of the World* had illegally hacked into voicemails on the cell phone of Milly Dowler, a 13-year-old girl who vanished in 2002, interfering with the police investigation of her disappearance. "As her friends and parents called and left messages imploring Milly to get in touch with them, the *News of the World* was listening and recording their every private word," *The Guardian* said. Scotland Yard detectives were believed to have found out about the hacking of the girl's phone by parsing the 11,000 pages of notes they found in the earlier phone-hacking investigation.[50]

The next day, Glenn Mulcaire told *The Guardian* he wanted to apologize "to anybody who was hurt or upset by what I have done," and said he had never intended to interfere with a police investigation. He said that working for the *News of the World* "was never easy. There was relentless pressure. There was a constant demand for results ... A lot of information I obtained was simply tittle-tattle ... but sometimes what I did was for what I thought was the greater good, to carry out investigative journalism."[51]

On July 6, Rupert Murdoch and his son James announced that they would shut down the *News of the World*, ending a 168-year run for the tabloid. James Murdoch said the paper had "a proud history of fighting crime, exposing wrongdoing and regularly setting the news agenda for the nation." Now, he said, that record had been sullied. "The *News of the World* is in the business of holding others to account. But it failed when it came to itself."[52]

The Murdochs appeared later in July before a parliamentary hearing and said they were unaware of what had been going on at the *News of the World*.[53]

The British government decided to conduct a separate investigation into the phone-hacking. That led to eight people being charged with crimes in July 2012. One of these was Andy Coulson, the former top editor of the *News of the World*, who had gone on to become the communications chief for Prime Minister David Cameron, before resigning in January 2011.[54] Another was the former UK News Corporation chief executive, Rebekah Brooks.

In June 2014 Coulson was found guilty of "conspiracy to hack phones" and was sentenced in July to 18 months in prison. Brooks was found not guilty of all charges.[55]

Coulson's "wasn't the only conviction at the high-profile hacking trial in London," Rem Rieder wrote in his column in *USA Today*: "A guilty verdict was entered against a certain approach to journalism, one where all that matters is getting the scoop, the sexy, often salacious story that no one else has."[56]

Confronting the Problems of Plagiarism and Fabrication

Craig Silverman is the author of *We Regret the Error*, the title of both a blog and a 2007 book cataloguing mistakes in the news media. He also writes a column on Poynter, and in the summer of 2012 he was (as he later wrote) worn out. "It seemed like every week brought a new, awful incident of plagiarism or fabrication at news organizations large and small." Trying to galvanize the profession into action, he posted a list of every known incident and called it "Journalism's Summer of Sin." He called out newsroom leaders "for being unwilling to engage and show accountability." Having vented his frustration, Silverman didn't think anything was going to happen. But then he got an email from Teresa Schmedding, president of the American Copy Editors Society. It basically said, "Let's do this."[57]

Under Schmedding's leadership, 14 media companies, 10 organizations of journalists, and 10 journalism education institutions produced a manual titled *Telling the Truth and Nothing But*. William G. Connolly, a retired *New York Times* editor, headed a task force consisting of 23 volunteers working in print, broadcasting, and digital. Norman Lewis' doctoral dissertation became the starting point for the project, and Lewis himself – by then an award-winning professor at the University of Florida – was recruited as an adviser.[58]

Telling the Truth and Nothing But was rolled out at a National Summit to Fight Plagiarism and Fabrication in St. Louis in April 2013. The free book defines and explains plagiarism and fabrication. It advocates having a system of checks to prevent them from happening, and it outlines what to do when they do happen. It encourages each newsroom to establish a policy. Such a policy should have the following components:

- There's no room for confusion.
- It's widely available.
- It involves random checks.
- It addresses attribution and linking.
- It's clear about discipline.
- It treats everyone equally.[59]

The book offers detailed definitions, which Lewis' 2007 dissertation had said were remarkably lacking for transgressions that the profession regarded so seriously. The following is an excerpt from the book's definition of plagiarism:

> Plagiarism is presenting someone else's language or work as your own. Whether it is deliberate or the result of carelessness, such appropriation should be considered unacceptable because it hides the sources of information from the audience. Every act of plagiarism betrays the public's trust, violates the creator of the original material and diminishes the offender, our craft and our industry.
>
> The best way to avoid plagiarism is to attribute information, a practice available in any medium. Credit should be given for information that is not common knowledge: facts, theories, opinions, statistics, photos, videos, graphics, drawings, quotations or original wording first produced by someone else. ...
>
> [W]e affirm a golden rule of attribution: Principled professionals credit the work of others, treating others as they would like to be treated themselves.[60]

And here is an excerpt from the book's definition of fabrication:

> Fabrication is often linked to plagiarism but in some ways is its opposite. Whereas plagiarism is using without attribution material produced by someone else and assumed to be factual, fabrication is making up material and publishing it in the guise of truth. Both are acts of deception. Both are wrong, but fabrication is especially egregious.
>
> Journalists are committed to seeking and presenting the truth. Knowingly creating false material, or deliberately altering reported material, therefore violates the most fundamental functions of journalism. Regardless of the platform, fabrication destroys the credibility of offending journalists, calling into question the validity of all their previous work.[61]

Fighting Plagiarism: A Q&A Based on the Book

Why is attribution the solution?

"Attribution is both a professional responsibility and a good business practice. ... In an era when all media institutions are suspect, heeding the ethic of transparency on all platforms reinforces the position of professional journalists as credible sources of information."[62]

Why is it important to provide relevant links in digital stories?

This gives readers and viewers the opportunity "to examine the sources of the information they're being given. Links are a digital form of attribution. In newsrooms where they are routinely provided in digital stories, the absence of links is a red flag to editors on the alert for plagiarism and fabrication."[63]

Does intent matter?

"An unavoidable complication in any discussion of plagiarism is intent. Was the plagiarism deliberate? Was it inadvertent? Plagiarism harms the creator of the original material, our craft, our industry – but just as crucially, it is a violation of the audience's trust. Whatever the motivation, the outcome is the same: Everyone suffers." Although intent matters in how a news organization deals with transgressors, "it's time to reject the all-too-common defense – 'I didn't mean it' – and to focus on education, training and the setting of clear standards."[64]

How much copying is too much?

"That's the wrong approach. It is more productive to look for reasons to attribute information more often, more clearly, more generously."[65]

Is it plagiarism to copy from a news release?

Not if it is quoted. Using it without disclosing its source "is misleading, suggesting that it came from an interview or that it is the first-hand knowledge of the reporter."[66]

Can someone self-plagiarize?

Referring specifically to Jonah Lehrer's "serial reuse" of what he had written previously for other publications, the book suggests a better way to frame the discussion is to consider the term *recycling material without disclosure*. This calls for common sense: In a running news story that is being followed up frequently, background material generally would not require attribution. "On the other hand, the older the material, the greater are the risks and thus the need for clear attribution," such as "the *Journal* reported at the time of his conviction."[67]

What about aggregation on the Web?

"Online aggregation is the reposting of another's work, generally wholesale through automatic scraping or parsing of an RSS feed, without additional reporting. … Automatic aggregation, even with attribution, should never cross the boundaries of fair use and professional respect. The reproduction of inappropriately large portions of text may discourage a reader from visiting the original work."[68]

What about curation?

"Curation is the individual selection and posting of a portion of another's work, usually with added material. … Curated work should also be clearly attributed. Curators should strive to go beyond merely reporting another's work, possibly including references to multiple news sources or original reporting, context, or commentary."[69]

What about user-generated content and social-media content?

The very fact that the information comes from outside the news organization "raises additional issues that can best be met by attribution and respect for copyright. The challenges in verifying such content make transparency in sourcing necessary – not just ethically but practically. … It is best to identify the work's creator in the clearest possible manner. The use of platform credit alone does not suffice – for example, sourcing a video clip to YouTube rather than the poster is akin to sourcing a print news story to the press that reproduced it. … On Twitter, for example, another's authorship can be indicated through the use of RT and MT ("retweet" and "modified tweet") with an @ link to the creator's profile."[70]

How can a reporter avoid inadvertent plagiarism?

"Cutting and pasting blocks of text can ensure that a source is quoted accurately, but it's a practice that should be used with great caution. Quoted material should never be pasted into notes or stories without being designated immediately as quotation. One helpful technique is to add quotation marks, the attribution and a link ... Another technique is to highlight quoted material (again with attribution and link) in a distinctive color in notes and drafts."[71]

Detecting Plagiarism and Fabrication

Newsroom leaders have been perplexed over how to curb plagiarism and fabrication. Their editing procedures are designed to catch and correct the human errors of honest journalists. Anyone who sets out to fabricate probably will succeed, at least for a while.

For the managers, then, the question is: Should we continue to operate on the basis of mutual trust? Or should we modify our procedures in order to catch the occasional rogue?

Trust is vital in a newsroom, and leaders could undermine it if they treat everyone as a likely fabricator. Professor Russell Frank of Pennsylvania State University, a former newspaper journalist, has said it would be hard to imagine the effect on morale in a newsroom in which every statement in every story is questioned. He told Lori Robertson of *American Journalism Review* that, if a reporter were asked if he really went to the places mentioned in his story, he probably would respond: "Well for crying out loud, I wrote it. Of course I did."[72]

Still, newsroom leaders need to be alert to patterns of fabrication and, when they spot them, to investigate. They need to edit with a healthy sense of skepticism that picks up on quotes and scenes that seem too good to be true. The essence of skeptical editing is that reporters, veterans and rookies alike, are asked about crucial facts: "How do you know that?" This is a reality check for honest reporters who may be jumping to conclusions. It also could catch the rare fabricator.

Copy editors, whose professional duties routinely involve asking questions of their reporting colleagues, are crucial in defending against plagiarism and fabrication, according to the authors of *Telling the Truth and Nothing But.* Like other editors, they "weigh details of the story against their own logic and judgment." As an example, the book mentions an opportunity missed: "Had the *Washington Post* editors who handled 'Jimmy's World' asked how an 8-year-old truant could be in fourth grade, they could have stopped Janet Cooke's fabrication before it was published."[73]

As for plagiarism, leaders likewise should investigate promptly and thoroughly when they receive any hints of violations. Equally important, they should be clear to their staffs about how they define plagiarism. They should examine whether they are fostering plagiarism by condoning, for example, sports notebook columns based on notes shared by beat reporters in other cities.

The authors of *Telling the Truth and Nothing But* take a stand for systematic, random testing of reporters' copy with online tools such as LexisNexis. This is the only reliable way, they say, "to identify the serial fabricators who otherwise operate undetected for years or decades."[74]

The Toronto Star has bought access to plagiarism software but does not use it for spot checks. Kathy English, the paper's public editor, said that "would suggest to writers that *The Star* does not trust them. We operate in an environment of trust. We must." The software is intended to be used if there is an accusation of plagiarism. In such a case, English said,

> I do the preliminary work the old-fashioned way: I take yellow highlighter and highlight all the similar passages in the two works, look at structure etc. Once we determine that what we have is indeed plagiarism, we would turn to the software to look at other examples of that person's work to see if there is a pattern.[75]

Telling the Truth and Nothing But devotes an entire chapter to "Responding to lapses." It contains practical suggestions, including tips on skeptical editing. It also advocates the appointment of a "standards editor" to take the lead in checking out any charge of plagiarism and fabrication, and even outlines a protocol for interviewing a suspected plagiarist or fabricator.

The starting point, the book emphasizes, is "a newsroom culture that values attribution, accuracy, transparency, and credibility." Staff members should "not only know the rules but take personal responsibility for them."[76] Anyone should feel comfortable telling management in confidence when ethical violations are suspected, even if they are only hunches. In the Janet Cooke case, several *Washington Post* staff members doubted her story but did not go to the top editors. One of the doubters was reporter Jonathan Neumann, himself a Pulitzer winner. Neumann told the National News Council investigators in 1981, "[W]e felt it wouldn't be fair to put her on the carpet when we couldn't prove anything."[77] In the Jack Kelley case, *USA Today* staff members who challenged his veracity were rebuffed by editors, the blue-ribbon investigative panel concluded.[78]

In its 2005 ethics code, the *Los Angeles Times* told staff members that they have a duty to report unethical behavior. According to the code:

> If you know of anything that might cast a shadow on the paper's reputation, you are expected to inform a supervising editor. This can be an uncomfortable duty; under some circumstances, it can do harm to one's relationships with others in the newsroom. It is a duty nevertheless.[79]

Journalists who make wrong choices about plagiarism and fabrication may lose their jobs and careers. The pain of humiliation could last a lifetime.

Consider the lament of a journalist fired for plagiarism, a woman who was interviewed on condition of anonymity for Norman Lewis' research. Anyone doing a Google search of the journalist's name, Lewis wrote, will find "not a quarter-century of achievement, but the one time she forgot to paraphrase." The journalist told Lewis: "With it out there on the Internet, it's out there forever."[80]

Notes

1   Leonard Pitts Jr., "Chris Cecil, plagiarism gets you fired," *The Miami Herald*, June 3, 2005.

2   Norman P. Lewis, *Paradigm Disguise: Systemic Influences on Newspaper Plagiarism*, 2007, 162–166. In an adaptation of his thesis, Lewis published "Plagiarism antecedents and situational influences," *Journalism and Mass Communication Quarterly*, 85:2 (Summer 2008), 313–330. In the adaptation, Lewis revised the number of appropriation plagiarism cases from five to four, and the number of research plagiarism cases from 66 to 67.

3   Lewis, *Paradigm Disguise*, 58–59.

4   Ibid., 166–182.

5   Ibid., 183–185.

6   Ibid., 182–183.

7   Roy Peter Clark, "The unoriginal sin." Originally written for the March 1983 issue of *Washington Journalism Review* (now *American Journalism Review*), the article was posted on the Poynter website in July 2000.

8   Cynthia Gorney, "Getting it right," *American Journalism Review*, Mar. 2001.

9   Howard Kurtz, "Ethics pressure squeezes a few out the door," *The Washington Post*, May 2, 2005.

10 Ibid.

11 Roy Peter Clark, "Why we should stop criminalizing practices that are confused with plagiarism," Poynter, Mar. 27, 2013.

12 Jack Shafer, "The Romenesko effect," *Slate*, Apr. 18, 2005.

13 Two surveys were conducted by the Freedom Forum Media Studies Center in September and October 1998. One survey involved a national sample of 1,016 adults, with a margin of error of ±3 percentage points. The other surveys were separate random samples of 400 adults in Boston and Cincinnati, with a margin of error of ±5 percentage points. The results were reported by Michael White, "Survey: public thinks journalists often guilty of ethical lapses," The Associated Press, Oct. 16, 1998.

14 Peter Johnson, "Media weigh in on 'journalistic fraud,'" *USA Today*, May 12, 2003.

15 Associated Press Managing Editors, "Readers respond: why we don't alert media to mistakes," Poynter, May 19, 2003.

16 Lewis, *Paradigm Disguise*, 90.

17 Clark, "The unoriginal sin."

18 Janet Cooke, "Jimmy's world: 8-year-old heroin addict lives for a fix," *The Washington Post*, Sept. 28, 1980.

19 *After Jimmy's World: Tightening Up in Editing* (New York: The National News Council, 1981), 16–25.

20 Buzz Bissinger, "Shattered Glass," *Vanity Fair*, Sept. 1998; Lori Robertson, "Shattered Glass at *The New Republic*," *American Journalism Review*, June 1998; Howard Kurtz, "Stephen Glass waits for prime time to say 'I lied,'" *The Washington Post*, May 7, 2003.

21 Eugene Volokh, "Court denies Stephen Glass admission to the California bar," *The Washington Post*, Jan. 27, 2014.

22 Sinéad O'Brien, "Secrets and lies," *American Journalism Review*, Sept. 1998.

23 O'Brien, "For Barnicle, one controversy too many," *American Journalism Review*, Sept. 1998.

24 O'Brien, "Secrets and lies."

25 Matthew V. Storin, "Some practical advice from a crisis-buffeted editor," in Robert H. Giles (ed.), *Media Mistakes of '98*, a booklet published by the Freedom Forum Media Studies Center.

26 Jacques Steinberg, "*Times* reporter resigns after questions on article," *The New York Times*, May 2, 2003; Howard Kurtz, "Reporter resigns over copied story," *The Washington Post*, May 2, 2003.

27 "*Times* reporter who resigned leaves long trail of deception," *The New York Times*, May 11, 2003.

28 Ibid.

29 Blake Morrison, "Ex-*USA Today* reporter faked major stories," *USA Today*, Mar. 19, 2004.

30 Kurtz, "*USA Today* found hoax before writer confessed," *The Washington Post*, Jan. 13, 2004.

31 Blake Morrison, "Ex-*USA Today* reporter faked major stories," *USA Today*, Mar. 19, 2004.

32 Rita Rubin, "Material without attribution," *USA Today*, Mar. 21, 2004.

33 Bill Hilliard, Bill Kovach, and John Seigenthaler, "The problems of Jack Kelley and *USA Today*," a memorandum to publisher Craig Moon, published in *USA Today*, Apr. 22, 2004.

34 Jim Romenesko, "Jonah Lehrer's NewYorker.com 'Smart people' post borrows from earlier *WSJ* piece," JimRomenesko.com, June 19, 2012.

35 Joe Coscarelli, "*New Yorker* writer Jonah Lehrer plagiarizes himself repeatedly," NYmag.com, June 19, 2012.

36 Jennifer Schuessler, "Lehrer apologizes for recycling work, while *New Yorker* says it won't happen again," *The New York Times*, June 20, 2012.

37 Jon Friedman, "New Yorker editor: Lehrer won't be exiled," MarketWatch, June 21, 2012.

38 Michael Moynihan, "Jonah Lehrer's deceptions," *Tablet*, July 30, 2012.

39 Julie Bosman, "Jonah Lehrer resigns from *The New Yorker* after making up Dylan quotes for his book," *The New York Times*, July 30, 2012.

40 Leslie Kaufman, "Publisher pulls a 2nd book by Lehrer, 'How We Decide,'" *The New York Times*, Mar. 1, 2013.

41 Charles Seife, "Jonah Lehrer's journalistic misdeeds at Wired.com," *Slate*, Aug. 31, 2012.

42 Evan Hanson, "Violations of editorial standards found in WIRED writer's blog," Wired.com, Aug. 31, 2012.

43 R. Foster Winans, *Trading Secrets* (New York: St. Martin's Press, 1986), 140–161, 301–306.

44 Nicholas Bender, "Damage report: after the Chiquita story," *Columbia Journalism Review*, May–June 2001.

45 Kimball Perry, "Fired reporter has criminal record erased," Cincinnati.com, July 24, 2012.

46 Don Van Atta Jr, Jo Becker, and Graham Bowley, "Tabloid hack attack on royals, and beyond," *The New York Times*, Sept. 1, 2010.

47 Ibid.

48 Ibid.

49 Ibid.

50 Nick Davies and Amelia Hill, "Missing Milly Dowler's voicemail was hacked by *News of the World*," *The Guardian*, July 4, 2011.

51 Nick Davies, "Phone hacking: Glenn Mulcaire blames 'relentless pressure' by *NoW* for actions," *The Guardian*, July 5, 2011.

52 Karla Adam and Paul Farhi, "*News of the World* to close amid phone-hacking scandal," *The Washington Post*, July 7, 2011.

53 Robert Hutton and Alex Morales, "Rupert Murdoch denies knowledge of phone-hacking, vows to 'clean this up,'" Bloomberg News, July 19, 2011.

54 Patrick Wintour and Nick Davies, "Andy Coulson resigns as phone-hacking scandal rocks Downing Street," *The Guardian*, Jan. 21, 2011.

55 BBC News, "Andy Coulson jailed for 18 months over phone hacking," July 4, 2014.

56 Rem Rieder, "A guilty verdict for sleazy journalism," *USA Today*, June 24, 2014.

57 Craig Silverman, "Journalism orgs launch free ebook for preventing, detecting and handling plagiarism and fabrication," Poynter, Apr. 5, 2013.

58 *Telling the Truth and Nothing But*, created in 2013 by the National Summit to Fight Plagiarism and Fabrication, 3–4.

59 Ibid., 25–26.

60 Ibid., 5.

61 Ibid., 8–9.

62 Ibid., 7–8.

63 Ibid., 28.

64 Ibid., 8.

65 Ibid., 12.

66 Ibid.

67 Ibid., 13.

68 Ibid., 14.

69 Ibid., 14–15.

70 Ibid., 15.

71 Ibid., 30.

72 Lori Robertson, "Confronting the culture," *American Journalism Review*, Aug.–Sept. 2005.

73 *Telling the Truth and Nothing But*, 32.

74 Ibid.

75 Kathy English, email to the author, Sept. 10, 2014.

76 *Telling the Truth and Nothing But*, 31.

77 *After Jimmy's World*, 22.

78 Hilliard, Kovach, and Siegenthaler, "The problems of Jack Kelley and *USA Today*."

79 "*Los Angeles Times* Ethics Guidelines," *Los Angeles Times*, July 13, 2005.

80 Lewis, *Paradigm Disguise*, 138.

10 Conflicts of Interest: Appearances Count

Journalists should leave no doubt of their primary loyalty to the audience

---

Learning Goals

This chapter will help you understand:

- the damage that a conflict of interest inflicts on a journalist's credibility;
- the definition of a conflict of interest, and the distinction between an *actual* and an *apparent* conflict;
- the potential for conflicts in journalists' use of social media;
- guidelines for avoiding conflicts of interest, actual or apparent; and
- situations that can lead to conflicts.

As election day approached in 2012, Robert Vickers wrestled with the question of whether to vote for Barack Obama or Mitt Romney. When he finally made his choice, he decided he would explain to the readers of *The Patriot-News* in Harrisburg, Pennsylvania, why he thought Romney deserved to be elected.

Vickers was *The Patriot-News'* political writer, and he had just finished covering the presidential campaign. In an op-ed column published on the Friday before the election, Vickers said he was publicly sharing his choice "as a catharsis of how I came to my decision, not to influence anyone else." He said he had never registered as a Republican or Democrat and had never before made a public statement about how he was voting. "Even close friends have a hard time trying to figure out my personal views."[1]

It was not easy getting his editors to agree to the column. The first answer was no. Vickers himself was ambivalent, but finally he concluded he should go public with his choice. He was able to convince the editors that he would be showing readers how someone was deliberating the important decision that they themselves were going to make – "someone who has greater access to the political machinations than everyday citizens."

His managing editor, Mike Feeley, said he liked the idea of demonstrating the kind of transparency that people demand of public officials. Besides, he said, Vickers primarily writes columns.[2]

It was a remarkable departure from journalism tradition: A journalist who had covered two candidates was announcing publicly which of the two he preferred.

The Ethical Journalist: Making Responsible Decisions in the Digital Age, Second Edition. Gene Foreman.
© 2016 John Wiley & Sons, Inc. Published 2016 by John Wiley & Sons, Inc.

On the day the column was published, Vickers responded to questions from readers in an online chat. He pointed to a new environment: "[T]he journalistic/political landscape has changed, and I reckon this is a step toward existing in that landscape. ... The wall of opinion and hard news was blown open long before my piece today."[3]

Robert Vickers' column, as well as his reference to the mingling of opinion and news, doubtlessly resonated with some in the profession who contend that journalists gain credibility if they reveal what they think about the people and events they cover.

In a 2007 column in the *National Journal*, William Powers proposed that news organizations post their staff members' biases online so the audience could take them into account. With blogging, podcasting, and other kinds of "citizen journalism," he wrote,

> the curtain has been pulled back, revealing actual human beings. To the extent that media outlets deny this by pretending that their employees have no views on politics and other topics – or that those views don't influence the coverage – they come off as charlatans.[4]

In contrast, the ethics codes of most news organizations continue to instruct journalists to keep their opinions to themselves. That also is the position this author takes.

Perception is crucial. What may be intended by journalists as an honest disclosure could lead the public to deduce instead that they are putting loyalty to partisan causes ahead of their duty to report the news fairly and impartially.

That perception is what is known as an **apparent conflict of interest**. By revealing whom he favors, the *Patriot-News* political writer could appear to be vested in the outcome. In the eyes of a public that tends to view journalism cynically, that revelation invites suspicions of bias.

Consider this analogy: A football referee announces before the big game, "I'm going to call this game fair and square, but Team A is the best on the field today. No question about it." Late in the game, a close play decides the outcome in favor of Team A. The referee called the play fairly – exactly the way he saw it – but he's not going to convince the fans of Team B that they weren't robbed.

Think about it: What did this hypothetical referee gain by announcing his opinion? What did he lose? Is it any wonder that referees keep their opinions to themselves? Shouldn't journalists, who wear the striped shirts in the news arena, be just as discreet?

Defining Conflict of Interest

The issue of journalists' political preferences offers an insight into the sometimes complex subject of conflict of interest.

Journalists owe their primary loyalty to the audience – readers, listeners, viewers, and digital users. Nothing should divert them from serving this audience to the best of their ability. Journalists have a *conflict of interest* if they allow self-interest, or a loyalty to any other person or organization, to take precedence over their duty to the audience.

A journalist who allows self-interest to interfere with his or her reporting is committing a flagrant violation of trust. Given the level of integrity in the profession, such instances are rare.

More often, what the audience sees is *the appearance* of a conflict. But appearances count.

Consider another analogy: If you are sick, you trust your physician to do what is best to help you get well. The physician owes primary loyalty to you. Several drugs might be effective in treating your condition, and let's say the physician chose the one he or she honestly thought to be most effective. Later, you learn that the physician earned a free vacation trip by writing a certain number of prescriptions for the drug you were given. Wouldn't you be suspicious? (In 2002 the federal government warned pharmaceutical companies not to offer financial incentives to doctors to prescribe certain drugs.[5])

Just as a patient deserves the doctor's best medical judgment, the journalist's audience deserves news judgment that is not influenced by anything other than the journalist's own professional skill, reporting, and experience. Avoiding conflicts of interest is all about carrying out the SPJ code's guiding principle of "act independently."

Some journalists think an *apparent* conflict is nothing to worry about. Their reasoning is that only an *actual* conflict poses a problem.

This author presumes that an editor or news director will not tolerate a journalist who is *not* trustworthy – that is, someone who commits an *actual* conflict of interest by distorting the news to fulfill a self-interest. However, the public usually lacks the concrete facts to judge whether a journalist is trustworthy. So, if a journalist *appears* to have a conflict, many news consumers will conclude that he or she *does* have a conflict. For that reason, the majority view in the profession is that any hint of a conflict should be avoided.

The profession collectively made that decision in the 1970s, when emerging newsroom codes banned accepting gifts from news sources. Invariably, journalists who had been taking the gifts rationalized that they could still act independently. By banning so-called freebies, the profession was saying that the only convincing way to assure the public of journalists' independence was to say no to gifts. The concept of an apparent conflict, of course, applies to many situations besides the acceptance of gifts.

"We journalists, knowing that we are pure in heart, may dislike having to meet the unreasonable test of others' perceptions of us," the distinguished broadcast commentator Daniel Schorr wrote in 1983. "But isn't that the test we invented for those who wield influence in the society?"[6]

John L. Hulteng wrote in *Playing It Straight*, "Men and women in the news business cannot allow their motives to become suspect."[7]

Both the news organization and the journalist bear a responsibility to act independently. They owe each other integrity.

To avoid conflicts, the news organization has an obligation to insulate its journalism from the commercial function, especially the sale of advertising, and to be careful that the company's civic activities do not compromise its journalism. Business-side conflicts are discussed in Chapter 11.

For the journalist, the responsibility to act independently means forgoing some privileges and even constitutional rights that other people enjoy. "Journalists have no place on the playing fields of politics," *The New York Times* declares in its ethics code. *Times* staff members may not run for office. They may not campaign for or give money to candidates, ballot causes, or efforts to enact legislation. They may not wear campaign buttons. They may not march in support of public movements or sign ads taking a position on public issues.[8]

"We have no ideology in this newsroom," Leonard Downie Jr. said in an online chat with readers after he had announced his retirement as editor of *The Washington Post* in 2008:

> Our only bias is for a good story and accountability journalism. The only political activity our journalists are allowed to engage in is voting, and even that I don't do. No personal or financial support for candidates or issues. No demonstrating. No petition signing.[9]

The journalist might be conflicted – or appear to be conflicted – because of activities in these principal areas:

- statements about controversial issues in a public forum, such as in postings on social media;
- personal financial interests such as accepting gifts, holding a secondary job, or making investments;
- involvement in off-the-job civic activities; and
- relationships with the subjects of news coverage.

Avoiding Conflicts of Interest

Journalists should be keenly aware that their acquaintances and news subjects see them in their professional role on a 24/7 basis. Even when they are off duty, they are judged by what they say or do.

"One unfortunate obligation of being a journalist is the limit it automatically imposes on your personal life," Rick Tulsky, a Pulitzer Prize-winning investigative reporter, wrote on the Medill Watchdog blog. The limitations may be frustrating, "but most journalists conclude their journalistic work can have a greater impact than any other thing they can do, and so the tradeoff makes sense."[10]

Most newsrooms give their staffs written conflict-of-interest codes. Although such codes cannot cover all situations that might arise, they are valuable because: (1) they provide guidance on dealing with the most common problems and set a tone for resolving problems that are not explicitly covered; and (2) they inform the journalist in advance of the conduct that is expected, so he or she is less likely to violate the code or to take personal offense when activities are questioned.

Typically, newsroom codes emphasize that staff members can comfortably choose to be involved in community activities that are unlikely to attract news coverage – activities like parent–teacher associations, Little League sports, and neighborhood associations. However, the journalist should be conscious of his or her 24/7 professional role and use common sense to avoid likely conflicts. For example, it is perfectly acceptable for a journalist to be an active member of a church, synagogue, mosque, or other religious group. But he or she should avoid serving on a committee protesting the location of a casino near the parish, because the committee's actions may well become a subject of news coverage.

When a conflict is unavoidable or insignificant, it should be disclosed to the audience. For example, the law firm representing a newspaper or broadcast station might receive news coverage for its work on behalf of other clients and, when that happens, it is appropriate to advise the audience that the firm also represents the news outlet. This brief mention tells the audience: "We're going to be fair in how we cover our law firm, but we're informing you of the association so that you can be the judge." This is called a **disclosure**.

If a conflict can be avoided, it should be. A disclosure in such a case is insufficient. Airlines and resorts might provide a free trip to a travel writer – an experience that the writer is supposed to evaluate for the benefit of potential paying customers. The writer's disclosure of the arrangement, while better than hiding it, does little to reassure readers. In the first place, the people providing the complimentary flight, lodging, and meals know that the writer is going to describe the experience, so they likely will lavish more attention on him or her than on the average customer. Another reason for the reviewer to be upbeat is the desire to get invitations to future junkets.

News organizations recognize that the actions of a staff member's spouse or significant other are beyond their control, but they require the staff member to inform them of any conflict that might arise from the relationship. "Some of our family members – including spouses, companions, and children – may be involved in politics or advocacy," the *NPR Ethics Handbook* says:

> We are sensitive to the perception of bias. So we inform our supervisors and work with them to avoid even the appearance of conflicts of interest. NPR journalists recuse themselves from covering stories or events related to their family members' political activities. We may go so far as to change job responsibilities (for instance, moving off the "politics desk" to an area of coverage well removed from that subject).[11]

Online, NPR's code cites the case of Michele Norris to illustrate how accommodations may be made because of a spouse's activity. In October 2011 Norris wrote to the NPR staff:

> I need to share some news and I wanted to make sure my NPR family heard this first. Last week, I told news management that my husband, Broderick Johnson, has just accepted a senior adviser position with the Obama Campaign. After careful consideration, we decided that Broderick's new role could make it difficult for me to continue hosting [*All Things Considered*]. Given the nature of Broderick's position with the campaign and the impact that it will most certainly have on our family life, I will temporarily step away from my hosting duties until after the 2012 elections. ... I will be wearing a different hat for a while, producing signature segments and features and working on new reporting projects. ... I will of course recuse myself from all election coverage.[12]

Guidelines for Journalists' Use of Social Media

Social media are well established as newsgathering tools. They also enable journalists to engage with their audience to a degree that was impossible before the digital era. An Indiana University survey of journalists in 2013 showed that 40 percent of US journalists regarded social media as very important to their work; 54 percent regularly used Twitter and other microblogs to gather news and report their stories; and 69 percent saw themselves as more engaged with their audiences.[13]

News organizations are encouraging their staff members to use social media professionally, but the opportunities of social media are accompanied by new challenges. For one thing, individual journalists have to be counted on to use judgment and restraint. Reporting the news via Twitter may not permit an editor's review of each tweet. (Chapter 12 of this text explores the newsgathering issues involved in social media, primarily the essential duty to verify before reporting anything found there. This chapter deals with potential conflict-of-interest problems arising from journalists' use of social media in their professional and personal lives.)

Many news organizations have issued guidelines that strive to maintain a delicate balance. The American Society of News Editors described that fine line in a 2011 report on 10 *Best Practices for Social Media*: "Putting in place overly draconian rules discourages creativity and innovation, but allowing an uncontrolled free-for-all opens the floodgates to problems and leaves news organizations responsible for irresponsible employees."[14]

The following are excerpts from the "best practices" report that the ASNE study committee wrote after reviewing various news organizations' policies:

- *Traditional ethics rules still apply.* "Reporters should act the same way online as they would in person. They shouldn't say anything they wouldn't want to see on the front page of their newspaper, and they shouldn't post anything that would embarrass them personally or professionally or their organization."
- *Assume everything you write online will become public.* "That's true even if it's on an account that's not explicitly linked to your employer. ... If something goes on a private page, employees should know they need to be ready to defend it publicly."
- *Engage with readers, but professionally.* "Too many news executives see social media platforms as merely a way to broadcast what they're doing. It's a two-way form of communication. Reporters have an obligation to interact and respond. ... Policies should encourage reporters to not get into flame wars with trolls or unreasonable readers."
- *Beware of perceptions.* "Reporters should make clear that retweeting or linking to items that might interest their followers is not an endorsement of the content. ... This can be cleared up by modifying the tweet or with a simple disclaimer, such as 'RT's don't = endorsements.' ... As Facebook has become more ubiquitous and the connotation of the verb 'friend' has been diluted, being 'friends' with someone you cover is more acceptable than it might have looked a few years ago."

- *Always identify yourself as a journalist.* "Anonymity is no more acceptable in online forums than it is at a political event or other traditional reporting venues. One can linger online in public places, but they should not misrepresent themselves to obtain access to material that is not public. When asking someone for information, especially if they plan to publish it, there's an expectation that reporters will be up front in identifying themselves. ... Don't pretend to be someone else to obtain information."
- *Keep internal deliberations confidential.* "Social media networks can threaten the integrity of the editorial process. Painstaking editorial decisions were traditionally made behind closed doors. ... Twitter and Facebook offer windows into reporting that make some editors nervous. ... Some reporters tweet through the reporting and editing process."

Guidelines from individual news organizations amplify the best practices identified by the ASNE committee. Most guidelines emphasize that, on social media, staff members must avoid expressions of opinion on contentious issues. The AP counsels in its 2013 guidelines: "AP staffers must be aware that opinions they express may damage the AP's reputation as an unbiased source of news."[15] *The New York Times* advises its staff: "Be careful not to write anything on a blog or a personal Web page that you could not write in *The Times* – don't editorialize, for instance, if you work for the News Department."[16] Reuters tells its journalists: "We want to encourage you to use social media approaches in your journalism but we also need to make sure that you are fully aware of the risks – especially those that threaten our hard-earned reputation for independence and freedom from bias."[17] *The Washington Post* instructs its staff not to "accept or place tokens, badges, or virtual gifts from political or partisan causes on pages or sites."[18] NPR's ethics code tells journalists, "You should conduct yourself in social media forums with an eye to how your behavior or comments might appear if we were called upon to defend them as a news organization."[19]

News organizations generally recognize that it is necessary for reporters to "follow" or "friend" their news sources on social media, even those who represent political parties and advocacy groups. NPR's code says, "But we do so to monitor their news feeds, not to become participants, and we follow and friend sites created by advocates from all sides of an issue. It's as basic a tool as signing up to be on mailing lists used to be."[20]

Several organizations emphasize the admonition – found in the ASNE list of best practices above – that social media are no place for reporters to complain about how their stories were edited or for photographers to complain about whether the photo editor selected the best image. Disagreements of this kind occur from time to time in any newsroom, but they have to be worked out within the organization. Going public with grievances ("you should have seen what I wrote before the editors censored it") is unprofessional behavior. On the other hand, newsroom leaders should be prepared to defend publicly anything they tell their staffs in electronic memos because, if it is controversial, someone will forward it to JimRomenesko.com or another media blog.

Problem Areas for Conflicts

This section discusses several situations in which conflicts might occur. The case studies accompanying this chapter are intended to give you a better understanding of the issues.

Freebies

Accepting gifts from people they cover is a onetime journalistic tradition now banned by newsroom codes.

To get an idea what it was like in the heyday of freebies, consider the tradition of "the divvy" among members of the Pennsylvania Legislative Correspondents' Association, an organization of Capitol reporters in Harrisburg. Every year, during the holidays, the association received gifts of liquor from state officials, which the reporters then divided among themselves. The association ended "the divvy" in 1972, much to the dismay of veteran reporters who called themselves "the old guard." In a history, former reporter Gary Tuma reminisced:

> To most of the old guard, the divvy was one of the most cherished customs of a job they loved. The newsroom used to sponsor a legendary Christmas party in the Capitol, and in that season of good cheer the reporters annually received plenty of it, sent over from the Liquor Control Board by the case, brought in by lobbyists, and carried by state officials who strolled in smiling with both fists wrapped around the neck of a bottle. It was the good stuff, too.[21]

An editor who pioneered in the banning of freebies was J. Russell Wiggins, who was successively managing editor, executive editor, and editor of *The Washington Post* between 1947 and 1968. When Wiggins died on November 19, 2000, Katharine Graham, chair of *The Post*'s executive committee, wrote a tribute that was published in the paper. Graham wrote that, on his arrival in 1947,

> Russ immediately made several changes that had a significant impact on the quality and integrity of the paper. First, he eliminated favors – free tickets for sports reporters, free admissions to theaters for critics, and parking tickets fixed by police reporters for people all over the building. This sounds elementary, but in those days it was done everywhere.[22]

The Associated Press instructs its staff:

> We do not accept free tickets to sports, entertainment or other events for anything other than coverage purposes. … Associated Press offices and staffers are often sent or offered gifts or other items – some of them substantial, some of them modest, some of them perishable – by sources, public relations agencies, corporations, and others. Sometimes these are designed to encourage or influence AP news coverage or business, sometimes they are just "perks" for journalists covering a particular event. Whatever the

intent, we cannot accept such items; an exception is made for trinkets like caps or mugs that have nominal value, approximately $25 or less. Otherwise, gifts should be politely refused and returned, or if that is impracticable, they should be given to charity.[23]

Secondary income

Newsroom codes generally allow journalists to do freelance work on their own time, with significant exceptions. Although freelancing is common, journalists must scrupulously avoid assignments that might interfere with their work for their primary employer.

Typically, the codes prohibit working for a competitor, or for a person or institution that the news organization covers.

Payments to a journalist from a third party pose a troubling question of divided loyalties. Kelly McBride of the Poynter Institute said, "Any time anyone gives you money, you have a loyalty to them, and that's a conflict."[24] The *New York Times'* code says:

> Staff members may not accept employment or compensation of any sort from individuals or organizations who figure or are likely to figure in coverage they provide, edit, package or supervise. ... Staff members may not accept anything that could be construed as a payment for favorable coverage or as an inducement to alter or forgo unfavorable coverage.[25]

The following examples show how journalists have undertaken what seem to be competing interests in their professional lives.

Jay Glazer balances two careers dealing with the same group of people: National Football League players. In one job, he covers the league for Fox Sports. In the other, he is a mixed martial arts trainer for some of the players he covers on television. Richard Sandomir wrote about Glazer's dual careers for *The New York Times* in 2011 and asked Ed Goren, president of Fox Sports, about how Glazer was balancing those careers. "Jay knows what his primary business is, and it's the business of journalism," Goren said. "If there's an issue, he's going to report it, whether it's about a friend or someone he doesn't know." The players and their teams seemed satisfied, too. At the time Sandomir was reporting his story, coach Mike Smith hired Glazer and his partner to train 16 Atlanta Falcons players in wrestling, boxing, and muay thai during the off-season.[26]

Another journalist-entrepreneur is Sara Hopkins, a reporter for WWAY in Wilmington, NC, who supplements her income by pitching major brands on social media. In 2014, "Sayhop" – as she is known on her commercials – had more than 10,000 followers on Twitter, 44,000 on Instagram, and 280,000 on Vine. Interviewed on NPR's *Marketplace*, Hopkins said Old Navy paid her $2,000 for a Vine ad and a tweet, and she also had a deal with Coca-Cola. WWAY's news director at the time, Scott Pickey, told Deborah Potter of NewsLab that Hopkins "was active on social media before we hired her" and that she does her commercials on her own time.[27]

Erin Andrews, a star sidelines reporter for ESPN, reported to viewers on New Year's Day 2011 that Texas Christian University players were slipping on the Rose Bowl turf in their game against the University of Wisconsin. She explained that the TCU players' problem was the new model of Nike shoes they were wearing. Two weeks later, Reebok announced that Andrews would be featured in the company's promotion of its new ZigTech exercise sneaker. Allan Brettman of *The Oregonian* in Portland asked an ESPN spokesman, Michael C. Humes, about what he saw as Andrews' conflict of interest. Humes responded, "It's rare she would ever cover stories involving shoes in her new role. With that said, if something relevant comes up, she would disclose her Reebok connection."[28] ESPN announced a new policy in April 2011 that would allow analysts – who are mostly former players and coaches – to have endorsement deals. Anchors, writers, and reporters, whose duties are journalistic, could have a deal only if there was no conflict of interest or appearance of a conflict. Andrews would not be permitted to renew her Reebok contract, but she could continue her Diet Mountain Dew commercials.[29] Andrews has since moved to Fox Sports.

Taking a public position on controversial issues

Codes discourage or prohibit journalists from taking a public stand on controversial issues or getting involved in politics other than by voting. Defining "controversial issues" is, of course, a judgment call. Can a garden columnist take part in a debate over a public school's sex-education course?

While it is conceivable that a journalist might publicly express an opinion on relatively minor issues that he or she does not cover or make news decisions about, those exceptions should be rare. When members of the audience find journalists expressing opinions, they are not apt to make distinctions about who covers what.

In several instances since the explosion of Facebook and Twitter, journalists' social-media conduct has been called into question.

Raju Narisetti, then *The Washington Post*'s managing editor overseeing features and the website, tweeted commentary on news developments in 2009. One tweet read, "We can incur all sorts of federal deficits for wars and what not. But we have to promise not to increase it by $1 for healthcare reform? Sad." And another: "Sen Byrd (91) in hospital after he falls from 'standing up too quickly.' How about term limits. Or retirement age. Or commonsense to prevail." After his commentary drew protests, including several from within the newsroom, he met with then executive editor Marcus Brauchli. Narisetti closed his Facebook account and explained that, while he had intended to convey his thoughts privately to about 90 friends and associates, "I also realize that … it's a clear perception problem." *The Post* then accelerated the release of new social media guidelines, one of which reads:

When using these networks, nothing we do must call into question the impartiality of our news judgment. We never abandon the guidelines that govern the separation of news from opinion, the importance of fact and objectivity, the appropriate use of language and tone, and other hallmarks of our brand of journalism.[30]

In 2010 Octavia Nasr was fired by CNN from her job as senior Middle East editor after she tweeted a tribute to a spiritual leader of Hezbollah who had died. On her CNN account, Nasr tweeted: "Sad to hear of the passing of Sayyed Mohammad Hussein Fadlallah. One of Hezbollah's giants I respect a lot."

Although the tweet was soon removed, outraged supporters of Israel recirculated it. The Simon Wiesenthal Center in the United States demanded that Nasr apologize "to all victims of Hezbollah terrorism whose loved ones don't share her sadness over the passing of one of Hezbollah's giants."

Nasr blogged that her message had been "simplistic" and "an error in judgment," explaining that her respect for the Hezbollah leader was due to his stand for women's rights. However, an internal CNN memo quoted by *The New York Times* said, "At this point we believe that her credibility in her position as senior editor for Middle Eastern affairs has been compromised going forward."[31]

Nasr, who started her own media consulting company, said in 2012 in an interview with Mallary Jean Tenore of the Poynter Institute that newsroom guidelines on social media give journalists direction but not protection. "I see them as a way to protect the employer's back, but they don't protect the employee." She said employers often react to how reporters' statements are perceived. "What's happening now is that it's not about what you say and what you mean, but it's about the perception of what you said and what you meant."[32]

As she began her assignment in 2012 as Jerusalem bureau chief for *The New York Times*, Jodi Rudoren "broke news, wrote with sophistication and nuance about what was happening, and endured difficult conditions," *The Times*' public editor, Margaret Sullivan, wrote in her column. Rudoren also was posting personal impressions on Facebook and Twitter that drew intense criticism from both sides of the Israeli–Palestinian conflict. The comment that caused the most controversy was this one on Facebook:

> While death and destruction is far more severe in Gaza than in Israel, it seems like Israelis are almost more traumatized. ... The Gazans have a deep culture of resistance and aspiration to martyrdom. ... They have such limited lives tha[t] in many ways they have less to lose. ... When I talk to people who just lost a relative, or who are gathering belongings from a bombed-out house, they seem a bit ho-hum.

Rudoren said later she regretted using the phrase *ho-hum*. She told Sullivan by phone, "I should have talked about steadfastness or resiliency." Sullivan said Rudoren was "a reporter who likes to be responsive to readers, is spontaneous and impressionistic in her personal writing style, and not especially tuned to how casual comments may be received in a highly politicized setting."

As a solution, *The Times*' foreign editor, Joseph Kahn, assigned an editor on the foreign desk in New York to help Rudoren with her social media posts. The idea was to allow her to engage with readers on the Web while "not exposing *The Times* to a reporter's unfiltered and unedited thoughts," as Sullivan put it in her column.[33]

The Times' decision to edit Rudoren's posts drew scorn from writers who contend that journalists are more credible if they reveal their opinions of the people and events they cover. Typical was this comment from John Cook on Gawker:

[T]he paper didn't want to be "*exposed to a reporter's unfiltered and unedited thoughts*." Mercy me! What newspaper would ever want to be exposed to the unfiltered and unedited thoughts of the people it pays to think and write? The very notion of an unfiltered and unedited thought is anathema to the conception of reporting and writing that the *New York Times* currently suffers from, one that places power in multiple layers of editors whose jobs consist primarily of hammering life, point of view, serendipity, and wit out of the stories their reporters write. One that filters and edits.[34]

In 2011 Thomas Kent, deputy managing editor of the Associated Press, messaged the staff:

In at least two recent cases, we have seen a few postings on social networks by AP staffers expressing personal opinions on issues in the news. This has happened on the New York Senate vote on gay marriage and on the Casey Anthony trial. These posts undermine the credibility of our colleagues who have been working so hard to assure balanced and unbiased coverage of those issues.[35]

On August 1, 2012, thousands descended on Chick-fil-A restaurants to buy food and express their appreciation to Dan Cathy, the chain's CEO, for his opposition to gay marriage. "Chick-fil-A Appreciation Day" was the idea of former Arkansas governor Mike Huckabee, a Fox News commentator, who urged people to "affirm a business that operates on Christian principles." Mark Krzos, among the reporters whom the *Fort Myers* (Florida) *News-Press* assigned to cover the event locally, posted on Facebook: "I have never felt so alien in my own country as I did today while covering the restaurant's supporters. The level of hatred, unfounded fear and misinformed people was astoundingly sad." Executive editor Terry Eberle called the comments "completely inappropriate" and said they "violate our policies." At Eberle's request, Krzos deleted the comments, but they had already been shared widely by his critics. Later in the day, after meeting with executive editor, Krzos resigned.[36]

On March 26, 2013, the Human Rights Campaign urged users of social media to show their support for marriage equality – that is, to support gay marriage – by changing their Facebook profile pictures to the campaign's logo, a red equal sign. Thousands of people quickly responded, some of them journalists. That prompted Nisha Chittal to conduct a survey for Poynter, investigating whether the journalists were "blurring the line between personal views and professional objectivity." Chittai found that the journalists who changed their avatars tended to be "affiliated with entrepreneurial, digital, and nontraditional media outlets." In comparison, "journalists from traditional media outlets such as *The New York Times, The Wall Street Journal,* Associated Press, and others largely appeared to refrain from participating."[37]

Shad Olson, a news anchor for KOTA-TV in Rapid City, South Dakota, made a speech on April 15, 2010, at a "tax day" rally staged by the Citizens for Liberty, a tea-party affiliate. After his supervisors at the station learned about the speech by reading a newspaper account, they suspended him from his on-air duties at KOTA-TV, though he continued to produce news shows there and to appear on air at a sister station in Scottsbluff, Nebraska. Olson said he made the speech because he thought Americans have "a flabby understanding of the history of the founding of our country," adding that his personal beliefs coincide with the tea party's. The station's news director, John Petersen, said Olson was entitled to those beliefs, but "a journalist should report the news, not make the news."[38] Three weeks into the suspension, Olson resigned to work as a paid political consultant and to launch a syndicated radio talk show.[39]

Reporters who appear on television and radio talk shows are frequently invited to express their opinions on the news and to speculate on outcomes. *The New York Times'* code, in addition to stating that journalists may not say things they could not write under their bylines, discourages appearances on "strident, theatrical forums that emphasize punditry and reckless opinion-mongering."[40] Amy Goldstein, a Pulitzer Prize-winning reporter for *The Washington Post*, observed:

> It has become fashionable for reporters to go on TV and, when they do, they often are asked to give their opinions. There is a lot of pressure to do that. A reporter needs to say up front, "I don't want to get those questions. If I do get them, I'm going to duck them."

Goldstein said she preferred the practice of broadcast hosts, like Gwen Ifill on Public Broadcasting Service, who invite guests "to tell what they know, not what they think."[41]

A manifestation of political opinion can be embarrassingly unprofessional even when it occurs within the confines of the newsroom. David Boardman, then the editor of the *Seattle Times,* admonished his staff after there was cheering at the August 13, 2007, daily news meeting over the news that Karl Rove had resigned as a White House adviser. Boardman wrote:

> I ask you to leave your personal politics at the front door for one simple reason: A good newsroom is a sacred and magical place in which we should test every assumption, challenge each other's thinking, ask the fundamental questions those in power hope we will overlook. … [I]f we allowed our news meetings to evolve into a liberal latte klatch, I have no doubt that a pathological case of group-think would soon set in.[42]

Civic activities

News organizations face complaints of favoritism if staff members cover organizations in which they or their bosses are members. This has led some journalists to refrain from joining anything. As a result, these journalists — whose career tracks usually have led them far from the places they grew up — find themselves isolated from their communities. They become distant from the people their news organizations are trying to serve.

In a manner similar to most newsroom codes, *The New York Times'* code states:

> Staff members of *The Times* are family members and responsible citizens as well as journalists. *The Times* respects their educating their children, exercising their religion, voting in elections and taking active part in community affairs. Nothing in this policy is intended to infringe upon those rights. But even in the best of causes, *Times* staff members have a duty to avoid the appearance of a conflict.[43]

The question, then, is where to draw the line in community involvement. The first principle is that journalists should not cover or make news decisions about organizations in which they are members. In addition, they should avoid situations that could reasonably be expected to result in news coverage.

Jayne Miller, a reporter for WBAL for more than a quarter-century, was deeply involved in helping Baltimore's poor. She has served on boards of several not-for-profit groups that provide job training and promote homeownership in the city. In 2001 she told David Folkenflik, then a reporter for *The Baltimore Sun*:

> I can't imagine living in this city and not getting involved as a citizen, because those are my true colors. Life is way too short to spend it working and going home here at night and closing the door and saying, "I'm done." I would be a poorer reporter if I weren't active as a citizen, because it brings perspective.[44]

Folkenflik's story raised questions about the possibility of conflicts stemming from her board roles. The organizations lobby for and spend tax dollars, and several of Miller's fellow board members have been newsmakers she covers for the station.[45]

Miller said in a telephone interview in 2008 that she could avoid conflicts in her board work because she insists on three caveats. First, she will not ask for donations from people she covers or might be expected to cover; second, if a board's agenda includes a topic she covers, she will recuse herself; and, third, she will not report on any issues involving the organizations she serves.

But what about the *appearance* of a conflict, since the public may not know of these caveats? Miller said that was not a concern. "My reputation is well established," she said. "People know I'm a no-nonsense reporter who is honest, open, and fair."

She said she had no problem covering her fellow board members. She said she could keep those relationships separate. "It's no different than if I lived next door to them as a neighbor."[46]

Relationships with sources and subjects of coverage

The *New York Times'* code takes note of the balancing act that reporters, especially beat reporters, must perform in their relationships with the people they write about:

> Cultivating sources is an essential skill, often practiced most effectively in informal settings outside of normal business hours. Yet staff members, especially those assigned to beats, must be aware that personal relationships with news sources can erode into

favoritism, in fact or appearance. … Though this topic defies firm rules, it is essential that we preserve professional detachment, free of any whiff of bias. Staff members may see sources informally over a meal or drinks, but they must keep in mind the difference between legitimate business and personal friendship. … Scrupulous practice requires that periodically we step back and look at whether we have drifted too close to sources we deal with regularly. The acid test of freedom from favoritism is the ability to maintain good working relationships with all parties to a dispute.[47]

Reporter–source relationships are discussed in detail in Chapter 13.

In recent years, newsrooms have been looking more closely at the relationships between journalist organizations and the industries they cover. Max Frankel, as executive editor of *The New York Times*, was among the first news executives to take action in this area. In his memoir, *The Times of My Life and My Life with The Times*, Frankel wrote:

A great uproar followed my discovery in 1989 that the reviewers of other papers were engaged in blatant politicking over the annual honors awarded by the New York drama and film critics. Since our critics routinely listed their favorite films, books and stage plays at season's end in *The Times*, I saw no reason why they should also join in a rival listing that provoked such unseemly behavior. … By the same logic, I rejected the appeal of our leading sportswriters, who wanted to go on electing retired baseball players to the Hall of Fame.[48]

Frankel's bans on voting for those awards are embodied today in *The Times'* code.

This kind of voting puts journalists in the position of making the news that they then are expected to cover. The problem is compounded when huge sums of money ride on their decisions. The Associated Press has for years conducted a sportswriters' poll of the top college football teams, and it is popular with readers. In 2004 the AP told the Bowl Championship Series that it could no longer use the AP poll in its mathematical calculations of which teams would play in its bowl games, the most lucrative in the sport.[49] Member newspapers of the AP had complained that coaches were lobbying sportswriters for their votes.

Many baseball players have clauses in their contracts that entitle them to bonuses if the Baseball Writers' Association of America gives them the Most Valuable Player Award or the Cy Young Award for pitching. But the biggest problem is the Hall of Fame. Because the association determines who goes into the hall, the sportswriters now find themselves adjudicating the question of whether to grant the honor to players tainted by allegations of steroids-inflated statistics. Phil Sheridan, then at *The Philadelphia Inquirer*, wrote a column in 2005 calling for the writers to bow out:

The process has always been problematic. Writers have been known to snub players they didn't like or who didn't cooperate with them. Writers have deliberately left obvious Hall of Famers off their ballots because they wanted to prevent the dreaded unanimous selection. … A lot of very questionable achievements are going to come before Hall of Fame voters in the next decade or so. There is no way that supposedly objective journalists should serve as arbiters who legitimize some careers and dismiss others.[50]

Questions of independence also come into play when industries hand out awards to journalists assigned to cover them. An example is the Eclipse Award, given for "outstanding coverage of thoroughbred racing." This award is conferred by the National Thoroughbred Racing Association, the National Turf Writers Association, and the *Daily Racing Form*.[51] In this instance, journalists not only vie for the approval of the people they cover, but they also help run the contest. The collaboration does not inspire an expectation of fearless coverage.

Case Study

Covering Police, Wearing Their Uniform

One evening in 1999, television reporter Caroline Lowe was speaking before a group of police trainees when one asked her what educational credentials she had to qualify her to speak about criminal justice. "He was glaring at me," she said.

Lowe, who had reported on the crime beat since 1977 for WCCO-TV in Minneapolis–St. Paul, was bothered by the question because she had dropped out of college to go to work. "I rattled off how many ride-alongs I had been on and that I done this for 20 years," she said in a telephone interview in 2003. "But he wanted to know what formal training I had had. I had to admit I had none."

The next day Lowe walked into the Metropolitan State University's School of Law Enforcement and signed up for her first criminal justice course. She planned then to take only a few courses to help her better understand the beat she covered. But four years and 61 credits later, Lowe graduated with a degree in criminal justice. As the outstanding student of her class, she made a speech at commencement exercises.

While she was working on her degree, Lowe went through eight weeks of training, separate from the degree program, that would enable her to be certified as an officer. During training she learned how to shoot a gun and how to fill out police paperwork. WCCO broadcast a four-part series as she progressed through "cop school."

In August 2003 Lowe took a 12-day leave of absence to work as a police officer at Minnesota's State Fair. She walked around the fairgrounds in uniform. In advance of the fair she also spent a few days getting familiar with the area so that she could direct people and get to places quickly. Nothing eventful happened while she walked the beat. She said that, if she had encountered a crime, she would have responded like any other officer, but "I mainly just helped lost kids find their parents."

Lowe said she walked the beat at the fair to fulfill a requirement for becoming a certified police officer. "To get your Minnesota peace officer's license activated, you must actually have a job," she said. While walking the beat, Lowe was not paid by WCCO. She paid for her uniform and borrowed a gun and nightstick from another officer.

Her dual role stirred controversy in the Twin Cities journalism community in 2003. Some argued that walking the beat was a conflict of interest. Others maintained that she had proved her independence through her reporting, which includes reporting on corrupt police officers.

"I think I have a history in this town," said Lowe, an award-winning reporter. "I've done more tough stories on cops than anyone else." She said she was only increasing her expertise in the beat she covers. "I weighed the pluses and minuses of doing this and the pluses outweighed the negatives." She said that, to avoid a conflict of interest, she decided never to cover any story involving an officer with whom she has worked or who works at the State Fair. "We don't usually cover the State Fair anyway, so it isn't really an issue," she said.

The Star-Tribune in Minneapolis conducted an online poll asking viewers how they felt about a reporter working in the beat she covers. Almost 70 percent either endorsed the idea or didn't care. Thirty percent thought it was a bad idea. Rob Daves of *The Star-Tribune* cautioned that the results could not be considered scientific. "Those polls are only for those who are motivated enough" to respond, Daves said.

Brian Lambert of *The* (St. Paul) *Pioneer Press* wrote two columns supporting Lowe. In the first column he dismissed the idea that "a reporter who covers the beat should never, ever assume the role of any person on that beat," saying it was "a one-size-fits-all view of the issue." His second column said Lowe's action was acceptable because she took unpaid leave, she didn't have access to any secret files while on the job, and she had an established reputation as a reporter.

Another *Pioneer Press* columnist, Ruben Rosario, sent Lowe an email that said, "We need more journalists and newsroom decision-makers with diverse life experiences and backgrounds and less of the journalism school textbook-café latte crowd, which seems to dominate so many newsrooms I see."

Jane Kirtley, Silha Professor of Media Ethics and Law at the School of Journalism and Mass Communication at the University of Minnesota, said she knows and respects Lowe but disagrees with her decision. "Be a journalist or be a police officer," she told Lambert for one of his columns. "Either is fine. But not both at once. There are good reasons why the two don't overlap. Journalists have gone to jail to maintain separation between the two."

Lowe said she was aware that, although certain WCCO colleagues "probably don't support what I did," most of those she works with have reacted positively. Maria Reitan, Lowe's news director at the time, supported her decision. The station's online biography of Lowe mentioned her work as a police officer at the fair and said she may be the only reporter in the country who is also a certified police officer.

WCCO anchor Don Shelby also supported her. "For me, there's absolutely no difference in this case than having your court reporter get a law degree," Shelby told Lambert. "You can twist the argument any way you want if you're so inclined, but I see no difference."

After walking the beat in 2003, Lowe returned to the fairgrounds for police stints in each of the next seven years. "Having the education, training, and experience have helped me ask better questions of the subjects ... I encounter on the criminal justice beat," she said.

Lowe earned a master's degree in police leadership and taught police–media relations classes to Minnesota law-enforcement officers. In 2011 she moved to California and became Santa Barbara County news manager for KSBY.

This case is adapted, with permission, from a paper Lindsay Bosslett wrote in 2003 as a student at Pennsylvania State University. Bosslett graduated in 2004 and is now managing editor of the Health Monitor Network at Montvale, New Jersey.

(Continued)

Sources

Bosslett's original sources included:

Interview with Rob Daves, Nov. 23, 2003.

Kimball, Joe, "Working as a cop, she'll keep a Lowe profile," *The Star Tribune*, July 18, 2003.

KSBY, "About Caroline Lowe," http://www.ksby.com/pages/caroline-lowe/.

Lambert, Brian, "Reporter-turned-copy walks thin blue line," *The Pioneer Press*, July 22, 2003.

Lambert, Brian, "Reporter conflict is in the eye of the beholder," *The Pioneer Press,* July 25, 2003.

Interview with Caroline Lowe, Nov. 18, 2003.

Lowe, Caroline, "Covering the crime beat," The School of Law Enforcement, Criminal Justice and Public Safety newsletter, Metropolitan State University, Spring 2001.

Minnesota State Colleges and University performance newsletter, "Crime reporter shares 'cop school' training," Fall 2002.

The case includes these additional sources:

Kahle, Shannon, telephone interview with Caroline Lowe, Apr. 10, 2008.

Lowe, Caroline, "Crime notes: a crime reporter's reflections on 30 years at WCCO TV," CBS Minnesota, Mar. 15, 2007.

Lowe, Caroline, email message to Shannon Kahle, Apr. 15, 2008.

Questions for Class Discussion

- Do you think that Caroline Lowe, as a police reporter, was in a conflict of interest when she took college courses in law enforcement?
- Was she in a conflict when she went through eight weeks of training and was certified as a police officer?
- Was she in conflict when she walked a beat in uniform at the State Fair?
- If you think she had a conflict, was it an actual conflict or an apparent conflict?
- What do you think of the arguments of Lambert, Rosario, Kirtley, and Shelby?

Case Study

Carrying the Torch, Stirring Controversy

When Dick Rosetta, a sportswriter for the *Salt Lake Tribune*, was asked if he would like to carry the Olympic torch for a ceremonial quarter-mile before the 2002 Winter Games, he accepted. "I've been a patriot from the get-go, and this is the American thing to do," Rosetta told the Associated Press. "You don't turn down carrying the torch for the Olympics. I don't care who you work for."

Rosetta's editor at the *Tribune*, James E. Shelledy, did care. He gave Rosetta the option of either covering the games – he was scheduled to cover figure skating – or carrying the torch. Rosetta, who at age 60 had intended to retire before the Olympics but stayed on at his editor's request, chose the torch. He was relieved of his figure-skating coverage.

"Our ethical guidelines state if you are directly involved in reporting or editing a news story, you can't be part of that event," Shelledy told The Associated Press.

Rosetta saw a distinction in the fact that the torch run was under the auspices of the US Olympic Committee while the Olympic athletic events, which he was supposed to cover, were overseen by the International Olympics Committee.

The Olympic torch-carrying ceremony, one of the most beloved rituals in sports, dates back to the 1936 Games in Munich. Prior to its arrival in Salt Lake City, the torch had traveled more than 13,500 miles across the United States in 65 days in the hands of 11,500 bearers.

Many other media organizations allowed journalists to carry the torch, including NBC, whose *Today* show host Katie Couric made the run. Even the *Tribune* had runners in the event. A columnist and the publisher carried the torch, and the paper defended this by saying the two were sufficiently distanced from reporting to maintain the paper's objectivity.

NBC telecast the Olympics from Salt Lake City. Brink Chipman, news director for KSL, the local NBC affiliate, told The Associated Press that NBC's role in televising the Olympics caused "an awkward situation" for the station's news staff. "We are a sponsor, but that has not stopped us from doing broad, intense coverage of the Olympics. If we didn't cover them honestly and legitimately, people would write about it … we'd be killed." KSL allowed "personalities" like the weatherman and anchors to carry the torch, but not reporters or editors.

Reporters for Salt Lake City's other newspaper, the *Deseret News*, got to carry the torch.

Deseret News managing editor Rick Hall told the Associated Press, "The torch is not graft or bribery or a gift. … We didn't see this as a conflict because it won't change the way we cover the Olympics."

Deseret News columnist Lee Benson criticized Shelledy for removing Rosetta from the Olympics coverage. Benson wrote: "[T]aking ourselves too seriously is a journalist's nature. We spend so much time taking everybody else to task, we don't know honest from sincere. Give us long enough to think about it, and we probably wouldn't vote."

Mike Reilley, who runs *Journaliststoolbox.com*, called the Olympic torch run "a rolling PR event" for the International Olympic Committee, the United States Organizing Committee, and the Salt Lake Olympic Committee. In a posting on the Society of Professional Journalists' online ethics forum, Reilley wrote that the *Tribune* made the right decision: "If it wants to maintain credibility in its community, it must maintain a distance from the event."

Herb Strentz, a professor at the Drake University School of Journalism in Des Moines, Iowa, expressed this opinion on the SPJ forum: "Really, not a thing is lost by *not* being involved, and that tips the scales for me."

Rosetta, who was inducted into the Utah Sports Hall of Fame in 2002, said he weighed the consequences of his decision. But in the end, he said, he

> looked at all those people carrying the torch, holding it high … people who battled leukemia, people dying of cancer, the guy who coached the soccer team for 40 years, the World Trade Center survivors, and I said, "Hey, maybe I do fit," and I'll carry it with pride.

This case is adapted, with permission, from a paper Jeff Rice wrote as a student at Pennsylvania State University. Rice graduated in 2003 and is now senior writer for Lions247, a website covering Penn State sports. The case was updated after Gene Foreman's September 30, 2008, email exchange with Dick Rosetta.

(Continued)

Sources

Rice's sources included:

Benson, Lee, "Torch run just isn't conflicting," *Deseret News,* Jan. 9, 2002.

Lake, Catherine S., "Newspapers, TV struggle with ethics of reporters carrying Olympic torch," The Associated Press, Jan. 11, 2002.

Questions for Class Discussion

- What are the arguments in favor of allowing the reporter to carry the Olympic torch? What are the arguments against?
- Do you agree with Rosetta that the paper should have recognized a distinction between the US Olympic Committee and the International Olympic Committee?
- If the conflict guidelines of *The New York Times* were applied in this case, what would the decision have been?

- Why do you think the Olympic officials asked sports reporters to carry the torch? Why do you think they asked Katie Couric?
- Do you think *The Tribune's* decision on Rosetta was compromised by the fact that two other employees carried the torch?

Case Study

A Love Triangle on the Evening News

At 4 p.m. on June 8, Los Angeles Mayor Antonio Villaraigosa issued a terse statement announcing that he and his wife, Corina, were separating after 20 years of marriage.

Two hours later, Telemundo television anchor Mirthala Salinas delivered the story to her Spanish-language viewers on the Friday evening news.

"The rumors were true," she declared of the split after an introduction that described the story as a "political scandal" that had left "many people with their mouth open."

What Salinas, 35, did not say in the newscast was that she was the other woman. She and Villaraigosa, 54, had been in a relationship even though she had previously been the political reporter assigned to cover local politics and the mayor.

Los Angeles Times, July 4, 2007

In separate announcements on July 3, Villaraigosa and Salinas confirmed the romance, which had been the subject of Internet chatter. "I have a relationship with Ms. Salinas, and

I take full responsibility for my actions," the mayor said at a news conference. Later in the day, Salinas said: "I first got to know the mayor at a professional level, where we went on to become friends. The current relationship grew out of our existing friendship."

Salinas was suspended, along with her station's news director and general manager. In September she was reassigned to the station's bureau in Riverside, and the news director was reinstated. The general manager was replaced. Salinas resigned – "I wasn't going to Riverside," she told *Los Angeles Magazine* the next spring – and four months later she was hired for a talk show on AM radio.

Telemundo president Don Browne said that allowing Salinas to deliver the news about the separation of the Villaraigosa couple was a "flagrant" violation of the network's news guidelines.

Salinas had previously asked not to be assigned to cover the mayor any more. She said in the interview with Shawn Hubler of *Los Angeles Magazine* that she was filling in for an anchor at the station who was on maternity leave, so she got the assignment of reading the story about the Villaraigosas. "There was no way I could get out of it," she said. "I was shaking. I didn't want to be there. ... I pretended I wasn't reading it. At that moment, it was like it wasn't me sitting at the news desk, doing the newscast."

Salinas had worked for 10 years at Telemundo's KVEA, which ranked second in number of viewers among Los Angeles' Latino stations. She had won a Golden Mike broadcasting award, and the newscast she anchored had won two local Emmies.

Salinas said in the magazine interview that she and the mayor had a romantic relationship for six months, after she and Villaraigosa had

seen each other frequently in social settings involving mutual friends. Villaraigosa visited her terminally ill mother and attended the mother's funeral in Phoenix in January 2007. Salinas said that, when she returned to work after the funeral, she told her supervisors at the station "she should not do any more reporting on the mayor because he had done so much for her family that she could no longer be objective about him," according to the magazine. The station moved her off the politics beat to an assignment as backup anchor and general correspondent.

Salinas told the magazine her romance with mayor began in April 2007, several weeks after she made the request to her supervisors, and ended that October. "I think it just got to the point where we both realized that it wasn't working out as that kind of a relationship," she said. She and Villaraigosa remain friends, she said.

Although Salinas had disclosed a close relationship with the mayor and was moved off the politics beat, she still was in the position of being the anchor who read the news story on Villaraigosa's marital breakup.

Many newsroom codes assert that a romantic relationship with a news subject is an apparent conflict of interest, one generally resulting in a change of assignment for the reporter. *The New York Times'* code says, in paragraph 24: "Clearly, romantic involvement with a news source would foster an appearance of partiality. Therefore staff members who develop close relationships with people who might figure in coverage they provide, edit, package or supervise must disclose those relationships" to their editors.

In a memorable case, Laura Foreman was dismissed by *The Times* in 1977 after she was found to have been involved romantically with Pennsylvania State Senator Henry J. "Buddy" Cianfrani while covering politics for *The*

(Continued)

Philadelphia Inquirer. A. M. Rosenthal, then *The Times'* executive editor, explained the firing by saying, in so many words, that he didn't care if reporters slept with elephants as long as they were not covering the circus.

Sources

Helfand, Duke, and Steve Hymon, "Mayor reveals romantic link with TV newscaster," *Los Angeles Times,* July 4, 2007.

Helfand, Duke, and Meg James, "Telemundo reassigns mayor's girlfriend," *Los Angeles Times,* Sept. 25, 2007.

Hubler, Shawn, "The mayor and his mistress," *Los Angeles Magazine,* May 2008.

Kaiser, Charles, "A. M. Rosenthal, 1922–2006," *The New York Observer,* May 21, 2006.

KNBC.com, "Mayor acknowledges relationship with TV anchor," July 3, 2007.

The New York Times, *Ethics in Journalism,* paragraph 26.

Questions for Class Discussion

- Why was Mirthala Salinas' relationship with the mayor an apparent conflict of interest for the reporter and her station?

- What should station executives have done when she reported the relationship to them?

Notes

1 Robert Vickers, "Why I'm voting for Mitt Romney," *The Patriot-News,* Nov. 2, 2012.

2 Andrew Beaujon, "*Patriot-News* M.E. says column about Romney vote was 'a hard sell,'" Poynter, Nov. 2, 2012.

3 Andrew Beaujon, "Robert Vickers: 'The wall of opinion and hard news' fell long before he endorsed Romney," Poynter, Nov. 2, 2012.

4 William Powers, "Who are we?," Nationaljournal.com, July 6, 2007.

5 Robert Pear, "Drug industry is told to stop gifts to doctors," *The New York Times,* Oct. 1, 2002.

6 Schorr is quoted in Charles W. Bailey, *Conflicts of Interest: A Matter of Journalistic Ethics* (Washington, DC: National News Council, 1984), 6.

7 John J. Hulteng, *Playing It Straight* (Washington, DC: American Society of Newspaper Editors, 1981), 25.

8 The New York Times, *Ethical Journalism: A Handbook of Values and Practices for the News and Editorial Departments* (New York: The New York Times, Sept. 2004).

9 "*Post* newsroom leader to retire," online chat between readers and Leonard Downie Jr., *The Washington Post,* June 24, 2008.

10 Rick Tulsky, "How journalists' personal lives create problems," Medill Watchdog, Feb. 28, 2014.

11 "Guideline: be aware that a loved one's political activity may create a perception of bias," *NPR Ethics Handbook.*

12 "Case study: when a spouse becomes involved in politics," *NPR Ethics Handbook.*

13 *The American Journalist in the Digital Age: Key Findings,* a representative survey of US journalists conducted by Lars Willnat and David H. Weaver from the Indiana University School of Journalism. The findings come from online interviews conducted Aug. 7–Dec. 20, 2013, with 1,080 US journalists working in print, broadcast, and digital media.

14 James Hohman and ASNE, *10 Best Practices for Social Media: Helpful Guidelines for News Organizations* (American Society of News Editors, May 2011).

15 "Social media guidelines for AP employees," The Associated Press, May 2013.

16 *The New York Times* social media policy, provided to Poynter on Jan. 19, 2009.

17 *Reuters Online Handbook.*

18 The Washington Post, *Digital Publishing Guidelines,* Sept. 1, 2011.

19 "Guideline: social media outlets are public spaces," *NPR Ethics Handbook*.

20 "Honesty," *NPR Ethics Handbook*.

21 Gary Tuma, *Covering the Capitol: A Century of News Reporting in Pennsylvania: Centennial History of Pennsylvania Legislative Correspondents' Association, 1895–1995* (Harrisburg: Pennsylvania Legislative Correspondents' Association, 1996), 28–30.

22 Katharine Graham, "The evocation of excellence: Russ Wiggins, good steward, farseeing guide of *The Post* for 21 years," *The Washington Post*, Nov. 20, 2000.

23 "Free tickets" and "Gifts," "News Values and Principles," The Associated Press.

24 Jim Drinkard and Mark Memmott, "HHS said it paid columnist for help," *USA Today*, Jan. 27, 2005.

25 The New York Times, *Ethical Journalism*, paragraphs 34–35.

26 Richard Sandomir, "Fox's Glazer straddles jobs as N.F.L. reporter and trainer," *The New York Times*, May 27, 2010.

27 Deborah Potter, "Should a journalist ever be a paid spokesman?," NewsLab, July 14, 2014.

28 Allan Brettman, "ESPN's Erin Andrews endorses Reebok shoe, two weeks after her damaging report on Nike football shoe," Jan. 25, 2011.

29 Kelly McBride and Regina McCombs, "So close, yet so far," Poynter Review Project for ESPN, Apr. 20, 2011.

30 Andy Alexander, "*Post* editor ends tweets as new guidelines are issued," *The Washington Post*, Sept. 25, 2009.

31 Peter Walker, "Octavia Nasr fired by CNN over tweet praising late ayatollah," *The Guardian*, July 8, 2010.

32 Mallary Jean Tenore, "Nasr: newsroom guidelines protect employers, not employees," Poynter, Feb. 10, 2012.

33 Margaret Sullivan, "Problems with a reporter's Facebook posts, and a possible solution," *The New York Times*, Nov. 28, 2012. The extended quotation from Rudoren's Facebook post appeared in Glenn Greenwald, "*Times* bureau chief in Jerusalem will now have her Facebook entries edited," *The Guardian*, Nov. 28, 2012.

34 John Cook, "*New York Times* bureau chief isn't chief of her own tweets," Gawker, Nov. 28, 2012.

35 Thomas Kent, "Expressing personal opinions on social networks," July 6, 2011.

36 Fidel Martinez, "Reporter resigns after expressing his opinion about Chick-fil-A on Facebook," *Daily Dot*, Aug. 13, 2012.

37 Nisha Chittal, "Journalists share arguments for, against using same-sex marriage symbols on social media profiles," Poynter, Mar. 27, 2013.

38 Kevin Woster, "KOTA anchorman temporarily sidelined after tea party appearance," *Rapid City Journal*, Apr. 28, 2010.

39 Kevin Woster, "KOTA anchorman who was suspended over tea party speech resigns," *Rapid City Journal*, May 12, 2010.

40 The New York Times, *Ethical Journalism*, paragraph 102.

41 Author interview with Amy Goldstein, Oct. 22, 2007.

42 Jim Romenesko, "Seattle Times editor elaborates on newsroom cheering memo," Poynter, Aug. 15, 2007.

43 The New York Times, *Ethical Journalism*, paragraph 60.

44 David Folkenflik, "Citizen Jayne: Baltimore's best TV journalist believes she can balance her on-air reporting and her off-camera activism. But should she?," *The Baltimore Sun*, Feb. 25, 2001.

45 Ibid.

46 Author's telephone interview with Jayne Miller, June 3, 2008.

47 The New York Times, *Ethical Journalism*, paragraphs 22–23.

48 Max Frankel, *The Times of My Life and My Life with The Times* (New York: Random House, 1999), 515–516.

49 The Associated Press, "AP made call with poll's integrity in mind," ESPN.com, Dec. 21, 2004.

50 Phil Sheridan, "Baseball writers wrong to exercise their right to vote," *The Philadelphia Inquirer*, Oct. 8, 2005.

51 National Turf Writers Association, "Guidelines for 2013 Media Eclipse awards are announced."

11 The Business of Producing Journalism

In a turbulent era of transition, news companies seek financial stability

---

Learning Goals

This chapter will help you understand:

- the tensions caused by technological and economic transition in today's news media;
- the fundamental elements of the business of journalism, and their ethical implications;
- how advertisers pay for journalism but cannot be allowed to influence journalism;
- how some efforts to increase revenue for the media company – and to reduce expenses in the news department – have led to ethically questionable practices; and
- the delicate relationship between news and business executives of media companies.

Many readers of *The Atlantic*'s website were puzzled and then angered by what they saw on their screens on January 14, 2013. First there was a headline that read "David Miscavige Leads Scientology to Milestone Year." Below that was a photograph of a beaming Miscavige, followed by two paragraphs of text that looked like a news story and asserted that Miscavige was the "driving force" behind a period of "unparalleled growth." Then came six pages of photographs of crowds celebrating newly opened Scientology churches and offices around the world.[1]

The Scientology spread was an example of "native advertising." Using this technique, an advertiser presents its message in a format that is *native* to the website. In other words, the ad resembles the site's editorial content. The impression was reinforced in the Scientology case by "user comments" that read much like endorsements of the feature's content.

If they looked carefully, readers could find disclaimers. Above the headline on the first page were the words "SPONSOR CONTENT" on a yellow background, and at the bottom of the concluding page was the statement "Sponsor content presented by The Church of Scientology."[2]

The Ethical Journalist: Making Responsible Decisions in the Digital Age, Second Edition. Gene Foreman.
© 2016 John Wiley & Sons, Inc. Published 2016 by John Wiley & Sons, Inc.

"Within a few hours, *The Atlantic* was steeped in ridicule and outrage via Twitter," Paul Farhi wrote in *The Washington Post*.[3] At 11:30 p.m., 11 hours after the Scientology package was posted, *The Atlantic* took it down. The next day, an apology appeared:

> We screwed up. It shouldn't have taken a wave of constructive criticism – but it has – to alert us that we've made a mistake, possibly several mistakes. We now realize that as we explored new forms of digital advertising, we failed to update the policies that must govern the decisions we make along the way. … We are sorry, and we're working very hard to put things right.[4]

The apology did not say what the mistakes were, but six weeks later, an Atlantic Digital executive elaborated at an ad-industry event in New York. "The biggest mistake in retrospect was that it wasn't harmonious to our site, and it didn't bring any value to our readers," vice president and general manager Kimberly Lau said. "The second mistake was allowing the marketing team to moderate comments in a way that wasn't transparent."[5]

A more fundamental problem is that native advertising – like its predecessors, **advertorials** in print and **infomercials** on television – undermines the credibility of the website's real editorial content. Native advertising blurs the distinction between a journalist's effort to inform the public and an advertising copywriter's effort to promote a brand. In the long term, ads camouflaged as news could lead consumers to stop reading a website at all.

David Dobbs assessed the *Atlantic* case in *Wired*: "It was a zero-sum game that created winners and losers. The Church of Scientology bought the right to siphon credibility from *The Atlantic*'s writers and editors."[6]

Zero-sum game or not, native advertising has generated dollars for an industry eager to find a revenue strategy that works. In May 2013 IPG Media Lab said that its research showed consumers "looked at native ads 53 percent more frequently than banner ads."[7] In July 2013 the Online Publishers Association and Radar Research reported that 73 percent of US publishers were offering native advertising to clients, and that 17 percent were considering whether to offer it.[8]

In the abstract, there is an industry consensus that transparency is crucial in the use of native advertising – that it has to be labeled so clearly that readers will not be confused about what they are reading. Yet the most commonly used labels are ambiguous; few contain the words "paid" or "advertising." Instead, the most popular phrases are "sponsor content," "sponsored by," "presented by," or the like. Forbes.com, a pioneer in native advertising, signals an ad by placing the label "BrandVoice" at the top of a post that otherwise resembles the site's editorial content.

People tend not to read labels and, when they do, they may not understand them, said David Franklyn, a University of San Francisco law professor who conducted a study of 10,000 people in the United States and abroad. "When people are presented with a story that looks like a story, they think it's a story," he said. "What we've found is that there is deep confusion about the difference between paid and unpaid content."[9]

Franklyn spoke at a workshop conducted on December 4, 2013, by the Federal Trade Commission in Washington, an event with the stated purpose of helping the

FTC better understand native advertising. But, as *Advertising Age* noted, "the commission's power to bring lawsuits to protect consumers seemed to be the impetus for the hearing's strong arguments."[10]

The New York Times departed from industry practice by actually delivering transparency when it began running native advertising on its website in January 2014. Its first native advertiser was Dell, the computer manufacturer. A box on *The Times'* home page displayed Dell's logo and linked to the "paid posts," as they are called in *The Times*. The reader was guided to a new window with a different URL, paidpost. nytimes.com. That page itself was labeled "Paid For and Posted by Dell." At the bottom of the page was this statement: "This page was produced by the Advertising Department of *The New York Times* in collaboration with Dell. The news and editorial staffs of *The New York Times* had no role in its preparation."[11] Before *The Times* began running native advertising, publisher Arthur Sulzberger assured staff members in a letter: "Our readers will always know that they are looking at a message from an advertiser."[12]

To try to understand the native-advertising phenomenon, the American Press Institute convened a "thought leader summit" in November 2013. From that conversation the institute identified four reasons for its growth. First, readers of news sites are receptive to "sponsored content that … educates and entertains, rather than a display ad trying to sell a product." Second, although companies have learned how to tell the stories of their brands, they need to put those stories in the mainstream media where customers would see them. Third, native advertising is well suited to the small screens of mobile devices. Fourth, the native-advertising model "highly values a premium publisher's unique environment."[13]

In a 2014 article in *Nieman Reports*, Joshua Benton explained that "publishers love native advertising because it plays to their strengths," essentially that highly valued "unique environment" mentioned in the American Press Institute's study. The publishers also recognize that the "digital giants" can give advertisers so much more information about the consumers they are trying to reach. Benton wrote:

> [T]he kings of online advertising – Google, Facebook – are swimming in user data. Google knows what you're searching for, what you're e-mailing about, where you're looking for directions – even what products you almost-but-not-quite bought online. Facebook knows who your friends are, where you went to school, whether you're single, what brands you like. All that data means they can target ads at you far more effectively than a newspaper website that doesn't know much more than the fact you're interested in news about Kansas City. … So native advertising – which is fundamentally about brands, both the news organization's and the advertiser's – is seen as a place where publishers can still have something to offer.[14]

Edward Wasserman, dean of the Graduate School of Journalism at the University of California, Berkeley, sees a "near-total absence of resistance from the news business" to the allure of native advertising. "This may not be the media world we want," he wrote in his blog, "but it sure looks like the one we're going to get."[15]

How Will News Be Paid For?

The era in which native advertising has thrived is one in which news organizations on all delivery platforms – print, broadcast, and digital – are undergoing a painful transition.

News consumers are moving to digital, but advertising dollars have not followed. The traditional advertising model, in which news coverage attracts an audience that is then rented out to advertisers, is not adapting well to digital.

In the absence of robust revenue, few digital news sites have assembled large reporting staffs. Digital may be the delivery medium that enjoys growing popularity, but it draws most of its news content from the legacy media, especially newspapers, whose popularity is shrinking along with the size of their news staffs. This dependence has continued even as newspapers' circulation and advertising decline to the point that their survival is at stake.

So the overarching question is: If newspapers vanish or shrink to irrelevancy, who will cover the news?

It is a question that pivots on money. It is not about the potential of the technology, or of a new generation of journalists who have grown up with the Web and have the skills to exploit its advantages in reporting and delivering the news. Journalism can flourish in the digital environment if entrepreneurs can figure out how to pay for covering the news while protecting the integrity of the news itself.

Historically, advertisers have paid for the news. Before cable, when television signals were captured by home antennas, broadcast news was entirely free to the consumer. People have always had to pay for mainstream newspapers, but the cost of subscriptions or of buying single copies merely defrays the true cost, and advertising pays the rest.

As for how the news is being underwritten during the transition, the Pew Research Center, Journalism & Media (previously Pew Research Journalism Project), provided this snapshot for 2013:

- *Advertising pays for 69 percent, but the picture is changing fast.* "Print advertising continues its sharp decline. Television advertising currently remains stable, but the steady audience migration to the Web will inevitably impact that business model, too. Digital advertising is growing, though not nearly fast enough to keep pace with declines in legacy ad formats."
- *The audience pays for 24 percent, mainly through subscriptions and cable fees.* The Pew researchers reported that, as 2013 ended, around 500 newspapers – a third of the total – either were charging for digital access or were planning to do so.
- *News companies' ancillary enterprises such as event hosting, marketing services, and Web consulting pay for 7 percent.* This "could become a critical component to the broader, long-term picture," the researchers wrote.[16]

About 1 percent of total revenue was attributed to capital investment and philanthropy, including foundation support for public radio.

The researchers projected the amount of money generated annually by news in the United States: $63 billion to $65 billion. To give a sense of scale, they listed the amounts generated by the global video game industry ($93 billion), Starbucks ($15 billion), and Google ($58 billion).

In an encouraging aside, the Pew report took note of these major investments in news in 2013: "the viral content website BuzzFeed's investment in original investigative and foreign reporting, Amazon founder Jeff Bezos' purchase of *The Washington Post* with the promise of 'runway' money to allow the newspaper to grow, Vox Media's capital investment in Ezra Klein's explanatory journalism project, and eBay founder Pierre Omidyar's projected $250 million investment in the creation of *First Look Media*."[17]

Aspiring journalists reading this text need to be aware of the unsettled nature of media economics, not so that they are frightened away from the profession but to help them bring their worldly wisdom when they enter it.

As this text has discussed, journalism performs a vital public service, and a journalism career has incalculable psychic rewards. But it should also be recognized that journalists' paychecks are drawn on the bank accounts of companies that cannot survive if they do not make a profit.

Although the news media are not the only industry under pressure in today's economy, theirs is an industry in which the public has an extraordinary stake.

Former newspaper editor Gene Roberts, in his Point of View essay "Tangoing without a Partner," which accompanies this chapter, contends that the public interest must be a factor in the debate:

> Almost no one seems to be grappling with the fundamental questions of publishing and broadcast in a democratic society: What are a newspaper's (or television station's) obligations to its community? Does it have a societal duty to cover local government, state government, schools, courts and the major social and political issues of the day? What about foreign news and national news? … Is there some point beyond which a publisher will not cut? Is there any public obligation at all, other than to public stockholders?

In Roberts' opinion, "staff reductions reduce a paper's ability to cover the news. And they raise the question of a paper's obligations to its community. … It is an ethical question."

The Role of Advertisers

To understand the role that advertisers play in the mainstream news media, consider two kinds of publications that exemplify the two extremes in the advertiser–news relationship. Call them the shopper model and the *Consumer Reports* model.

The shopper model

In most communities, people find their mailboxes stuffed with magazines that contain feature stories as well as a disproportionate volume of advertising. These are so-called "shoppers." Although the stories purport to give consumer advice, they are uniformly uncritical – or, to be more accurate, gushing in their enthusiasm – about the businesses that have bought ads. The stories are advertisements in a news-story format.

To the extent that you read shoppers, you take them on their own terms. Reading the display ads, you assume a "buyer beware" attitude. Reading the accompanying feature stories, you look only to find services you want to check out for yourself. You are not fooled into thinking that the stories can be trusted as an independent evaluation of merchandise and services.

The *Consumer Reports* model

At the other end of the spectrum are a few niche magazines that depend entirely on the subscriptions paid by their readers. The reputation of *Consumer Reports'* product evaluations, for example, is built around the magazine's policy of accepting no advertising. Since there are no advertisers, readers can assume that what the magazine publishes is its own best judgment about the products. To head off any suspicion that *Consumer Reports* might be secretly paid by manufacturers, the magazine prohibits companies and stores from using its product evaluations in posters or ads.

Today, news organizations increasingly are applying a version of the *Consumer Reports* model by charging for access to their digital news coverage. However, consumers have historically resisted paying directly for news; newspaper executives know that when they raise subscription prices, circulation will go down. It remains to be seen whether consumers' subscription dollars will make up the difference created by the decline in advertising revenue on the Web.

John Cassidy reported in *The New Yorker* magazine that "subscription-based journalism (encompassing digital and print) is rapidly becoming financially viable, at least for national publications." Cassidy wrote that, in the fall of 2014, *The New York Times* had 875,000 digital subscribers and *The Wall Street Journal* had 900,000. Pointing to the top-of-the-line subscription prices of $455 a year for *The Times* and $348 for *The Journal*, Cassidy commented that, to some extent, "newspapers are turning into luxury goods." He also cautioned: "None of this means that journalism is out of the woods. Regional newspapers, which by definition have smaller markets than national ones, have been hit particularly hard by the decline in print advertising."[18]

The mainstream media

Like the shoppers, the news media depend financially on advertising. But, like their counterparts at *Consumer Reports*, journalists who work for good news organizations demonstrate, day in and day out, that they owe their first loyalty to readers, listeners, viewers, and digital users. They follow the SPJ code's guiding principle of "act independently." They put the audience ahead of the company that issues their pay-checks – and ahead of the advertisers that provide the money to cover salaries and overhead. Moreover, the presence of advertising is so transparently evident that it serves as a daily disclosure of an unavoidable conflict of interest. The audience can and does hold the news organization accountable for being editorially independent of its advertisers.

In that respect, the companies that produce news are drastically different from other businesses. That difference is not easy for advertisers to understand or accept. The owners of a restaurant, for example, are accustomed to being treated with effusive courtesy by the company from which it buys food supplies. But when the same owners buy an ad in a newspaper, they might be rewarded by a critic's negative review or news coverage of a city inspector's devastating hygiene report.

Advertisers who try to influence news coverage – and executives of news organizations who allow them to do so – ignore the unique, fragile nature of the news business. That can be expressed as follows (and in Figure 11.1):

- First, thanks to the honest, fair news policies of the organization and the talent and energies of its journalists, a newspaper, broadcast station, or digital news site attracts a loyal audience.
- Then, the audience becomes attractive to advertisers because they are potential consumers of their products. Renting the audience to advertisers is a business transaction with benefits for both parties: The advertisers reach their potential customers, and the news company acquires the money it needs to pay expenses and make a profit.
- However, if advertisers tamper with the news policies and manipulate coverage, the audience dwindles as more and more consumers realize that the news coverage lacks integrity. The audience then is less valuable to the advertisers who did the tampering. In the end, both the advertisers and the news organization lose.

Figure 11.1   A news company's traditional business model.
GRAPHIC COURTESY OF BILL MARSH

In its code of ethics and professional conduct, the Radio Television Digital News Association declares that "professional electronic journalists should … vigorously resist undue influence from any outside forces, including advertisers, sources, story subjects, powerful individuals and special-interest groups." In its "guidelines for balancing business pressures and journalism values," RTDNA says: "Journalists, news managers and business-side managers must develop shared values, clear guidelines and practical protocols that serve the dual goals of journalistic independence and commercial success."[19] Under the "act independently" principle, the SPJ code says journalists should "deny favored treatment to advertisers, donors or any other special interests, and resist internal and external pressure to influence coverage."

Questionable Ways to Increase Revenue

The Washington Post's salon initiative

In July 2009 a colorfully printed flier purported to invite lobbyists to "underwrite and participate" in an "off-the-record dinner" to discuss health care at the home of The Washington Post's publisher, Katharine Weymouth. The flier continued:

> Spirited? Yes. Confrontational? No. The relaxed setting in the home of Katharine Weymouth assures it. What is guaranteed is a collegial evening, with Obama Administration officials, Congress members, business leaders, advocacy leaders and other select minds typically on the guest list of 20 or less.

Also attending, the flier said, would be "the publisher, executive editor and health-care reporters of The Washington Post." Attendees could "build crucial relationships with Washington Post news executives in a neutral and informative session."

The price of sponsoring the "salon" would be $25,000, with a maximum of two sponsors. A lobbyist could sponsor 11 salons over a year for $250,000.

The existence of the flier was reported in Politico by a former Post reporter, Mike Allen. Immediately, The Post cancelled the first salon. Executive editor Marcus Brauchli sent a message to the news staff saying, "We will not participate in events where promises are made that in exchange for money The Post will offer access to newsroom personnel or will refrain from confrontational questioning." Publisher Weymouth issued a statement saying that the flier was prepared by The Post's marketing department and "was never vetted by me or by the newsroom," and that, if it had been, it would have been summarily killed. "We are always looking for new revenue streams," she said, "but we will pursue only avenues that uphold our high standards of journalism."[20]

David Carr quipped in his Media Equation column in The New York Times: "Theoretically, you can't buy Washington Post reporters, but you can rent them."[21]

No salons ever took place. Yet the incident was, as Post ombudsman Andy Alexander wrote in his own column, "a public relations disaster."[22]

Like the *Los Angeles Times'* decision in 1999 to share profits from a special magazine issue with the subject of the issue, the Staples Center (see Case Study at the end of this chapter), *The Post's* experience illustrates the problems that can ensue if business-side executives lack sensitivity to the importance of integrity in news coverage.

Other problematic revenue innovations

Success in the marketplace is essential to both the news and business sides of news outlets, of course. There also is no question that, in the industry's difficult economic transition, innovation is called for. Unfortunately, innovation has led to apparent conflicts of interest, such as:

- Television interview shows in which advertisers pay for the privilege of being interviewed, while the commercial transaction is disclosed subtly, if at all.
- A newspaper business-news column sponsored by a bank, with the bank's name in the column title and its distinctive advertising color in the page layout. Readers may think the bank has also bought special treatment in the news.
- Radio stations that sell the naming rights to their studios, so that each news broadcast is announced as if the commercial sponsor owns the news. This too can create the perception that news about the sponsor will get special treatment.
- Television newscasts from a studio set that displays coffee cups with a sponsor's logo, an example of "product placement" borrowed from the movies.
- "In-text" advertising, in which two green lines beneath a word in an digital news story contain embedded advertisements that appear if the user moves the cursor over it. The reporter may have used the word legitimately – in fact, he or she does not know what keywords have been sold – but users might think the word was placed in the news story simply to sell an ad.

How Newsrooms Are Coping with Hard Times

Questionable targets in job reductions

A grim fact of economics is that, if a company's revenue shrinks over an extended period, costs have to be cut. In the newspaper business, that reality has produced a dramatic reduction in jobs, including those in the newsroom. The American Society of News Editors reported in 2014 that its annual newsroom census showed 36,700 newsroom jobs, down one-third from a pre-recession peak of 55,000 in 2006.[23]

In deciding where to cut, editors have generally chosen to keep as many reporters in the field as they can, and this means a sharp reduction in the number of editors. The intuitive basis for that choice is that editors don't produce content; reporters do. Still, it is a questionable strategy. It ignores the damage to a news outlet's authority resulting from the prevalence of errors that an adequately staffed copy desk could have prevented. "Copy editors are to writers as nets are to trapeze artists," Pulitzer Prize-winning reporter David Cay Johnston has written.[24] Accuracy, of course, is an ethical value, because faulty reporting misinforms the audience and can harm the subjects of news coverage.

Sometimes, reductions in editing have been presented as a virtue. For example, *The Asbury Park* (New Jersey) *Press* told readers on August 6, 2014, that it was "flattening our management structure to be more nimble, with fewer hierarchical lines and fewer managers." As a result, the announcement promised, "[r]eporters will be able to post to APP.com directly, cutting layers to give you the news more quickly and efficiently."[25] To this, columnist Will Bunch responded satirically in a column in the *Philadelphia Daily News*. The airline experience could be improved by cutting out air traffic controllers, he wrote, so that "pilots will be able to fly directly to the airport, cutting layers to get you on the ground more quickly and efficiently."[26]

The publisher of *The St. Augustine* (Florida) *Record* informed readers on January 19, 2014, that one of her New Year's resolutions was to eliminate typos and grammar mistakes in the newspaper. "I hear from some readers that part of the entertainment value of *The Record* is counting the number of errors," she wrote. Her solution was to invite readers to come to the newsroom any night between 8 and 11 o'clock and proofread pages. "We'll keep a tally of the proofreading volunteers," she wrote, "and award a nice dinner or two to the person who helps us catch the most typos and errors."[27] That initiative also prompted satire, including a mention on *Saturday Night Live*. John McIntyre, who runs the copy desks at *The Baltimore Sun*, wrote on his blog: "If the publisher is really serious, rather than indulging in a stunt, there is a ready solution: Staff the copy desk with qualified editors."[28]

In percentage terms, visual journalists have been the target for more job reductions than reporters and copy editors. In May 2013 the *Chicago Sun-Times* laid off all 28 employees in its photography department, saying it would rely on wire services, freelancers, and reporters using iPhone cameras.[29] (Four *Sun-Times* photojournalists were rehired in 2014 in a settlement with the newsroom union.[30]) The American Society of News Editors' census showed that photographers, artists, and videographers declined by 43 percent from 6,171 in 2000 to 3,493 in 2012. An analysis by the Pew Research Center said: "Shrinking budgets play a significant part, but so does the explosion of mobile technology and social media, making it easier for citizens and nonprofessionals to capture and share images."[31]

The trend toward multimedia journalism

In today's newsroom, cross-platform journalism requires its practitioners to possess multimedia skills. Reporters might be called on to take photographs, either still or video. Print journalists might do "talkbacks" on television in which they discuss the stories they have covered. Television reporters might write stories for print.

Importantly, all of these print and broadcast journalists might provide multimedia reports throughout the day for the affiliated website.

In the past, a sound news organization has been built by journalists who specialize. If a news organization expects every journalist to do everything, the risk is that the acceptable level of performance will no longer be "excellence" but "good enough." A world-class reporter may be an incompetent photographer, and vice versa. "Newsrooms aren't little Lake Wobegons, where everyone is above average and can do everything well," Deborah Potter wrote in *American Journalism Review*.[32]

Another problem with **multimedia journalism** is that there often isn't time for one person to do everything. The *Los Angeles Times* sent two stellar journalists to Iraq in 2006 to report on how the military was providing emergency medical treatment to those wounded in combat. Reporter David Zucchino and photojournalist Rick Loomis collaborated on a three-part series in the newspaper and a multimedia report on its website.

Zucchino said he had taken acceptable photographs for publication in the past, but he could never have matched Loomis' stunning images, which were the first in an American newspaper to show wounded soldiers on the battlefield in Iraq. "If I had tried to report the articles *and* take the photos, the reporting would have suffered as well," Zucchino said. "Reporting a complicated story under stressful circumstances takes a certain single-mindedness and attention to detail." Even so, the two journalists shared the duty of recording interviews and ambient sound for the website. "Between us, I think we got some very dramatic audio that enriched the project," Zucchino said. "But holding out a tape recorder while interviewing someone or while observing a situation is far less distracting than trying to shoot photos."[33]

To be clear: Today's journalists need to be conversant with the latest technology of reporting for the Web. Journalism students should be learning multimedia skills, both to qualify themselves for the job market and to gain the hands-on experience with varied technology that helps them to understand its capabilities. Ideally, however, journalists ultimately should specialize in the kind of work they can do best.

A decline in Statehouse coverage

As news outlets cover the news with fewer reporters, they understandably are focusing on local news. Residents of small towns and rural areas can get national and international news from networks and the Internet, but they must depend on local papers and broadcast stations to report the news close to home.

However, a significant gap has developed: coverage of state government. Even as much policy-making has shifted from the federal government to governors and state legislatures, fewer statehouse reporters are watching. The Pew Research Center reported in July 2014 that fewer than a third of US newspapers assign any kind of reporter, full- or part-time, to the statehouse. As for local television stations, Pew reported that 86 percent do not have even one statehouse reporter, either full- or part-time. Wire services try to compensate, and Pew said The Associated Press was increasing the size of some of its state capitol bureaus.[34]

Patrick Marley, statehouse reporter for the *Milwaukee Journal Sentinel*, told the Pew researchers: "We have scads of reporters in Washington covering every bit of news that Congress makes. State legislators have more effect on people's lives. We need to have eyes on them, lots of eyes."[35]

Relations between News and Business

There has always been tension between the two sides of a business entity that reports the news. The tension centers on competing needs. On one side is the need – essential for credibility – for the newsroom's independence, so that it can decide how to cover the news. On the other side – essential to survival in the marketplace – is the need to make a profit.

Amid that tension, two metaphors dealing with the relationship of business and news executives have attained mythical status. One metaphor holds that there should be a separation of church and state – with news as the church and business as the state. The second declares that a wall should separate the two.

Understandably, business executives take exception to the church–state metaphor. Jack Fuller, who was both an editor and a business executive, has expressed his scorn for it: "The establishment of journalists as a kind of priesthood has introduced an element of insufferable self-righteousness in newsrooms that has aggravated the journalists' natural inclination to see themselves as living in a world apart from ordinary, mercenary concerns."[36]

The idea of a wall is impractical because there has to be communication between the news department and the business departments. An appropriate level for a discussion of policy matters is the top managers in each department. For example, advertisers' complaints about news, if they are deemed worthy of the newsroom's attention, should be communicated only from the top advertising manager to the top newsroom manager. It is inappropriate for, say, an advertising manager who has lost a restaurant account to air his grievances with the restaurant critic he blames for having alienated the advertiser.

Continual skirmishing between news and business executives can exact a heavy toll on the executives involved. When John Carroll became editor of the *Los Angeles Times* in April 2000, he was eagerly welcomed by a newsroom staff reeling from the trauma of the Staples Center scandal and uneasy about the new ownership by the Tribune Company. Under Carroll, the *Times* had an astonishing turnaround. In the next five years, the resurgent staff won 13 Pulitzer Prizes – meaning that, in the opinion of the Pulitzer judges, almost one-fifth of the nation's best newspaper journalism during this period was being produced by the staff of a single paper.

And then Carroll quit.

While the *Times* was enjoying its profound journalistic success, Carroll was being worn down behind the scenes in grueling battles that he and the publisher, John Puerner, were waging with Chicago executives who repeatedly demanded staff reductions. In deciding in July 2005 to retire at age 63, Carroll followed Puerner out the door; the publisher had resigned a few months earlier to take a "self-imposed career break."[37]

It is not surprising that some newsroom veterans fondly remember a day when owners didn't bother their editors with the problems of commerce. In *The Vanishing Newspaper*, Philip Meyer reminisced:

> The reason newspapers were as good as they were in the golden age was not because of the wall between church and state. It was because the decision-making needed to resolve the profit-service conflict was made by a public-spirited individual who had control of both sides of the wall and who was rich and confident enough to do what he or she pleased. In today's world, most leaders of the press do not have that kind of functional autonomy.[38]

Jack Fuller, for one, remembers the past differently. In his *News Values* (written eight years before Meyer's book, so he wasn't responding to Meyer personally), Fuller asserted:

> Odd as it seems to some of us who can still remember what it was like to work for privately owned newspapers, there are journalists who appear to have forgotten some of its worst qualities: the authoritarian management system in which editors were like children before the powerful father; the use of the paper's coverage for the owners' personal needs; ... the commingling of resources so that a photographer might find himself detailed to shoot the picture for the owner's Christmas card; the shameless willingness to give advertisers (and personal favorites of the owner) privileged access to the newspaper's news columns.[39]

In 1973 Ridder Publications bought the morning *Wichita Eagle* and the afternoon *Wichita Beacon* from local owners. In 1974 Ridder merged with Knight Newspapers to form Knight Ridder (Knight Ridder was bought by McClatchy Newspapers in 2006). In 1975 Davis "Buzz" Merritt was sent from Knight Ridder's Washington bureau to be the editor of the two Wichita newspapers. What Merritt found in the editor's desk drawer – artifacts from the days of the authoritarian local ownership – offers a glimpse of how journalism can be distorted to serve commercial interests:

> A folder marked "newsroom policies" contained a series of memos outlining some of the rules ... One, noting that *The Eagle* had reported the rape of a woman in the downtown Macy's department store parking garage, declared that henceforth, the address and location of crimes related to businesses would not be reported. ...
>
> Another rule: Wichita's economy is heavily dependent on four aviation plants, Boeing, Beech, Cessna, and Learjet – and in the event of an airplane crash, the paper would not report the make of the plane, unless it was a Piper or some other brand built elsewhere.
>
> Another was a list of ... prominent people whose names would not appear in a negative light in the newspaper without clearance from "the second floor." The newsroom was on the third floor; the business office on the second.

And there were instructions to make sure that some "good news" was on the front page of the newspapers every day, adorned with the round, yellow smiley-face icon then popping up elsewhere. Pointedly, the definition of "good news" included store openings and important new building permits.[40]

When he became chief executive of Time Inc. in 2013, Joseph A. Ripp erased the line dividing business and editorial. He reorganized the company's magazines (including such titles as *Time*, *Sports Illustrated*, *People*, and *Fortune*) so that editors would report to division presidents. Ripp said in a memo that the new structure would "create a strong partnership between business and editorial" and would "result in a cohesive vision for each of our brands."[41]

In 2014 Ripp told Bloomberg TV that, with the reorganization, editors were "happier": "No longer are we asking ourselves the question, 'Are we violating church and state,' whatever that was. We are now asking ourselves the question, 'Are we violating the trust with our consumers?' We're never going to do that."[42]

Also in 2014, in discussions with union leaders over staff layoffs, Time Inc. turned over a form showing that one of the criteria for evaluating SI.com reporters and editors was: "Produces content that [is] beneficial to advertiser relationship." Other criteria included "quality of writing," "impact of stories/newsworthiness," "productivity/ tenacity," "audience/traffic," "video," "social," and "enthusiasm/approach to work."

Anthony Napoli, a union representative, told Gawker that Time Inc. used the rating form in deciding which staff members on the *Sports Illustrated* website would be laid off. Napoli said, "Writers who may have had high assessments for their writing ability, which is their job, were in fact terminated based on the fact that the company believed their stories did not 'produce content that is beneficial to advertiser relationships.'"

A spokesman for *Sports Illustrated* responded that the union's interpretation of the rating form "takes one category out of context." He said the form "encompasses all of the natural considerations for digital media," and it "starts and ends with journalistic expertise."[43]

A March 2014 internal report by *The New York Times*, titled "Innovation," suggested that *The Times* is at a competitive disadvantage because the social-media experts from the editorial and marketing divisions are too separated. The report urged that they join forces to engage the organization's digital audience. The report says, "The very first step should be a deliberate push to abandon our current metaphors of choice – 'The Wall' and 'Church and State' – which project an enduring need for division. Increased collaboration, done right, does not present any threat to our values of journalistic independence."[44]

Although today's publishers ultimately make the decisions, policy for the newspaper company typically is influenced by an "operating committee," which consists of the vice presidents representing the company departments, including news. In this environment, the editor is outnumbered; all the other vice presidents are oriented toward the company's business function and tend to dismiss newsroom concerns about ethics and credibility.

Maxwell King, who was editor of *The Philadelphia Inquirer* between 1990 and 1997, said his business colleagues were disdainful of the arguments that he and Zachary Stalberg, editor of the *Philadelphia Daily News*, made in the operating committee's meetings:

> Zack and I argued that the public's trust in the newspaper has a commercial value. We pointed out that in their relationship with advertisers, they would see that the customer's trust would deliver something of value. They wouldn't lie or misrepresent to an advertiser, so we should not do that to our readers. We said that if we are honest and ethical, people will buy our product. The business executives saw us as prissy and insulated from the harsh realities of the business world.[45]

Publishers' and station managers' civic activism sometimes places them at odds with their newsroom leaders. The business executives consider it an essential civic duty to be "good citizens" in the community like the top executives of other businesses. The newsroom leaders worry that the audience will associate the company's activism with news coverage and perceive favoritism toward the publishers' or station managers' causes.

In the worst form of the news–business relationship, some publishers and station managers abuse their authority by manipulating news coverage. Fortunately, that kind of direct interference is relatively rare today, far removed from the era that produced the policies Buzz Merritt found in the folder in the editor's desk at *The Wichita Eagle* in 1975.

Point of View

Tangoing without a Partner

Gene Roberts

Having journalists discuss ethics and standards without the participation of business executives is like tangoing without a partner. No matter how expert, no matter how serious, half of the act is missing.

Business executives, of course, control the money and, without firm commitments from these executives, journalists cannot set meaningful standards on what they cover in a community and what they pass on to the readers in the news columns. And there is also the question of treating readers fairly and without confusion by clearly delineating news from advertising. Again, it takes two to tango.

It is more important today than in the past for key players on the business side to get exposure to discussions on ethics and professional standards. Why? The hierarchy of newspapers has changed dramatically in just a generation or so. As recently as the 1950s and 1960s, most daily newspapers were family-owned local institutions. There were good owners and bad owners in terms of feeling a sense of public responsibility, but they were in overall charge of both the newsroom and the business side and usually had to give at least some thought to the problems of each side. Usually, the owner had an editor to run the newsroom and a general manager to head up the business operations. The owners could be absolute monarchs, but found it in their interest to have a separation of church and state.

Today, more than 80 percent of America's approximately 1,500 dailies are owned by groups and chains. And the chief executives of these organizations appoint publishers to run each local newspaper. Increasingly, as profit pressures mount, these publishers are far more likely to come out of accounting departments or advertising than out of newsrooms. And usually they have authority over the editor, but without having nearly as much exposure to the overall quandaries of publishing as the old local owners had.

As newspaper revenues fall, the business executives cope with one financial emergency after another and make little time, if any, for discussions of publishing ethics and standards. Almost no one seems to be grappling with the fundamental questions of publishing and broadcast in a democratic society: What are a newspaper's (or television station's) obligations to its community? Does it have a societal duty to cover local government, state government, schools, courts, and the major social and political issues of the day? What about foreign news and national news?

For well over two decades now, the overall trend line at newspapers is down in newsroom staff and the space devoted to news coverage.

Obviously this has an impact on a newspaper's ability to collect the news and pass it on to the readers. Is there some point beyond which a publisher will not cut? Is there any public obligation at all, other than to public stockholders?

Newspapers operate under unique constitutional protections. Do these protections obligate newspapers to make any sort of minimal commitments to news coverage? None that America's publishers are willing to acknowledge through their professional organizations. Neither the Newspaper Association of America, which represents most dailies in the United States, nor the National Newspaper Association, which represents most weeklies and some family-owned dailies, have ethical codes or any sort of written standards of professional obligations. The National Funeral Directors Association has a code of ethics. So do airline pilots. And interior designers. And booksellers. And professional organists. And professional hypnotists. And wedding professionals. The fabric of civilized society is not likely to unravel if a wedding is mishandled or if an interior designer botches an apartment makeover. But if a newspaper fails to properly cover local government or the public schools?

We need codes. We need standards. But above all we need a sober assessment of our obligations to supply the news and enough of it to ensure that our readers can be knowing participants in our democracies.

This essay is an excerpt from the Neal Shine Lecture on Ethics delivered at Michigan State University, November 12, 2007. Gene Roberts, now retired, was executive editor of *The Philadelphia Inquirer*, managing editor of *The New York Times*, and a professor at the Philip Merrill College of Journalism at the University of Maryland.

Case Study

Sharing Ad Profits, Creating a Crisis

The $400 million Staples Center, home of the Lakers and Clippers basketball teams and the Kings hockey team, was completed in 1999. To commemorate the arena's impact on Los Angeles' downtown, the *Los Angeles Times* published a 164-page special issue of its Sunday magazine on October 10, 1999.

Two weeks later, the *Times* news staff was in revolt. It had been discovered that the *Times* had shared the magazine's considerable advertising profit with the Staples Center. That created a huge conflict-of-interest problem for the reporters and editors who worked on the section, because to the public it appeared that they were giving all that space to a business partner.

Although the magazine's content was not influenced by the Staples Center or the *Times'* advertising department, it had been unpopular in the newsroom from the beginning. Many of the journalists who worked on the special magazine considered it excessive. Alice Short, editor of the magazine, said, "I put in a couple of months of my life working on an issue of the magazine I didn't want to do. We were told it was tough luck; we had to do it anyway."

The *Los Angeles Business Journal* broke the news of the deal, and *The New York Times* followed with a detailed article. Within hours of receiving the news, more than 300 *Times* staff members had signed petitions in protest. "In one swift blow," the petition said, "we communicated to our readers that we have undisclosed financial ties with our editorial subjects."

The staff got moral support from the paper's retired publisher, Otis Chandler, who had in the 1960s and 1970s led the *Times* to a national reputation for quality journalism. In a letter that was read in the newsroom, Chandler denounced the profit-sharing deal as "unbelievably stupid and unprofessional." His statement said: "Respect and credibility for a newspaper is irreplaceable. Sometimes it can never be restored." Immediately, photographs of Chandler were posted throughout the newsroom.

Kathryn Downing, a lawyer with no newspaper experience before she was appointed publisher less than two years earlier, addressed a meeting of 200 angry staff members and acknowledged that the deal had been a mistake. She said she had thought she was "protecting the line" between the business and news sides of the paper, but "I missed completely the fallout from sharing revenue."

The Staples Center episode occurred in the context of a five-year campaign by Mark Willes, a former cereal executive who had been hired as chief executive of the *Los Angeles Times'* parent company, to demolish the so-called wall between the business and news sides. Willes appointed "general managers" for each news section and directed that the general managers and section editors work together on ideas to create new revenue streams. Robert G. Magnuson, a former *Times* business editor, assessed the Willes innovation afterward: "However well intentioned, the system broke down when overzealous GMs, intent on strutting their stuff and showing off their P&L [profit-and-loss] prowess, waltzed into the newsroom barking orders to editors and reporters."

Although editor Michael Parks initially opposed the idea of an internal investigation that would result in a detailed report for readers, he gave in and assigned the task to the paper's media critic, David Shaw. Shaw's 14-page report, edited by retired managing editor George Cotliar, was published on December 20. Shaw faulted publisher Downing for failing to comprehend the deal's ethical ramifications, and editor Parks for not stopping the magazine's distribution or disclosing the conflict when he became aware of the deal.

Shaw also criticized Willes' campaign to demolish the wall between the business offices and the newsroom and replace it with a line that could be easily crossed: "Many in the *Times*' newsroom see the Staples affair as the very visible and ugly tip of an ethical iceberg of ominous proportions – a boost-the-profits, drive-the-stock-price imperative that threatens to undermine the paper's quality, integrity and journalistic purpose." Shaw conceded that a wall has its flaws, but "a wall is also impregnable and immovable; a line can be breached much more easily, moved so gradually that no one knows it has actually been moved until it's too late, and principles have been irrevocably compromised." Willes was quoted in Shaw's story as saying that the Staples Center incident argues for more communication between newspaper departments, not less. People didn't talk to each other when they should have, Willes said.

The profit-sharing deal grew out of an agreement that the *Times* signed on December 17, 1998, making it a "founding partner" of the Staples Center. The *Times* would get exclusive signage rights to the arena, exclusive rights to sell the *Times* inside the arena, a news kiosk in the main entrance, and a 16-seat suite for all events. The *Times* agreed to pay the Staples Center $1.6 million a year for five years –

$800,000 in cash and the rest from "ideas" that would generate revenue. The special magazine was one of those revenue-generating ideas.

The day before the Shaw report was published, Downing and Parks published a "To our readers" statement on the front page acknowledging that the Staples deal was a mistake and announcing a new set of ethical principles to guide the *Times*. The following are excerpts from the principles:

- The *Times* will not engage in any dealing with advertisers or other groups that require or imply coverage or restrict it in any way.
- The publisher will fully and promptly disclose the nature of relationships (partnerships, sponsorships) to the editor.
- Themed advertising sections must be readily distinguishable from news.
- The *Times* will not contribute to political candidates, parties or causes or to ballot measures.
- Editorial staff will not be involved in managing or promoting [events or festivals] but may provide advice on speakers and panelists.
- Contact between editorial and the business side is essential to publish on a daily basis. These contacts should come at a level appropriate to the function. On larger issues, such as themes of coverage, decisions require the approval of the editor or a managing editor.

In March 2000 the *Times* and other media holdings of the Times Mirror Company were sold to the Tribune Company of Chicago. Willes, Downing, and Parks all left the company.

Sources

Barringer, Felicity, "Newspaper magazine shares profits with a subject," *The New York Times*, Oct. 26, 1999.

(Continued)

Barringer, Felicity, "Ex-publisher assails paper in Los Angeles," *The New York Times*, Nov. 4, 1999.

Hiltzik, Michael A., and Sallie Hofmeister, "Remorseful, *Times* publisher promises changes," *Los Angeles Times*, Oct. 29, 1999.

Magnuson, Robert G., "How do we protect integrity in an increasingly complex world?," in *Embracing Journalism's Real Value: Building the Business, Protecting the Principles* (Poynter Institute, Jan. 2001).

Risser, James, "Lessons from L.A.," *Columbia Journalism Review*, Jan.–Feb. 2000.

Shaw, David, "Crossing the line: a *Los Angeles Times* profit-sharing arrangement with Staples Center fuels a firestorm of protest in the newsroom – and a debate about journalistic ethics," *Los Angeles Times*, Dec. 20, 1999.

Winokur, Scott, "L.A. *Times* ad deal labelled a 'fiasco,'" *San Francisco Examiner*, Nov. 28, 1999.

Zacchino, Narda, "Staples incident rocks *Times*, inside and out," *Los Angeles Times*, Nov. 9, 1999.

Questions for Class Discussion

- What is meant by the traditional "wall" between a news organizations news and business staffs? Do you think Mark Willes' effort to remove the wall was a contributing factor to the Staples Center episode?
- What was the ethical issue in the decision to share advertising profits from the special magazine with the Staples Center? What guiding principle of the SPJ ethics code is involved?

- What do you think of the *Times*' decision to publish a 14-page critical analysis of the affair? What guiding principle of the SPJ code is involved in this decision?
- Read the *Times*' new advertising/news guidelines in the Case Study. What do you think is the reasoning behind each of the guidelines?

Notes

1 "Sponsor content: David Miscavige leads Scientology to milestone year," *The Atlantic*, Jan. 14, 2013.

2 Ibid.

3 Paul Farhi, "*Atlantic* fiasco renews ethics concerns about advertorials," *The Washington Post*, Jan. 15, 2013.

4 "Statement from *The Atlantic*," *The Atlantic*, Jan. 15, 2014.

5 Jeff John Roberts, "What the *Atlantic* learned from Scientology: native advertising is harder for news brands," GigaOm, Feb. 28, 2013.

6 David Dobbs, "*The Atlantic*, Scientology, and the theft of credibility," *Wired*, Feb. 28, 2013.

7 IPG Media Lab, "Ad effectiveness reveals native ads drive more attention and brand lift over banner ads," May 3, 2013. IPG said it surveyed 4,770 consumers and used eye-tracking technology to assess the attention of 200 consumers. The research was

conducted in collaboration with Sharethrough, a company specializing in native advertising.

8 Ginny Marvin, "73% of online publishers offer native advertising, just 10% still sitting on the sidelines," Marketing Land, July 22, 2013.

9 Tracie Powell, "Native ads aren't as clear as outlets think," *Columbia Journalism Review*, Dec. 5, 2013.

10 "Arguments fly during FTC workshop on native advertising," *Advertising Age*, Dec. 4, 2013.

11 "Five things to know about *The New York Times*' new native ads," *Advertising Age*, Jan. 8, 2013.

12 Sam Kirkland, "Sulzberger: 'Our readers will always know that they are looking at a message from an advertiser,'" Poynter, Dec. 19, 2013.

13 Jeff Sonderman and Millie Tran, "Understanding the rise of native content," American Press Institute, Nov. 13, 2013.

14 Joshua Benton, "What would David do?," *Nieman Reports*, Summer 2014, 50–51.

15 Edward Wasserman, "'Sponsored content' gets a new push for legitimacy," Unsocial Media, Aug. 5, 2013.

16 Jesse Holcomb and Amy Mitchell, "The revenue picture for American journalism and how it is changing," Pew Research Center Journalism & Media, Mar. 26, 2014.

17 Ibid.

18 John Cassidy, "A bit of good news about journalism," *The New Yorker*, Dec. 11, 2014.

19 Radio Television Digital News Association, "Guidelines for balancing business pressures and journalism values."

20 Andy Alexander, "*The Post*'s 'salon' plan: a public relations disaster," *The Washington Post*, July 2, 2009.

21 David Carr, "A publisher stumbles publicly at *The Post*," *The New York Times*, July 4, 2009.

22 Alexander, "*The Post*'s 'salon' plan."

23 Rick Edmonds, "Newspaper industry lost another 1,300 full-time editorial professionals in 2013," Poynter, July 29, 2014.

24 David Cay Johnston, "Honoring the word police," The National Memo, Jan. 3, 2014.

25 Hollis R. Towns, "We're creating a newsroom of the future," *Asbury Park Press*, Aug. 6, 2014.

26 Will Bunch, "It's a true fact!!! People who edit things no longer neeeded," *Philadelphia Daily News*, Aug. 11, 2014.

27 Delinda Fogel, "'Catch the typos' contest kicks off 2014," *The St. Augustine Record*, Jan. 19, 2014.

28 John McIntyre, "Accept no substitutes," *The Baltimore Sun*, Jan. 27, 2014.

29 Monica Anderson, "At newspapers, photographers feel the brunt of job cuts," Pew Research Center, Nov. 11, 2013.

30 Robert Feder, "Amid more layoffs, *Sun-Times* rehires four photographers," RobertFeder.com, Mar. 4, 2014.

31 Anderson, "At newspapers, photographers feel the brunt of job cuts."

32 Deborah Potter, "Doing it all: having the same person report and shoot the stories may save money, but at what cost?," *American Journalism Review*, Oct.–Nov. 2006, 94.

33 David Zucchino, email to the author, May 30, 2008.

34 Jodi Enda, Katerina Eva Matsa, and Jan Lauren Boyles, "America's shifting statehouse press," Pew Research Center, July 10, 2014.

35 Ibid.

36 Jack Fuller, *News Values* (Chicago: University of Chicago Press, 1996), 200.

37 Lori Robertson and Rachel Smolkin, "John Carroll bows out in L.A.," *American Journalism Review*, Aug.–Sept. 2005.

38 Philip Meyer, *The Vanishing Newspaper* (Columbia: University of Missouri Press, 2004), 206–207.

39 Fuller, *News Values*, 197.

40 Davis Merritt, *Knightfall* (New York: American Management Association, 2005), 67.

41 Michael Sebastian, "Time Inc. shakeup: editors to report to business side, editor-in-chief Martha Nelson exits," *Advertising Age*, Oct. 31, 2013.

42 Jim Romenesko, "Time Inc. CEO says editors are happier reporting to business side," JimRomenesko.com, June 20, 2014. The article refers to a transcript provided by Bloomberg TV.

43 Hamilton Nolan, "Time Inc. rates writers on how 'beneficial' they are to advertisers," Gawker, Aug. 18, 2014.

44 Mashable, "The full *New York Times* innovation report," May 16, 2014.

45 Author's telephone interview with Maxwell King, Nov. 12, 2007.

12 Getting the Story Right and Being Fair

Newswriting skills of accuracy and fairness are ethical skills, too

---

Learning Goals

This chapter will help you understand:

- the ethical importance of being accurate and fair in news reporting;
- the importance of verification as the mainstream media broaden their use of user-generated content;
- the need to be on guard against hoaxes; and
- the value of acknowledging and correcting errors in the news.

In retrospect, the pace of reporting in the twentieth century seems almost casual. Newspapers had only a few deadlines, and for morning papers those deadlines were at night, hours after most of the news had happened. Broadcast reporters usually worked toward a few scheduled newscasts. The only reporters who had a deadline every minute were those who worked for the wire services, whose far-flung client newspapers might be going to press at any time of the day or night.

Now, in the digital era, everybody is on deadline all the time. In the scramble to get the news first, it is easy to forget that the reporter's first duty is to get the story right. That human weakness may help explain errors in reporting the news, but it cannot excuse them.

Journalism students can benefit from analyzing the torrent of errors that news consumers witnessed in a series of high-profile, breaking-news reports – five involving deadly violence and one a crucial Supreme Court ruling – in a period of less than three years.

On January 8, 2011, outside a supermarket in Tucson, Arizona, Congresswoman Gabrielle Giffords was greeting constituents when a 22-year-old man began firing into the crowd. Twenty people were shot and six died, including a federal judge and a nine-year-old girl. Giffords, shot in the head, survived. However, NPR reported on the air and on Twitter that Giffords had been killed. The false report was quickly retweeted thousands of times and picked up by other news organizations.[1]

On June 28, 2012, when the Supreme Court issued its crucial ruling on the constitutionality of President Barack Obama's Affordable Care Act, CNN and Fox News reported incorrectly that the court had struck down the law's individual mandate.

The Ethical Journalist: Making Responsible Decisions in the Digital Age, Second Edition. Gene Foreman.
© 2016 John Wiley & Sons, Inc. Published 2016 by John Wiley & Sons, Inc.

That is the section requiring most Americans to have medical insurance or pay a penalty. Actually, in a 5–4 decision, the court had upheld the individual mandate.[2]

On July 20, 2012, a man wearing combat gear and a gas mask threw tear gas into a theater in Aurora, Colorado, during a midnight showing of a new Batman movie, *The Dark Knight Rises*. Then he began shooting into the crowd with multiple weapons, killing 12 and wounding 58. A 24-year-old man, James Holmes, was arrested outside the theater after the shooting.[3] On the air, ABC News' chief investigative reporter, Brian Ross, speculated about Holmes' background: "There is a Jim Holmes of Aurora, Colorado, page on the Colorado Tea Party site …. Now, we don't know if this is the same Jim Holmes, but it is a Jim Holmes of Aurora, Colorado."[4] The man accused of being the shooter was not, however, the same Jim Holmes.[5]

On December 14, 2012, a young man fatally shot 20 first graders and six adults at Sandy Hook Elementary School in Newtown, Connecticut, and then killed himself. The first reports contained numerous errors, starting with the identity of the shooter; it was Adam Lanza, 20 years old, not his brother Ryan Lanza, 24. Their mother was not a teacher and she was not killed at the school; Adam had shot her to death at their home before going to the school. Adam was not recognized by the principal and buzzed through the locked door of the school; he forced his way in.[6] As the news circulated that Ryan Lanza was a mass murderer, he posted frantically on Facebook from Hoboken, New Jersey: "IT WASN'T ME I WAS AT WORK IT WASN'T ME."[7]

On April 15, 2013, near the finish line of the Boston Marathon, two pressure-cooker bombs filled with nails and metal pellets exploded within seconds of each other, killing three people and injuring at least 264.[8] Two days later, CNN reported incorrectly that a suspect had been arrested, and several other news organizations made the same mistake. The cover of the *New York Post*'s print edition on April 18 displayed a photograph of two men with backpacks and the headline "Bag Men." (*The Post* ran a story inside saying that the photo of the men was being circulated within law enforcement, and "there is no direct evidence linking them to the crime." The men were not the bombers.[9]) Reddit, doing its own sleuthing, concluded falsely that the bomber was a Brown University student who had been missing for about a month.[10]

On September 16, 2013, a Washington Navy Yard worker named Aaron Alexis walked through the fourth, third, and first floors of Building 197, shooting people he encountered and killing 12 before being shot to death by law-enforcement officers.[11] Tweets by CBS and NBC reporters gave the wrong name for the shooter. Other initial reports gave varying numbers of shooters (as many as three).[12]

In the aftermath of those errors, several of the offending news organizations sought to correct the errors and to try to discover what had caused them. From those exercises, lessons were learned – or, more properly, lessons were reinforced. Here are a few:

- *Ask the key question: "How do you know that?"* You have to be sure your source has first-hand information. Alicia C. Shepard, NPR's ombudsman at the time of the Giffords story, found that NPR had two unnamed sources who said Giffords had been killed, but that both were relying on other people. Robert Garcia, leader of NPR's Newscast Unit, told Shepard that "in reporting a death, the best valid confirmation comes from the hospital or family – people with first-hand knowledge."[13]

- *If you are reporting a court's opinion, read the entire opinion.*   The error in reporting the Supreme Court's decision on the Affordable Care Act stemmed from reckless haste. Chief Justice John Roberts' opinion began by laying out the court majority's judgment that the act's individual mandate was not justified by Congress' power to regulate interstate commerce. The tenor of Roberts' statements led some to conclude that the court was striking down the law. But the opinion went on to hold that the penalty imposed on people who do not buy insurance could reasonably be characterized as a tax, which the opinion said was permissible under the Constitution.[14]

- *Do your reporting before publishing, broadcasting, or posting.*   When a reporter finds a name on the Web that is similar to that of someone accused of mass homicide, the next step is to check it out. Don't speculate. The on-air statement about a possible Tea Party connection to the Aurora shooter was premature and wrong. A statement from the network read, "ABC News and Brian Ross apologize for the mistake, and for disseminating that information before it was properly vetted."[15]

- *Remember that the police working a chaotic crime scene are just as likely to be confused as anyone else.*   The multiple factual mistakes in the Newtown massacre came from unnamed police at the scene.[16] In this case, the essential question, "How do you know that?," could have been directed by reporters to the officers dispensing the information, particularly as to how they had identified the killer.

- *Be wary of sources who won't be identified.*   The false report that an arrest had been made in the Boston Marathon bombing – a report based on sources who would not be named – was immediately denied by the FBI, which warned that such unverified reporting could have "unintended consequences" for its investigation.[17] CNN's John King, who broke the arrest story, told a radio station the following week: "When you do something like this, it's embarrassing. ... The one thing you have to do is look straight in the camera and say, 'We were wrong.'"[18]

- *When you are reporting on Twitter without a backup reading from an editor, be especially careful.*   In the Washington Navy Yard case, as had happened at Newtown, some news organizations named an innocent person as the shooter. "You would think it would be pretty basic," Rem Rieder wrote in *USA Today*: "When it comes to naming someone as the person who committed a horrific crime, you wait until it's completely nailed down, no matter how fierce the competition pressure."[19]

- *What you hear on a police scanner is only a tip.*   In *The Washington Post*, Paul Farhi wrote that reports at the Navy Yard were "hopping from law-enforcement scanners to Twitter to traditional media reports, all within minutes." He quoted Jim Farley, the top news executive at WTOP, an all-news station: "A scanner does give you information; it tells you who to call."[20]

Competitive pressure is just one of the factors that create a news environment in which errors can flourish.

Another factor is the Web's interactivity with the audience and the relative ease of changing content, so the temptation is to put your first draft out there and let the audience correct it. The ethicist Bob Steele scorns this approach as "morally bankrupt," noting that the initial posting, even if corrected later, could cause serious harm.[21] Because search engines like Google and Yahoo! crawl the Web and archive content, original versions of stories may stay online even if they have been corrected.

Yet another factor is diminished editorial oversight. Online news sites may not need a large copy desk like a newspaper's, but they do need skilled copy editors on duty throughout the day and night to place a critical second set of eyes on every story before it is posted. Today, newspapers are downsizing or even eliminating copy desks. Steele has urged a recommitment to high standards of quality control to "build and protect the integrity of the journalism as it morphs into new forms of reporting, storytelling, and delivery."[22]

In a Point of View essay that accompanies this chapter, "Decision-Making in the Digital Age," the late James M. Naughton advocated for the timeless values of sound judgment in covering the news on any platform. "Sound judgment," Naughton wrote, "pays homage to speed but reveres accuracy."

Accuracy and Fairness: Standards of Ethical Reporting

Accuracy and fairness are the essence of journalism. The two virtues are intertwined. Accuracy and fairness start with the basic reporting skills of getting the facts right and presenting them in context. In the following standards for *accuracy* in the Society of Professional Journalists' code, under the principle of "seek truth and report it," journalists are told to:

- Take responsibility for the accuracy of their work. Verify information before releasing it. Use original sources whenever possible.
- Remember that neither speed nor format excuses inaccuracy.
- Provide context. Take special care not to misrepresent or oversimplify in promoting, previewing or summarizing a story.
- Gather, update and correct information throughout the life of a news story.
- Provide access to source material when it is relevant and appropriate.[23]

Journalists should not be satisfied with merely being accurate – that is, correctly reporting facts. They should strive for a human's best possible rendering of *truth*, presenting the facts in a context that fosters an understanding of the event or issue. Truth may not emerge from a single day's reporting. The Watergate case, for example, took more than two years (1972–74) to unfold.

Some news organizations spot-check their reporting by sending a questionnaire to the story subjects. Bill Marimow, a two-time Pulitzer Prize-winner as a reporter before becoming a newspaper editor, "audited" his own stories by phoning the subjects after the stories were published to make sure he got the facts right. Marimow said his audits often produced added benefits:

> If something has happened since your last conversation [with the source], the audit may yield a followup story for the Web or the next day's newspaper. Most important – and this is a subtle benefit – your sources will begin to trust you and respect you more than most of the other journalists who cover them. … That trust and respect, in time, eventually lead to more exclusive stories for your news organization because, when your sources want to disclose something, they'll think of calling you first.[24]

Some magazines employ fact-checkers who essentially re-report the stories. They contact sources to ask if they were quoted correctly, and they conduct research to verify facts from archives. Time constraints make it impractical for newspapers, broadcast, and online sites to employ fact-checkers, but good editors develop a sixth sense that alerts them to facts in news stories that need to be double-checked. Editors, too, ask: "How do you know that?"

Fairness revolves around the journalist's moral obligation to follow the facts, to reject favoritism or bias, and to consider the viewpoints of the subjects of their reporting. The Golden Rule is a good test of fairness. Not only news reporters but also commentators have a duty to be fair; an ethical journalist's commentary is grounded in fact, not conjecture.

The following standards for fairness appear under two SPJ principles – "seek truth and report it" and "minimize harm" – and tell journalists to:

- Show compassion for those who may be affected by news coverage. Use heightened sensitivity when dealing with juveniles, victims of sex crimes, and sources or subjects who are inexperienced or unable to give consent.
- Diligently seek subjects of news coverage to allow them to respond to criticism or allegations of wrongdoing.
- Balance a suspect's right to a fair trial with the public's right to know. Consider the implications of identifying criminal suspects before they face legal charges.
- Realize that private people have a greater right to control information about themselves than public figures and others who seek power, influence or attention. Weigh the consequences of publishing or broadcasting personal information.[25]

Framing – the term that journalists use to define or interpret events they report on – is subjective, and it can be a fairness issue. Steven A. Smith, former editor of *The Spokesman-Review* in Spokane, Washington, describes the frame as "the context or narrative theme through which the story is told."[26] When they write about the daily ups and downs of the stock market, journalists frame stories in terms of what likely caused the changes. Thomas Patterson and Philip Seib wrote:

> A news story would be a buzzing jumble of facts if journalists did not impose meaning on it. At the same time, it is the frame, as much as the event or development itself, which affects how the citizen will interpret and respond to news developments.[27]

In choosing the frame, journalists should be alert to two traps – first, allowing their opinions to get in the way, and, second, choosing a frame solely on the basis of audience appeal. Conflict is a popular story frame but one that can be exaggerated. Although the conflict frame may result in provocative stories, it could ignore nuances and mislead the audience about context. An example is a tendency to frame stories about proposed business and residential construction projects as "environmentalists versus developers."[28]

Another element of fairness is to make sure to seek a response from a person or institution criticized in a news story. In its manual of style and usage, *The New York Times* emphasizes that if an attack "is detailed or occurs in a deeply researched article, time and space must be allowed for the subject's thoughtful comment." If a reporter cannot find those criticized, "the article should say what effort was made, over how long a time, and tell why it did not succeed."[29]

Fairness also means that news organizations should be conscious of how they handled comparable news developments in the past. If A's announcement of candidacy for mayor leads the evening newscast, so should B's. If a person is charged with a crime on the front page, his or her acquittal also should appear on the front page.

Completeness is an essential reporting standard. Bill Marimow makes the point that a good news story is accurate, fair, and *thorough*.[30]

Investigative reporters in particular must be aware of a trap called "falling in love with the story." Without realizing it, they could reach a conclusion that relies too much on evidence that supports their thesis and too little on evidence that indicates the thesis is not true. Like anyone in love, they magnify the positives and dismiss the negatives about the object of their passion. To use another metaphor, reporters instead should apply the *scientific method*. They should start with a hypothesis, then test it to see if it is valid. Their goal, like that of scientists in the laboratory, should be to find the truth, not necessarily to prove the hypothesis.

Two case studies accompanying this chapter illustrate issues of accuracy and fairness: "Richard Jewell: He Really Was a Hero" and "A Story of Rape at Mr. Jefferson's University."

Harnessing the Power of the People

In the digital age, ordinary citizens are helping to report and photograph the news. Smart news organizations are creating social-media units that comb Twitter, Facebook, and other networks for content that the public needs – but only if that content is authentic. In a process called crowdsourcing, these organizations also reach out to the audience for help on specific stories.

Verification of any **user-generated content** is an ethical duty. The information or image on the Internet may be newsworthy, but is it real or is it fake? A professional news organization knows and trusts its staff journalists and the freelance contributors it deals with regularly. People who post on social media are, in contrast, largely unknown to the organization. Thus the organization relies on the new social-media units staffed by journalists who separate truth from fiction, and do it on deadline.

Eric Carvin, The Associated Press' social media editor, wrote that gathering user-generated content "is an indispensable tool in the modern journalist's arsenal." With contributions from members of the public, Carvin said, AP can make major news events "come to life – and in some cases, has made them possible to cover at all."[31]

David Carr of *The New York Times* praised Twitter's role in drawing attention to the racially charged standoff in August 2014 in Ferguson, Missouri, between the police and civilians protesting the fatal shooting of an unarmed black teenager by a white officer. "Twitter," Carr wrote, "has become an early warning service for news organizations, a way to see into stories even when they don't have significant reporting assets on the ground."[32] Mark Little, who founded Storyful in 2010 as a news agency that verifies social-media content and creates narrative from it, wrote that sources of information in the digital age are nothing like journalists' sources of yesteryear. Those traditional sources were valued for their power and authority.

"Authority has been replaced by authenticity as the currency of social journalism," Little wrote:

> The key to engaging with a community is to seek out those closest to the story. They rarely have a title but are people of standing within a community. They are guides to the wisdom within their crowd and interpreters of nuance: if you are verifying video from Syria you don't want a foreign policy wonk, you want someone who can distinguish between a Damascus and a Homs accent.[33]

Photography by members of the public can be extremely valuable because only by chance would a professional be present when a major accident or crime occurs. Although citizens have long contributed images to the mainstream news media, that is happening almost routinely now, thanks to social media.

An amateur photographer, Virginia Schau, won the 1954 Pulitzer Prize for spot photography with her picture of a man being rescued from a truck dangling from a bridge.[34] George Holliday's 1991 video of the police beating of an African American man named Rodney King became a media sensation when broadcast on a Los Angeles television station, and when the officers charged in the beating were acquitted a year later, six days of rioting broke out.[35]

In the aftermath of the bombing of the federal building in Oklahoma City on April 19, 1995, Charles H. Porter IV, a 25-year-old bank clerk, photographed a firefighter tenderly cradling a blood-stained child who was among the 168 people killed that morning. Three hours later, as a photo-service clerk handed over his prints, she happened to see the image of the firefighter and child, and she began to cry. The clerk's reaction convinced Porter he had something special.[36] He took it to a photographer friend, who put him in touch with The Associated Press' Oklahoma City bureau. His photograph went onto the AP wires and onto the front pages of newspapers worldwide. It too won a Pulitzer Prize.[37]

For the digital era, a defining moment for citizen news photography occurred during a wave of suicide bombings that killed 52 people in London on July 7, 2005. Three bombers attacked different trains in the London Underground within 50 seconds of each other and, about an hour later, another bombing occurred on a double-decker bus. Yuki Noguchi wrote in next morning's issue of *The Washington Post*:

> Some of the most intimate images of yesterday's bomb blasts in London came from cell phones equipped with cameras and video recorders, demonstrating how a technology originally marketed as entertainment has come to play a significant role in up-to-the-minute news.[38]

However, the journalist's sense of healthy skepticism is vital in screening social-media content. When Hurricane Sandy hit the East Coast in October 2012, an image of an ominous, circular cloud above the Statue of Liberty was tweeted thousands of times. Professionals debunked the image as a composite that had appropriated a cloud photographed in Nebraska in 2004 by a stormchaser, Mike Hollingshead. Another faked cloud photo, this one over the Manhattan skyline, was popular on Instagram. Even a real photo being circulated was phony in another way. A picture of soldiers guarding the Tomb of Unknown Soldier in a driving rain was presented as having been taken during the hurricane, but an image search showed that it was taken a month before Sandy hit.[39] Two images of sharks swimming in flooded streets in New Jersey after the hurricane also went viral on Twitter but were exposed as Photoshopped fakes.[40]

In 2013 a photograph of a giant beach ball on a London street during a driving rain was offered to *The Guardian*'s open-journalism platform, which allows readers to share their images and stories. It put the editors on guard against being hoaxed, because, as they said, the picture looked "too good to be true." Yet, after a rigorous check, they found it was indeed true. Until the storm, the ball – as tall as a double-decker bus – had been tethered to a building nearby. The bizarre image made for fascinating photojournalism.[41]

A Case Study accompanying this chapter, "Verifying a Key Boston Video," shows how professionals go about the task of testing the authenticity of social-media content that, if true, would be of news value.

Crowdsourcing is helping journalists develop important stories. In 2013 Elisabeth Rosenthal of *The New York Times* undertook a series of articles investigating why health costs in the United States were so much higher than in other developed countries. After her first story, about a woman who paid more than $6,000 for a routine colonoscopy that would cost under $1,000 elsewhere, the rest of Rosenthal's series told the personal stories of people who sent her online comments.[42] Those comments were solicited with the reporter's direct questions, such as "Tell us about an experience in a hospital that you thought was – or wasn't – worth the charges." Rosenthal told Margaret Sullivan, the paper's public editor, that she had received tens of thousands of comments: "They are a wonderful and intelligent resource for me, as a reporter. And they do keep you honest, as people bring up interesting objections to your ideas."[43]

In covering a tornado that hit their city on April 27, 2011, and killed 53 people, journalists of *The Tuscaloosa* (Alabama) *News* coped with an active rumor mill: "Bodies in the lake. Bodies on top of the mall. Bodies hidden by city officials in a locker somewhere outside of town." None of the stories were true. To investigate the most persistent rumors, *The News* created a blog that tried to find out where they came from, to get the facts from public officials, and to update information quickly. "The blog also gave readers a space to weigh in with their own evidence, which proved very useful," the paper's city editor, Katherine K. Lee, wrote in *Nieman Reports*. One of the most persistent rumors was that several children had died when the local Chuck E. Cheese was destroyed by the tornado. That rumor was disposed of when the restaurant's manager posted on the blog that she herself had closed the place before the storm hit.[44]

In a Point of View essay accompanying this chapter, "Declaring What You *Won't* Report," Craig Silverman, who has written extensively on accuracy in journalism, urges journalists to let the audience know in breaking-news situations "why a given piece of information hasn't met their standards." Before the digital age, news organizations tended to ignore information that they have checked out and discredited, even if the false story had been circulated widely. Silverman's approach could help news consumers sort fact from rumor in a fast-moving situation in which reporting by professionals and amateurs may run side by side in social media: "Rather than remaining silent about what they refuse to report, or cannot verify, news organizations should be vocal about where they stand."

Be on Guard against Hoaxes

The news media have always been a target of pranksters. In small towns across America, local papers and radio stations have learned to double-check obituaries and announcements of engagements and weddings. Failing to do so can result in embarrassment for the news organization, not to mention the anguish suffered by the subjects of the fake reports.

Sometimes the stakes are higher and the media victims bigger. The *Los Angeles Times* had to retract and apologize for a 2008 story based on purported FBI records in which a confidential informant accused two men of helping to arrange a 1994 attack on Tupac Shakur in which the rap star was pistol-whipped and shot three times. In the face of threats of lawsuits by the two accused men and a critical review by the investigative website The Smoking Gun, the *Times* concluded 10 days later that the FBI records appeared to be fakes.

The Smoking Gun showed that the records, which had been filed in court by a federal prisoner, looked as if they had been produced on a typewriter, though the FBI had been using computers for three decades. The *Times'* retraction said the website also pointed out "numerous misspellings and unusual acronyms and redactions that could have cast doubt on the documents' authenticity." The misspellings were similar to those in a lawsuit the same prisoner had filed.[45]

Today, as Craig Silverman has pointed out, "the complexity of verifying content from myriad sources in various mediums and in real time" is a formidable challenge. "This content can provide critical information during conflicts and natural disasters and provide clarity and color to a local event," he wrote for *Nieman Reports*:

> But it also takes the form of fraudulent messages and images engineered by hoaxers, manipulators and propagandists. Rumors and falsehoods spread just as quickly as, if not faster than, facts. In many cases they prove more compelling, more convincing, more clickable.[46]

Today, some of those "more clickable" stories that go viral on Twitter are finding their way into mainstream outlets that seem to have found the stories too good to check. Ryan Grim, Washington bureau chief for *The Huffington Post*, was quoted in a *New York Times* story about the phenomenon:

> The faster metabolism puts people who fact-check at a disadvantage. If you throw something up without fact-checking it, and you're the first one to put it up, and you get millions and millions of views, and later it's still proved false, you still got those views. That's a problem. The incentives are all wrong.[47]

In 2014 at least 30 news outlets spread the news that an organization named the Buckhead Neighborhood Coalition had been formed to protest the rock star Justin Bieber's supposed intention to move to Atlanta, saying Bieber would be "nothing but bad for our children." It turned out to be a hoax manufactured by a morning radio talk show, *The Regular Guys*.[48]

Another widely circulated story centered on an escalating exchange of rude notes on a Thanksgiving Day 2013 airline flight. The feud was supposedly between Elan Gale, a producer for *The Bachelor* television show, and a woman who irritated him by complaining loudly about her flight delay.[49] Gale's live tweets were picked up by BuzzFeed, which got more than 1.4 million reads, and then by other outlets. After Gale revealed that the story was fiction – and after BuzzFeed's update said it was a hoax – Gale took exception to the word *hoax* and said he was just "broadcasting to my followers who know what I do."[50]

A Case Study accompanying this chapter, "The Football Star's Fictitious Girl-friend," presents an elaborate hoax that went unchallenged by the mainstream news media. It is yet another situation in which someone should have asked, "How do you know that?"

Correcting the Record

Corrections of fact are routine in the news media today. The duty to acknowledge error was well established before the digital era arrived, an example of the maturing of journalism in the second half of the twentieth century. Until then, journalists disdained corrections because they did not want the public to think they made mistakes.

When errors occur in online reporting, news organizations should correct the mistakes and indicate what was wrong in an earlier version. Simply removing the error without flagging the story means that users who saw the earlier version are not cautioned that they were misinformed. In their book *Advancing the Story: Broadcast Journalism in a Multimedia World*, Debora Halpern Wenger and Deborah Potter recommended that news sites make their corrections policy clear to their users and provide an email address for reporting errors.[51]

Regarding errors committed on Twitter, Rachel E. Stassen-Berger of the *Star-Tribune* in Minneapolis has pointed out that if a journalist simply deletes a tweet, "that method does not acknowledge the error and can leave misinformation uncorrected, allowing it to spread." In a paper she wrote for the Online News Association's ethics code project, she cited this example of a Twitter correction by *The Washington Post*:

@washingtonpost
   Correction: Senate voted 68 to 32 to approve farm bill. Vote count was wrong in previous tweet wapo.st/1fsb1zV

"The correction clearly says the original information was wrong, notes the original tweet was deleted, and includes the correct information and a photo of the incorrect tweet," Stassen-Berger wrote: "The deletion means that the incorrect tweet can no longer be shared."[52]

For newspapers, a "best practice" is to publish corrections in an anchored position – that is, in the same location each day, to be easier for readers to find. If the essence of a front-page story is proved wrong, the corrective story should also appear on the front. This was the case on March 27, 2008, when the *Los Angeles Times* apologized for and corrected its Tupac Shakur story mentioned earlier.[53]

It is important to write corrections clearly. The reader should be able to understand what was wrong in the original story and what the story should have said. Some newspapers perpetuate the myth that a correction must not repeat the error, with the result that their corrections often are incomprehensible. *The Washington Post*'s policy states, "We generally do say exactly what was wrong, to make it absolutely clear what is being corrected."[54]

If an editor inserts a mistake in a reporter's story, some newspapers state in the correction that the misinformation was "due to an editing error." That is what Kathy English, public editor of the *Toronto Star*, thinks her paper should do. She wrote a column in 2014 urging reconsideration of a policy that states, "Publishing the *Star* is a team effort and published corrections do not ascribe blame within the *Star*." She mentioned a case in which an editor inserted the word *sarcastically* in reporting a tweet evidently sent sincerely by a candidate. As a result, English wrote, the *Star* reporter "was attacked on Twitter for a mistake he never made."[55]

For broadcast journalism, a problem is how to get a correction to the people who likely saw or heard the error, since the audience for subsequent newscasts may be different. In *Advancing the Story*, Wenger and Potter recommended correcting the mistake in the next newscast and then repeating the correction the next day in the newscast aired in the same time slot that the mistake was broadcast: "The goal is to make sure the correct information reaches the widest possible audience as well as to let people know that accuracy matters to the news organization."[56]

The late David Shaw, media critic for the *Los Angeles Times*, traced the history of news-media corrections in an article in the *Times* in 2004. Shaw reminisced about how, early in his career, editors regarded corrections as

> the airing of dirty laundry that would, they feared, undermine their papers' credibility. Thus, newspapers generally printed corrections only when they were threatened with libel suits or when their errors were so egregious that they had no choice – and then they tried to bury those corrections in the back of the paper, next to the ads for athlete's foot powder.

Shaw credited the Louisville *Courier-Journal* and *Times* as the first US newspapers, in 1967, to "institutionalize the practice of routinely publishing corrections in a prominent, designated place." By 1973, a quarter of the newspapers with circulations of over 100,000 had such a policy. The number grew in the 1990s, and the American Society of Newspaper Editors reported in 1999 that the practice was embraced by 93 percent of newspapers with a circulation of over 5,000.[57]

Point of View

Declaring What You *Won't* Report

Craig Silverman

It started with confusion at the scene of the crime in the schoolhouse in Newtown, Connecticut. A source told CNN the killer was named Ryan Lanza.

Soon several news organizations published images from a Facebook profile belonging to a man with that name. Some of them declared he was the killer.

He wasn't. It was his brother, Adam.

After we learned the caliber of the weapon used in the shooting, people began circulating images of large assault weapons, saying this was the gun used. Those early weapons were off the mark as well.

The errors continued. Adam Lanza's mother, whom he killed before going to the school,

didn't work at the school; the students who died were in first grade, not kindergarten.

In breaking-news situations, journalists must play a constructive role, rather than amplifying false information and adding to speculation.

One thing that struck me in the Newtown case was the news organizations that didn't spread the Facebook profile, the ones that showed restraint.

When information is abundant, rumors are easy to stoke and disseminate. When others have already put speculative information out there, showing restraint may seem difficult. But at that moment it can be a competitive differentiator.

During real-time news events, quality sources of information are sometimes characterized by

(Continued)

what they *aren't* reporting. They are the ones holding back while others rush ahead. The ones sticking to a verification process and not being swayed by speculation or a desire for traffic and attention.

The value of restraint is difficult to quantify. You don't get more traffic for what you don't report. It therefore seems like a losing proposition. As is often said, people remember who got it wrong, not who got it right. Or who held back.

During events such as the shooting in Newtown, one way to realize the value of restraint is to talk about what you *aren't* reporting. Carefully acknowledge the speculation ("A Facebook profile is circulating, but we are not confident it is the shooter and that's why we are not sharing it").

This seems counterintuitive to the value of restraint, but today's information environment requires that restraint itself be shared, be publicized. It must become part of the process of real-time journalism, and part of the conversation. That way people know who is and isn't reporting a given piece of information, and

why. It will help bring a measure of order and explanation by reminding people that information is not universally verified.

Rather than remaining silent about what they refuse to report, or cannot verify, news organizations should be vocal about where they stand.

I'd like to see restraint practiced and publicized, and to see more journalists speak up about why a given piece of information hasn't met their standards.

It also means we have to provide the kind of background and context that can help the public understand the new rules and practices that drive our work.

Craig Silverman is the author of *Regret the Error: How Media Mistakes Pollute the Press and Imperil Free Speech* (New York: Sterling, 2007) and an adjunct faculty member at the Poynter Institute. This is excerpted, with his permission, from an article he wrote for Poynter on December 17, 2012, reflecting on coverage of the fatal shooting of 20 children and six adults at Sandy Hook Elementary School three days earlier.

Point of View

Decision-Making in the Digital Age

James M. Naughton

We tend in newsroom discussions to separate news judgment from other aspects of the craft, as if it were something only a few people can master and for which they should be paid extra.

But making sound judgments is a responsibility of every journalist at every level in broadcast, print, or new media. We constantly

exercise news judgment in choosing what to report, whom to interview, whom to trust, how to illustrate, what to amplify, what to omit, how to make the story interesting, when to quote or paraphrase, when and where – or whether – to run the article, what the headline should be, when to follow up, and how to correct inevitable errors.

The problem nowadays is that we're expected to make the right calls on the run. We used to spend some of our time working to double- or triple-check information, to verify, to research context, to scour complementary and contradictory data, to think and then to craft an accurate and coherent account. Many journalists now spend valuable time scanning the Web and surfing cable channels to be sure they're not belated in disclosing what someone else just reported, breathlessly, using sources whose identity we'll never know.

The digital age does not respect contemplation. The deliberative news process is being sucked into a constant swirl of charge and countercharge followed by rebuttal and rebuttal succeeded by spin and counterspin leading to new charges and countercharges.

Now there are no cycles, only *Now*. A journalist today is apt to be wedging someone else's information into a story nanoseconds before air time or press run, without the debate about tone and propriety we Watergate geezers could have with our editors.

When it's all-news-all-over, the demand is too often for the *new*, not necessarily for *news*. We need to elevate, not debase, news judgment. Sound judgment pays homage to speed but reveres accuracy. News judgment can abet courage or invoke caution. News judgment is conscious and conscientious. It is authoritative but not judgmental. It relates the new to the known.

And it must not go out of fashion, no matter how difficult the circumstances now. Ignore "Hard Copy." Read Matt Drudge for entertainment, not sourcing. Muster courage to pursue your own story, one that can be vouched for. Tell the viewer or reader what we don't know, can't prove, didn't have time to figure out.

This is excerpted from an essay that the late James M. Naughton, then the president of the Poynter Institute, wrote for *The New York Times* on February 16, 1998.

Case Study

Richard Jewell: He Really Was a Hero

Richard Jewell, a security guard stationed in Atlanta's Centennial Park during the 1996 Summer Olympics, seemingly was in the right place at the right time in the early morning of July 27. Police had received an anonymous call at 12:58 a.m. warning that a bomb would explode in 30 minutes. Near his station in the park, Jewell noticed a suspicious backpack. After notifying an agent of the Georgia Bureau of Investigation, who summoned bomb technicians, Jewell helped to evacuate the area. The bomb exploded at 1:20 a.m., killing one person and injuring 111.

His rescue efforts made Jewell a media hero. Katie Couric interviewed him for NBC's *Today* show and told him, "You did the right thing, Richard."

His hero image was short-lived. On the afternoon of July 30, *The Atlanta Journal-Constitution* published an extra edition with the front-page

(Continued)

headline: "FBI suspects 'hero' guard may have planted bomb."

In the interim, a former employer of Jewell's had tipped the FBI about Jewell's erratic behavior as a college campus security guard. One possibility the FBI was examining in its investigation was whether Jewell, who aspired to be a police officer, might have set the bomb himself in order to be seen as a hero in clearing people out of the area. *Journal-Constitution* reporters soon picked up tips from law-enforcement officers that Jewell was being viewed as fitting "a profile." Those tips led to the July 30 extra edition.

Jewell never was charged. The FBI notified him three months later that he was not a target of its investigation. The Centennial Park bomb was actually planted by Eric Rudolph, who had also carried out other bombings in the South, including one in Birmingham, Alabama, that killed a police officer and maimed a nurse. Charged in the Centennial Park bombing in 1998, Rudolph eluded capture for five years in the mountains of North Carolina. He pleaded guilty and is serving life in prison.

On August 1, 2006, Governor Sonny Perdue honored Jewell at the Georgia State Capitol for having saved lives at Centennial Park. On August 30, 2007, Jewell died at age 44 after battling diabetes.

The *Journal-Constitution*'s July 30, 1996, story about Jewell presents two ethical questions. First, should he have been named, given that he had not been charged? Second, if the answer to the first question is yes, was the resulting story accurate and fair?

As for the first question, there is an element of risk whenever an uncharged suspect is identified in the media. Foremost, there is the risk to the subject of the story, whose reputation may be tarnished by the publicity, and this should be of grave concern to the journalists. And for the news organization, there is the possibility of a libel suit if the suspect is never charged; Jewell reached financial settlements with *The New York Post*, CNN, and NBC, and his suit against the *Journal-Constitution* was pending when he died.

In most cases editors and news directors wait to see if law-enforcement officers have enough evidence to file a charge. However, an argument can be made that identifying Jewell on July 30 was appropriate given the case's high profile and the *Journal-Constitution*'s solid information that Jewell was under suspicion. (Not only did the paper receive multiple tips, but a reporter read the story before publication to a law-enforcement agent who did not object to any of the statements about the investigation. The agent also assured the journalists that publishing the story would not hinder the investigation.) In any case, Jewell's status as a suspect would have become known the next day when FBI agents with a search warrant combed his home for evidence of bomb-making. The *Journal-Constitution*, whose elaborately detailed coverage of the Olympics was widely admired in the profession, obviously felt under pressure not to be beaten by competitors in any news story pertaining to the Olympics.

If Jewell were to be identified, then the newspaper had a special obligation to be fair to the uncharged suspect. To begin with, its story should have prominently noted two important facts: that Jewell had not been charged and that investigators had not revealed any physical evidence linking him to the crime.

The *Journal-Constitution*'s headline and 10-paragraph story did not make those disclaimers. It contained other problems of fairness, accuracy, and completeness. Those problems were discussed in a case study that *Los Angeles Times* journalist Ronald J. Ostrow wrote in 2003 for the Pew Research Center's Project for Excellence in Journalism. Ostrow wrote that the *Journal-Constitution*'s reporting that day was "coverage being shaped to support a conclusion."

The story did not quote any sources; instead, it employed what the paper calls "the voice of God." Ostrow wrote: "The voice of God approach means that the paper would not attribute the story to unnamed sources. Rather it would take the responsibility on itself, implying that not only has the paper learned these things, but vouches for their accuracy."

The lead paragraph's description of Jewell as "the focus" of the investigation lent itself to interpretation that he was the only person under suspicion. Ostrow said the reporters and editors struggled over how to describe Jewell before settling on this wording; one thought "focus" was a less damning description than "suspect." The journalists were aware that law-enforcement agents were looking at other possible suspects.

The story said Jewell "fits the profile of the lone bomber," including the characteristics of "a frustrated white man" and "a police wannabe." These prejudicial descriptions were gleaned from the reporters' conversations with investigators. The paper made a factual error in stating that Jewell had "approached newspapers … seeking publicity for his actions," overtures that would have fit the presumed profile.

The story said the warning call was made "on a phone a few minutes' walk from the park," an imprecise measurement given that 22 minutes elapsed between the call and the explosion. In fact, law-enforcement investigators had already concluded that the distance was too great for Jewell to have made the call and returned to the park to report spotting the backpack, Ostrow wrote. Later, Jewell's attorney said, "The theory of a person setting off a bomb to become a hero doesn't work if you have an accomplice."

The story contained subtle juxtapositions of fact that invite conclusions – including statements that, as a onetime deputy sheriff, Jewell had received bomb training, and that he owned a backpack similar to the one that contained the bomb. A conclusion is also suggested by conspicuously attributing to Jewell certain statements about his actions that were already established fact – that he spotted the backpack, that he pointed it out to a law-enforcement officer, and that he helped move people from the area. The story stated ominously, "Agents have not seen Jewell in NBC tape of the 20 minutes following the blast."

The story does not include a comment from Jewell, although the paper did try to talk with him. A reporter was sent to his apartment complex, which was being watched through binoculars by several men in plain clothes, but Jewell would not come to the door when she knocked. The reporter said he asked her to come back later when his mother returned. Before the story was published, another reporter made several unanswered phone calls to Jewell's apartment.

The *Journal-Constitution*'s story set off a media frenzy. On talk shows, commentators did not hesitate to speculate on Jewell's guilt.

L. Lin Wood, Jewell's attorney, later filed court papers describing a news environment in which "the media struggles to fill air time with different faces, different stories or different angles to known stories. The competition is intense and the profit potential is enormous." As a result, Wood said, "mistakes about individuals are published with increasing frequency and instantaneously broadcast and published to the world."

Even in such an environment, Ostrow wrote in his case study, the news media must continue "to meet their traditional standards

(Continued)

of fairness, accuracy and professional responsibility." If they do not, he wrote, "then news reporting as we have known and honored it would almost certainly disappear. There would no longer be a compelling reason for it to exist."

Sources

The Associated Press, "Richard Jewell honored at Georgia Capitol for heroism during 1996," Aug. 2, 2006.

BBC News, "Man admits Atlanta Olympics bomb," Apr. 13, 2005.

The New York Times, "Richard Jewell: The Wrong Man," Retro Report, Oct. 7, 2013. Contains a video. Retrieved on Sept. 3, 2014, from http://retroreport.org/richard-jewell-the-wrong-man/.

Ostrow, Ronald J. "Richard Jewell and the Olympic Bombing," Pew Research Center, June 13, 2000. The case study includes the text of the headline and story in The Atlanta Journal-Constitution's extra edition on July 30, 1996. The bombing killed one person, not two as stated in the case study.

Sack, Kevin, "Richard Jewell, 44, hero of Atlanta attack, dies," The New York Times, Aug. 30, 2007.

Questions for Class Discussion

- What lessons can journalists learn from studying this case?
- Do you agree with the journalists' decision to identify Jewell as someone who was being investigated?
- What do you think of "the voice of God" approach to writing the news story?
- Should "presumption of innocence" be a journalism principle as well as a judicial one?

Case Study

A Story of Rape at Mr. Jefferson's University

Magazine writer Sabrina Rubin Erdely knew she wanted to write about sexual assaults at an elite university. What she didn't know was which university.

So, for six weeks starting in June, Erdely interviewed students from across the country. She talked to people at Harvard, Yale, Princeton and her alma mater, the University of Pennsylvania. None of those schools felt quite right. But one did: the University of Virginia, a public school, Southern and genteel, brimming with what Erdely calls "super-smart kids" and steeped in the legacy of its founder, Thomas Jefferson.

What Erdely eventually found in Charlottesville shocked her, and it eventually shocked the nation.

Paul Farhi, "Sabrina Rubin Erdely"

Erdely's blockbuster story was posted on *Rolling Stone*'s website on November 19, 2014, and in the December 4 issue of the magazine.

In searing detail it described a gang rape of a Virginia student named Jackie, who had been introduced to the writer by a leader of a rape survivors' group.

In her narrative Jackie told how, as a first-year student in the fall of 2012, she and her date – "Drew," a pseudonym for a fellow lifeguard at the university aquatic and fitness center – went to a loud, boisterous party at the Phi Kappa Psi house on the University of Virginia's fraternity row. Lured to an upstairs room, she said, she was knocked to the floor and raped by seven men over three hours while "Drew" and another man "gave instruction and encouragement." She said she remembered the men urging on one of their group, "Don't you want to be a brother?" and "We all had to do it, so you do, too."

Adding to the horror, Jackie related that she was discouraged from reporting the incident when two men and a woman answered her call for help that night. At first, she said, one of the men, "Randall" (a pseudonym), suggested taking her to a hospital, which presumably would have led to a report to police. But, as they talked, the three decided the social price would be too high. The article quoted the female in the group, referred to as "Cindy": "She's gonna be the girl who cried 'rape,' and we'll never be allowed into any frat party again."

The account of rape and the indifference of Jackie's friends established the theme of Erdely's 9,000-word article. "At UVA rapes are kept quiet," Erdely wrote, "both by students – who brush off sexual assaults as regrettable but inevitable casualties of their cherished party culture – and by an administration that critics say is less concerned with protecting students than it is with protecting its own reputation from scandal."

When Erdely's story went online, the reaction at the university was immediate. Students and faculty took to the streets to demand reforms in how the administration handles rape complaints. Someone spray-painted "Suspend Us" on the Phi Kappa Psi house, and windows were shattered. The university president, Teresa Sullivan, who said the school "is too good a place to allow this evil to reside," suspended fraternity and sorority activities for the rest of the calendar year. The university's board of visitors voted for a zero-tolerance position on sexual assault. At the university's request, Charlottesville police began investigating Jackie's report of gang rape in 2012.

When *Washington Post* reporter Paul Farhi interviewed Erdely for a November 28 article, the magazine writer said she was surprised and gratified. "I was concerned, very late in the game, that no one would be willing to read this story. I thought the reaction would be 'We know about this problem,' and they'd turn the page."

Skepticism over the story

Even then, there was growing skepticism among journalists about an explosive story that relied on a single source.

"Something about this story doesn't feel right," Richard Bradley, editor and author, blogged on November 24. "One must be most critical about stories that play into existing biases," he wrote. "And this story nourishes a lot of them: biases against fraternities, against men, against the South; biases about the naivete of young women, especially Southern women; pre-existing beliefs about the prevalence – indeed the existence – of rape culture; extant suspicions about the hostility of university bureaucracies to sexual assault complaints that can produce unflattering publicity."

Critics called attention to the fact, reported by Farhi, that Erdely had not confronted Jackie's

(Continued)

alleged assailants to give them a chance to respond to her accusation. They also questioned why Erdely failed to interview the three friends who came to Jackie's aid on the night of the alleged assault, and why she decided to mask their identities.

In *The New York Times* on December 2, Ravi Somaiya reported that it was at Jackie's request that *Rolling Stone* had not contacted her assailants. Quoting "people familiar with the reporting process who declined to be publicly identified," Somaiya wrote: "*Rolling Stone* decided her situation was too delicate to risk acting against her wishes." (This was ultimately confirmed by the magazine.)

In Farhi's November 28 article for *The Post*, Erdely was quoted as saying that she found Jackie to be "completely credible." She said: "It's impossible to know for certain what happened in that room, because I wasn't in it. But I certainly believe that she described an experience that was incredibly traumatic to her."

Erik Wemple, *The Post*'s media critic, blogged on December 2 about the decision to rely on a single source: "For the sake of *Rolling Stone*'s reputation, Sabrina Rubin Erdely had better be the country's best judge of character."

In an article for *The Post* on December 1, Farhi wrote that Erdely was declining to answer specific questions about her reporting. He wrote that she told *The Post* in an email: "[B]y dwelling on this, you're getting sidetracked." According to Farhi, she said that, when Jackie told her account of the gang rape to the UVA administration, it "chose not to act on her allegations in any way – i.e, the overarching point of the article. THAT is the story: the culture that greeted her and so many other UVA women I interviewed, who came forward with allegations, only to be met with indifference."

The Post put together a team, led by reporter T. Rees Shapiro, to re-report *Rolling Stone*'s story.

The story collapses

On December 5 Shapiro wrote in *The Post* that, as their interviews raised questions about the story, it "began to unravel." Jackie's friends who are advocates for sex-assault awareness, he wrote, "believe that something traumatic happened to her, but they also have come to doubt her account. … The friends said that details of the attack have changed over time and that they have not been able to verify key points in recent days."

A key interview was with one of the three students who came to Jackie's aid on the night in question. This student insisted on anonymity but said Jackie "did not appear physically injured at the time but was visibly shaken" and said she "had been at a fraternity party and had been forced to have oral sex with a group of men." This student also said that, rather than discouraging Jackie from reporting the incident, "they offered to get her help and she said she just wanted to return to her dorm."

Phi Kappa Psi issued a statement, also on December 5, saying it had been cooperating with a police investigation and had reached the conclusion that the *Rolling Stone* account was untrue. The statement said that no "date function or social event" was scheduled on the night the rape was supposed to have occurred; no member of the fraternity was a lifeguard at the aquatic and fitness center or otherwise matched Jackie's description of her date in the *Rolling Stone* story; and, in keeping with interfraternity rules, there were no pledges during the fall semester. The statement said, "Moreover, no ritualized sexual assault is part of our pledging or initiating process. This notion is vile, and we vehemently refute this claim."

Shapiro wrote that in recent days Jackie had given her close friends the name of the man identified in the *Rolling Stone* article as "Drew," but the name was that of a student who belonged to a different fraternity. Reached by phone, this man, by then a UVA graduate, said he had been a lifeguard at the aquatic and fitness center and was familiar with Jackie's name, but he said he had never taken her on a date or even met her.

In the face of the revelations, *Rolling Stone* apologized for its story. In a statement posted on December 5 on the magazine's website, managing editor Will Dana explained:

> We published the article with the firm belief that it was accurate. Given all of these reports, however, we have come to the conclusion that we were mistaken in honoring Jackie's request to not contact the alleged assaulters to get their account. In trying to be sensitive to the unfair shame and humiliation many women feel after a sexual assault, we made a judgment – the kind of judgment reporters and editors make every day. We should not have made this agreement with Jackie and we should have worked harder to convince her that the truth would have been better served by getting the other side of the story.

As originally posted, Dana's statement included this sentence: "In the face of new information, there now appear to be discrepancies in Jackie's account, and we have come to the conclusion that our trust in her was misplaced."

The line about misplaced trust ignited another round of media criticism: Was *Rolling Stone* blaming its reporting failures on an apparently traumatized college student? Dana quickly responded by tweeting: "That failure is on us – not on her." In the magazine's online statement, the line was deleted and the following words

inserted: "These mistakes are on *Rolling Stone*, not on Jackie."

In the days that followed, more information came out. When Matt Stroud of The Associated Press interviewed the three students who answered Jackie's call, they agreed to allow him to use their real names. "Kathryn Hendley, Alex Stock, and Ryan Duffin are still trying to get the record straight," Stroud wrote on December 14, adding that they particularly wanted it known that they had not discouraged her from reporting the attack. In their interview with Stroud, the three students elaborated on what they had told *The Post* earlier in separate interviews without allowing their real names to be used.

The students said they had met Jackie at a picnic table outside Fitzhugh dormitory, a 20-minute walk from the fraternity house. Hendley (portrayed in *Rolling Stone* as "Cindy") told Stroud that, when she arrived, Jackie said she didn't want her to be a part of the conversation, and she "watched from afar while Stock and Duffin talked with Jackie."

Duffin ("Randall" in the *Rolling Stone* story) told Stroud that Jackie was shaking and "it looked like she had been crying. Her lip was quivering, her eyes were darting around." Eventually, Duffin said, Jackie told him and Stock that she had been forced to perform oral sex on five men at a fraternity house. Stroud's story quoted Duffin: "My first reaction was, 'We need to go to police,'" he said. "I wanted to go to police immediately. I was really forceful on that, actually. And I almost took it to calling [the police] right there." He said he had his phone out, prepared to call 911, "but she didn't want to, and," he remembers thinking, "I can't do that if she doesn't want to do it." Stroud wrote that Stock corroborated this version of events. "Jackie's response was, 'I don't want to,'" Stock

(Continued)

said, "'I don't want to do that right now. I just want to go to bed.'"

After *Rolling Stone* apologized for its story, one of Jackie's first-year dormitory suitemates, Emily Clark, wrote a letter that was published in *The Cavalier Daily*, UVA's student newspaper. She wrote that Jackie "came to UVA bright, happy and bubbly," but later that fall "I, as well as others, noticed Jackie becoming more and more withdrawn and depressed." Much later, she wrote, Jackie told her that "multiple men had assaulted her at this party. She didn't say anything more. It seemed that was all she'd allow herself to say." Declaring that Jackie's account "is not a hoax, a lie or a scheme," Clark asserted:

> Something terrible happened to Jackie at the hands of several men who have yet to receive any repercussions. Whether the details are correct or not, and whether the reporting was faulty, or the hazy memories of a traumatizing night got skewed … the blame should never fall on the victim's shoulders.

On December 5, the same day *Rolling Stone* apologized, university president Teresa Sullivan issued a statement reaffirming UVA's focus on the problem of sexual violence. She said, "The university remains first and foremost concerned with the care and support of our students and, especially, any survivor of sexual assault. Our students, their safety, and their well-being, remain our top priority."

Sources

Bradley, Richard, "Is the *Rolling Stone* story true?," Shots in the Dark, Nov. 24, 2014.

Clark, Emily, "A letter from a friend: Jackie's story is not a hoax," *The Cavalier Daily*, Dec. 7, 2014.

Erdely, Sabrina Rubin, "A rape on campus: a brutal assault and struggle for justice at UVA," *Rolling Stone*, Nov. 19, 2014. Includes the note to readers posted by Will Dana on Dec. 5 and revised on Dec. 7.

Farhi, Paul, "Sabrina Rubin Erdely, woman behind *Rolling Stone*'s explosive U-Va. alleged rape story," *The Washington Post*, Nov. 28, 2014.

Farhi, Paul, "Author of *Rolling Stone* article on alleged U-Va. rape didn't talk to accused perpetrators," *The Washington Post*, Dec. 1, 2014.

Farhi, Paul, "How *Rolling Stone* failed in its story of alleged rape at University of Virginia," *The Washington Post*, Dec. 5, 2014.

Shapiro, T. Rees, "Key elements of *Rolling Stone*'s U-Va. gang rape allegations in doubt," *The Washington Post*, Dec. 5, 2014.

Shapiro, T. Rees, "U-Va. students challenge *Rolling Stone* account of alleged sexual assault," *The Washington Post*, Dec. 10, 2014.

Somaiya, Ravi, "Magazine's account of gang rape on Virginia campus comes under scrutiny," *The New York Times*, Dec. 2, 2014.

Stroud, Matt, "Friends say they pushed U.Va. 'Jackie' to call cops," *The Washington Times*, Dec. 14, 2014.

The Washington Post, "In statement, U-Va. fraternity 'vehemently' denies rape claims," Dec. 5, 2014. Text of the statement by Phi Kappa Psi's Virginia Alpha chapter.

Wemple, Erik, "*Rolling Stone* whiffs in reporting on alleged rape," *The Washington Post*, Dec. 2, 2014. Includes a partial transcript of Erdely's interview with *Slate* in a Nov. 27, 2014, podcast.

Wemple, Erik, "Updated apology digs deeper hole for *Rolling Stone*," *The Washington Post*, Dec. 7, 2014.

Questions for Class Discussion

- Do you think *Rolling Stone* would have run the story as written if the reporter had found any of the alleged perpetrators and asked them to respond to Jackie's allegations? If the reporter had interviewed the three students who responded to Jackie's distress call?
- How should *Rolling Stone* have responded to Jackie's request that the alleged perpetrators not be contacted?

- In general, what ethics issues are involved when a story is based on a single source, particularly if that source's identity is to be withheld?
- How can news organizations guard against erroneous stories short of sending out a second reporter to re-report everything that might be controversial?

Case Study

The Football Star's Fictitious Girlfriend

As linebacker Manti Te'o was leading his Notre Dame football team to an undefeated regular season in 2012, some sportswriters were attracted to an off-field saga involving the young Hawaiian who had made All-America both athletically and academically. It was a prototypical human-interest story, one that was hard to resist.

These reporters wrote about how Te'o was involved in a long-distance relationship with a 22-year-old Stanford graduate who had been in a horrific automobile accident in California and then diagnosed with leukemia. And how, days after learning that the girlfriend and his grandmother had both died, a determined Te'o collected a dozen tackles in Notre Dame's 20–3 victory over Michigan State on September 15, 2012.

In one of its stories, the *South Bend Tribune* described the scene as the couple met after the Notre Dame–Stanford game in 2009: "Their stares got pleasantly tangled, then Manti Te'o extended his hand to the stranger with a warm

Figure 12.1   Manti Te'o at Notre Dame.
PHOTO BY JOE RAYMOND. REPRINTED BY PERMISSION OF THE ASSOCIATED PRESS.

(Continued)

smile and soulful eyes." Detailed accounts of the star-crossed romance also appeared in *Sports Illustrated* and on ESPN and CBS, among other media outlets.

On January 16, 2013, Deadspin shattered the myth. The sports website posted a 4,000-word investigative story headlined "Manti Te'o's dead girlfriend, the most heartbreaking and inspirational story of the college football season, is a hoax."

Piece by piece, the writers Jack Dickey and Timothy Burke dismantled the story lines. The girlfriend, Lennay Kekua, had never existed. She had been created by a male acquaintance of Te'o's who later admitted having impersonated Lennay in hours-long phone calls with Te'o night after night. Lennay never went to Stanford, was never in a car wreck, and did not get leukemia – nor did she ever meet Manti Te'o.

After Deadspin's revelations, the Notre Dame athletic director, Jack Swarbick, and Te'o issued statements decrying the hoax. The statement from Te'o said in part: "To realize that I was the victim of what was apparently someone's sick joke and constant lies was, and is, painful and humiliating."

Notre Dame had been aware of the hoax since December 26, when, university officials said, Te'o came to them and revealed that Lennay never existed and that he had been duped. The university immediately hired outside investigators, and their report confirming the hoax came back on January 4. (That was three days before the national championship game, which Notre Dame lost to Alabama, 42–14.) With the report in hand, Notre Dame decided there was no violation of laws or NCAA rules, and Swarbick said the hoax would be Te'o's "story to tell."

Ned Zeman, recounting the Deadspin investigation for *Vanity Fair* in June 2013,

wrote that the website was tipped to the hoax on January 11 by an anonymous email purportedly from someone in Laie, Hawaii, the Te'o family's hometown. "The story about his girlfriend dying is completely made up," the tipster wrote. The tipster also reported a rumor circulating on Oahu that Te'o had been duped by "a man pretending to be this girl, Lennay Kekua." Dickey and Burke took only four days to uncover the hoax and another day to write their story.

They started with a Google search of "Lennay Kekua," which showed that she existed only in stories about Manti Te'o; "otherwise, she was a person without any digital footprint of her own aside from one thumbnail avatar photo that appeared in every news story," Zeman wrote. The reporters also discovered that the news accounts disagreed about details such as when her accident had occurred, when she had died of leukemia, and where her funeral was held.

"You can learn a lot about what happened by looking at the contradictions between other journalists' stories," Burke said afterward in an email Q&A with Mallary Jean Tenore of the Poynter Institute. "That was what tipped us off, after all, that something was weird here. Major news organizations disagreed on the date of a person's death by up to four days."

The reporters also checked with Stanford and learned that Lennay Kekua had never been enrolled. They found sources who led them to Ronaiah Tuiasosopo, a 22-year-old onetime high school quarterback who was leading the band at a California church where his father was pastor. The reporters confirmed that he was acquainted with T'eo and that the two had exchanged messages on Twitter. One of Deadspin's sources said that Tuiasosopo created Lennay in 2008 and that, before Te'o was involved, he "introduced" her online to another man. That relationship lasted about a month "before family members grew suspicious that Lennay could never be found on the telephone, and that wherever one expected Lennay to be, Ronaiah was there instead," according to the Deadspin story.

When the reporters traced the avatar photo to someone who was not Lennay Kekua, the hoax was confirmed.

As Dickey and Burke wrote in their January 16 story, they used "an exhaustive related-images search of each of Lennay's images (most of which had been modified in some way to prevent reverse image searching)." They determined that the avatar was an image of a California woman whom they assigned the pseudonym "Reba" to protect her identity. She confirmed that the avatar photo was "a picture of me from my Facebook account." "Reba," it turned out, was a high school classmate of Tuiasosopo and unaware that she had become the face of Lennay. When the reporters sent her photos that had appeared on Lennay's Twitter account, they wrote, "one picture in particular brought Reba to a start." She said she had sent that photo to Tuiasosopo at his request. Now she called Tuiasosopo to ask questions – questions to which he responded by "acting weird" – and the photo was quickly deleted. After that, the reporters wrote, "Reba" had a series of lengthy phone calls in which "she told us everything she knew" about Tuiasosopo. (Since the Deadspin article, "Reba" has come forward under her real name, Diane O'Meara.)

Dickey and Burke's story suggested that Te'o was a willing participant rather than a victim of the hoax, but in doing so they relied on anonymous sources. The story quoted a friend of Tuiasosopo as saying he was "80 percent sure" Te'o was "in on it" because Tuiasosopo's

Instagram account contained photos of him and Te'o together. The story said "the sheer quantity of falsehoods" led the friend and "another relative of Tuiasosopo" to believe Te'o "had to know the truth." However, Te'o's claim that he was an innocent victim has never been disproved.

While Dickey and Burke employed the tools of sophisticated technology, their investigation was driven mainly by a sense of skepticism and the basic reporting skill of asking good questions. They took an anonymous tip and checked it out.

Tommy Craggs, editor-in-chief of Deadspin, told Mallary Jean Tenore of Poynter that Dickey and Burke compiled their notes in a Google Docs file that became "a skeleton" for the final story. "They asked themselves the obvious questions, socratically: Who is the person in the photos? Where was Lennay Kekua born? When was Lennay Kekua born? Where did Lennay Kekua live? Did Lennay Kekua attend Stanford? When was Lennay Kekua's car accident? When did Lennay Kekua die?" He said they tried to answer those questions through public records, where they found nothing, and media reports, where they found plenty, "contradictions and all."

From there, Craggs said, "the story wrote itself. That's all pretty obvious, and anyone who reports a story like this goes through at least a mental catechism like this. But putting it all on the page made the holes in the Lennay story plain to see."

Why didn't other reporters do that kind of checking before they wrote about Lennay? Actually, two of them did make inquiries but did not follow up when they could not verify basic facts.

Pete Thamel, who wrote a cover story on the Manti–Lennay romance for the October 1, 2012,

(Continued)

issue of *Sports Illustrated*, acknowledged on Dan Patrick's syndicated radio show that he found "small red flags" when he tried to check out the girlfriend. He said he could not find an obituary or any record of her on LexisNexis. Since the existence of the girlfriend was taken as a given at Notre Dame, and since he had talked about Lennay with a Notre Dame priest, Te'o's teammates, and Teo's father, he decided to "write around it." Thamel said in an NPR telephone interview: "It's a great lesson for me, for anyone who's a journalist, to keep being skeptical, even in stories that are not at the start inherently ones that make you skeptical."

Gene Wojciechowski, who reported on the romance on ESPN, said in an interview on his network that he tried unsuccessfully to find an obituary on Lennay and, when he asked Te'o how to get a photo of his girlfriend, he was persuaded not to intrude on the family's grief. "It's easy to say now, but at the time it never enters your mind that somebody was involved in that kind of hoax," Wojciechowki said. "We wanted to believe it so much."

For the journalism profession, what lessons are to be learned from the Manti Te'o story?

John McIntyre of *The Baltimore Sun* wrote on his blog: "[W]hile reporters are supposed to be responsible for the factual accuracy of their accounts, other responsible parties are involved in these fiascoes. There are supposed to be editors who ask hard questions. There is supposed to be skepticism."

Ken Armstrong, a Pulitzer Prize-winner for *The Seattle Times*, in an interview with Richard Deitsch of *Sports Illustrated*'s website, said that "this kind of mythologizing – 'Win one for the Gipper,' the Babe's called shot to center field – is not limited to sports." In the wars in Iraq and Afghanistan, he said, the US Army got the media to buy into false stories about Jessica Lynch and Pat Tillman. (Lynch was wounded and briefly captured in Iraq in 2003; she did her duty honorably but was not the hero the army made her out to be. Tillman, the former pro football player who enlisted in the Rangers, was reported by the army to have been killed as he attacked the enemy in Afghanistan in 2004; he was actually killed accidentally by fire from American soldiers.) Armstrong said, "The lessons of the Te'o story – the need to be wary of inspirational tales with details that run light or are contradictory – extend beyond the playing field."

Amy Nutt of *The Newark Star-Ledger*, another Pulitzer winner, said in an interview with Deitsch: "The real problem was quite simple: the story of the girlfriend's death, like so many stories today that turn out not to be true, was a single-source story. … [A]ll you knew was what a college football player just told you."

Steve Buttry, who blogs on journalism issues, wrote that if the journalists covering the story had used an accuracy checklist, they "would have found lots of red flags and no verification." In the online versions he also noted a lack of links to related content to provide context and attribution; a journalist who wanted to link to Lennay's obituary would have found nothing. And that should have signaled caution.

Jack Shafer, the Reuters media critic, wrote that "the cumulative force of repetition" may have dissuaded reporters from being suspicious. In other words, the same story had been told many times before, so it must be true. In a column after the Deadspin story came out, Shafer wrote: "[R]eporters tend to believe – but shouldn't – things that get retold."

Josh Levin, executive editor of *Slate*, saw "confirmation bias" – the tendency of humans to accept information that confirms their existing belief and to dismiss any information to the contrary. "This was journalism as fill-in-the-blank exercise," he wrote in his critique, "the creation of a simple story that tells you what you already know. In this case, what we already knew happened not to be the truth."

Sources

Burke, Timothy, and Jack Dickey, "Manti Te'o's dead girlfriend, the most heartbreaking and inspirational story of the college football season, is a hoax," Deadspin, Jan. 16, 2013.

Buttry, Steve, "Linking and checklists could have prevented journalists from Manti Te'o 'girlfriend' hoax embarrassment," The Buttry Diary, Jan. 17, 2013.

Cacciola, Scott, "After inquiry, Notre Dame decided revealing Te'o hoax was up to him," *The New York Times*, Jan. 17, 2013.

Cherry, Kendra, "What is confirmation bias?," About.com/Psychology.

Deitsch, Richard, "Pulitzer Prize-winners discuss Manti Te'o story," *Sports Illustrated*, Jan. 21, 2013.

Folkenflik, David, "The Manti Te'o story: why the news media let its guard down," NPR, Jan. 18, 2013.

Koblin, John, "How *Sports Illustrated*'s Manti Te'o story got published," Deadspin, Jan. 17, 2013. This story links to Pete Thamel's six-minute telephone interview on the syndicated *Dan Patrick Show*.

Levin, Josh, "The fake girlfriend experience," *Slate*, Jan. 16, 2013.

McIntyre, John, "We're supposed to be skeptical," *The Baltimore Sun*, Jan. 17, 2013.

Rieder, Rem, "A colossal hoax," *American Journalism Review*, Dec. 2012–Jan. 2013.

Shafer, Jack, "Manti Te'o and the press get blitzed," Reuters, Jan. 17, 2013.

Sonderman, Jeff, "Notre Dame football player Te'o girlfriend hoax 'became truth through the media,'" Poynter, Jan. 16, 2013.

Tenore, Mallary Jean, "Deadspin's Burke: Te'o story shows 'diminished role' of investigative journalism," Poynter, Jan. 17, 2013.

Tenore, Mallary Jean, "Deadspin's editor-in-chief explains editing, reporting behind Manti Te'o story," Poynter, Jan. 17, 2013.

Zeman, Ned, "The boy who cried dead girlfriend," *Vanity Fair*, June 2013.

Questions for Class Discussion

- How does this case demonstrate the importance of skepticism in journalism?
- Why is it important to pay attention to a tip, which, if true, could result in a significant news story?
- What were the technological tools the Deadspin reporters used?
- How did the reporters use basic reporting skills?
- Should Deadspin have quoted anonymous sources speculating on whether Te'o was involved in the hoax?
- What can editors do to head off the reporting of stories that may be hoaxes?
- What is your reaction to Shafer's theory of "the cumulative force of repetition" in the case?
- What is your reaction to Levin's theory of "confirmation bias"?

Case Study

Verifying a Key Boston Video

Malachy Browne

One of the iconic videos of the tragic bombings at the Boston Marathon on April 15, 2013, was filmed by an athlete running her final mile of the marathon. As she approached the finish line on Boylston Street, the second bomb detonated meters ahead. It was a compelling video, but we at Storyful needed to verify it.

One photo showing the moment of the blast was posted by Boston journalist Dan Lampariello, a member of one of our pre-curated Twitter lists, and someone familiar to Storyful. Lampariello's tweet was geolocated to Boylston Street; this information, which came from a reliable source, helped to confirm the location of the explosion. It also gave us a reference point to use with what was shown in the runner's video.

A Google Street View of Boylston Street confirmed both Dan Lampariello's photo and the athlete's point of view as she approached the finish line. Indeed, some of the athletes filmed in the video could be seen in Lampariello's photo upon close inspection.

That process confirmed the content of the video. Finding the original source of this video was less straightforward.

The video itself was uploaded to a YouTube account with no giveaway details and an obscure username, NekoAngel3Wolf. Searching Twitter for the unique video code led us to someone sharing it under the handle NightNeko3, again with no personal details. The "Neko" reference in both profiles suggested they were related.

Searching for similar social profiles, we found a Pinterest account also registered as NightNeko3, giving the real name Morgan Treacy. Our team at Storyful quickly located a Facebook account for Morgan Treacy, a teenager whose posts were geolocated to Ballston Spa, in upstate New York.

Morgan described the video on Twitter as her mother's perspective of the explosion. Knowing that a prestigious marathon like Boston's would likely track athlete times, we checked the surname "Treacy" on Boston Athletic Association's registrant page. A single result was returned: Jennifer Treacy, age 45–49, from New York State. Jennifer Treacy's time split shows her passing the 40-kilometer mark at 2:38 p.m. but failing to cross the finish line two kilometers later. Jennifer was averaging 10 minutes per mile, placing her in the vicinity of the blast at 2:50 p.m., when the bombs exploded.

The social people search website Spokeo gave us an entry for Jennifer L. Treacy, 47, with an address at Ballston Spa, New York. LinkedIn also gave us a profile for Jennifer Treacy from Ballston Spa, who is employed by the New York State Department of Health.

One final piece of evidence confirmed our investigation. A man named Gerard Quinn is a Facebook friend of Morgan Treacy, who we were now almost 100 percent sure was Jennifer's daughter. Quinn previously commented on family videos posted by Morgan. So there was a link between him and the family. We saw on Quinn's Facebook profile that he had expressed pride that his niece, Jennifer, was running the Boston Marathon. He'd linked to her marathon map and time splits. He also later commented on Facebook that Jennifer was OK after the blast and on her way home.

A public telephone directory produced a phone number that allowed us to speak directly to Jennifer Treacy. She confirmed that the video was hers and that news organizations were permitted to use it. She had also informed law enforcement agencies of the video, she said.

In summary, all of the information supporting the veracity of this video was available online via free tools – location information, corroborating accounts of the event, the uploader's digital history, and the owner's contact details. Familiarity with these tools allowed us to verify the video in around 10 minutes.

Malachy Browne is an editor at the Dublin headquarters of Storyful, the first news agency of the social-media age. This Case Study is reprinted, with permission, from *Verification Handbook: An Ultimate Guideline on Digital Age Sourcing for Emergency Coverage* (Maastricht, The Netherlands: European Journalism Centre, 2014). The video was retrieved on Sept. 4, 2014, from https://www.youtube.com/watch?v=WIAfyYQzZaM.

Questions for Class Discussion

- Why did Storyful need to verify the authenticity of the video?
- What were the two kinds of verification Browne was seeking?
- Why was it important to Browne that he talk with Jennifer Treacy herself?
- Are you surprised that the video was verified so quickly?

Notes

1 Alicia C. Shepard, "NPR's Giffords mistake: relearning the lesson of checking sources," NPR, Jan. 11, 2011.

2 Jeff Sonderman, "CNN, Fox err in covering Supreme Court health care ruling," Poynter, June 28, 2012.

3 "Timeline: Colorado theater shooting," CNN.

4 Dylan Byers, "ABC News apologizes for 'incorrect' tea party report," *Politico*, July 20, 2012.

5 Ibid.

6 David Folkenflik, "Coverage rapid, and often wrong, in tragedy's early hours," NPR, Dec. 18, 2012.

7 Doug Stanglin, "ID mixup of shooter prompts Facebook plea: 'It wasn't me,'" *USA Today*, Dec. 15, 2012.

8 "Boston Marathon terror attack fast facts," CNN.

9 Jon Terbush, "*N.Y. Post* under fire for misidentifying Boston bombing 'suspects,'" *The Week*, Apr. 18, 2013.

10 Erik Martin, "Reflections on the recent Boston crisis," Reddit Blog, Apr. 22, 2013. Martin is general manager of Reddit.

11 "What happened inside Building 197?," *The Washington Post*, updated Sept. 25, 2013.

12 Byers, "CBS, NBC retract Navy Yard shooter reports," *Politico*, Sept. 16, 2013.

13 Shepard, "NPR's Giffords mistake."

14 Details of the Supreme Court ruling from Adam Liptak, "Supreme Court upholds health care law, 5–4, in victory for Obama," *The New York Times*, June 28, 2012.

15 Byers, "ABC News apologizes for 'incorrect' tea party report."

16 Jack Shafer, "Newtown teaches us, once again, to discount early reports," Reuters, Dec. 17, 2012.

17 Rem Rieder, "On Boston bombing, media are wrong – again," *USA Today*, Apr. 18, 2013.

18 Amy Hunter, "CNN's King says mistakes last week were 'embarrassing,'" WTOP, Apr. 23, 2013.

19 Rieder, "Big errors in Navy shooting coverage," *USA Today*, Sept. 17, 2013.

20 Paul Farhi, "When news breaks, scanners and social media can create a cloud of errors for news outlets," *The Washington Post*, Sept. 16, 2013.

21　Author's telephone interview with Bob Steele, Sept. 7, 2007.

22　Steele, "Ethical values and quality control in the digital era," *Nieman Reports*, Winter 2008.

23　"SPJ Code of Ethics," SPJ, revised Sept. 6, 2014.

24　Bill Marimow, email to the author, Nov. 10, 2007.

25　"SPJ Code of Ethics," SPJ.

26　Quoted in Robert J. Haiman, *Best Practices for Newspaper Journalists* (Arlington, VA: Freedom Forum's Free Press/Fair Trial Project, 2008), 58.

27　Thomas Patterson and Philip Seib, "Informing the public," in Geneva Overholser and Kathleen Hall Jamieson (eds.), *The Press* (Oxford: Oxford University Press, 2005), 193.

28　Richard Oppel, former editor of the Austin (Texas) *American-Statesman*, made this point in a quotation in Haiman, *Best Practices for Newspaper Journalists*, 58.

29　Allan M. Siegal and William G. Connolly, *The New York Times Manual of Style and Usage* (New York: Times Books, 1999), 127–128.

30　Marimow, email, Nov. 10, 2007.

31　Eric Carvin, "User-generated content," paper written for the Online News Association (2014).

32　David Carr, "View of #Ferguson thrust Michael Brown shooting to national attention," *The New York Times*, Aug. 17, 2014.

33　Mark Little, "Finding wisdom in the crowd," *Nieman Reports*, Summer 2012.

34　Dan Gillmor, "Rodney King and the rise of the citizen photojournalist," Mediactive, Mar. 2, 2011.

35　Ibid.

36　Dean Lucas, "Oklahoma City bombing," Famous Picture Collection.

37　Joe Strupp, "The photo felt around the world," *Editor & Publisher*, May 13, 1995.

38　Yuki Noguchi, "Camera phones lend immediacy to images of disaster," *The Washington Post*, July 8, 2005.

39　Fiona McCann, "How to spot a fake," in Claire Wardle (ed.), *Social Newsgathering: A Collection of Storyful Blog Posts* (Dublin: Storyful, 2013), 28–32, online book retrieved on Sept. 3, 2014, at http://blog.storyful.com/wp-content/uploads/sites/5/2013/02/SocialNewsgather.pdf.

40　Tom Phillips, "Verifying two suspicions 'street sharks' during Hurricane Sandy," in Craig Silverman (ed.), *Verification Handbook: An Ultimate Guideline on Digital Age Sourcing for Emergency Coverage* (Maastricht, The Netherlands: European Journalism Centre, 2014), 44–46, online book retrieved on Sept. 3, 2014, at http://verificationhandbook.com/downloads/verification.handbook.pdf.

41　Philippa Law and Caroline Bannock, "Verifying a bizarre beach ball during a storm," in Silverman (ed.), *Verification Handbook*, 42–43.

42　Paul Raeburn, "Elisabeth Rosenthal's dazzling series on healthcare costs at the *New York Times*," Knight Science Journalism at MIT, Apr. 7, 2014.

43　Margaret Sullivan, "For some, reader contributions become a new reporting tool," *The New York Times*, Mar. 17, 2014.

44　Katherine K. Lee, "Taking on the rumor mill," *Nieman Reports*, Summer 2012.

45　James Rainey, "The *Times* apologizes over article on rapper," *Los Angeles Times*, Mar. 27, 2008.

46　Craig Silverman, "A new age for truth," *Nieman Reports*, Summer 2012.

47　Ravi Somaiya and Leslie Kaufman, "If a story is viral, truth may be taking a beating," *The New York Times*, Dec. 9, 2013.

48　Sydney Smith, "Justin Bieber Atlanta protests: 30+ news outlets hoaxed," iMedia Ethics, Feb. 24, 2014.

49　David Weigel, "If you want reporters to check stories before they publish, you're a hater," *Slate*, Dec. 3, 2013.

50　Somaiya and Kaufman, "If a story is viral, truth may be taking a beating."

51　Debora Halpern Wenger and Deborah Potter, *Advancing the Story: Broadcast Journalism in a Multimedia World* (Washington, DC: CQ Press, 2007), 276.

52　Rachel E. Stassen-Berger, "Corrections," paper written for the Online News Association (2014).

53　Rainey, "The *Times* apologizes over article on rapper."

54　Romenesko, Jim, "*Washington Post* updates its online correction policies," JimRomenesko.com, Jan. 16, 2013.

55　Kathy English, "Do we need more transparency in corrections?," *Toronto Star*, May 30, 2014.

56　Wenger and Potter, *Advancing the Story*, 275.

57　David Shaw, "Papers must write it up when they get it wrong," *Los Angeles Times*, June 13, 2004.

13 Dealing with Sources of Information

The fine line between getting close but not too close

Learning Goals

This chapter will help you understand:

- ethical issues in reporter–source relationships;
- a journalist's ethical obligation to protect a confidential source;
- the challenges of cultivating sources while maintaining independence in beat reporting; and
- recurring situations that pose ethical issues in dealing with sources.

For more than five years, Nancy Phillips had cultivated Len Jenoff as a source in her reporting for *The Philadelphia Inquirer* about the 1994 murder by bludgeoning of Carol Neulander, a rabbi's wife in suburban Cherry Hill, New Jersey. She had bought meals for Jenoff, had listened endlessly to his stories, and had given his wife her recipe for latkes. The couple sent her postcards from vacation resorts and holiday cards at Hanukkah.

Now, on December 9, 1999, Jenoff was giving her electrifying news: The rabbi, Fred J. Neulander, had paid him to arrange the murder.

But there was no story in the next morning's paper. At Jenoff's insistence, Phillips' conversation with the self-styled private investigator had been *off the record*, meaning that she was bound by a reporter's honor not to publish what he told her. "I can't believe I'm telling you this," Jenoff said. Moments later, he pleaded: "Please don't hurt me with this, Nancy. … I may have to take this to the grave."

Phillips left his house shaken, suspecting that he might be telling the truth even though his conversations in the past had been riddled with lies. "But I was in a bind," she wrote in a first-person story in *The Inquirer* much later: "He would not give me permission to tell the story, and because I had agreed to keep his confidence, I had to honor that and could not tell the authorities." In keeping with the paper's policy, she did tell her editors what Jenoff had told her. They agreed that she should honor the confidentiality commitment, and they shared her skepticism of Jenoff.

Four months passed as Phillips anguished over the secret. She prodded Jenoff to go to the authorities. On April 28, 2000, after she and Jenoff shared a pizza at a Cherry Hill restaurant, he asked her to ride with him to visit two places in Philadelphia

---

The Ethical Journalist: Making Responsible Decisions in the Digital Age, Second Edition. Gene Foreman.
© 2016 John Wiley & Sons, Inc. Published 2016 by John Wiley & Sons, Inc.

that had figured in the crime. As he drove, she urged him to go to the prosecutor's office right then. With his consent, she called Prosecutor Lee A. Solomon on her cell phone.[1] For three hours, a hit man, a reporter, a prosecutor, and a homicide detective sat in a booth at a diner. They drank coffee (the prosecutor had six cups). And they talked about murder.[2]

Jenoff's confession broke the case. He implicated the rabbi and named his accomplice, Paul Michael Daniels. The authorities had filed murder charges in 1998 against Rabbi Neulander, for arranging his wife's murder. But they had never found the weapon and had not charged anyone with carrying out the fatal bludgeoning. After the confession in the diner, police wired Jenoff and monitored a conversation he had with Daniels. When they heard the two men discuss the crime, they moved in and arrested them.[3]

Jenoff told Phillips at the end of the meeting in the diner: "You can now tell the story."[4] Nine days later, *The Inquirer* published Phillips' first-person account. It was the last story she wrote about the case she had covered so long with skill and persistence. Having become a participant in the story, she could no longer cover it for *The Inquirer*.

Neulander, Jenoff, and Daniels all went to prison. The rabbi's motive for plotting his wife's murder was that he wanted to marry another woman but avoid the scandal of a divorce, which would probably have caused him to lose his synagogue. The hit men testified at his trial that Neulander had paid them $30,000 to kill his wife, and they had beaten her to death with metal pipes. Neulander was convicted and sentenced to life. Jenoff and Daniels pleaded guilty and were sentenced to a maximum of 23 years each.[5] In January 2014, having served his mandatory minimum of 10 years, Jenoff walked out of Mid-State Correctional Facility in Wrightstown, New Jersey.[6]

For all its drama, the episode illustrates the ethical issues that reporters face regularly in dealing with their **sources**.

The first issue is Phillips' conviction that she should respect Jenoff's confidence. It would have been easy for her to rationalize that, because he was certainly a liar and quite likely a murderer, she had no moral obligation to keep her off-the-record promise. That is not the way Nancy Phillips saw it. "In this profession, we live and die on our ability to keep every promise we make to everybody, large and small," Phillips told Howard Kurtz, then *The Washington Post's* media writer. "This, of course, was an extreme circumstance. … When we laid down the rules, I obviously didn't know what was going to come out of his mouth."[7]

The second issue is the question of who is entitled to the journalist's first loyalty. Prosecutor Solomon said that, when journalists learn someone has committed a murder, they "have a moral and ethical obligation to step forward," Alicia C. Shepard reported in *American Journalism Review*. But Robert J. Rosenthal, then the editor of *The Inquirer*, told Shepard that journalists' duty is to publish stories for the people, not to help the police: "It's crucial for our long-term credibility to not be seen as a branch of law enforcement." Ethics scholar Louis W. Hodges of Washington and Lee University agreed that sources would evaporate if journalists were seen as working for the police, although there are exceptions, such as if a journalist knows that someone is about to commit a serious crime.[8]

The third issue is the matter of cultivating a source who might, as Jenoff eventually did, tell the reporter something of importance to the public. As discussed in Chapter 10, cultivating sources is "an essential skill, often practiced most effectively in informal settings outside of normal business hours … but [reporters] must keep in mind the difference between legitimate business and personal friendship."[9] The process is something of a paradox – the journalist needs to get close enough to gain the source's confidence even while maintaining sufficient distance from the source to be able to report as an independent observer. (Jeffrey Fleishman's Point of View essay "Sometimes, Different Rules Apply" poignantly relates a rare exception to the rule.)

Phillips' long conversations with Jenoff covered a range of subjects, including their shared Jewish religion. But throughout, she said, she made it clear to Jenoff that she was a reporter and not his friend. Even so, there were nasty insinuations. Before Neulander's trial, the rabbi's lawyers said Jenoff had told fellow jail inmates of having "a personal, physical relationship" with Phillips. To this, the reporter responded: "Let me be clear: As a reporter, I have conducted myself at all times as a professional."[10]

The Jenoff episode also raised a question that is unusual in reporter–source relationships. Though unintentionally, the reporter became part of the story she was covering. The circumstance of Jenoff's off-the-record murder confession ultimately required Phillips to cross the line between observer and participant. She decided that she had to become an adviser to Jenoff, pushing him to tell the authorities what he had done. When he finally did this – and when he released her from her pledge of confidentiality – she wrote her detailed account of the entire episode for *Inquirer* readers, disclosing her own participation in the story.

Ethics in Reporter–Source Relationships

Unless they witness a news event themselves, journalists depend on other people for the information they report to their readers, viewers, listeners, and online users. Some of these *sources* saw the event themselves. Others possess expertise that could help the journalists' audience evaluate what is known about the event. This chapter discusses ethical issues in journalists' dealings with sources.

The SPJ code of ethics, under the guiding principles of "seek truth and report it," "minimize harm," and "act independently," tells journalists to:

- Identify sources clearly. The public is entitled to as much information as possible to judge the reliability and motivations of sources.
- Realize that private people have a greater right to control information about themselves than public figures and others who seek power, influence or attention.
- Use heightened sensitivity when dealing with juveniles, victims of sex crimes, and sources or subjects who are inexperienced or unable to give consent. Consider cultural differences in approach and treatment.

- Boldly tell the story of the diversity and magnitude of the human experience. Seek sources whose voices we seldom hear.
- Consider sources' motives before promising anonymity. Reserve anonymity for sources who may face danger, retribution or other harm, and have information that cannot be obtained elsewhere. Explain why anonymity was granted.
- Be cautious when making promises, but keep the promises they make.
- Be wary of sources offering information for favors or money; do not pay for access to news.

In selecting sources, journalists look for authority. They have to find sources who have first-hand knowledge, who are not merely repeating what they heard from others. Because a one-source story likely would be self-serving and reflect only a single perspective, journalists test a source's information by interviewing a diversity of people. A wide range of sources provides checks and balances.

Journalists have a responsibility to screen their sources on behalf of the audience, especially when the sources are nameless in their stories. "If your sources are wrong, you are wrong" was Judith Miller's explanation for her "totally wrong" stories about the likelihood that weapons of mass destruction would be found in Iraq when the United States invaded in 2003.[11] Miller's explanation offers little comfort for *New York Times* readers who were misled by her reporting. It also leaves the impression that reporters are stenographers who uncritically pass along what they are told.

Journalists must act independently, not allowing a relationship with a source, whether adversarial or friendly, to influence the story. Journalists have a moral duty not to exploit a vulnerable person for their own purposes, and their audience depends on them to resist a crafty source who would deflect them from the pursuit of the truth.

Sources who seek to manipulate may provide useful information; as the saying goes, bad people can give us good information. Mark Feldman, a former broadcast journalist and later a college journalism professor, observed: "The public is the poorer if reporters get high-and-mighty and say, 'We accept only leaks with pure motives.'"[12] What is essential in these situations is a heavy dose of skepticism; journalists need to check out the information while being conscious of the source's motive. "[J]ournalists must take motive into account in weighing what sources tell them," Jack Fuller wrote in *News Values*. "Motive gives a clue to the source's biases and reasons for lying or telling the truth only selectively."[13]

In general, a journalist should identify himself or herself to a person being interviewed. It is the journalist's responsibility to make clear what ground rules apply to reporting on the conversation. When interviewing ordinary citizens unfamiliar with the routine, the journalist should emphasize that what they say could appear in the newspaper, on the air, or on the Internet. If the story is to appear in multiple media, the source should know that, too.

The person being interviewed might ask what kind of story the journalist intends to write. That is a fair question, one deserving an honest answer. In outlining the premise that is being investigated, the journalist should also pledge to keep an open mind until all relevant facts have been gathered.

Should a source ever be deceived? There is sometimes a fine line between shrewd, resourceful reporting and unethical reporting. A deontologist-journalist would never deceive, of course. A teleologist-journalist might argue for misleading (read *deceiving*) a source if the stakes are high enough – that is, the story is vitally important to the audience, and there is no other way to obtain it. This topic is discussed in Chapter 16.

Often, reporter–source issues revolve around confidentiality. Ideally, sources agree to be named and to allow their statements to be conveyed to the public. However, it might be useful, as in the Jenoff case described above, for a reporter to listen on an off-the-record basis in the hope that the source will later go on the record or that the information can be confirmed by named sources or by documents.

Protecting Sources in Jeopardy

Some people who secretly provide information for journalists' stories may be vulnerable professionally, economically, even physically. Journalists have a moral obligation not to place them in jeopardy.

Time and again, journalists have been threatened with jail or fines for contempt for refusing a judge's order to give up the identity of a source to whom they have pledged confidentiality. State shield laws provide some protection, but a journalist still might be ordered to identify a source if a judge determines that the information is vital in a criminal case and cannot be obtained in any other way. In addition, the federal government does not have a shield law.

The prospect of jail time is real. In July 2014 *Columbia Journalism Review* listed 10 reporters since 2001 who had protected their sources while facing the possibility of going to jail. Four were actually deprived of their freedom: freelancer Joshua Wolf, who served more than seven months for refusing to give prosecutors a video he had made of a street protest in San Francisco in 2005; Judith Miller of *The New York Times*, who was jailed for three months in 2005 for refusing to reveal who had given her the name of Valerie Plame, a CIA operative; Jim Taricani, a television reporter in Providence, Rhode Island, who was confined to his home for six months in 2004 after refusing to say who had given him an FBI video of a city official taking a bribe; and freelancer Vanessa Leggett, who was jailed for 168 days in 2001 for refusing to give a Texas grand jury the notes she had taken while researching a murder case.[14]

"Our word is binding," the NPR code tells the radio network's journalists. "As an ethical matter, we would not want to reveal the identity of an anonymous source unless that person has consented to the disclosure. That's why we take the granting of anonymity seriously."[15]

The use of **confidential sources** places a heavy burden on journalists in addition to the duty to protect their identity. Journalists must go to extra lengths to corroborate information provided by confidential sources, because the audience has no way of assessing their authority or likely bias. Journalists should be reluctant to grant anonymity, agreeing only when convinced that the source is in jeopardy, that the source is reliable, and that the source's information is both overwhelmingly important and unobtainable elsewhere on the record.

Confidentiality could reasonably be invoked to protect a whistle-blower who comes forward to report abuse of power in government or business. It would be unfair, however, to give the cover of anonymity to someone who wants to damage the reputation of a rival.

Steve Buttry, an editor at Digital First Media who blogs about ethics, advises journalists to be wary of granting anonymity to people who possess power in society. "Powerful sources who demand confidentiality are often eager to tell their stories," he said: "They just don't want to be responsible for them. The more willing a source is to tell a story, the more insistent a reporter should be that the source stand by the story."[16]

The New York Times tightened its guidelines on anonymous sources in 2004. Bill Keller, who was then *The Times'* executive editor, explained why journalists should have the discretion to grant anonymity:

> The ability to offer protection to a source is an essential of our craft. We cannot bring readers the information they want and need to know without sometimes protecting sources who risk reprisals, firing, legal action, or, in some parts of the world, their lives when they confide in us.

Keller pointed out that some editors prohibit the use of anonymous sources: "This is high-minded foolishness. Without the option of protecting sources, with recourse only to an increasingly redacted public record, the coverage of government and other powerful institutions would tend more and more toward press-conference stenography."[17]

Keller emphasized that anonymous sources, if they are to be quoted by *The Times*, must be in a position to know what they are talking about – that is, they must have first-hand information. Reporters should ask questions like these: "Was he in the room? Did she read the document?"

Keller also advocated quality of sources over quantity. Instead of a "two-source rule" or a "three-source rule," he would rely on journalists' judgment in a given situation: "One actual participant in an event may be better than three people who heard about it third-hand, or from one another. One neutral witness may be more valuable than a crowd of partisans."[18]

The Associated Press says in its reporting standards that anonymous sources may be used only to convey information, "not opinion or speculation."[19] Likewise, the NPR code says that anonymous sources "should never be heard attacking or praising others in our reports."[20]

Without divulging sources' identity, reporters should give the audience as much information as possible to inform readers why those sources should be believed. They should negotiate in advance with the source about how he or she is going to be described. For example, "a source in the administration" is better than "a government source"; "a source who works in the White House" is even better; and "a White House source with access to the memos in question" is better than any of the others.

Journalists must not mislead the audience about where their information came from. It is wrong to say that an official was "unavailable for comment" and then quote the official anonymously. And it is wrong to say that a statement came from "a league official" rather than an official of a certain team (it is rationalizing to argue that there is no deceit because the team is a member of the league).

The Challenges of Beat Reporting

Most journalists are generalists. They have a broad range of knowledge and are quick learners, but they lack specialized knowledge in a given subject. To develop that kind of expertise, news organizations typically assign some of their reporters to what is known in the profession as "beats." Beat reporters cover a certain category of news: city hall, the police, the courts, a professional baseball team, the pharmaceutical business, and so forth. In addition to gaining an expertise in the subject matter, the reporter gets to know the newsmakers far better than a general-assignment reporter making a cold call on deadline to someone he or she has never met.

Emilie Lounsberry has covered courts nearly all of her newspaper career, starting when she was a college sophomore and a part-time court reporter for *The Daily Intelligencer* in Doylestown, Pennsylvania. Since 1982, she has reported on the courts for *The Philadelphia Inquirer*. She is sold on the value of beat reporting:

> Being in a courtroom is as comfortable, for me, as being in my own living room. I know how events will unfold. I can recognize good lawyering and good judging. I am familiar with the language of the law – and it does not frighten me. The confidence and ease I've developed from covering the law have enabled me to go deeper and deeper into complex issues and investigative matters.
>
> Along the way, I've also built up a pretty good working list of sources – with cell phone numbers, home numbers, and even an occasional parent's phone number. Like building a beat, developing good sources is an essential component of good journalism. A good source is someone who can help a reporter figure out what is happening behind the scenes.[21]

When ethics scholar Edward Wasserman, now dean of the Graduate School of Journalism at the University of California, Berkeley, looks at the beat-reporting system, he sees an inherent conflict of interest regarding sources. "If you deliberately set out to invent an arrangement less conducive to tough adversarial reporting, it would be hard to beat beats," Wasserman wrote in his column in *The Miami Herald*:

> The wisdom of beats rests on the idea that journalism can flourish in a setting where a journalist's professional success utterly depends on the continuing cooperation of the same people that the journalist is supposed to badger, provoke, expose and, in sum, hold accountable on the public's behalf. And that is totally illogical.[22]

Wasserman identified a genuine problem, but the crucial question is whether the problem is outweighed by the benefits of the beat reporter's expertise and wholesome source relationships. Lounsberry thinks a conscientious reporter can cope. "I try to keep a fair degree of independence from sources," she said. "I do not consider sources as 'friends'; when I meet with them, it is usually over lunch or coffee, rather than dinner or a social event. This helps keep some distance."[23]

Lounsberry's *Inquirer* colleague, Tommy Gibbons, a police reporter for almost 33 years, said mutual trust is the key to successful relationships on the beat. Even if the job occasionally requires writing a story that will reflect unfavorably on a valued source, he said, "you'll be OK if you are trusted as being fair." When Gibbons retired, the Philadelphia police commissioner told a gathering of well-wishers that he "didn't always agree with what I wrote, but I was fair." That comment, Gibbons said, "was worth a million compliments."[24]

Should Sources Be Paid?

The SPJ code takes a stand against payments, which mirrors the prevailing attitude in the profession.

Philip Seib and Kathy Fitzpatrick laid out the case against **checkbook journalism** in *Journalism Ethics*:

> Digging for facts might require more effort than writing a check, but it is more honest. Buying news will create a marketplace for untruths in which the more lurid the story, the higher the payment. Money-hungry sources will be likely to embellish and fabricate to drive their prices higher. Also, this practice is likely to damage even further the public's opinion of how journalists do their job.[25]

A few journalists argue to the contrary. "It seems to me that news outlets need to get beyond their discomfort with paying *any* sources for *anything*," Tom Goldstein wrote in *Journalism and Truth*. He noted that some news organizations have paid "consultants" for information, and said the practice of paying for quality information is well established in investing, the law, and other occupations. "Paid sources may have an incentive not to tell the truth. But this does not seem terribly different from what is already the case: sources who are not paid may also have an incentive not to tell the truth."[26]

Gizmodo, a technology site owned by Gawker Media, obtained the prototype of a new iPhone model in 2010 by paying $5,000 to an unidentified person who said an Apple engineer had inadvertently left it in a bar. Nick Denton, founder and owner of Gawker Media, said he was pleased by the Web traffic generated by exclusives purchased by Gizmodo and his other sites, Gawker and Deadspin. "I'm content for the old journalists not to pay for information. It keeps the price down," he told Paul Farhi of *The Washington Post*.[27]

Farhi wrote that television networks were saying they did not pay for interviews but were "devising ways to compensate high-profile news subjects anyway." A favored tactic, he wrote, was "to pay sources for the right to air personal photographs or home videos. Since the payments technically aren't for interviews, the networks say this doesn't constitute an ethical breach."[28]

The Society of Professional Journalists criticized the networks in 2010 for what it called "the growing trend of checkbook journalism." It issued a news release listing five instances in which exclusive access to news subjects was arranged through gifts, free travel, and payments for photographs.[29]

SPJ's criticism was focused on ABC News' $200,000 payment to the family of Casey Anthony, who was on trial in Orlando, Florida, on a charge of murdering her two-year-old daughter, Caylee, two years earlier. The payment became public in 2010 when Anthony's attorney mentioned it in a pretrial hearing. (Anthony was acquitted in 2011.) After the payment became known, ABC News said that in 2008 it had bought exclusive rights to "an extensive library of photos and home video for use by our broadcasts, platforms, affiliates, and international partners. No use of the material was tied to any interview." An ABC spokesman said that paying for "licensing exclusive rights" was a common practice in broadcast, but that the payment should have been disclosed to the audience.[30]

Chris Cuomo, then the co-anchor of ABC News' *20/20* magazine show, candidly defended his decision in 2011 to pay $10,000 to $15,000 for photos that Meagan Broussard sent to Representative Anthony Weiner of New York. Broussard was among several women involved in online relationships with Weiner in a "sexting" scandal that forced him to resign from Congress. On *20/20*, Cuomo conducted an exclusive interview with Broussard. Later, on CNN's *Reliable Sources*, Cuomo told the program's host, Howard Kurtz:

> The commercial exigencies of the business reach into every aspect of the reporting now. … [I]t is the state of play right now. I wish it were not. I wish money was not in the game. But you know, it's going to go somewhere else. You know someone else is going to pay for the same things.[31]

Six weeks later, Kurtz reported on *The Daily Beast* that ABC News had quietly decided to get out of the business of paying for exclusive interviews. Jeffrey Schneider, an ABC News spokesman, confirmed the change of policy, telling Kurtz: "We can book just about anyone based on the strength of our journalism, the excellence of our anchors, correspondents, and producers, and the size of our audience. These licensing deals had become a crutch."[32]

American correspondents have made payments abroad, though not without soul-searching. When Steve Stecklow was in Nicaragua covering the Sandinista–Contra conflict for *The Philadelphia Inquirer* in the 1980s, "I had to bring a carton of cigarettes to bribe soldiers at checkpoints to let me through." Stecklow, now with *The Wall Street Journal,* said that bribing the guards was "the only way to get through. Also, many foreign news organizations routinely pay for information, and so the sources expect to be paid. It's hard to explain that we can't pay."[33]

Compassion is another reason that correspondents have paid for information. In Zambia, Michael Wines of *The New York Times* interviewed a group of stone-crushers, "a class of laborers who cling to the lowest social rung even in this, one of the world's poorest nations." He decided to pay them for their help on his story describing the misery of their lives.

After the interviews, Wines drove to a grocery store and bought $75 worth of cornmeal, cooking oil, rice, orange concentrate, bread, milk, and candy. "I returned and unloaded it to undiluted pandemonium – mothers' riotous joy; youngsters mobbing for sweets: actual dancing in the street for 30 people, a real live Christmas in July."[34]

Interviewing Children

Watching television coverage of the aftermath of the schoolhouse massacre in New-town, Connecticut, James Poniewozik was angered by what he saw. Poniewozik is not an ordinary television viewer; he happens to be a columnist for *Time* magazine, and this is what he wrote on December 14, 2014:

> Whatever the ultimate casualty count at Sandy Hook Elementary School, every student there Friday was a victim. These kids – 10 years old, 5 years old – had been through an experience ghastlier than most adults have ever survived.
>
> Minutes after they made it to safety outside the school, having heard and seen unspeakable things, cable, network and local TV crews were waiting to interview them, live on camera, about things a kid should never have to talk about. Flanked by their parents, boys and girls too young to see an R-rated movie described being hustled to safety as bullets whizzed by them in the halls of their school.
>
> It was arresting. It was heartbreaking. And it was rash, unnecessary and wrong.[35]

Poniewozik quoted guidelines prepared by the Dart Center for Journalism & Trauma about interviewing children in tragedies: "Avoid interviewing children at the scene. They are very likely in shock and need comfort, not questioning." The Dart Center urges that journalists "be willing to wait until the parents and child are ready to talk, even if that is weeks or months after the crisis. You will likely get a much bet-ter interview." If interviews are conducted immediately, find a quiet place "away from the chaos of emergency personnel and other victims."[36]

The tragedy at Columbine High School near Denver on April 20, 1999, also resulted in questionable television interviews, even though the students there were about a decade older than their Newtown counterparts in 2014.

Journalists rushed to the school after two students, armed with guns, killed 12 stu-dents and a teacher, then themselves. The TV crews conducted live interviews with young people fleeing the school, many of them traumatized. In one of the interviews, a girl blurted out the name of the one of the killers; fortunately, she had it right. A consensus "best practice" in conducting live interviews with juveniles is to conduct pre-interviews without cameras, in recognition of the fact that these young subjects can become emotional and make unpredictable statements. Because pre-interviews were skipped to save time, the interviewers put teenagers on the air without having any idea of what they would say.[37]

In an essay for Poynter, Al Tompkins wrote: "Understanding how young people see the world around them often demands that we hear what they have to say." While giving young people a chance to be heard, journalists should be aware of their vulnerability. Tompkins noted that, especially in breaking-news situations, juveniles may not be able to recognize the ramifications of what they say.[38]

Tompkins suggested that the journalist try to secure parental permission for a child to be interviewed:

> Is it possible to have the parent/guardian present during the course of the interview? What are the parents' motivations for allowing the child to be interviewed? Are there legal issues you should consider, such as the legal age of consent in your state? If you conclude that parental consent is not required, at least give the child your business card so the parents can contact you if they have an objection to the interview being used.[39]

Showing Copy to Sources Before Publication

Showing copy in advance is a taboo in many newsrooms. No matter how clearly the journalist stipulates that only questions of accuracy will be considered, the practice can open the door to haggling. The source or story subject may feel betrayed if the story is changed in the editing process, even if he or she is cautioned about that possibility.

In spite of these hazards, a significant number of journalists consider some kind of source review – reading back quotations or showing entire story drafts – to be a valuable protection against inaccuracy. "I first showed a story to a source in 1985," Jay Mathews wrote in *The Washington Post*:

> He was an old friend who worked as an economist for a Montana Indian tribe I was writing about, and I wanted to make sure I made no errors that might cause him grief. I woke up the next morning to find that the newsroom bogeyman had not gotten me and the story was better for having had that numerical error in the 19th paragraph corrected.[40]

If a reporter is writing about a highly technical subject, such as a complex surgical procedure, checking at least part of the story with the source seems a defensible practice. The goal is to get the facts right. A reporter, however, needs to comply with his or her news organization's policy on source review.

NPR's code restricts how much its journalists can share with outsiders before a report is broadcast:

> For purposes of accuracy and fairness, there are times when we may want to review portions of a script with a source or read back a quotation to ensure we captured it correctly. We may also play audio or read transcripts of an interview to a third party if the purpose is to get that party's reaction to what another person has said. Otherwise, however, the public is the first audience for our work.[41]

A controversy flared up in July 2012 over a widespread practice in Washington of allowing government officials and their aides to review – and often demand changes in – quotations reporters wanted to attribute to them. Jeremy W. Peters wrote in *The New York Times*: "From Capitol Hill to the Treasury Department, interviews granted with quote approval have become the default position. ... The quotations come back redacted, stripped of colorful metaphors, colloquial language and anything even mildly provocative." The practice had spread to the presidential campaign, where Mitt Romney's aides would not allow the Republican candidate's five sons to be quoted without prior approval from the campaign team.[42]

After Peters' story appeared, one Washington bureau after another renounced quote approval. In September, *The Times* said it was drawing "a clear line" against the practice because, then executive editor Jill Abramson said, it "puts so much control over the content of journalism in the wrong place."[43]

Ironically, quote approval stemmed from an effort to reduce the number of anonymous quotes in stories from Washington. Peter Baker, White House correspondent for *The Times*, told public editor Margaret Sullivan:

> [D]uring the late Clinton era ... editors pushed us to go back to sources who spoke on background and get permission to use their names with specific quotes we were planning to use anyway but anonymously. Sources generally found that being on the record was not so worrisome (or career-threatening) once they knew what we actually wanted to use ... As a result, stories that traditionally were filled with anonymous quotes began having more named sources.[44]

Interviewing by Email

Journalistically, using email is inferior to interviewing in person, Professor Russell Frank of Pennsylvania State University wrote in a 1999 *Quill* magazine article. Frank wrote that reporters "don't get enough of a sense of the person they're dealing with; email doesn't lend itself to give-and-take, follow-up questions or serendipitous digressions; and email responses sound canned, unspontaneous."[45]

However, the practice of email interviews has grown because of its sheer convenience. Reporters and sources don't have to take time to arrange an in-person interview or to play phone tag. Undoubtedly, some sources prefer email because it gives them a chance to write measured responses.

The problems Frank identified persist today, and in terms of reporter preference, email interviews generally take third place to in-person interviews and telephone interviews. As a matter of disclosure to the audience, reporters should state if an interview was conducted by email or telephone rather than in person. In addition, reporters using information sent to them by email have an obligation to verify that the message was actually sent by the person whose name is signed.

The Debate over Verbatim Quoting

When sources are quoted for print or online news outlets, journalists have three choices. They can:

- *Quote directly.* The words the source used are placed inside quotation marks. The quotation is, at least in theory, a verbatim transcript.
- *Quote indirectly.* The reporter paraphrases the source's statement, usually for brevity or clarity, but faithfully conveys the essence of what the source said. Quotation marks are not used.
- *Use partial quotations.* This is a combination of the first two. The quotation is paraphrased except for a few words of direct quotation that appear between quotation marks.

From the standpoint of news-writing technique, each of the three choices has strengths and weaknesses. This text deals only with their ethical implications.

Indirect and partial quotations are ethically sound if they are faithful to the essence of the source's statements, and if the phrases placed within quotation marks are the precise words the source used.

The ethics of direct quotations is a subject of debate in the profession. In theory, a direct quotation is verbatim; it is exactly what the source said, nothing more and nothing less. The controversy centers on whether practice follows theory.

Most newsroom ethics codes state the theory in unequivocal terms. In its online News Values & Principles, The Associated Press states: "We do not alter quotations, even to correct grammatical errors or word usage."[46] *The New York Times Manual of Style and Usage* says: "Readers have a right to assume that every word between quotation marks is what the speaker or writer said. *The Times* does not 'clean up' quotations."[47] *The Washington Post*'s policy is: "When we put a source's words inside quotation marks, those exact words should have been uttered in precisely that form."[48]

Strictly following those rules, a journalist would write direct quotations that record the source's every false start or stutter, every "you know," every "um" or "ah." In addition to humiliating the source, that would distract the reader. The policy manuals offer a solution for the conundrum – use indirect quotations or partial quotations, or use direct quotations but insert an ellipsis (…) to indicate that something inconsequential is missing. Usually those alternatives solve the problem.

Occasionally, though, the source's less than perfect utterance would, from a journalistic standpoint, make a highly desirable direct quotation. What is the ethical journalist to do? The betting here is that in such a situation the journalist will, in the words of Roy Peter Clark of the Poynter Institute, "tidy up the quote rather than make someone look stupid."[49] Clark wrote, "I believe every writer, every journalist that I know, whether they're willing to admit it or not, cleans up quotes in some way."[50]

Regardless of how they feel about tidying up quotations, journalists reporting on news conferences should quote verbatim, false starts and all. Otherwise they may have to answer to an annoyed audience about why their quotations differ from what was heard on a broadcast sound bite or what was written in another journalist's account of the same news conference.

Some reporters drop "gonna" and "gotta" into direct quotations to add spice to their stories. Since almost no one slows down to pronounce "going to" and "got to" with perfect diction, reporters who selectively quote in this manner are unfairly portraying certain of their news subjects as being less than articulate.

It also is unfair to pick on people who are relatively uneducated, or for whom English is a second language. To grasp how humiliating quoting in dialect can be, consider the way Roberto Clemente, a Puerto Rican who became one of major league baseball's early Latino stars, was quoted by some sportswriters when he joined the Pittsburgh Pirates in the 1960s:

> I say, "I 'ope that Weelhelm [Hoyt Wilhelm] peetch me outside, so I could hit to right," but he peetch me inside and I meet it and hit it to right field. Willie runs to third and to home plate and the game is over. That make me feel real good."[51]

The headline over that story in the *Post-Gazette* was: "I Get Heet, I Feel Good." Clemente, who was an eloquent public speaker in Spanish, was angered and hurt by the exaggerated phonetic spellings, biographer David Maraniss wrote. The player told another sportswriter: "I know that I don't have the good English pronunciation because my tongue belong to the Spanish. But I know where the verb, the article, the pronoun, whatever it is, go."[52]

Athough repeated verbatim quotations should be avoided in these situations, lest they embarrass the story subject, neither should the subject be portrayed as an erudite speaker in English. In such a situation, indirect quotations with an occasional partial quotation are a better choice.

Occasionally, inserting a bracketed clarification into a direct quotation helps a reader understand the context, but this device tends to be overused. Liberally sprinkling bracketed phrases into extended direct quotations can produce two undesirable results. One is that the reader is distracted from the substance of the quotation. The other, more damning, is that the reporter seems to be suggesting that the speaker is so inarticulate that he or she needs the reporter's help to compose an intelligent sentence.

Quoting in slang and dialect should be avoided because it comes across as condescending. This stricture does not apply, however, when a speaker purposely uses slang or dialect. When Sylvester Croom took over as football coach at Mississippi State University in 2003, he acknowledged that he was the first of his race to hold that job in the Southeastern Conference. *The New York Times* cleaned up one of his remarks, quoting him: "'I am the first African American coach in the S.E.C., but there is only one color that matters here and that color is maroon,' referring to the Bulldogs' official colors, maroon and white, as the crowd applauded." Three days later, *The Times* published a correction. The coach, *The Times* reported, had said "there *ain't but* one color that matters here and that color is maroon."[53]

National Public Radio cleans up after people who are interviewed on the network and even its own correspondents in the field.

In a good-natured *On the Media* show in 2007, NPR reporter John Solomon revealed that a producer working on the audio recording at an editing console can make a speaker sound more articulate without changing what he or she meant to say. With just a few strokes of the keyboard, Solomon said, the producer "tightened the sound bites I was going to use, taking out sentences, words and even some of the pauses, making what are called internal edits. Then the various thoughts were woven together technically in a way that would be totally hidden to the listener." Also on the show, Solomon framed the larger debate over tidying up quotations:

> By making everyone sound better and increasing the amount of content in the broadcasts, it would seem to be a win–win–win for the network, its sources, and, most importantly, its listeners. Yet is there a small sin of omission? NPR may not be actively misleading listeners, but we all know that they don't know how we create the cleaner and more articulate reality.[54]

Point of View
Sometimes, Different Rules Apply
Jeffrey Fleishman

I hated being in Children's Hospital of Oklahoma. I kept my notebook deep inside my pocket. When the mother next to me was told her child was dead, blown completely out of his sandals, some of her grief crawled inside of me.

What if it would have been one of my children? I quickly put that thought away, back someplace where I could collect it later. I looked at the clock: 5 p.m. Deadlines. I kept the notebook buried; to pull it out, I thought, would have been some kind of sin. My eyes took in the details: Parents, their faces raw from worry, held up snapshots of infants and smiling toddlers. Nurses whisked by, their white shoes squeaking, their clip charts scant with answers.

Then she spoke. Jannie Coverdale spoke. "I need to know about my babies, no one's telling me anything about my babies." No one did. She had been to five other hospitals trying to find out about her grandsons Aaron, 5, and Elijah, 2. They had been in America's Kids day-care center. But where were they now? She walked outside with a cigarette. I followed. We talked for a few minutes. She asked who I was. I told her. There was that heavy silence reporters are used to. Then she said it was OK to tell her story. I reached for my notebook, slowly. Every word she spoke seemed to matter. In such agony, there is no falseness.

I thanked her. Deadlines. She said God would take care of her.

I rushed toward the hotel to file. All the way there I kept thinking that I have a 5-year-old son. His name is Aaron.

(Continued)

That night Dan Meyers, another *Inquirer* reporter, and I ate dinner together. His son, Jackson, had recently turned 1. We talked about Jackson and my kids, Aaron and Hannah. But soon we spun the conversation in another direction. Talking about our kids meant thinking about the bloody children from the day-care center, the ones zipped in body bags.

Before I went to bed that night I pulled out a picture of Aaron and Hannah. They were alive, small, in my palm. I turned the light off and sat with them in darkness.

It's strange to write like this. In the first person, no scenery to hide behind. We so often live out of our notebooks, using them as shields for feelings. Somewhere amid the truth-gathering, we've lost — necessarily so or not — a little of the ability to imagine. I guess that's why Hemingway said journalism is fine training for a writer, so long as the writer knows when to quit it. But Jannie Coverdale didn't have to imagine. She knew how to fit words to pain. And every time she spoke of her Aaron, I thought of mine.

Over the next five days I spent time with Jannie Coverdale. I stayed at a distance, coming only when invited, and found I was invited often. I saw worry wear her brown eyes down. I saw God lift her with hope, a spark across her wide, smooth forehead. I saw her, for a moment with clenched hands, grow strong in the belief that Aaron and Elijah were alive under some steel beam. Her fortitude rubbed off on me. And at times I hoped that when Jannie's ordeal was over, I'd write a story about how two little kids had survived in some crevice, some pocket of air.

"When I'm in bed and everything is quiet I see things," said Jannie. "I see the babies. One night I dreamt I saw Aaron and Elijah and there were angels holding them and God was blowing breath in their faces to give them life."

The angels had other plans.

Saturday night Jannie was told.

Aaron and Elijah were dead.

I had a picture of those boys in my hotel room. Every day I got up and looked at it. I placed it beside my computer when I wrote. They were the faces of my words, the boys who filled up my days. They held 90.53 inches of news space. Four days of coverage. Now, they were gone. There is power in innocent blood, whether it's that of the Coverdale boys or the thousands of children — shrivelled, hacked and dead — in Rwanda. You don't have to be a parent to feel that sorrow. You only have to be human.

On Sunday I did a story of Jannie picking out a casket. The funeral was on Wednesday. At the cemetery, the gravedigger twirled a hand-crank and the casket holding Elijah and Aaron descended into the clay with a mechanical finality.

Jannie cried: "They're taking my babies."

I put my sunglasses on.

I stood among the tombstones on the rim of the hundred or so people gathered around Jannie. My notebook was in my pocket. One of Jannie's sons came over to me. "My mom wants to see you," he said. I followed him through the crowd and stopped in front of Jannie. She opened her arms. I walked into them. A bomb had ripped away her grandsons, but her compassion was undiminished.

Jeffrey Fleishman's essay about covering the 1995 bombing of the federal building in Oklahoma City was written for *The Philadelphia Inquirer*'s in-house newsletter. It is reprinted with the permission of the writer.

Notes

1 Phillips, Nancy, "Tale of murder took years to unfold long before confessing …," *The Philadelphia Inquirer*, May 7, 2000, supplemented by an email exchange with the author on Feb. 2, 2009.

2 Alicia C. Shepard, "The reporter and the hit man," *American Journalism Review*, Apr. 2001.

3 Ibid.

4 Howard Kurtz, "Reporter kept her promise," *The Washington Post*, May 11, 2000.

5 Robert Hanley, "2 hit men get 23-year terms for killing wife of rabbi," *The New York Times*, Jan. 31, 2003.

6 Rita Giordano, "Hit man in killing of rabbi's wife to be freed from prison," *The Philadelphia Inquirer*, Jan. 25, 2014.

7 Kurtz, "Reporter kept her promise."

8 Shepard, "The reporter and the hit man."

9 *Ethical Journalism* (New York: The New York Times), paragraphs 22–23.

10 Shepard, "The reporter and the hit man."

11 Don Van Natta Jr., Adam Liptak, and Clifford J. Levy, "The Miller case: a notebook, a cause, a jail cell and a deal," *The New York Times*, Oct. 16, 2005.

12 Bob Egelko, "BALCO case has journalism in a quandary," *San Francisco Chronicle*, Feb. 18, 2007.

13 Jack Fuller, *News Values* (Chicago: University of Chicago Press, 1996), 41.

14 "A look at the last nine reporters who faced the possibility of jail time," *Columbia Journalism Review*, July 1, 2014.

15 "Anonymous sourcing," NPR Ethics Handbook.

16 Steve Buttry, "Power and eagerness should guide reporters' confidentiality decisions," The Buttry Diary, June 30, 2010.

17 Bill Keller, "Keller memo on anonymous sources," *The New York Times*, June 9, 2008.

18 Ibid.

19 "Standards: anonymous sources," Associated Press.

20 "Anonymous sourcing," NPR Ethics Handbook.

21 Emilie Lounsberry, "Beats, courts and sources," paper written for this book (Aug. 20, 2007). (*The paper is available in the Student Resources section of the website.*)

22 Edward Wasserman, "The insidious corruption of beats," *Miami Herald*, Jan. 8, 2007.

23 Lounsberry, "Beats, courts and sources."

24 Author's telephone interview with Tommy Gibbons, Sept. 18, 2007.

25 Philip Seib and Kathy Fitzpatrick, *Journalism Ethics* (Fort Worth, TX: Harcourt Brace, 1997), 109–110.

26 Tom Goldstein, *Journalism and Truth: Strange Bedfellows* (Evanston, IL: Northwestern University Press, 2007), 118.

27 Paul Farhi, "Up for audit: 'checkbook journalism' and the news groups that buy big stories," *The Washington Post*, Nov. 17, 2010.

28 Ibid.

29 Kevin Smith and Andy Schotz, "SPJ Ethics Committee condemns major broadcast networks' practice of 'checkbook journalism,'" SPJ, Mar. 23, 2010.

30 Ibid.

31 Julie Moos, "ABC's Chris Cuomo defends checkbook journalism: 'It is the state of play right now,'" Poynter, June 12, 2011.

32 Howard Kurtz, "ABC bans paying news subjects," *The Daily Beast*, July 25, 2011.

33 Author's interview with Steve Stecklow, Oct. 19, 2007.

34 Michael Wines, "To fill notebooks, and then a few bellies," *The New York Times*, Aug. 27, 2006.

35 James Poniewozik, "Kids at tragedies: turn off the cameras," *Time*, Dec. 14, 2012.

36 The Dart Center for Journalism & Trauma, a project of the Graduate School of Journalism at Columbia University, offers tip sheets for journalists. The advice quoted by James Poniewozik is in "Covering Children and Trauma" by Ruth Teichroeb.

37 Alicia C. Shepard, "Columbine shooting: live coverage," in Tom Rosenstiel and Amy S. Mitchell (eds.), *Thinking Clearly: Cases in Journalistic Decision-Making* (New York: Columbia University Press, 2003), 64.

38 Al Tompkins, "Guidelines for interviewing juveniles," Poynter, May 17, 1999.

39 Ibid.

40 Jay Mathews, "Sources of accuracy," *The Washington Post*, May 31, 2003.

41 "Independence," NPR Ethics Handbook.

42 Jeremy W. Peters, "Latest word on the trail? I take it back," *The New York Times*, July 15, 2012.

43   Margaret Sullivan, "In new policy, *The Times* forbids after-the-fact 'quote approval,'" *The New York Times*, Sept. 20, 2012.

44   Ibid.

45   Russell Frank, "You've got quotes!," *Quill*, Oct. 1999.

46   "Quotations," AP News Values & Principles.

47   Allan M. Siegal and William G. Connolly, The *New York Times Manual of Style and Usage* (New York: Times Books, 1999), 278.

48   The policy was quoted in Deborah Howell, "Quote, unquote," *The Washington Post*, Aug. 12, 2007.

49   Quoted in Fawn Germer, "Are quotes sacred?," *American Journalism Review*, Sept. 1995.

50   Quoted in Hallie C. Falquet, "Verbatim: when good people use bad grammar," *American Journalism Review*, Oct.–Nov. 2006.

51   David Maraniss, *Clemente: The Passion and Grace of Baseball's Last Hero* (New York: Simon & Schuster, 2006), 155.

52   Ibid., 174.

53   Ray Glier, "College football: pioneer sees a coach first and foremost," *The New York Times*, Dec. 3, 2003, with correction appended on Dec. 6, 2003.

54   John Solomon, "Pulling back the curtain," National Public Radio, May 25, 2007.

14 Making News Decisions about Privacy

The public may need to know what individuals want hidden

Learning Goals

This chapter will help you understand:

- the tension between the public's legitimate need to have certain information and the desire for privacy by the individuals involved;
- the legal restraints on publicizing private information;
- a three-step template for making decisions in privacy cases; and
- how journalists should approach situations in which privacy is central to decision-making.

The noise level at the Hetzel Union Building – the HUB, as the student union at Pennsylvania State University is fondly known – got on the nerves of a 19-year-old white sophomore on a fall afternoon in 2013. She'd had enough, and she decided to register a complaint on Twitter.

"Dear most of the African American community at Penn State," the student tweeted, "the hub is not your playground, please stop shouting and dancing and playing music."

On the 45,000-student campus, the tweet caused consternation. It was quickly retweeted more than a hundred times by people who viewed it as inappropriate. About thirty of those retweets were sent to *The Daily Collegian*, alerting the staff to the news.

Within hours, *The Collegian* tweeted, "Earlier today, a #PennState student tweeted an offensive comment regarding black students in the HUB that garnered a backlash on social media." That was followed by a tweet naming the student. A screenshot of the sophomore's tweet, showing her name and photograph, graced the front page of the student daily the next morning.

A *Collegian* reader who was disturbed by the staff's handling of the story was Russell Frank, a former newspaper reporter and editor who teaches journalism at Penn State. In an op-ed essay published in *The Collegian* a few days later, he wrote that the paper "could have used the foolish tweet as a jumping-off point to gather additional evidence of racist attitudes among Penn State students and revisit the question of whether the university is doing enough to combat such attitudes." Instead, he wrote, "the paper decided to make an example of the tweeter."

The Ethical Journalist: Making Responsible Decisions in the Digital Age, Second Edition. Gene Foreman.
© 2016 John Wiley & Sons, Inc. Published 2016 by John Wiley & Sons, Inc.

Frank argued that the news was the tweet, not the tweeter. "For most of us, I suspect, it was more important to know what was said than who said it." He thought the tweeter should have been given a break because of her age. "If a Penn State faculty member had been the source of the tweet, I would say, by all means, name him and shame him. Holding people with power accountable is exactly what journalists should be doing. But an undergraduate?"

Two days after her controversial tweet, *The Collegian* published an email from the sophomore: "I sincerely apologize for my actions and words. The tweet in question is inappropriate, and I am truly sorry to those who I have offended."

Brittany Horn, editor in chief of *The Collegian*, defended her decision in a telephone interview with Libbi Heinz and Kristin Odell, graduate students at the University of Arkansas who were preparing a case study for the university's Center for Ethics in Journalism.[1] Horn said that *Collegian* editors had "wrestled with the same issues" that Professor Frank raised, but they were persuaded that, because students' negative reaction to the tweet was so strong, the tweeter had become a "public figure." She went on to observe that students were aware that their social media activity "is part of their resume now" and that "there are consequences for what you say."

Horn said the *Collegian* editors wanted to avoid making the story "only about her." She was not named in subsequent news stories nor in an editorial proposing that the tweet afforded an opportunity to discuss the broader issue of diversity on campus. In the original online news story, Horn pointed out, the comment function was deactivated because the editors did not want the news organization to be "a forum for hurt."

The tweeter declined to be interviewed by the Arkansas students, but she did send them an email repeating her apology. She acknowledged getting "a lot of negative attention on Twitter" and said the *Collegian* story "seemed to fuel the fire." The newspaper, she said, "forgot that I was just a 19-year-old girl who said the wrong thing, at the wrong time, on a public media site, and it just went viral." She assessed the long-term consequences of her tweet:

> [F]or the rest of my life when I go to apply to jobs, I'm going to have to explain what happened in college. My future kids will search me on Google and ask me what these articles are about. One tweet, that I truly regret, will now haunt me for the rest of my life."[2]

Public Interest versus Individual Desire for Privacy

The question of whether to name the Penn State tweeter illustrates an important ethical issue for journalists, who frequently must decide whether the public has a legitimate need for information that the people involved would prefer to keep private.

Those decisions are rarely clear-cut. In this case, a private individual committed a public act that was clearly newsworthy. The *Collegian* editors were within their legal rights to publish the tweeter's name and photograph. And only on rare occasions do journalists withhold the identity of a story's subject. Professor Frank, however, made a case for telling the story about the incendiary tweet without naming the student who wrote it (the tweeter is anonymous in this textbook for the same reason).

Privacy cases present a conflict between the Society of Professional Journalists code's guiding principles of "seek truth and report it" versus "minimize harm." The tensions were summed up by Philip Patterson and Lee Wilkins in *Media Ethics: Issues and Cases*: "The challenge for journalists is to be courageous in seeking and reporting information, while being compassionate to those being covered."[3]

The law does give individuals an ability to sue if certain kinds of private information are publicized, and of course journalists must be aware of these legal limits. However, as a practical matter in these decisions, as in the case of the Penn State tweeter, journalists look to their ethical standards rather than to a rule of law.

In privacy cases, the audience's perception of journalists' conduct again comes into play. The audience appears jaded by the slogan "the public's right to know," seeing it as an excuse to invade someone's privacy to sell newspapers or raise broadcast ratings. Nevertheless, journalists frequently do have a responsibility to inform the public of matters that the participants could argue are none of the public's business.

Like "the public's right to know," an individual's "right to privacy" is a phrase that does not appear in the Constitution. However, emeritus professor Louis W. Hodges of Washington and Lee University considers it "reasonable to claim that privacy is assumed as necessary to the guarantee of other rights."[4] Hodges wrote about an individual's *moral right to privacy* and defined the term as "the power to determine who may gain access to information about oneself."[5] He argued, "Privacy plays a central role in human affairs. Without some degree of privacy, civilized life would not be possible."[6] However, he also asserted:

> But the right of privacy is not absolute. It stands beside a countervailing right of others to know quite a lot about us as individuals. Those two legitimate rights – the individual right to a measure of privacy and the right of others to know something about the individual – frame the moral issues.[7]

In the broadest sense, an individual's desire for privacy is trumped by the media's duty to report on the public performance of public officials, crimes, and accidents:

- *Public performance of public officials.* Although the officials may try to evade the media's scrutiny, it is an axiom of our democracy that the people's business should be conducted in public. Governments at all levels have enacted laws to enforce this concept – laws that require governing bodies to debate and vote in public, and courts to be open.
- *Crimes.* Citizens need to know about crimes in order to protect themselves and to evaluate the performance of the police. But coverage of crimes could result in some invasion of privacy.
- *Accidents.* For the same reasons that they need to be informed about crimes, citizens have a clear interest in knowing about events that cause loss of life, injuries, and property damage. As in the case of crimes, news coverage could divulge facts that those involved want to keep private.[8]

The issues, however, are more complex than might appear from the above list, a reality illustrated in the Case Study "Tracing the Source of Web Comments," which accompanies this chapter.

Journalists have to decide questions like these: Should public officials have some zone of privacy in their personal lives and, if so, how wide should it be? What entitlement to a zone of privacy do celebrities have? When their decisions affect the public welfare, should not the owners of private businesses be scrutinized just as office holders are? When journalists report on crimes and accidents, how much private information should they make public? If an ordinary citizen commits suicide in private, should the death be reported as a suicide?

Legal Restraints in Privacy Cases

Although the courts commonly rule in favor of the news media in privacy cases, practicing journalists need to know how privacy law might restrict their reporting. The legal concept of privacy was articulated in 1890 in a *Harvard Law Review* article by Samuel D. Warren and Louis D. Brandeis. Reacting to scandal-mongering in American newspapers of the period, they proposed that citizens be able to sue a press that is "overstepping in every direction the obvious bounds of propriety and of decency."[9] Over the next century, the law on privacy evolved into four distinct categories, or torts, in which subjects of news coverage might sue news organizations for intrusion into a person's solitude or private affairs; publication of embarrassing facts; false light; and appropriation:

- *Intrusion into a person's solitude or private affairs.* Journalists cannot trespass into a person's home or personal papers. The tort takes place with the act of intruding, even if nothing is published. In his memoir, the late *New York Times* executive editor Turner Catledge reminisced about how "picture snatching" was an accepted practice when he was a reporter in the 1920s: "The best way to get the pictures [of murder victims] was just to snatch them off the walls and tables and mantels and out of family albums at the scene of the action."[10] In modern times, the courts have held that even when invited by police to accompany them on a raid on private property, journalists can be sued by the property owners. This category of law also bars the harassment of a person or disrupting his or her private life.
- *Publication of embarrassing private facts.* Journalists cannot delve into a person's past to report notorious information if that information has no bearing on the person's present life, or if it is something that the public has no legitimate interest in. In today's computerized society, that kind of information is particularly easy to find in the databases of government and business. (See *public records* below.)
- *False light.* Journalists cannot create an erroneous, unattractive impression about a person. Newspapers sometimes do this when they use a file photo to illustrate a current story with an entirely different context – for example, using a routine

classroom photo of students taking an exam to illustrate a story about cheating on exams. Television stations have the same problem with file video.

- *Appropriation.* If a person's name or photograph is going to be used for commercial purposes, the subject must give approval (and presumably be compensated). For example, Tiger Woods has to agree to the use of his likeness to sell golf apparel and automobiles.

The law, otherwise, is permissive. As a result, the journalist has to discern the difference between legally acceptable conduct and truly ethical conduct. In *Ethics in Media Communications: Cases and Controversies*, Louis A. Day addressed two areas in which these decisions frequently are made: public places and public records:

- *Public places.* "The general rule is that anything that takes place in public view can be reported on. The idea is that activities that transpire in public are, by definition, not private." Day cautioned that journalists ought to use restraint. Before taking a photo of two lovers on a bench in a public park, he suggested, a news photographer first ought to ask permission: first, as a matter of decency, because the photographer is intruding in a private moment; and, second, to avoid acute embarrassment, if the lovers happen to be married, but not to each other.[11]
- *Public records.* Day noted that journalists have a right to report embarrassing information that appears in the public record. "Any citizen could conceivably examine this record," he wrote; "Thus, the press is merely providing publicity for what individual citizens could see for themselves if they wished. This is a convincing argument from a legal standpoint. From an ethical perspective, it is less so. The reality is that most private facts committed to public records remain unknown to society unless publicized by the media."[12] This is an issue involved in the Case Study "Mapping the Locations of Gun Owners," which accompanies this chapter.

Either by mining free sites or by subscribing to a search website, journalists and others can access huge quantities of sensitive information on the Internet, including the amount of mortgages people owe on their homes, the salaries of public employees in some jurisdictions, the amount of taxes people have paid (or failed to pay), bankruptcies, criminal records, marriages and divorces, and political contributions. The availability of this information confers power on the journalist, along with the responsibility of deciding whether the benefit of disseminating the information outweighs the potential embarrassment to the individuals involved.

Making Decisions: A Three-Step Template

Journalists must recognize that their decisions about intruding into people's privacy can cause profound harm in their lives. In these situations, there is a conflict between the two guiding principles in the Society of Professional Journalists' code, "seek truth and report it," and "minimize harm."

Box 14.1   Making Decisions in Privacy Cases

Step 1: Analyze the information

- Is the information something the public needs to know, or is it merely something the public is curious about?

Step 2: Analyze the likely harm

- Does the publication, broadcasting, or posting of the information inflict harm? If so, how much?
- Is harm inflicted by merely gathering the information?

- What degree of privacy can the news subject reasonably expect?
- Did the news subject intentionally do something to create news?

Step 3: Make the decision

- Does the value of the information to the public outweigh the harm that might be inflicted on the news subject?
- If certain harmful details are omitted, would the public be sufficiently informed?

The decision-making process (Box 14.1) calls for a careful, sensitive application of ends-based thinking and the Golden Rule. The process involves three steps: (1) assess the information; (2) calculate the likely harm; and then (3) weigh those two factors against each other to arrive at the decision.

Step 1: Analyze the information

Journalists should first evaluate the public's need to know the information that the subjects of the news coverage want to keep private. In doing so, they distinguish between what the public is *interested in* and what it has a legitimate *need to know*. While this decision obviously is subjective, a simple test is to ask whether the information fulfills journalism's primary duty – providing citizens with the information they need to go about their daily lives and to make governing decisions about their community.

People are interested in a lot of things that they do not have a need to know. Louis Hodges observed that people are capable of such things as morbid curiosity and prurient interest – factors that "are not grounds for invading someone's privacy, although they are the criteria that gossip sheets use." In Hodges' standard, the reported information should be "of overriding public importance" and "the public need cannot be met by any other means."[13]

The fact that something is "a good story" – which in newsroom parlance is any story, good news or bad, that people will eagerly receive – is not a sufficient criterion. Working under intense deadlines and competitive pressure, journalists may not make a sound distinction between what the public is interested in and what it needs to know.

Applied ethics in journalism is *not* about reflexive decision-making; it is about critical thinking. To arrive at a decision they can defend, journalists must go beyond reflex and weigh concrete factors, pro and con, about whether to use a story.

Especially in their decision-making about privacy, journalists must be on their guard against rationalizations. Their passion is to tell good stories. They feel pressure from their bosses and colleagues to deliver good stories. It is tempting to reveal private information, even if it harms the subjects. It takes discipline to test whether a decision to publish is self-serving.

Step 2: Analyze the likely harm

If the information is deemed to have met the importance standard in some degree, journalists next assess the harm that the reporting might inflict on the subjects of the story. The *gathering* of the information, aside from the *publication* of it, can itself be intrusive and cause harm. Louis Day has cautioned that journalists need to respect their news subjects as autonomous individuals whose dignity "should not be arbitrarily compromised for the sake of some slogan such as 'the people's right to know.'"[14]

This step also involves balancing the degree of harm caused by a disclosure against the degree of privacy that the news subject can reasonably expect. Public officials doing the public's business have the least claim to privacy, and ordinary citizens have the greatest.

Celebrities – "public figures" in legal terms – often protest that the media invade what they consider to be a zone of privacy. During the 1980 World Series, *The Philadelphia Inquirer* sent a reporter to the suburban neighborhood of the Phillies' star third baseman, Mike Schmidt. The resulting feature story portrayed Schmidt as a friendly neighbor who, among other kind gestures, autographed the cast of a teenager's broken arm. Although he was portrayed in favorable terms, Schmidt was not pleased. *Write what you want about what I do at the ballpark*, he told sportswriters emphatically, *but leave my private life alone.*[15]

It also is pertinent whether the subjects deliberately decided to create news or were involuntarily drawn into the news.

Step 3: Make the decision

In this step, journalists consider what they have learned in steps 1 and 2, and arrive at a decision they can defend. They construct a scale in which the importance of the news is weighed against the harm inflicted on the subject of the coverage, as modified by the degree of privacy the subject can expect under the circumstances. They consider whether they can fulfill their duty to inform the public while omitting some of the harmful private details.

News Situations in which Privacy Is a Factor

Ordinary people thrust into the news

People who involuntarily become newsmakers typically have survived some sort of disaster, or they are relatives of people who have been tragically killed. Of all the people journalists deal with, this group has both the greatest entitlement to privacy and the least experience in coping with the media. Under the principle of "minimize harm," the SPJ code cautions: "Realize that private people have a greater right to control information about themselves than public figures and others who seek power, influence or attention."

News consumers *want* to know how these news subjects are coping with their ordeals, but this does not meet the *need* standard. The same consumers are likely to be scornful of reporters who appear to violate privacy. In *Best Practices for Newspaper Journalists*, Robert J. Haiman wrote:

> The public … disapproves of newspaper photographers and television camera crews who "catch" private citizens in moments of grief and shock. [The public character-izes] spot news photography as often unnecessarily invasive, insensitive, and unfair. That powerful images of sorrow or tragedy are newsworthy and are captured openly, utilizing traditional photojournalism practices, does not persuade those who believe people in such circumstances are entitled to a zone of privacy from the press. The public sym-pathizes strongly with victims of tragedy who sometimes seem to be revictimized by their encounters with reporters and photographers at a moment when they are most vulnerable.[16]

Victims of sex crimes

A common practice in journalism is to withhold the names of victims of sex crimes. This practice is based on the principle of minimizing harm. Kelly McBride of the Poynter Institute, writing in *Quill* magazine, gave these specific reasons:

- "Rape is different from any other crime. Society often blames the victims. Studies show rape victims suffer from the stigma of being 'damaged' by the experience."
- "Rape victims are less likely to report the crime if they know their names will appear in the newspaper. Rape is already the most underreported crime in the country."
- "Because rape victims are treated with insensitivity by society, they deserve a level of privacy not afforded other crime victims."[17]

Exceptions to the rule have been made if the victim is murdered, if the victim has been abducted, or if the victim agrees to be identified. The Case Study "Identifying a 13-Year-Old Rape Victim," which accompanies this chapter, presents questions that journalists should consider in an abduction/sexual molestation case, especially when the victim is a juvenile.

Journalists who disagree with the prevailing standard make these points:

- It is not fair to name the accused without also naming the accuser, since the accusation may prove false.
- Names are part of the story and add credibility, and journalists should not allow the person making the news to dictate how the news will be covered.
- By withholding names in these cases, journalists reinforce the notion that the victims have disgraced themselves.

These arguments obviously have merit, and there is no absolute answer. The author sees the principle of minimizing harm as more compelling. In an effort to offset the unfairness implicit in naming only the accused, news organizations are obliged to report with equal prominence if the accused is acquitted. As for the argument that the newsmaker is dictating the terms of coverage, there is no indication that the public sees a sinister departure from normal reporting standards when sex-crime victims go nameless. Finally, while it makes sense to combat the idea that a stigma attaches to rape victims, it is ethically questionable to enlist an unwilling victim in that cause.

Politicians' sexual affairs

Until the 1980s, politicians' affairs outside marriage were generally ignored unless they affected the politicians' performance of official duties. That was the policy that the Washington press corps followed when President John F. Kennedy engaged in multiple affairs; these drew no press notice, even though one of his partners was a girlfriend of a Mafia leader. Professor Larry Sabato of the University of Virginia wrote, "In the press reports, Jack Kennedy, champion philanderer, became the perfect husband and family man."[18] In retrospect, even by the standards of the 1960s, Kennedy's promiscuous conduct exacted a cost in his performance of official duties, and by omission the press created a false impression of the president.

Sometimes, politicians' affairs did make news when the old standard prevailed.

In 1974 Arkansas Representative Wilbur D. Mills' affair with a burlesque dancer, Fanne Foxe, was reported because Washington police stopped him one night for speeding and driving with his headlights out, and Foxe dashed from his car and jumped into the Tidal Basin. Although reporters had been aware that Mills — who chaired the House Ways and Means Committee — had a drinking problem, they did not cover his personal life until he became a police item.[19]

In 1976 journalists reported on Ohio Representative Wayne L. Hays' affair with Elizabeth Ray, because she was paid $14,000 a year as a staff member without having to do any Congress-related work. That was news because Hays had abused his office by paying his mistress with taxpayers' money. "I can't type. I can't file. I can't even answer the phone," Ray told *The Washington Post*.[20]

The climate changed in 1987 when *Miami Herald* journalists staked out the Washington townhouse where Colorado Senator Gary Hart, a leading candidate for the 1988 Democratic presidential nomination, met with an aspiring actress named Donna Rice. Amid the ensuing publicity, Hart withdrew from the race. Alicia C. Shepard reported in *American Journalism Review* about what happened in the years after that:

> An obscure lounge singer named Gennifer Flowers held a press conference in 1992. Flowers claimed that for 12 years she had carried on an affair with Bill Clinton, at the time a presidential candidate. The story paralyzed the Clinton campaign briefly. The source, Flowers, had been paid by the *Star*, a supermarket tabloid, and the story was not entirely verifiable. It played itself out after the candidate, with wife Hillary Rodham Clinton at his side, deflected the charges on "60 Minutes." (In 1998 Clinton admitted that he had sex with Flowers, but just once.)
>
>   Two years later, an Arkansas state employee named Paula Jones accused Clinton of crudely propositioning her when he was governor of the state. Jones' press conference was largely ignored by the media, although her charges gained attention after she filed a suit against the president. Then, on January 21, 1998, Monica Lewinsky entered our lives. Before long, semen-stained dresses, kinky acts with cigars, oral sex performed on a president while he chatted with a congressman – all found their way into print and onto broadcasts. Some news organizations relied on firsthand reporting; others picked up what was being reported elsewhere.[21]

Contemporary journalists continue to debate whether a politician's sex life is a private matter or a public concern. Journalists who say it is a legitimate subject of coverage argue that it illuminates a character issue that their audience is entitled to know about. Journalists also point to hypocrisy if the office holder has campaigned as happily married or is an ardent supporter of so-called family values. Other journalists contend that the old standard should continue to apply – an extramarital affair by a politician is none of the public's business unless there is a pattern of sexual harassment or a problem with the way the politician conducts his or her public office.

During the 1996 presidential campaign *The Washington Post* prepared a story about an affair that Bob Dole, the Republican candidate, had in the late 1960s with a university employee while he was a congressman and still married to his first wife, Phyllis Holden. Several editors at *The Post* wanted to publish the story because of what they said was the Dole campaign's effort to cast him as a morally superior alternative to Bill Clinton. Ultimately, *Post* editor Leonard Downie Jr. killed the story. Downie decided that the story did not meet his standard – that "the revelation of a love affair from a quarter century earlier had to be justified by its relevance to the candidate's suitability for the presidency or his past conduct in public office."[22]

North Carolina Senator John Edwards' affair with Rielle Hunter presents a noteworthy case study because the mainstream news media did not mention the affair for months after the *National Enquirer* reported it. Finally, in August 2008, Edwards admitted in an ABC News interview that he had been involved in 2006 with Hunter, a videographer then working in his campaign for the Democratic presidential nomination. He denied that he was the father of Hunter's child, born in February 2008. He acknowledged meeting with Hunter in a California hotel room in July 2008 at her request because "she was having some trouble; she just wanted to talk," and "I wanted her not to tell the public what had happened."[23]

Although the *National Enquirer* had been reporting on the affair since October 2007, Edwards had denied the allegations, dismissing one *Enquirer* story as "tabloid trash."[24] The *Enquirer* disclosures were followed by silence in the mainstream media, but not in the blogosphere and on talk shows, where "the MSM" was denounced for seeming to protect Edwards. "The new media really kept this story alive," *Enquirer* editor David Perel said.[25] Although some mainstream organizations chose not to pursue the story – "I'm not going to recycle a supermarket tabloid's anonymously sourced story," said executive editor Bill Keller of *The New York Times*[26] – others tried to check it out, with little to show for their efforts. Then, in August 2008, *The Charlotte Observer* and *The* (Raleigh) *News & Observer* in Edwards' home state started publishing stories; *The Charlotte Observer* found the birth certificate of Hunter's child with no father's name listed. As ABC News investigated the case, Edwards agreed to the interview in which he confessed.[27]

Media writer Howard Kurtz wrote in *The Washington Post* about "the box" that mainstream journalists found themselves in: not reporting on a subject that was common knowledge: "When critics, especially on the right, accused the media of protecting a Democrat because of liberal bias, journalists were unable to respond, because to do so would be to acknowledge the very thing they were declining to report."[28]

One reason the traditional media were leery of the Edwards story is that the *Enquirer* paid for information on Edwards. Perel said the paper's policy was no different from that of police, who have been known to pay informants. "The thing to remember is we only pay for information once it's verified and accurate," Perel said. "So, if somebody tells us that John Edwards is going to show up at the Beverly Hilton to meet Rielle Hunter, and he does, well, that information is verified."[29]

Ombudsman Michael Getler of Public Broadcasting Service criticized PBS's *NewsHour with Jim Lehrer* for making no mention of the Edwards story on August 8, 2008, the day he admitted the affair. To Getler, that didn't make sense, especially when, three days later, *NewsHour* broadcast a lengthy segment examining why the mainstream media had remained silent on the story for so long. When Getler asked why the newscast itself had declined to report the story once Edwards confirmed it, he was told that Edwards was no longer a candidate for public office and was not on a short list for the vice presidential nomination. In his ombudsman column, Getler explained why he disagreed:

> a startling, nationally televised confession by a very high-profile public and political figure; a former senator who has twice campaigned for the presidency and who was campaigning at the time of the affair; who was the vice-presidential candidate in 2004; who withdrew from the 2008 race only early this year; who used campaign funds to hire the filmmaker; [whose] wife is suffering from cancer; who used his family and the importance of character and values in his campaigns; who was a possible speaker at the forthcoming Democratic nominating convention; and who campaigned surely knowing that this affair could blow up the party if he became successful and if it became known, which it almost always does.[30]

Suicides

Journalists generally agree that a suicide ranks low on the scale of news, particularly when the person involved is not a news figure and when the suicide occurs in private. There also is a consensus, however, that coverage is necessary if a suicide takes place in public or if the person involved is well known.

The suicide of Budd Dwyer in Harrisburg, Pennsylvania, on January 27, 1987, met both criteria: Dwyer, the state treasurer, shot himself to death in front of reporters and photographers at a news conference after he had been sentenced to prison for fraud. Even given those powerful news values, many news consumers objected to the broadcast of an unedited video by one station and to front-page coverage with graphic photographs in newspapers. The objections focused not on privacy but on matters of taste. News coverage of the Dwyer suicide is discussed in detail in the Case Study "Covering a Public Official's Public Suicide" in Chapter 15.

When noncelebrities commit suicide in a spectacular way – say, by leaping from a bridge while a crowd watches – most editors and news directors will opt for subdued coverage rather than appearing to glamorize the act and thus encouraging copycats.

A more common problem faced by news outlets of all sizes is deciding whether to include the cause of death in the obituary of a private citizen who has committed suicide in private. The anguish of the deceased's family is intensified when the obituary mentions suicide, even if it is a single sentence: "Police said the cause of death was a self-inflicted gunshot wound." Seeking to minimize harm, some journalists readily omit any reference to suicide, even if they list the cause of death in other obituaries. Other journalists object that this is censoring the news and that credibility suffers because, by omission, the news outlet is implying the death was due to natural causes. They reason that relatives and friends are well aware of the cause of death and might infer from the omission that other news may have been censored as well.

However, a news organization intent on reporting suicides may be thwarted by funeral directors and medical examiners who suppress the cause of death as a gesture of compassion to the families.

The way that the news media report suicide can contribute to copycat suicides, according to a study published in August 2001 by the American Foundation for Suicide Prevention, the American Association of Suicidology, and the Annenberg Public Policy Center of the University of Pennsylvania. The study found that people in the audience might identify with the suicide victim if the news media:

- portray suicide as a heroic or romantic act;
- report the suicide method, especially if the description is detailed; or
- present suicide as the inexplicable act of an otherwise healthy or high-achieving person.

The study showed that more than 90 percent of suicide victims have a significant psychiatric illness, which often is undiagnosed, untreated, or both. "The cause of an individual suicide is invariably more complicated than a recent painful event such as the break-up of a relationship or the loss of a job." An example of a problematic headline cited in the study was: "Boy, 10, kills himself over poor grades."

The study's authors urged the news media to produce more stories on such topics as trends in suicide rates, recent treatment advances, myths about suicide, and warning signs of suicides.[31]

Juveniles accused of crimes

Advocates in the criminal justice system urge that underage offenders should be shielded from publicity. Although names of the accused are routinely publicized in other crimes, these advocates argue that this is inappropriate when the defendants are juveniles. They contend that the public's desire to know the names should yield to the possibility that these young people can rebuild their lives if they do not also have to cope with the notoriety.

Few journalists disagree with that principle, and the practice is to withhold names (even in the rare instances that authorities provide them) when crimes like burglary or shoplifting are involved.

The decision-making is more complicated when children are accused of homicides or other major felonies. These situations do not lend themselves to a blanket rule, but many editors and news directors will identify children who are accused of multiple murders, as in the 1998 case of two boys who fatally shot four students and a teacher at a school in Jonesboro, Arkansas. The reasoning is that in such high-profile events, the need of the public to be completely informed outweighs the desire not to interfere with the rehabilitation of the offenders. Bill Keller, then managing editor of *The New York Times*, said that in the Jonesboro case, the boys' lives were forever "turned upside down," making their identification in the newspaper "inconsequential."[32]

Personal lives of public figures

It is accepted that a price of fame is the loss of the kind of privacy that ordinary people enjoy. Still, a legitimate question for journalists is: Aren't even celebrities entitled to some kind of privacy? The two cases below illustrate the different ways that question has been answered.

The public learned that George W. Bush had become a painter in February 2013 when The Smoking Gun posted images of two of his works that he had sent to his sister Dorothy via email.[33] One painting showed a man showering and another depicted a man in a bathtub. The images, which were rather discreet, turned out to be of the former president himself.[34]

The website had obtained the images, along with other private data, from a hacker who had intercepted the family's emails, which included lists of cell-phone numbers, home addresses, and email addresses. In addition to the artwork, the messages revealed concerns about the health of former President George H. W. Bush, including a message from George W. Bush soliciting relatives' ideas for a eulogy to his father. The Smoking Gun did not post the confidential lists turned over by the hacker. A photo of the elder Bush in the hospital was posted briefly, then taken down. On social media, the Bush paintings went viral.

William Bastone, editor and co-founder of The Smoking Gun, told Paul Farhi of *The Washington Post* that "we certainly thought hard about using some of the stuff," and said the site used only a small part of what the website received from a hacker identified only as "Guccifer." Bastone said, "The nature of the hack was so extensive and extraordinary – considering that two presidents had their emails illegally accessed – that we clearly thought it was newsworthy." The story was framed as a report on the security breach.

The Post reported the hacking but its website did not link to the original report, and *The Post* did not print the hacked photos. *The Post's* executive editor, Martin Baron, told Farhi there was no reason to print the photos because "this is all private to the Bush family; there are no public policy implications here whatsoever."[35]

George W. Bush, incidentally, exhibited 30 oil-on-board paintings of world leaders at the George Bush Presidential Library and Museum in Dallas in April 2014. Art critic Roberta Smith wrote in *The New York Times* that he "is something of a natural when it comes to making oil paintings, a decent amateur."[36]

When Michael Sam, the University of Missouri's All-America defensive end, stunned the sports world on February 9, 2014, with the announcement that he is gay, it wasn't news to the sports editor of the *Columbia Missourian*. But the story broke in the national media – ESPN, *The New York Times* – and not in the hometown paper that students publish under the supervision of professionals affiliated with the university's journalism school.

Greg Bowers, the sports editor, said that a graduate student, Erik Hall, had learned of Sam's sexual orientation six months earlier. In a column published after Sam's announcement, Bowers wrote that Hall had called Sam and asked if he could interview him about his sexuality. Three times, Sam agreed to the interview. Three times, he changed his mind. "The interview didn't happen," Bowers wrote. "So the story didn't happen. We could've written the story. Other journalists might have written the story. But it wasn't the right thing to do."

Bowers said it wasn't hard to discover that Sam was gay: "A simple Internet search turned up more than enough rumors. Chat rooms buzzed. He revealed his sexuality to his fellow defensive players back in the preseason. He frequented local gay bars."

Sam would not, however, be outed in the Missourian. "As far as we were concerned," Bowers wrote, "only one person could out him and that was Sam."[37]

Reporting social-media content

Facebook, Instagram, Twitter, and other social networking websites provide an online connection for groups such as college students, business colleagues, extended families, and friends. They also have become a routine source of background and tips for many journalists, especially when young people are involved in the news. It is smart reporting, but it also presents ethical questions of accuracy and fairness. The posting may not be authentic, and probably was intended for a private audience even though it is in a public space. Under its principle of "minimize harm," the SPJ code contains this standard: "Weigh the consequences of publishing or broadcasting personal information."

In today's environment, "what was once inaccessible conversation between small groups of ordinary people can be very accessible" to journalists, Monica Guzman of *The Seattle Times* wrote in a paper for the Online News Association's do-it-yourself ethics code. She recommended restraint:

> There might be news value to these conversations, particularly if they appear to reflect a buzzworthy trend in public sentiment. But pulling out particular quotes by particular people … might put a big spotlight on a comment never meant for such exposure.[38]

In an article for *American Journalism Review*, Jason Spencer of the *Herald-Journal* in Spartanburg, South Carolina, advised fellow reporters to email "friends" on social media to verify information or arrange interviews. "Always identify yourself as a reporter," Spencer wrote. "Remember: The information people post on a social networking page is self-selected. It could be biased, exaggerated or just plain wrong."[39]

Butch Ward of the Poynter Institute wrote an essay for Poynter about the need for verification. The essay was inspired by his daughter Caitlin's experience in having her Web comment used by the news media. Caitlin Ward, then a student at Lafayette College, posted a memorial message on the MySpace page of a friend who was killed in the Virginia Tech massacre on April 16, 2007. A few days later, a friend told her she had been quoted on *The New York Times'* website. No one from *The Times* had called for confirmation before her message was included in one of its mini-profiles of the Virginia Tech victims.

When Butch Ward contacted *The Times* while preparing his essay, an editor responded that the newspaper had concluded the risk in this instance was low. Ward ended his essay with the question: "Are we really willing to risk even further damage to our credibility by abandoning traditions as old and honored as verification?"[40]

Case Study
Tracing the Source of Web Comments

When reporter James Ewinger at *The Plain Dealer* in Cleveland read a comment about one of his relatives in an anonymous posting on his newspaper's website in March 2010, he was disturbed by its inflammatory nature. He also wondered how the writer could have acquired

(Continued)

certain inside knowledge reflected in the comment.

The comment, which discussed the relative's mental health, violated the site's rules prohibiting personal attacks. It was signed "lawmiss." Ewinger told a senior editor that the posting invaded his relative's privacy. The editor agreed that it was out of bounds and had the comment removed from the site.

But Ewinger continued to wonder who had posted the comment, so he conducted a publicly available computer search to find all the comments that lawmiss had posted on *Plain Dealer* news stories. What he saw in those comments was an intimate knowledge of the law, leading him to the conclusion that lawmiss was a lawyer, very likely a judge. He informed his editors of his suspicion.

"A day or two later, a senior editor came to me and told me that I was right," Ewinger said later. "He said he knew because a Web editor tracked down the identity."

As editor Susan Goldberg told Bob Garfield on NPR's *On the Media* program on April 2, the paper at that time had the ability "to connect people's handles online with their email addresses." She said the Web editor had run the email address through a Google search and had found that it belonged to Cuyahoga County Judge Shirley Strickland Saffold.

The Web editor had also reported that lawmiss had made more than 80 comments on the website in the previous three years – and that lawmiss had commented on three cases in Judge Saffold's court, including two capital cases.

Goldberg told Garfield that one of the cases involved a firefighter who shot and killed three people, and "lawmiss was complaining that he didn't get the death penalty because he was white, rather than black." Judge Saffold is an African American.

The other capital case was pending in Judge Saffold's court at the time. The attorney for Anthony Sowell, who was accused of killing 11 women in serial murders, was described in one lawmiss posting as someone who acts like a buffoon.

Goldberg said that, with a public-records request, the newspaper determined that "Judge Saffold's computer at the courthouse had been used to connect to [Cleveland.com] when several of the comments were made." In a filing later with the Ohio Supreme Court, Judge Saffold said: "[L]ike thousands of other Clevelanders, I do visit the Cleveland.com site, which is the online version of the Cleveland *Plain Dealer*. The fact that my computer was open to Cleveland.com at the same time that lawmiss posted comments is merely coincidence – two things happening at the same time, but with no causal relationship between them."

The newspaper decided to tell its readers the identity of lawmiss and the comments about cases before Judge Saffold. It wasn't an easy decision, Goldberg told Garfield: "We didn't, in fact, publish the next day. We made sure we got lots of comment, and we made sure the stories were fair. We also did a companion story that also ran on page one about our decision to do it and sort of the ethical firestorm we knew this was going to kick up."

The Plain Dealer published its findings on March 26. Judge Saffold filed suit for at least $50 million on April 7 against the newspaper, its website, affiliated companies, and nine staff members, including editor Goldberg, Ewinger, and the unidentified Web editor who had traced the identity of lawmiss. Among other torts, the lawsuit alleged that the defendants had defamed Judge Saffold and violated her privacy and its own privacy policy by revealing that the lawmiss comments were linked to her email address. Her daughter Sydney, then 23 and living in

Columbus, Ohio, was co-plaintiff. The lawsuit said that Shirley and Sydney shared a "family email address" that had been created by the judge's former husband, Oscar Saffold.

The judge's attorney, Brian Spitz, told Dan Bobkoff of NPR that she didn't deny that she sometimes used the pseudonym "lawmiss." But he said that she had not commented on anything that had come before her court. Spitz said those comments were written by Sydney Saffold. The daughter told reporter James F. McCarty of *The Plain Dealer* that she is an active blogger with an interest in the court system. She said she had made "quite a few, more than five" of the lawmiss comments.

Spitz told NPR: "Either *The Plain Dealer* breached its promise to keep that information confidential, or it never intended to keep it confidential. So it's either breach of contract or fraud."

The Plain Dealer said in an April 8 news story that Cleveland.com's privacy policy was written by Advance Internet, a separate entity affiliated with the newspaper's owner, Advance Publications Inc. The news story noted that the privacy policy states in part, "[W]e reserve the right to use the information we collect about your computer, which may at times be able to identify you, for any lawful business purpose."

Countering that assertion, Judge Saffold's lawsuit said the website promised users in its privacy policy that it would "protect your privacy" and that "personally identifying information is protected." In addition, the lawsuit said, the policy implicitly acknowledged that comments would be anonymous and that multiple users might use a single account, as Shirley and Sydney Saffold had done.

The lawsuit also alleged that the reason that lawmiss' identity was traced was not because of comments made about cases in Judge Saffold's court, but was instead "a result of a vendetta

against lawmiss for publishing comments about a relative of *Plain Dealer* reporter Ewinger." Continuing that vendetta, the lawsuit said, *The Plain Dealer* falsely linked Judge Saffold to racist comments posted anonymously on other websites. The lawsuit also said the paper recounted a quotation attributed to the judge in a 1996 news story that had no relevance to the lawmiss postings but instead served only "the malicious purpose of casting Shirley Saffold in a negative light."

On December 31, 2010, *The Plain Dealer* reported that the lawsuit had been dismissed and that a financial settlement had been reached with Advance Internet. Although details of the settlement were not disclosed, Judge Saffold said Advance Internet had agreed to make a charitable contribution to Olivet Institutional Baptist Church choir in the name of her mother, Retha Morris, who died in April. The judge said, "This episode was very difficult for my mother to deal with in her last days."

Advance Internet now blocks *Plain Dealer* reporters and editors from access to the email addresses of commenters. John Hassell, vice president of content for Advance Internet, said in a statement, "We take privacy very seriously and believe our users should feel confident that private information shared with us will not be made public."

As she explained in her NPR interview with Garfield (which occurred before the lawsuit was filed), editor Goldberg divided the series of events into two distinct components:

- *The decision to trace the identity of lawmiss.* The Web editor didn't consult Goldberg about this: "it was just something he went ahead and did. … Maybe it wasn't a good decision. To me, okay, the decision was made. Now we've got to go forward, and what do we do?"

(Continued)

- *The decision to report that lawmiss had made comments about cases before Judge Saffold.* "[W]hat keeps getting lost in this debate is the right of this defendant who is on trial for his life to a fair and impartial judge," Goldberg said. "I would imagine that those cases could be subject of appeal. I would imagine that *The Plain Dealer* would be just devastated by criticism about sitting on relevant and important information."

After *The Plain Dealer*'s revelations about lawmiss, the attorney for murder defendant Anthony Sowell asked the Ohio Supreme Court to remove Judge Saffold from the Sowell case. Acting Chief Justice Paul E. Pfeifer did so on April 22. He wrote in his order, "An objective observer who has read the online postings might reasonably question why comments about a defendant and defense counsel appearing before the judge were posted on the judge's personal online account, even if the judge did not make the comments herself."

Discussion of the case

This case can be approached as two separate cases, each with its own moral agent. The class could consider what its decision would be in each case.

In the first case, the moral agent is the Web editor who decided to use internal software to determine the email address of lawmiss. Goldberg has said in an interview for her own newspaper published on March 26: "You can argue we should not have uncovered lawmiss' identity, and maybe we shouldn't have."

The same *Plain Dealer* story, written by reporter Henry J. Gomez, also quoted media ethicist Bob Steele of the Poynter Institute and DePauw University as being troubled by the decision to investigate who was using the lawmiss pseudonym. He said that at the time the investigation began that there was "no immediate, profound danger to someone" and "no clear suspicion of judicial misconduct."

Gomez also interviewed Rebecca Jeschke of Electronic Frontier Foundation, an online privacy rights group. Jeschke said, "I would think twice before participating in a message board where I had to give my email address knowing that management could access it at any time. It seems appropriate in this case, but … it's hard not to imagine scenarios where it's abused."

Gomez also found that other news organizations already were hiding online commenters' identity from their news staffs. Steve Yelvington of Morris Digital Works, the online division of a company with 13 daily newspapers, said: "We are careful to firewall our business records from our journalists."

Gomez's story noted that in a May 2009 column in *The Plain Dealer*, editor Goldberg encouraged "freewheeling conversation" on blogs and stories at Cleveland.com. His story said: "She also wrote that she was not in favor of requiring posters to use their real names because she feared that, given the culture of the Internet, doing so would stifle online conversation."

In the second case, Goldberg is the moral agent. After consulting with the paper's lawyers and other editors, she made the decision to tell the public that the lawmiss comments came from Judge Saffold's email address.

Goldberg said she felt compelled to act once she knew lawmiss was linked to a judge and that some of the comments dealt with capital cases heard by that judge.

"I don't know how you can pretend you don't know that information. How can you put that genie back in the bottle?" the editor told Gomez for his March 26 story:

What if it ever came to light that someone using the email of a sitting judge made comments on a public Web site about cases she was hearing, and we did not disclose it? These are capital crimes and life-and-death issues for these defendants. I think not to disclose this would be a violation of our mission and damaging to our credibility as a news organization.

In his interview with Gomez, ethicist Steele agreed with Goldberg's decision to report the information, despite his objections to the way the newspaper had discovered lawmiss' identity. Steele said: "Should *The Plain Dealer* be shining light on this? I say yes. I don't think *The Plain Dealer* could walk away from the puzzle with so many pieces turned face up right now."

Sources

Atassi, Leila, "Cuyahoga County Judge Shirley Strickland Saffold files $50 million lawsuit against *The Plain Dealer* and others," *The Plain Dealer*, Apr. 8, 2010.

Bobkoff, Dan, "Judge takes paper to court over online comments," NPR, Apr. 10, 2010.

Ewinger, James, email exchange with Gene Foreman, July 2014; telephone conversation, July 28, 2014.

Farkas, Karen, "Judge Shirley Strickland Saffold is removed from the Anthony Sowell murder trial," *The Plain Dealer*, Apr. 22, 2010.

Gomez, Henry J., "*Plain Dealer* sparks ethical debate by unmasking anonymous cleveland. com poster," *The Plain Dealer*, Mar. 26, 2010.

McCarty, James F., "Anonymous online comments are linked to the personal email account of Cuyahoga County Common Pleas Judge Shirley Strickland Saffold," *The Plain Dealer*, Mar. 26, 2010.

NPR, "Anonymous justice," On the Media, Apr. 2, 2010. Transcript of Bob Garfield's interview with Susan Goldberg on NPR.

Plain Dealer staff, "Saffolds dismiss lawsuit against *Plain Dealer*, settle with Advance Internet," *The Plain Dealer*, Dec. 31, 2010.

Schultz, Connie, "Web site posters' anonymity an invitation to mischief," *The Plain Dealer*, Mar. 28, 2010.

Court filings in the lawsuit "Shirley Strickland Saffold et al. vs. Plain Dealer Publishing Company et al."

Case Study

Mapping the Locations of Gun Owners

In the days after the shootings that left 28 people dead in Newtown, Connecticut, editors and reporters at *The Journal News* in New York City's northern suburbs talked about news coverage of the issue of guns. They discussed how neighbors of Nancy Lanza were surprised that she kept in her home the high-powered weapons that her son Adam used to kill her, 20 children, and six adults at Sandy Hook Elementary School, and himself. Because much of *The*

(Continued)

Journal News' market looks a lot like Newtown, they focused on what the newspaper could tell its readers about the weapons in their neighborhoods and who owned them.

Reporter Dwight R. Worley proposed a story exploring whether existing laws gave the public enough information about gun owners in their community. As part of his investigation, he intended to gather pistol-permit data from public records.

On December 23, 2012, nine days after the Newtown massacre, *The Journal News* published Worley's story, along with data from public records about 33,614 handgun owners in two suburban counties. Online, it posted an interactive map. Although the map was not searchable by name or address, it allowed readers to hover over neighborhoods and streets and see who had permits in those locations.

Worley's news article was accompanied by an editor's note disclosing that the reporter "owns a Smith & Wesson 686.357 Magnum and has had a residence permit in New York City for that weapon since February 2011."

Gun owners responded angrily to what they perceived as a reckless and unwarranted invasion of privacy.

Christine Haughney reported on the outcry in *The New York Times* on January 6:

> Personal information about editors and writers at the paper has been posted online, including their home addresses and information about where their children attended school; some reporters have received notes saying they would be shot on the way to their cars; bloggers have encouraged people to steal credit card information of *Journal News* employees; and two packages containing white powder have been sent to the newsroom and a third to a reporter's home (all were tested by the police and proved to be harmless).

Publisher Janet Hasson said later that a total of five suspicious packages were received either in the newspaper's White Plains office or in employees' homes. Hasson hired armed guards to patrol two of the newspaper's offices.

The Journal News' December 23 article was headlined "The Gun Owner Next Door: What You Don't Know about the Weapons in Your Neighborhood."

Worley introduced the article with three paragraphs about a shooting that had occurred in 2012 in the Westchester County town of Katonah. A 77-year-old man who had shot and wounded a female neighbor was found to have accumulated a number of weapons, including two handguns that had not been registered. Worley wrote that neighbors were surprised to learn of the cache, and one was quoted as saying: "Would I have bought this house knowing somebody (close by) had an arsenal of weapons? No, I would not have."

Worley's fourth paragraph read: "In the wake of the mass shooting at the Sandy Hook Elementary School … and amid renewed nationwide calls for stronger gun control, some Lower Hudson Valley residents would like lawmakers to expand the amount of information the public can find out about gun owners."

The newspaper had obtained the information about handgun ownership through Freedom of Information requests to the three counties in its circulation area: Westchester, Rockland, and Putnam. Westchester and Rockland responded with names and addresses but declined to give information about the types of weapons owned; Putnam defied the FOI request. Explaining why only handgun owners were listed, the newspaper said New York laws allow people to buy rifles and shotguns without getting a permit.

Reviewing *The Journal News'* project and the public response a year and a half later, Worley said the map wound up overshadowing the story he proposed and wrote. His idea, he said, was not to "simply publish names and addresses on a map and tack a story onto it." He said that, "while the public, for obvious reasons, focused on the map, for the newspaper the story came first."

In an email, he elaborated on his purpose:

[T]he story asked questions about the type of information that should be made public about gun owners; whether names and addresses are enough or should the public have access to more information, including the types of permits issued and the type/number of weapons owned. Most people I interviewed, including gun-control advocates, said names and addresses are enough and information beyond that should remain private. My story reflected those views. The map accompanied the story.

Worley's December 23 article contained gun owners' criticism of the newspaper's intention to publish the gun-ownership data. A certified gun instructor, licensed to carry firearms and the owner of an AR-15 automatic rifle, one of the firearms used by the Newtown shooter, was quoted: "Why do my neighbors need to know that? I'm not a threat to my neighbors." The president of the New York Rifle and Pistol Association said publishing the data would endanger gun owners, noting that some of them owned valuable weapon collections. "You're giving a shopping list to criminals," he told Worley.

The Journal News published a follow-up story on June 15, 2013, asserting that no gun-theft spree had occurred:

Four months and 593 Westchester and Rockland burglaries later, there's little to suggest those fears materialized. A *Journal News* review of burglaries in the two counties found that

11 handguns were stolen in six break-ins – four of those plus a rifle from one residence – through May 1. Three of those homes were not on the map, and police said they found no link between the map and the three that were, despite widespread media reports and statements from public officials that the map was to blame.

Publisher Hasson defended the newspaper's original report at the time it was published. "Frequently the work of journalists is not popular," she said in a prepared statement. "One of our roles is to report publicly available information on timely issues, even when unpopular. We knew publication of the database (as well as the accompanying article providing context) would be controversial, but we felt sharing information about gun permits in our area was important in the aftermath of the Newtown shootings."

The map was planned from the beginning as the digital component to the story, Hasson said in an email. That is "our standard approach to any story we do, to provide the richest, most detailed digital assets available."

Hasson said it was worth noting that the gun permit story received 234,652 page views and 98,386 visits. The map, which was taken down on January 18, 2013, after New York changed its gun laws and allowed permit holders to shield their identifying information, received 1,149,813 page views and 672,947 visits. Hasson said, "Beyond the controversy and discounting a good portion of that traffic to outside the newspaper's market, local readers were still highly interested in finding out who owned guns in their neighborhood."

The publisher said the staff was surprised by "the ferocity and the highly organized nature of the opposition" from the National Rifle Association and other gun-rights groups. "We had published a story in 2006 about what happens

(Continued)

to the weapons of permit holders after they die," she said. "That included a list of the permit holders' names and their hometowns. That story sparked intense opposition as well, but not at the same intensity level." What was the difference? She concluded that it was the role social media played in 2012 and the fact that the story appeared right after Newtown, "when gun-rights groups were on high alert for any perceived negative publicity."

Journalists who commented on *The Journal News'* project were generally disapproving.

Al Tompkins of the Poynter Institute argued that the newspaper had failed to justify what the gun owners saw as an intrusion. "Journalistic invasions of privacy ought to produce outstanding insights into an issue and problem," Tompkins wrote on the Poynter website. Timeliness – that is, publishing the lists immediately after the Newtown shootings – "is not reason enough to publish this information," he wrote.

In a *New York Times* column headlined "Invasion of the Data Snatchers," Bill Keller asked rhetorically: "[W]hat is the boundary between a public service and an invasion of privacy?"

David Carr, a *Times* colleague of Keller's, also wrote a critical column: "[W]as it really journalism? Not so much. The accompanying article was about whether gun permits should be public, but the newspaper seemed to have all but decided that debate by publishing the map." The decision, Carr wrote, "lacked a rationale."

For his blog on Washingtonpost.com, Erik Wemple consulted James Grimaldi, an investigative reporter for *The Wall Street Journal*. He quoted Grimaldi: "Really, it is a data dump with little analysis. They should have looked to see what the patterns are. Any criminals who got guns and shouldn't have them? School teachers? Preachers? I'd run the list against other databases – get creative. Vs. other licenses? School bus drivers? Grocers? Seems an opportunity lost."

The Journal News was defended by Geneva Overholser, former editor of *The Des Moines Register* and at the time the director of the Annenberg School for Communication and Journalism at the University of Southern California. In an interview with David Folkenflik on NPR, she said the paper had performed a service. "Public information like this," she said, "can give somebody living in a given neighborhood a more accurate view of what life is like around them."

Dylan Byers, media reporter for *Politico*, defended the newspaper against criticism that its work lacked context. He wrote, "In the highly charged debate over guns that followed the shooting, the extent of ownership was highly relevant. The shooting, known to anyone in this country not living under a rock, *was* the context. By publishing the 'gun map,' *The Journal News* gave readers a visceral understanding of the presence of guns in their own community." Jack Shafer made a similar point in a column for Reuters: "Surely it was considered vital news to many in Westchester and Rockland that their neighbors were packing portable heat."

Sources

Byers, Dylan, "In defense of the 'Journal News' gun map," *Politico*, Jan. 14, 2013.

Carr, David, "Guns, maps and data that disturb," *The New York Times*, Jan. 13, 2013.

Folkenflik, David, "Journalists thrust into heart of gun story," NPR, Dec. 27, 2012.

Haughney, Christine, "After pinpointing gun owners, paper is a target," *The New York Times*, Jan. 6, 2013.

Keller, Bill, "Invasion of the data snatchers," *The New York Times*, Jan. 13, 2013.

Shafer, Jack, "Let's not go crazy over publishing gun lists," Reuters, Jan. 2, 2013.

Tompkins, Al, "Where *The Journal News* went wrong in publishing names, addresses of gun owners," Poynter, Dec. 27, 2012.

Wemple, Erik, "The 4 mistakes of the *Journal News*," *The Washington Post*, Jan. 2, 2013.

Worley, Dwight R., "The gun owner next door: what you don't know about the weapons in your neighborhood," *The Journal News*, Dec. 24, 2012.

Questions for Class Discussion

- What are the arguments for publishing and mapping the names and addresses of handgun owners? What would you have done?
- Is a publication justified by the fact that the information is in the public record? To borrow hypotheticals from Bill Keller's column, would you publish other lists that possibly could be obtained legally: The personal details of all the employees of local clinics that perform abortions? The names and addresses of food-stamp recipients in your community? Addresses of homes where pit bulls are kept?
- When a news organization makes a decision of this kind, is it appropriate to weigh the subjects' perception of harm against the value of the information to the public?

Case Study

Identifying a 13-Year-Old Rape Victim

On New Year's Day 2002, 13-year-old Alicia Kozakiewicz walked out of her house in suburban Pittsburgh and got into a car driven by a Virginia man she had met in an online chat room. That was the beginning of a nightmare. For the next four days, she was tortured, sexually assaulted, and chained to the floor of the basement of the man's townhouse.

While she was missing, Pittsburgh news media outlets ran her photograph and stories about her disappearance. Those media notices helped lead to her rescue. A Florida man saw an online video of Alicia being held captive, then found the missing-person news stories. The tipster notified the FBI. Agents traced the abductor's screen name, determined her location, and came to her rescue.

Returning home after her rescue, Alicia and her parents, Mary and Charlie Kozakiewicz, found the place surrounded by reporters and photojournalists. Before going inside, they spoke briefly with the media. Mary Kozakiewicz said their only purpose was to allow Alicia "to say thank you because everyone had done their job. In this community, when you get help, you say thanks."

She added, "But many said that by allowing her to say thanks ... we gave a press conference."

Indeed, that was the way some of the journalists saw it, and the perception contributed to their decision to continue naming the girl in their coverage of her abduction and rescue,

(Continued)

even though her abductor had been accused of sexual assault. (The abductor, Scott Tyree, then 38, was convicted and sent to prison.)

Johnna A. Pro, a *Pittsburgh Post-Gazette* staff writer, told student journalist Alissa Wisnouse in 2002: "I think they thought this was her 15 minutes of fame. I think we might have hesitated had her parents brought her back and hidden her at her grandmother's house. But they were making no attempt to shield her from the onslaught of the media."

It would be years before any members of the Kozakiewicz family spoke to journalists again. As the incessant coverage continued in the print and broadcast media, they disconnected their telephones and would not answer the door. Mary Kozakiewicz said her daughter felt she was "being forced into hiding."

This Case Study focuses on the *Post-Gazette*, although the *Pittsburgh Tribune-Review* and at least some of the local broadcast outlets also continued using the girl's name.

Like most news media, the *Post-Gazette*'s policy is to shield the identity of sexual-assault victims. But in this case, reporters and editors were already inclined to continue using her name because it was "out there" as a result of the two missing-person stories. They reasoned that it would have been futile to try to pull her name back.

The parents' behavior seemed to assuage any doubts. Pro said in 2002 she felt bad for the girl "because I think she was wronged by her parents, not us. It's her parents' job to protect her, not ours. I think once she was found, they could have and should have shielded her from the media. And they didn't." Put simply, Pro said, "I'm not her mother, I'm not her dad. I'm a journalist with a job to do."

After the initial stories about rescuing the girl, the *Post-Gazette* stopped using her photograph. However, the newspaper continued to

use her name in 13 news stories, five columns, and two letters to the editor, according to the numbers Wisnouse reported in a thesis at Pennsylvania State University that spring.

The coverage continued for a month. The topics included updates on criminal proceedings against Tyree, Internet safety for teens, and whether the girl's parents owed tuition payments for Alicia because she was attending a public school outside her home district. (Mary Kozakiewicz said they did not owe tuition.) One column discussed how, before her abduction, the girl had a website "replete with sexually provocative phrases and pictures of herself." (Mary Kozakiewicz characterized the pictures as "simple family photos.")

On January 20, more than two weeks after the girl was rescued, the *Post-Gazette*'s then editor, the late John Craig, wrote a column discussing the newspaper's decision to name her:

> If the *Post-Gazette* has a firm policy on not identifying the names of victims of sexual crimes, and is at particular pains to protect the identity of children, how is it that the newspaper continues to print [her] name and picture? We had a lively internal debate on that question over several days last week. ...
> I acknowledged that withholding the names of sexual-abuse victims of all ages is a popular position and it was unlikely that there would be complaints if we stopped using her name. ... In my opinion, electronic databases being what they are, unless there is a fundamental change in the laws of the United States, anyone visiting the *PG*'s files years from now will be able to find the name and the stories. That is a long-term privacy risk.

Craig invited readers to share their thoughts with him, and Pro said there was no public outcry about using the girl's name: "People were upset with her parents. The public reaction was against her parents, not the media." The parents, of course, were not talking, so that perception went unchallenged.

Looking back on the case in 2008, Pro said:

Did we do a disservice to Alicia? The nurturing, empathetic side of me says yes. Even so, I believe my job as a journalist covering the story was to report it fairly and accurately, which I did; to debate the necessity of using her name with my colleagues and superiors, which I did; and serve my readers, which I did.

The disconnect between the parents and the journalists proved to be emotionally costly. After a girl has been rescued from a predator, Mary Kozakiewicz said, "you should not use her name. Give her time to heal."

Mrs. Kozakiewicz said, "Things would die down a bit, but every time her name was mentioned on television or in the newspaper, people would be pointing again." As a result, she chose to home-school Alicia for the remainder of the school year. "When she attended a public high school the following year, kids still treated her differently."

In the fall of 2007 college freshman Alicia Kozakiewicz began conducting weekly multimedia presentations at elementary and middle schools in the Pittsburgh region. "Given the awful power of her tale, she's been inundated with requests to speak," Nicole Weisensee Egan wrote in *People* magazine. Egan described a presentation she made before 400 students: "Projected behind her on a screen is her missing poster. 'That's me about five years ago,' she tells the kids, who listen with rapt attention. 'I was almost another body in the morgue. So please: Listen to me.'"

Mary Kozakiewicz said her daughter's experience with the news media was a factor in her decision to speak to the school groups. Mrs. Kozakiewicz said she, too, is speaking out. She travels with Alicia to speak with law-enforcement officers, educators, and legislators. To families with missing children, she said her message is: "Be very careful of the media because though they may be instrumental in the recovery of your child, you must also be aware of the harm they can do."

Should the *Post-Gazette* and other Pittsburgh media have continued using Alicia's name in 2002?

In an email to Wisnouse, Bill Mitchell of the Poynter Institute addressed the question of whether the parents invited publicity: "The parents' views should certainly be considered but not necessarily considered determinative. A parent in such case might urge a newsroom to use a child's name – who knows why? – but the newsroom would still be faced with making its own best decision in the interest of the child and its own principles."

This case is adapted, with permission, from an honors thesis that Alissa Wisnouse (now Alissa Barron Stranzl) wrote while a senior at Pennsylvania State University. The case uses Alicia Kozakiewicz's name because she is now an adult and has made public presentations on her experience.

Sources

Alissa Wisnouse's original sources included:

Chute, Eleanor, "Girl reunited with grateful parents who 'feel blessed,'" *Pittsburgh Post-Gazette*, Jan. 6, 2002.

Craig, John G., Jr., "To name or not to name: sex-crime cases pose a privacy concern," *Pittsburgh Post-Gazette*, Jan. 20, 2002.

Geisler, Jill, "You can't unring a bell, but you can stop ringing it," Poynter, Mar. 16, 2000.

(Continued)

Gigler, Dan, "Crafton Heights girl, 13, missing," *Pittsburgh Post-Gazette*, Jan. 3, 2002.

Kalson, Sally, "Alicia's web sites pose a very disturbing question," *Pittsburgh Post-Gazette*, Jan. 9, 2002.

Pittsburgh Post-Gazette Stylebook, 1997.

Pro, Johnna A., "Teen's parents fear Internet link in disappearance," *Pittsburgh Post-Gazette*, Jan. 4, 2002.

Roddy, Dennis B., and Jon Schmitz, "Suspect Scott Tyree: 'A classic long-haired computer guy'," *Pittsburgh Post-Gazette*, Jan. 5, 2002.

Wisnouse, Alissa, email exchanges with Bill Mitchell (Apr. 4, 2002) and Jill Geisler (Apr. 5, 2002).

Wisnouse, Alissa, telephone interviews with Tom Birdsong (Mar. 11, 2002) and Johnna A. Pro (Mar. 22, 2002).

The Case Study also draws on the following sources:

Egan, Nicole Weisensee, "Abducted, enslaved – and now talking about it," *People*, Apr. 16, 2007.

Foreman, Gene, telephone interview with Mary Kozakiewicz, Dec. 10, 2008; email exchange, Dec. 8–11, 2008.

Kahle, Shannon, telephone interview with Mary Kozakiewicz, Sept. 5, 2008.

Pro, Johnna A., email to Shannon Kahle, June 20, 2008.

Questions for Class Discussion

- Do you think the fact that the girl's name was "out there" in the missing-person stories gave the *Post-Gazette* no choice but to continue using her name?
- If you favor continuing to use her name, do you think it was appropriate to write enterprise stories on such topics as her Internet site and whether the girl's family owed tuition payments?
- If you think the *Post-Gazette* should have stopped using her name, how would you have explained your decision to the readers?
- Should the parents' apparent willingness to allow the girl to be interviewed have guided the journalists' decision to continue covering her?
- In writing his column, was editor John Craig being accountable to *Post-Gazette* readers?

Notes

1 This section of the chapter is based on "Naming a tweeter," a case study developed by Libbi Heinz and Kristin Odell from the University of Arkansas Center for Ethics in Journalism. Disclosure: The reporting and writing of the case was overseen by the author of this textbook, who was serving in fall 2013 as the university's first distinguished visiting professor in journalism ethics. The case was retrieved on Oct. 23, 2014, from http://journalism.uark.edu/wp/?p=3095.

2 Heinz and Odell, "Naming a tweeter."

3 Philip Patterson and Lee Wilkins, *Media Ethics: Issues and Cases*, 5th edn. (New York: McGraw-Hill, 2005), 135.

4 Louis W. Hodges, "The journalist and privacy," *Journal of Mass Media Ethics*, 9:4 (1994), 202.

5 Ibid., 197.

6 Ibid., 200.

7 Ibid., 202.

8 The three topics were identified in Jay Black, Bob Steele, and Ralph Barney, *Doing Ethics in Journalism:*

A Handbook with Case Studies, 3rd edn. (Boston: Allyn & Bacon, 1999), 238.

9 Warren, Samuel D., and Louis D. Brandeis, "The Right to Privacy," *Harvard Law Review*, 4:5 (Dec. 15, 1890).

10 Turner Catledge, *My Life and The Times* (New York: Harper & Row, 1971), 38.

11 Louis A. Day, *Ethics in Media Communications: Cases and Controversies*, 5th edn. (Belmont, CA: Thomson Wadsworth, 2006), 139.

12 Ibid.

13 Hodges, "The journalist and privacy," 203.

14 Day, *Ethics in Media Communications*, 153.

15 Author's recollections as managing editor of *The Philadelphia Inquirer*.

16 Robert J. Haiman, *Best Practices for Newspaper Journalists* (Arlington, VA: Freedom Forum's Free Press/Fair Press Project, 2000), 29.

17 Kelly McBride, "Rethinking rape coverage," *Quill*, Oct.–Nov. 2002, 9.

18 Larry J. Sabato, *Feeding Frenzy: How Attack Journalism Has Transformed American Politics* (New York: Free Press, 1991), 40.

19 Gail Collins, "A candidate's 'irrelevant' past," *The American Editor*, Dec. 1999, 16.

20 Marion Clark and Rudy Maxa, "Closed session romance on the Hill," *The Washington Post*, May 23, 1976.

21 Alicia C. Shepard, "Gatekeepers without gates," *American Journalism Review*, Mar. 1999.

22 Leonard Downie Jr. and Robert G. Kaiser, *The News about the News* (New York: Alfred A. Knopf, 2002), 56–62.

23 Rhonda Schwartz, Brian Ross, and Chris Francescani, "Edwards admits sexual affair; lied as presidential candidate," ABCNews, Aug. 8, 2008.

24 Michael Calderone, "Why I also didn't write on John Edwards," *Politico*, Aug. 10, 2008.

25 Russell Adams and Shira Ovide, "Mainstream media notes *Enquirer* scoop," *The Wall Street Journal*, Aug. 11, 2008.

26 Clark Hoyt, "Sometimes, there's news in the gutter," *The New York Times*, Aug. 10, 2008.

27 Adams and Ovide, "Mainstream media notes *Enquirer* scoop."

28 Howard Kurtz, "Affair put press in a touchy situation," *The Washington Post*, Aug. 11, 2008.

29 David Perel's comment on *Reliable Sources* on Cable News Network, Aug. 10, 2008.

30 Michael Getler, "The Edwards confession: unfit for *NewsHour* viewers?," PBS, Aug. 13, 2008.

31 "Recommendations for reporting on suicide," American Foundation for Suicide Prevention.

32 Keller was quoted in "Naming kid criminals," *Columbia Journalism Review*, July–Aug. 1998, 18.

33 Paul Farhi, "Publication of hacked George W. Bush e-mails raises journalism ethics questions," *The Washington Post*, Feb. 8, 2013.

34 Alex Seitz-Wald, "The four most interesting revelations from the hacked Bush emails," *Salon*, Feb. 8, 2013.

35 Farhi, "Publication of hacked George W. Bush e-mails."

36 Roberta Smith, "The faces of power, from the portraitist in chief," *The New York Times*, Apr. 6, 2014.

37 Greg Bowers, "Behind the story: the Michael Sam story began brewing in August," *Columbia Missourian*, Feb. 9, 2014.

38 Monica Guzman, "Privacy/reporting on personal lives," paper for the Online News Association.

39 Jason Spencer, "Found in (My)Space," *American Journalism Review*, Oct.–Nov. 2007, 36–39.

40 Butch Ward, "From MySpace post to NYT quote," Poynter, May 21, 2007.

15 Making News Decisions about Taste

The conflict between reflecting reality and respecting the audience

---

Learning Goals

This chapter will help you understand:

- the choices that journalists have to make when reporting the news could offend a significant segment of the audience, and why those choices have ethical implications;
- a two-step process for making decisions about news content that is likely to offend;
- the problem of perceived insensitivity by the media;
- the problem of offensive words in the news; and
- the problem of offensive images in the news.

Author's note: Because of the nature of the subject, this chapter contains strong language and images.

Two days after Seung-Hui Cho massacred 32 fellow Virginia Tech students and shot himself dead, a package arrived at NBC news headquarters in New York at 11 a.m. on Wednesday, April 18, 2007.[1] The package contained 25 minutes of video, 45 photographs, and a 23-page manifesto in which the mass murderer sought "to use the media as his personal platform."[2]

Cho mailed the package during the two hours between his murder of two people in a dormitory and of 30 others in a classroom building. He sent it by overnight delivery, but the package was delayed because he had entered the wrong zip code. The network notified the FBI and held off reporting on the package until the agency's experts could examine it.

That evening on *NBC Nightly News*, the network broadcast two minutes of video, seven photographs, and 37 sentences from Cho's manifesto. The images showed Cho pointing guns at the camera and profanely denouncing rich "brats" and their "hedonistic needs." In an excerpt shown by NBC, Cho said:

> You had a hundred billion chances and ways to have avoided today. But you decided to spill my blood. You forced me into a corner and gave me only one option. The decision was yours. Now you have blood on your hands that will never wash off.

Anchor Brian Williams told viewers, "We are sensitive to how all of this will be seen by those affected and know we are, in effect, airing the words of a murderer here tonight."[3]

The Ethical Journalist: Making Responsible Decisions in the Digital Age, Second Edition. Gene Foreman.
© 2016 John Wiley & Sons, Inc. Published 2016 by John Wiley & Sons, Inc.

Parts of the same video appeared on cable news programs that evening and on the three networks' morning shows on Thursday, April 19. Newspaper front pages displayed photographs of Cho waving the guns. Online news sites around the world posted various versions of Cho's package.

The reaction of the public was swift and overwhelmingly angry. In protest, the families of several Virginia Tech victims cancelled scheduled appearances on the NBC *Today* show.[4] One comment posted on NBC's website, expressing the view of many, read: "I am totally appalled that NBC News has chosen to broadcast the videos of a psychopath according to his wishes."[5] A reader wrote to the *Houston Chronicle* to object to its front-page photo of Cho: "Are you trying to glorify or vilify this tormented young man? And are you giving fodder for others who might … get their '15 minutes of fame'[?]"[6]

A theme of the public's outrage was that the news media were paying too much attention to the killer and not enough to the innocent victims. Some made the point that the image of Cho with his guns was the last thing those victims ever saw.

As the complaints poured in on Thursday, April 19, television outlets sharply reduced their use of the video. According to a content analysis by the Project for Excellence in Journalism,

> By Thursday night, some of the cable shows were showing brief excerpts of the videos while others were not showing anything at all. And by Friday morning, April 20, it appears that almost all of the TV outlets decided to stop airing the footage.[7]

NBC anchor Williams said he would broadcast more material only if it shed more light on the killings.[8] Fox News announced that it would stop showing the video, saying, "Sometimes you change your mind."[9] ABC News spokesman Jeffrey Schneider said, "It has value as breaking news, but then becomes practically pornographic as it is repeated ad nauseam."[10]

WSLS-TV, the NBC affiliate in Roanoke, decided after the first day to stop airing audio of Cho's "ranting death tape" or images of Cho pointing weapons. "We realize that would only further cause pain to the Virginia Tech community," executive producer Jessica A. Ross said in a statement.[11]

On April 24, Williams and NBC News president Steve Capus flew to Chicago to appear on *The Oprah Winfrey Show* to defend their decision. "Sometimes good journalism is bad public relations," Capus said. "Remember, this was days after the incident. The largest question out there was 'Why?'" Williams said the images were too much for his own family to watch but too important not to give to the public. He and Capus said the network showed restraint in selecting which of Cho's material it would broadcast.[12]

The ethical issue that journalists faced in Cho's hate-filled package pivoted on balancing the fundamental principles of truth-telling and minimizing harm. It involved choices about *taste* – choices between reporting certain information because it is in the public interest, and withholding it or toning it down out of respect for the sensibilities of the audience. Respect for the audience is an ethical responsibility. So is a concern for the people involved in the stories and pictures. And, on the opposite side of the coin, so is the news media's obligation to report the news.

Despite the protests, journalists were right to inform the public about the contents of Cho's multimedia package, although the quantity of coverage is open to debate. "I believe that the video and Cho's so-called manifesto add pieces to a complex puzzle, albeit a very painful puzzle," said the ethicist Bob Steele: "We may not know more about why he did what he did, but his tape and his writings might give us more understanding of what happened on Monday and why it happened as it did."[13]

What is beyond dispute in the Cho case is that many in the audience thought their values were not shared by the news media. This may be a gross misreading of the media's intent, but it reinforces the axiom that editors and news directors should approach taste decisions with care and explain those decisions thoughtfully. Even then, they can expect complaints.

A Two-Step Decision Process on Taste Issues

To make decisions about taste – how to handle offensive content – journalists should be aware that the media can offend in three ways:

1   with words or images that can be perceived as insensitive, as the Cho package was;
2   with words that are obscene, vulgar, or profane, are sexist, or disparage ethnic or racial groups; and
3   with images that portray graphic violence and nudity.

In general, the mainstream news organizations police their content to avoid *unnecessarily* offending their audiences. Editors and news directors want to build a loyal audience. They know that many news consumers will go elsewhere if they are regularly offended by what they read, see, or hear, or if they are concerned about exposing their children to content of this kind. That is a powerful incentive for news organizations to avoid offensive content. Unlike the motion-picture industry, whose rating system cautions customers about the kind of language and scenes they will see if they go to a certain movie, mainstream news outlets assume that their audience expects nothing more startling than a PG or PG–13 product.

A two-step process (Figure 15.1) can guide you to a thoughtful decision on whether to publish, broadcast, or post offensive content.

Figure 15.1
Making decisions on offensive content.
GRAPHIC COURTESY OF BILL MARSH.

STEP 1 Recognize words or images that likely will offend a significant number of the audience.

STEP 2 Assess the news value of the content. Is the news value outweighed by the offense likely to be taken? Or is the news is so valuable that the public needs to be told even though many will be offended?

News value

Offense

Step 1: Recognize words or images that are likely to offend a significant number of the audience

The three categories of potentially offensive words and images listed above should help you identify problematic material. So should your observations about audience reaction in the past to material that your organization and other organizations have used. Pay attention to a furor like that generated by the Cho package, because the audience is sending a message.

Apply what some journalists call "the Wheaties test": deciding whether a typical news consumer can handle watching, hearing, or reading the news while eating breakfast. Rule-based thinking would lead you to discard any content that fails the Wheaties test. That could be the easiest choice, but it might not fulfill your responsibility to inform the public.

Step 2: Assess the news value of the content

In this step, ends-based thinking is involved. You may decide that the news value does not outweigh the offense likely to be taken. Or you may decide that the news is so valuable that the public needs to be told, even though many will be offended.

If you decide to use the offensive content, make careful decisions about how to present it – that is, apply Aristotle's Golden Mean. Consider the length of time to allot on a broadcast; the size and location of photographs in a newspaper; and cautionary notices that can be posted with links used in online coverage. Think about how to explain your decision.

When the Audience Might See Insensitivity

As discussed, the Cho multimedia package offended a sizable segment of the audience primarily because of the perception that news organizations were glorifying a mass killer. The media were criticized for perceived insensitivity, not for vulgar language or obscene images (Cho's profanities in his videotape were bleeped by broadcasters).

Another example of what some perceived as insensitivity was CBS's decision to broadcast on *60 Minutes* the videotaped moment of death for a terminally ill man whom Dr. Jack Kevorkian had injected with potassium chloride, after the man confirmed that he wanted to die. CBS's broadcast of Kevorkian's video on November 22, 1998, was widely criticized, and six network-affiliated stations refused to air the segment. The criticism was two-pronged: First, CBS was faulted for giving Kevorkian a platform for airing his views on euthanasia (the network said it was illuminating the debate). Second, CBS was accused of using exclusive video of a man's death to boost ratings during a sweeps week (CBS said the show was not rushed).[14] "That this death was staged for the cameras is the most unsettling aspect of the story, a dark corollary to the growing assumption that the untelevised life is not worth living," Caryn James wrote in *The New York Times*.[15]

Later, Kevorkian was convicted of second-degree murder in Michigan and served eight years in prison before being paroled in 2007.[16] He died in 2011.

Words can be insensitive in context even if they are not vulgar. Examples are *trailer trash* and other terms of class identification. This excerpt from a story about public schools is gratuitously hurtful:

[S]tudents are "tracked," grouped by their perceived abilities into separate classes. And it doesn't take an education expert to see when a teacher … is stuck in a class period where the school's discipline problems, throwaways and dumb kids have been sent to learn."[17]

Offensive Words in the News

Although their decisions on taste questions are more often a matter of judgment than of law, broadcast news organizations are subject to the scrutiny of the Federal Communications Commission. The Supreme Court has ruled that "obscenity" is not protected under the First Amendment, and the FCC bans it on broadcast television and radio at all times. What the FCC calls "indecent" or "profane" material is prohibited between the hours of 6 a.m. and 10 p.m. local time, when the FCC says there is "a reasonable risk" that children will be in the audience. (See Box 15.1.) There is no FCC list of words that are always indecent or profane; the FCC says it decides on a case-by-case basis and is influenced by the context in which the words are uttered.[18]

Box 15.1   FCC Definitions of Offensive Content

The following summary is based on the Federal Communications Commission's "Consumer guide: obscene, indecent and profane broadcasts."

Obscenity is not protected by the First Amendment and cannot be broadcast at any time. The Supreme Court has established that, to be obscene, material must meet a three-pronged test:

- An average person, applying contemporary community standards, must find that the material, as a whole, appeals to the prurient interest.
- The material must depict or describe, in a patently offensive way, sexual conduct specifically defined by applicable law.
- The material, taken as a whole, must lack serious literary, artistic, political, or scientific value.

Indecency has been defined by the FCC as "language or material that, in context, depicts or describes, in terms patently offensive as measured by contemporary community standards for the broadcast medium, sexual or excretory organs or activities. Indecent programming contains patently offensive sexual or excretory material that does not rise to the level of obscenity." Broadcasts that fit the indecency definition are prohibited between 6 a.m. and 10 p.m.

Profanity has been defined by the FCC as "including language so grossly offensive to members of the public who actually hear it as to amount to a nuisance." Like indecency, profanity is prohibited on broadcast radio and television between 6 a.m. and 10 p.m.

Print and online news outlets answer exclusively to their audiences, and their policies are guided by what they think their audiences will deem appropriate.

Newspapers and magazines seeking a mass-circulation audience have the greatest reluctance to use offensive content.

Alternative papers and certain magazines allow themselves greater freedom to use offensive content in describing the people and events they cover. The reasoning is that their audiences are composed of adults willing to tolerate coarse language if that results in realistic reporting and robust commentary.

On the Internet, there are widely varying standards. The websites of mainstream news organizations generally reflect the same standards as the originating newspaper or broadcast organization. In contrast, online magazines tend to follow the policy of comparable print magazines; for example, *Salon* has been described by one of its top editors as being aimed at an adult audience and consequently "reflects the vernacular of the general population."[19]

Journalists producing the mass-circulation publications are confronted with a delicate balancing act when news of importance has an unsavory element. Clarity may be sacrificed as they try to convey news while minimizing offense. The Case Study "Reporting on a Vulgar List in the News," which accompanies this chapter, illustrates the compromises that have been made.

To be sure, there are critics who say that the concern about shielding audiences from coarse language goes too far. When that happens, they say, it is may be impossible for those audiences to understand what a news story is about.

"Our society's comfort level with offensive language and content has drastically shifted over the past few decades, but the stance of our news media has barely changed at all," Jesse Sheidlower, president of the American Dialectical Society, wrote in an op-ed essay in *The New York Times* on March 30, 2014:

> Even when certain words are necessary to the understanding of a story, the media frequently resort to euphemisms or coy acrobatics that make stories read as if they were time capsules written decades ago, forcing us all into wink-wink-nudge-nudge territory. …
>
> Taste is a legitimate concern. But this isn't a matter of sprinkling salty words around to spice up the content. These circumlocutions actually deprive readers of the very thing these institutions so grandly promise: news and information.[20]

As an example to illustrate his point, Sheidlower mentioned the "impolitic" comments about the European Trade Union that a US assistant secretary of state, Victoria Nuland, made while talking on the telephone with the American ambassador to Ukraine. When her comments wound up on the Web – the result, the British Broadcasting Corporation reported, of an apparent bugging of the call[21] – news organizations reported what Nuland said. Except, Sheidlower observed in his essay, many of them really *didn't* report what she said:

> Reuters and *The Guardian* printed her most notable comment in full. Most major news organizations, including *The Washington Post*, *Time* magazine, *The Wall Street Journal*, CNN and The Associated Press, reported the actual phrase Ms. Nuland used, but replaced some letters of the particularly offending word (which began with the letter F)

with dashes or asterisks. The *Los Angeles Times* reported that Ms. Nuland used "a blunt expletive when expressing frustration." And [*The New York Times*] stated that she had "profanely dismissed European efforts in Ukraine as weak and inadequate."[22]

Thomas Kent, deputy managing editor of the Associated Press, blogged in response to the Sheidlower essay: "I'm not sure everyone's OK with news media keeping up with the latest vulgarities. For instance, if our stories were as laced with things 'sucking' as common speech is, readers might find it very tedious very fast."

Kent also wrote that AP was regularly using language that it once considered unprintable. He defended the use of dashes in the Nuland story, and in other instances, by saying that the wire service believed most of its subscribers preferred it that way. "It's also our own opinion," Kent said, "that loading up our services with gratuitous obscenities cheapens our work and is of service to no one."[23]

The New York Times issued new guidelines on profanity and vulgarity in 2014, including one that states:

> If the precise nature of an obscenity, vulgarity, or other offensive expression is essential to the reader's understanding of a newsworthy event – not merely to convey color or emotion – editors should consider using the term or a close paraphrase; readers should not be left uninformed or baffled about the nature of a significant controversy.[24]

The Wall Street Journal also announced that it was relaxing its rules. Its in-house critique, Style & Substance, reported: "The sentence in a March 7 article about a besieged law firm jumped out at us: '*We kicked ass!*' an *employee, who wasn't named in the indictment, wrote…* There was a time when the Journal might have scrubbed the language with a long dash: '*We kicked a–!*' What has changed? Standards Editor Neal Lipschutz says it is a matter of slightly redrawing the line between being classy and being Victorian."[25]

News organizations tend to agree in the abstract that, when offensive language is used by a ranking public official in a public place, they need to report it. However, the consensus appears to stop there. Different organizations use different approaches in those situations, just as they did in the State Department phone call cited by Sheidlower.

An incident on the floor of the United States Senate on June 24, 2004, illustrates the diversity of opinion.

The Washington Post reported that Vice President Dick Cheney told Senator Patrick Leahy of Vermont: "Go fuck yourself." In its version, *The New York Times* said Cheney had used "an obscenity." The *Los Angeles Times* reported that Cheney said, "Go … yourself."[26]

Media writer Howard Kurtz told his *Post* readers that the paper's executive editor, Leonard Downie Jr., explained the decision to use the vulgarity:

> When the vice president of the United States says it to a senator in the way in which he said it on the Senate floor, readers need to judge for themselves what the word is because we don't play games at *The Washington Post* and use dashes.[27]

The three newspapers diverged again when the Reverend Jesse Jackson said bitterly on July 6, 2008, that Barack Obama was "talking down to black people" and

"I want to cut his nuts off." The vulgarity was captured by a Fox News microphone that Jackson thought was turned off, and Jackson subsequently apologized. The *Los Angeles Times* printed in full what Jackson said; *The Washington Post* said "he wanted to castrate the presumptive Democratic nominee"; and *The New York Times* described Jackson's remarks as "critical and crude" without specifying what was crude. *The Post's* website provided a link to the video of Jackson's remarks.[28]

An emotionally charged crime is another situation in which journalists might conclude that a journalistic purpose is served by reporting the language used. In a front-page story on July 7, 2007, *The Plain Dealer* in Cleveland quoted verbatim what witnesses said a man shouted before he shot three neighbors to death: "I'll bet you guys won't be doing this shit again." The editors thought that, given the violence that followed, readers were entitled to know exactly what the man said.[29] Some readers objected. "Does this mean all bars are down at *The PD* and we can expect to see other obscenities and vulgarities in the paper now?" a Cleveland reader asked.[30]

Obviously, the concept of "journalistic purpose" can be, and is, fiercely debated. Reporting, in some manner, the statements of Assistant Secretary of State Nuland, Vice President Cheney, the Reverend Jackson, and the angry shooter in Cleveland fulfills a journalistic purpose. Reporting verbatim the locker-room comments of a professional athlete, uttered in an environment where vulgarity is commonplace, clearly does not. Unfortunately for the decision-makers, there are many cases between those extremes.

In 1998 many newspapers printed "sexual descriptions and slang" that appeared in documents that independent counsel Kenneth Starr submitted with his recommendation that President Bill Clinton be impeached. *The New York Times* included the expressions in texts of the Starr documents but omitted them from its news stories.[31] "The Starr Report raised questions about what content is suitable for family newspapers and live broadcasts," online expert J. D. Lasica wrote: "Many news organizations resolved this dilemma by heavily editing its content in print and on air and then making the entire report available on their websites, accompanied by prominent warnings about the report's graphic content."[32]

Offensive Images in the News

Photographs or video showing graphic violence, nudity, or perceived invasion of privacy are more likely than coarse words to disturb members of the audience. If everything else is equal, images affect people more viscerally. People can be expected to react angrily when they encounter offensive images without warning, on television or on the front page of a newspaper. The subject of offensive images is discussed in more detail in Chapter 19.

The Case Study, "Covering a Public Official's Public Suicide," accompanying this chapter, is a notable example. In this case, the public protested instances in which broadcast or print media were thought to have gone too far in depicting what happened at the convicted Pennsylvania state treasurer's news conference in 1987. There also was widespread self-restraint, as nearly all the Pennsylvania television stations stopped the videotape before R. Budd Dwyer fired the fatal shot, and few newspapers published the still photograph showing that moment.

Live coverage of breaking news could result inadvertently in televising a death on camera. In 1998 a KTLA-TV helicopter covered an incident in which a man with a rifle was sitting in a truck on a Los Angeles freeway, standing off police and backing up traffic for miles. Suddenly the truck burst into flames and the man, later identified as Daniel Jones, a 40-year-old AIDS patient, emerged and took off his scorched pants. Then he ran back to the truck and pulled out the rifle, while news managers at the station screamed to pull the cameras back. "But the order came too late, as KTLA viewers saw Jones blow his brains out," the magazine *Brill's Content* reported.[33]

The Radio Television Digital News Association has created guidelines for evaluating graphic video and sound. The RTDNA notes, "Television news managers understand that the visual images always overpower the spoken word. Powerful pictures can help explain stories better or they can distort the truth by blurring the important context of the report." The RTDNA guidelines urge journalists to identify their journalistic purpose in broadcasting graphic content and to consider alternative ways to tell the story.[34]

On questions of taste, online news sites have another advantage over the older media. When these sites post offensive but newsworthy images, they can require users to click a hyperlink in order to access them.

"TV, radio, and print don't allow the audience to avoid the content if they so choose," said Jonathan Dube, editor of Cyberjournalist.net and a president of the Online News Association. "If you air a video or print a large photo, your audience will see it. The Web, on the other hand, enables the news organization to post the video, but behind a warning, so that only those who seek it out will see it."[35]

Case Study

Reporting on a Vulgar List in the News

When a document circulating among students at Mt. Lebanon High School rated the school's "Top 25" girls, the episode made the front page of the *Pittsburgh Post-Gazette*. The document's vulgar language did not.

Challenged to depict the document accurately but within the bounds of taste that restrain a family oriented newspaper, the *Post-Gazette* wrote on April 26, 2006:

> The document, titled "Top 25 in 2006," ranks the girls in order from 1 to 25. It includes their names, grade levels and photos.
>
> Each girl is assigned a letter grade for her breasts, buttocks and face, followed by a brief

description of each girl in crude and vulgar terms.

There are references to girls performing oral sex and comments about their height and weight.

The paper quoted the father of one of the girls rated in the list – not named to protect the girl's identity – calling it "the equivalent of a written rape on our daughter."

The *Post-Gazette* put its coverage online in the same form that appeared in the print version. That attracted a volume of reader postings exceeded only by comments on major stories about the Steelers, Pittsburgh's pro football team. The reader reaction was fairly evenly divided between people expressing outrage over the list and those baffled by why such adolescent conduct was reported at all, much less on the front page.

The online magazine *Salon*, with more liberal standards for an audience it considers primarily of adults, reported on May 5 that "while the *Post-Gazette*'s description was technically accurate … it had the effect of downplaying the list's vulgarity." *Salon* continued:

(Heads-up: The next couple of paragraphs quote from the list itself, including graphic and offensive descriptions.) The list actually awards each girl a "titty grade" and an "ass grade" along with her face grade, and gives an approximate 100-word "Reason Top 25" explanation for each. A representative description notes that "Despite her egocentric views," one top scorer's "beauty and her big round ass makes this quality easily forgettable. … We all know we want to lather up that ass with some ketchup and dip our hot dog into it." Another girl is praised for doing "a great job in using the brain cells she has to cordially select her outfits to illustrate her many positive aspects of her body. All the boys in the senior class are just counting the days when her and [name deleted by *Salon*] break up so they can move

in for the kill on her luscious, fresh, and splendid vagina."

Other girls are described as being "a strong 'freshman 15' candidate," "the perfect height to suck a dick" and, in the case of a Latina on the list, using "a perfume to keep the taco smell off of her." The list also includes an entry for the girl voted least attractive, who's described as a "cottage cheese filled disgusting thing" with a "maggot filled pussy."

The *Post-Gazette*'s managing editor, Susan L. Smith, said the staff wrestled with the list's terminology before arriving at "a fairly clear consensus' that the paper had to adhere to its language standards. Executive editor David Shribman ruled: "I can identify no real journalistic purpose at this time in violating our own standards of good taste by publishing these crude and demeaning personal descriptions, no matter how shocking the impact of those words might be on our own readers."

Columnist Sally Kalson said she understood the editors' decision. But, she wrote in her column: "we still have a dilemma. Anyone who dismisses the list with 'boys will be boys' has not seen the actual document. … Comments from readers on our website indicate that some are defending the boys in a vacuum. If they knew the actual content, many would hang their heads in shame."

The *Post-Gazette* considered putting the list online with a link from its website warning users of its explicit content. Deputy managing editor Mary Leonard said that idea was discarded, noting that for mainstream media like the *Post-Gazette*, "standards for the Web are still evolving."

The newspaper and its website continued to cover the Mt. Lebanon incident through the spring and summer. A single male student was suspended, and his name was published in the *Post-Gazette* after the parents of one of the girls sued him for defamation. The police

(Continued)

investigated but did not file criminal charges. The school district conducted a day-long sexual harassment training session for its teachers. The district was cleared in a sexual harassment complaint, filed by a parent, when the US Department of Education's Office of Civil Rights found that district officials had investigated the incident promptly and thoroughly.

In a May 15 editorial, the *Post-Gazette* wrote:

> Students, and not just those in Mount Lebanon, must learn two … lessons. One is to leave their vulgarity at home – along with guns, knives and other weapons. The other is that cyberspace, for good or evil, gives them the kind of power wielded by any media mogul. Like the owner of a newspaper chain or a TV network, list makers are protected in this country by free-speech guarantees. What students may not know, however, is they lose some of those rights when they walk through schoolhouse doors. Courts have ruled that schools may prohibit lewd, profane and vulgar speech.

Sources

Chute, Eleanor, "DA says no charges over Mt. Lebanon 'Top 25' list," *Pittsburgh Post-Gazette*, May 25, 2006.

Chute, Eleanor, and Torsten Ove, "Discipline in Mt. Lebanon 'list' furor may be soon," *Pittsburgh Post-Gazette*, Apr. 28, 2006.

Foreman, Gene, telephone interviews with Susan L. Smith and Mary Leonard, Apr. 18, 2008.

Fuoco, Linda Wilson, "Mt. Lebanon schools clearing in handling of explicit 'Top 25' list," *Pittsburgh-Post Gazette*, July 8, 2006.

Goldstein, Sarah, "Top 25 reasons to hate high school," *Salon*, Apr. 27, 2006.

Kalson, Sally, "Cake-eaters gone vile: the Mt. Lebanon High School 'Top 25' list is worse than you might think," *Pittsburgh Post-Gazette*, Apr. 30, 2006.

Niederberger, Mary, "Family files suit over Mt. Lebanon High School 'Top 25' list," *Pittsburgh Post-Gazette*, June 24, 2006.

Niederberger, Mary, and Laura Pace, "Harassment session result of sex list," *Pittsburgh Post-Gazette*, May 10, 2006.

Niederberger, Mary, and Nikki Schwab, "Explicit ranking of high school girls sparks outrage in Mt. Lebanon," *Pittsburgh Post-Gazette,* Apr. 26, 2006.

Pittsburgh Post-Gazette, "Editorial: posting profanity/schools have Internet lessons yet to teach," May 15, 2006.

Rockwell, Page, "Another look at top-25 lists: turns out the Mt. Lebanon High School 'Top 25 of 2006' is grosser than we thought," *Salon*, May 5, 2006.

Questions for Class Discussion

- Why does a mainstream newspaper like the *Post-Gazette* adopt restrictive standards on language?
- Did the *Post-Gazette*'s language standards result in imprecise or ineffectual reporting of the offensive nature of the list?
- If you think it did, is this an acceptable tradeoff for a mainstream newspaper?
- Do you think the *Post-Gazette* should have put the list online for readers to see its contents for themselves? If so, would you have required that readers be presented with a disclaimer warning them of the vulgar language before linking to the list's explicit content? Would you have deleted the names?
- Why do you think *Salon* decided to go beyond the boundaries that the *Post-Gazette* thought it had to observe?
- Do you agree with *Salon*'s decision?

Case Study
Covering a Public Official's Public Suicide

A day before he was scheduled to be sentenced to prison for fraud, Pennsylvania state treasurer R. Budd Dwyer called a news conference. The three dozen reporters and photographers who assembled at Dwyer's Harrisburg office on Thursday, January 22, 1987, were expecting Dwyer to announce his resignation. Still and video cameras recorded the scene as the embattled treasurer read a rambling, half-hour-long statement criticizing the criminal justice system.

When members of a camera crew started to pack up their equipment, Dwyer told them to stay, saying, "We're not done." Dwyer reached inside a manila envelope and pulled out a .357 Magnum. After waving back the horrified journalists, Dwyer placed the pistol in his mouth and fired.

The public suicide of the disgraced public official presented television news directors and newspaper editors around Pennsylvania with a grim decision: What images of the incident should they pass along to their viewers and readers?

The raw video showed Dwyer reading the statement, taking the gun from the envelope, cautioning the people in the room to stay back, putting the pistol in his mouth, and pulling the trigger. In some versions, he falls out of the frame; in others, the cameras follow him to the floor. The versions showing him on the floor are the most graphic, as blood pours from his mouth, nose, and forehead.

Photographers of the print media also kept their cameras trained on Dwyer. Paul Vathis of the Associated Press wrote for *Editor and Publisher* magazine that he acted instinctively: "From professional experience, I just kept taking pictures."

In addition to head-and-shoulders "mug shots" of Dwyer, images offered to editors for newspapers that afternoon and the next morning showed Dwyer reaching into the envelope; holding the pistol in his right hand while waving people back with his left; holding the pistol in both hands in front of his chest; placing the pistol in his mouth; collapsing in a blurred moment immediately after the gunshot; and lying dead on the floor while his aide directs the journalists to leave the room.

Deciding for television

The suicide occurred just after 11 a.m. and tape was fed by satellite to television stations around the state within 30 to 40 minutes, according to a study by Professors Patrick R. Parsons and William E. Smith of Pennsylvania State University.

Their analysis, published in the *Journal of Mass Media Ethics*, showed a remarkable similarity in the way that the videotape was edited by 16 of the 20 stations that broadcast news:

> They showed a soundbite from the news conference followed by the moments just before the actual suicide. Most stations stopped the tape as Dwyer held the gun pointing upward in front of him. Half a dozen stations froze the video at that point, letting the audio track continue through the gunshot; the rest cut back to the anchor or went to black. At least two stations, during their noon newscasts, showed Dwyer placing the gun in his mouth, but stopped the tape before that point on subsequent newscasts.

(Continued)

Three stations showed the moment of death in the noon newscasts. They ran the tape until just after Dwyer pulled the trigger but did not follow his body to the floor, thus eliminating a scene of gore. The stations defended their decision on the grounds of newsworthiness and immediacy, and they noted that the images they showed were, in the words of the researchers, "not particularly graphic or bloody."

Two of these stations, WPXI in Pittsburgh and WPVI in Philadelphia, did not show the gunshot on their later newscasts. The news director of WPXI, who was out of state at the time, said later he regretted that this part had been shown at noon. He phoned from the West Coast to order that the gunshot be eliminated in the subsequent newscasts.

The other station showing the gunshot was WHTM in Harrisburg. Its initial bulletin, without a cautionary disclaimer, broke into children's programming, which had a larger audience than usual because many schools were closed as a result of a heavy snowstorm. The station later apologized. The station showed the videotape again at its regular newscasts in the evening, this time warning viewers about its graphic nature. The video then was accompanied by a studio discussion of suicide by mental health officials.

The twentieth station did not run video on any of its newscasts. This was WLYH of Lancaster, whose news director, Cliff Esbach, said the pictures did not add anything to the description in the story. He also said that showing the tape "just wouldn't be the decent thing to do."

Professors Parsons and Smith concluded that the "standard version" – stopping the video before the gunshot – was an easy decision for the news directors. "There was little agonizing over the issue. Even those journalists who did have trouble making the decision eventually came to the majority conclusion." The news directors who chose this standard version said the moment of death was in bad taste. "We want good video," one news director told the researchers, "but we want the video for its news value. We're not looking to shock people."

Deciding for newspapers

For their Thursday afternoon and Friday morning editions, editors at Pennsylvania daily newspapers selected from the images supplied by the Associated Press and United Press International. Their choices were tabulated in a study published in the *Newspaper Research Journal* by Professor Robert L. Baker of Pennsylvania State University. For this case study, Baker's totals for similar images offered by both AP and UPI are combined.

The most frequently used image, on front pages and overall, was a photograph of Dwyer holding the pistol in his right hand while waving with his left hand to warn anyone who would intervene (Figure 15.2(b)). Baker's study showed that the AP and UPI versions were used in 43 papers, including 31 on the front page. From a taste standpoint, this image has the advantages of suggesting the tension and violence of the incident but without showing anything graphic.

Thirty-eight newspapers chose a head-and-shoulders portrait of Dwyer, including 28 that used such a picture on the front page. Nearly all these newspapers also published one or more additional photographs from the news conference.

The third most frequently used image was that of Dwyer with the pistol in his mouth before he pulled the trigger (Figure 15.2(d)). Thirty-nine newspapers used that photo, including 18 on the front page. Many readers deemed this photo to be too graphic, especially if it appeared on the front page. The other images, in order of frequency of use, were:

- *Reaching into the envelope* (Figure 15.2(a)): 35 newspapers, including 8 on the front page.
- *Pistol in both hands* (Figure 15.2(c)): 19 newspapers, including 7 on the front page.

- *Collapsing after the impact* (Figure 15.2(e)): 6 newspapers, including 5 on the front page; this is the most graphic of the still pictures of the news conference.
- *Body on the floor* (Figure 15.2(f)): 12 newspapers, including 2 on the front page.

The largest newspaper in the state, *The Philadelphia Inquirer*, ran two photographs on the front page. One showed Dwyer holding the pistol and waving people away, and the other showed him with the pistol in his mouth. On an inside page, *The Inquirer* ran the

Figure 15.2(a)   Reaching into the envelope

Figure 15.2(b)   Waving back intervention

Figure 15.2(c)   Pistol in both hands

Figure 15.2(d)   Pistol in the mouth

Figure 15.2(e)   Collapsing after the impact

Figure 15.2(f)   Body on the floor

PHOTOS 15.2(A), (C), (D), (E), AND (F) BY PAUL VATHIS.
PHOTO 15.2(B) BY GARY MILLER.
ALL PHOTOS REPRINTED BY PERMISSION OF THE ASSOCIATED PRESS.

(Continued)

body-on-the-floor image. About 500 readers telephoned the newspaper the next day to complain, especially about the image of Dwyer with the pistol in his mouth. A common complaint was that, if a graphic photo runs on the front page, there is not much parents can do to shield their young children from seeing it.

The two Pittsburgh dailies, the *Post-Gazette* and *The Press*, both decided against showing the photos of either the pistol in the mouth or of the collapse after impact. "I thought both of those were sensational and gruesome, without much value," said Madelyn Ross, managing editor of *The Press*.

The *Meadville Tribune*, published in Dwyer's hometown, ran only a portrait. Managing editor John Wellington told a researcher, Professor Robert C. Kochersberger of North Carolina State University, that the paper's decision was immediate and instinctive. "Would anyone with half a whit of common sense want graphic suicide pictures imposed on his children?"

Questions for Class Discussion

- This text has made the point that suicides generally are not treated as significant news stories. In the case of R. Budd Dwyer's suicide, what news values argued for extraordinary treatment?
- Are you surprised that 16 of the 20 stations chose to edit the raw videotape in a similar fashion (stopping before the gunshot)? Why do you think all those news directors came to the same conclusion independently of each other?
- Do you think WHTM made a mistake in how it broadcast its initial news bulletin on the suicide? If so, why?
- Do you agree with WLYH's decision not to show any of the video?
- Why do you think so many newspapers chose the image of Dwyer holding the

Sources

Baker, Robert L., "Portraits of a public suicide: photo treatment by selected Pennsylvania dailies," *Newspaper Research Journal*, 9:4 (Summer 1988), 11–23.

Biance, Robert, and Ken Guggenheim, "Use of suicide film debated at news, television desks," *The Pittsburgh Press*, Jan. 23, 1987.

Kochersberger, Robert C., Jr., "Survey of suicide photos use by newspapers in three states," *Newspaper Research Journal*, 9:4 (Summer 1988), 1–10.

Parsons, Patrick R., and William E. Smith, "R. Budd Dwyer: a case study in newsroom decision making," *Journal of Mass Media Ethics*, 3:1, 84–94.

Vathis, Paul, "Eyewitness account by the AP's photographer," *Editor & Publisher*, Jan. 31, 1987.

Warner, Gary A., "Invitation to suicide leaves newsmen wondering why," *The Pittsburgh Press*, Jan. 23, 1987.

pistol and waving for people to stand back (Figure 15.2 (b))?
- Do you think a newspaper should have run the image of Dwyer holding the pistol in his mouth (Figure 15.2(d))? If so, should the newspaper run the photo on the front page or on an inside page?
- Was the *Meadville Tribune* right to run only a portrait of Dwyer? Regarding the editor's statement about children, consider: Should a newspaper be edited for children, or should it be edited for adults with the likelihood that children may see it? (To use the movie industry's terminology, the difference is between editing for a G audience or a PG audience.)

Notes

1   The Associated Press, "NBC News: airing Cho video 'good journalism,'" *The Washington Post*, Apr. 24, 2007.

2   Kim Pearson, "Cho manifesto highlights challenges for online journalism," *Online Journalism Review*, May 3, 2007.

3   David Folkenflik, "NBC cites an obligation to air Cho materials," NPR, Apr. 19, 2007.

4   Ibid.

5   Pearson, "Cho manifesto highlights challenges for online journalism."

6   James T. Campbell, "Right choice to use killer's photos on Page One," *Houston Chronicle*, Apr. 22, 2007.

7   "Campus rampage is 2007's biggest story by far: PEJ news coverage index for April 15–20, 2007," Pew Research Center, Apr. 23, 2007.

8   Folkenflik, "NBC cites an obligation to air Cho materials."

9   David Bauder, "Backlash leads to pullback on Cho video," The Associated Press, Apr. 19, 2007.

10 Ibid.

11 Jessica A. Ross, executive producer of WSLS-TV in Roanoke, VA, statement issued Apr. 19, 2007.

12 The Associated Press, "NBC News: airing Cho video 'good journalism.'"

13 Campbell, "Right choice to use killer's photos on Page One."

14 Franklin Foer, "Death in prime time," *U.S. News & World Report*, Dec. 7, 1998.

15 Caryn James, "'60 Minutes,' Kevorkian and a death for the cameras," *The New York Times*, Nov. 23, 1998.

16 Kathy Barks, "Kevorkian leaves prison after 8 years," The Associated Press, June 1, 2007.

17 Cited in Doug Kim, Melissa McCoy, and John McIntyre, "Charged language," paper presented to the American Copy Editors Society in Portland, OR, Sept. 1998.

18 Federal Communications Commission, "Consumer guide: obscene, indecent and profane broadcasts." Retrieved on Feb. 9, 2015, from http://transition.fcc.gov/cgb/consumerfacts/obscene.pdf.

19 Lori Robertson, "Language barriers," *American Journalism Review*, Nov. 2000, 41.

20 Jesse Sheidlower, "The case for profanity in print," *The New York Times*, Mar. 30, 2014.

21 BBC, "Ukraine crisis: transcript of leaked Nuland–Pyatt call," Feb. 7, 2014.

22 Sheidlower, "The case for profanity in print."

23 Thomas Kent, "Too vulgar to print," The Definitive Source, Apr. 9, 2014.

24 The guidelines were quoted in Margaret Sullivan's public editor blog for *The New York Times*, "Dicey language at *The Times*, a view from Venezuela's president and coverage of women's basketball," Apr. 3, 2014.

25 Style & Substance, "The law on 'ass,'" Mar. 30, 2014.

26 Howard Kurtz, "*Post* editor explains decision to publish expletive," *The Washington Post*, June 26, 2004.

27 Ibid.

28 Clark Hoyt, "When to quote those potty mouths," *The New York Times*, July 13, 2008.

29 Ted Diadiun, "The s- word," *The Plain Dealer*, July 15, 2007.

30 Ibid.

31 Allan M. Siegal and William G. Connolly, *The New York Times Manual of Style and Usage* (New York: Times Books, 1999), 241.

32 J. D. Lasica, "The Starr investigation," in Tom Rosenstiel and Amy Mitchell (eds.), *Thinking Clearly: Cases in Journalistic Decision-Making* (New York: Columbia University Press, 2003), 39.

33 D. M. Osborne, "Overwhelmed by events," *Brill's Content*, 1998, 67–68.

34 Radio Television Digital News Association, "Guidelines for graphic content."

35 Quoted in Pearson, "Cho manifesto highlights challenges for online journalism."

16 Deception, a Controversial Reporting Tool

When values collide: Lying while seeking the truth

Learning Goals

This chapter will help you understand:

- the importance of recognizing an intention to deceive and not rationalizing it;
- the exacting conditions that a news organization should meet before engaging in undercover reporting;
- examples of undercover reporting;
- other situations, short of going undercover, in which journalists deceive or could be perceived as deceiving; and
- why journalists almost universally are opposed to deceiving the audience.

He was lying on the floor, curled up in a ball, his knees doubled into his stomach and his hands clasped over his head.

Then the big, black leather shoe came crashing down on top of his shaved head and his face ricocheted off the shiny, gray concrete floor.

Another foot slammed into his stomach with all the force of a football kicking specialist. Another foot dug into his back and another into his legs and another into the top of his head.

For nearly three minutes, the four white-suited attendants – three stood more than 6 feet tall – towered over the huddled figure on the floor, kicking every part of his defenseless body.

On a spring day in 1965, readers opened their copies of *The Plain Dealer* in Cleveland to find this vivid account of what happened to a young man incarcerated at Lima State Hospital for the Criminally Insane. They also learned what had led to the punishment: The man had *whispered* in a ward where the "patients" were forced to sit together for 11 hours a day, a rule of utter silence enforced by beatings or by cancelling a man's privilege to buy candy or tobacco "and other small things that are his last tie with the outside world."[1]

Plain Dealer readers learned this – and much more disturbing information about Lima State Hospital – because reporter Donald L. Barlett had gained employment as an attendant at the hospital.

The Ethical Journalist: Making Responsible Decisions in the Digital Age, Second Edition. Gene Foreman.
© 2016 John Wiley & Sons, Inc. Published 2016 by John Wiley & Sons, Inc.

As a new employee, Barlett was assigned an orientation tour of nine wards. He and another attendant were with a group of patients who were sweeping out cells and mopping halls on a ward's first floor when a teenage patient rushed up and shouted, "Someone's gettin' it upstairs." With that, the other attendant raced up the stairs to the second floor, and Barlett followed. They arrived to find the beating under way.

Barlett's job brought him in contact with the hospital's assortment of criminals and teenage runaways. He talked with patients and other attendants. After working days in the hospital, he spent his evenings writing notes about what he had seen and heard.

Those notes were turned into a series of stories in *The Plain Dealer* that revealed a practice of housing young runaways with adult sex criminals; treatment for mental illness that consisted almost entirely of heavy doses of sedatives; incarceration based on psychiatric evaluations lasting all of 10 minutes; therapy that consisted of spending all day tying bits of string together; punishment meted out to patients who had epileptic seizures; and almost nonexistent educational and occupational training programs.

"For nearly seven weeks, a *Plain Dealer* reporter worked in the dark imprisoned world of Ohio's most troublesome criminals and sex criminals," the newspaper announced in a sidebar to the first story in the series. The newspaper also disclosed that, to get hired, Barlett had used a version of his own name "but a fictitious background."[2]

It wasn't Barlett's idea to pose as a hospital attendant. His city editor simply told him what he was going to do. "See what's going on inside," Barlett remembers the editor's instructions. He was told to collect information and follow where it led.[3] After Barlett's series of stories, the governor of Ohio ordered institutional reforms at Lima State Hospital.

What Barlett did at Lima State Hospital is known as undercover reporting. Gathering information while pretending to be someone else is the ultimate act of journalistic deception.

Deception is a paradox in journalism: The profession's purpose is to reveal truth, and deception is making someone else believe what the deceiver knows to be untrue.

A strictly *deontological* journalist would never practice deception, because a universal rule of behavior requires truth-telling at all times. A *teleological* journalist, considering the potential results of the reporting, might conclude that deception is acceptable if it will lead to a greater good. Anecdotal and some empirical evidence suggests that most journalists take the teleological approach.

Retired editor Reid MacCluggage is on the teleological side. In the president's column for the newsletter of the Associated Press Managing Editors in 1998, MacCluggage wrote:

> Readers will support editors who make intelligent, thoughtful and empathetic decisions, and they will condemn editors who shoot from the hip. ... There are times when we need to bend the rules to break an important story. But those times should be rare, the stories must be profound, and editors need to proceed with great caution.[4]

Ethics scholars also refrain from an absolute position on deception. Louis W. Hodges has expressed the journalist's moral choice in these terms: "[D]eceit is morally wrong … but … circumstances can arise in which deceit is relatively less wrong than other possible courses of action." In some newsgathering situations, then, "deceit is morally acceptable." However, journalists must not deceive unnecessarily, and they have a moral obligation to give good reasons for deceiving. In contrast, Hodges says, a decision not to deceive requires no justification.[5]

As Don Barlett sees it, however, a failure to deceive could itself be morally wrong. He thinks that if deception is the only way that journalists can inform the public about important facts — such as the sweeping dysfunction at Lima State Hospital — they have a moral obligation to deceive.

Barlett said, "A decision to withhold critical information from readers by refusing to document it is every bit as deceitful as gaining access to information under false pretenses — but without serving any greater good."[6]

Defining Deception, Avoiding Rationalizations

Whether a certain act of journalistic deception is acceptable can only be decided on a case-by-case basis. The decision must take into consideration both the degree of deception and the news value of the information that might be obtained.

To make a reasoned decision, journalists must first acknowledge that they are contemplating deception. Then they should ask themselves if the information to be gained for the public is important enough to justify the deception. Applying the Golden Rule, they should ask themselves how they would feel if they were deceived in the same way. They should consider what they would do if their deception is discovered. When they report to the audience, they should be willing to disclose their deception.

The first step in the decision process — acknowledging an intention to deceive, whether verbal or nonverbal — is not easy. It is human nature to rationalize, to call it something else, like "smart reporting." At one of his ethics seminars for journalists, Michael Josephson posed a hypothetical question, and the give-and-take went like this:

> JOSEPHSON: What would you do if someone stole a highly newsworthy document from the mayor and gave it to you?
> REPORTER: I prefer to say that my newspaper "obtained" the document.
> JOSEPHSON: Then you don't know the definition of stealing?[7]

So, definitions are needed.

In her seminal book, *Lying*, the ethicist Sissela Bok defined *deception*:

> When we undertake to deceive others intentionally, we communicate messages meant to mislead them, meant to make them believe what we ourselves do not believe. We can do that through gesture, through disguise, by means of action or inaction, even through silence.[8]

For a communication to be deceitful, the deception must be intentional. Giving someone misinformation through honest error does not meet Bok's definition.[9]

In their Watergate investigation in 1972–74, Carl Bernstein and Bob Woodward falsely told potential sources that "a friend [at the Nixon re-election committee] told us that you were disturbed by some of the things you saw going on there, that you would be a good person to talk to." Bernstein and Woodward acknowledged that this approach, though it seemed to work best, was "less than straightforward." Right or wrong under the circumstances, it was deception.[10]

To the extent that journalists will consider deception, deceiving the audience is not what they have in mind. "Never lie to the audience" is as close to an absolute rule as you will find in journalism ethics, an example of Kantian deontology. That is because seeking truth for the public is the profession's reason for existence.

Deceiving a journalist's colleagues, likewise, is out of the question, because the resulting lack of trust would make that journalist ineffective and, quite likely, soon out of a job.

By a process of elimination, then, the only acceptable targets of journalistic deception are sources and story subjects. Does that mean it is open season on these people?

It had better not be, the ethics scholars say. They argue that acts of deception damage journalism's credibility and that, consequently, the bar for engaging in them must be high.

Sissela Bok wrote in *Lying* that journalism is one of several professions – others include medicine, the law, and the military – in which practitioners find themselves "repeatedly in straits where serious consequences seem avoidable only through deception." But resorting to deception in a crisis can lead to using those tactics more casually, she warned. In journalism and the other professions she mentioned, achievements in a competitive environment are rewarded. "Cutting corners may be one way to such achievements, and if deception is pervasive and rarely punished, then it will be all the more likely to spread. The accepted practices may then grow increasingly insensitive, and abuses and mistakes more common."[11]

For Deni Elliott, sleight of hand is a tool for a magician, not a journalist. She has written that deceptive newsgathering techniques "cause more harm than good to the profession of journalism as a whole."[12]

Michael Josephson cautions that journalists' credibility and trustworthiness can be undermined by misrepresentations, trickery, impersonation, and the use of hidden audio recorders or cameras in newsgathering. These practices, he has written, "are outside the bounds of generally accepted journalistic behavior" and require thorough discussion.[13]

As Josephson advocates, any undercover reporting project should require the approval of the highest authority in the newsroom. That makes sense because that person – the editor or news director – ultimately may have to answer to the public for the deception. In addition, the decision-making process should allow all arguments, pro and con, to be heard, and that is what is supposed to happen when the decision is brought to the highest authority.

A High Threshold for Undercover Reporting

Although today's print media rarely engage in undercover reporting, the technique has flourished – in the form of hidden cameras – in television reporting.

In *The Elements of Journalism*, Bill Kovach and Tom Rosenstiel outlined three formidable standards that should be met for undercover reporting:

1   The information is vital to the public interest.
2   There is no other way to get the story.
3   The deception is disclosed to the audience.[14]

Louis Hodges added this standard: The deception must not "place innocent people at risk." A journalist posing as a firefighter probably would fail this standard by being unable to deliver as a firefighter in case of an actual fire, endangering other firefighters and possibly civilians in a burning building.[15]

The authors of *Doing Ethics in Journalism* added other caveats:

- The journalists and the news organization must "apply excellence" through solid reporting and by committing the time and money needed to be thorough.
- The harm prevented by the deception must outweigh any harm caused by the act of deception.
- The journalists must conduct "a meaningful, collaborative and deliberative decision making process" in which they weigh such factors as their motivation and the consequences of the deception.[16]

A half-century later, Don Barlett's cameo role as an attendant at Lima State Hospital passes those tests. His information was vitally important, as he documented that the hospital was a dumping ground for more than a thousand people who, under the law, could be incarcerated wrongly and indefinitely. To report in a convincing way, he had to get inside and see the abuses firsthand. *The Plain Dealer* told its readers how he got inside, including lying in his employment application. Barlett's job as an attendant did not put other people at risk. Excellence in reporting and writing are in evidence throughout the series, as Barlett demonstrated the skills that later would make him a two-time recipient of the Pulitzer Prize. The subsequent reforms at Lima State Hospital are evidence that his masquerade prevented harm. Barlett thinks that his superiors considered the possible consequences of his assignment and found them outweighed by the value of giving their readers an eyewitness account. Almost certainly, however, an undercover assignment would be undertaken with much more deliberation in a newsroom today.

The Society of Professional Journalists' code contains this standard under the guiding principle of "seek truth and report it": "Avoid undercover or other surreptitious methods of gathering information unless traditional, open methods will not yield information vital to the public."

Memorable Examples of Undercover Reporting

Undercover reporting was a tradition in newspaper investigative reporting through the 1970s. A familiar name in journalism lore is that of Nellie Bly, the intrepid reporter who got herself committed to Blackwell's (now Roosevelt) Island in 1887 and reported for *The New York World* about what she saw in the notorious asylum. Brooke Kroeger described Bly's feat in her definitive book, *Undercover Reporting: The Truth about Deception*:

> As a "girl reporter" in her early twenties, she accepted a life-imperiling, man-size assign-ment to feign insanity and get herself committed to the Women's Lunatic Asylum … On release, she quickly filled two pages of the World's Sunday feature section with her heavily detailed account, starting with her step-by-step preparation for the ruse and then her encounters with the judges and doctors who sent her across the river to endure the inedible food, filth, harsh treatment, and stark-raving boredom.[17]

Kroeger, a New York University professor, wrote that Bly gave undercover report-ing "instant credence as a sure-fire circulation-building gimmick," encouraging any competitor to hire its own "stunt girl." For journalism, Kroeger observed, "[t]he trick then and thereafter was to use the construct selectively, and for high purpose, so as not to wear it out."[18]

The noted journalist Ben Bagdikian persuaded the Pennsylvania attorney general in 1972 to allow him to be a prisoner in the state prison at Huntingdon so that he could take "a serious look at the whole system." After three months of observing men behind bars, Bagdikian wrote an eight-part series about the experience for *The Washington Post*. In the series, he wrote that other kinds of research – interviewing former prisoners and reading books and reports – "had not prepared me for the intellectual impact of maximum security incarceration."[19]

The reluctance of today's print media to use undercover reporting can be traced to the anti-deception arguments made by two influential editors in blocking a Pulitzer Prize for an elaborate ruse staged by the *Chicago Sun-Times* for a series of 25 articles published in 1978.

To document its suspicions about shakedowns by city inspectors, the paper oper-ated a bar – aptly named The Mirage – for four months in late 1977. The *Sun-Times* history of the episode tells what happened next:

> There was a payoff parade of city and state inspectors, hands out, in search of health and safety violations to wink at. Six accountants offered to keep, and kept, endless crooked books for the tax man. It was all put down on paper by the reporters … and made vivid by *Sun-Times* photographers … snapping quietly from a hidden loft.

The *Sun-Times* history credits the series with "serious" reforms – new procedures in city inspections, revisions of the city code, and investigations by the city, state, and federal agencies.[20]

When the Mirage story became a finalist for a Pulitzer Prize, it was vigorously and successfully opposed by two members of the prize board. Benjamin Bradlee of *The Washington Post* and Eugene Patterson of *The St. Petersburg Times* argued that reporters ought to operate in the open. Patterson said the *Sun-Times* reporters could have interviewed bar owners.[21] That was not practical, according to the *Sun-Times* history, which states that the paper's investigative reporters had been hearing for years from business people complaining about being shaken down: "But … nobody would go on record. Everyone was afraid of City Hall."[22]

Such was the influence of Bradlee and Patterson that undercover reporting went out of favor in newspapers in the years that followed. There were exceptions, however, and when Tony Horwitz posed as a worker in a chicken-processing plant in 1994, his account in *The Wall Street Journal* won a Pulitzer Prize. Horwitz's bosses ordered him to tell no lies, and on his application form he listed Columbia University as his education and Dow Jones & Company as his employer, without specifying that it published *The Journal*. He was hired immediately.[23]

In the spring of 1992 ABC producers lied about their work experience and gave phony references to gain employment as meat wrappers at Food Lion supermarkets, where they used cameras hidden in wigs to expose unsanitary food handling and labor-law violations. ABC broadcast its findings on *PrimeTime Live* in November 1992 during a sweeps period.

Food Lion sued the network, not for libel but for fraud and trespass. A North Carolina jury returned a $5.5 million judgment, and jury foreman Gregory Mack said afterward: "You didn't have any boundaries when you started this investigation. … You kept pushing on the edges … It was too extensive and fraudulent."[24] First Amendment lawyer Bruce W. Sanford observed: "The jury felt that reporters shouldn't misrepresent themselves or use other deceptive practices to obtain news, even when the 'news' amounted to truthful reporting about serious health and safety violations at one of America's largest grocers."[25] On appeal, the Food Lion verdict was overturned.

Walter Goodman defended ABC's deception in a *New York Times* essay after the jury verdict:

> Yes, the reporters were out to catch instances of unappetizing behavior and the most flagrant and unfragrant of them were played up, as is the way in exposes. But the program made a strong case that tricks like repackaging outdated fish and prettifying unsold chicken with barbecue sauce were common at two Food Lion stores at least. Employees seemed to be doing such refurbishment as a matter of course.

Goodman said ABC could have bought the food and subjected it to laboratory analysis, but such findings "would have been no substitute for the on-the-spot evidence of malpractice."[26]

Beginning in the 1980s, undercover reporting became a staple on television, Susan Paterno wrote in "The Lying Game" in *American Journalism Review* in May 1997. "Local news teams try to outdo one another during sweeps weeks," she wrote, while national newsmagazines have proliferated on the networks. "[T]elevision needs pictures. And pictures drive reporters undercover for dramatic, indisputable evidence of wrongdoing." Paterno quoted Ira Rosen, ABC's senior producer in the Food Lion case: "In television, pictures provide a level of truth as much as the spoken word. You can't separate the two. People need to see."[27]

The authors of *The Elements of Journalism* cautioned that journalism's watchdog role can be diminished as the networks' prime-time magazines and local stations' newscasts focus on consumer topics instead of monitoring the powerful:

> [T]oo much of the new "investigative" reporting is tabloid treatment of everyday circumstances. … Consider the Los Angeles TV station that rented a house for two months and wired it with a raft of hidden cameras to expose that you really can't get all the carpeting in your house cleaned for $7.95. … [E]xposing what is readily understood or simply common sense belittles investigative journalism. The press becomes the boy who cried wolf. It is squandering its ability to demand the public's attention because it has done so too many times about trivial matters.[28]

The ethicist Bob Steele also has deplored "the glut of hidden camera stories focusing on small-scale consumer scams, 'gotcha' pieces targeting someone for a minor breach of behavior, or weak investigative reports that don't justify deception." In contrast, he praises hidden-camera reporting that has "exposed systemic racial discrimination, critical weaknesses in airport security, gross incompetence by law enforcement officers, and abhorrent patient care in nursing homes and hospitals."[29]

Steele would limit hidden cameras to stories that reveal "exceptionally important information … of vital public interest, such as preventing profound harm to individuals or revealing great system failure." Hidden cameras should be a tool of last resort, after journalists have tried or have ruled out obtaining the information through conventional techniques. When hidden-camera reporting accuses someone of wrongdoing, Steele cautioned, "we must ensure that the tone and emphasis of hidden camera video meet standards for factual accuracy and contextual authenticity." He also noted that hidden-camera journalism sometimes traps "the little guy who happens to be easily accessible," instead of the higher-ranking people who are truly responsible.[30]

Working "Beneath the Radar" and Other Episodes

When Anne Hull and Dana Priest conducted the investigation in 2007 that revealed horrendous neglect of wounded soldiers and marines at Walter Reed Army Medical Center, they did not go undercover. That would have broken *The Washington Post*'s rules. What they did, in Hull's words, was to work "beneath the radar."

Specifically, they carefully avoided doing anything that might bring their presence at the medical center to the attention of army officials for more than three months while they gathered information for the series of articles that won 2008 Pulitzer Prize for public service. As Hull said later:

> [W]e needed to see the problems at Walter Reed with our own eyes. We needed to roam around the 110-acre facility at various hours of the day or night and talk to soldiers and Marines without the interference of Army public affairs. We needed to connect with wounded soldiers that were not pre-selected by the Army.
>
> So we bypassed the normal protocol of requesting permission to visit Walter Reed and be accompanied by an escort. We simply went onto post on our own. We never lied about our identity. We presented our driver's licenses at the guard gates as all visitors do. Once on the post, we made sure to not bring attention to ourselves while reporting. We tried to never put ourselves in the position where someone might ask, "Who are you?" As with any reporting, you try not to stand out from your subjects.[31]

Once they got acquainted with soldiers, marines, and family members, they identified themselves as *Post* reporters. All the sources they quoted in their stories were aware of why the reporters were there. The sources kept their secret from the higher-ups. Hull said, "We stressed with each person we talked to, please don't tell anyone you're talking to us, especially your supervisor ... And if you see us in public, don't acknowledge us."[32]

Priest said they would brief a soldier on "phraseology" to use if they were asked about their presence, "so they don't lie about who you are, but maybe they don't disclose who you are, either."[33]

Priest also said that, to avoid being identified as journalists, she and Hull usually didn't carry cameras, and they kept their notebooks out of sight.[34] They were, however, ready to acknowledge their identity as reporters if anyone in authority asked them, but no one did. "Lying about this was not an option," Hull said. "In fact, it would have been a breach of ethics."[35] Hull also said, "We often went there separately, because we could accomplish twice as much work and, if one got caught, it's better than two getting caught."[36]

In the introduction to her book tracing the history of undercover reporting, Brooke Kroeger told the story of the Walter Reed investigation. She asked "whether there is really a difference for a journalist between not ever telling a lie – emphasis on the word *telling*, because lies, to qualify as lies, are verbalized – and the deliberate projection of a false impression with a clear intent to mislead, to deceive."[37] She wasn't criticizing the *Post* team. To the contrary, she argued that their approach was legitimate, "even unavoidable, given the circumstances and the stakes." Their tactics, Kroeger wrote, did not "undermine the value of the enterprise or call it into question."[38]

Like Tony Horwitz's reporting on a chicken-processing plant, the *Post* reporters were able to get their story because their true roles were not discovered by the people in charge, who could have thrown them out. Incidentally, when the truth became known in each case, those bosses were gracious. After his story was published,

Horwitz tried to send back his $5.10-an-hour earnings, but the poultry company refused it. A company official told him that, based on the working conditions he had written about, "you earned it." Horwitz donated the money to charity.[39] And when Hull and Priest confronted a general and eight colonels with their findings at Walter Reed, Priest said their reception was cordial. "They realized we really knew what we were talking about."[40]

There are other noteworthy examples of how journalists, by not being perceived as journalists, were able to do their jobs better. In some cases the journalists encouraged the misperception.

Reporter Jack Nelson flew to Orangeburg, South Carolina, in February 1968 to investigate a melee at South Carolina State College in which police and National Guardsmen killed three black students and wounded more than two dozen others. The authorities said they had fired when students charged at them, throwing bottles and bricks. As Gene Roberts and Hank Klibanoff wrote in their book *The Race Beat*, Nelson went directly to the hospital where the wounded students had been treated.

> With an air of authority underpinned by his business suit and crew-cut hair, he introduced himself as "Nelson, with the Atlanta bureau. I've come to see the medical records." Nelson's bureau was, of course, the *Los Angeles Times* bureau, not the FBI's Atlanta bureau.
>
> The records Nelson inspected showed that sixteen students had back wounds, and that some who had lain on the ground to escape the gunfire had wounds on the soles of their feet. Nelson's story in the *Times* authoritatively disputed the official version that the shots were fired in self-defense.[41]

While covering a murder case around 1960 for *The News and Observer* in Raleigh, North Carolina, Gene Roberts picked up a stethoscope from a desk and "walked nonchalantly into the emergency room where police were interrogating a suspect who confessed." Years later, as executive editor of *The Philadelphia Inquirer*, Roberts told the story to Pennsylvania State University professor H. Eugene Goodwin for his ethics textbook. "I didn't lie to anyone," he said. "We're not obligated to wear a neon sign."[42]

In his 1985 book *The News at Any Cost*, Tom Goldstein described how Athelia Knight of *The Washington Post* reported in 1984 on the ease with which drugs could be surreptitiously taken into Lorton Reformatory near Washington. Knight sat silently on a bus that was headed for the prison and listened as other passengers talked about smuggling marijuana and other illegal drugs to inmates. She said, "I must have seemed like just another woman with a husband or boyfriend locked up." If asked, she would have identified herself as a reporter. Her editor, Ben Bradlee, considered the situation different from the Mirage reporting he had criticized in 1978. He said, "I see a really seminal distinction between planning any kind of deception, however much the end might seem to justify the means, and embarking on a project where your occupation as a journalist is not advertised."[43]

Jack Fuller wrote in *News Values*:

> I do not believe that the journalistic obligation of truth-telling requires reporters to wear their press passes on their chests. When a reporter in the course of his ordinary human activity and without lying gets into a position to witness newsworthy events (when a building inspector solicits a bribe at the reporter's own home, for example, or if a city work crew goes to sleep on the job along his route to the office) he does not need to interrupt the action with a disclosure of his affiliation.[44]

Mayhill Fowler, a blogger for *The Huffington Post*, was invited to a fundraiser in San Francisco for presidential candidate Barack Obama two weeks before the important Pennsylvania primary in April 2008. She got the invitation because she was an Obama contributor. It was at this gathering that Obama said small-town Pennsylvania voters "cling to guns or religion or antipathy to people who aren't like them" as a way of expressing their bitterness over economic hardships. After Fowler reported the statement in her blog, the mainstream media picked it up. Obama had to explain, especially to voters in Pennsylvania, that "I didn't say it as well as I should have."[45]

Fowler was hardly concealed as she did her reporting at the fundraiser. Obama, she said later, "was looking at 350 strangers, many of whom were using cell phones and small video cameras and flips to record the event." Her invitation, press critic Jay Rosen noted in his own blog, didn't say "you can't blog about this."[46]

Many journalists have long held the position that they have no moral obligation to identify themselves at a gathering as large as the one Obama addressed in San Francisco. At an occasion like that, they reason, it is absurd for speakers to expect to keep secret what they say. (Although some Obama followers complained that Fowler was unfair to report his remark, Rosen gave the candidate credit for neither challenging Fowler's right to report nor questioning her accuracy.)

Reporters also have been known to give an interview subject the wrong impression about how much the reporter already knows. It is a tactic to elicit information that the reporter needs.

"You don't always tell all you know," said Roy Reed, a retired *New York Times* reporter. "At other times, you indicate that you know more than you do. The public needs to know the information, and the source may not be forthright."[47]

In a *New Yorker* article titled "The Writing Life: Elicitation," John McPhee revealed how he sometimes gets interview subjects to open up: a technique he calls "creative bumbling." He elaborated: "You can develop a distinct advantage by waxing slow of wit. Evidently you need help. Who is there to help you but the person who is answering your questions?"[48]

Homer Bigart of *The New York Times* was a reporter who habitually pretended to know less than he did. Bigart practiced the technique when he was sent to Philadelphia, Mississippi, in 1964 to cover the investigation into the killing of three civil rights workers. "Couldn't have a normal conversation with the man," one of his interview subjects complained to another *Times* reporter. "He didn't know anything. I had to explain *evvvverything* to him."[49]

Testing Security: A Problematical
Use of Undercover Reporting

When journalists go undercover to test security at airports and schools, their efforts may lead to security improvements. But there is also the possibility that the suspected dysfunctional security will be functional enough to ensnare them – with unpleasant consequences. Journalists have been arrested while carrying out such tests.

In a 2006 article, Al Tompkins of the Poynter Institute suggested that, before undertaking tests at schools, journalists should answer questions like these: How will the journalists' intrusion affect the students? If a school has armed police officers, how can the journalists be sure there is no violent confrontation? Could the journalists be charged with trespassing?[50]

When a reporter for television station KSDK was testing security at Kirkwood High School near St. Louis on January 16, 2014, he inadvertently caused a lockdown. Jessica Bock reported in the *Post-Dispatch*: "Students and teachers at the school were huddled in classroom with the lights off for about 40 minutes … after a man came into the school and asked to speak with security, then left." Students were told to stand against the walls in order to stay out of sight of anyone walking the halls.

Ginger Cayce, a spokeswoman for the school district, told *The Post-Dispatch* that school officials "learned some things" from the test but were disappointed they had not been alerted in advance. She said the reporter gave his name and cell-phone number at the school office, but administrators were alarmed when he asked for the location of a restroom and then walked in the opposite direction. Although the cell-phone number's voicemail identified the owner as a KSDK reporter, Cayce said, the lockdown had to be ordered as a precaution because she could not immediately confirm his identity with the station.[51] KSDK issued an on-air apology three days later.

Deceiving the Audience
Is Rejected Almost Universally

Journalism's purpose is to inform the public; to achieve that purpose, news organizations must gain the public's trust. That hard-earned trust is squandered if the organization knowingly circulates misinformation.

That journalists reject deceiving the audience was confirmed in a survey of 740 members of Investigative Reporters and Editors in 2002. Those experienced journalists were asked about 16 deceptive practices on a seven-point scale, from "not at all justified" to "very justified," based on the question, "Given an important story that is of vital public interest, would the following be justified?"

Asked if they would make an untrue statement to readers/viewers, 99 percent rated the practice "not all justified" or "mostly" not justified. The respondents also rejected other scenarios in which the audience would be deceived: "using nonexist-ent characters or quotes in a story" (97 percent) and "altering quotes" (96 percent).

In contrast to the near-unanimous rejection of making an untrue statement to readers/viewers, a significantly lower 80 percent rejected making an untrue statement to news sources. Forty percent rejected withholding information from readers/viewers, compared to 10 percent rejecting withholding information from sources.

Analyzing the survey results, Seow Ting Lee of Illinois State University saw a pattern: that journalists "reacted more favorably to deceptive practices targeting news sources than to those targeting news audiences." Lee also noted another pattern: that the journal-ists generally "were more approving of deceptive practices that involved *omission* (with-holding information, surreptitious recording of information) than of deceptive practices involving *commission* (impersonation, lying, tampering with or falsifying information).[52]

When journalists are asked to lie to their audience, the request most often comes from police who seek their help in solving crimes or protecting innocent people from harm.

One newspaper that intentionally published a false story was the *King County Journal* in Washington State. In 2003 the authorities had been tipped by a jailhouse informant that a former prisoner supposedly had been hired for arson by his cellmate, a man in prison for murdering his wife. If the former prisoner burned the house where the murderer's mother-in-law and his 13-year-old son lived, the murderer would pay even more to have the family of his prosecutor killed. Before placing the second contract, the murderer wanted to see a story in the paper stating that the arson had been carried out.

Acting on the informant's tip, authorities arrested the former prisoner, who coop-erated to avoid a murder-conspiracy charge. Then a deputy prosecutor and the sheriff's office told *Journal* editor Tom Wolfe that they could trap the murderer if the paper published a story stating falsely that the house was torched. Lives were at stake, they said.

Wolfe's first reaction was that deliberately publishing the fake story would erode the paper's credibility. But he concluded that what he was being asked to do was not very different from withholding certain information about a crime that might endanger someone. "We know the people involved quite well," he said. "It was not a theoretical concern, it was an actual concern."

The sheriff's office said the ruse helped them trap the murderer, who was caught discussing his plans in a secret recording after reading the fake story.[53] "We very much appreciate the *King County Journal* for printing [the story] for us," a spokeswoman for the sheriff said.[54]

Journalism ethics teachers criticized the *Journal*. "It was a lie. The newspaper delib-erately told a falsehood, not just to the guy in the prison cell, but to all its readers," said Michael Parks, then the director of the School of Journalism at the University of Southern California's Annenberg School for Communication. Publishing a bogus story undermines "the foundation of trust the newspaper has with its readers," said Aly Colon, then of the Poynter Institute's ethics faculty.[55]

Later, the top King County prosecutor said that, if he had known about it, he would have vetoed his subordinates' decision to ask the *Journal* to publish the fake story. "It was not sensitive to the traditional role of the press," Prosecutor Norm Maleng's spokesman said. "It just wasn't appropriate."[56]

Point of View

The Truth about Deception

Brooke Kroeger

Even the most cursory analysis of a century and a half of significant undercover investigations by journalists makes clear how effective the practice can be. Repeatedly, they have proved their worth as producers of high-impact public awareness or as hasteners of change.

Like almost no other journalistic approach, undercover reporting has a built-in ability to expose wrongs and wrongdoers or perform other meaningful public service. It can illuminate the unknown, it can capture and sustain attention, it can shock or amaze.

The criticism that has bedeviled the practice in more recent years comes from the ethical compromises it inevitably requires, its reliance on some of journalism's most questionable means, and the unacceptable excesses of the few. Deception not only happens in the course of reporting undercover, it is intrinsic to the form. For would-be truth tellers, this is shaky ground.

Yet at its best, undercover reporting achieves most of the things great journalism means to achieve. At its worst, but no worse than bad journalism in any form, it is not only an embarrassment but can be downright destructive. The capacity of undercover reporting to bring important social issues to public attention and thus to motivate reformers to act far outweighs the objections against it, legitimate though they may be. Its benefits, when used selectively, far outweigh the lapses, which, it turns out, are more of a preoccupation only in some quarters of the profession than they are with the public.

Professor Kroeger is director of Global and Joint Program Studies in the journalism department at New York University, where she was department chair from 2005 to 2011. The above is excerpted from her book *Undercover Reporting: The Truth about Deception* (Evanston, IL: Northwestern University Press, 2012), xv–xvi. Copyright © 2012 by Brooke Kroeger. Published 2012 by Northwestern University Press. All rights reserved.

Case Study

Rumsfeld's Q&A with the Troops

Secretary of Defense Donald Rumsfeld took questions from the troops on December 8, 2004, while visiting Iraq and Kuwait. One question in Kuwait made worldwide news: Why, asked Specialist Thomas Wilson of the Tennessee National Guard, "do we soldiers have to dig through local landfills" for makeshift armor for their humvees?

(Continued)

Rumsfeld's response proved controversial. He said that the army was trying to upgrade the armor on its vehicles in Iraq, and that the delay was not a matter of money or of intent, but of production limitations. In the days afterward, army suppliers disputed the statement about production limitations. One result of the question – and the public attention focused on it – was that the shipment of armored humvees to the troops was speeded up.

Rumsfeld also said in his response: "As you know, you go to war with the Army you have. They're not the Army you might want or wish to have." His critics back in the United States saw this comment as condescending and pointed out that Rumsfeld had had many months to prepare for the invasion of Iraq.

The question was popular with the troops assembled for the secretary's visit. From the audience of 2,300 soldiers came an outburst of "hooahs" and applause so loud that Rumsfeld had to ask Specialist Wilson to repeat his question.

A day later, there was a postscript: The question that the soldier had asked turned out to have been written for him by a *Chattanooga Times Free Press* reporter who was "embedded" with the soldier's unit. The question's origin became known because the reporter, Edward Lee Pitts, wrote about it in an email to a colleague at the paper, and someone leaked the email to Internet sites. That led to criticism of the reporter. "He created news in order to cover it," Rush Limbaugh said on his radio talk show. Limbaugh called it "a setup." In the story Pitts wrote for his newspaper about the question and Rumsfeld's answer, Pitts did not disclose that he had been the author of the question.

In his email, Pitts said he had wanted to ask the question himself but was denied a chance to speak to Rumsfeld at what the Pentagon called a town hall meeting for GIs. In his email, he wrote: "I just had one of my best days as a journalist today. As luck would have it, our journey North was delayed just long enough so I could attend a visit today here by Defense Secretary Rumsfeld." Pitts wrote that he and two soldiers "worked on questions to ask Rumsfeld about the appalling lack of armor their vehicles going into combat have." Pitts said he "found the Sgt. In Charge of the microphone for the question and answer session and made sure he knew to get my guys out of the crowd." Pitts wrote that Wilson told him he "felt good b/c he took his complaints to the top."

President George W. Bush and Secretary Rumsfeld said they welcomed the pointed questions that the soldiers raised. Bush said the military was addressing the issue of lack of armor for its vehicles in the combat zone and said he didn't blame the soldier for asking the question. "If I were a soldier overseas wanting to defend my country," the president said, "I would want to ask the secretary of defense the same question." Rumsfeld said it was "good for people to raise questions."

Tom Griscom, publisher and executive editor of the *Times Free Press*, supported the way Pitts handled the situation. "I am supportive of his trying to find a way to get the question asked," he said. He said it was a mistake, however, not to have told readers about the question's origin. The paper disclosed Pitts' role on the front page of the next day's paper.

Griscom said "the soldier asked the question" although he could have turned Pitts down. "Because someone's in the media who's embedded with them, does that mean they don't have the same opportunity to make a suggestion of something that might be asked?" Griscom said. "Is that what makes it wrong, because a journalist did it? … That response from the troops was a clear indication that this is an issue on their minds."

Don Fost wrote in the *San Francisco Chronicle* that the incident "raised questions about journalistic objectivity and whether the press manipulates the coverage of events." Jane Kirtley, professor of media ethics and law at the University of Minnesota, told Fost that Pitts broke the rules. "I don't like it," she said. "Not because they're not good questions, but because we have to play by the rules."

On his network's *Reliable Sources* program, Jamie McIntyre of CNN said he might have suggested a question for a soldier who asked, but he thought actually writing the question "does cross a line." On the same program, Matt Cooper of *Time* magazine supported Pitts, calling the question "clever" and saying it was validated by the troops' enthusiastic reaction. McIntyre and Cooper both said Pitts should have told readers about his involvement.

Other ethics experts supported Pitts.

Tom Rosenstiel, then director of the Pew Research Center's Project for Excellence in Journalism, said that Pitts "may have emboldened soldiers to ask questions that citizens are often a little more timid about asking." He said that Pitts may have helped frame the question "in a more provocative way" but that there was "no sleight of hand."

Alex Jones, director of Harvard University's Joan Shorenstein Center for Press, Politics and Public Policy, said Pitts' role "makes me uncomfortable" but "I don't consider this to be a setup because it was a legitimate question as far as the soldier was concerned."

Stuart Loory, who holds the Lee Hills Chair in Free Press Studies at the University of Missouri, observed: "Reporters don't have the same access any longer that they did to ask their own questions. And planting a legitimate question with somebody who may have the access, I think, is an acceptable practice. The question is whether or not the soldier who asked the question really believed in it, and my guess is that he did, or he wouldn't have asked it."

Bob Steele, then of the Poynter Institute, said the question was legitimate. "The soldiers were not deceived. They knew what was going on."

Pentagon spokesman Larry Di Rita had a different view. He said in a news release: "Town hall meetings are intended for soldiers to have dialogue with the secretary of defense. ... The secretary provides ample opportunity for interaction with the press. It is better that others not infringe on the troops' opportunity to interact with superiors in the chain of command."

Sources

Bandler, James, "Reporter discloses his help to soldier on armor question," *The Wall Street Journal*, Dec. 10, 2004.

CNN, "Reporter planted GI's question for Rumsfeld," Dec. 10, 2004.

CNN, transcript for *Reliable Sources*, Dec. 12, 2004.

Fost, Dan, "Reporter helped orchestrate GI's query to Rumsfeld," *San Francisco Chronicle*, Dec. 10, 2004.

Gibson, Gail, "A guardsman's question has continuing effect," *The Baltimore Sun*, Dec. 9, 2004.

Hansell, Saul, "G.I.'s query to Rumsfeld prompted by reporter," *The New York Times*, Dec. 10, 2004.

Kurtz, Howard, and Thomas E. Ricks, "Reporter prompted query to Rumsfeld," *The Washington Post*, Dec. 10, 2004.

Mink, Eric, "The question that saved lives," *St. Louis Post-Dispatch*, Dec. 15, 2004.

Page, Clarence, "'Just answer the question, Mr. Rumsfeld,'" *Chicago Tribune*, Dec. 12, 2004.

(Continued)

Poynter, "Chattanooga reporter's email to colleagues," Dec. 9, 2004.

Rutten, Tim, "Free to shoot from the hip," *Los Angeles Times*, Dec. 11, 2004.

Strupp, Joe, "Editor backs embed in Rumsfeld incident but criticizes aftermath," *Editor & Publisher*, Dec. 9, 2004.

USA Today, "Publisher: reporter needed to tell of Rumsfeld Q&A role," Dec. 10, 2004.

Questions for Class Discussion

- Did Edward Lee Pitts engage in deception by helping the soldiers write their questions and arranging for the sergeant at the microphone to call on them? If you think it was deception, do you think it was justified?

- In his first story on the town hall meeting, should Pitts have told readers that he had written Specialist Wilson's question?
- If you were Pitts, how would you respond to Rush Limbaugh's criticism that you had "created news in order to cover it"?

Case Study

Spying on the Mayor in a Chat Room

Reporters for *The Spokesman-Review* in Spokane, Washington, interviewed an 18-year-old high school graduate in the fall of 2004 about a dinner date the teenager said he had had a few months earlier with a 53-year-old man he had met in an online gay chat room.

This is what the teenager told the reporters: After dinner, he was given the keys to a convertible in the restaurant parking lot. As he drove curvy roads north of the city, he asked the older man what he did for a living. "[H]e says, like, I'm the mayor of Spokane." Until that moment, the teenager had no idea he was on a date with Mayor Jim West — a date that ended with consensual sex.

When reporters interviewed the high school graduate after police tipped them about him, *The Spokesman-Review* had spent two years investigating West, a Republican with an anti-gay rights record. But the newspaper did not immediately publish the teenager's account of a date with West.

At the time, the newspaper was seeking interviews with two men who had told police that West had sexually abused them when they were children and West a sheriff's deputy and Boy Scout leader. In the winter and spring of 2005, reporters interviewed those men and heard the accusations themselves.

Steven A. Smith, then editor of *The Spokesman-Review*, wanted proof of West's conduct "beyond a shadow of a doubt." In an online Q&A with readers later, Smith reviewed the evidence that the paper had at the time:

- The account of the 18-year-old who said that he had chatted with a person while on Gay.com, that the person turned out to be Mayor West, and that the conversations resulted in a date and a sexual encounter.

- And the accounts of the two men alleging that West had abused them as children. But both were felons and one was in prison at the time on a drug conviction.

"The problem in the cyberworld is that there was no backup evidence," Smith said in the Q&A: "If we had published that allegation [of the teenager who had the date with West], it would have elicited an immediate denial from the mayor, and that would have been that. The screen names would have disappeared, the mayor would have dropped out of the chat rooms, and we'd be guilty of either improperly sullying his reputation or guilty of letting him off the hook."

Smith said the only way to confirm the story was to go online and engage the mayor in the chat room. To do this, *The Spokesman-Review* hired a forensic computer expert, a former federal agent whom it did not identify.

For a 2006 documentary on the investigation of Mayor West, the PBS program *Frontline* asked Bill Morlin, the *Spokesman-Review* reporter who had been investigating the mayor, about the decision to hire a consultant to go undercover on Gay.com. Morlin responded in the on-camera interview, "I knew I couldn't do it," because the paper's ethics code prevented staff members from pretending to be someone they were not. But, Morlin said, the paper could hire consultants who did: "What those consultants do to accomplish their jobs, as long as it is legal, I don't have a problem with that."

The consultant registered on Gay.com as "Moto-Brock," a fictitious high school senior questioning his own sexuality and eager to meet older gay or bisexual men.

"It took two months of chatting with the mayor online in a variety of ways to get him to the point where he trusted us enough to reveal himself," Smith said. Ultimately West thought he was communicating with a teenager, Smith said, adding: "He showed up for a meeting that he set up, and at that point, we knew we had the mayor."

On May 5, 2005, *The Spokesman-Review* published its story reporting the 18-year-old high school graduate's 2004 date with the mayor, the allegations of the two men who said West had abused them as children, and the details of his online conversations with the paper's computer expert.

"Once in the chat room, which has a policy that all participants be 18, the consultant changed his age to 17 because the newspaper wanted to know whether West was using the Web to meet underage children," the newspaper reported. "Within two months, Moto-Brock and RightBi-Guy [who turned out to be the mayor] were discussing sex in the Gay.com chat room, and the dialogues were being recorded by the newspaper's consultant."

The paper said that, when West was interviewed the day before its story was published, he admitted his online relationships with the 18-year-old and Moto-Brock. After a long pause in the interview, he said, "They were both adults, and I was in public office when I dated women in this community. So what's your point?"

The paper said the transcripts of the online conversations showed that RightBi-Guy was the first person to raise the issue of sex. The *Spokesman-Review* report continued:

> He also suggested that he and Moto-Brock switch their conversations from the Gay.com chat room to America Online instant messaging, which is transitory in nature and disappears quickly unless steps are taken to record chats. Over a period of several months, RightBi-Guy offered Moto-Brock autographed sports memorabilia, prime seats

(Continued)

for Seahawks and Mariners games, help getting into college, an internship job in the Spokane mayor's office and the promise of trips to Washington, DC. In mid-March, Moto-Brock told RightBi-Guy that he'd turned 18.

The paper confirmed West's identity when he showed up for a golf date with Moto-Brock at Indian Canyon at 10 a.m. on April 10. Earlier, in order that Moto-Brock would know whom to look for, RightBi-Guy had emailed him his picture. "The picture was of West," the paper reported.

He also emailed Moto-Brock a link to the mayor's Web page on the Spokane City Hall site. Three people affiliated with *The Spokesman-Review* reported seeing West arrive at the course in his blue Lexus at 9:45 a.m. April 10. ... The two never met in person. Shortly after that failed meeting, the consultant was asked by the newspaper to stop communicating online with RightBi-Guy. But West subsequently sent the consultant two more emails, including a final message sent April 28. Sent from the mayor's office, the e-mail has "internship" in its subject line. The email asks Moto-Brock, "Still interested?"

Days after publishing its story, *The Spokesman-Review* reported that Ryan Oelrich, 24, said he had been appointed by West to the city's Human Rights Commission in April 2004 after apparently meeting him in a Gay.com online chat room. Oelrich said that, after he was appointed to the commission, West made several sexual advances online and once offered him $300 to swim naked with him. Oelrich said he had declined the offer.

Oelrich, who heads a gay youth organization in Spokane, said he knew of five or six young gay men who had also received inappropriate sexual advances from West. Oelrich said

that he left the Human Rights Commission in January 2005 after West "hounded me for months, telling me I was cute and asking me out on dates."

At a news conference, West said: "I categorically deny any allegations about incidents that supposedly occurred 24 years ago as alleged by two convicted felons and about which I have no knowledge. The newspaper also reported that I had visited a gay Internet chat room and had relations with adult men. I don't deny that."

An ethical issue for *The Spokesman-Review*, in addition to its use of deception, was the question of whether West's sexual activity warranted news coverage. Editor Smith said in an online Q&A with readers on May 9:

This is not about being gay. As we were working on our actual stories, I kept rewriting them in my mind as if the issues involved hetero sex — that is, a scenario in which the 50-plus-year-old mayor was chatting up 17- and 18-year-old high school girls and then initiating cyber-sex and soliciting real-life sex when they turned 18. As a parent of teenagers, including a teen-age daughter, I decided it would absolutely be a story. ... I think this story is about behavior most in our community would find repulsive — gay or straight.

Another questioner wanted to know why the paper faked the age — 17, almost 18. Smith responded:

The website requires a simple declaration of age to register. And those who use the site tell us it is replete with youngsters. If you go into the chat rooms, you'll often find more underage kids than adults. We're also told this is a site where older men seek out minors. We wanted to know if the mayor would approach someone underage (he did without prompting), if he'd turn the conversations to sex (he did, without prompting). But as soon as we moved the character to 18, the mayor's intent became overtly sexual.

When *Editor & Publisher* magazine asked 10 top editors about *The Spokesman-Review*'s decision to use the computer expert to engage the mayor online, no one endorsed the idea. That led the late Steve Lovelady, then managing editor of *CJR Daily*, an online service of *Columbia Journalism Review*, to defend *The Spokesman-Review*'s reporting on West as "public service journalism at its best." He criticized other editors who

> piously declare that they wouldn't have taken the measures that Smith took to make his story airtight. … What exactly is Steve Smith supposed to be guilty of? Having the prudence and caution to hire an expert to ascertain the mayor's online identity before *The Spokesman-Review* went into print? Where I come from, we don't call that entrapment; we call it responsible journalism.

After the newspaper's revelations, a petition was circulated to oust Mayor West. The recall petition contended that West used his political office for personal benefit by offering a city internship to someone he thought was an 18-year-old man he had met in a gay online chat room and with whom he had conducted sexually explicit chats. West, who was not charged with any crime, acknowledged making mistakes in his personal life but asked voters to give him a second chance. On December 6, 2005, the mayor was recalled from office in a special election, with the electorate voting by two to one to oust him. On July 22, 2006, West died of colon cancer.

Sources

Frontline, "A hidden life," PBS, Nov. 14, 2006.

Graff, E. J., "The line on sex: when is a scandal merely voyeurism?," *Columbia Journalism Review,* Sept.–Oct. 2005, 9.

Morlin, Bill, "West tied to sex abuse in the '70s, using office to lure young men," *The Spokesman-Review,* May 5, 2008.

The Spokesman-Review, "Spokesman-Review investigation of Jim West: *Spokesman-Review* editor Steven A. Smith addressed your questions about our series of stories on the mayor," May 9, 2005; May 17, 2005; June 23, 2005.

Strupp, Joe, "Truth our mission?," *Editor & Publisher,* June 2005, 62.

Tu, Janet I., "Newspaper's ruse raises issue of journalism ethics," *The Seattle Times,* May 6, 2005.

Questions for Class Discussion

- Was *The Spokesman-Review* justified in investigating and reporting on Mayor West's sex life?
- If you think the paper was right to report on that subject, would you have published the story solely on the basis of the statements of the 18-year-old high school graduate and the two men who said West had abused them as children?
- If you didn't think that was enough evidence, would your decision have changed when Ryan Oelrich, whom West had appointed to a city commission, made his statements to reporters?
- Was the paper justified in using deception by hiring a computer expert to pose as a high school student and engage in an online conversation with the mayor? What do you think about Bill Morlin's statement that, in essence, staff members could not ethically go undercover but it was all right for a consultant to do so?
- Was the paper accountable to its readers after publishing the allegations?

Notes

1   Donald L. Barlett, "Patient at Lima beaten and kicked for whispering," *The Plain Dealer*, May 27, 1965.

2   "PD reporter got job 'inside Lima' for data," *The Plain Dealer*, May 23, 1965.

3   Author's telephone interview with Donald L. Barlett, Apr. 23, 2007.

4   Reid MacCluggage, "Should we ever deceive?," *APME News*, Winter 1997–98.

5   Louis W. Hodges, "Undercover, masquerading, surreptitious taping," *Journal of Mass Media Ethics*, Fall 1988, 26–36.

6   Barlett, email to author, June 24, 2008.

7   Author's recollections as managing editor of *The Philadelphia Inquirer*, for which Josephson conducted seminars in the early 1980s.

8   Sissela Bok, *Lying: Moral Choice in Public and Private Life* (New York: Vintage Books, 1978), 13.

9   Ibid., 8.

10 Carl Bernstein and Bob Woodward, *All the President's Men* (New York: Touchstone, 1974), 60.

11 Bok, *Lying*, 120.

12 Deni Elliott, "Journalists' con games can backfire," *Montana Journalism Review*, 26 (Summer 1997), 3–6.

13 Michael Josephson, "Declaration of ethical standards," unpublished paper written for the Associated Press Managing Editors (1993).

14 Bill Kovach and Tom Rosenstiel, *The Elements of Journalism: What Newspeople Should Know and the Public Should Expect*, 3rd edn. (New York: Crown, 2014), 121.

15 Hodges, "Undercover, masquerading, surreptitious taping."

16 Jay Black, Bob Steele, and Ralph Barney, *Doing Ethics in Journalism: A Handbook with Case Studies*, 3rd edn. (Needham Heights, MA: Allyn & Bacon, 1999), 163.

17 Brooke Kroeger, *Undercover Reporting: The Truth about Deception* (Evanston, IL: Northwestern University Press, 2012), 194–195.

18 Ibid., 195.

19 Stephen Klaidman and Tom L. Beauchamp, *The Virtuous Journalist* (New York: Oxford University Press, 1987), 195.

20 *Chicago Sun-Times* history, accessed on its website in 2008 but no longer available.

21 Philip Seib and Kathy Fitzpatrick, *Journalism Ethics* (Fort Worth, TX: Harcourt, Brace, 1997), 90.

22 *Chicago Sun-Times* history.

23 Susan Paterno, "The lying game," *American Journalism Review*, May 1997.

24 Ibid.

25 Bruce W. Sanford, *Don't Shoot the Messenger: How Our Growing Hatred of the Media Threatens Free Speech for All of Us* (New York: Free Press, 1999), 145.

26 Walter Goodman, "Beyond ABC v. Food Lion," *The New York Times*, Mar. 9, 1997.

27 Paterno, "The lying game."

28 Bill Kovach and Tom Rosenstiel, *The Elements of Journalism*, 1st edn. (New York: Crown, 2001), 121–122.

29 Bob Steele, "High standards for hidden cameras," Poynter, Aug. 25, 2002. This article was originally published in *Hidden Cameras/Hidden Microphones: At the Crossroads of Journalism, Ethics and Law* (Radio-Television News Directors Foundation, 1998).

30 Ibid.

31 Al Tompkins, "Anatomy of a Pulitzer: Q&A with Hull and Priest," Poynter, Apr. 6, 2008.

32 Anne Hull, in "Creating an investigative narrative: excerpts from a presentation by Anne Hull and Dana Priest," *Nieman Reports*, 62:2 (Summer 2008).

33 Dana Priest, in "Creating an investigative narrative."

34 Ibid.

35 Hull, email to the author, Aug. 18, 2014.

36 Hull, in "Creating an investigative narrative."

37 Kroeger, *Undercover Reporting*, 7.

38 Ibid., 7.

39 Paterno, "The lying game."

40 Priest, in "Creating an investigative narrative."

41 Gene Roberts and Hank Klibanoff, *The Race Beat: The Press, the Civil Rights Struggle, and the Awakening of a Nation* (New York: Alfred A. Knopf, 2006), 363.

42 Ron F. Smith, *Ethics in Journalism*, 6th edn. (Malden, MA: Blackwell, 2008), 195. Roberts' account of walking into the emergency room wearing a stethoscope is familiar to the author and other *Philadelphia Inquirer* editors from the period (1972–90) when Roberts led the paper.

43 Tom Goldstein, *The News at Any Cost: How Journalists Compromise Their Ethics to Shape the News* (New York: Simon & Schuster, 1985), 143–144.

44 Jack Fuller, *News Values: Ideas for an Information Age* (Chicago: University of Chicago Press, 1996), 51–52.

45 Jay Rosen, "The uncharted: from off the bus to *Meet the Press*," *Huffington Post*, Apr. 14, 2008.

46 Ibid.

47 Author's telephone interview with Roy Reed, Sept. 10, 2007.

48 John McPhee, "The writing life: elicitation," *The New Yorker*, Apr. 7, 2014.

49 Roberts and Klibanoff, *The Race Beat*, 402.

50 Al Tompkins, "Tuesday edition: reporters testing school security," Poynter, Oct. 9, 2006, updated Mar. 3, 2011.

51 Jessica Bock, "KSDK reporter working on school safety story prompted Kirkwood High lockdown," *St. Louis Post-Dispatch*, Jan. 17, 2014.

52 Seow Ting Lee, "The ethics of journalistic deception," in Lee Wilkins and Renita Coleman, *The Moral Media: How Journalists Reason about Ethics* (Mahwah, NJ: Lawrence Erlbaum, 2005), 98–100. Lee's web survey was conducted Feb. 2–23, 2002. Of the 3,795 members of the Investigative Reporters and Editors to whom the survey was delivered, 740 responded, a rate of 19.4 percent.

53 Aly Colon, "Faking the news: weighing the options when the stakes are high and important principles are at stake," Poynter, Apr. 22, 2003.

54 Sara Jean Green and Ian Ith, "Ethics of paper's fake arson story debated," *The Seattle Times*, Apr. 18, 2003.

55 Ibid.

56 Robert L. Jamieson Jr., "A question of ethics: fake story is news not to print," *Seattle Post-Intelligencer*, Apr. 25, 2003.

17 Covering a Diverse, Multicultural Society

An ethical duty to be sensitive in reporting on minority groups

---

Learning Goals

This chapter will help you understand:

- the ethical dimensions of covering a diverse, multicultural society;
- the complexity of stories about racial and ethnic conflict;
- techniques that help journalists do a better job of covering cultures other than their own;
- ethical issues in the coverage of new immigrants;
- when racial identifications in news stories are justified, and when they are not;
- ways to make coverage more inclusive of the entire community;
- the need to eliminate any disparity in how different races and ethnicities are covered; and
- the need for accuracy and sensitivity in covering gays and lesbians in the news.

On December 14, 1995, 17-year-old Cynthia Wiggins rode a local transit bus from the east side of Buffalo, New York, to her job at a fast-food restaurant in the Walden Galleria Mall in suburban Cheektowaga. The bus stop was on Walden Avenue, a seven-lane highway that went past the mall. The curb where the bus stopped was covered by a snowdrift eight feet high, and there was no crosswalk. Threading her way through the busy Christmas-season traffic, Wiggins walked alongside an 18-wheel dump truck. The driver couldn't see her.

As she started to cross in front of the truck, the traffic light turned green. The driver of a nearby van watched helplessly as "both sets of tandems went over the girl." The witness said, "[T]here's no way she could get out of the way of the wheels."

To many people – particularly those who are white – nobody was to blame for Cynthia Wiggins' tragic death.

To many other people – particularly those who are black, as Wiggins was – she was surely a victim of racism.

A few months after Wiggins was fatally injured on Walden Avenue, Ted Koppel of ABC News took his *Nightline* camera crews to Buffalo to try to sort out the controversy.

The Ethical Journalist: Making Responsible Decisions in the Digital Age, Second Edition. Gene Foreman.
© 2016 John Wiley & Sons, Inc. Published 2016 by John Wiley & Sons, Inc.

"Remember now, we're talking about a traffic accident," Koppel told his viewers when the *Nightline* report aired on May 22, 1996. "No one has charged that Cynthia Wiggins was run down deliberately. No one has even suggested that she was killed intentionally because of her race. So why do feelings run so high?"

The ABC journalists interviewed white residents who said the accident had nothing to do with race. One of these, radio talk-show host Gary MacNamara, said: "There have been many cases, many things that happen in our society, where automatically racism is thrown out, that it's got to be racism, it's got to be racism, without any proof. Well, that's crying wolf."

This is what *Nightline* reported in its documentary, titled "The Color Line and the Bus Line":

After giving birth to a son, Wiggins was studying part-time to get her high school diploma. She received some public assistance but needed a part-time job. With no jobs available in her depressed neighborhood, she found work in the Galleria in the nearly all-white Cheektowaga. To get there required a half-hour ride on the Number 6 bus.

But the Number 6 bus did not stop in the mall, a circumstance that became the crux of the controversy over Wiggins' death.

Koppel told his viewers that, when the Galleria was built in 1988, "there was clearly some nervousness about the crime rate at the Thruway Mall, just down the road."

Ken Cannon, a former executive of the company that developed the Galleria, said in reference to Thruway Mall: "There had been some knifings, and there had been some other instances related to drugs, and alcohol, which we were not interested in moving down the highway. And nor was the town, for that matter."

"I was surprised," said Gordon Foster, a former transit official, "but they had mentioned one route that they did not want to have serve the mall, which was Route 6, which … at that time, went right by the area where they were building the mall, and had been there for many years."

Cannon said the transit officials "did ask us about access for the bus traveling down Walden Avenue, and I said to them that we had these concerns about security."

Also interviewed for *Nightline* was Bud White, a merchant who had talked with the Galleria's managers about locating a store in the mall. He said that, at a meeting with Tim Ahern and Mark Congell of the mall management, he asked about "the black community" and was told: "You know, don't worry about the black communities. … We don't want 'em, and we're not going to let 'em … [W]e're not going to let the buses come in."

Ahern said he and Congell remembered the meeting with White, and "those statements are emphatically false."

Professor Henry Taylor of Buffalo University, an African American, told ABC:

It sounds so innocent. Don't let the buses roll into the suburban regions. Don't let the buses roll into the malls. Don't let the buses roll into the industrial parks. But there are major consequences to this. That's why I refer to those transportation issues as racist. Sanitized, guiltless racism, the kind of … racism that people can engage in in the quietness of their suburban homes.

At the end of the documentary, Koppel told his viewers that after Cynthia Wiggins' death, the transit company and the mall had agreed on a new bus stop on the grounds of the Galleria. "Passengers on the Number 6 bus will no longer have to dodge traffic on Walden Avenue," Koppel said. "It is, in a manner of speaking, Cynthia's legacy."[1]

The *Nightline* editor and producer who had initiated the Buffalo story was Eric Wray, an African American, who had immediately sensed its importance. Until the reporting in Buffalo began, Koppel himself had doubts about whether the story about a traffic accident was worthy of national attention.

Wray wrote later that ABC's reporting in Buffalo was an example of the "Rashomon approach," named for the film of the same name by the Japanese filmmaker Akira Kurosawa. It involves looking at a story through multiple perspectives. Each observer has "a different perspective that leads to differing conclusions and reveals different 'truths' about what actually happened."

Wray saw the Rashomon approach as especially important in stories involving racial or ethnic conflict:

> In many ways, the Cynthia Wiggins tragedy is its own Rashomon. Clearly, white and black Buffalo area residents had different opinions about the circumstances that led to her death. Differing notions about the placement of the bus stop – sinister to some; incidental to others – point up different perceptions of racism. Buffalo's, and to some extent, America's stance on racial justice issues appears quite adequate to some but unfair to others.
>
> For journalists, this is a major point of conflict in the story. The same event was viewed by many people differently and was clearly based on their vantage points. ...
>
> Each perspective has its own biases and prejudices. The "truth," if there is such a thing in journalism, can only be determined by looking at an event from multiple points of view.[2]

In 2006 the *Nightline* documentary was praised by the authors of a book that celebrated and analyzed exemplary reporting on America's cultural diversity. "The story teaches how to question assumptions by using a variety of voices and perspectives to examine a racially divisive issue," wrote Arlene Notoro Morgan, Alice Irene Pifer, and Keith Woods in *The Authentic Voice*: "It also teaches the value of using street reporting to combine a variety of conflicting viewpoints, creating a narrative that allows the audience to reach its own conclusion through the facts that are laid out."[3]

Ethics in Reporting on a Multicultural Society

Providing accurate, fair, and sensitive coverage of a diverse, multicultural society is an essential dimension of ethical journalism.

Until the last half of the twentieth century, that kind of coverage was rarely an acknowledged goal of the American news media. In 1947 the Hutchins Commission challenged the news media to "give a comprehensive picture of constituent groups in society, avoiding stereotypes."[4] In 1968 the Kerner Commission painted a picture of an American society divided along racial lines and said the division was strikingly evident in the news media, whose workforce then was nearly all white and nearly all male.[5] The civil rights movement of the 1960s put pressure on news media executives to end hiring discrimination and to begin actively recruiting members of racial and ethnic minority groups.

Today, most news organizations are consciously striving to bring members of those minority groups into the ranks of journalists and to broaden their news coverage to include all elements of a diverse community.

In general, the news media still have a long way to go before they truly are representative of society as a whole. Members of minority groups made up 22.4 percent of the television news workforce and 13.0 percent of the radio news workforce in 2014.[6] Among journalists working at daily newspapers in 2014, 13.3 percent were members of minority groups.[7] Among online-only news sites, about 20 percent were members of minority groups.[8] Contrast this with the Census Bureau's estimate that on July 1, 2013, members of minority groups accounted for 37.4 percent of the national population of 316.1 million.[9]

Still, diversity in hiring has done much to inform the reporting by newspapers, broadcast stations, and online sites. Although no journalist should be expected to speak for his or her entire ethnic group, journalists of color exert a valuable influence on newsroom decision-making that was missing in decades past. And, increasingly, journalists of color are the people making the decisions. In 2014, 15 percent of daily newspapers said one of their top three editors was a person of color.[10] The same year, people of color composed 13.6 percent of television news directors and 11.6 percent of radio news directors.[11]

The Society of Professional Journalists' ethics code, under the guiding principle of "seek truth and report it," tells journalists to:

- "Boldly tell the story of the diversity and magnitude of the human experience. Seek sources whose voices we seldom hear."
- "Avoid stereotyping.[12] Journalists should examine the ways their values and experiences may shape their reporting."

The Challenge of Covering Other Cultures

A challenge for journalists, irrespective of their own racial or ethnic groups, is to write knowledgeably about another culture. Specifically, the challenge is to rise above "superficial, ordinary and, in important ways, harmful journalism," wrote Keith Woods, NPR's vice president for diversity.[13] It requires conversation about a subject that makes many journalists uncomfortable. It means taking the initiative.

As the United States' population continues to diversify, the ability to report on multiple cultures becomes an ever more important skill. The Census Bureau predicted in

2012 that so-called minority groups would collectively become a majority in 2043, although non-Hispanic whites would remain the largest demographic component. The bureau's projection of 2060 populations is shown in Figure 17.1.[14]

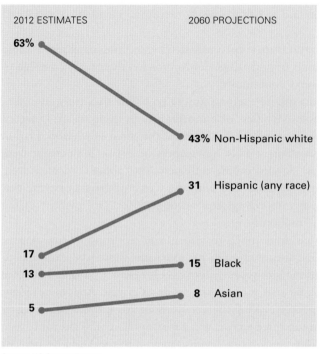

Figure 17.1
Projected changes in the US racial/ethnic make-up: The chart shows the percentage of population for each of the four largest demographic groups in 2012 and 2060.
GRAPHIC COURTESY OF BILL MARSH.

Source: US Census Bureau

Joann Byrd, former ombudsman of *The Washington Post*, wrote *Respecting All Cultures: A Practical Ethics Handbook for Journalists* in April 2002 when she was chair of the Ethics and Values Committee of the American Society of Newspaper Editors. Here is some of the advice she gave:

> *Challenge our stereotypes.*   These scraps of shorthand are often pejorative, and since stereotypes are almost never accurate, they can be counted on to get in the way of a trustworthy report. The cure for stereotypes is becoming informed about people as individuals.
>
> *Ask about cultural traditions.*   Remember that cultural values influence each of us. ... [S]hared ideas can reveal what the people themselves see as their "community." And if they serve as glue for families and groups of people, traditions are inherently interesting to people who practice them and those who have different traditions of their own. Besides, talking about values can move us beyond the superficial in short order.
>
> *Learn protocols and courtesies.*   Appropriate dress and customs about such things as shaking hands and eye contact will help us avoid inadvertently insulting a new acquaintance.[15]

For more of Joann Byrd's recommendations for covering other cultures, read her Point of View essay in this chapter, "Gaining Respect by Showing Respect."

Aly Colon, Knight Professor of Ethics in Journalism at Washington and Lee University, has suggested ways that a journalist could connect with people of other cultures:

> Make it a point to go out into the many different communities in your city. Stroll their streets. Shop in their stores. Eat in their restaurants. Study their history. Learn their culture. Show them your face. Have a conversation with them. Listen. Listen. Listen.[16]

Techniques for coverage of race relations and ethnic diversity have been refined through a "Let's Do It Better!" program launched in 1999 at the Graduate School of Journalism at Columbia University. The program, led first by Professor Sig Gissler and later by associate dean Arlene Notoro Morgan, recognized the nation's best reporting on the subject. As winning journalists discussed their projects in conferences conducted by Columbia, they shared their successes and failures. From their experience, teaching tools for the profession evolved.

A group of journalists led by Keith Woods and Morgan met at the Poynter Institute in 2001 to analyze about 150 of the best entries in the Columbia program, a trove that included print, radio, and television journalism. The panel wanted to identify the techniques that worked best in this sensitive area of reporting.

Woods summarized what they had learned: "The best stories ... seem to be written *from* communities, not *about* them. The stories are intellectually curious, not merely voyeuristic. They answer some questions and raise others. They challenge, inform, and are delivered with authority."[17] Woods identified four fundamental measures of excellence that emerged from the study:

1 *The story provides context*, offering historical and supporting information that helps the audience understand. The reporter assigns race its appropriate place in the story.
2 *The story embraces complexity*. It rises above "one-dimensional explanations and the polarized, black-or-white, saints-or-sinners framing to reveal the gray truths of race relations."
3 *We hear the voices of the people*. The quotes and sound bites are "purposeful and clear"; they "advance the story, convey character and personality, reveal new truths, or otherwise add value to the piece."
4 *The story has the ring of authenticity*. The reporting is "broad and deep enough, the details fine enough, the opinions open enough to provide true insight." The writing is clear, direct, and free of euphemisms. The sources are representative of the group, not "assigned an undue leadership role by the media or by themselves."[18]

When Freedom Forum researchers conducted town meetings with news consumers in its Free Press/Fair Press Project in 1998–99, they repeatedly encountered complaints from members of minority groups that news outlets were sending reporters into black and Hispanic communities mostly to cover crime, violence, poverty, or drugs. They said positive development efforts in minority communities rarely were covered.

Robert J. Haiman, whose *Best Practices for Newspaper Journalists* drew on the ideas gathered in the town meetings, wrote that minority participants were disturbed that newspapers persisted in "anointing" minority community leaders. These presumed leaders, Haiman wrote, were not necessarily regarded as leaders by the people who lived in those communities, nor had they been empowered to speak for the communities.

Haiman quoted one black participant:

> You have got to stop looking for two or three people to speak for the black community; it can't be done any more than two or three people can speak for the entire white community. And, besides, too often you get the wrong ones, anyway.[19]

For newspaper editors and broadcast directors, a perplexing question is which reporters and photojournalists should cover minority communities. One goal is to *get the story right*, with all its nuances. Another is to *get the right story*, because stories can be technically accurate, yet lacking the diverse viewpoints that are critical to completeness.

So who should get the assignment?

It would seem logical that an African American reporter would be more likely to gain rapport with African American news subjects than a white reporter. Or that a Latino reporter would be more successful with Latinos, especially in overcoming a language barrier.

But journalists who are members of minority groups can feel isolated and stereotyped if they only, or usually, cover their own communities. Some of these journalists told Haiman they felt pressured to "conform to dated newsroom standards that hampered them in suggesting or assigning stories outside traditional white awareness and sensitivities."[20]

Deciding who gets a certain assignment "can be a controversial judgment call," former network producer Av Westin wrote in *Best Practices for Television Journalists*. Westin would not assign stories automatically on the basis of race. But, he also wrote,

> In newsrooms where racial and ethnic diversity exists, take advantage of the mix of backgrounds and interests, because the issues in their communities will then work their way back into the broadcasts ... A well-rounded reporter should be able to handle any subject matter. On the other hand, in a complex story involving sensitive community feelings, it can be productive to assign a reporter who brings special insights or experience to the story. The decision of whom to assign should be influenced, finally, by who can do the best job.[21]

Issues in Covering Immigrants

Gabriel Escobar, managing editor of *The Philadelphia Inquirer* and himself an immigrant from Colombia, reported extensively on immigrants for *The Washington Post*.

"These stories are a way to shed light on the complex process of assimilation, and executed well, they will add texture and dimension," he wrote in an essay for *The Authentic Voice*.

This coverage "will not always be greeted with applause," Escobar wrote. People in the immigrant community complain that the media seldom go beyond the superficial feature. But these same people, he observed, will object "when the attention becomes probing and, in the process, reveals something that someone will construe as a negative." Escobar offered a case in point:

> Several years ago, I suggested to a colleague who covered transportation that he examine why so many Latino immigrants were getting killed crossing streets in suburban Washington. His analysis proved something irrefutable: immigrants were far more likely to die than any other group.
>
> Several theories were offered, and one of the most perceptive was that these immigrants had settled in neighborhoods built and designed for commuters. By necessity and circumstance, they were pedestrians in places ill suited for walking.
>
> When the story ran, [*The Post*] received numerous complaints from Latino activists and others who said the reporters had stooped to a new low: accusing immigrants of being so ignorant that they did not understand something as elementary as crossing the street. Instead of pressing local communities to improve pedestrian access and educate the public, the reaction to the story removed any impetus to address what clearly was a safety issue.[22]

Escobar also found that, while his Spanish fluency could be an asset, it had a downside. Instead of perceiving him as a neutral reporter, the people he was covering saw him as an ally: "To them, I was on their side, and the bond was sealed by my ability to talk to them in Spanish. What I saw as a very effective tool employed in the act of reporting, they saw as some manifestation of cultural solidarity."[23]

In a situation in which his news subjects regarded his neutral reporting as a betrayal, Escobar learned a lesson: "It was part of my job, paradoxically, to maintain some distance even as language brought us closer. Just as critical, however, was recognizing that cultural perceptions often trumped the ability to communicate in the language of the subjects being covered."[24]

The issue of immigrants who are in the United States illegally is one of the nation's most important news stories. A wave of immigration that gained momentum in the 1970s has made Hispanics the country's largest minority group, constituting about 17 percent of the population as of 2013, according to Census Bureau estimates.[25] The Pew Research Center estimated that 11.7 million immigrants were in the United States illegally in 2012.[26]

When journalists report on people who have immigrated illegally, they run the risk that their story subjects may be deported. This presents an ethical dilemma. The Society of Professional Journalists' principle of "seek and report truth" would argue that the names should be used, and there is no question that credibility suffers when the people in news stories are nameless. But the SPJ principle of "minimize harm" would guide journalists to omit names in order that their sources not be penalized for giving them information.

Although private citizens may choose to notify authorities if they encounter an undocumented immigrant, journalists must not. As neutral observers gathering information, they do not take sides in the dispute over illegal immigration. They avoid being perceived as an arm of law enforcement (a concern discussed in Chapter 13). At the opposite extreme, they could be seen as protecting lawbreakers. So, the question remains: How much information should journalists tell the audience about someone who is in the United States illegally – and how much should be withheld?

Reporters who cover immigration are struggling with that question.

Daniel Gonzalez, who covers the immigration beat for *The Arizona Republic* in Phoenix, told Lucy Hood of *American Journalism Review* that he always tries to name people – but he doesn't always give the full names: "Mexican people have two last names. Sometimes we might use the least common of the two names." On other occasions, Gonzalez said, he uses the first name only, or the first name and an initial.[27]

For "Enrique's Journey," a series of articles tracing a Honduran boy's arduous trip to join his mother in North Carolina, Sonia Nazario of the *Los Angeles Times* omitted the last names of the boy and his mother. The decision was made reluctantly after the *Times* ran their names through a computer search and determined that the two could be located online. Nazario's account, which won the 2003 Pulitzer Prize for feature writing, was accompanied by this explanation: "The *Times'* decision in this instance is intended to allow Enrique and his family to live their lives as they would have had they not provided information for this story." Nazario said:

> The readership reaction confirmed that we made the right decision. I didn't get any response from the readers asking why we hadn't put his last name in. I did get messages saying: "Thank you for not listing his last name. That was the right thing to do."[28]

Kelly McBride of the Poynter Institute told *American Journalism Review*'s Lucy Hood that journalists must be aware of the risks when they report on undocumented immigrants, and they need to ask themselves questions: Is the source likely to be fired, deported, or harassed? Is the source capable of assessing the risk? Does he or she understand the legal implications? "You have to ask a lot of questions," McBride said, "including what your journalistic purpose is."[29]

It is essential that the subject of the story give what is known as "informed consent" – that is, the subject fully understands how he or she will be identified and quoted. Gonzalez, of *The Arizona Republic*, said he always tells his sources what his story is about and clearly explains the possible consequences to them. "Once you've done that," he said, "you've done your job."[30]

The Case Study "When a Story Gets Its Subject Arrested" tells about a grocery worker, Julio Granados, who was arrested by the Immigration and Naturalization Service after he was the subject of a detailed, illustrated feature story in *The News & Observer* of Raleigh, North Carolina.

The very terminology that the news media use in reporting on immigration has been called into question. Latinos have objected to the term *illegal immigrant* as offensive, saying that no human being should be called "illegal."

The Associated Press announced on April 3, 2013, that it would stop using the term "illegal immigrant." Kathleen Carroll, executive editor and senior vice president, said the wire service's stylebook "no longer sanctions the term 'illegal immigrant' or the use of 'illegal' to describe a person. Instead, it tells users that 'illegal' should describe only an action, such as living in or immigrating to a country illegally." Thus, AP continues to use the term "illegal immigration" and phrases such as "people who entered the country illegally" or "someone living in the country on an expired visa."[31]

The New York Times shifted its policy on "illegal immigrant" on April 23, 2013. The newspaper planned to continue to allow the phrase to describe "someone who enters, lives in or works in the United States without proper legal authorization." However, reporters and editors were encouraged to "consider alternatives when appropriate to explain the specific circumstances of the person in question, or to focus on actions." Philip B. Corbett, associate managing editor for standards, said, "'Unauthorized' is also an acceptable description, though it has a bureaucratic tone. 'Undocumented' is the term preferred by many immigrants and their advocates, but it has a flavor of euphemism and should be approached with caution outside quotations."[32]

On another language issue, Phuong Ly asked in an essay on Poynter whether it was time to stop using the term *minorities*: "The term has long been used to describe people who are not white. But changing demographics make the term outdated and oxymoronic." As an example, Ly quoted an AP story: "For the first time, minorities make up the majority of babies in the US …"

Looking for an alternative, Ly did not find a consensus in her survey of journalists. Among those she talked with was David Minthorn, deputy standards editor at the AP, who said the wire service uses "minority" as a dictionary defines it: "a racial, ethnic, religious, or political group smaller and different from the larger group." Minthorn added, "I have no doubt other precise terms will emerge as the situation evolves."[33]

When to Identify News Subjects by Race

Through the mid-twentieth century, newspapers – especially in the South – routinely identified people by race in all kinds of news situations. More precisely, nonwhite people were identified by race; a person whose race was not mentioned was understood by readers to be white. The practice both reflected and encouraged stereotypes.

Although routine racial identification has disappeared, journalists sometimes are confused about when it serves a purpose to specify the race of the people involved in the news.

Keith Woods has urged journalists to "flag every racial reference" and ask these questions:

1   *Is it relevant?*   Race is relevant when the story is about race. Just because people in the conflict are of different races does not mean that race is the source of their dispute. A story about interracial dating, however, is a story about race.

2 *Have I explained the relevance?*   Journalists too frequently assume that readers will know the significance of race in stories. The result is often radically different interpretations. That is imprecise journalism, and its harm may be magnified by the lens of race.

3 *Is it free of codes?*   Be careful not to use *welfare, inner-city, underprivileged, blue-collar, conservative, suburban, exotic, middle-class, Uptown, South Side,* or *wealthy* as euphemisms for racial groups. By definition, the White House is in the inner-city. Say what you mean.

4 *Are the racial identifiers used evenly?*   If the race of a person charging discrimination is important, then so is the race of the person being charged.

5 *Should I consult someone of another race/ethnicity?*   Consider another question: Do I have expertise on other races/cultures? If not, broaden your perspective by asking someone who knows something more about your subject. Why should we treat reporting on racial issues any differently from reporting on an area of science or religion that we do not know well?[34]

Physical descriptions of suspects in crimes are a nettlesome issue. If a description includes race and little else, minority-group news consumers often protest that the description is merely a device for mentioning the race of a person who supposedly committed a crime.

For this reason, many news organizations have adopted a policy of using descriptions of suspects only when they are sufficiently detailed to be of help in apprehending the suspect. This calls for applying common sense. If the police say the suspect is "a black male adult wearing a yellow sweatshirt," the description could fit many people.

If a description is to be published, broadcast, or posted online, skin color is an essential element. It is illogical to list gender, age, height, weight, attire, and other identifying characteristics while omitting race. Though often misunderstood by even seasoned journalists, the purpose of the policy is not to keep race out of a description but to establish a high standard for using a description in the first place.

When the *Eagle-Tribune* in Lawrence, Massachusetts, announced such a policy in 2005, internal emails denounced the policy as misguided political correctness. One of the newsroom dissenters wrote: "Are we to write that 'Three men from east Texas were convicted of dragging James Byrd behind a pickup truck until he was decapitated' without mentioning that the thugs were white and the victim black?"[35]

This reference to a 1998 murder in Jasper, Texas, revealed a misunderstanding of the policy and its intent. No responsible news organization would have published a news account of the racially motivated Texas killing that failed to identify the race of the killers and the victim.

Making Coverage More Inclusive

For reporters, an important dimension of achieving diversity in news coverage is to broaden their so-called Rolodex list – the expert commentators they consult about news developments – to make sure that they are truly representative of the community.

Members of racial and ethnic minorities still tend to be quoted most often in stories about race or ethnicity. Robert J. Haiman's *Best Practices in Newspaper Journalism* recounted a comment by a black participant in one of the Freedom Forum's workshops: "Where is the story that quotes a black doctor on some medical [advance] that has nothing to do with race?"[36]

"Look closely at your Rolodex," Professor Yanick Rice Lamb wrote in *Quill* magazine: "If you sorted your sources roughly by age, gender, race, geography and so on, where would you come up short? … This is not about being politically correct; it's about doing good journalism." Lamb, a former reporter who teaches journalism at Howard University, wrote that "good experts are everywhere, and they're easy to find." Among her suggestions: visit neighborhood churches, restaurants, community centers, and schools; ask existing sources for other contacts; and check out community papers, radio stations, and websites.[37]

Encouraging reporters to diversify their source lists should be a goal of newsroom managers, but experience suggests that an informal approach is best. Applying quotas — such as quoting a minimum of one minority-group member on a newspaper's front page each day — can be counterproductive.

Keith Woods says the goal should be "mainstreaming," or the inclusion of oft-excluded groups in stories that are not about their race or ethnicity. "Journalists have complained at times — legitimately — that the mindless pursuit of mainstreaming has led to tokenism, where people with little expertise and less to say have been forced into stories simply because they fit a demographic quota," he said. A better course, he said, is for journalists to learn enough about their communities to be able to "draw on a fuller palette of people."[38]

Eliminating Racial and Ethnic Disparity in Coverage

After half a century of striving for diversity and enlightened news coverage, the news media still occasionally reveal a double standard.

Cynthia Tucker, then the editorial-page editor of *The Atlanta Journal-Constitution*, wrote a column in 2005 noting the disparity in news coverage of two young, middle-class women who vanished after planning a wedding. Jennifer Wilbanks, a Georgia white woman, drew intense media attention when she ran away before her wedding. In contrast, there was only media silence about Stacy-Ann Sappleton of Tecumseh, Ontario, a black woman who disappeared after flying into New York City's LaGuardia Airport and catching a taxi that was supposed to have taken her to her future in-laws' home in Queens. Her fiancé, his parents, and Sappleton's mother spent a frantic weekend searching before her bullet-riddled body was found in a trash receptacle in Queens. "When she first disappeared, we tried to contact the media, and they wouldn't help us," the fiancé told *The New York Times*.[39] Tucker wrote:

> The frenzy surrounding Wilbanks' disappearance once again highlights a peculiar feature of early 21st century American culture: a fixation on pretty, young, middle-class

white women. … Heaven knows, my industry ought to come in for a heaping dose of criticism for the sensationalist coverage given one small drama – the Wilbanks disappearance – without broader societal implications. But the fact is that the runaway-bride soap opera attracted loads of interest from readers and viewers. As American news consumers, are we discriminating about the sort of victims worthy of our concern: pretty, middle-class, young, white – yes; old, ugly, poor, black, brown – apparently not.[40]

On August 30, 2005, soon after Hurricane Katrina devastated New Orleans, two wire services sent their clients similar photographs of people wading through chest-high water and carrying food and belongings. The caption for an Associated Press photograph of an African American man said he was photographed after "looting a grocery store."[41] The caption of an Agence France-Presse/Getty Images photograph, showing two white people, a young man and woman, said they were photographed after "finding bread and soda from a local grocery store."[42] Bloggers quickly protested the disparity.

Three Pennsylvania State University researchers analyzed 1,160 photographs relating to five weeks of Katrina coverage in four newspapers: *The New York Times*, *The Washington Post*, *USA Today*, and *The Wall Street Journal*. The researchers concluded:

> Photographs consistently put Anglos [non-Hispanic white people] in the role of helper and African-Americans in the role of helpless victim, supporting previous stereotyping. … The overwhelming representation of White military and social service personnel "saving" the African-American refugees may be one of the most significant themes in images of people in the coverage.[43]

Covering Gays and Lesbians in the News

When *The Washington Post* wrote in 2008 about the burial at Arlington National Cemetery of an army intelligence officer killed in an explosion in Baghdad, the paper reported poignantly on many aspects of the soldier's life.

Donna St. George's story recounted that Major Alan G. Rogers had been awarded two Bronze Stars; that in the fatal explosion he shielded two fellow soldiers who survived; and that his commanding officer in Iraq called him "an exceptional, brilliant person – just well-spoken and instantly could relate to anybody."[44]

What the published story did not say was that Rogers was gay.

St. George's story originally had mentioned that Rogers was a former treasurer of the American Veterans for Equal Rights and that several of his friends had confirmed his sexual orientation. These friends told St. George that he hadn't been allowed to share that information in the military because of the "don't ask, don't tell" rule then in effect. (The military, which once discharged service members found to be gay or lesbian, adopted a policy in 1993 saying that it would not ask members about their sexual orientation and that members would not be permitted to tell others about their orientation. A law ending the "don't ask, don't tell" policy was passed by Congress and signed by President Barack Obama in 2010.)

The late Deborah Howell, then *The Post*'s ombudsman, wrote that, after an "agonizing" newsroom discussion, *Post* executive editor Leonard Downie Jr. made the decision to omit the information about Rogers' sexual orientation. According to Howell's account, Downie concluded "there was no proof that Rogers was gay and no clear indication that, if he was, he wanted the information made public."[45]

The editor's ruling was in line with *The Post*'s stylebook policy, which states:

> A person's sexual orientation should not be mentioned unless relevant to the story. ... Not everyone espousing gay rights causes is homosexual. When identifying an individual as gay or homosexual, be cautious about invading the privacy of someone who may not wish his or her sexual orientation known.[46]

The debate that *Post* staff members had about the Rogers story is an example of how a stylebook provides a valuable starting point for discussion but does not necessarily dictate a final decision. In her column, Howell wrote that *The Post* was right to be cautious, but she differed with the decision: "[T]here was enough evidence – particularly his feelings about 'don't ask, don't tell' – to warrant quoting his friends and adding that dimension to the story of his life. The story would have been richer for it."[47]

The Post's experience illustrates a problem that many gay men and lesbians say they have with the news media. They perceive a double standard: If people are "straight," spouses and families are typically mentioned in stories about their lives; if they are openly gay or lesbian, the comparable basic facts tend to be omitted.

Robert Dodge, who in 2001 was the president of the National Lesbian and Gay Journalists Association (NLGJA), made the double-standard argument about stories about heroes of September 11. He wrote that the media should have mentioned their sexual orientation while recounting the lives of a priest who was killed while administering the last rites to injured rescue workers at the World Trade Center; one of the passengers aboard United Airlines Flight 93 who tried to overpower hijackers planning to crash the plane into targets in Washington, DC; and the first officer of the airliner that hijackers crashed into the Pentagon. Dodge continued:

> Some journalists may embrace outdated ideas that identifying openly gay and lesbian heroes will cast a negative image on their memory. This decision is based on a presumption that being gay or lesbian is wrong, a bias that works completely against news objectivity. Withholding relevant details about their lives, their partners and families is unfair and hurtful to the people they loved. In our mission as journalists, it also denies readers and viewers information about the true identity of those who are in the news. It is the same as withholding information about the spouse, children and other features about the heterosexual heroes.
>
> What about legitimate concerns about "outing" someone, or disclosing the sexual orientation of someone who deserved privacy? We suggest more and better reporting.
>
> Instead of asking whether the victim was married, it might be better to ask if he or she had a partner. This basic question may open the door to find out more about the subject of your story – including the chance that they were heterosexual and had a significant, romantic relationship outside of traditional marriage.[48]

Biographical stories like the one about Major Rogers and the gay heroes of 9/11 call for a level of personal detail that is not appropriate in routine news accounts, where a person's sexuality – along with his or her race, ethnic background, or religious beliefs – is usually irrelevant.[49] Because this is an issue of equitable treatment, it deserves the attention of journalists.

Ruling on a related issue, the Associated Press revised its stylebook in 2013 to state that, "regardless of sexual orientation, *husband* or *wife* is acceptable in all references to individuals in any legally recognized marriage." The AP said *spouse* or *partner* may be used if requested.[50]

Resources for Reporters Covering Diversity Issues

Educating fellow journalists to be fair and sensitive in covering their demographic groups is a top priority for the professional organizations formed in recent decades by journalists of color. Through their websites, these groups offer stylebook supplements and background information. The groups include:

- The National Association of Black Journalists (NABJ), founded in 1975.
- The Asian American Journalists Association (AAJA), founded in 1981.
- The National Association of Hispanic Journalists (NAHJ), founded in 1982.
- The Native American Journalists Association (NAJA), founded in 1984.
- The South Asian Journalists Association (SAJA), founded in 1994.

The National Lesbian and Gay Journalists Association was founded in 1990. Like the professional organizations of journalists of color, NLGJA offers online resources to help fellow journalists – in this case, when they report on stories involving lesbian, gay, bisexual, and transgender issues.

Another resource for journalists covering lesbian, gay, bisexual, and transgender issues is GLAAD, an advocacy organization founded in 1985. Its website states: "GLAAD works with print, broadcast and online news sources to bring people powerful stories from the LGBT community that build support for equality. And when news outlets get it wrong, GLAAD is there to respond and advocate for fairness and accuracy."

Established in 1994, UNITY is an umbrella organization that tries to raise the news media's awareness of diversity issues, both in news coverage and in recruiting. It began as UNITY: Journalists of Color, and its first gathering drew 6,000 journalists to Atlanta in 1994. The charter members were the Asian American Journalists Association, the National Association of Black Journalists, the National Association of Hispanic Journalists, and the Native American Journalists Association.

UNITY's member organizations have fluctuated over the years. In 2014 there were three: the Asian American Journalists Association, the National Lesbian and Gay Journalists Association, and the Native American Journalists Association. It now is known as UNITY: Journalists for Diversity.

Point of View

Gaining Respect by Showing Respect

Joann Byrd

Let's say that among people in this particular community, common courtesy requires an exchange of gifts. Enter American journalists who've been told it's unethical to accept gifts, and to offer anything as payment for information.

This is a collision of values.

Here's another one: Most people we want to interview expect to build trust over a long period before they tell us anything; they don't respond favorably to a stranger demanding a quote for the first edition.

Whether they are white business people or Native American tribal elders or Vietnamese immigrants, their expectations and our journalistic needs do not seem, at the moment anyway, compatible.

Such conflicts occur when we are defining news in our communities, when we are pursuing enterprise, and when we are racing the clock.

But the fact that there may be conflicts ahead cannot deter us from covering stories across cultures. Unless we do those stories, we are not meeting our ethical obligation to reflect all the people who live in the region where we report the news. The trick will be providing that coverage with a minimum of damage to anybody's values.

It's our responsibility as journalists to make this work.

To begin, let's define culture, also known as "community." This is a group of people who share an ethnic heritage or a language, a faith, a physical characteristic, a history, a profession, an interest, or some other quality that brings them together.

It might clarify things if we think of journalism as a culture. Journalism certainly has unique rules and procedures, assumptions, and values. Those conventions are the reasons we run into ethical challenges when we are acting as journalists in a world inhabited by people who aren't.

This is actually the lede: *Show respect. When we respect people, we hold them in esteem and treat them as honorable equals.*

The people we are meeting, interviewing, writing about, and photographing are worthy of our respect just because they are human beings.

These new sources, then, are not merely means to our own journalistic ends. They are autonomous individuals with their own interests and integrity.

Unless they're elected officials, public employees, or executives of publicly traded companies, the people we encounter as we cover the news are not obligated to talk to us, to have their picture taken, or to do even one thing to help us tell a story. And if they decline – which seems more likely in a community not thoroughly immersed in the ways of the mainstream news media – we just find someone else.

We demonstrate respect by honoring the courtesies expected in a culture, by being straightforward with people about what they are getting into, and by acknowledging their concerns. We treat them as thinking adults who deserve a voice in what transpires.

Showing respect is the minimum behavior that people require of each other. To build relationships, we should do more than what's required.

(Continued)

We've wisely absorbed the caution that no culture is a monolith, and that all the people in a group we define will never – OK, *almost never* – act or think alike.

If we're behaving with respect toward the individuals we are covering, we will naturally use the right framework. If we respect an individual, we don't think of her as merely a part of a whole, as a carbon copy of anyone else.

And if we cover individuals, their stories will convey the complexity of their culture.

The goal is not happy, lightweight stories. Our audience knows when we are pandering to them, and they're apt to be pretty skeptical about our expanding our coverage to produce fluff.

No source objects to looking good, but candy-coated pieces also can feel patronizing to the subjects of the stories who are grownups with serious lives and concerns.

Holding back on serious journalism in other cultures does not demonstrate respect.

Quality journalism does.

Adapted from Joann Byrd, *Respecting All Cultures: A Practical Ethics Handbook for Journalists* (American Society of Newspaper Editors, April 2002).

Case Study

When a Story Gets Its Subject Arrested

Sharyn Vane

Julio Granados allowed *News & Observer* reporter Gigi Anders to come into his life – to the bodega where he worked, to the home he shared with other Mexican immigrants, to the shrine he'd built in a nearby thicket of trees. He told her all about sending money home to his family in Mexico and his lonely life in America.

On March 8, 1998, the Raleigh, North Carolina, daily published "Heart without a Home," two full pages on Julio's life (Figure 17.2). And, two weeks later, readers learned of the postscript: Granados, 21, and five others at the El Mandado market had been arrested by the Immigration and Naturalization Service. Agents in Charlotte had seen *The News & Observer*'s article – which mentioned Granados' undocumented status and included details about where he lived and worked – and decided to arrest him.

Incensed, the Hispanic community blamed *The News & Observer*. And some of the paper's own reporters and editors were asking whether the newspaper had weighed the ramifications of its actions before publishing the story.

In the weeks after the story ran and Granados was arrested, Anders received dozens of calls – including death threats – at home and at work. The paper published letters decrying the story as "irresponsible journalism" that had "destroyed this young man's life." Anders and her editors met with the staff, as well as with members of the Latino community, to talk

Part of a surge of Latino immigration to North Carolina, Julio Granados sought to help his family in Mexico. But his success has a price — a life often alone.

As a young teen, Julio Granados learned to play the guitar while attending seminary. Although he left behind the dream of being a priest, he finds playing his acoustic guitar a familiar, comforting way to pass the time.

STAFF PHOTOS BY ROBERT MILLER

Heart without a home

BY GIGI ANDERS
STAFF WRITER

RALEIGH

On this Monday, as he does on alternate weeks, Julio Granados is sending $500 to his mother, Amalia, in Mexico. It's half of what he has made in the past two weeks of 11-hour days, but it's much more than that, too. The money — and the opportunity to earn it — is what brought Granados to Raleigh almost 20 months ago, and it's what sustains him.

"It's a good feeling not to have to depend on your parents," Granados says. "Without my help, they'd have to sacrifice a lot."

Granados and his family have been apart since he left Guadalajara on foot on a soft Friday evening, late in June 1996. He kissed and embraced his parents and stepped into the night, carrying a battered duffel bag with only a change of clothes. He had his Mexican voter ID and 600 pesos in

Granados looks at an old family picture taken at a birthday party; he is the boy at left in the snapshot. Now 21 and living in North Carolina, he finds that recalling the good times eases his loneliness.

his wallet, not even $100. But it was enough.

Walking along the road, his brown leather work boots kicking up the yellow dust, Granados looked at the slowly darkening sky, trying to memorize this twilight and what it held: the long, thin cirrus clouds that turned from pale to deepest gray, a thousand white stars that shared their scattered light with the yellow moon. Mexico is yellow, he thought, and America will be green.

Granados knows that working in America without proper papers is a risk. But he's willing to take it on.

He works six-day weeks at La Bodega El Mandado, a Hispanic supermarket in North Raleigh that is one of the busiest sites of electronic money transfers in the Triangle. It sends thousands of dollars a day by wire to mothers, fathers, wives in towns and cities throughout Mexico and Central America.

This morning, Granados already has alerted Amalia that the money is coming, using a prepaid phone card he bought at the bodega. At

SEE **GRANADOS**, PAGE 20A

Figure 17.2   The opening page of the "Heart without a home" feature story.
REPRINTED BY PERMISSION OF *THE NEWS & OBSERVER*.

(Continued)

about what the paper did and why it had done it. Executive editor Anders Gyllenhaal (later vice president/news of McClatchy Newspapers) wrote a column praising the piece but acknowledging there were things editors might do differently next time.

Central to the story of Julio Granados and its aftermath is the paper's role. How much responsibility do journalists have in ensuring that their sources – particularly those who aren't media savvy – fully understand the potential consequences of a page one story? "Our goal here was not to do anything but try and explain this person's life," Gyllenhaal said. "We certainly didn't mean for this to happen."

News & Observer features editor Felicia Gressette had noted an increase in the numbers of immigrants working in and around the city. Gressette thought it made sense to humanize these faceless workers. "[F]or an awful lot of people, middle-class whites, it's outside of their frame of reference," she said. "We wanted to do a story that would get inside the life and world of someone who had come to the Triangle," as the cities of Raleigh, Durham, and Chapel Hill are called.

Gressette assigned the story to Anders, a Cuban-born features reporter fluent in Spanish who had profiled other Hispanics in the community. Anders knew exactly where to look: the El Mandado bodega in north Raleigh, a sort of crossroads for the area's growing Hispanic population. Over lunch, she explained to proprietress Ana Roldan what she was looking for and asked Roldan if she knew anyone who might fit that description. "She didn't hesitate," Anders recalled. "She said, 'Julio. He's perfect. He's exceptional.'"

And he *was* exceptional, Anders would find out. Though a bit bemused as to why *The News & Observer* would be interested in him, he gamely let Anders and photographer Robert Miller join him at work at El Mandado as he unpacked crates of mangoes and stocked shelves with stacks of tortillas, at home as he strummed his acoustic guitar and hummed "Ave Maria," and in the woods behind his house as he struggled through the brambles to a makeshift altar with a statue of the Virgin of Guadalupe. A former seminary student, he was articulate and thoughtful in their Spanish-language interviews, detailing memories of Mexico made painful by their distance from his current life.

Anders knew she had the makings of a great profile. But she admitted to being worried when she asked Granados about his US work status and he told her he had no papers. Anders recalled:

> I felt my heart sinking because I thought, "He's going to pull out." But he didn't. I said, "OK, do you understand that your name is going in this story? And your picture? Do you understand what this means?" And he asked, "Do they read the *N&O* in Charlotte?" Charlotte is a synonym for the INS. And I said, "Yes."
>
> He said, "Might I get deported?" I said, "You might." And he said, "Well, if that's what happens, then I guess it's my destiny." That's the word he used – destiny.

Granados said he didn't remember it that way: He told another *News & Observer* reporter in April that he gave Anders permission to use his name but not his status. "My name, yes. But not the fact that I'm here without papers."

Anders responded that she had given Granados fair warning. "This is, to my mind, a full-grown person making his own decision," she said.

When Anders' story became a contender for Sunday front-page play, projects editor Rob Waters wondered aloud at a meeting exactly what Granados had been told. "I remember thinking that this would be at least an implicit invitation to the INS to come get this guy," Waters said. "I was simply raising one question, and I think I remember being told that those questions were being raised."

The story went to press.

"I think that there was some naiveté on our part about what the reaction would be," executive editor Gyllenhaal said. "Part of what happened was that a lot of people in the community are divided on the whole question of undocumented workers, and some of them who are opposed called the INS and said, 'You look at this, you've gotta do something about this.' … We just didn't think the thing through."

Sixteen days after the story ran, INS agents arrived mid-morning at El Mandado, loading Granados and the five others into a van for the trip to jail. Anders got a hysterical call at home from Roldan and promptly called Gressette to let her know what had happened. Word began filtering through the newsroom, and Gyllenhaal and managing editor Melanie Sill called a meeting. Fifty to 60 staffers showed up for the hour-long session.

"It was not a relaxed meeting," Anders says, describing pointed queries on how much Granados really understood about what might happen to him after the story ran. Had a trusting 21-year-old immigrant been exploited? How much had she talked with Granados about the INS? And what had she told the Roldans?

One of those who had concerns was state government editor Linda Williams. She said that, when she read Anders' story that Sunday morning, she instantly thought, "Oh my God, he's going to be deported." While Anders may have discussed the potential repercussions of the profile with Granados, Williams said, she also should have talked with Roldan and her husband, Marco, about the story's implications for them.

"The people who own the store – why were they not quoted in the story about why they were hiring people illegally? How do they justify hiring him?" Williams asked.

If the newsroom was concerned, some readers were downright angry. They barraged the paper with letters, and they weren't fan letters. "Irresponsible journalism resulted in the arrest of Julio Granados, the hard-working Mexican featured in your March 8 article," fumed Eunice Brock and Charles Tanquary. "This feature story could have been written equally forcefully without showing Granados' face or revealing his name and place of employment." Charlie Ramirez wrote, "I am sure he will enjoy being back in his homeland, courtesy of the *N&O*. Whatever happened to journalistic integrity?"

The Roldans said Anders misled them about how much detail she would include in her story. "She said, 'I will not write something like that. I will not write something to put Julio or your business in any trouble,'" Marco Roldan insisted. Anders said she had made no such pronouncements to the couple.

INS agents said they received copies of the Granados article from two sources. But Charlotte-based agent Scott Sherrill said it was more than just the front-page play that had triggered action. "There were some things in there that made us feel like it was important that we do this," Sherrill said. "The fact that he claims he was smuggled across the border … It implies in there that he eluded arrest by the

(Continued)

Border Patrol by running after he was smuggled across the border. That makes it a little more of a serious violation."

Gyllenhaal tackled the controversy in a column on March 29, "Lessons in a story gone wrong." He defended the piece as a "powerful package." But he acknowledged that the fact that the story was so detailed led INS agents to Granados at El Mandado. And he said that *The News & Observer* hadn't thought hard enough about the impact of such a story on "one largely powerless, fairly ordinary young Mexican."

He said the paper could have left out the name of the market, a crucial detail that might have kept the INS from acting. However, Anders pointed out that, because the story was indeed so acutely detailed, leaving out the name of the market would have made the newspaper look as if it was deliberately trying to hide Granados from the INS – something the paper wouldn't do for other lawbreakers.

Roberto Suro, author of *Strangers among Us: How Latino Immigration Is Transforming America*, said:

One thing that makes me uncomfortable is this idea that someone who is just a straightforward illegal alien, basically for economic reasons, somehow deserves some kind of protection. How much do you get in the business of making judgments? What if you're writing about people who use and sell drugs – you won't ID a user, but you would ID a seller? You're making a judgment that one violation of the law is somehow less serious than another.

Suro also questioned whether someone like Granados was truly ignorant of the backlash potential of such a story:

He was certainly conversant with the law as it applies to be here illegally. To have gotten as far as he did – to go across the border all the way to North Carolina, he had to have had a fair knowledge of the law as it applies to the foreign-born and what's required to avoid getting caught. I mean, he may not have understood the U.S. tax code, but where it mattered, he knew.

This case is excerpted, with permission, from Sharyn Vane, "Too much information?," *American Journalism Review*, June 1998.

Questions for Class Discussion

- How does this case illustrate a conflict between reporting truth and minimizing harm?
- What responsibility did *The News & Observer* owe to Julio Granados?
- What responsibility did the paper owe to the owners of the market where he worked?
- Should journalists protect their sources and story subjects even though they are violating the law?
- Is there an Aristotle's Golden Mean in this case? Would it have been practical to omit some crucial details, as the executive editor says? Or would that have signaled to readers that the paper was trying to hide Granados from the INS, as the reporter says?
- What ideas do you have about how the paper could have reported this story without endangering Granados or appearing to go out of its way to protect him?
- In the aftermath of the arrest of Granados and the others, what did *The News & Observer* do to be accountable to its readers? To its staff?

Notes

1 This account of the Cynthia Wiggins case is constructed from "The color line and the bus line," in Arlene Notoro Morgan, Alice Irene Pifer, and Keith Woods (eds.), *The Authentic Voice* (New York: Columbia University Press, 2006), 105–126. The chapter includes the transcript of the *Nightline* broadcast on May 22, 1996.

2 Eric Wray, "Reporting the Rashomon way," in Morgan, Pifer, and Woods (eds.), *The Authentic Voice*, 126.

3 Morgan, Pifer, and Woods (eds.), *The Authentic Voice*, 106.

4 Commission on Freedom of the Press, *A Free and Responsible Press: A General Report on Mass Communication: Newspapers, Radio, Motion Pictures, Magazines, and Books* (Chicago: University of Chicago Press, 1947), 26–27.

5 United States National Advisory Commission on Civil Disorders, *Report of the National Advisory Commission on Civil Disorders* (Washington, DC: US Government Printing Office, 1968), 211–212.

6 Bob Papper, "Women, minorities make newsroom gains," Radio Television Digital News Association, July 28, 2014.

7 "2014 census: Minorities in newsrooms increase; 63 percent have at least one woman among top-three editors," American Society of News Editors, July 29, 2014.

8 Ibid.

9 "As the nation ages, seven states become younger, Census Bureau reports," US Census Bureau, June 26, 2014.

10 "2014 census," ASNE.

11 Papper, "Women, minorities make newsroom gains."

12 A stereotype is "a fixed mental image of a group that is frequently applied to all its members" (Charles Zastrow and Karen Kirst-Ashman, *Understanding Human Behavior and the Social Environment* (Chicago: Nelson-Hall, 1987), 553).

13 Keith Woods, "The essence of excellence: covering race and ethnicity (and doing it better)," report for Columbia University, 2001, 3.

14 "US Census Bureau projections show a slower growing, older, more diverse nation a half century from now," US Census Bureau, Dec. 12, 2012.

15 Joann Byrd, *Respecting All Cultures: A Practical Ethics Handbook for Journalists* (Washington, DC: American Society of Newspaper Editors, 2001), 9, 10, 11.

16 Aly Colon, "Making connections with diverse communities," *Quill*, July 2000, 70–71.

17 Woods, "The Essence of Excellence," 4.

18 Ibid.

19 Robert J. Haiman, *Best Practices for Newspaper Journalists* (Arlington, VA: Freedom Forum's Free Press/Fair Press Project, 2000), 43–44.

20 Ibid.

21 Av Westin, *Best Practices for Television Journalists* (Arlington, VA: Freedom Forum's Free Press/Fair Press Project, 2000), 23–24.

22 Gabriel Escobar, "The making of 'The Other Pro Soccer,'" in Morgan, Pifer, and Woods (eds.), *The Authentic Voice*, 326.

23 Ibid., 328.

24 Ibid., 328–329.

25 "As the nation ages," US Census Bureau.

26 Jeffrey S. Passel, D'Vera Cohn, and Ana Gonzalez-Barrera, "Population decline of unauthorized immigrants stalls, may have reversed," Pew Research Center, Sept. 21, 2013. Pew's methodology is to subtract legal immigration from the adjusted foreign-born population to arrive at the total for unauthorized immigrants.

27 Lucy Hood, "Naming names," *American Journalism Review*, Apr.–May 2006.

28 Sonia Nazario, "Ethical dilemmas in telling Enrique's story," *Nieman Reports*, Fall 2006, 29.

29 Hood, "Naming names."

30 Ibid.

31 Paul Colford, "'Illegal immigrant' no more," The Definitive Source, Apr. 2, 2013.

32 Christine Haughney, "*The Times* shifts on 'illegal immigrant,' but doesn't ban the use," *The New York Times*, Apr. 23, 2013.

33 Phuong Ly, "As people of color become a majority, is it time for journalists to stop using the term 'minorities'?" Poynter, Aug. 4, 2011.

34 Keith Woods, "Guidelines for racial identification," Poynter, Feb. 25, 2000.

35 Jay Fitzgerald, "Paper's edict draws dissent," *Boston Herald*, July 15, 2005.

36   Haiman, *Best Practices for Newspaper Journalists*, 44.

37   Yanick Rice Lamb, "Take time to examine your sources," *Quill*, Oct.–Nov. 2002, 38.

38   Woods, "The Essence of Excellence," 7.

39   Shaila K. Dewan and Sherri Day, "Police wonder if cabby erred before a killing," *The New York Times*, May 14, 2004.

40   Cynthia Tucker, "Our opinion: media blackout for this bride," *The Atlanta Journal-Constitution*, May 8, 2005.

41   The Associated Press caption read: "A young man walks through chest deep flood water after looting a grocery store in New Orleans on Tuesday, Aug. 30, 2005."

42   The AFP/Getty Images caption read: "Two residents wade through chest-deep water after finding bread and soda from a local grocery store."

43   Shannon Kahle, Nan Yu, and Erin Whiteside, "Another disaster: an examination of portrayals of race in Hurricane Katrina coverage," *Visual Communications Quarterly*, 14 (Spring 2007), 86.

44   Donna St. George, "Army officer remembered as hero," *The Washington Post*, Mar. 22, 2008.

45   Deborah Howell, "Public death, private life," *The Washington Post*, Mar. 30, 2008.

46   Ibid.

47   Ibid.

48   Robert Dodge, "Gays and lesbians on September 11," Ryerson University School of Journalism's Diversity Watch.

49   Bao Ong, "When sexuality is part of the story," NLGJA: The Association of LGBT Journalists.

50   Jennifer Vanasco, "AP's first usage guidelines on 'husband, wife,'" *Columbia Journalism Review*, Feb. 21, 2013.

18 Ethics Issues Specific to Digital Journalism

Online, there are huge opportunities and some problems

Learning Goals

This chapter will help you understand:

- the dilemma over how to handle requests to "unpublish" archival content that is embarrassing the subjects of long-ago news coverage;
- the value of an Internet "conversation" with the audience and the problems that unmonitored comments can cause;
- the value of providing hyperlinks in online stories, and the question of whether to link to problematical websites;
- the benefits and possible ethical consequences of blogging and social media activity by journalists; and
- the relationship of journalists and citizen bloggers.

Imagine that you are the editor of *The Toronto Star*, Canada's largest-circulation newspaper, and you receive this request:

> My name was mentioned in two *Toronto Star* articles discussing a bomb threat at [a public location].
>
> The articles state that I am charged with a number of offenses including false message, common nuisance and mischief interfering with property. I had no involvement in this criminal activity, and as a result, these charges were withdrawn against me on December 16th, 2008.
>
> I am currently an articling student [lawyer intern] at a law firm and face serious damage to my reputation as a result of my name being mentioned in these articles. Searches of my name in online search browsers immediately link to these articles, which unfairly stigmatizes me and prevents me from pursuing my professional goals. As a result, I would like to request to have my name removed from these articles.
>
> Please feel free to contact me if you have any questions.
>
> Sincerely, [name redacted][1]

Before news went on the Internet, editors didn't get requests like this. People throw away (or, we hope, recycle) newspapers after they are read. Nearly everybody who reads articles in print like those about the Toronto bomb threat quickly forgets

---

The Ethical Journalist: Making Responsible Decisions in the Digital Age, Second Edition. Gene Foreman.
© 2016 John Wiley & Sons, Inc. Published 2016 by John Wiley & Sons, Inc.

about them. If people want to read a story published in a newspaper years earlier, they have to go to a public library and scroll through microfilm. Even then they need to have a good idea where to find what they are looking for.

Of course, things are different when news is online. "Life in the age of Google means that just about everything published by news organizations is now just a few clicks away from anyone with a computer," Kathy English, public editor of *The Star*, wrote in a definitive report on the problem of "unpublishing" requests. "A news organization's journalism can now reach more people, in more places around the world, at greater speed than ever before. And news published online, seemingly, never dies."[2]

The young lawyer's case illustrates how, when a news organization grapples with requests to unpublish, it is torn between conflicting ethical duties. On the one hand, the organization has a duty to preserve the integrity of its archives, part of its implicit contract with the public. On the other hand, the organization has a duty to be fair to people like the lawyer who was cleared of criminal charges but really is being hurt by those indelible news stories.

This chapter discusses the unpublishing dilemma and other ethics issues that relate specifically to journalism as it is practiced on the Web. In addition, the chapter expands on earlier discussions of how traditional ethics standards have been applied as journalism moved online. In Chapter 10, which examined problems of perceived conflicts of interest, the text discussed the obligation of journalists to be discreet in posts on Facebook, Twitter, and other social media. In Chapter 12, which examined issues relating to accuracy and fairness, the text discussed the need to verify user-generated content gathered from social media or in crowdsourcing, as well as ways of correcting news tweets found to be in error.

Maintaining Integrity (and Fairness) in the Archives

Clark Hoyt, who was then the public editor of *The New York Times*, noticed in 2008 that nearly every day someone would contact the paper to ask that the digital archives be erased or changed. He wrote in a column that the people making the requests were saying "they are being embarrassed, are worried about losing or not getting jobs, or may be losing customers because of the sudden prominence of old news articles that contain errors or were never followed up."

Times editors told Hoyt that if they had to re-report every story challenged as incorrect, there would be no time to report that day's news.

Bob Steele of the Poynter Institute told Hoyt that he would be cautious about removing or altering content from the archives. "The public would have every reason to say: 'What else is missing? What else is altered?'"

Viktor Mayer-Schönberger, an associate professor of public policy at Harvard's John F. Kennedy School of Government, had a different answer for Hoyt: Newspapers should program their archives to "forget" some information, allowing low-profile content like news briefs to vanish from public access after a certain period. Significant stories could be kept longer, even indefinitely. The professor said computers should be like humans, who remember the important and forget the trivial.

The Times decided to correct errors in archived articles when a person can offer proof. This solved the problem raised by a woman who worried that prospective employers would think she was guilty of resumé inflation because her *Times* wedding announcement, published 20 years earlier, incorrectly listed the university where she got her degree.[3]

College newspapers also began to field the same kind of requests. *The Daily Collegian*, the independent student newspaper at Pennsylvania State University, was asked about three times a week in 2007–8 to remove or alter content in its archives. Devon Lash, a senior who was editor in chief of *The Collegian*, stated the paper's policy: "Our online archives act as a history of the events at Penn State and the surrounding community, and removing any content would go against our mission to inform and practice ethical journalism."

Lash's solution was similar to the one reached by editors at *The Times*. She wrote that content could be corrected or amended – and the original item flagged to indicate the alteration – if the person making the complaint submitted proof of an error.

The policy worked in favor of a man who had been charged with possession of child pornography while a Penn State student. He persuaded *The Collegian* to note in its archives that his record as a first offender was expunged after he completed an accelerated rehabilitation program.

But *The Collegian* refused the request of one of its former staff members to delete certain opinions he had expressed in his *Collegian* columns. He said he had changed his mind about those issues, and the years-old opinions were now embarrassing him in his job with the State Department.[4]

In 2009 *The Toronto Star*'s Kathy English undertook a project for the Associated Press Managing Editors (now the Associated Press Media Editors), seeking to identify the profession's "best practices' in handling unpublishing requests. The centerpiece of her research was a questionnaire sent to news organizations throughout North America, to which 110 organizations responded. English consulted with lawyers, with members of the Organization of News Ombudsmen, and with members of the Canadian Newspaper Association. She visited three newsrooms: Gatehouse Media, then based in Downers Grove, Illinois, near Chicago; the *Chicago Sun-Times*; and the *Chicago Tribune*.

English found that, when people approach Google directly with their requests to make unfavorable content disappear, Google refers them to the news organizations. Google's Webmaster Central states: "In order for information in Google's results to change, the information must first change on the site where it appears, and this is a change that Google is unable to make for you." Google advises people that the webmasters of those sites "can remove the concerning information, take the page down from the Web entirely, or block Google from including the page in Google's index."

English's survey showed that, while there was a clear consensus against unpublishing, four out of five editors had unpublished online articles. Two out of three said they might unpublish an article that was inaccurate or unfair. Only half of the organizations had formulated policies, but two out of three organizations said only the top newsroom editor could make the decision to unpublish.

When English compiled a list of best practices, the first was: "News organizations should start from the principle that published content is part of the historical record and should not be 'unpublished' from the online archive. News organizations do not rewrite history or make news disappear." The following were among other best practices she identified in her research:

- *Put a clear policy in place.* Such a policy stipulates the principle against unpublishing. It also "makes clear that while the online archive is more accessible to the public and can be altered easier than print content, it is no different from the newspaper archives that have always existed." The policy "should be transparent and must be applied consistently."
- *Take time to explain your policy to readers.* Those readers "may not understand the media's journalistic reasons to resist unpublishing. Many see the online article as an easily altered version of the story." The organization should help them understand that "this is an issue of integrity and credibility and reflects our sense of responsibility to our readers, our community and the historical record."
- *Unpublish for the right reasons.* "There may be some *very rare* circumstances where it is deemed necessary to remove content"; in most cases, this would be for legal reasons, including defamatory material. "Serious consideration … should be given when someone's life may be endangered."
- *Source remorse is not a right reason to unpublish.* Accurate and fair reporting should not be altered "because sources change their minds about what they told a journalist, or decide, following publication, that they do not want to be identified in the news."
- *Unpublish by consensus.* Decisions should be made not by an individual but by a consensus of several ranking news executives. "This provides recourse for those publishers and editors who may field such requests from advertisers and powerful people in their community who seek to influence the public record."
- *Ongoing accuracy is our responsibility.* "In some cases, further reporting may be necessary to verify new information, especially in cases involving charges against individuals named in the news. If we err, or if new relevant facts emerge, we should correct and update online articles. Transparency with our readers demands that we indicate that an article has been edited to correct or update."
- *Unpublish content that violates commenting rules.* "Online user-generated comments that violate an organization's commenting policies can be freely removed from the organization's website at the discretion of the news organization."
- *Before publication, consider the implications.* "In a digital world in which all news and information is easily available to anyone with a computer and Internet access, the onus to publish ethical and excellent journalism relevant to the community is more important than ever. … [W]e should be considering the implications of what we publish well before words and images are committed to paper or Web space. This is especially important in relation to the reporting of criminal charges,

and particularly those of misdemeanors such as shoplifting and public mischief."[5] [On this point, the Society of Professional Journalists' ethics code states under the "minimize harm" principle: "Consider the long-term implications of the extended reach and permanence of publication. Provide updated and more complete information as appropriate."]

So, how did *The Star* handle the unpublishing request from the young lawyer?

English said the man made a compelling argument: He "was with a friend who left a note in a public place making a joke about a bomb. He did not know that the friend was going to do this, and he did not participate in the prank." Police charged him as well as the woman who left the note, but the charges against him were dropped before the case came to court.

After verifying that the charges had been dropped – something *The Star* had not reported at the time – the newspaper decided to flag the online archives. A note was appended to the top of the online articles stating that his record had been cleared.

The young man was not satisfied with the decision, and he worried about how his career would be affected. English herself wondered whether it would have been humane to grant a policy exception. But "in fairness to others who had made similar requests in recent months," she wrote, the paper chose not to remove the stories. Although those stories have been flagged and corrected, they will continue to be "the first thing anyone would read about him – well above reports of awards he had won as a law student and in high school."[6]

If he were living in Europe, rather than in Canada or the United States, the Toronto lawyer might have had legal recourse. The European Court of Justice, whose jurisdiction extends to the 28 members of the European Union, ruled on May 13, 2014, that individuals have a right to force Google and other search engines from linking to matters that are "inadequate, irrelevant or no longer relevant, or excessive in relation to the purposes for which they were processed and in the light of the time that has elapsed."[7]

A fact sheet issued by the European Commission stressed, however, that the court decision would be applied on a case-by-case basis:

> Neither the right to the protection of personal data nor the right to freedom of expression are absolute rights. A fair balance should be sought between the legitimate interest of Internet users and the person's fundamental rights. Freedom of expression carries with it responsibilities and has limits both in the online and offline world. This balance may depend on the nature of the information in question, its sensitivity for the person's private life and on the public interest in having that information. It may also depend on the personality in question: the right to be forgotten is certainly not about making prominent people less prominent or making criminals less criminal.[8]

Jeffrey Toobin, writing in *The New Yorker*, observed that "[t]he consequences of the court's decision are just beginning to be understood." He noted that, in the first several months after the decision, Google received about 128,000 requests for deletions "and granted about half of them."[9]

The Benefits of Interactivity – and a Problem

Before the Internet, "Big Media" treated the news as a lecture, Dan Gillmor wrote in his 2004 book *We the Media*. Now, what Gillmor calls "the former audience" can talk back, and the news has become a conversation.[10]

Eagerly embracing the idea of a conversation, news sites have invited user comments. They want to take advantage of the Web's interactivity to create a lively forum on current events, and they want to fulfill the expectations of site visitors who are accustomed to having their say on the Web. Jim Brady, former executive editor of *The Washington Post* online, said it is "absolutely essential" to engage readers interactively: "It builds immense loyalty with readers, it allows communities to form around common interests, it makes readers feel like they're participating and not watching from the outside."[11]

Sadly, allowing reader comments makes news websites vulnerable to mean-spirited, profane, uninformed postings, including the following:

- On CNN's website, a 2010 story reporting the rescue of 33 Chilean miners after being trapped underground for 69 days drew comments like these: "How much longer is the media going to milk this beyond tired story?" "These guys are frauds."[12]
- On the website of *The Indianapolis Star*, some users posted comments ridiculing an army reservist from Indianapolis who had been killed in Iraq.[13]
- On the website of the *Orange County* (California) *Register*, the target was an obese woman who gave birth to a son she had not known she was carrying until two days before his arrival. The comments contained made-up "facts" about her: that her house was a mess because she was too lazy and fat to clean it, that she ate Krispy Kremes all day, and that the state was trying to take her baby away because she was an unfit mother.[14]
- On the website of *The Cincinnati Enquirer*, some users responded to a story about a woman killed by a drunken driver in a bar parking lot by demanding to know why she was out at 2 a.m. on a school night.[15]

Consider the difference in how reader commentary typically is handled in newspapers and online.

Before publishing a letter to the editor, the newspaper verifies that the letter actually was written by the person whose signature appears on it. Letters are then edited, and the writer is not permitted to use coarse language, make personal attacks, or misstate facts.

On the Web, in contrast, many sites allow screen names, which may be pseudonyms. Electronic filters block vulgarities but not personal attacks and factual misstatements. Few sites screen comments before they are posted; on most sites, it is up to users to flag questionable comments. Only then are they reviewed and, if found to be offensive, taken down.

David Zeeck, editor of *The News Tribune* in Tacoma, Washington, is not troubled that the standards for online comments are looser than those for letters to the editor: "Online, expectations are different. The conversation is more casual. The discussion is at a very different level." He offered this analogy:

At a town meeting, people meet together to decide issues, and there are clear rules of order. Later, when the same people gather at the local tavern, the discussion is more spirited and free-wheeling. That's what we are seeing in the online postings: a more robust exchange.

The two kinds of conversations are depicted by the late Tony Auth, Pulitzer Prize-winning cartoonist, in Figure 18.1.

Figure 18.1 Two kinds of conversation.
CARTOON COURTESY OF TONY AUTH.

Like most news sites, Zeeck's *News Tribune* asks readers to flag inappropriate language, defamation, and inaccuracy: "Then we read it and may take it down. If someone is repeatedly abusive, we will delete the user's account."[16]

When *The New York Times* opened its website to reader comments about news coverage and editorials in 2007, it hired a staff of editors to screen the comments before they went online. This was a substantial investment that most websites say they cannot afford. *The Times* wanted to avoid a lack of civility while engaging in a conversation with the readers.

It should come as no surprise that some readers objected to *The Times'* efforts to curb racism, name-calling, and other examples of rudeness. One reader objected to censoring of speech, "however derogatory, mean-spirited, or offending it is. We need an open dialogue." Another wrote, "Mandating tepid civility in blog comments has an ideological component. 'Politeness' bars sharply worded disagreement by dissenters against those who claim to be authority, but [doesn't] usually bar dismissive or patronizing arguments by authorities against the dissenters."[17]

In 2005 the *Los Angeles Times* experimented – for one day, as it turned out – with the idea of a "wikitorial," in which online readers were invited to rewrite the paper's editorial on the subject of the Iraq War. Instantly the site was flooded with vulgar messages. The *Times* suspended the feature and expressed "thanks and apologies to the thousands of people who logged on in the right spirit."[18]

Editors who advocate anonymity contend that it makes the conversation more egalitarian, attracting vulnerable people who would abstain if they had to use their names. In 2008 Carole Tarrant, then the editor of *The Roanoke Times*, wrote a column about the people who wrote regularly for the paper's website using screen names such as Roenoke, Ziranthia, TripleActionJones, Justafan, and Georgia Boy:

> [W]ho are these people who so expressively pound their keyboards?
>
> I've never met a one of them. I can't tell you their hometowns, their genders or their occupations – or, for that matter, their real names.
>
> I don't need to know. What's important to me are their real-time, unfiltered ideas. To me, the anonymous comments on message boards represent a truly democratic snapshot of ourselves, one stripped of any status or "Well, you know who he is" sniping.[19]

Research, however, confirms the abundant anecdotal evidence of a correlation between anonymous online comments and lack of civility. Arthur Santana, a communications professor at the University of Houston, examined comments that readers wrote in 2013 on stories about immigration on two groups of news websites. On websites that permitted anonymity or screen names, Santana judged 53 percent of the comments to be uncivil. On websites that required commenters to use their real names, 29 percent were uncivil.[20]

Julie Zhuo, a Facebook executive, wrote a *New York Times* op-ed essay in 2010 urging websites to ban anonymous comments and to moderate their forums. She argued that psychological research has repeatedly shown that "anonymity increases unethical behavior":

> Road rage bubbles up in the relative anonymity of one's car. And in the online world, which can offer total anonymity, the effect is even more pronounced. People – even ordinary, good people – often change their behavior in radical ways. There's even a term for it: the online disinhibition effect.

Zhou wrote that, at Facebook, a public-commenting widget she had helped design was aimed at "replicating real-world social norms by emphasizing the human qualities of conversation. People's faces, real names and brief biographies ('John Doe from Lexington') are placed next to their public comments, to establish a baseline of responsibility."[21]

Many news websites have turned to Facebook Comments, which requires commenters to sign on with a Facebook account. These sites are seeing a higher quality of discussion, Jeff Sonderman reported in 2011 for Poynter. Sonderman noted that the *Los Angeles Times* was using Facebook Comments, requiring real names, on its blogs while continuing to allow pseudonyms in comments on its news articles. Jimmy Orr, the paper's online managing editor, said he had seen a "stunning" difference in the level of discourse. He told Sonderman that the people posting through Facebook Comments on the blogs did not require heavy moderating of their conversation even when there was anger. On the articles, he said, comments plunged "into the lowest common denominator – racism, threats, vulgarity. It was night-and-day." Orr's conclusion: "Trolls don't like their friends to know that they're trolls."[22]

In a Point of View essay accompanying this chapter, Dean Edward Wasserman of the Graduate School of Journalism at the University of California, Berkeley, calls on news organizations to establish rules to keep their online forums honest and respectful.

Journalists' Use of Blogs and Social Media

As part of the job

News sites are employing blogs, as well as Facebook, Twitter, and other social media, to gather and report news and to promote their work. Curt Chandler, who teaches multimedia reporting at Pennsylvania State University, observed: "Especially in a breaking-news situation, reporters are expected to be able to post clean, accurate content directly online, just as photographers are expected to post photos with full captions."[23]

After a tornado hit Tuscaloosa, Alabama, on April 27, 2011, killing 53 people, *The Tuscaloosa News* took advantage of the immediacy of social media to tweet information and post photographs of the destruction. The paper's city editor, Katherine K. Lee, described the Pulitzer Prize-winning coverage for *Nieman Reports*:

> Reporters' tweets were aggregated to the paper's website and Facebook page so people could see a continuous stream of information in the minutes immediately after the storm hit. Within the first 24 hours, we also created a Google Docs spreadsheet on the website to allow readers to post their own information, whether they were seeking missing loved ones or hoping to reassure their families that they were safe. … People knew where the destruction was, what streets to avoid, where to go for help.[24]

Four years earlier, *The Roanoke Times* used a blog to report the Virginia Tech massacre in which a deranged student shot and killed 32 people on April 16, 2007. Rather than taking the time to put their information into the format of news stories, *Times* reporters filed bulletin after bulletin. The time-stamped items were posted on Roanoke.com with the most recent always at the top. In a paper prepared for the

Associated Press Managing Editors in October 2007, *Times* reporter Mike Gangloff gave these tips for a breaking-news blog:

> Don't be afraid to flood the site with info. That's what the readers are coming for. … [G]ive a snapshot of how our community is being affected. … Work in vignettes from around the community that show how people are responding.[25]

A blog can help a news organization be accountable to the audience. *The New York Times* posted an explanation in 2008 about how the newspaper was covering the resignation of Governor Elliot Spitzer after his involvement with a prostitute was made public.[26]

One of the early journalist bloggers, *Chicago Tribune* columnist Eric Zorn, considers blogging to be the purest form of journalism. He told *American Journalism Review* in 2003 that he carries his notebook everywhere so he can share his thoughts instantly in his "Change of Subject" blog for ChicagoTribune.com. "You start thinking about life in this whole new way," Zorn said. "Your brain is turned on all the time."[27]

As a columnist, Zorn also expresses opinions in the print *Tribune*. Most of the journalist bloggers, however, are expected to write from a neutral point of view for their newspapers or to report neutrally in broadcasts. Aiming for a gossipy tone in their blogs, some of these journalists have been known to express opinions about the people and events they cover. This issue is explored in the Case Study at the end of this chapter, "For a Reporter-Blogger, Two Personalities."

Consider this paradox as to how the same organization treats print and online copy. When a newspaper reporter writes a just-the-facts news story for the print edition, the copy may be reviewed by three or more editors checking factual accuracy, quality of prose, spelling and grammatical correctness, and inadvertent expressions of bias. When the same reporter writes a blog in which risk-taking commentary is encouraged, the reporter quite likely posts it directly to the Internet with no editorial intervention.

To Bob Giles, retired editor and former curator of the Nieman Foundation, putting blogs on the Web without editing poses a threat to credibility. If the reporters reveal their biases in the blogs, the audience may perceive bias in the supposedly neutral news stories that appear in the print edition. "Blogs can be very effective, giving behind-scenes information and more information, but they have to be kept in bounds," Giles said: "There has to be a review process. There has to be accountability."[28]

Kinsey Wilson, former executive editor of *USA Today* and director of its website, said candidly that online journalism requires reporters who can function without the backstopping of layers of editors:

> In the traditional newspaper model, there are checkpoints along the way to publication of the story. Online, you have to rely on the individual to take more care. You need people with high degrees of judgment, maturity, and training. People who know when they can safely work solo and who know when they need another set of eyes on a story or a blog post.[29]

These are the reasons that editors most frequently give for posting blogs first and editing later:

- editing detracts from the spontaneity of the blog (editors would "beat the life out of them," one blogger said);
- writers are encouraged to blog at all times of day and night, and editors are not always available;
- there is a bottleneck as blogs await editing; and
- bloggers know the guidelines and can be trusted to follow them.

In an article for *American Journalism Review*, Carl Straumsheim, then a journalism graduate student at the University of Maryland, wrote that the BBC's 2012 social-media guidelines stated "the golden rule for our core news" was that "whatever is published – on Twitter, Facebook or anywhere else – *must have a second pair of eyes prior to publication*" [emphasis original]. In contrast, *The Washington Post*'s 2011 social-media guidelines give reporters a "measure of autonomy," in the words of assistant managing editor Peter Perl, to tweet breaking news without editorial review: "Our choice is basically that we would rather encourage our journalists to get the news out quickly and carefully rather than to put a roadblock in their way."

Ken Paulson, then the president of the American Society of News Editors, told Straumsheim that Twitter was entitled to no exemption from journalism's accuracy standard. Paulson said, "People kind of shrug and say it's the nature of the medium. I think you need to apply the same standard to tweets as you apply for articles. It's just journalism – it's just more succinct."

Straumsheim quoted Mathew Ingram, a senior writer at the media technology blog GigaOm, as saying that pre-editing of tweets is an example of imposing old standards on social media. "Not taking advantage of social media or trying to hand-cuff or hamper your journalists' ability to take advantage of social media is really shortsighted," Ingram said. "It's basically handicapping yourself in a race in which you're already handicapped."[30]

A 2012 incident involving the Cleveland Browns beat reporter at *The Plain Dealer* in Cleveland shows how easy it is to stumble while using the technology.

Tony Grossi, who had covered the Browns for two decades, was reassigned because he pushed the wrong button and inadvertently mass-tweeted this assessment of the Browns' owner, Randy Lerner: "a pathetic figure, the most irrelevant billionaire in the world." What Grossi intended as a snarky, insider comment to a single colleague was instead dispatched to his more than 15,000 Twitter followers. Although he realized his mistake and retracted the tweet within 60 seconds, he couldn't stop his words from reverberating around the football world.

Grossi apologized profusely, and so did his editors on the paper's website. The publisher sent a letter of apology to Lerner and the Browns organization. *The Plain Dealer*'s public editor, Ted Diadiun, wrote in a column that the editors decided they had no choice but to give Grossi a different assignment, "not as punishment but because the editors decided he could no longer credibly remain on that beat." As Diadiun summed up the problem, the paper's reporter "had revealed to the world his utter disdain for the owner of the team he was covering. How would the paper's readers be able to have faith in the objectivity in his reports following that?"[31]

As a hobby

Blogs written for a journalist's pleasure are a genre that have occasionally caused problems for the employers of the bloggers.

Steve Olafson, a reporter for the *Houston Chronicle*, was fired in 2002 because a blog he wrote under the pseudonym Banjo Jones expressed opinions about the people and events he covered.[32] After leaving the paper, Olafson continued his blog and, in an ironic twist, the *Chronicle* website decided in 2006 to post a link to his blog.[33]

After his column at the *Hartford Courant* was ended and he was reassigned as travel editor in 2003, Denis Horgan started a personal blog. Editor Brian Toolan saw a conflict of interest and forced him to stop blogging. This set off a firestorm of protests on the Internet, leading Toolan to explain his action in a *Nieman Reports* article. Toolan's reasoning was that the public identified Horgan with the *Courant*, and therefore it was inappropriate when the ex-columnist "created a new journalistic platform for himself and began opining on issues, institutions and public officials that reporters and columnists at the paper must cover."[34] For his part, Horgan argued that Toolan had infringed on his freedom of speech: "[T]he soldiers and police can't come into my house to tell me what to think and what to write on my own time but my editor can."[35]

While Bobby Caina Calvan was reporting for *The Sacramento Bee* and its parent, McClatchy Newspapers, from Iraq in 2007, he quarreled with an American soldier who questioned his identification at a Baghdad checkpoint. Calvan expressed his frustration about the incident – "in a snarky, arrogant way," as *The Bee*'s public editor characterized it – in a personal blog he was using to stay in touch with his family and friends. The blog wasn't private, of course; almost nothing on the Internet is. For his complaint about a soldier, Calvan and his employer were bombarded with hate email, and one blogger nominated the reporter for a "Jerk of the Year" award. His editors in McClatchy's Washington bureau, who hadn't known about his blog, promptly announced a new rule: "No personal blogs allowed."[36]

Shea Allen was fired as a reporter at WAAY in Huntsville, Alabama, in 2013 because she blogged light-hearted comments about her job, such as "I've gone braless during a live broadcast and no one was the wiser" and "If you ramble and I deem you unnecessary for my story, I'll stop recording but let you think otherwise." Allen said her managers were particularly upset by her revelation that she took naps in the news car.[37]

Hyperlinks in Online News Stories

One of online journalism's unique advantages is the ability to provide hyperlinks directing readers to pertinent material elsewhere on the Web.

Linking contributes to transparent journalism by giving readers a chance to see source documents for themselves. Ken Sands of *Congressional Quarterly* urged journalists to inform readers about what they know and how they know it: "They should publish transcripts of interviews. Audio clips are even better. You avoid accusations of 'taking something out of context' if you provide the raw information."[38]

Providing background information – for the old media, always a problem of broadcast time or newspaper space – is as easy as providing links to earlier stories. In a 2008 speech to journalism students, former newspaper editor John Carroll said: "[Y]ou can write accordion-like stories that can be expanded to match each reader's degree of interest. One person might give your story ten seconds; another might spend a rewarding half day with it."[39]

In a 2010 article for Nieman Lab, Jonathan Stray, a journalist and computer scientist, listed four advantages that links give to online journalism:

- *Links are good for storytelling.* "Links give journalists a way to tell complex stories concisely … offering context and depth. … The journalist can break a complex story into a non-linear narrative, with links to important sub-stories and background."
- *Links keep the audience informed.* "[J]ournalists have always depended heavily on the reporting of others. … A link is a magnificently efficient way for a journalist to pass a good story to the audience. Picking and choosing the best content from other places has become fashionably known as 'curation,' but it's a core part of what journalists have always done."
- *Links are a currency of collaboration.* "When journalists use links to 'pay' people for their useful contributions, they encourage and coordinate the production of journalism. Anyone who's seen their traffic spike from a mention on a high-profile site knows that links can have an immediate monetary impact. But links also have subtler long term value, both tangible (search rankings) and intangible (reputation and status)."
- *Links enable transparency.* "A link is the simplest, most comprehensive, and most transparent method of attribution."[40]

An ethical issue is whether to link to graphic, hate-mongering, or otherwise offensive content. The concern is that the link will be interpreted as an endorsement. But search engines will enable users to find the site anyway, and these users may think the news site is being coy if it omits the link.

In *Advancing the Story: Broadcast Journalism in a Multimedia World*, Debora Halpern Wenger and Deborah Potter offered a hypothetical example:

> Let's say you're doing a story on the increase in hate crimes in your community. One of the people included in your story is a member of the Creativity Movement, which

believes Caucasians are meant to rule the world. Do you link to the organization's Web page to offer people more information about it? If so, do you need to link to a site that condemns such groups?

The best solution, these authors suggest, "is to make sure that you clearly identify each link for users to make sure they know where they are going when they click on it. At that point, the user can make an informed choice."[41]

News sites have generally avoided linking to unspeakable violence, such as videos of terrorists beheading their hostages. In a paper for Poynter, Steve Outing wrote that, by omitting such links, the news sites are "expressing their publishing standards" even though their users can find the videos quickly:

> News organizations … no longer are effective gatekeepers, shielding their audiences from material deemed too sensitive, controversial, or disgusting. All they can do on the internet – using whatever ethical guidelines they choose – is to regulate their own small slice of cyberspace.[42]

Journalists and Citizen Bloggers

Journalists share cyberspace with the blogosphere, as the realm of citizen bloggers is called. To put it mildly, their relationship often has been contentious. But each of the two groups unquestionably has a strong influence on the other, and they share a need to gain the trust of the audience.

In her 2002 book, *The Weblog Handbook: Practical Advice on Creating and Maintaining Your Blog*, Rebecca Blood called blogs "the mavericks of the online world." From a "position outside the mainstream of mass media," she wrote, blogs have an ability to "filter and disseminate information to a widely dispersed audience."[43]

Several blogging experts have urged citizen bloggers to accept voluntary standards. "The weblog's greatest strength – its uncensored, unmediated, uncontrolled voice – is also its greatest weakness," Blood wrote in *The Weblog Handbook*.[44] Like other leaders in the blogosphere, she emphasized transparency: "It is unrealistic to expect every weblogger to present an even-handed picture of the world, but it is very reasonable to expect them to be forthcoming about their sources, biases, and behavior."[45]

Bloggers take delight in catching mistakes in the or mainstream media, or MSM. Kelly McBride of the Poynter Institute has called bloggers "the watchdog guarding the watchdog." Bloggers, she wrote, "question and criticize the professional media, who question and criticize the powerful."[46] The bloggers themselves are less delicate, informing the MSM: "We can fact-check your ass."[47]

Fact-checking bloggers pounced on CBS's *60 Minutes Wednesday* program of September 8, 2004. Dan Rather cited four memos, purportedly written by George W. Bush's commanding officer, as evidence that the future president received preferential treatment while a Vietnam-era pilot in the Texas Air National Guard. Bloggers said the memos were forged. CBS ultimately conceded that it could not prove they were authentic.[48]

Bloggers also have discovered news that the traditional media have overlooked. A prime example is the birthday party on December 5, 2002, that led to Mississippi Republican Trent Lott's departure as Senate majority leader. In remarks on the occasion of Strom Thurmond's hundredth birthday, Lott said the country would not have "all these problems" if Thurmond had been elected president.

Reporters present at the party failed to recognize the significance of Lott's statement. When Thurmond was a candidate for president in 1948, he had run on a segregationist platform. But it was not lost on bloggers watching on C-SPAN. They wrote about it on the Internet until the traditional media started paying attention. A few weeks later, Lott stepped down.[49]

Point of View
Let's Have Rules for Online Comment
Edward Wasserman

In the pre-Internet world of TV and newspapers, public comment wasn't a problem. Broadcast news didn't have any – aside from the weekly guest spot, usually some hapless civic association president reading from a prompter and staring terrified into the camera. Papers had their letters pages, but allowed only enough space for a few dozen a week, and they were generally written with care and were easy to prune for taste and diction.

Things were nicely under control.

But on the Internet, public comment isn't kitchen-table talk, it's saloon brawl. Postings are sharp and rough-and-tumble. Harsh and derisive exchanges are common. So are personal attacks. Chat rooms and message boards routinely allow people to post comments anonymously. Only when postings are so egregious, so outrageous, racist, or vile that other participants cough up hairballs do managers strike the comments and banish the authors.

That's the cyber pond traditional news organizations are diving into. They understand that their own futures hinge on reestablishing online the central role in civic life that they've played offline. So they are eager to host forums where people in the communities they serve go first to offer comment.

So they embrace the rambunctious discourse of the Internet with the zeal of the convert – and the sweaty fervor of the desperate: Got something to say? Tell us!

Editors who would never dream of running an unsigned letter-to-the-editor now argue for promiscuous anonymity.

And taste and civility, respectfulness? Old-line values of a discredited media elite. I exaggerate, but not that much. The new guiding principle is hands-off. At an editors' workshop I attended, some very good and high-powered online journalists – not the consensus, admittedly – suggested that even screening postings would drive commentators to other websites, where they could speak their minds without restraint. And that would be ruinous to newspapers' online strategies.

(Continued)

The Organization of News Ombudsmen, a group I admire and to which I belong, solicited email input on how news organizations should handle public comment: Is to OK to block anti-immigrant rants, to weed out defamation, to protect privacy and attempt to enforce some standards of reasonable expression? What about unsigned comment?

Some organizations argue that they are providing a public space, which they don't have the right, let alone the duty, to regulate. It will look after itself.

But is the marketplace of ideas self-regulating? Is defamation canceled out by testimonials, false-hoods by truth? Or does Internet talk promise another sad case of what the late ecologist Garrett Hardin called the "tragedy of the commons": each individual herdsman benefits from putting one more head of cattle onto public pasture, and suffers little from cumulative overgrazing.

In time, though, community disaster ensues.

In this case, the extreme license given individuals to vent, dissemble, excoriate and indulge their hates verbally, winds up destroying the expressive freedom that other people, less bold and less opinionated, need. Venturing an opinion, even a sound one, just isn't worth the risk. The overall result is a less expansive, less robust sphere of expression – and sound, worthwhile thoughts aren't shared.

Public conversation – exchanging ideas about what a community is and ought to be – is something that has to be learned. Unfortunately, mainstream media have made a fortune teaching people the wrong ways to talk to each other, offering up Jerry Springer, *Crossfire*, Bill O'Reilly. People understandably conclude rage is the political vernacular, that this is how public ideas are talked about.

It isn't. Now that it is online, journalism has the opportunity to morph into a practice based not just on information gathering and narrative skill, but of stewardship, of presiding over a community-wide conversation about what's going on and what matters.

Those message boards and chat rooms aren't just market-extension opportunities for media owners. They're warm and busy spaces where a new world of expression and communication is incubating. To say there should be rules, that communicants should be admonished to strive for honesty and civility and respect, is not to justify elitism. It's not even to prescribe the rules.

But it's to acknowledge that rules are needed, and to kick off the process of writing them.

Edward Wasserman, now dean of the Graduate School of Journalism at the University of California, Berkeley, wrote this column on March 17, 2008. It is reprinted with permission.

Case Study

For a Reporter-Blogger, Two Personalities

On his day job for *The Morning Call* in Allentown, Pennsylvania, John L. Micek reported on politics in the State Capitol while scrupulously striving to avoid any a hint of bias.

But this reporter liked to have a little fun, too. Most days, before he started work on stories for the newspaper, Micek discarded his objective-reporter mode and became – in his words – a "snarky smartass." In this persona he wrote a "devious" political blog skewering the very politicians he would report on that day. "It's bizarre," Micek said. "It's almost like I'm two different people."

The blog was called "Capitol Ideas," and its readership consistently ranked in the top three of the website's 17 blogs.

Like many newspaper reporters, Micek took up blogging as a side job. Except that it soon was no longer a side job; blogging became part of his duties.

And Micek loved it.

The content and style of the blogs were foreign to the decades-old conventions of journalism – be fair, be objective, and verify, verify, verify. Online, there is wide acceptance of the notion that the rules are not the same as they are in print and broadcast.

Micek said his blogging approach was to spice his notebook leftovers with what he calls a "tabloidy attitude," a knowing voice he picked up from being a fan of the *New York Post*. The Capitol in Harrisburg has "news breaking out all over the place," Micek said. Before the blog, 90 percent of the material he gathered stayed in his notebook. Then there wasn't a place for it in the paper. But once he had a blog, there was a place for it: on the website.

Micek posted his blog directly onto the Web. His editor, Peter Leffler, said he asked Micek and the other staff bloggers to give him a sense of what they planned to do in their blogs, and he went online a couple of times a day to check their postings. He said that, when the blogs were started, the intention was to edit them before posting. That soon proved "unworkable" because of the volume of copy and the time pre-editing would require.

The two personalities of Micek were on display in his coverage of Vice President Dick Cheney's speech to Republican activists in Harrisburg on September 8, 2007.

Micek's blog report began:

We're just back from VP Dick Cheney's utterly news-free speech at the Harrisburg Hilton. With just a year left to go dictating the affairs of the universe, Cheney contented himself with taking a valedictory lap in front of the 140 or so party faithful who had, depending on their degree of faithfulness, paid $250 to $2,500 for the pleasure of hearing him speak and/or having their picture taken with him.

By the time the next morning's paper was printed, Micek had shed the irreverent tone and found enough substance in Cheney's remarks to lead his *Morning Call* story with: "Vice President Dick Cheney called Friday for extension of the Bush administration's tax cuts, warning of 'one of the largest money grabs in American history' if congressional leaders allow them to expire."

Micek said he treated blogging responsibly. "But I think you can do online journalism with snark and humor. That makes things interesting." He added that most subjects of news coverage didn't hold his blog against him when he was reporting for the paper, and he attributed that to his practice of "fair abuse; I try to smack everybody equally." Micek said it helped that he has been on the beat for nearly a decade and had established a reputation for fairness. "I think my sources are sophisticated enough to know that a mild spanking on the blog does not equate to unfair treatment and/or bias in the dead-tree product."

Not that he lacked critics. Micek said that when he poked fun at Republican gubernatorial candidate Lynn Swann's campaign in 2006, the ex-football star's staffers bristled. "It took

(Continued)

them some time to figure out I was messing with them in the blog but would give them a fair shake during the day," he said.

As a by-product of the blog, Micek said, he got tips that led to news stories for the print edition, as well as "back-channel discussions that have enriched my knowledge and added new dimensions to my understanding of my beat."

Micek also said his blog broke down the wall between him and his readers. If he got something wrong, people would tell him quickly. "I don't have to wait until next day's paper to fix it." He saw his goal as getting readers to go from the blog to the paper and then back to the blog. Reeling people in, he said, is what the business is about.

Ardith Hilliard, then editor of *The Morning Call*, said she saw the Web as an entirely different medium, one that "invites a chatty, personality-laden form of communication" and "involves instant interaction with the audience." She said Micek and his editors had agreed that he should not take "editorial-like stances on issues but instead focus on the funny, the absurd, the atmospheric material about the State Capitol" that rarely appears in newspapers.

To illustrate how Micek can assume an edgy tone on his blog without taking an editorial position, Hilliard mentioned his handling of a parliamentary maneuver by Philadelphia Senator Vince Fumo in a Senate committee. Fumo, trying to head off a constitutional amendment banning same-sex marriages and civil unions, made a tongue-in-cheek proposal to outlaw divorce. His point was that if the amendment's backers really wanted to protect the institution of marriage, the best way would be to make it impossible for couples to dissolve their unions.

"This is why we so totally love this place," Micek blogged. "Just when you think the General Assembly has run out of ways to surprise you, someone comes along and introduces a measure so nuts that the affairs of state get turned on their head and the political process becomes a piece of performance art."

Hilliard said Micek was being irreverent but without taking an editorial position on same-sex unions. "It is true that infusing one's writing with personality and attitude can come dangerously close at times to expressing opinion," Hilliard said. "Blogging by a reporter, therefore, is not without risk, and some surely stray over the line. I believe that John and our other bloggers have avoided that mistake."

The ethicist Bob Steele said reporters' revealing their opinions was a problem before the Internet, and it "can be problematic for the readers who may question the independence and fairness of the reporter." Tensions are exacerbated with blogs, he said, because of an expectation that they will be edgy and because they are edited with less rigor than the content of the print newspaper.

Tom Rosenstiel, now the president of the American Press Institute, said a reporter who adopts a different personality online is comparable to one who goes on a television talk show and spouts opinion. "You can't go on ranting and raving about the president and your opinion of him; then you've become something other than a reporter," Rosenstiel said. "You can't go back and say, 'Now I'm covering you, Mr. President, and I'm objective.'" Rosenstiel said that same reporter could go on television and maintain credibility by behaving within journalistic standards. The same goes for blogs, he said.

In January 2013, Micek took a new job that calls for expressing opinion full time both in print and on the Web. He left *The Morning Call* and became editor of the editorial and opinion pages of *The Patriot-News* in Harrisburg and its website, PennLive. In a news story announcing his appointment, the Harrisburg organization noted his experience as the "Capitol Ideas" blogger.

This case is based on a report that Sara Ganim, a senior at Pennsylvania State University, wrote for *The Lion's Roar*, a publication of Penn State's College of Communications in Fall 2007, and is used by permission of Ganim and the College. As a reporter for *The Patriot-News*, Ganim won the 2012 Pulitzer Prize for local reporting.

Sources

Ganim's report on the reporter-blogger included interviews with John L. Micek, Tom Rosenstiel, and Bob Steele. Additional reporting by this textbook's author included interviews and/or email exchanges with Micek; Ardith Hilliard, then editor of *The Call*; and Peter Leffler, who supervised staff blogs at *The Call*. For this textbook's second edition, Steve Bien-Aime updated the case study after interviewing Micek about his new job with *The Patriot-News*.

Questions for Class Discussion

- If you were a reader of *The Morning Call* when Micek worked there, would you have suspected a bias in Micek's reporting in the newspaper, based on what he wrote in his blog?
- If you were a subject of John Micek's reporting, would it affect your relationship if he expressed a negative opinion about you in his blog? Would you be satisfied with his statement that he tries to "smack everybody equally"?
- Do you think the verification standards for journalist-written blogs are different from those for print and broadcast reporting?
- Do you think blogs should be edited before they are posted?

Notes

1   Kathy English, *The Longtail of News: To Unpublish or Not To Unpublish* (APME Online Journalism Credibility Project, Oct. 2009).
2   Ibid.
3   Clark Hoyt, "When bad news follows you," *The New York Times*, Aug. 26, 2007.
4   Devon Lash, email to the author, Sept. 4, 2008.
5   English, *The Longtail of News*.
6   Ibid.
7   Jeffrey Toobin, "The solace of oblivion," *The New Yorker*, Sept. 29, 2014.
8   European Commission, "Factsheet on the 'right to be forgotten' ruling (C-131/12)."
9   Toobin, "The solace of oblivion."
10 Dan Gillmor, *We the Media: Grassroots Journalism by the People, for the People* (Sebastopol, CA: O'Reilly Media, 2004), xxiv, xxv.
11 Jim Brady, quoted in Pat Walters, "Dealing with comments: a few interesting approaches," Poynter, May 31, 2007.
12 Julie Zhuo, "Where anonymity breeds contempt," *The New York Times*, Nov. 29, 2010.

13 Dennis Ryerson, "We don't want a few to spoil community conversation," *The Indianapolis Star*, Mar. 17, 2008.

14 Kelly McBride, "Dialogue or diatribe: one woman's story," Poynter, May 17, 2007.

15 Bob Steele, "Baggy pants, drunken driving and day care: Cincy's challenges with user comments," Poynter, May 24, 2007.

16 Author's telephone interview with David Zeeck, Oct. 26, 2007.

17 Clark Hoyt, "Civil discourse, meet the Internet," *The New York Times*, Nov. 4, 2007.

18 Cecilia Friend and Jane B. Singer, *Online Journalism Ethics: Traditions and Transitions* (Armonk, NY: M. E. Sharpe, 2007), 137–138.

19 Carole Tarrant, editor's column in *The Roanoke (Virginia) Times*, May 18, 2008.

20 Arthur D. Santana, "Virtuous or vitriolic?," *Journalism Practice*, 8:1 (July 18, 2013), 18–33.

21 Zhuo, "Where anonymity breeds contempt."

22 Jeff Sonderman, "News sites using Facebook Comments see higher quality discussion, more referrals," Poynter, Aug. 18, 2011.

23 Author's email exchange with Curt Chandler, Oct. 2014.

24 Katherine K. Lee, "Taking on the rumor mill," *Nieman Reports*, Summer 2012.

25 Mike Gangloff, presentation to Associated Press Managing Editors, Oct. 5, 2007.

26 *The New York Times*, "The Times answers Spitzer scandal questions," City Room: Blogs from the Five Boroughs, NYTimes.com, Mar. 13, 2008.

27 Jill Rosen (ed.), "Bloggin' in the newsroom," *American Journalism Review*, Dec. 2003–Jan. 2004, 10.

28 Author's telephone interview with Bob Giles, Sept. 10, 2007.

29 Author's telephone interview with Kinsey Wilson, Sept. 26, 2007.

30 Carl Straumsheim, "Who gets it first: Twitter or the editors?," *American Journalism Review*, Mar. 16, 2012.

31 Ted Diadiun, "Tony Grossi's reassignment was a painful necessity," *The Plain Dealer*, Jan. 28, 2012.

32 Steve Olafson, "A reporter is fired for writing a weblog," *Nieman Reports*, Fall 2003, 91.

33 Joe Strupp, "*Houston Chronicle* links to ex-reporter's blog that got him fired," *Editor & Publisher*, Feb. 24, 2006.

34 Brian Toolan, "An editor acts to limit a staffer's weblog," *Nieman Reports*, Fall 2003, 92–93.

35 Mark Glaser, "Will Denis Horgan blog again?," *Online Journalism Review*, May 9, 2003.

36 Armando Acuna, "Green reporter, Green Zone dispute, red-hot rhetoric," *The Sacramento Bee*, Nov. 11, 2007.

37 Paul Gettis, "Huntsville reporter Shea Allen fired from WAAY-31 for blogging about working braless and other 'confessions,'" AL.com, July 29, 2013. See also NBC video, "Revealing too much: reporter fired for controversial blog post," *Today*, July 30, 2013.

38 Ken Sands' email to author, May 30, 2008.

39 John Carroll, "The future (we hope) of journalism," Creason Lecture at the University of Kentucky, Apr. 1, 2008. (*An excerpt is available in the Student Resources section of the website.*)

40 Jonathan Stray, "Why link out? Four journalistic purposes of the noble hyperlink," Nieman Lab, June 8, 2010.

41 Debora Halpern Wenger and Deborah Potter, *Advancing the Story: Broadcast Journalism in a Multimedia World* (Washington, DC: CQ Press, 2007), 278.

42 Steve Outing, "The thorny question of linking," Poynter, Oct. 21, 2004.

43 Rebecca Blood, *The Weblog Handbook: Practical Advice on Creating and Maintaining Your Blog* (Cambridge, MA: Perseus, 2002), 114.

44 Ibid., 115.

45 Ibid., 116.

46 Kelly McBride, "Journalism in the age of blogs," Poynter, Sept. 15, 2004.

47 Jeff Jarvis, "My *New York Post* op-ed on Rathergate," BuzzMachine, Sept. 19, 2004. Jarvis credits a blogger, Ken Layne, for creating the slogan in 2001.

48 Friend and Singer, *Online Journalism Ethics*, 18.

49 Ibid., 136. See also Thomas B. Edsall, "Lott decried for part of salute to Thurmond," *The Washington Post*, Dec. 7, 2002.

19 Ethics Issues Specific to Visual Journalism

Seeking truth with the camera while minimizing harm

Learning Goals

This chapter will help you understand:

- why it is essential that the public be able to trust the truthfulness of the news media's photographs and video;
- how a news photograph can be distorted either by stage-managing the scene or by manipulating the image;
- the standards that photojournalists have adopted to ensure the integrity of their images;
- how photojournalists make decisions about using photographs whose content may be offensive to the audience; and
- the psychological harm that can be caused merely by taking photographs, even if they are not disseminated to the public.

Brian Walski was sunburned, hungry, and sleep-deprived on April 1, 2003, as he sat down with his laptop computer to send the *Los Angeles Times* photographs he had taken on the battlefield in Iraq.

The *Times* photojournalist selected two images of a British soldier standing in front of a group of Iraqi civilians, most of whom were seated. The soldier was instructing the civilians to take cover from Iraqi gunfire. In one image, the soldier gestured with an outstretched left arm while holding his weapon in his right. In the other, the soldier was not pointing, but among the civilians there was action that the other image lacked: a man holding a child seemed to be approaching the soldier.

On his computer screen, Walski combined the image of the gesturing soldier with the one in which the man and child were prominent in the center of the frame. It appeared that the soldier and the man were interacting, making the composite a more powerful news image than either of the originals. Walski transmitted the composite without telling his editors in Los Angeles what he had done. The *Times* published the photo three columns wide on its front page and shared it with other Tribune Company newspapers.

At the *Hartford Courant*, Walski's photo impressed assistant managing editor Thom McGuire so much that he ran the photo the full six columns across the *Courant*'s front page.

The Ethical Journalist: Making Responsible Decisions in the Digital Age, Second Edition. Gene Foreman.
© 2016 John Wiley & Sons, Inc. Published 2016 by John Wiley & Sons, Inc.

Later, a *Courant* employee was searching for some images in a computer and came across the Walski photo. He noticed that some of the seated civilians seemed to appear twice. When McGuire was notified, he magnified the image 600 percent. What he saw made him "sick to my stomach." He phoned his counterpart at the *Times*, Colin Crawford, with the grim news that the photo was a fake.

Crawford was shocked. "I said out loud, 'No way! There must be a technical, digital … satellite glitch explanation,'" he later told Kenneth Irby of the Poynter Institute.

It took a day for Crawford to track down Walski, who was still shooting and transmitting photographs from southern Iraq. Walski confessed that he had combined the images – an act that violated both *Times* policy and the profession's widely accepted standard of zero tolerance of altered images. In a satellite-phone conversation, he was fired.

The *Times* ran an editor's note the next day along with the two original images and the composite. The *Courant* did the same. The *Chicago Tribune*, which had published the composite on an inside page, also notified its readers.[1]

Photojournalists generally empathized with Walski's drive to produce excellent photography while enduring gunfire, desert heat, and a shortage of food, water, and sleep. But they did not condone what he had done. "The only thing we have to offer the public is our credibility," said a former president of the National Press Photographers Association, John Long of the *Courant*. "We can say that it is awful once, but if happens again and again we'll destroy ourselves. … We have to have accurate information."[2]

Walski, a veteran of 25 years as a photojournalist and a staff member of the *Times* for nearly five years, sent his colleagues an email apology. "This was after an extremely long, hot and stressful day, but I offer no excuses here," he wrote:

> I deeply regret that I have tarnished the reputation of the *Los Angeles Times*. … I have always maintained the highest ethical standards throughout my career and cannot truly explain my complete breakdown in judgment this time. That will only come in the many sleepless nights that are ahead.[3]

Reporting, and Distorting, through Images

Photography dates from two inventions announced in 1839–40 after years of experimentation: Louis-Jacques-Mandé Daguerre's daguerreotype and William Henry Fox Talbot's calotype. In France, in 1839, Daguerre announced that he had discovered how to create a permanent image using a box camera and a highly polished, silver-plated sheet of copper on which the image was "fixed," or stabilized, with salt water.[4] In England the following year, Talbot reported his discovery of a negative/positive process that shortened exposure times and allowed multiple prints to be made from a single negative.[5] The inventions created a technology with great potential for science, art, and journalism.

Professor Louis W. Hodges of Washington and Lee University has described photography's essential role in modern journalism:

> Though their messages overlap, pictures and words communicate different things. In conveying feeling and eliciting emotions (sympathy, anger, horror), pictures are usually superior to words. … On the other hand, words are inherently superior to pictures in communicating concepts, propositions or ideas. Thus the right words coupled with the right pictures can communicate ideas as well as strong feelings about those ideas. A written statement about the concept of freedom, for example, can carry greater meaning when it is accompanied by a picture of newly released hostages.

For these reasons, news photographs are not mere adjuncts or appendages that just accompany stories. Pictures are integral to the larger journalistic function of telling people about their world. Pictures can grab attention in ways that a lead paragraph cannot, and that is part of their journalistic purpose. But their more important communicative function is to tell a story, to communicate meaning.[6]

However, the miraculous technology of photography can be abused to give journalism's audience an image depicting a scene that never happened. Photojournalists can deceive the audience by:

- stage-managing (posing or "setting up") the scene being photographed; or
- altering the content or context of an otherwise authentic photograph.

Tampering with reality "is a violation of everything journalism stands for," Professor Russell Frank of Pennsylvania State University wrote in an essay published in the *Los Angeles Times* a few days after Brian Walski's transgression in the desert. Frank explained why the stakes are so high:

> Whoever said the camera never lies was a liar. Photographers – including some news photographers – have always arranged scenes and posed subjects. They also have been known to cut and paste one image onto another for comic or dramatic effect. Computers have just made it easier.
>
> Photo editors have zipped up open flies (*Orange County Register*), grafted Oprah's head onto Ann-Margret's body (*TV Guide*), moved the Great Pyramids of Egypt (*National Geographic*), and covered immodest women (Louisville *Courier-Journal* and *The New York Times*).
>
> Despite all this fakery, readers continue to believe that what they see in a news photo really happened. They almost have to. They need to feel as if they can get reliable information somewhere.
>
> But journalists know very well that this trust is a fragile thing. Try to persuade people that fakes are real enough times and they'll start thinking that the real ones are fake. That is why the *Times* moved so quickly after Walski's fake was discovered.[7]

As Professor Frank observed, photographers have tampered with reality ever since the beginning of the craft. One of Daguerre's rivals, Hippolyte Bayard, was frustrated by the French government's failure to recognize his own considerable contributions to photography. To protest, he posed as a corpse for a fake photograph and, on the back, wrote that "the unhappy man threw himself into the water in despair."[8]

In the third decade of the age of photography, the American Civil War produced examples of fakery using both stage managing and image manipulation. Photographers posed the same soldiers for photographs showing them fighting the enemy or lying dead in the battle's aftermath. A popular full-length photograph of President Abraham Lincoln was created by placing Lincoln's portrait on the body of Senator John C. Calhoun of South Carolina.[9]

In the twenty-first century, Professor Hany Farid of Dartmouth College has developed electronic tools to detect tampering with photographs and images. He began his research after discovering that federal rules of court evidence gave digital images the same credence as those on film, even though digital photography is easier to manipulate in ways that are harder to detect. "While I was primarily motivated by the issue of photographic evidence in the courts," he said in an interview with author Ron Steinman, "my hope is that our work will also help the media, among others, contend with the issue of digital manipulation."[10] Farid's online gallery, "Photo tampering throughout history," provides a valuable, illustrated history of photo manipulation, digital or otherwise.[11]

Integrity Standards for Still Images

It can be argued that, even though digital technology makes the **manipulation** of photographs easier today, the integrity of journalistic images has never been greater. This is due mainly to the near-universal acceptance of the principle that *no* digital manipulation can be tolerated. Transgressions receive enormous publicity within the profession – thanks mainly to the Internet – because they are rare and thus noteworthy.

The zero-tolerance concept is based on two factors. First, because the public is well aware of computer software that can easily be used to alter images, the only way to maintain trust is for journalists to ban any alterations, no matter how benign (such as zipping the fly of a boy's pants). And, second, *zero* is an easily understood, inflexible number; once photographers and photo editors start making exceptions, these exceptions can only lead to a loss of perspective that results in more significant exceptions.

The ethics code of the National Press Photographers Association, as well as the photo policies of many newsgathering organizations, explicitly prohibits tampering with what is known as documentary photography – that is, news photographs. The NPPA's code says: "Editing should maintain the integrity of the photographic images' content and context."[12] The Associated Press states in its policy that it will never alter the content of photographs, adding: "Our pictures must always tell the truth."[13] In prohibiting any alteration of a photo's content, *The Washington Post*'s policy explains: "This means that nothing is added or subtracted from the image such as a hand or tree limb in an inopportune position."[14] *The New York Times*' policy prohibits adding, rearranging, distorting, or removing people or objects.[15]

It is more important for photojournalists today to be schooled in ethics because they work with less oversight than in the past, John Beale, former award-winning chief photographer for the *Pittsburgh Post-Gazette*, tells his photojournalism students at Pennsylvania State University. Beale explained how the profession has changed in the digital era:

> With film, most photographers returned to the newspaper office to develop the film and make prints. At many papers, photo editors reviewed every image that was made for the assignment. Photographers worked together in darkrooms. Digital changed all that. Often, photographers complete an assignment and transmit from their cars or their homes. There's little oversight until an image is questioned.[16]

Most newsroom codes permit the computer equivalent of what was known in yesterday's chemical darkrooms as "burning" and "dodging." Parts of the image can be darkened or lightened to improve reproduction, so that what the audience sees is closer to what the photographer saw. (In the darkroom, a technician would focus the enlarger's beam on an area of the image that needed to be darkened by "burning," or shield an area that needed to be lightened by "dodging.") The technique of "toning," or improving contrast, is similarly allowed to compensate for detail lost in mass printing.

However, even burning, dodging, and toning are ethically wrong if they change the context of a news photograph. When O. J. Simpson was arrested on murder charges in 1994, his police photo ran on the cover of *Time* after being deliberately darkened by the magazine's artists, who also added a five o'clock shadow. The alteration was readily apparent to the public because *Newsweek*'s cover used the same photo without retouching.

A normally acceptable editing technique is "cropping" – removing extraneous parts of an image at its borders. This focuses the viewer's attention on the most important part of the picture, which can be printed larger because insignificant details on the edges of the photograph have been removed. Cropping is necessary because it is impractical for photographers to frame scenes precisely as they shoot; even with digital cameras, which enable them to instantly see the images they have captured, they must allow a margin of error.

Cropping can be used for questionable purposes. During Franklin D. Roosevelt's tenure as president (1933–45), sympathetic photographers and photo editors never showed the public the wheelchair and leg braces he required for mobility as a result of having been stricken years earlier by polio. As historian Doris Kearns Goodwin wrote:

> In twelve years, not a single picture was ever printed of the president in his wheelchair. No newsreel had ever captured him being lifted into or out of his car. When he was shown in public, he appeared either standing behind a podium, seated in an ordinary chair, or leaning on the arm of a colleague.[17]

Contemporary photojournalists probably would not emphasize Roosevelt's disability, but they would not hide it either.

Until the late decades of the twentieth-century, "flopping" portrait photos was routine in newspapers. Rather than have a person appear to gaze off the page, the editor producing the layout would order the engraver to reverse the photo. That resulted in the image that the subject sees in a mirror (but not the image that others see). No wonder that this technique came to be rejected as borderline fakery.

Most print photojournalists reject the stage-managing of news photographs – that is, directing the people being photographed to do something for the benefit of the camera. These photojournalists argue that a posed photograph cannot ethically be presented as a "found moment." A noteworthy example of stage-managing occurred in the *Los Angeles Times* in 1993. While covering a fire scene, *Times* photographer Mike Meadows suggested that a firefighter go to a swimming pool and pour water over his head to cool off. The result was a stunning photograph, but when photo director Larry Armstrong discovered the circumstances in which it had been taken, he suspended Meadows. "When you manipulate the situation," Armstrong said, "you manipulate the news."[18]

Under the profession's standards, posing can be acceptable if the resulting image is not a documentary news photograph and the posing is obvious to the viewer. For example, a story about a new chief executive officer of an automobile company might be accompanied by a photograph of the executive in business attire, wearing a hard hat and standing in front of an assembly line. No one will reasonably assume that the CEO actually works in the factory. In cases where there may be a question, the caption should make clear that the photograph was posed.

In 2011 the White House stopped a practice that evidently had been in effect since Harry S. Truman's administration. After a televised speech, the president used to walk into the room again and pretend to begin reading the speech for the benefit of photographers who had not been allowed to shoot while the real speech was being delivered. That was supposed to solve two problems: the lack of room for even a small pool of photographers, and the sound of the clicking shutters disrupting the speech. Photojournalists had objected to the re-enactment; "anytime you take a photo that looks real and isn't, you're perpetrating a visual lie," said Sean Elliot, president of the National Press Photographers Association. As an alternative for still photography, the news media would have to use a frame taken from the television screen.[19]

Right or wrong, magazine art directors grant themselves leeway in modifying photographs that news photo editors do not. "The general feeling," said Robert Newman, art director for *Inside.com*, "is that the covers of magazines are commerce, they're selling tools, a commodity. … The image has become another graphic element, like type and color, to be altered at will to fit an editorial and graphic concept."[20]

A liberal interpretation of that rationale presumably led to such extreme examples as darkening the Simpson mug shot in *Time* on June 27, 1994; to straightening the teeth of Bobbi McCaughey, the Iowa mother of septuplets, in *Newsweek* on December 1, 1997; and to superimposing Martha Stewart's head on a model's body in *Newsweek* on March 7, 2005, when Stewart was released from prison, where she had lost weight.[21]

Lynn Staley of *Newsweek* said her magazine might retouch cover photos to remove blemishes or small wrinkles, "but after a bad experience with Mrs. McCaughey's teeth a few years ago, we won't do anything that will require surgery in real life."[22]

The Economist attracted criticism for a 2010 cover photograph that showed President Barack Obama, his head bowed and standing alone on a Louisiana beach, an oil rig dimly seen in the distance, after a massive oil spill in the Gulf of Mexico. When he was photographed by a Reuters photographer, Obama was in conversation with two people. Reuters' policy prohibits manipulation. Emma Duncan, deputy editor of *The Economist*, acknowledged that Charlotte Randolph, a local parish president, was "edited out of the image" and that Coast Guard Admiral Thad W. Allen "was removed by the crop." She wrote, "We don't edit photos in order to mislead. I asked for Ms. Randolph to be removed because I wanted readers to focus on Mr. Obama, not because I wanted to make him look isolated. That wasn't the point of the story."[23]

Margaret Sullivan, *The New York Times*' public editor, discovered in 2014 that the paper's monthly style magazine, *T*, allows manipulation of fashion photographs. "Fashion is fantasy," Sullivan was told by Michele McNally, assistant managing editor for photography. "Readers understand this. It's totally manipulated, with everything done for aesthetics." Deborah Needleman, editor of *T*, said fashion magazines routinely allowed retouching: "Red taken out of someone's eye, a wrinkle in a skirt smoothed, a model's tattoo removed." In her column, Sullivan was unconvinced. "It would be best," she said, "if all the photography produced by the *Times* newsroom could be held to the same standard."[24]

Concerns have been raised about the veracity of photographs taken with smartphones using apps, such as those on Hipstamatic and Instagram, that impart an artistic finish to an image. Not just amateurs but some professionals are using them. Nick Stern, a photojournalist who has covered news in 40 countries, wrote on CNN. com, "With an app typically costing no more than $1.99, everyone is becoming a news photographer – creating dramatic, emotive images with subdued tones, vignette edges and selective focus." The problem, Stern wrote, is that the image is not what the photographer saw:

> Every time a news organization uses a Hipstamatic or Instagram-style picture in a news report, they are cheating us all. It is not the photographer who has communicated the emotion into the images. It's not the pain, the suffering, or the horror that is showing through. It's the work of an app designer in Palo Alto who decided that a nice shallow focus and dark faded border would bring out the best in the image.[25]

Newspapers and magazines alike use photo illustrations, which can either be a posed photograph (usually in a studio with no digital alteration) or a digitally altered photograph. Kenneth Irby of the Poynter Institute says that a photo illustration "is illustrative in nature and is clearly out of the realm of reality. Traditionally, it is an approach used for fashion, food, and product photographs."[26]

The Washington Post allows "a work of fictional imagery," but the fiction must be self-evident. "If a caption is necessary to explain that the content is not real, then we should not use the image," *The Post*'s policy states.[27]

To illustrate the story "How the Right Went Wrong" for its issue of March 15, 2007, *Time* magazine published a cover photo of President Ronald Reagan that had been altered to make it appear that he was crying. The alteration was subtly acknowledged inside the magazine, where David Hume Kennerly was credited for the photograph and Tim O'Brien for the "tear."[28] After its contrived cover photo of Martha Stewart, which was acknowledged in the table of contents, *Newsweek* changed its policy so that future photo illustrations would be labeled on the cover.[29]

The very term *photo illustration* is newsroom jargon that readers may not understand. Rather than using the term as a label, editors would be more transparent if they explained exactly what had been done to the photograph.

Even so, it is the image and not the accompanying text that makes the greatest impression on the audience. Deni Elliott and Paul Martin Lester wrote in a column for *News Photographer* magazine: "[I]t should come as no surprise that, for almost all viewers, when visual and textual messages are in conflict, readers will remember the visual. The visual message wins out."[30]

A 1994 incident illustrates the point made by Elliott and Lester. *New York Newsday* published a composite photo placing Olympic figure skater Nancy Kerrigan and her rival Tonya Harding together on the ice six weeks after Kerrigan had been clubbed on the right knee by an associate of Harding. The image overwhelms the caption's disclosures that the two "appear to skate together" and that the image is a "composite photo." Steven R. Knowlton wrote in *Moral Reasoning for Journalists*, "The reader is angry for having been fooled, however briefly, and for being so gullible as to be taken in. And the newspaper now has a reader who will look at what it publishes hereafter with a new suspicion. Or, maybe, not look at it at all."[31]

Integrity Standards in News Video

While print journalists have reached a consensus against stage-managing their subjects, the line for television has been less clear.

The late Travis Linn, a CBS bureau chief and then a professor at the University of Nevada, Reno, wrote in 1991, "In the minds of most television journalists, there is innocent staging and there is blatant and unethical staging." His article in *Journal of Mass Media Ethics* identified three "basic motivations" for staging: convenience of editing, convenience of time, and convenience of story. While writing that all three are dangerous ethically, Linn said they could be arranged in that order as "a hierarchy of ethical transgression."

In staging for *convenience of editing*, a videographer might ask a subject to walk into a building twice, allowing the camera to capture the action from both outside and inside the building.

For *convenience of time*, the subject of a news story is asked "to repeat an action that occurred before the camera arrived or to carry out an action that is expected to occur later, because the reporter does not have time to wait for the real action." For example, if the camera is not present at a news conference when a person announces his or her candidacy for mayor, the candidate usually will agree to reread the announcement.

The most objectionable staging on Linn's list is for *convenience of story*. The journalist gives "instructions or directions to the subject of a news story to cause the story to develop in a certain way, when there is no reason to believe it would develop in that way otherwise." This practice, Linn wrote, is unacceptable. While at CBS, he spotted a video from the Rio Grande that seemed – and was – too good to be true. "Just as a border patrol truck pulled to a stop and the officers got out, a border patrol plane swooped low overhead, momentarily blotting out the image of the rising sun." Linn called for the raw tape, which showed the scene being enacted three times:

> On the soundtrack I could hear a voice cueing the patrolmen in the truck just as the plane was swooping down, "Okay now! Walk to the gate!" If the labor movement had been stronger in Texas, the border patrolmen would have been entitled to the Screen Actors Guild minimum for their performance.[32]

In their 2008 online book *Photojournalism, Technology and Ethics*, Scott Baradell and Anh D. Stack pointed out that the difference in standards between print and video takes on new importance in today's converged media environment. Newspaper photographers are shooting news video for their papers' websites. Baradell and Stack wrote: "[I]n the minds of many print photojournalists, TV's justifications for setting up shots represent a slippery slope, one that starts with the relatively innocent staging for editing purposes, but can eventually descend into changing the nature of the story."[33]

Al Tompkins of the Poynter Institute said that "still photographers, generally, have a harder line than TV folks have had." Rather than softening the line for television, Tompkins said, "I would strengthen it. As more people learn to shoot and edit video using their phone, iMovie, and other home edit programs, they will understand the deception more and will be less and less tolerant of it." He also noted that the National Press Photographers Association's code of ethics "forbids staging – period. It applies to video and still equally."[34]

Editing video and sound for television presents another set of ethical hazards. The Radio Television Digital News Association's ethics code states that an electronic journalist should not "manipulate images or sounds in any way that is misleading." The code also counsels the journalist to "use technological tools with skill and thoughtfulness, avoiding techniques that skew facts, distort reality, or sensationalize events."[35] The National Press Photographers Association's code says: "Do not manipulate images or add or alter sound in any way that can mislead viewers or misrepresent subjects."[36]

In its publication *Newsroom Ethics: Decision-Making for Quality Coverage*, RTDNA's educational foundation lists guidelines created by Poynter's Al Tompkins. Among the guidelines are these: "Don't add sounds that did not exist unless it is clear to the audience that they have been added in the edit room. Don't add sounds that you obtained at another scene or from another time or place if adding the sounds might mislead the audience."[37]

RTDNA's *Newsroom Ethics* cautions electronic journalists to be judicious in adding music to video. Music "has the ability to send complex and profound editorial messages," and journalists contemplating whether to add music "must ask themselves whether the music adds an editorial tone to the story that would not be present without the music."[38]

Restraint in adding special effects also is urged by *Newsroom Ethics*. "Slow motion, slow dissolves, tight cropping and framing, dramatic lighting, and unusual angles can all send subtle or even overt messages to the viewer about a person's perceived guilt, power or authority."[39]

Brooke Barnett and Maria Elizabeth Grabe of Indiana University conducted an experiment in which audiences watched videos of news events in both standard speed and slow motion. All the events shown were of disturbing content: a flood in a small town, a house fire, a protest at an abortion clinic, and a gang-related shooting. The research yielded three major findings: First, viewers are more likely to blame suspects shown in slow motion than those shown in standard speed. Second, slow motion makes news stories "seem less fair and informative and more sensational." Third, slow motion magnifies the negative nature of certain news stories, "making viewer experiences of bad news feel worse." Barnett and Grabe regard slow-motion video as a distinctive feature of "tabloid news packaging," along with "obtrusive voice inflection, excessive use of zoom movements, and sound."[40]

Making Decisions about Offensive Content

Photojournalists regularly confront questions of how to report the news with authenticity while avoiding giving offense to the audience. This subject was discussed in Chapter 15 and is elaborated on here.

The public can be expected to react negatively to images depicting graphic violence, gore, dead bodies, nudity, indecent behavior, perceived invasion of privacy, and juveniles doing things that might endanger them.

Decisions on this kind of content have to be on a case-by-case basis. These decisions weigh the degree of offense and the news value of the specific photograph or video.

Sherman Williams, assistant managing editor/visual journalism of the *Milwaukee Journal Sentinel*, considers the following factors in deciding whether to use a graphic image:

- *The scale of the event.* The bigger the news – think 9/11, Hurricane Katrina – the more likely Williams will run it. There were few reader complaints, for instance, about the photograph of the firefighter holding a dead child in the aftermath of the bombing of the Oklahoma City federal building on April 19, 1995, in which 168 people were killed. "The event was huge," Williams said, "and the photo summed it up."

- *Who is involved.*   If the image is graphic and the people involved are ordinary people involuntarily thrust into the news, Williams is less likely to run it. In addition, the audience may be tolerant of a graphic image if the subject survives, but decidedly offended by the image if the subject dies.
- *Whether the event is close to home.*   There are two competing considerations. The first is that proximity argues for running the image. The other is that the photo is more likely to hurt someone in the audience, and readers will identify with the photo subject.
- *Whether the image will appear in print or online.*   "I don't know why," Williams said, "but people react more to what they see in the print newspaper than what they see online. When we have run the same photo in print and online, we have gotten many more complaints from the print readers."[41]

When journalists conclude that the news value of a sensitive photograph obliges them to use it, they may also consider ways of minimizing the likely offense. In print, these considerations are running the photo on an inside page rather than on the front page, running it small rather than large, and running it in black and white rather than in color. Depending on the photo's composition, it might also be possible to crop out an offensive detail while preserving the newsworthy elements of the image. Online, an editor could run a cautionary note suggesting user discretion and then require the user to click on a link in order to see the photograph. On television, an announcer could warn viewers of the graphic nature of the image and give them time to turn away.

The Case Studies accompanying this chapter offer an opportunity for a class to debate whether a sensitive image should be disseminated to the public: "The Falling Man, World Trade Center, 2001," "Photographing a Man Pushed to His Death," and "A Marine Is Mortally Wounded."

Newspapers sometimes have sought to explain in a caption or an editor's note why they used a photograph that they expect many readers to find offensive. Those who favor this technique say that explaining the decision is a matter of transparency and accountability. One of these is Kenneth Irby of the Poynter Institute, who wrote: "[W]e should be willing to disclose why we make a decision. ... We should share a certain level of reflective thinking and even our vulnerability."[42] The ethicist Michael Josephson, who favors explanations, suggests wryly that the practice makes journalists appear "a little less arrogant."[43] Vin Alabiso, former Associated Press vice president and executive photo editor, would run the explanation because readers tend to assume that journalists do not consider readers' sensibilities. "We shouldn't think that what we do is so complicated and mysterious that we can't give them our thinking," Alabiso said. "I'm influenced by my experience of appearing on panels with readers to examine photos. The readers are often won over by the arguments of the professionals."[44]

Photo editors should be wary of images that show people doing something that appears dangerous, because parents fear that their children will mimic what they see. The *St. Paul Pioneer Press* learned that lesson on January 24, 2000, when readers protested a photograph of a 16-year-old boy peering into the barrel of a pistol. "It shocked me. The first rule is that every gun is loaded," one reader said. "What were you thinking?" another demanded to know.

The photograph illustrated a feature about a police officer's demonstration of fake and real guns. The officer tries to make the teenagers aware of how powerful guns are and of how easy it is to confuse fake and real guns. The pistol that the boy was examining in the photograph had been modified to make it inoperable, a fact that the caption failed to mention. However, as the ethicist Bob Steele noted, the photograph should not have been used even with a complete explanation. "It still would be about a young man pointing a weapon in his face, which is not what the story is about," Steele said.[45]

Another category of sensitive images is known in the profession as "public grief." These photos – showing ordinary people in public under horrifying circumstances, such as the distressed mother in the Case Study in Chapter 7, "The Death of a Boy" – are often scorned by the audience as callous intrusions into privacy. These photos, which may be quite poignant, are a source of controversy in the profession because of the competing emotions they evoke – empathy for the subjects or anger with the news media for the perceived intrusion.

Full frontal nudity, whether of adults or children, rarely appears in the mainstream news media, probably because editors and news directors sense that such images will provoke anger in the audience. To borrow a phrase often used by people complaining about the news, journalists could ask themselves whether they would want members of their families to be depicted in such an embarrassing manner.

An exception was made by many editors in 1972 when photographer Huynh Cong "Nick" Ut photographed terrified children who had endured a napalm bombing in Vietnam; one of the children was nine-year-old Phan Thi Kim Phuc, who was burned, crying, and completely nude. Decades later, Ut's photograph is regarded as one of the iconic images of the Vietnam War and a powerful statement about the ravages of war.

When a story is about nudity – as, for example, the fad of "streaking" at public events in the 1970s – print photo editors generally take care in selecting or cropping images to avoid showing genitals or female breasts. Television discreetly blurs part of the video. KXTV of Sacramento, California, used that editing technique in June 2000 when an 18-year-old woman celebrated receiving her diploma by taking off her graduation robe, while wearing nothing underneath.[46]

Intrusion by Photojournalists

Photojournalists make the compelling argument that, if they take a picture, there is time later to make a calculated decision about whether to use it; if they do not take the picture, any discussion back at the newsroom will be pointless. However, the act of taking a photograph can cause harm, whether or not the image is disseminated to the public.

In *Photojournalism: An Ethical Approach*, Paul Martin Lester described the photographer's ethical quandary:

> During a controversial news event, when a father grieves visibly over the loss of a drowned child, a writer can stay behind the scenes with pen and paper hidden. A photographer is tied to a machine that must be out in the open and obvious to all who are present. …
>
> Long lenses or hidden-camera techniques can be used, but the results are usually unsatisfactory. Focus, exposure, and composition problems are increased with the use of telephoto lenses or hiding a camera. …
>
> The photographer, unlike the hidden writer, can be the target of policemen, family members, and onlookers who vent their anger and grief on the one with the camera. …
>
> Because photographers must be out in the open to take pictures, the photographer's ethical orientation must be more clearly defined than with writers who can report over the telephone. A photographer must have a clear reason why an image of a grieving parent is necessary.[47]

The authors of *Doing Ethics in Journalism* suggest that photojournalists ask themselves questions like these: "Is this a private moment of pain and suffering that needs to be seen by our readers or viewers?" "Am I shooting at a distance that is not obtrusive or potentially revictimizing individuals?" "Am I acting with compassion and sensitivity?"[48]

After teacher Christa McAuliffe was killed along with six other crew members when the space shuttle Challenger exploded shortly after launch on January 28, 1986, her church in Concord, New Hampshire, scheduled a memorial service that evening. Journalists crowded into St. Peter's Roman Catholic Church to cover the service.

Quoting eyewitnesses, editor Mike Pride of the *Concord Monitor* described what happened: "Reporters, photographers, and television camera people commandeered the first ten rows. They shot back at the few mourners. TV cameras moved down the aisles filming weeping people. A reporter tried to question a praying mourner."

Pride was present the next night when his own church, St. John's Roman Catholic, held a memorial service. He wrote:

> [T]he Rev. Dan Messier, a young priest, descended from the sanctuary to comfort a young boy in the front pew. It was as though a single duck had flown into a blind occupied by 50 hunters. Rapid-fire clicks and flashes zeroed in on the scene as the boy buried his head in Messier's shoulder.

Pride wrote that he had to separate his personal feelings from his professional feelings. His paper used the photograph of the priest hugging the child. "I'm not sure it was worth a thousand clicks of the shutter, but it told a touching story. The mourner in me felt abused by the media in the church, but the editor in me had to run the picture."[49]

Case Study

The Falling Man, World Trade Center, 2001

On the morning of September 11, 2001, Associated Press photographer Richard Drew was taking pictures at a fashion show when his cell phone rang with an urgent call from his office. Instructed to hurry to the World Trade Center, Drew took a chance and caught a subway train, which he found to be eerily deserted.

Drew walked to a spot where ambulances were gathering. He heard people gasping in horror because people in the towers were jumping to escape the flames and smoke. With a 200-millimeter lens, he started photographing the falling bodies in sequences of 10 to 12 frames each. "It's what I do," he explained later to *CBC*

Newsworld: "It's like a carpenter, he has a hammer and he builds a house. I have a camera and I take pictures."

After taking his pictures, Drew walked north to the Associated Press headquarters, then in Rockefeller Plaza. Inserting the disc of his digital camera into his laptop, he zeroed in on the picture you see in Figure 19.1. "You learn in photo editing to look for the frame," he told *Esquire* magazine. "You have to recognize it. That picture just jumped off the screen because of its verticality and symmetry. It just had that look."

AP sent the photo around the world. Many American newspapers used it, drawing

Figure 19.1   A man falls from the World Trade Center, September 11, 2001.
PHOTO BY RICHARD DREW. REPRINTED BY PERMISSION OF THE ASSOCIATED PRESS.

complaints from their readers about the horror of the image and the disrespect that they thought journalists were showing by recording a man's death plunge.

The New York Times devoted nearly a full inside page to the photograph. The paper's then executive editor, Howell Raines, said the image of the one man "showed the magnitude of the situation and the loneliness." Although another editor expressed concern that "perhaps it's too close – close enough that people might be able to tell who it is," Raines ordered the photograph into the paper. He told the authors of *Running toward Danger: Stories behind the Breaking News of 9/11*: "The picture was about human suffering. In a tragic moment, you cannot be dishonest or evasive. ... I thought the picture told a story our readers needed to see. To suppress that picture would be wrong."

The Morning Call in Allentown, Pennsylvania, published the photo on the back page of the front section. Photo editor Naomi Halperin told her colleagues, "You know going into this that you're going to get reader response and it's going to be heavy and it's going to be angry." The outraged response was the largest *The Call* had ever received over a photo. Managing editor David Erdman told *CBC Newsworld* that he thought the photo forced anybody who looked at it to "think about 'what would I do?' ... 'what choice would I make?' and the absolute horror of making that choice."

Brian Storm, then the multimedia director at MSNBC.com, said he and his team decided that the jumpers were an "essential part of the story," although they worried that a loved one could recognize a jumper. *Quill* magazine said Storm decided to create a site for the photos so that they could be accessed by users who, by linking to the site, had made a conscious decision to look at them.

Estimates of the number of people who jumped from the towers range from 50 (*The New York Times*) to 200 (*USA Today*). "How do you portray such a horrific event, in which thousands are killed?" asked AP's then photo chief, Vin Alabiso. "Graphic images are often integral to visually reporting a graphic story. Otherwise, photographically, the severity of the news is misrepresented."

Reflecting on his experience in an interview with Peter Howe of *The Digital Journalist*, Drew said: "It wasn't just a building falling down; there were people involved in this. This is how it affected people's lives. ... I didn't capture this person's death. I captured part of his life."

Sources

Author's telephone interview with Vin Alabiso, Sept. 21, 2007.

CBC Newsworld, "Passionate Eye Showcase: The falling man."

Howe, Peter, "Richard Drew," The Digital Journalist.

Junod, Tom, "The falling man," *Esquire*, Sept. 2003.

Kim, Connie, "A single day, a thousand images," *Quill*, Nov. 2001, 22–23.

Trost, Cathy, and Alicia C. Shepard, *Running toward Danger: Stories behind the Breaking News of 9/11* (Lanham, MD: Rowman & Littlefield, 2002), 44, 210.

Questions for Class Discussion

- Why do you think so many people were disturbed by this photograph?
- Considering that dozens of World Trade Center victims, possibly hundreds, died in this manner, should your visual coverage of the day's event include this element?
- Would you run the photograph?

Case Study

Photographing a Man Pushed to His Death

R. Umar Abbasi, a freelance photographer traveling to an assignment for the *New York Post*, was holding his camera as he waited for a subway train at the 49th Street platform on December 3, 2012. The loudspeaker announced that the train was approaching, and then – Abbasi recalled later – "I suddenly heard people gasping … and out of the periphery of my eye, I saw a body flying through the air and onto the track."

Ki-Suck Han, 58 years old, had been pushed off the platform, witnesses said, by a deranged man. For a brief time, estimated by Abbasi as 22 seconds though by other witnesses as somewhat longer, Han struggled to escape the oncoming train. But he couldn't climb back onto the platform, and the train's driver could not stop. Han was fatally crushed.

What Abbasi did in those fleeting seconds made him the target of outraged criticism in social media. "I just started running," he said in a first-person account published in the *Post* two days later. "I had my camera up – it wasn't even set to the right settings – and I just kept shooting and flashing, hoping the train driver would see something and be able to stop."

Abbasi's critics argued that he should have put the camera down and tried to help Han get back on the platform. Abbasi said he was too far away, even at the instant he started running. He said people closer to the victim "watched and didn't do anything."

One of the images captured by Abbasi's camera (Figure 19.2), showing Han in the train's path, occupied the entire front page of the next edition of the *Post* with a caption in large type: "DOOMED: Pushed on the subway track, this man is about to die."

The *Post*'s choice of photograph and caption provoked criticism both on social media and in professional photojournalism circles.

Figure 19.2   Pushed onto the subway track, a man struggles to get back onto the platform as a train approaches.

Abbasi said the decision to publish was the editors', not his. "When it was over, I didn't look at the pictures," he wrote in his account. "I didn't even know I had even captured the images in such detail. I didn't look at them. I didn't want to."

The train driver was quoted by the *Daily Mail* of London as saying that he saw Han but couldn't stop. "I did what I was trained to do," he said. "You're hopeful you're going to stop, but you don't have control of the train at that point." After the impact, the driver rushed to the victim wedged between the train and the platform. Afterward the driver, in shock, was taken away in a wheelchair and wearing an oxygen mask. Two bystanders were treated for shock.

Police arrested Naeem Davis, a 30-year-old street vendor, and charged him with second-degree murder. They said he admitted that he and Han had argued, and he had pushed Han onto the track.

Bystanders' accounts differed as to whether Davis or Han started the argument. Abbasi said a video of the argument, recorded by a bystander on her smartphone, showed Davis unsuccessfully trying to get Han to leave him alone.

Leigh Weingus, trends editor of *The Huffington Post*, who happened to be waiting for the train on her way to work, wrote a first-person article for her website. In her account, Han confronted Davis. She wrote that Davis said calmly to Han, "I don't know you. Get out of my face," but that Han "continued to scream angry words." She noticed that the two men were standing dangerously close to the edge of the platform as they continued to argue. Then she heard a thud and a public-address announcement that the Q train was approaching, followed by a woman's yell, "Stop the train! There's a man on the tracks!" Weingus wrote: "Terrified, I looked down and saw the Asian man lying face down on the tracks. *He has a family!* I thought as I too started shrieking, 'Stop the train!'"

On NBC's *Today* two days after the incident, Abbasi acknowledged to Matt Lauer and Savannah Guthrie that the *Post* was paying him for the photographs on the camera memory card he had turned over to the newspaper. However, he didn't want to call it "selling" an image. "I would call it licensing to use it," he said on television. "Selling a photograph of this nature sounds morbid. I licensed these photographs."

Abbasi said later that, under his contract with the *Post*, he receives a daily pay rate and the *Post* has exclusive rights for a limited time to any photos he takes while on assignment. When he was being interviewed on *Today*, Abassi said, "I chose the term 'licensing' to keep the discussion abstract. My intention was to avoid discussing details about my contract while on the air and to indicate I had not rushed out to market the photo to the *Post*."

Discussion of the case

This case presents two ethical questions:

- Rather than triggering his camera, which resulted in a remarkable news photograph, should Abbasi have tried to pull Han out of the train's path?
- Should the *Post* editors have published that particular image on its front page with a caption that could be perceived as exploiting Han's impending death?

To make his decision, Abbasi would have had to ask himself if he were in a position to pull Han back onto the platform. The decision would have had to have been made instantly. By his own account, he could not, and dozens of people waiting on the platform were much closer to Han than he was. Also by his own account, Abbasi was not intentionally shooting pictures but instead doing what he could to save Han – flashing his camera in the direction of the train's driver.

(Continued)

In contrast to the certainty expressed by Abbasi's social-media critics, the actual situation was ambiguous.

John Long, a longtime member of the ethics committee of the National Press Photographers Association, wrote in an NPPA blog: "If the photographer thought in the panic of the moment that flashing his strobe would alert the train driver, so be it. I do not know how far he was from the victim or how fast the train was going or if he could have pulled the man up … I cannot and will not pass judgment on another man's motives."

A. D. Coleman, blogging on Nearby Café, considered how difficult it would have been for Han to save himself or for anyone to rescue him. "There's a recess beneath the platform, which means no foothold or surface against which to brace oneself for the climb," he wrote. "Unless one had unusual upper-body strength, hauling oneself onto the platform from the tracks would prove difficult. For the same reason, it would take considerable strength and extraordinary effort to stand or lie on the platform while pulling up to safety someone of adult size; once that person's feet left the railbed, they'd become dead weight."

As for the *Post*'s front page, professionals were highly critical.

Kenneth Irby, senior faculty member at the Poynter Institute, said the editors had several images to choose from and they had picked "the most disturbing." He wrote on Poynter: "The moment before death is a delicate fraction of a second and the *NY Post* print edition and cover screen image lacks compassion for the victim, his family, his friends and the *Post*'s audience. In a few words it is disgusting, disconcerting, insensate and intrusive."

In an interview with Jeff Bercovici on Forbes.com, John Long cited examples of horrifying images of combat casualties and drowned bodies in the aftermath of Katrina, which he said were published because they were relevant to important public debates. The photo of Han on the subway track would not rise to that level, he said. "If I was the night editor, I don't think I would run it."

Writing on the NPPA blog, another ethics committee member, Steve Raymer, described the image as "tasteless and inflammatory." He said the photograph could cause "additional pain and trauma, including aggravating symptoms of post-traumatic stress syndrome in individuals who have experienced trauma in the past."

In his Media Decoder blog on NYTimes.com, David Carr wrote: "The treatment of the photo was driven by a moral and commercial calculus that was sickening to behold."

At the University of Pennsylvania, as the 14 students in his "writing from photographs" seminar arrived for the final class of the semester, Professor Paul Hendrickson projected the *Post*'s cover photo on the screen. From the class debate emerged a consensus that the photograph could have been published but not the way the *Post* did it. One of the students, Joe Pinsker, wrote in an essay published on Forbes.com: "Most of us thought that with a more tasteful presentation – one that honored Han's life and paid diligence to the terror of the situation – this photograph could have justifiably been printed. Some even argued that we have an obligation to look at it, because it forces us to question the motivations of ourselves and our society. Maybe, certain photographs demand that we ask these questions."

Sources

Email exchange between the author and R. Umar Abbasi, Sept. 2014.

Bercovici, Jeff, "*New York Post*'s subway death photo: was it ethical photojournalism?," Forbes, Dec. 4, 2012.

Carr, David, "Train wreck: the *New York Post*'s subway cover," *The New York Times*, Dec. 5, 2012.

Coleman, A. D., "The photographer as citizen," Photocritic International, Dec. 28, 2012.

Collins, Laura, Daniel Bates, Louise Boyle, Daniel Miller, and Beth Stebner, "'There was no way I could have saved him': photographer claims he was too far away to pull 'doomed' subway rider off train tracks," *The Daily Mail* (London), Dec. 5, 2012.

Conley, Kirstan, "Suspect confesses in pushing death of Queens dad in Times Square subway station," *New York Post*, Dec. 4, 2012.

Lauer, Matt, and Savannah Guthrie, interview with R. Umar Abbasi, *Today*, Dec. 5, 2012.

Moos, Julie, "Irby: blame *NY Post* editors, not photographer, for subway death photo," Poynter, Dec. 4, 2012.

National Press Photographers Association, "Subway photo," Dec. 5, 2012.

Pinsker, Joe, "*NY Post* subway death photo: a real-world final exam," Forbes, Dec. 6, 2012.

Weingus, Leigh, "Witnessing a tragedy on my way to work," *The Huffington Post*, Dec. 4, 2012.

Questions for Class Discussion

- What do you think of R. Umar Abbasi's conduct in the subway station when he realized that a man had been pushed onto the track?
- Given that he was a professional photographer on assignment for the *New York Post*, do you think it was wrong for him to be paid for the images he shot?
- What do you think of the *Post*'s front page? Consider the choice of photograph, its placement on the cover, and the wording of the caption.

- If you disagree with the *Post*'s treatment, would you have used the same photograph but handled it differently? If so, how?
- Consider Steve Raymer's comment that the photograph could cause "additional pain and trauma." Can you think of any photographs whose news value could argue for publication even though they might make news consumers uncomfortable?

Case Study

A Marine Is Mortally Wounded

DAHANEH, Afghanistan – The pomegranate grove looked ominous.

The U.S. patrol had a tip that Taliban fighters were lying in ambush, and a Marine had his weapon trained on the trees 70 yards away. "If you see anything move from there, light it up," Cpl. Braxton Russell told him.

Thirty seconds later, a salvo of gunfire and RPGs – rocket-propelled grenades – poured out of the grove. "Casualty! We've got a casualty!" someone shouted. A grenade had hit Lance Cpl. Joshua "Bernie" Bernard in the legs.

A Marine and son of a Marine, a devout Christian, Iraq war veteran and avid hiker, home-schooled in rural Maine, Bernard was about to become the next fatality in the deadliest month of the deadliest year since the U.S.-led invasion of Afghanistan in 2001.

The Associated Press, Sept. 4, 2009

(Continued)

When 21-year-old Corporal Bernard and his fellow marines were ambushed on August 14, 2009, they were accompanied by three Associated Press journalists. The AP's Julie Jacobson, crouching under fire 10 yards away, photographed the scene with a telephoto lens as two of the corporal's buddies scrambled to his aid (Figure 19.3).

One of Bernard's legs was blown off by the grenade and the other was mangled. While heavy fire continued, the wounded marine was carried on a stretcher to an armored vehicle. After more first aid was administered 500 yards from the firefight, he was evacuated to a field hospital. There he died on the operating table from a blot clot in his heart. His death was one of 51 among American service members in Afghanistan that month.

Later, some of the marines asked Jacobson if they could see her photographs. They flipped through the images in her computer. When they came to the one in which Bernard was mortally wounded, she recalled, they stopped.

"But none of them complained or grew angry about it," she wrote in her journal. "They understood that it was what it was. They understand, despite that he was their friend, it was the reality of things."

The Associated Press did not immediately distribute Jacobson's photographs. That would have been a violation of the military's rules under which journalists are "embedded" with combat units. The identity of troops who become casualties cannot be reported until the Defense Department officially releases the names.

Figure 19.3   A marine is mortally wounded in Afghanistan.
PHOTO BY JULIE JACOBSON. REPRINTED BY PERMISSION OF THE ASSOCIATED PRESS.

The AP took another step before publication. After Corporal Bernard was buried on August 24 in Madison, Maine, an AP reporter went to the home of his parents to show them the photographs. It was, as an AP executive said later, a gesture of courtesy.

The corporal's father, retired marine First Sergeant John Bernard, opposed the publication of the image showing his son mortally wounded. He said it would be disrespectful to his son's memory and would only hurt the family more. In a phone call to the AP later, he reiterated his objection.

On the morning of September 3, while acknowledging the family's anguish, and after much deliberation, the Associated Press sent to its member news organizations the still photographs (including the image of the mortally wounded marine), video, and an article co-written by Alfred de Montesquiou and Julie Jacobson. The package of images and text showed Corporal Bernard before the ambush and also the memorial service conducted by his unit. The news service set a release time of 12:01 the following morning, giving editors an entire day to decide whether to use the package.

After the material had been distributed but before the release time, Defense Secretary Robert Gates phoned the AP's president, Tom Curley, to urge him to change his mind. Unsuccessful, Gates sent the AP a letter deploring its decision:

Why your organization would purposefully defy the family's wishes knowing full well that it will lead to yet more anguish is beyond me. Your lack of compassion and common sense in choosing to put this image of their maimed and stricken child on the front page of multiple American newspapers is appalling. The issue here is not law, policy or constitutional right – but judgment and common decency.

The AP issued a statement of explanation.

"AP journalists document world events every day," said Santiago Lyon, vice president and director of photography. "We feel it is our journalistic duty to show the reality of the war there, however unpleasant and brutal that it sometimes is."

"We believe this image is part of the history of this war," said John Daniszewski, vice president and senior managing editor for international news. "The story and photos are in themselves a respectful treatment and recognition of sacrifice."

"To ignore a moment like that simply … would have been wrong," Jacobson, the photographer, wrote in an entry in her journal that appeared in the AP's statement. "Death is a part of life and most certainly a part of war. Isn't that why we're here? To document for now and for history the events of this war?"

The New York Times reported on September 5 that "a few newspapers have published the picture, and many more have not." *The Times* itself published the photograph of the wounded Corporal Bernard on its website but not in its print edition.

The London *Daily Mail* reported on September 7 that at least 20 newspapers used some of the AP's package on its front page, but they put the wounding photo on an inside page or did not run it at all.

After "hours of debate," *The Wheeling* (West Virginia) *Intelligencer* used the photo on an inside page. The paper wrote in a statement to readers, "Too often, we fear, some Americans see only the statistics, the casualty counts released by the Department of Defense. We

(Continued)

believe it is important for all of us to understand that behind the numbers are real men and women, sometimes making the ultimate sacrifice, for us."

In the Bernards' home state, the *Portland* (Maine) *Press-Herald* published the story with an editor's note saying that it would be "in poor taste" to run the photo.

Aside from the criticism aimed at the AP for distributing the photographs, some people questioned why, instead of taking photographs, Jacobson did not try to help the wounded marine. She wrote this entry in her journal: "I kept trying to gauge whether or not to drop the camera and help the Marines with the injured man. I remember feeling that as my first instinct when we had first approached him, but saw that there were two guys with him and I decided I was not needed."

Lyon, the AP photo director, said Jacobson "immediately recognized that this image would require special handling." He said she sent it to AP's New York headquarters with clear instructions to hold it for review. That, Lyon said, started "a wider internal discussion that ultimately led to the full package of text, photos, and video designed to put the young Marine's death into context."

In an interview with David W. Dunlap for a September 5 posting on Lens, the visual journalism blog of *The New York Times*, Lyon discussed the behind-the-scenes deliberations at AP. His assessment was that the photograph shows

> in a very unequivocal and direct fashion, the real consequences of war, involving in this case a U.S. Marine. And that becomes very personal and very direct in some way, because we have a name, we have a home town, we have a shared nationality and we have, to a certain extent, a shared culture and some common values. So I think it really

becomes a very immediate visual record of warfare that, in and of itself, is compelling, and that becomes more compelling because of its rarity.

Lyon explained that photographs like this one were rare because so few journalists were covering the war in Afghanistan.

Dunlap's posting drew more than 650 reader comments. In a follow-up posting on September 21, Dunlap wrote:

> [R]eaders felt passionately about the question. But many did not see it as a black-and-white issue. There weren't really two sides to the discussion as much as there was a continuum of opinion. Many who strongly favored the AP's decision acknowledged that the additional suffering brought to Corporal Bernard's family was a high price to pay for public enlightenment. Many who strongly opposed the AP's decision to release the picture conceded that the news organization was within its lawful right to do so.

One of the readers who disapproved was Army Major Amanda Rossi, who wrote: "No one debates that A.P. did not have a constitutional right to publish the photo. However, just because you can does not always mean that you should. ... In this case, it was possible to tell the story without compromising the truth and without the controversial photo in question."

Marine Corporal Jerry Wilson was among the Lens readers who did not find the photograph inappropriate, posting this comment: "Embedded journalists and photographers are not there to paint a pretty picture for everyone. They are there to report the news they see. After almost eight years of combat, this is the first picture that has actually captured a real part of both wars."

The ethicist Bob Steele wrote on Poynter on September 4 that the AP had gone through "a purposeful, thoughtful process." He concluded that its decision was "journalistically sound and ethically justifiable."

Steele acknowledged that the AP was obliged to give very serious consideration to the father's wishes. "Yet, no matter how important that request from the father, the final decision sits with the AP. It means the journalists had to have a competing journalistic purpose and an overriding ethical justification to go against the family's wishes."

Steele observed that, while journalists endure a backlash almost every time they show the horror of war, they also get criticism for not showing the horror of war more often:

> Journalism's obligation is to inform the public about significant issues in our society. That includes telling stories – with images, words and sound – that meaningfully describe both the horror and heroism of the battlefield. … The images and words of war reporting may cause pain. But we owe it to Lance Cpl. Joshua Bernard and to all those who fight our wars to try to comprehend what happens in battle.

Questions for Class Discussion

- What two cornerstone principles of the Society of Professional Journalists' code are in conflict in this case?
- What is the main argument for publishing the photographs?
- How would you weigh the family's wishes against that argument?
- What steps did the AP take to mitigate harm?
- In a situation like this, does the AP have a different obligation than its member newspapers that receive its material? That is, is the AP obliged to distribute photos that

are *potentially* newsworthy, while each paper, considering its own audience, can then make its own decision about whether to publish those photos? After all, it is the member papers that are paying to put that photographer in the field. Don't they have a right to make that choice?
- Given all the circumstances, if you were in charge of the AP, would you have distributed the photograph of the mortally wounded marine?

Sources

Associated Press, "Why AP published photo of slain Marine," Sept. 4, 2009.

Daily Mail, "Pictured: the heartbreaking image of a dying U.S. marine that has reignited American divisions over the Afghan war," Sept. 7, 2009.

de Montesquiou, Alfred, and Julie Jacobson, "Death of a Marine," Associated Press, Sept. 4, 2009. The article was accompanied by 11 photographs by Jacobson.

Dunlap, David W., "Behind the scenes: to publish or not?," Lens: Photography, Video and Visual Journalism, *The New York Times*, Sept. 4, 2009.

Dunlap, David W., and Beth Flynn, "Readers' voices: public and private trauma," Lens: Photography, Video and Visual Journalism, *The New York Times*, Sept. 21, 2009.

Seelye, Katharine Q., "Gates assails news agency for publishing photo of Marine killed in Afghanistan," *The New York Times*, Sept. 4, 2009.

Steele, Bob, "AP made right call in publishing photo, story of fallen Marine," Poynter, Sept. 4, 2009.

Notes

1   This account of the Walski incident is based on Kenneth Irby, "*L.A. Times* photographer fired over altered image," Poynter, Apr. 2, 2003.

2   Cheryl Johnston, "Digital deception," *American Journalism Review*, May 2003, 10–11.

3   Irby, "*L.A. Times* photographer fired over altered image."

4   "Daguerre (1787–1851) and the Invention of Photography," Heilbrunn Timeline of Art History, Metropolitan Museum of Art.

5   "William Henry Fox Talbot," J. Paul Getty Museum.

6   Louis W. Hodges, "The distorting mirror: ethics and the camera," unpublished paper (2003). (*The paper is available in the Student Resources section of the website.*)

7   Russell Frank, "Altered photos break public's trust in media," *Los Angeles Times*, Apr. 7, 2003.

8   Paul Martin Lester, *Photojournalism: An Ethical Approach* (Hillsdale, NJ: Lawrence Erlbaum, 1991), 92.

9   Ibid., 95–97.

10 Ron Steinman, "An interview with Dr. Hany Farid," The Digital Journalist, Feb. 2008."

11 Farid, Hany, "Photo Tampering throughout History," Four and Six. http://www.fourandsix.com/photo-tampering-history/

12 "NPPA code of ethics," National Press Photographers Association.

13 Kenneth Irby, "Associated Press letter on photo editing policy," Poynter, Sept. 5, 2003.

14 Kenneth Irby, "*Washington Post* policy on manipulation of photographic images," Poynter, Sept. 5, 2003.

15 Kenneth Irby, "*New York Times* guidelines on our integrity," Poynter, Sept. 5, 2003.

16 Author's email correspondence with John Beale, Aug. 12–13, 2014.

17 Doris Kearns Goodwin, *No Ordinary Time: Franklin and Eleanor Roosevelt: The Home Front in World War II* (New York: Simon & Schuster, 1994), 586.

18 Howard Kurtz, "*L.A. Times* gets burned by disaster photograph," *The Washington Post*, Feb. 2, 1994.

19 Paul Farhi, "White House reenactments stir debate over photographic practice," *The Washington Post*, May 13, 2011.

20 Kenneth Irby, "Magazine covers: photojournalism or illustration?," Poynter, Jan. 2, 2003.

21 Sherry Ricchiardi, "Distorted picture," *American Journalism Review*, Aug.–Sept. 2007, 40.

22 Irby, "Magazine covers."

23 Farid, "Photo tampering throughout history."

24 Margaret Sullivan, "Tattoo removal on the photo desk," *The New York Times*, May 18, 2013.

25 Nick Stern, "Why Instagram photos cheat the viewer," CNN, Feb. 23, 2012.

26 Kenneth Irby, "The art and language of photography: a photojournalism glossary," Poynter, Aug. 26, 2002.

27 Irby, "*Washington Post* policy on manipulation of photographic images."

28 Ricchiardi, "Distorted picture," 41.

29 Jay DeFoore, "*Newsweek* changes crediting policy following cover flap," *Photo District News*, Mar. 8, 2005.

30 Deni Elliott and Paul Martin Lester, "Manipulation: the word we love to hate (part 3)," *News Photographer*, Oct. 2003.

31 Steven R. Knowlton, *Moral Reasoning for Journalists: Cases and Commentary* (Westport, CT: Praeger, 1997), 189.

32 Travis Linn, "Staging in TV news," *Journal of Mass Media Ethics*, 6:1 (1991), 47.

33 Scott Baradell and Anh D. Stack, *Photojournalism, Technology and Ethics: What's Right and Wrong Today?* (New York: Black Star, 2008), 35–36.

34 Al Tompkins, email to author, Nov. 18, 2008.

35 "RTDNA code of ethics," Radio Television Digital News Association, Jan. 24, 2014.

36 "NPPA code of ethics."

37 *Newsroom Ethics: Decision-Making for Quality Coverage*, 4th edn. (Washington: Radio Television News Directors Foundation, 2006), 81.

38 Ibid., 82.

39 Ibid.

40 Brooke Barnett and Maria Elizabeth Grabe, "The impact of slow motion video on viewer evaluations of television news stories," *Visual Communication Quarterly*, Summer 2000, 4–7.

41 Quotations from author's telephone interview with Sherman Williams, Oct. 12, 2007.

42 Irby, quoted in Bill Marvel and Manuel Mendoza, "Gruesome images: does taste trump newsworthiness?," *The Dallas Morning News*, Apr. 1, 2004.

43 Josephson's comment to the author.

44 Author's telephone interview with Vin Alabiso, Sept. 21, 2007.

45 Quoted in Nancy Conner, "Critics take aim at decision to use photo of youth looking into gun," a reader advocate's column originally published in *St. Paul Pioneer Press*, Jan. 30, 2000; reprinted in Michele McLellan, *The Newspaper Credibility Handbook: Better Ways to Build Reader Trust* (Washington, DC: American Society of Newspaper Editors, 2001), 158.

46 *Newsroom Ethics*, 23–24.

47 Lester, *Photojournalism: An Ethical Approach*, 4.

48 Jay Black, Bob Steele, and Ralph Barney, *Doing Ethics in Journalism: A Handbook with Case Studies*, 3rd edn. (Needham Heights, MA: Allyn & Bacon, 1999), 207.

49 Mike Pride, "A grieving Concord repelled by media misbehavior," *presstime*, Mar. 1986, 12–14.

20 Some Thoughts to Take with You

Capsules of advice for aspiring journalists

As you complete this study of news media ethics, reflect on what you have learned – and what you should take with you as you enter the journalism workplace, where your decisions will affect the lives of others.

The most important lesson is to *stop and think*. When you are confronted with an ethical question, think carefully. Identify the values involved in possible courses of action, analyze them dispassionately, and reach a decision that you can defend.

Some journalists may say that in a deadline environment there is no time for a process of critical thinking. The reality is that only rarely must a decision be made in an instant. Even if you do have to decide in an instant, your practice in this course can guide you to a sound decision. In addition, the ethical question can often be anticipated, when there is time to consider your options more deliberately.

As you enter the journalism profession, please remember the fundamental lessons this textbook has sought to impart:

- In any decision, practice critical thinking – a systematic, logical approach. That does not mean you should dismiss your emotional response to a situation; if it *feels* wrong, it may well *be* wrong. But go beyond your reflexes to rationally consider arguments for or against a proposed course of action.
- The Golden Rule remains the best single rule. Even though it will not solve every problem, putting yourself in the place of the person affected is a good way to assess the rightness of your decision.
- You owe your first allegiance to your audience – the readers, the viewers, the listeners, the online users. That allegiance must be a vital factor in any decision you make.
- Your mission is to give your audience the truth as best you can determine it. That requires more than simply getting the facts right. Provide the context that gives meaning to the facts.
- Although you may not be able to report the story *completely* in a single day, be sure that *everything* you do report is true and in context. In the spirit of transparency, tell the audience about the key questions that are still unanswered.
- You owe your audience respect. However, practicing journalism is not like running a store; the customer is *not* always right. When your reporting or your decisions are challenged, carefully review them. If the complaint is right, correct your mistake and reform your procedures if necessary. If you think the complaint is wrong, explain your decision.

The Ethical Journalist: Making Responsible Decisions in the Digital Age, Second Edition. Gene Foreman.
© 2016 John Wiley & Sons, Inc. Published 2016 by John Wiley & Sons, Inc.

- In the newsroom, people trust each other. Plagiarism, fabrication, and manipulation of images could – and should – be a death sentence for your career.
- Be fair to your sources. Identify yourself as a journalist and make it clear that your purpose is to obtain information to be disseminated to the public. *You* are responsible for making sure your sources understand any ground rules about how information will be attributed.
- Deceiving a source is acceptable only in rare cases. Deception can be justified only when there is no other way to obtain information that is vital to the public, and when that information cannot be obtained through conventional reporting techniques. You must disclose your methods to the audience.
- Do not manipulate the people you report on, treating them as the means to achieve your own ends. Likewise, as the surrogate for the audience, do not allow yourself to be manipulated by your sources and diverted from the truth.
- Your reporting must be free of bias. Although you will form opinions about the people and events you cover, it is a test of your professionalism that you filter these biases from your news accounts.
- Do not take public positions on controversial issues or the people and events you cover. To tell others of your opinions is to invite them to find those opinions in your reporting. Remember that people see you as a journalist 24/7; in their eyes, you are never off duty.
- Be independent of those you cover. Your loyalty is to the audience.
- Avoid the appearance of a conflict, and disclose any unavoidable appearance of conflict. Turn down gifts or perquisites offered because of your occupation. Ask yourself: Would the average person be offered this gift or perk? If the answer is no, turn it down.
- Remember that a journalist is an observer, not a participant. Generally, it is only in a crisis – when you are *the only person or the best person to save a life or avoid an injury* – that you should you put down your notebook or camera and become a participant.
- Be compassionate. Recognize that people may be hurt when you report the truth. In those cases, minimize harm. Never use your power as a journalist to inflict harm gratuitously.
- When your reporting would expose private information that would embarrass the subjects of the news coverage, weigh the value of the information to the public against the degree of harm that the subject might suffer. Consider what degree of privacy the subject can reasonably expect: A public official doing public business deserves the least privacy; an ordinary person involuntarily thrust into the news deserves the most.
- It is not acceptable for you to publish something just because someone else will publish it or has published it. Do not lower your standards to those of your least ethical competitor.
- Practice the scientific method in your reporting: Start with a thesis, then conduct research to see if that thesis is valid. Your goal is to find the truth, not necessarily to validate your thesis. Falling in love with your story could blind you to evidence that your thesis is not true.

- Ask your sources: *How do you know that?*
- The burden is on you, the journalist, to prove the truth of what you publish, broadcast, or post online – not for an adversary to prove that your reporting is false.

Now, a final piece of advice: Your education in journalism ethics will help you determine the morally correct course to take in a given situation. As you have learned, however, defining what is right and wrong is only half the battle. You can expect powerful pressures to follow a different course of action. It will require courage to resist these pressures and to do what is right. Be ready to stand on principle. *Be an ethical journalist.*

Glossary

accountability The obligation of journalists to treat their audience with respect and to respond constructively to criticism. Essential to accountability is a willingness to correct errors and to explain news decisions.

advertorial/infomercial/native advertising All of these are advertisements resembling news. An advertorial is print advertising that uses headlines, news stories, photographs, and captions suggesting news ("editorial") content. An infomercial is television advertising that resembles a news feature or documentary. Native advertising is paid content on a news website that closely resembles – is "native" to – the site's own news content.

apparent conflict of interest Something that a journalist does – or says publicly – that causes the audience to *perceive* a conflict of interest or a bias, even though the journalist's reporting is appropriate. For example, if a journalist contributes to a political candidate or cause, the audience can be expected to perceive bias in that journalist's reporting – and to attribute the same bias to the journalist's entire news organization. See **conflict of interest** for a discussion of an *actual*, rather than an apparent, conflict.

applied ethics The branch of moral philosophy that deals with making decisions about concrete cases in a business or profession. Its purpose is to put ethical theory into action.[1]

Aristotle's Golden Mean A moderate but ethically defensible solution in a situation in which the extreme choices are unacceptable.[2] This concept is based on the ancient Greek philosopher's belief in moderation as a virtue – for example, courage as the mean between recklessness and cowardice.[3] Aristotle's Golden Mean is at work, for example, in the US government's policy on the sale of tobacco. At the extremes, the government might have banned tobacco because its health dangers have been clinically proved, or it might have permitted unregulated sales because citizens should have the civil liberty of deciding for themselves whether to buy it. Instead, the government chose a Golden Mean: to tax tobacco heavily, regulate advertising, require warning labels, and bar sales to children.[4]

audience The readers, viewers, listeners, and digital users who consume the news that journalists produce. It is to the audience that journalists owe their first allegiance.

checkbook journalism Paying news sources for their information.

citizen journalism See **user-generated content.**

confidential source Someone who provides information to a journalist on the condition that he or she not be identified.

conflict of interest A journalist's self-interest or loyalty to another person or organization that the journalist permits to alter, influence, or take precedence over his or her duty to the audience. For example, if a film critic has a side job to promote the work of a movie producer, he or she would be unlikely to write unfavorable reviews of that producer's films. The critic's tainted reviews would cheat the audience, which expects and is entitled to an honest appraisal of the films. Likewise, a news company is in a conflict of interest if it produces puff pieces about an advertiser or suppresses legitimate news that is unfavorable to the advertiser. These are *actual* conflicts of interest, in which the journalism is subverted; for comparison, see **apparent conflict of interest**. See also **disclosure**.

The Ethical Journalist: Making Responsible Decisions in the Digital Age, Second Edition. Gene Foreman.
© 2016 John Wiley & Sons, Inc. Published 2016 by John Wiley & Sons, Inc.

consequentialism See **ends-based thinking.**

critical thinking The systematic process of analyzing ethical problems – a process that involves applying logic to the available information. It is crucial to sound decision-making. Critical thinking is the opposite of an emotional response.[5]

crowdsourcing Systematically gathering information from members of the public. Although citizens represent a valuable pool of information, professional journalists have a duty to verify any information before distributing it.

deception Communicating "messages meant to mislead others, *meant to make them believe what we ourselves do not believe.* We can do that through gesture, through disguise, by means of action or inaction, even through silence" (Sissela Bok's classic definition).[6]

deontology See **rule-based thinking.**

disclosure Informing the audience of something that might be perceived as a **conflict of interest.** A disclosure may be warranted if the conflict is unavoidable or insignificant. Disclosing the possible appearance of conflict makes members of the audience aware of the connection and allows them to decide whether the content is biased. For example, the law firm that represents the news organization happens to make the news in its representation of another client; the resulting news story notes the relationship of the law firm and the news organization. A disclosure is not an antidote to a conflict that is both avoidable and significant. For example, a disclosure that a travel writer has received free travel, lodging, and meals does not allay the audience's skepticism about the validity of the writer's review of the trip; instead, the writer's employer should pay the expenses of the trip, and the writer should represent himself or herself as a typical traveler.

duty-based thinking See **rule-based thinking.**

ends-based thinking An ethical theory that allows the decision-maker to weigh competing values according to the consequences that may occur.[7] It directs a choice in favor of the course of action that brings the most good to the most people.[8] This theory is also called *teleology, consequentialism,* and *utilitarianism.*

ethical dilemma A situation in which a person's *ethical* values are in conflict, forcing him or her to choose one ethical value over another. For example, in Lawrence Kohlberg's hypothetical Heinz's dilemma, Heinz must choose between compassion and honesty – stealing the drug to save his wife's life, or allowing her to die. However, not every difficult decision is an ethical dilemma. See also **false ethical dilemma.**

ethical values Values that directly relate to beliefs about what is right and proper: honesty, promise-keeping, fairness, compassion, respect for the privacy of others.[9] See **nonethical values.**

ethics A set of moral principles, a code – often unwritten – that guides a person's moral conduct. Ethics is more than just discerning the difference between right and wrong; it requires acting on what is right.[10]

fabrication Making things up and passing them off as genuine.

false ethical dilemma A situation requiring a person to choose between an ethical value and a nonethical value. The false ethical value can be expressed as a clash between *what you should do* and *what you would like to do* – for example, the choice between respecting a news subject's privacy (ethical value) and getting a news story before the competition does (nonethical value). The ethical person rejects the nonethical value and acts on the ethical value, choosing ethics over expediency. Thus, doing the right thing may require a sacrifice in the short term.

framing The context or narrative theme through which a news story is told. Framing represents the journalist's effort to interpret and give meaning to the news. Conflict is a common – and commonly abused – story frame. Journalists should recognize that choosing a frame is a subjective decision in which they must guard against injecting their biases.

gatekeeping Once, editors decided what information was worthy of passing along to the public, and what was not. The Internet changed this so-called gatekeeping function. Today, society depends on journalists to be its surrogates in sifting the huge volume of information available, testing it for accuracy, and helping citizens understand it.

Golden Rule Doing unto others as you would have them do unto you. The Golden Rule appears in various forms in all the world's major religions. Also known as the *rule of reversibility*, it is a powerful decision-making tool because it allows you to imagine yourself in the place of the person affected by your decision and, from that perspective, to assess the fairness of the decision.

independence Journalists' freedom of obligation to any interest that would interfere with their duty to serve the public. Journalists are detached observers of the people and events they cover. See **conflict of interest**.

infomercial See **advertorial/infomercial/native advertising.**

infotainment The blending of news and entertainment as a marketing strategy aimed at attracting an audience with sensationalism. This phenomenon is illustrated by cable television's fixation on a single story, such as the death in 2007 of Anna Nicole Smith, the *Playboy* centerfold model who had become a rich widow and then a star on reality TV.

intervention A decision by a journalist to become involved in a news situation that he or she is covering. The journalist's traditional role is as an observer rather than a participant, for two reasons: intervention changes the nature of the event, and the intervention could persuade the audience of bias on the journalist's part. However, in certain rare situations, a journalist might intervene for humanitarian reasons. In general, a journalist should act to save a life or prevent injury if he or she is the best or only person in a position to intervene.

journalism (1) The *independent act* of gathering and disseminating information, in which the practitioner (2) *is dedicated to seeking the truth* and (3) *owes first loyalty to the consumers* of the information.[11]

manipulation Distorting what purports to be documentary news photography either by stage-managing the scene or by altering the content of otherwise authentic images.

moral agent The person who makes the decision in a given situation. A moral agent's goal is to make a decision that can be defended as having been rationally chosen by a caring individual.

multimedia journalism In today's newsroom, cross-platform journalism requires its practitioners to possess multimedia skills. Reporters might be called on to take photographs, either still or video. Print journalists might do "talkbacks" on television in which they discuss the stories they have covered. Television reporters might write stories for print. Importantly, all of these print and broadcast journalists might provide multimedia reports throughout the day for the affiliated website.

native advertising See **advertorial/infomercial/native advertising.**

nonethical values Values that relate not to moral duty but to desire: wealth, status, happiness. Note that these are not *un*ethical values; instead, they are morally neutral. For a journalist, nonethical values could be getting an important news story before the competition does, or increasing website traffic, newspaper circulation, or broadcast ratings. Seeking these goals is not morally wrong unless an ethical value is violated in the process.[12] See **ethical values**.

op-ed In newspapers, this is an adjective denoting commentary – in columns or essays – that is distinguished from the newspaper's impartial news reporting. The name derives from "opposite editorial," because op-ed content is placed next to the editorials that express the newspaper's own institutional opinion.

plagiarism Taking credit for phrases, sentences, paragraphs, or even an entire story that someone else has created.

rationalization A temptation in the decision process. In choosing a course of action that is self-serving, the decision-maker deludes himself or herself into thinking that the choice is an ethical one. For example, an employee who cheats on an expense account may conclude that the stealing is justified because he or she was denied a raise.

rule-based thinking An ethical theory holding that a person always has an absolute duty to follow a universal rule of conduct, such as telling the truth. It permits no exceptions and no excuses, and has no concern for the consequences. This theory also is called *deontology* or *duty-based thinking*.

socialization The process by which a new generation absorbs the values of the community. These values are most commonly transmitted by family, peer groups, role models, and societal institutions.

social responsibility A business concern's moral duty to strive to make its community better. This obligation to the public requires more than merely complying with the law. For companies that report the news, a critical social responsibility is to provide the fair, accurate, reliable information that a community needs to be self-governing.

source Someone who gives a journalist information about a news matter.

teleology See **ends-based thinking.**

transparency Being open to any reasonable question that members of the audience could raise: why a certain story was done; how the story was produced; who the sources were; any conflict of interest that might be perceived about the news organization or the reporter; gaps in the story's content that the reporter has not been able to fill.

truth To report – to the degree that it is humanly possible – what actually happened in a given news situation. This process begins with getting the facts right through a process of verification. Truth-seeking also involves an ability to find sources with firsthand knowledge, to filter out the biases of those sources, and to use subjective judgment to provide context to the facts.

user-generated content Information and images provided to news organizations by members of the audience and then presented to the audience as a whole. Although this kind of content is called citizen journalism by some, it does not meet the definition of journalism unless the provider acts independently, is dedicated to seeking truth, and renders first loyalty to the audience. However, members of the audience can be a valuable resource in generating news-coverage ideas and providing information or photography that is subsequently verified by professional journalists. See **journalism.**

utilitarianism See **ends-based thinking.**

values Deeply held convictions and beliefs about what is effective, desirable, or morally right. These values may or may not be ethical values. Our character is defined by the values – ethical or not – that we consistently rank higher than the others. See **ethical values** and **nonethical values.**

Notes

1   Louis A. Day, *Ethics in Media Communications: Cases and Controversies*, 5th edn. (Belmont, CA: Thomson Wadsworth, 2006), 5.

2   Ibid.

3   Rushworth M. Kidder, *How Good People Make Tough Choices: Resolving the Dilemmas of Ethical Living* (New York: HarperCollins, 1995), 70.

4   Clifford G. Christians, Kim B. Rotzoll, Mark Fackler, Kathy Brittain McKee, and Robert H. Woods Jr., *Media Ethics: Cases and Moral Reasoning*, 7th edn. (Boston: Allyn & Bacon, 2005), 13.

5   Derived from Barry Beyer, *Critical Thinking* (Bloomington, IN: Phi Delta Kappa Educational Foundation, 1995), 8–9.

6   Sissela Bok, *Lying: Moral Choice in Public and Private Life* (New York: Vintage Books, 1978), 13.

7   Michael Josephson, *Ethical Issues and Opportunities in Journalism* (Marina del Rey, CA: Josephson Institute, 1991).

8   Kidder, *How Good People Make Tough Choices*, 24.

9   Michael Josephson, "Definitions in ethics," unpublished paper (2001). (*The paper is available in the Student Resources section of the website.*)

10   Michael Josephson, *Becoming an Exemplary Police Officer* (Los Angeles: Josephson Institute, 2007), 21.

Although the book was written for police officers, it offers Josephson's thinking on ethics in a general sense.

11   In composing his definition of journalism, the author derived its components from Bill Kovach and Tom Rosenstiel, *The Elements of Journalism: What Newspeople Should Know and the Public Should Expect*, 3rd edn. (New York: Three Rivers Press, 2014).

12   Josephson, "Definitions in ethics."

Index

The Ethical Journalist: Making Responsible Decisions in the Digital Age, Second Edition. Gene Foreman.
© 2016 John Wiley & Sons, Inc. Published 2016 by John Wiley & Sons, Inc.